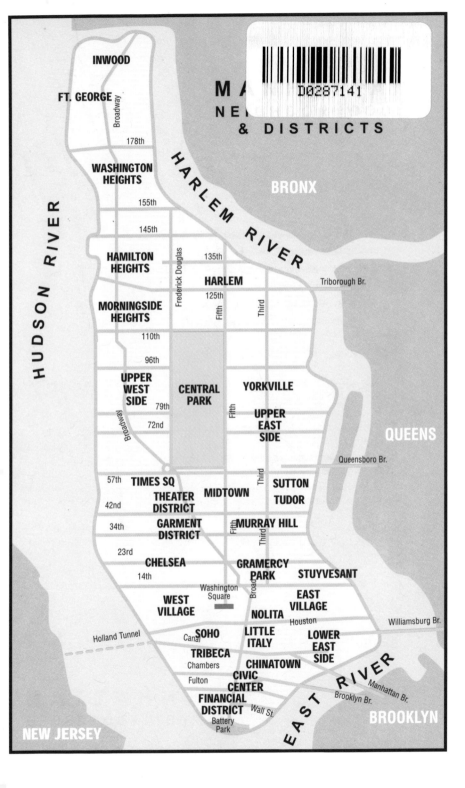

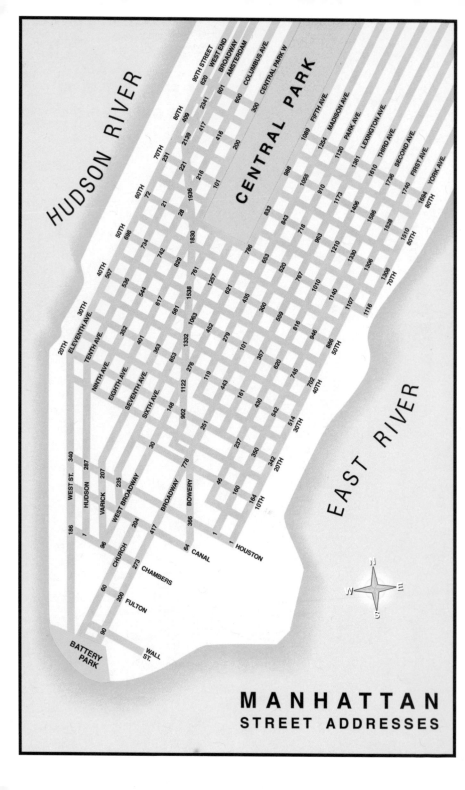

MANHATTAN
STREET ADDRESSES

GERRY FRANK'S

Where to Find It, Buy It, Eat It in New York

GERRY FRANK'S

Where to Find It, Buy It, Eat It in New York

Gerry's Frankly Speaking

P.O. Box 2225
Salem, OR 97308
503/585-8411
800/NYC-BOOK (800/692-2665)
Fax: 503/585-1076
E-mail: gerry@teleport.com

Gerry Frank's Where to Find It, Buy It, Eat It in New York
Copyright (c) 1980, 1981, 1983, 1985, 1987, 1989, 1991,
1993, 1995, 1997, 1999, 2001, 2003, 2005, 2007
by Gerald W. Frank.

All rights reserved. No part of this book may be reproduced in any
form or by any electronic or mechanical means, including information
storage and retrieval systems, without permission in writing from the
author, except by a reviewer who may quote brief passages in a review.

Printed in the United States of America
Library of Congress Catalog Card Number 80-7802

ISBN (13): 978-1-879333-19-2
ISBN (10): 1-879333-19-8

First Edition 1980
Second Edition 1981
Third Edition 1983
Fourth Edition 1985
Fifth Edition 1987
Sixth Edition 1989
Seventh Edition 1991
Eighth Edition 1993
Ninth Edition 1995
Tenth Edition 1997
Eleventh Edition 1999
Twelfth Edition 2001
Thirteenth Edition 2003
Fourteenth Edition 2005
Fifteenth Edition 2007

No fees were paid or services rendered in exchange for inclusion in
this book.

Although every effort was made to ensure that all information was
accurate and up-to-date at the time of publication, neither the publisher
nor the author can be held responsible for any errors, omissions, or
adverse consequences resulting from the use of such information. It is
recommended that you call ahead to verify the information contained in
individual business listings.

Contents

III. WHERE TO FIND IT: MUSEUMS, TOURS, TICKETS, AND MORE

IV. WHERE TO FIND IT: NEW YORK'S BEST FOOD SHOPS

V. WHERE TO FIND IT: NEW YORK'S BEST SERVICES

VI. WHERE TO BUY IT: NEW YORK'S BEST STORES

VII. WHERE TO "EXTRAS"

From the Author . . .

Dear Readers,

It doesn't matter whether you're a native New Yorker, a seasoned traveler who has been here a hundred times, or someone visiting for the very first time. New York is the most exciting, interesting, and diverse city in the world! There's something here for everyone—and the same holds for my account of it in the following pages.

I first began writing this book on a whim almost 30 years ago. As an executive for my family's department store chain in the Pacific Northwest, I had been coming to New York on a regular basis since the 1950s. Turning my notes into a book seemed like a natural thing to do, but no publisher thought an Oregonian could possibly write a worthwhile guidebook to New York. Undeterred by their lack of enthusiasm, I published it myself. Little did I know when I began begging the owners of the bookstores that used to line Fifth Avenue for a little shelf space that **Where to Find It, Buy It, Eat It in New York** would become the best-selling complete guidebook to New York, with over a million copies sold!

My volume offers different things to different people. To native New Yorkers, it's a chance to reminisce and learn a few secrets about their city that they didn't know before. For those who live here, it's a great resource for everything from rug cleaners to consignment stores. And for the millions of people who visit every year as tourists, it's a one-stop source for everything the title suggests: where to find it, buy it, and eat it in this remarkably rich and diverse city.

Men wore hats and women wore gloves back when I first started coming to New York more than six decades ago. When I published the first edition of this book, New York had just emerged from bankruptcy and whole sections of the city were dirty wastelands where tourists would never think of going. In the intervening years, the city has seen great sadness and great joy, shared tragedy and savored triumph, and has changed dramatically in many ways. Whole neighborhoods have been altered, and several generations have come and gone. New York is an even greater city today!

The heart of this book has always been a collection of personal notes and opinions. Nobody pays for inclusion, and I am solely the judge of what goes in and what stays out. This could not happen without the terrific team that, like New York's neighborhoods, has morphed over the years. Cheryl Johnson has been with me since I first began putting **Where to Find It . . .** together. Between the two of us there are tales to tell, and I could not have done it then or continued producing the book now without her patience and dependable expertise. Her husband, Jim Johnson, is in on the fun as well. Carrie Klein is my editor-at-large and a fine researcher who helps with particular chapters. Linda Chase has helped "detail" several editions and continues in that vein. Parke Puterbaugh is my superb editor who has been with me through many editions. We have a new terrific graphic artist, Nancy Chamberlain, whose debut is this 2008-2009 cover. Tom and Carole Stinski still typeset and are incredibly conscientious about producing the best product possible. Last, but not least, is my executive assistant and friend, Linda Wooters, who oversees the many facets of my life, as well as this book.

For all the changes over the years, New York remains for me what it was the first time I visited: magic. That's what I hope you'll find in these pages. To quote an old marketing line: I love New York! I hope you do, too.

Gerry Frank

I. In and Around the World's Greatest City

GETTING TO NEW YORK

So you're headed for New York! Whether you're traveling 90 miles from Philadelphia or 9,000 miles from Singapore, you're in for a wonderful treat. But first you'll need to get here.

AIRPORTS—New York City is served by three major airports, and more than 90 million people pass through them every year. **LaGuardia Airport** is the most frequently used for domestic flights, while **John F. Kennedy International Airport** (also referred to as "JFK" or "Kennedy") has both domestic and international flights to and from just about every nation. Both airports are in the borough of Queens, although LaGuardia is much closer to Manhattan than Kennedy is. **Newark Liberty International Airport** (commonly called "Newark"), across the Hudson River in New Jersey, handles both domestic and international flights as well. The most common ways of traveling between Manhattan and these airports are by taxicab, shuttle bus, and private car or limousine.

Taxi lines form in front of most terminals at all three airports, and the exits to them are usually well marked with signs that say "Ground Transportation." These lines are legitimate and generally move quickly. Assuming you don't run into bad traffic, a cab trip between LaGuardia and midtown will take about half an hour and cost roughly $25, plus bridge toll and tip. The trip between Kennedy and anywhere in Manhattan can take as long as an hour and costs a flat fee of $45, plus bridge or tunnel toll and tip. A taxi between Newark and Manhattan can also take as long as an hour and can be really costly: as much as $60 (the metered fare plus a $5 surcharge for any destination on the East Side of Manhattan and another $5 surcharge anywhere in New York during rush hour or on weekends between noon and 6), plus tolls and a $1 surcharge for each piece of luggage over 24 inches. If you have a preference for which route to take into or out of Manhattan from any of these airports, tell the driver in advance. And be forewarned: although they are required by law to do so, cab drivers in Manhattan don't like taking people to the airports because it's sometimes hard to get quick fares back. (In fact, they aren't even *allowed* to pick passengers up at Newark.) So give yourself a little extra time when you're getting ready to catch a cab to go to the airport.

If taxi fares seem a little steep, there are less expensive alternatives. Several companies run **shuttle buses** and **vans** between Manhattan and the airports. If you're alone and going to a major hotel in midtown, you can really save money by taking a shuttle. But it may not be worth it if there are others in your party to share a cab, if you're in a hurry, or if you're headed to a friend's apartment or an out-of-the-way hotel. Shuttle-bus tickets and schedules are available at the ground transportation desks at all three airports.

Of all the shuttle bus services in New York, I recommend **New York Airport Service** (212/875-8200, www.nyairportservice.com) for travel between LaGuardia or Kennedy and various midtown hotels as well as Grand Central Terminal, Penn Station, and Port Authority. In addition to reliable and convenient service, they offer discounts for round-trip tickets and special deals for families traveling with young children. If you're traveling from Newark, you might try **Newark Airport Express** (212/964-6233). The **SuperShuttle** (212/258-3826, www.supershuttle.com) also comes highly recommended and serves all three airports. For a complete list of options and prices, call the Port Authority's **Air-Ride** (800/247-7433). Between 8 a.m. and 6 p.m. on weekdays, you can talk to a live person. At other times, you'll get a comprehensive recording.

AirTrain is an affordable option from both Kennedy and Newark, although I would caution anyone with mobility limitations or lots of luggage against trying it. For $7 you can take AirTrain from Kennedy to the Howard Beach or Jamaica subway stops and then take a subway into Manhattan. If you're in a hurry and willing to pay a little more, you can also take the Long Island Railroad into Penn Station. From Newark, you can take AirTrain to the Newark Rail Link Station and then ride either Amtrak or New Jersey Transit into Penn Station. Call 800/626-7433 or go to www.panynj.gov/airtrain for detailed information.

Don't Say I Didn't Warn You

Under no circumstance should you follow someone who approaches to ask if you want a taxi or limousine ride. The crowd offering taxis and limousines can be quite daunting, and their offers may seem tempting if the airport is jammed; however, you'll end up paying far more than you should and will have absolutely no recourse. Check their credentials! Check their price!

If you really want to save money, are in no hurry, and don't mind schlepping your stuff, **public transportation** is also an option. For $3, you can take the M60 bus from LaGuardia to the corner of Lexington Avenue and 125th Street or Broadway and 116th Street and then any one of a half dozen subway lines into midtown and other parts of Manhattan. The same $3 will get you to Kennedy via subway (the E and F lines) and bus (the Green Line Q-10), but it takes almost two hours.

A fourth option is calling a private **car service** or **limousine** ahead of time. A driver will meet you at the gate or in the baggage claim area, holding up a sign with your last name on it. Depending on your personality, this will make you feel important, embarrassed, or a little bit of both. Be forewarned that a car or limo service can get pretty pricey, particularly if the driver has to wait because your flight is delayed. (They charge for waiting time.) Costs to and from LaGuardia run anywhere from $25 plus tip, if you want a sedan and everything goes smoothly, to well over $100, if there are delays or you request a limousine. Prices are higher to and from Kennedy and Newark. You can also secure a sedan or limousine after you've arrived by going to the ground transportation desks at any of the three airports. A consistently reliable, established company with a large fleet and published rate quotes is **Carmel** (212/666-6666 or www.carmellimo.com). **Carey** (212/599-1122, www.carey.com) is another well-respected company used mostly by corporate clients.

TRAINS—Dozens of Amtrak trains come in and out of New York City every day. Service is concentrated between Washington and Boston, but you can catch trains between New York and Florida, Chicago, or even Seattle and many cities in Canada. Although many people imagine themselves arriving by train at the historic and architecturally distinguished Grand Central Terminal, in actuality **Amtrak** runs in and out of the considerably less romantic Pennsylvania Station (commonly referred to as **Penn Station**). A major subway hub, Penn Station sits underneath Madison Square Garden between 31st and 33rd streets and Seventh and Eighth avenues.

You can choose between the Acela Express, sleeping cars, and other kinds of Amtrak service. Multi-day excursion passes are also available. Although the station is much improved from its dilapidated state a decade ago and actually includes an enclosed waiting area for ticketed Amtrak passengers in the middle of the main concourse, it's still not a place you will want to spend much time. (Call Amtrak at 800/872-7245 or go to www.amtrak.com for fare and schedule information.) Some **MetroNorth** commuter trains run in and out of Grand Central Terminal, although they are limited to stops in suburban Connecticut and New York. Call 800/638-7646 for schedules or stop by a ticket booth at Grand Central.

Don't Say I Didn't Warn You, Part Two

Single-occupancy vehicles are now banned from entering Manhattan between 6 a.m. and 10 a.m. on weekdays via all access routes. If you're traveling alone in Manhattan during those times, you can take a subway, bus, or taxi. Given the absence of below-ground traffic, the subway is definitely the fastest alternative.

DRIVING—If you can avoid driving to or in New York, by all means do so. Otherwise, you will end up paying exorbitant prices for tolls and parking (and your mental health will inevitably suffer, too). The fact that most New Yorkers don't own cars ought to tell you something! Traffic in and around the metropolitan area is horrendous, drivers are extremely aggressive, and the on-street parking rules are extraordinarily complicated. Once you're in New York, the only time you may possibly need a car is if you want to leave for a day or two—and then you can rent one, as many New Yorkers do. The public transportation system in New York is extremely efficient, inexpensive, and used frequently by just about everyone.

If you still aren't convinced or have no alternative, turn on your GPS or get a map before setting out and study it carefully. The three major approaches to the city involve the New England Thruway (I-95), the New York State Thruway (I-87), and the New Jersey Turnpike (I-95). Expect long waits during rush hour at the bridges and tunnels leading in and out of Manhattan. Turn to AM radio stations 770, 880, or 1010 for area traffic reports to help you decide which approach to take. Expect to pay a hefty toll for whichever bridge or tunnel you choose. And no matter what else you do, avoid rush hour (actually rush *hours*, as they occur through mid-morning and start again in mid-afternoon) and Sunday afternoon.

GETTING TO KNOW NEW YORK

In case you haven't already figured it out, this book isn't really about New York. It isn't even about New York City. It's about Manhattan. Most people (including me) use New York, New York City, "the city," and Manhattan synonymously. But New York is one of the 13 original colonies and among the Northeast's largest states, and New York City actually comprises five separate boroughs: Manhattan, Brooklyn, The Bronx, Queens, and Staten Island. Manhattan is one of the four boroughs that are islands (only The Bronx is attached to the mainland).

A Little History

Now that you know we're talking only about the island of Manhattan, a little history may help make sense of how the city is laid out. Native Americans were the first known residents of this area. Italian explorer Giovanni da Verrazano (for whom the Verrazano Narrows Bridge, linking Brooklyn and Staten Island, is named) sailed into New York Harbor in 1524 and "discovered" Manhattan for his French patron, King Francis I. In 1609, a trader for the Dutch East India Company named Henry Hudson sailed into the harbor and up the river that now bears his name. The first permanent European settlement in Manhattan, a Dutch trading post called Nieuw Amsterdam, was established in 1625 at the southern tip of the island, where Battery Park is today. The story you've heard since childhood about representatives of the Dutch East India Company "buying" the area from local Indians for inexpensive beads, cloth, and other trinkets is accurate, except, of course, the two sides had vastly different understandings of what their agreement meant. It was renamed New York in 1664 after the British—in the person of Charles II's brother, the Duke of York—gained control of the still-tiny settlement.

It's hard to imagine today, but such areas as midtown and even Greenwich Village were way out in the country for another 150 years. Indeed, Wall Street is so named because a wall of logs was erected there in the mid-17th century to protect the farms in lower Manhattan from the wilderness to the north. New York's population—which numbered only 60,000 as late as 1800—remained concentrated on the southern tip of the island, while most of Manhattan was used for country estates and farmland or just left as forests and wilderness. Indeed, pigs were roaming around Wall Street well into the 19th century. When a commission headed by engineer John Randall, Jr., laid out a grid system for the largely undeveloped area from Houston Street north to 155th Street in 1807, most residents thought it entirely unnecessary.

THE RANDALL PLAN—For those trying to find their way around Manhattan, the so-called Randall Plan is a godsend. The streets below Houston (pronounced *House*-ton), particularly those below Canal Street, meander like the Dutch farm trails they once were. Even the relatively straight ones were not built for 21st-century traffic. World-famous Wall Street, for example, is narrower than the typical suburban driveway. Truth be told, not much about the city's layout makes sense south of 14th Street. If you're ever at the corner of West 4th Street and West 10th Street in Greenwich Village, you'll know what I mean!

Thanks to the Randall Plan, however, everything north of 14th Street is just about as simple as a major city can be. With the exception of Broadway—originally a well-worn footpath and now one of the country's longest streets, extending from the southern tip of Manhattan to the capital city of Albany—and some of the streets in northern Manhattan, the streets and avenues are laid out in a north-south, east-west grid. All of the east-west streets are numbered, as are many of the north-south avenues. In general, most avenues are one-way and alternately northbound and southbound. Most streets are one-way as well: the even-numbered ones tend to be east-bound, and the odd-numbered ones westbound. Two-way exceptions include such major east-west thoroughfares as Canal, Houston, 14th, 23rd, 34th, 42nd, 57th, 72nd, 79th, 86th, 96th, 110th, and 125th streets. (See the "Key to Addresses" section for help with finding a specific address.)

EAST SIDE, WEST SIDE—Starting just north of Washington Square Park at about 8th Street in Greenwich Village, Fifth Avenue divides the city into east and west sides. Broadway, built on an old Native American trade route, acts as the east-west dividing line south of Washington Square, although it runs a little east of where Fifth Avenue would be. That east-west distinction is important, as most addresses in New York reflect it. For example, 125 East 52nd Street and 125 West 52nd Street are two distinct locations several blocks apart.

Let's start with the **East Side** of the city. Moving east from Fifth Avenue toward the East River, you'll cross Madison Avenue, Park Avenue (called Park Avenue South below 34th Street and Fourth Avenue below that), Lexington Avenue (called Irving Place between 14th and 20th streets), Third Avenue, Second Avenue, and First Avenue. Madison Avenue doesn't start until 23rd Street, while Lexington Avenue begins as Irving Place at 14th Street. Sutton Place starts at 51st Street between First Avenue and the river, turns into York Avenue at 60th Street, and stops at 92nd Street. East End Avenue runs between York Avenue and the river from 79th to 90th streets. All of these avenues run north-south, parallel to Fifth Avenue. FDR Drive ("The FDR" to locals) hugs the aptly named East River along the east side of the island.

The **West Side** of Manhattan is a bit more confusing. Moving west from Fifth Avenue toward the Hudson River, you'll find Avenue of the Americas (or Sixth Avenue, as everyone still calls it, despite the official name change in the 1950s), Seventh Avenue, Eighth Avenue (known as Central Park West north of 59th Street), Ninth Avenue (Columbus Avenue north of 59th Street), Tenth Avenue (Amsterdam Avenue north of 59th Street), and Eleventh Avenue (West End Avenue between 59th Street and its end at 107th Street). You'll also find Broadway meandering about the West Side above 23rd Street. Avenue of the Americas and Seventh Avenue both stop at the south end of Central Park. Riverside Drive runs parallel to West End Avenue near the Hudson River north of 72nd Street. All of these avenues run north-south and parallel to Fifth Avenue (except Broadway, which meanders diagonally before more or less straightening out around 79th Street). The Henry Hudson Parkway (also known as the West Side Highway and sometimes called Twelfth Avenue around midtown) runs along the far west side of the city.

Central Park occupies land between 59th and 110th streets, further dividing the East Side from the West Side north of midtown Manhattan. Fifth Avenue runs along the east side of the park, and everything east of it is known as the Upper East Side. Central Park West runs along the west side of the park, and everything west of it is known as the Upper West Side. Both the Upper East Side and Upper West Side are largely residential, although many of the north-south avenues have lots of shops, restaurants, and professional offices.

NORTHERN MANHATTAN—The avenues on the East Side remain fairly consistent as they move north of Central Park into the area known as East (or Spanish) Harlem. Lenox Avenue (which soon becomes Malcolm X Boulevard) picks up where Avenue of the Americas left off below the park. Adam Clayton Powell, Jr. Boulevard picks up where Seventh Avenue left off. Central Park West becomes Frederick Douglass Boulevard. Amsterdam Avenue, Broadway, and Riverside Drive all extend into Northern Manhattan, while such major roads as Convent Avenue, St. Nicholas Avenue, Edgecombe Avenue, and Fort Washington Avenue are exclusive to Harlem and the northern tip of Manhattan.

Every Street Has a Story

If I had nothing but time, I've always thought a great way to know New York would be to walk one street every day. Every street in this great city has a lot of stories to tell, some very personal, some woven into the city's history, and some unfolding right now. One of my favorite streets to walk is **West 12th Street** in Greenwich Village. In the nine blocks between **First Presbyterian Church**, on the corner of West 12th Street and Fifth Avenue, and **Hudson River Park**, on the west side of West Street, you can find everything from a thriving **Greenmarket** (at Abingdon Square on Saturday) to **S.F. Vanni**, a quirky Italian-language bookstore (30 W 12th St) to the home of the **James Beard Foundation** (167 W 12th St). Along the way, you'll also see some wonderful examples of Greek Revival and Neo-Federal architecture. **Barbuto** (at Washington St), **Jarnac** (at Greenwich St), and **Village Den** (at Greenwich Ave) are all great spots to grab a bite if you're down here.

Key to Addresses

So how do you find an address in Manhattan? Manhattan phone directories and other publications generally include cross-street information as part of their address listings. If you have an address without a cross street, however, here's a reliable system for figuring it out:

AVENUES—If you have a numerical address on one of the north-south avenues, you can determine the approximate cross street by dropping the last number, dividing the remainder by two, and adding or subtracting the number indicated.

Avenue A, B, C, or D	Add 3
First Avenue	Add 3
Second Avenue	Add 3
Third Avenue	Add 10
Lexington Avenue	Add 22

Fourth Avenue/Park Avenue South ..... Add 8
Park Avenue .... Add 35
Madison Avenue .... Add 26
Fifth Avenue
• addresses up to 200 .... Add 13
• between 201 and 400 .... Add 16
• between 401 and 600 .... Add 18
• between 601 and 774 .... Add 20
• between 775 and 1286 .... Subtract 18
• between 1289 and 1500 .... Add 45
• addresses up to 2000 .... Add 24
Avenue of the Americas/Sixth Avenue ... Subtract 12
Lenox Avenue/Malcolm X Boulevard ... Add 110
Seventh Avenue .... Add 12
Adam Clayton Powell, Jr. Boulevard ..... Add 20
Broadway
• addresses up to 754 are below 8th Street
• between 754 and 858 .... Subtract 29
• between 859 and 958 .... Subtract 25
• addresses above 1000 .... Subtract 30
Eighth Avenue .... Add 10
Ninth Avenue .... Add 13
Columbus Avenue .... Add 60
Tenth Avenue .... Add 14
Amsterdam Avenue .... Add 60
Eleventh Avenue .... Add 15
West End Avenue .... Add 60
Convent Avenue .... Add 127
St. Nicholas Avenue .... Add 110
Manhattan Avenue .... Add 100
Edgecombe Avenue .... Add 134
Fort Washington Avenue .... Add 158

Five area codes and 11 digits!

The proliferation of cell phones, pagers, and fax machines has meant that three new area codes—917, 347, and 646—have been added to 212 (Manhattan) and 718 (New York's other four boroughs). Whether you're calling across the street or out to Staten Island, all calls now require dialing 11 digits: the numeral 1, plus the area code and phone number, although calls may not be long distance.

Central Park West and Riverside Drive have formulas of their own. To find the cross street for a building on Central Park West, divide the address by 10 and add 60. To find the cross street for a building on Riverside Drive up to 165th Street, divide the address by 10 and add 72.

A word of caution: because certain addresses—particularly those on Fifth, Madison, and Park avenues—are thought to be particularly prestigious, many buildings use them even if their entrances are actually on a side street. This is most common in midtown and along Fifth Avenue on the Upper East Side. So if you can't find an address, look around the corner.

CROSS STREETS—Numbered cross streets run east-west. Addresses on them are easy to find. Allow for a little variation below 23rd Street (because Madison, Eleventh, and Twelfth avenues have yet to begin) and throughout the city whenever Broadway is involved.

EAST SIDE

1 to 49 .... between Fifth Avenue and Madison Avenue
50 to 99 .... between Madison Avenue and Park Avenue
100 to 149 ..... between Park Avenue and Lexington Avenue
150 to 199 ..... between Lexington Avenue and Third Avenue
200 to 299 ..... between Third Avenue and Second Avenue
300 to 399 ..... between Second Avenue and First Avenue
400 to 499 ..... between First Avenue and York Avenue

New York and Presidential History

Few places in our country have the rich history of New York. Whether you're interested in Colonial America, the Revolutionary War, the Civil War, the history of immigration, the labor movement, or the civil rights movement, New York is just brimming with stories and sights.

Presidential history buffs will want to know that:

- General George Washington used the **Morris-Jumel Mansion** (Edgecombe Ave at 160th St) as his headquarters during the Battle of Harlem Heights and gave his farewell address to his troops at **Fraunces Tavern** (54 Pearl St).
- President George Washington was inaugurated at **Federal Hall National Memorial** (26 Wall St).
- Republican presidential candidate Abraham Lincoln gave an historic anti-slavery speech that many consider the turning point in his campaign at **Cooper-Union** (30 Cooper Square) in 1860. Five years later, his body lay in state in the **City Hall rotunda** (Chambers St at Broadway).
- President Ulysses S. Grant and his wife are buried at **Grant's Tomb** in **Riverside Park** (Riverside Dr at 122nd St).
- President Theodore Roosevelt was born on East 20th Street (now the **Theodore Roosevelt Birthplace National Historic Site**, at 28 E 20th St).
- President Herbert Hoover lived in the tower at the **Waldorf-Astoria** (301 Park Ave) for many years after he left the White House.
- President Dwight Eisenhower was president of **Columbia University** (Broadway at 116th St) before he sat in the Oval Office.
- The offices of the **William J. Clinton Foundation** are located at 55 West 125th Street in Harlem. The former president's wife, of course, is the senior U.S. Senator from New York and a leading presidential candidate for the 2008 election as this book goes to press.

WEST SIDE BELOW 59th STREET

1 to 99 ...... between Fifth Avenue and Avenue of the Americas
100 to 199 ..... between Avenue of the Americas and Seventh Avenue

200 to 299 . . . . . between Seventh Avenue and Eighth Avenue
300 to 399 . . . . . between Eighth Avenue and Ninth Avenue
400 to 499 . . . . . between Ninth Avenue and Tenth Avenue
500 to 599 . . . . . between Tenth Avenue and Eleventh Avenue
600 and up . . . . . between Eleventh Avenue and Twelfth Avenue

WEST SIDE ABOVE 59th STREET
I to 99   . . . . . . between Central Park West and Columbus Avenue
100 to 199 . . . . between Columbus Avenue and Amsterdam Avenue
200 to 299 . . . . between Amsterdam Avenue and West End Avenue
300 and up . . . . between West End Avenue and Riverside Drive

Odd-numbered addresses on east-west streets are on the north (uptown) side, while even-numbered ones are on the south (downtown) side.

West *What* Street?

Even native New Yorkers would have trouble identifying all of the honorary street names scattered throughout the city. Leonard Bernstein Way? West 65th Street between Broadway and Amsterdam Avenue, just north of Avery Fisher Hall. But what about streets named for such less familiar eminences as Josh Rosenthal Way? West 72nd Street between Columbus Avenue and Central Park West. Joe Horvath Street? West 52nd Street between Tenth and Eleventh avenues. Abraham Kazan Street? Grand Street, down on the Lower East Side. R. Lonnie Williams Place? Uptown, on East 104th Street.

Neighborhoods

It may be hard for visitors to believe, given New York's size, but the city is really a collection of small neighborhoods. Some of these neighborhoods are more famous than others, and their borders may ebb and flow over the years, but each has a history and flavor all its own. To get a full sense of this wonderful city, I encourage you to visit as many neighborhoods as possible. From north to south, they include:

INWOOD AND WASHINGTON HEIGHTS—Home to General George Washington's forces during the Revolutionary War, these neighborhoods cover all of Manhattan north of about 151st Street. Racially and ethnically mixed, they have been home to generations of immigrants and now include everything from trendy to middle-class and poor areas. Several large and remarkably unspoiled parks, **Yeshiva University**, the **Dyckman Farmhouse**, **The Cloisters**, **Columbia-Presbyterian Hospital**, and **Audubon Terrace** are all in this area, as is the entrance to the **George Washington Bridge**. As the name implies, Washington Heights contains some surprisingly steep sections.

HARLEM—There are actually two Harlems: East Harlem (also called Spanish Harlem) and Harlem proper. East Harlem begins at about 96th Street and runs along the east side of the island to its northern tip. The population of this area is predominantly Latino, and Spanish is spoken more frequently than English here. **El Museo del Barrio** is on the southwestern edge of East Harlem.

Harlem itself occupies a small corridor in the middle of the island at the top of Central Park (at 110th Street) and then extends north and west of the famous and always busy 125th Street. That thoroughfare has again become a major shopping and entertainment hub, thanks in large part to the leadership of former NBA star Magic Johnson. The population of Harlem is largely African-American, and the historic neighborhood is known around the world as a center of African-American music, politics, and culture. Here you'll find the **Schomburg Center for Research in Black Culture**, the **Apollo Theater, Abyssinian Baptist Church**, and the **Studio Museum of Harlem**, as well as the offices of former President Bill Clinton.

MORNINGSIDE HEIGHTS—This relatively small but vibrant area runs between Morningside Drive and the Hudson River from 110th Street to 124th Street. The stretch of Broadway between those streets is the neighborhood's economic heart. The area is dominated by three large and well-known institutions: **Columbia University, Riverside Church**, and the **Cathedral Church of St. John the Divine**. **Grant's Tomb** is across from Riverside Church, at 122nd Street in Riverside Park. This politically liberal and wonderfully diverse neighborhood is full of students, professors, and visitors from all over the world.

UPPER WEST SIDE—This primarily residential area extends west of Central Park to the Hudson River from Columbus Circle at 59th Street all the way north to 110th Street. The Upper West Side is home to such famous apartment buildings as the **Dakota** and the **Ansonia**. The neighborhood is racially and ethnically mixed, and its residents pride themselves for being politically progressive and tending toward the bohemian (although by downtown standards, Upper West Siders are decidedly conventional).

Like a lot of Manhattan neighborhoods, the Upper West Side is brimming with children and families. Thanks in large part to entrepreneur Donald Trump, even the once grim Columbus Circle, at the southwest corner of Central Park, has been reborn with the **Time Warner Center** and its **Shops at Columbus Circle**. A little farther north, the **ABC Studio** (where talk shows and soap operas are taped) and **Lincoln Center** dominate the low and high ends of cultural life, respectively. The fabulous food stores **Fairway** and **Zabar's** are landmarks a bit farther north. So are the **American Museum of Natural History** and the **New-York Historical Society**, both located on Central Park West. **Barnes & Noble** at Broadway and 82nd Street has become a major fixture in the neighborhood as well. Columbus Avenue, Amsterdam Avenue, and Broadway are lined with stores, while Central Park West, West End Avenue, and Riverside Drive are almost exclusively residential. The most elegant living areas of the Upper West Side are on Central Park West and the cross streets in the high 60s, the 70s, and the low 80s. Although even many longtime New Yorkers may suppose there's little worth visiting between 96th Street and Harlem, that area—particularly on Broadway—is alive with good restaurants, neighborhood shops, and jazz clubs.

UPPER EAST SIDE—Best known for art museums, galleries, and upscale boutiques, the Upper East Side is also the city's most prestigious old-money residential neighborhood. It covers the area east of Central Park from Fifth Avenue to the East River between 59th and 96th streets. Fifth

Avenue (also known as **Museum Mile**) is dominated by such famous institutions as the **Metropolitan, Guggenheim,** and **Cooper-Hewitt** museums. It is also home to a large number of expensive apartment buildings, former mansions, and foreign consulates, as well as many of Manhattan's elite private schools. On Madison Avenue you'll find the **Whitney Museum** and lots of galleries, all sorts of chic international designers and retailers in the 60s and lower 70s, and upscale boutiques and shops in the upper 70s and lower 80s. Park Avenue and most of the cross streets are home to residential buildings and such institutions as the **Asia Society** and the **Americas Society**. From Lexington Avenue east to the river above 75th Street—an area known as **Yorkville**—rents go down a bit. You'll find **Gracie Mansion,** the mayor's residence in Carl Schurz Park, overlooking the river at about 88th Street. **Bloomingdale's** has long been a major retail force at the southern end of the Upper East Side.

Only in New York!
    The newsstand at the corner of Broadway and 32nd Street—an area close to the Diamond District and known for its sizable Korean business population—may be the only one in the world that sells newspapers in Hebrew, Korean, and English.

MIDTOWN—Squarely in the middle of the island south of 59th Street, midtown Manhattan is one of the busiest places on earth on weekdays and is less crowded, except for an ever-increasing number of tourists, on Sundays. (During Christmas season, tourists and natives alike flock to midtown.) The area extends from 42nd to 59th streets between Third and Seventh avenues. Fifth Avenue, home to the most expensive rental real estate in the world, is the heart of midtown and one of the world's most famous shopping areas. The flagship stores of **Tiffany's, F.A.O. Schwarz, Saks Fifth Avenue,** and **Bergdorf Goodman** are all here, as are such pop-culture icons as **Niketown** and **The Gap**. Many stately mansions once lined this part of Fifth Avenue, but only a few remain and none still serves as a residence.

    St. Patrick's Cathedral and several other famous churches are also on Fifth Avenue in midtown. **St. Bartholomew's** is on Park Avenue, and the stately **Central Synagogue** is on Lexington Avenue. Landmark buildings like the **Citicorp Center, Trump Tower, Rockefeller Center,** and the **Chrysler Building** dominate the skyline. **Carnegie Hall,** the **Ed Sullivan Theater,** and **Radio City Music Hall** occupy the western edge of midtown. The once-elegant 57th Street, on the north edge of midtown, is definitely a lot less exclusive these days, as stores like Swatch, Sunglass Hut, and Victoria's Secret sit side-by-side with Chanel, Prada, and Louis Vuitton. **Grand Central Terminal,** the **New York Public Library,** and the vibrant **Bryant Park** mark midtown's southern edge.

CLINTON—Home to the infamous Hell's Kitchen Gang a century ago, this neighborhood was long known as Hell's Kitchen and was once among the most violent and dangerous neighborhoods in the country. No longer! It stretches south from 59th Street to 34th Street between Eighth Avenue and the Hudson River. Led by the startling transformation of the **Times**

Square area into a family-friendly tourist mecca, much of Clinton has been gentrified. The always crowded and still scruffy **Port Authority Bus Terminal** is on Eighth Avenue in the southern part of this neighborhood. Ninth Avenue, particularly in the high 30s and 40s, is home to a lot of ethnic grocers, bakers, butchers, and restaurants. The west end of 42nd Street boasts some very good off-Broadway theaters. The **Jacob K. Javits Convention Center** and most of the city's passenger-ship terminals are located here along the Hudson River. Long considered one of the few "affordable" neighborhoods in New York, this area has seen lots of high-rise construction in recent years and plans are in the works for much more.

MURRAY HILL—Covering the East Side from 42nd Street south to 34th Street, Murray Hill begins at Park Avenue and runs to the East River. This area is almost entirely residential, and the nicest part can be found around Park Avenue in the upper 30s. The only real visitor attractions are the **Morgan Library** and the incredible **Science, Industry, and Business Library** in the old B. Altman Building at Madison Avenue and 34th Street.

Harlem is Hot!

In the nearly three decades that I've been writing this book, the fortunes of certain neighborhoods have risen and fallen dramatically. Property values have gone through the roof in the northern part of the Upper West Side in recent years, and Harlem is experiencing another renaissance. The renovated **Apollo Theater** (253 W 125th St) is full of energy almost every night, the **Studio Museum** (144 W 125th St) showcases luminaries in the art world, and the **Schomburg Center for Research in Black Culture** (515 Malcolm X Blvd) has become a world-class research institution.

Spend a day in Harlem and discover some lesser-known treasures like **The Brownstone** (2032 Fifth Ave), which is the cafe and boutique for independent clothing designers; **Hue-Man Bookstore and Cafe** (2319 Frederick Douglass Blvd), which stocks the city's best and biggest selection of African-American children's books; and **Wimps Southern Style Bakery, Sky Cafe and Martini Bar** (29 W 125th St), which offers a mouth-watering selection of fabulous baked goods and an upstairs bar. Former President Bill Clinton's offices are at 55 West 125th Street.

CHELSEA—This neighborhood began taking off more than a decade ago and hasn't looked back. Still a largely residential neighborhood, despite its influx of galleries, restaurants, and (lately) big-box stores, Chelsea extends from 34th Street down to 14th Street between Avenue of the Americas and the Hudson River. **Madison Square Garden** and **Penn Station** are in the northeast corner of Chelsea, but it's the southern part of the neighborhood that has really taken off. Surprisingly quiet and relatively clean, the southwestern part of Chelsea has turn-of-the-century townhouses and small apartment buildings. It's also home to the lovely grounds of the **General Theological Seminary** and the **Chelsea Piers** development. What's really gotten the city's attention, however, are the almost 200 galleries that have migrated to the western edge of Chelsea, between 20th and 26th streets. Meanwhile, the southeastern edge of Chelsea, particularly where Chelsea and the Flatiron District overlap along Avenue of the Americas in the high teens and low 20s, has become what it was a century ago: a retailing hub. Such superstores as **Bed Bath & Beyond, Barnes & Noble**, and **Burlington Coat Factory** occupy buildings that once housed famous department stores.

FLATIRON DISTRICT—Named for the historic Flatiron Building, an architectural curiosity at the intersection of Broadway and Fifth Avenue at 23rd Street, this area was known as Ladies' Mile in the late 19th century for its elegant department stores. (A famous jingle at the time: "From 8th Street down, the men are earning it/From 8th Street up, the women are spending it.") Those department stores went out of business a century ago, but the buildings and the neighborhood are again alive and well, thanks in large part to an influx of superstores. The Flatiron District runs between Park Avenue South and Avenue of the Americas from 23rd Street down to 14th Street. Avenue of the Americas is really thriving, and parts of Fifth Avenue in this area also have undergone a resurgence. The **Church of the Transfiguration** (affectionately known as "the Little Church Around the Corner"), the **Marble Collegiate Church**, and the **Empire State Building** are all just north of here.

GRAMERCY PARK—This aging but still pleasant neighborhood was once the city's most elegant residential area. It covers the area from Park Avenue South to Second Avenue between 34th Street and 14th Street. The nicest part is **Gramercy Park** itself. The city's only remaining private park, it is bounded by Park Avenue South, Third Avenue, and 20th and 21st streets. A stroll down Irving Place, which runs from the park south to 14th Street, can be very pleasant indeed. The Flatiron District and the Gramercy Park area meet at **Union Square**, a lively area that is home to the city's largest and most popular Greenmarket. The **New York Police Academy** and **Theodore Roosevelt's birthplace** are on the western edge of Gramercy Park, and **Stuyvesant Square Park** occupies both sides of Second Avenue between 15th and 17th streets. Two huge planned residential areas, Stuyvesant Town and Peter Cooper Village, abut the East River, as does Bellevue Hospital.

MEATPACKING DISTRICT—This is one of the city's most bizarre and fascinating neighborhoods. I'm not suggesting that the average tourist would want to wander around here. However, the neighborhood west of Ninth Avenue (from 15th Street south to Gansevoort Street, between Chelsea and the West Village) is being shaped by a collision of interesting forces. Traditionally this dirty, architecturally uninteresting area has been the home of New York's meatpacking industry, as well as a great deal of prostitution. But the number of meatpacking businesses has dropped precipitously and community action has forced much of the prostitution elsewhere. Meanwhile, artists, bar owners, ultra-trendy boutiques and fashion designers, and even young families are attracted by the neighborhood's relatively cheap rents. The result is a weird mix of trendy bars, fashionable boutiques, wholesale meatpacking plants, transvestites, and Midwestern tourists seeking to be chic. There's even an ultramodern (and ultra-costly) hotel—the Gansevoort —for the beautiful people.

EAST VILLAGE—In the middle of the 19th century, the Astors, the Vanderbilts, and much of the rest of fashionable New York called the area we now know as the East Village home. Two decades ago, it was known for its drugs, squatters, and general filth. Today the East Village is among the city's funkiest and, surprisingly, most livable neighborhoods. It lies between Avenue B and Broadway from 14th Street down to Houston Street. Alphabet City (the avenues in the eastern part of the East Village that have letters for names) and **Tompkins Square** are much tamer than they were a decade ago, and many parts have become gentrified to the point of being family-friendly, but they're still home to some offbeat and colorful nightclubs, shops, and people. The area along 6th Street between First and Second avenues is a thriving ethnic enclave known as Little India. The area around 7th Street and Third Avenue is home to a great many Ukrainian immigrants, and Stuyvesant Street is a gathering spot for young people from Japan. The **Ukrainian Museum**, **St. Mark's in the Bowery**, and **Grace Church** are all in the northern part of the East Village. **Old Merchant's House**, the last remnant of the East Village of yesteryear, is on its western edge.

New York Districts

The **Fulton Fish Market** is gone. The **Flower District** and the **Garment District** are pale imitations of their former selves. But while most of the dozens of distinct shopping districts that once defined New York are gone or in precipitous decline, a few "only in New York" areas—shopping and otherwise—are still worth noting:

- **Diamond District**—Jewelers and gem-cutters are concentrated on 47th Street between Fifth Avenue and Avenue of the Americas.
- **Financial District** (a.k.a. "Wall Street")—Banks, investment firms, and stock markets are headquartered between Broadway and Water Street from Maiden Lane to Exchange Place.
- **Museum Mile**—Some of New York's finest museums are strung along Fifth Avenue from 70th Street north.
- **Theater District**—Renowned on- and off-Broadway theaters occupy Broadway and Eighth Avenue from 44th to 48th streets and on 42nd Street between Ninth and Tenth avenues.
- **Crystal District**—The five-block stretch of Madison Avenue between 58th and 63rd streets is home to Steuben, Swarovski, Baccarat, Daum, and Lalique.

You'll also find a cluster of **kitchen-supply stores** on the Bowery north of Delancey and Grand streets; **women's shoes** on 8th Street between Fifth Avenue and Avenue of the Americas; some **bead and notions stores** on Avenue of the Americas in the high 20s and low 30s; and several good **paper stores** on 18th Street between Fifth Avenue and Avenue of the Americas.

GREENWICH VILLAGE—Although Greenwich Village is best known for the beatniks and jazz clubs of the 1950s and the folk scene of the 1960s, it's also true that Edgar Allan Poe, Walt Whitman, Edna St. Vincent Millay, Frederic Church, and Edward Hopper all lived here at one time or another.

In fact, this area has been among the city's most vibrant centers of culture (and *counter*culture) since relatively affluent New Yorkers began moving here in the early part of the 19th century to avoid the health epidemics of the increasingly crowded city to the south. Greenwich Village covers most of the area from Broadway west to the Hudson River between 14th Street and Houston Street. The section from Seventh Avenue to the river is known to locals as the West Village, and the part west of Ninth Avenue is the Meatpacking District. The beautiful **Jefferson Market Library**, the **Forbes Magazine Galleries**, **New York University**, and lots of interesting shops and nightclubs are located here, as is the always lively **Washington Square Park** and its famed arch. If you're going to spend time walking around here, relax and enjoy the Village without worrying about exactly what street you're on. The streets down here are confusing at best, but the area is small and you can't really get lost.

Where Is Little Italy?

Yes, it still exists—sort of. As Chinatown and Nolita expand and the few remaining Italian immigrants move elsewhere, Little Italy lives on really only for tourists. Mulberry Street (known to locals as Via San Gennaro) around Grand Street is still home to a few Italian restaurants and stores. But, like the Garment District and the bookstores of Fifth Avenue, Little Italy is largely just a memory now.

SOHO—Short for *South of Houston*, Soho went from being the center of New York in the middle of the 19th century to an almost entirely abandoned wasteland in the middle of the 20th century. Rediscovered by artists looking for inexpensive space in the 1960s and by upscale boutiques and retailers in the 1990s, it's now so trendy—that is to say, crowded and overrun with designer boutiques and tourists—that many artists, galleries, and now even some of the same high-end retailers who flocked to the area just a few years ago have moved to other parts of town. That said, it's still an energetic and dynamic neighborhood that's fun to walk around. Soho begins several blocks below Washington Square Park on Houston Street and runs south to Canal Street between Broadway and Avenue of the Americas. The neighborhood comes alive on weekends and in the evening. Almost everything down here stays open later than similar establishments in the rest of the city. Many of the neighborhood's commercial galleries are concentrated on and around West Broadway (a separate street located four blocks west of Broadway) between Houston and Broome streets.

TRIBECA—Shorthand for *Triangle Below Canal*, Tribeca used to be a rather dull and dirty commercial district but is becoming both residential and every bit as chic as Soho. It covers the area from Canal Street south to Chambers Street between Broadway and the Hudson River. Although it doesn't look as upscale as you might expect and can be very confusing for outsiders wandering around, Tribeca is home to emerging and established artists, commercial galleries, converted loft apartments, movie stars (Robert DeNiro's **Tribeca Film Center** has become a fixture), some good restaurants, and lots of boutiques.

CHINATOWN—This neighborhood's 150,000 residents, who occupy roughly 40 square blocks, make up the largest concentration of Chinese population outside of Asia. Because it is always growing and increasingly overlaps such neighborhoods as Little Italy and the Lower East Side, Chinatown has boundaries nobody can quite agree how to define. Roughly speaking, it runs from Grand Street south to Worth Street, between Broadway and Allen Street. Its busiest streets are Canal, Mott, and Pell. If you've ever been to Hong Kong or southern China, you'll be overwhelmed by the similarities between those places and this neighborhood. Look for all sorts of wonderful food stores, as well as the **Museum of Chinese in the Americas** and the marvelous Chinese New Year parade and celebration.

> If you know where you want to go but aren't sure how to get there, log on to **www.hopstop.com** for directions to any street address in New York via subway, bus, or on foot. This great website also includes itineraries proposed by readers and tips on where to go (and where *not* to go!). You can use it for cities like Chicago and Boston as well.

NOLITA—Short for *North of Little Italy*, Nolita is a tiny neighborhood packed with vibrant restaurants, galleries, and boutiques. The entire area lies between Houston and Kenmare streets on Mulberry, Lafayette, Mott, and Elizabeth streets.

LOWER EAST SIDE—Many people use the Lower East Side as a geographic umbrella for Chinatown, Little Italy, and the Bowery, but I know it as a distinct neighborhood where generations of Eastern European and other immigrants first settled in overcrowded tenements and worked in sweatshops so their children could have better lives. (Many newer immigrants still live and work here in conditions that are not as much improved as you might think, although the immigrants and longtime retailers are being pushed out by yuppies looking for "affordable" housing and the increasing rents that follow them.) I also know it as what has historically been the best place in Manhattan to shop for high-quality clothing, household goods, and accessories at a discount. Because some of the area's businesses are still run by religiously observant Jews, they are closed for Shabbat on Friday afternoon and Saturday. Sunday is the shopping day here. Canal and Orchard streets are the area's heart, but the Lower East Side extends broadly from Houston to Canal streets and from the Sara D. Roosevelt Parkway east to Ludlow Street. The area still looks pretty run-down and many of the old stores are really struggling, but some of the old-timers are becoming more retail-savvy as their shops are increasingly interspersed with hip clubs, chic boutiques, art galleries, and new restaurants. Make sure to stop by the **Lower East Side Tenement Museum** and the **Eldridge Street Synagogue** to get a sense of the area's rich history.

DOWNTOWN—This area is a little hard to define except to say that it's centered around **City Hall**. Very roughly speaking, it runs from Chambers Street south to Fulton Street and from West Broadway east to Pearl Street. Many mom-and-pop stores and major chains are sited here, and its streets are always busy. **St. Paul's Chapel**, the **Woolworth Building**, the entrance to the **Brooklyn Bridge** pedestrian walkway, and the beautifully restored City Hall Park are all reasons to spend a little time here. Despite lots of improvements recently, this area always seems dirtier than the rest of the city. The **South Street Seaport** is located just east of downtown, and it's an easy walk south to Wall Street and Battery Park.

LOWER MANHATTAN—Extending from Wall Street and other parts of the Financial District south to Battery Park, this is the oldest part of New York City and was home to the World Trade Center. The hardest hit by the lingering aftermath of the terrorist attacks of September 11, 2001, it remains a very somber place. Things are very compact and vertical down here, with the streets as narrow as the buildings are tall. The boat to the **Statue of Liberty** and **Ellis Island** leaves from near **Castle Clinton National Monument** in Battery Park, and the **Staten Island Ferry**'s terminal is just east of the park. While in Lower Manhattan, look for the exceptional **Museum of the American Indian**, **Trinity Church**, the **Federal Hall National Memorial**, **Fraunces Tavern Museum**, and the **Museum of American Financial History**.

BATTERY PARK CITY—A planned residential area built entirely on landfill created when the original World Trade Center site was excavated in the 1970s, this collection of high-rise apartment buildings sits on the western side of Manhattan's southern tip, starting a bit north of Battery Park itself. The **World Financial Center**, where a lot of its residents work, is planted squarely in the middle of this neighborhood, and the **Museum of Jewish Heritage** is at its southern tip. Of course it's important to note that the World Trade Center sat on this neighborhood's eastern edge, and its absence has created a devastating hole, both physically and psychologically. While work to build a memorial on the site and to rebuild some of the surrounding area is ongoing, that hole will be there for many years to come.

Attention Older Visitors!

If you have trouble climbing long flights of stairs, avoid the subway! Most stations have steep stairways and few have elevators. Buses, on the other hand, can kneel to ease access from the curb, and newer ones have ramps instead of stairs. By law, taxi drivers are required to help disabled passengers and cannot start the meter until passengers are safely settled.

GETTING AROUND NEW YORK

Because it is an island and cannot sprawl outward, New York is compact and easier to navigate than most of the world's other large cities. You have a range of choices for how to get around, listed here in order of personal preference.

WALKING—Without question, this is my favorite way to get around New York. It may seem a little overwhelming at first (particularly in midtown at rush hour), and you'll stick out like a sore thumb if you wait on the curb for the "walk" signs, but walking is definitely the best way to see the city and get a sense of its neighborhoods. Often, especially in midtown on a weekday, walking is also the fastest way to travel ten or more blocks. Walking north-south (uptown or downtown), 20 blocks are equivalent to one mile. Most east-west (crosstown) blocks, particularly those between Fifth and Seventh avenues, are much longer. Unless you have small children in tow or are trying to get from Columbia University (at 116th Street) to New York University (at 4th Street), walking is the least expensive and most interesting way to travel. Just be aware of traffic and wear comfortable walking shoes!

SUBWAY—Some visitors and natives love to ride the subway, while others will do anything to avoid it. The millions of people who ride subways every weekday know it's usually the fastest and most efficient way to travel in the city. The subway can get very crowded, so if you get claustrophobic, avoid it around rush hour. Always hold on tightly to the hands of children who are with you. Thanks to an ongoing anti-grafitti campaign, a beefed-up police presence, an increasingly well-enforced ban on panhandling, and lots of renovations, the experience also has become significantly more pleasant.

The subway system is the result of a merger of private lines like the BMT and the IRT that sprang up over a century ago. Some of the stations and cars are quite old, so don't expect the relative luxury of BART in San Francisco or the Metro in Washington, D.C. Its 714 miles of track connect every borough except Staten Island. In Manhattan, the system is concentrated south of 110th Street (particularly below 59th Street). Maps of the system are available at station booths and are posted in most subway cars and stations. If you need to study a map, I suggest doing so in your hotel room or some other private place so as not to advertise the fact that you don't know where you're going. You'll also find a detailed map of the subway system in the front section of the Manhattan Yellow Pages.

The stairs leading down to most subway stations are almost always on a corner, marked by signs with a big "M" or "MTA." It's important to know that some are closed on weekends and others are marked for "uptown" or "downtown" access only. Unlike those in some of the other boroughs, Manhattan's subway stations are underground. (This should be noted by anyone who has trouble climbing stairs, as there are lots of steep ones in the subway system and few elevators.) You'll typically find station booths at the bottom of the stairs. Inside the station, signs point to the appropriate platform for uptown (sometimes "Bronx-bound") or downtown (sometimes "Brooklyn-bound") trains. Keep an eye out for express trains—they're great timesavers if you want to go where they're going, since they make limited stops. Some trains, such as the F line, run "express" in Queens but become "local" in Manhattan. The line number or letter, the words "local" or "express," and the name of the last stop are written on the side of each subway car, but maps are the best source of such information.

If you haven't been to New York for awhile, you might be sad to learn that subway tokens have gone the way of the dodo bird. Thanks to the **Metro-Card** system, you can buy a plastic card that you swipe in the turnstiles for a single ride, multiple rides, or a one-day or seven-day pass. A single ride costs $2, 6 rides cost $10, 12 rides cost $20, a one-day unlimited "Fun Pass" costs $7, and a seven-day unlimited pass costs $24. (For information about how to qualify for half-price fares for riders 65 and older, go to www.mta. info.) The best deal for visitors who ride public transportation—and Metro-Cards are accepted on both the subway and bus system—is the seven-day unlimited pass. In fact, it's about the best deal you'll find in New York!

MetroCards can be purchased using credit or debit cards at automated, multilingual vending machines in all subway stations. Some of these machines take cash, but not all of them do. If you want to use cash, you can go to the station booth (for everything except the one-day Fun Pass) or to most grocery and drug stores.

For all its great features, the MetroCard has one drawback worth mentioning: to discourage misuse of unlimited-ride cards, you cannot use the Fun Pass or any multiday, unlimited-ride pass again within 18 minutes of entering or leaving a given subway station. That can be frustrating if you get off at the wrong stop or are running a quick errand.

Don't Try to Get a Cab at 5 p.m.!

As ridiculous as it sounds, the hardest time of day to catch a cab is late afternoon—right around quitting time and just before dinner. Why? Because cab drivers typically work a 12-hour shift, and 4:30 or 5 p.m. ends the day shift. If you're making early dinner reservations or need to be somewhere in late afternoon, plan accordingly!

Some general subway rules:

- Once you've passed through the turnstiles and are inside a station, you can transfer between lines or ride for as long as you like. And if you're using a MetroCard, you can even transfer for free onto a bus within two hours with the same card—or anytime you want if you're using an unlimited-ride card!
- Station names are written on the walls of the stations and are announced inside subway cars, but the former are sometimes obscured and the latter are often garbled, so stay on your toes. If you miss your stop, don't panic: you can get off and go back.
- Some lines stop running for a couple hours in the early morning, and many have less frequent or different service at night and on weekends. However, all stations in the system are served by some train on a regular basis 24 hours a day, seven days a week.

If you have questions or a problem, call the Metropolitan Transit Authority at 718/330-1234 between 6 a.m. and 10 p.m. every day. (Non-English speakers can call 718/330-4847.)

Two subway strategies worth mentioning:

- Take an express to the stop closest to your destination and then wait for a local to take you the rest of the way. You can always get on one line and then switch trains to get to your destination. This works particularly well on the 4, 5, and 6 lines on the East Side, for example, as only the 6 makes local stops in midtown while the 4 and 5 go all the way down to Bowling Green. So, for instance, you can board the 6 in midtown and switch to a 4 or 5 at 42nd Street, 34th Street, or wherever else the lines meet.
- Wait for the next train if an arriving one is packed. Chances are there's a less crowded train right behind it. Your ride could be significantly more pleasant if you wait a minute or two. This also holds true for buses.

Finally, a word about safety. The Metropolitan Transit Authority has worked hard to clean up stations and the graffiti in them, as well as significantly reduce the number of system breakdowns. Still, some subway stations and cars can be really dirty. Statistically, however, the system is no more dangerous than any other mode of transportation. In general, like crime in New York, subway crime has fallen sharply. But do use common sense.

- *Don't* ride late at night or very early in the morning, particularly if you're alone.
- *Don't* enter deserted stations.
- *Don't* ride in an otherwise empty car.
- *Don't* wear flashy jewelry.
- *Don't* wander around aimlessly.
- *Don't* stand too close to the tracks.
- *Don't* use any subway station bathroom.
- *Do* stick close to the designated off-hours waiting area if you're riding at an off-peak hour so that an attendant can keep an eye on you.
- *Do* watch your wallet or purse, particularly when in crowded cars.

TAXIS—All officially licensed medallion taxicabs in New York are yellow, have the words "NYC Taxi" and fare information written on their side doors, and post their medallion number in a box on the roof. Inside you'll see a meter and the driver's license (with his or her picture) and medallion number displayed on the dashboard, usually on the passenger's side. The city, particularly outside midtown, is full of unregulated "cars for hire" (a.k.a. gypsy cabs) that are not legally allowed to pick up people south of 96th Street. Still, they sometimes try to do just that.

I strongly encourage you to stick with medallion cabs. The cost of a ride in a medallion cab is calculated per trip rather than per person, which means that a short trip for four adults in a cab can actually be cheaper than a bus or subway ride. That said, however, fares can add up quickly, particularly if you're stuck in heavy traffic. The charge begins at $2.50 the moment you get in and costs 40 cents for every one-fifth of a mile driven and every 60 seconds the cab sits in traffic or goes slower than 12 miles per hour. In general, the meter should "click" every four blocks when you're going north-south and every block when you're going east-west, if traffic is moving smoothly. You pay for any tolls, and there's a 50-cent surcharge for rides made between 8 p.m. and 6 a.m. and a $1 surcharge on rides between 4 p.m. and 8 p.m. on weekdays. The meter in the front keeps a running total of the fare, and the driver is required to give you a receipt, if requested. A tip of between 15% and 20% of the fare is standard, and payment is generally expected in cash. Drivers often cannot make change for bills larger than $20 (and are not required to).

Drivers *are* required to take you anywhere within the five boroughs of New York City, to Westchester and Nassau counties, and to Newark Airport. That's the law, but the reality is that many cab drivers will make a fuss if you want to go to one of the airports, one of those suburban counties, or even to lower-income neighborhoods in Manhattan. Moreover, be forewarned that drivers can charge double the metered fare once they leave the city limits, plus tolls. (Special fees that apply to airports are covered earlier in this chapter.) If you have a problem, jot down the driver's name and medallion number and contact the New York City Taxi and Limousine Commission (write 40 Rector Street, New York, NY 10006, call 311, or go to www. nyc.gov/html/tlc) to complain. These folks take their oversight responsibilities seriously.

So how do you go about hailing a cab? Stand on or just off a curb and stick your arm up and out. If the number (but not the "off-duty" sign) is lit in the rectangular box on the roof, the cab is empty and looking for business. Finding a cab in a snowstorm, in midtown, on a rainy Friday afternoon or any day around 5 p.m. is difficult, but you usually won't have trouble finding one in most parts of the city at most times of day. If you do have trouble, go to a major hotel or join the cab line at Penn Station, Grand Central Terminal, or Port Authority Bus Terminal. If you want the driver to take a particular route (it's a good idea to know exactly where you're going), say so when you get in. Assuming it isn't raining, I also suggest giving the driver the closest intersection rather than a street address as your destination. Because some blocks, particularly crosstown ones in midtown, can be jammed with traffic, this will save both time and money. Passengers ride in the back seat, although the driver will usually let one person ride up front if there are four in your party. A final note: the law now requires drivers to help disabled passengers and prohibits them from starting the meter until such passengers are safely settled.

My Best Advice
- Everybody is in a hurry. You don't need to be. Slow down and savor the sights and sounds of Manhattan.
- Give yourself permission to wander without a plan or destination in neighborhoods like the West Village or the Upper East Side.
- The subway is by far the fastest and most efficient way to get around the city, but avoid it if you have trouble using stairs.

BUSES—In the earliest editions of this book, I wrote that the only reasons to take a city bus are if you have a lot of time and are afraid of the alternatives. A friend who rode the bus every day objected strongly. First of all, she pointed out, the city's blue-and-white buses are wheelchair-accessible (which the subway decidedly is not) and "elderly friendly" in that the driver can lower the stairs at the entrance for anyone who has trouble climbing high steps. Some of the city's newest buses are even "low-floor" models, with loading ramps instead of stairs. Buses are also "stroller friendly," insofar as the doors don't close automatically and there are only a few steps to climb and descend.

Precisely because people who take the bus aren't in a hurry, they tend to be friendlier than subway riders and often will give an older person or a harried parent their seat. Because there is a driver, you can ask questions or get directions. And because the bus stops frequently and you can always see where you're going, it's a relatively cheap way to get a flavor of the city. I still find the system frustratingly slow (the average speed of the M96, a bus traversing the length of 96th Street, has been clocked at 4.3 miles per hour at midday), but buses do have some redeeming features, and their popularity has increased so dramatically that there are now a number of double-length ("articulated") buses traveling busier routes.

Buses run up and down most avenues and on most major cross streets beween 6 a.m. and midnight. Uptown buses stop every two or three blocks, and crosstown buses stop on every block—assuming someone is waiting at a bus stop or a bus rider has pushed the yellow tape to alert the driver that a stop is requested. Many bus lines have a "limited stop" version that stops every ten blocks or so at major intersections; an orange "limited" sign is clearly visible in the front windshields. At a minimum, you can spot a bus stop by its blue sign and route numbers. The city has renovated and added more "Guide-a-Ride" signs, route maps, and bus shelters, making the system much more user-friendly.

Many stops are used by more than one route, so check the screen on the front or side of each bus for its route number or simply ask the driver. If you're using a fare-based MetroCard, you can transfer for free to a subway or bus line as part of the same trip within two hours. If you're paying in cash on the bus, you'll need to ask for a transfer and it's good only on another bus. Of course you're entitled to unlimited bus and subway rides going in any direction if you have an unlimited-ride MetroCard.

If you pay per ride, the bus costs $2 ($1 for senior citizens 65 and over with identification and free for up to three children under 44 inches tall with a fare-paying adult). You need exact change and the machine cannot accept bills. For more information, see the previous section on the subway or go to any subway station.

You can get a map of Manhattan bus routes on most buses (ask the driver or look for boxes by the front and back doors) and at most subway booths. You will also find a detailed map of the bus system in the Manhattan Yellow Pages. The map details bus routes, frequency of service, and which bus to take to major museums and other attractions. If you have questions about how to get from one place to another via bus, call the Metropolitan Transit Authority between 6 a.m. and 10 p.m. at 718/330-1234 or go to www.mta.info.

CAR SERVICES—If you're wondering about the large number of Lincoln Town Cars and other black sedans in midtown and the Financial District, they are car services. Unlike taxicabs, which cruise the streets looking for business, car services are available only by reservation and often are exclusively for corporate clients. If you're in New York on business, your company may arrange to have you picked up from the airport and shuttled around town by one of these services. Chances are you will be given an account number and pay with a voucher provided by either your company or the driver. A client's name and car number will typically be posted in the window of the car, and you'll be told in advance what to look for.

Some car services and limousine companies take reservations from individuals. **Carey** (212/599-1122, 800/336-4646, or www.carey.com) is among the larger and more reputable companies. You can have a car meet you at the airport, be shuttled around town for a day, or simply arrive and depart from the opera in style. The cost typically is calculated by the hour or the trip rather than by mileage, so make sure you agree on a price before making a commitment. Reservations are required. Make them at least a day in advance and call to confirm several hours before you expect to leave. If you want a specific type of car or limousine, say so when you're making reservations. These car services are on the high end of the business. You'll find lots of gypsy cabs and low-end car services in the outer boroughs and outside midtown, but I suggest avoiding them. Just so you know, licensed limousines are required to post a diamond-shaped decal on the right side of their windshield. On it will be an eight-digit number bookended by the letters T and C.

DRIVING—If you read my comments earlier in this chapter, you already know that I *strongly* recommend not driving in New York. Leave the hassles and headaches to cab and bus drivers. The parking regulations alone ought to discourage you. There are alternate-side-of-the-street rules, special rules for several dozen official holidays, and weekend rules. (For information, go to www.nyc.gov/html/dot.) And that's assuming you can find a parking space. (The average monthly cost of a parking space in an underground lot in midtown is more than $500!) Illegal parking can cost upwards of $200 per infraction—and that's *after* you've paid for the towing and impoundment of your vehicle. If you can't find a space on the street or want the security of a garage, you're going to pay big bucks. Forty dollars a day is not uncommon.

Hundreds of thousands of cars, taxis, trucks, and other vehicles come into Manhattan every day. While the speed limit on city streets is 30 miles per hour unless otherwise posted, it's little wonder that the average speed of traffic going uptown or downtown is less than 10 mph ... and the average crosstown speed is half that! If you must drive, I recommend becoming a member of AAA or some other major automobile club and getting all the information they have about traffic laws and driving in the city. Whatever else you do, make sure you know where you're going and be prepared for a lot of honking. Drivers in New York are not very patient or pleasant.

Don't Miss

Everyone has their list of favorites in New York, but here are a few places that you just *shouldn't* miss if you're visiting this great city:

- Ellis Island and the Statue of Liberty
- Lower East Side Tenement Museum and Orchard Street
- Frick Collection
- Metropolitan Museum of Art
- Grand Central Terminal
- American Museum of Natural History
- Museum of the City of New York (especially the Rockefeller Rooms)
- Museum of Modern Art
- Central Park
- The Cloisters
- St. Patrick's Cathedral
- Cathedral Church of St. John the Divine

WHAT TO EXPECT

I find that people often have a lot of preconceptions about New York. Some of them are accurate. It *is* big, bigger and more compact that any other city in North America. It *is* really, really, expensive. And it *does* bustle: people walk faster, drive more aggressively, and talk louder in New York than they do in other cities (at least in the United States). But a lot of preconceptions are wrong. New York is surprisingly clean and safe, and much easier to navigate than most people expect. Even people who haven't been to New York in ten years are surprised by how remarkably livable this great city has become.

Safety

As with so many other things about New York since I first started writing this book almost 30 years ago, crime has changed dramatically. The good news is that it has gone down. Way down. In fact, per capita crime in New York is lower than in any other major city in the United States. Both violent and petty crime are way down, and security is almost as tight here as it is in Washington, D.C.

All that said, it's still worth following a few common sense "don'ts":

- Don't display big wads of money or flashy watches and jewelry. In fact, avoid taking them with you. Leave most of your cash and all of your valuables at home or in the hotel safe.
- Don't open your wallet in public.
- Don't use ATMs when no one else is around.
- Don't leave ATMs until you've put your money in a wallet and then put the wallet in your pocket or purse.
- Don't keep your wallet in your back pocket unless it's buttoned. Better yet, carry your wallet in a front pocket, along with keys and other important items.
- Don't wear your purse slung over one shoulder. Instead, put the strap over your head and keep your purse in front of you or to the side.
- Don't doze off on the subway or bus.
- Don't take the subway late at night or very early in the morning.
- Don't jog in Central Park or anywhere else after dark.
- Don't let yourself believe that staying in "good" neighborhoods protects you from crime. The only time I was ever mugged was on Park Avenue at 62nd Street, and you can't find a better neighborhood than that!
- Don't let anybody in your hotel room, even if they claim to work for the hotel, unless you've specifically asked them to come or have checked with the front desk to verify their authenticity.
- Don't talk to strangers who try to strike up a conversation unless you're sure of their motivation.
- Don't ever leave bags unattended. If you're going to put a bag or backpack on the floor at a restaurant or bathroom stall, put your foot or a leg of your chair through the strap.
- Don't hang your purse or anything else on the back of the door in a public bathroom stall.
- Don't walk around with your mouth open, camera slung over your shoulder and map visible, while saying things like, "Gee, honey, we sure don't have buildings this tall back home!"
- Don't be afraid to cross the street if a situation doesn't feel right. Shout for help if somebody is bothering you.
- Move away from unattended packages and immediately report any suspicious items or behavior to authorities.

A final word of warning: watch where you walk. Manhattan has an incredible amount of traffic, and the struggle among cars, taxis, trucks, buses, and pedestrians is constant. It may sound silly to repeat a warning from childhood, but look both ways before stepping into the street, wherever you are.

If you're traveling with a group or family, it's always a good idea to plan a meeting place in case you get separated. If there's an emergency, call 911.

Tipping and Other Expenses

Be advised: New York is expensive. *Really* expensive. The city's hotels are among the most expensive in the country, often costing upwards of $300 per night for a basic double room. The average dinner at a decent restaurant (even vwithout wine) can easily run $50 or more per person; most theater and opera tickets are just plain outrageous (think $100 plus); and even a quick lunch under $10 is increasingly hard to find. Everybody expects a tip, too. It's up to you, of course, but $1 per bag to the bellman, between 15% and 20% of your fare to the cab driver, and between 15% and 20% of your pre-tax restaurant bill (double the tax—it's 8.25% on just about everything) to your waiter is typical. Most people also tip wine stewards (10% of the wine bill), parking valets ($2), private tour guides (at least $5 a day), and doormen who hail cabs ($1), among others.

The good news is that you can find cheaper hotels, less expensive restaurants, good deals, and even some free events and activities. You can also try to make wise choices. The difference between buying a single bagel through room service at one midtown hotel and a deli a block away, for instance, is more than $10! However, in general my advice is be prepared to spend money—and lots of it—if you're here for a special visit. Don't nickel-and-dime yourself out of enjoying a priceless experience!

Checklists

If you're planning a trip to New York, think ahead about what you want to do and read the relevant sections of this book carefully. Pay special attention to things that require advance planning, like tickets to certain events, Broadway shows, television show tapings, and tours. Special sales or events require that you visit at certain times of year. Weather is always a consideration. Average temperatures range from highs in the 30s and 40s in December, January, and February (with snow always a possibility) to highs in the 80s and 90s in June, July, and August (when the humidity can wilt even the sturdiest among us). Whenever you come and whatever you plan to do, I recommend packing these key items:

- comfortable walking shoes
- umbrella and raincoat (or warm coat, scarf, and boots)
- jacket and tie (still required in a few places) for men, nice dress or outfit for women
- opera glasses
- address book and postcard stamps
- prescriptions and an extra pair of glasses (in case you lose them)
- tickets (airplane and others)
- AARP and/or Medicare card if you qualify for a senior discount
- student ID card if you qualify for a student discount
- a government-issued picture ID card

All the little items that you may want in your hotel room or when you're out and about cost a lot less at home than in New York. Most hotels will supply small sewing kits, most now have in-room coffeemakers and hairdryers, and some will let you borrow an umbrella for free. But consider packing aspirin, snacks, and gum. Plan what you're going to need for the day before leaving the hotel room. Put a couple of credit cards, driver's license, and some money in a secure pocket or money belt and then stash everything else in a shoulder bag so there's no worrying about a stolen purse or wallet. Leave your room key at the front desk for the same reason. Depending on the time of year, here's a list of things I recommend taking with you for a day of exploring:

- addresses and phone numbers of places you plan to visit and details about how to get there
- address and phone number of your hotel
- bus and subway maps
- tissues
- list of public bathrooms in the areas you'll be visiting
- umbrella
- coat or sweater (and boots and gloves in winter)
- unlimited-use MetroCard (for subways and buses)
- loose change and small bills
- Finally, don't forget this book!

II. Where to Eat It: Manhattan a la Carte

New York is a restaurant town. Certainly it's the best restaurant town in the United States and possibly the world. You could eat every meal at a different restaurant for a year and still not come close to exhausting the possibilities. Hundreds of restaurants serve every imaginable kind of food, and new ones open every day.

These restaurant reviews, like everything else in this book, reflect my opinions. Restaurants that try to inflate their own standing by claiming not to have reservations for six weeks irritate me, as do those that don't pay attention to details like clean menus and bathrooms. Moreover, I don't care how good the food is if the staff is uninformed or snooty. You don't need to bother; you have literally hundreds of choices.

An unpleasant new attitude has permeated some of Manhattan's better (read: more expensive) restaurants. Chefs have stepped out of their kitchens at times to become celebrities in their own right. There's nothing wrong with that, as many of them really are! But when they project an attitude that they are doing diners a favor by allowing them to come to their "house" to eat, then it needs another look. Diners come to enjoy food and shouldn't be made to feel like beggars pleading for admission to some hallowed room. Reservationists are almost always unpleasant. Restaurant greeters are often young ladies more interested in showing their wares than showing diners to tables, and they're in need of training in manners and customer service. The bottom line is that we are guests in these fine restaurants, and we deservedly expect—given the prices we pay—to be treated with warmth and consideration.

I like restaurants that emphasize good service, quality food, and reasonable prices. One of my absolute musts is warm, fresh bread. The good news is that lots of restaurants have all of these qualities, although "reasonable" is a relative term when it comes to New York menu prices and clearly depends on what is being served. At the right restaurant, it's worth every penny! Some of my favorites are old-timers—restaurants that have been around for years and know how to do things right. Some are newcomers striving to find a following with tapas, barbecue, or whatever the latest hot trend happens to be. The following pages include hundreds of restaurants, from casual to upscale, that I consider to be worth your time and money.

Before I share my recommendations, keep these things in mind when dining out in New York:

- People in New York eat later than elsewhere in the country. Prime dinner hour is 8 p.m. Many are still eating at 10 p.m.
- Reservations matter! Make them, confirm them, honor them, and be nice to the person who takes them.
- Dress appropriately. New York is much less formal than it used to be, but a few restaurants still have dress codes and many others have basic expectations of appropriate attire. Whatever you do, please don't wear a baseball cap in any restaurant!
- *Old* doesn't necessarily mean *tired*. Some of the best restaurants in New York have been around for years. Don't overlook them just because they're not trendy.
- Go where New Yorkers go for dinner. Explore areas like the Lower East Side and the East Village. Stay away from touristy Times Square.
- Ask wine stewards and waiters for suggestions, but be wary of high-priced specials and don't order bottled water. New York's drinking water is among the best in the country!
- Tip appropriately. A good rule of thumb is to double the tax (which is 8.25%). For really good service, tip between 20% and 25%.

In the following pages, you'll find a list of restaurants by neighborhood as well as extensive lists of places I think offer the best in a given food category. In addition, I've written dozens of full-length reviews beginning on page 88. Those restaurants fall into one of four price categories (appetizer plus entree, not including drinks):

- Inexpensive: $15 and under per person
- Moderate: $16 to $34 per person
- Moderately expensive: $35 to $45 per person
- Expensive: $46 and up per person

If you have a particularly good or bad eating experience, don't hesitate to talk with the owner. And by all means, please let me know, as I value the input of my readers tremendously. That goes for suggesting your favorite restaurants as well!

Bon appetit!

Quick Reference Guide

Note: Reference to Sunday simply means that a given restaurant is open on Sunday.

CENTRAL PARK AREA

Landmarc (Time Warner Center, 10 Columbus Circle, 2nd floor): American, Sunday
Sarabeth's Kitchen (40 Central Park S): American/Continental, Sunday
Tavern on the Green (Central Park W at 67th St): Continental, Sunday

CHELSEA

Da Umberto (107 W 17th St): Italian
Del Posto (85 Tenth Ave): Italian, Sunday
F&B Güdtfood (269 W 23rd St): European street food, Sunday
Frank's (410 W 16th St): Steak, Sunday
Gascogne (158 Eighth Ave): French, Sunday

Klee Brasserie (200 Ninth Ave): Austrian, Sunday
La Bottega (Maritime Hotel, 88 Ninth Ave): Italian, Sunday
La Lunchonette (130 Tenth Ave): French, Sunday
Moran's Chelsea (146 Tenth Ave): American, Sunday
Porters New York (216 Seventh Ave): American, Sunday
Trestle on Tenth (242 Tenth Ave): Swiss, Sunday
T Salon (Chelsea Market, 75 Ninth Ave): Teahouse, Sunday
202 (Chelsea Market, 75 Ninth Ave): Mediterranean, Sunday

CHINATOWN
Golden Unicorn (18 East Broadway): Chinese, Sunday

EAST HARLEM
Rao's (455 E 114th St): Italian

EAST SIDE/UPPER EAST SIDE
Annie's (1381 Third Ave): American, Sunday
Arabelle (Hotel Plaza Athenee New York, 37 E 46th St): Continental, Sunday
Aureole (34 E 61st St): New American
Bravo Gianni (230 E 63rd St): Italian, Sunday
Cafe Boulud (20 E 76th St): French, Sunday
Cafe d'Alsace (1695 Second Ave): Alsatian, Sunday
Cafe Sabarsky (Neue Galerie, 1048 Fifth Ave): Vietnamese, Sunday
Daniel (60 E 65th St): French
davidburke & donatella (133 E 61st St): Continental, Sunday
Demarchelier (50 E 86th St): French, Sunday
Elio's (1621 Second Ave): Italian, Sunday
Etats-Unis (242 E 81st St): American, Sunday
Fred's at Barneys New York (660 Madison Ave, 9th floor): American, Sunday
Geisha (33 E 61st St): Japanese
Gino (780 Lexington Ave): Italian, Sunday
Il Riccio (152 E 79th St): Italian, Sunday
Il Vagabondo (351 E 62nd St): Italian, Sunday
Jackson Hole Burgers (various locations): Burgers, Sunday
Jacques Brasserie (204 E 85th St): French, Sunday
John's Pizzeria (408 E 14th St): Italian, Sunday
King's Carriage House (251 E 82nd St): Continental, Sunday
L'Atelier de Joël Robuchon (Four Seasons Hotel New York, 57 E 57th St): French, Sunday
Le Boeuf à La Mode (539 E 81st St): French, Sunday
Le Refuge (166 E 82nd St): French, Sunday
Nicola's (146 E 84th St): Italian, Sunday
Our Place (1444 Third Ave): Chinese, Sunday
Paola's (245 E 84th St): Italian, Sunday
Park Avenue Cafe (100 E 63rd St): American, Sunday
Payard Patisserie & Bistro (1032 Lexington Ave): French
Pinocchio (1748 First Ave): Italian, Sunday
Portofino Grille (1162 First Ave): Italian, Sunday
Post House (Lowell Hotel, 28 E 63rd St): Steak, Sunday

Primavera (1578 First Ave): Italian, Sunday
Sarabeth's at the Whitney (Whitney Museum of American Art, 945 Madison Ave): American/Continental, Sunday
Sarabeth's Kitchen (1295 Madison Ave): American/Continental, Sunday
Serendipity 3 (225 E 60th St): American, Sunday
Sette Mezzo (969 Lexington Ave): Italian, Sunday
Sfoglia (1402 Lexington Ave): Northern Italian
Sistina (1555 Second Ave): Italian, Sunday
Spigolo (1561 Second Ave): Italian, Sunday
Taste (1413 Third Ave): American, Sunday
Tini's (1562 Second Ave): Italian, Sunday
Tony's Di Napoli (1606 Second Ave): Italian, Sunday
Vinegar Factory (431 E 91st St): American, Sunday
Vivolo (140 E 74th St): Italian

EAST VILLAGE
Danal (90 E 10th St): French, Sunday
Gyu-Kaku (34 Cooper Square): Japanese BBQ, Sunday
Hearth (403 E 12th St): American, Sunday
I Coppi (432 E 9th St): Italian, Sunday
Jack's Luxury Oyster Bar (101 Second Ave): Seafood

FLATIRON DISTRICT/GRAMERCY PARK/LOWER BROADWAY/UNION SQUARE
A Voce (41 Madison Ave): Italian, Sunday
Blue Smoke (116 E 27th St): Barbecue, Sunday
Blue Water Grill (31 Union Square W): Seafood, Sunday
Bolo (23 E 22nd St): Spanish, Sunday
City Bakery (3 W 18 St): Bakery/Cafe, Sunday
craft (47 E 19th St): American, Sunday
Eleven Madison Park (11 Madison Ave): French/American, Sunday
Fleur de Sel (5 E 20th St): French, Sunday
Gramercy Tavern (42 E 20th St): American, Sunday
Houston's (378 Park Ave S): American, Sunday
La Petite Auberge (116 Lexington Ave): French, Sunday
MetroCafe & Wine Bar (32 E 21st St): American, Sunday
Olives New York (W New York Union Square, 201 Park Ave S): Continental, Sunday
Pump Energy Food (31 E 21st St): Health, Sunday
Rolf's (281 Third Ave): German, Sunday
Rosa Mexicano (9 E 18th St): Mexican, Sunday
Tabla (11 Madison Ave): Indian, Sunday
Tocqueville (15 E 15th St): American, Sunday
Union Square Cafe (21 E 16th St): American, Sunday
Veritas (43 E 20th St): Continental, Sunday

GREENWICH VILLAGE/WEST VILLAGE
Babbo (110 Waverly Pl): Italian, Sunday
Blue Hill (75 Washington Pl): American, Sunday
Blue Ribbon Bakery (35 Downing St): American, Sunday
Camaje (85 MacDougal St): French, Sunday

Chez Jacqueline (72 MacDougal St): French, Sunday
Cowgirl (519 Hudson St): Southwestern, Sunday
Cucina Stagionale (289 Bleecker St): Italian, Sunday
Gavroche (212 W 14th St): French, Sunday
Gonzo (140 W 13th St): Italian, Sunday
Good (89 Greenwich Ave): American, Sunday
Gotham Bar & Grill (12 E 12th St): American, Sunday
Il Mulino (86 W 3rd St): Italian
Jarnac (328 W 12th St): French, Sunday
John's Pizzeria (278 Bleecker St): Italian, Sunday
La Ripaille (605 Hudson St): French, Sunday
Le Gigot (18 Cornelia St): French, Sunday
Little Owl (90 Bedford St): New American, Sunday
Minetta Tavern (113 MacDougal St): Italian, Sunday
One If By Land, Two If By Sea (17 Barrow St): Continental, Sunday
Paris Commune (99 Bank St): French, Sunday
Pó (31 Cornelia St): Italian, Sunday
(The Famous) Ray's Pizza of Greenwich Village (465 Ave of the
  Americas): Pizza, Sunday
Strip House (13 E 12th St): Steak, Sunday
Tartine (253 W 11th St): Continental, Sunday
Wallsé (344 W 11th St): Austrian, Sunday
Waverly Inn & Garden (16 Bank St): Continental, Sunday

LINCOLN CENTER
Gabriel's Bar & Restaurant (11 W 60th St): Italian
Picholine (35 W 64th St): Mediterranean, Sunday
P.J. Clarke's at Lincoln Center (44 W 63rd St): American/Bistro,
  Sunday
Rosa Mexicano (61 Columbus Ave): Mexican, Sunday

LOWER EAST SIDE
A.O.C. Bedford (14 Bedford St): Continental, Sunday
Clinton St. Baking Co. & Restaurant (4 Clinton St): American, Sun-
  day
Freeman's (Freeman Alley): Continental, Sunday
Katz's Delicatessen (205 E Houston St): Deli, Sunday
Schiller's (131 Rivington St): American, Sunday
Tasting Room (72 E 1st St): Continental, Sunday
Thor (Hotel on Rivington, 107 Rivington St): Central European, Sunday

MEATPACKING DISTRICT
Pastis (9 Ninth Ave): French, Sunday
Spice Market (403 W 13th St): Asian, Sunday
Valbella (421 W 13th St): Northern Italian

MIDTOWN EAST
Angels Ristorante (1135 First Ave): Italian, Sunday
Aquavit (65 E 55th St): Scandinavian, Sunday
Artisanal (2 Park Ave): Bistro/Brasserie, Sunday
BLT Steak (106 E 57th St): Steak
Bottega del Vino (7 E 59th St): Italian, Sunday

Brasserie (100 E 53rd St): French, Sunday
Butterfield 8 (5 E 38th St): American, Sunday
Cafe Centro (MetLife Building, 200 Park Ave): Continental
Cafe Indulge (561 Second Ave): American/Bakery, Sunday
Capital Grille (Chrysler Center, 155 E 42nd St): Steak, Sunday
Chin Chin (216 E 49th St): Chinese, Sunday
Cucina & Co. (MetLife Building, 200 Park Ave, lobby): Italian
Dawat (210 E 58th St): Indian, Sunday
Delegates Dining Room (United Nations Headquarters, First Ave at 46th St): Continental
Dining Commons (City University of New York Graduate Center, 365 Fifth Ave, 8th floor): American
Docks Oyster Bar and Seafood Grill (633 Third Ave): Seafood, Sunday
El Parador Cafe (325 E 34th St): Mexican, Sunday
F&B Güdtfood (150 E 52nd St): European street food, Sunday
57 (Four Seasons Hotel New York, 57 E 57th St, lobby level): American, Sunday
Four Seasons (99 E 52nd St): Continental
Frank's Trattoria (371 First Ave): Italian, Sunday
Fresco by Scotto (34 E 52nd St): Italian
Grand Central Oyster Bar Restaurant (Grand Central Terminal, 42nd St at Vanderbilt Ave, lower level): Seafood
Hatsuhana (17 E 48th St and 237 Park Ave): Japanese
Houston's (Citicorp Center, 153 E 53rd St): American, Sunday
Il Postino (337 E 49th St): Italian, Sunday
La Grenouille (3 E 52nd St): French
Le Cirque (One Beacon Court, 151 E 58th St): French
Le Périgord (405 E 52nd St): French, Sunday
Les Halles (411 Park Ave S): French, Sunday
L'Impero (45 Tudor City Pl): Italian
Maloney & Porcelli (37 E 50th St): American, Sunday
Marchi's (251 E 31st St): Italian
Michael Jordan's The Steak House N.Y.C. (Grand Central Terminal, 23 Vanderbilt Ave): Steak, Sunday
The Morgan Dining Room (225 Madison Ave): New American, Sunday
Morton's of Chicago (551 Fifth Ave): Steak, Sunday
Mr. K's (570 Lexington Ave): Chinese, Sunday
Naples 45 (MetLife Building, 200 Park Ave): Italian
Oceana (55 E 54th St): Seafood
Palm One (837 Second Ave): Steak, Sunday
Palm Too (840 Second Ave): Steak, Sunday
Park Bistro (414 Park Ave S): French, Sunday
Pershing Square (90 E 42nd St): American, Sunday
Pietro's (232 E 43rd St): Italian
P.J. Clarke's (915 Third Ave): American/Bistro, Sunday
Pump Energy Food (805 Third Ave and 113 E 31st St): Health, Sunday
Rare Bar & Grill (Shelburne Murray Hill, 303 Lexington Ave): American, Sunday
Ristorante Grifone (244 E 46th St): Italian
Rosa Mexicano (1063 First Ave): Mexican, Sunday
San Pietro (18 E 54th St): Italian

Shun Lee Palace (155 E 55th St): Chinese, Sunday
Smith & Wollensky (797 Third Ave): Steak, Sunday
Sparks Steakhouse (210 E 46th St): Steak
Tao (42 E 58th St): Asian, Sunday
Tropica (MetLife Building, 200 Park Ave, lobby level): Seafood
Turkish Kitchen (386 Third Ave): Turkish, Sunday
Vong (200 E 54th St): Thai, Sunday
Water Club (500 E 30th St): American, Sunday
Wild Salmon (622 Third Ave): Seafood, Sunday

MIDTOWN WEST
Abboccato (136 W 55th St): Italian, Sunday
Bar Americain (152 W 52nd St): American, Sunday
Beacon (25 W 56th St): American, Sunday
Ben Benson's Steak House (123 W 52nd St): Steak, Sunday
Brasserie 8½ (9 W 57th St): French, Sunday
Brasserie Ruhlmann (45 Rockefeller Plaza): French, Sunday
Brooklyn Diner USA (212 W 57th St): Eclectic, Sunday
Bryant Park Grill (25 W 40th St): American/Continental, Sunday
Carmine's (200 W 44th St): Italian, Sunday
Carnegie Delicatessen and Restaurant (854 Seventh Ave): Deli, Sunday
Del Frisco's Double Eagle Steak House (McGraw-Hill Building, 1221 Ave of the Americas): Steak, Sunday
44 & X Hell's Kitchen (622 Tenth Ave): American, Sunday
Gaby (44 W 45th St): French, Sunday
Il Gattopardo (33 W 54th St): Italian, Sunday
John's Pizzeria (260 W 44th St): Italian, Sunday
Keens Steakhouse (72 W 36th St): American, Sunday
Kobe Club (68 W 58th St): Japanese/Steak
Le Bernardin (155 W 51st St): French
Le Biarritz (325 W 57th St): French
Mangia É Bevi (800 Ninth Ave): Italian, Sunday
McCormick & Schmick's (1285 Ave of the Americas): Seafood, Sunday
Michael's (24 W 55th St): California cuisine
Museum of Modern Art (9 W 53rd St): Continental, Sunday
Nobu 57 (40 W 57th St): Japanese, Sunday
Osteria del Circo (120 W 55th St): Italian, Sunday
Our Place Shanghai Tea Garden (141 E 55th St): Chinese, Sunday
Palm West Side (250 W 50th St): Steak, Sunday
Patsy's (236 W 56th St): Italian, Sunday
Pump Energy Food (40 W 55th St and 112 W 38th St): Health, Sunday
Quality Meats (57 W 58th St): New American/Steak, Sunday
Redeye Grill (890 Seventh Ave): American, Sunday
Remi (145 W 53rd St): Italian, Sunday
René Pujol (321 W 51st St): French
Round Table (Algonquin Hotel, 59 W 44th St, lobby): American, Sunday
Rue 57 (60 W 57th St): French, Sunday
Sea Grill (19 W 49th St): Seafood
Tony's Di Napoli (147 W 43rd St): Italian, Sunday
Trattoria Dell'Arte (900 Seventh Ave): Italian, Sunday
21 Club (21 W 52nd St): American

Uncle Jack's Steakhouse (440 Ninth Ave and 44 W 56th St): Steak,
  Sunday
Woo Chon (10 W 36th St): Korean, Sunday

SOHO/LITTLE ITALY
Balthazar (80 Spring St): French, Sunday
Barmarche (14 Spring St): New American, Sunday
Bistro les Amis (180 Spring St): French, Sunday
Blue Ribbon (97 Sullivan St): Eclectic, Sunday
Butter (415 Lafayette St): New American
Chinatown Brasserie (380 Lafayette St): Chinese, Sunday
Country Cafe (69 Thompson St): French/Moroccan, Sunday
Cupping Room Cafe (359 West Broadway): American, Sunday
Fiamma Osteria (206 Spring St): Italian, Sunday
Giorgione (307 Spring St): Italian, Sunday
Goblin Market (199 Prince St): Continental, Sunday
Il Cortile (125 Mulberry St): Italian, Sunday
Kittichai (60 Thompson St): Thai, Sunday
Le Jardin Bistro (25 Cleveland Pl): French, Sunday
Mezzogiorno (195 Spring St): Italian, Sunday
Onieal's Grand Street (174 Grand St): Continental, Sunday
Raoul's (180 Prince St): French/Bistro, Sunday
Savore (200 Spring St): Italian, Sunday
Spring Street Natural Restaurant (62 Spring St): Health, Sunday
Tasting Room (264 Elizabeth St): Continental, Sunday
Woo Lae Oak Soho (148 Mercer St): Korean, Sunday
Zoë (90 Prince St): American, Sunday

THEATER DISTRICT/TIMES SQUARE
Baldoria (249 W 49th St): Italian, Sunday
Barbetta (321 W 46th St): Italian, Sunday
Bond 45 (154 W 45th St): Italian, Sunday
DB Bistro Moderne (55 W 44th St): French, Sunday
Ellen's Stardust Diner (1650 Broadway): Diner, Sunday
Le Rivage (340 W 46th St): French, Sunday
Orso (322 W 46th St): Italian, Sunday
Ruby Foo's (1626 Broadway): Chinese, Sunday

TRIBECA/DOWNTOWN/FINANCIAL DISTRICT
Acappella (1 Hudson St): Italian
Blaue Gans (139 Duane St): Austrian/German, Sunday
Bouley (162 Duane St): French/American, Sunday
Bouley Bakery (120 West Broadway): Bakery, Sunday
Bridge Cafe (279 Water St): American, Sunday
Capsouto Frères (451 Washington St): French, Sunday
Cercle Rouge (241 West Broadway): French, Sunday
Chanterelle (2 Harrison St): French, Sunday
Danube (30 Hudson St): Austrian
Devin Tavern (363 Greenwich St): Rustic American, Sunday
Flames Steakhouse (5 Gold St): Steak
Fresh (105 Reade St): American

Il Bagatto (192 E 2nd St): Italian, Sunday
Mai House (186 Franklin St): Vietnamese
MarkJoseph Steakhouse (261 Water St): Steak
P.J. Clarke's on the Hudson (4 World Financial Center): American/Bistro, Sunday
Roy's New York (New York Marriott Financial Center Hotel, 130 Washington St): Pan-Pacific, Sunday
Scalini Fedeli (165 Duane St): Italian
Tribeca Grill (375 Greenwich St): American, Sunday
2 West (Ritz-Carlton New York, Battery Park, 2 West St): American, Sunday
Upstairs at Bouley (130 West Broadway): Eclectic, Sunday
Walker's (16 N Moore St): Pub, Sunday

WEST SIDE/UPPER WEST SIDE

Alouette (2588 Broadway): French, Sunday
Asiate (Mandarin Oriental New York, 80 Columbus Circle): French/Japanese, Sunday
Big Nick's (2175 Broadway): Burger/Pizza, Sunday
Café Gray (Time Warner Center, 10 Columbus Circle, 3rd floor): Continental, Sunday
Carmine's (2450 Broadway): Italian, Sunday
'Cesca (164 W 75th St): Continental, Sunday
Compass (208 W 70th St): American, Sunday
Docks Oyster Bar and Seafood Grill (2427 Broadway): Seafood, Sunday
Fairway Cafe & Steakhouse (2127 Broadway, upstairs): American, Sunday
Good Enough to Eat (483 Amsterdam Ave): American, Sunday
Jean Georges (Trump International Hotel and Tower, 1 Central Park W): Continental, Sunday
John's Pizzeria (260 W 44th St): Italian, Sunday
La Boite en Bois (75 W 68th St): French, Sunday
Métisse (239 W 105th St): French, Sunday
Ocean Grill (384 Columbus Ave): Seafood, Sunday
Ouest (2315 Broadway): American, Sunday
Picholine (35 W 64th St): French Mediterranean, Sunday
Ruby Foo's (2182 Broadway): Chinese, Sunday
Sarabeth's Kitchen (423 Amsterdam Ave): American/Continental, Sunday
Shun Lee Cafe/Shun Lee West (43 W 65th St): Chinese, Sunday
Telepan (72 W 69th St): New American, Sunday

OUTSIDE MANHATTAN
Brooklyn
   Peter Luger Steak House (178 Broadway, at Driggs Ave): Steakhouse, Sunday
   River Cafe (1 Water St, foot of Brooklyn Bridge): American, Sunday
Queens
   Park Side (107-01 Corona Ave, at 51st Ave): Italian, Sunday

An Exclusive List: Hundreds of the Best Taste Treats in New York City (Eat In and Takeout)

Antipasto bar: **Da Umberto** (107 W 17th St) and **Trattoria Dell'Arte** (900 Seventh Ave)

Appetizers, gourmet: **Russ & Daughters** (179 E Houston St)

Apple crisp: **Yura** (1645 Third Ave and 1292 Madison Ave)

Apple ring (holidays or special order): **Lafayette** (26 Greenwich Ave)

Artichoke: **La Lunchonette** (130 Tenth Ave)

Artichoke, fried: **Gusto** (60 Greenwich Ave)

Bacon: **The Kitchenette** (156 Chambers St and 1272 Amsterdam Ave)

Baguettes: **Amy's Bread** (75 Ninth Ave, 250 Bleecker St, and 672 Ninth Ave)

Bakery goods, kosher: **Crumbs** (321½ Amsterdam Ave)

Banana split: **Blue Ribbon Bakery** (33 Downing St)

Baskets, gift and corporate: **Manhattan Fruitier** (105 E 29th St) and **Petrossian Cafe & Boutique** (911 Seventh Ave)

Bean curd: **Fong Inn Too** (46 Mott St)

Beef, braised (when available): **Danube** (30 Hudson St)

Beef, cut to order (affordable): **Florence Meat Market** (5 Jones St)

Beef, fillet of (when available): **King's Carriage House** (251 E 82nd St)

Beef and veal (premium): **Lobel's Prime Meats** (1096 Madison Ave)

Beef cheeks (when available): **Fleur de Sel** (5 E 20th St)

Beef Wellington: **One If By Land, Two If By Sea** (17 Barrow St)

Belgian nut squares: **Duane Park Patisserie** (179 Duane St)

Bialys: **Kossar's Bialys** (367 Grand St)

Blintzes: **Cafe Edison** (228 W 47th St) and **Veselka** (144 Second Ave)

Boeuf Bourguignon (menu special): **Country Cafe** (69 Thompson St)

Bomboloncini (fried doughnuts with fillings): **Osteria del Circo** (120 W 55th St)

Bouillabaisse: **Payard Patisserie** (1032 Lexington Ave) and **Pearl Oyster Bar** (18 Cornelia St)

Bratwurst: **Schaller & Weber** (1654 Second Ave)

Bread, banana: **O Mai** (158 Ninth Ave)

Bread, Brazilian cheese: **Puff & Pao** (105 Christopher St)

Bread, chocolate cherry: **Amy's Bread** (75 Ninth Ave and 672 Ninth Ave)

Bread, focaccia: **Falai Panetteria** (79 Clinton St)

Bread, Indian: **Dawat** (210 E 58th St)

Bread, Irish soda: **Zabar's** (2245 Broadway)

Bread, *Malawah* (Yeminite fried flat bread): **PressToast** (112 MacDougal St)

Bread, Semolina raisin fennel: **Amy's Bread** (75 Ninth Ave and 672 Ninth Ave)

Bread, sourdough *boule* (small round loaf): **Silver Moon Bakery** (2740 Broadway)

Bread, whole wheat: **Dean & Deluca** (560 Broadway and 1150 Madison Ave)

Brioche: **Chez Laurence Patisserie** (245 Madison Ave)

Brownies: **Fat Witch Bakery** (75 Ninth Ave) and **Sarabeth's Kitchen** (1295 Madison Ave, 423 Amsterdam Ave, 945 Madison Ave at Whitney Museum, and 40 Central Park S)

Buns, sticky: **William Greenberg Jr. Desserts** (1100 Madison Ave) and **Sarabeth's Kitchen** (423 Amsterdam Ave)

Burrito, breakfast: **Kitchen/Market** (218 Eighth Ave)

Burritos: **Burritoville** (1487 Second Ave and other locations) and **Harry's Burrito Junction** (241 Columbus Ave and other locations)

Burritos (to go): **Benny's Burritos** (113 Greenwich Ave)

Butcher: **Balducci's** (155-A W 66th St)

Butcher, Eastern European: **Kurowycky Meat** (124 First Ave)

Cabbage, pickled with pork and noodles: **Ollie's Noodle Shop and Grill** (200 W 44th St)

Cacik (iced cucumber yogurt soup): **Turkish Kitchen** (386 Third Ave)

Cake: **E.A.T.** (1064 Madison Ave), **Edgar's Cafe** (255 W 84th St), and **Ferrara Bakery and Cafe** (195 Grand St)

Cake, Belgian chocolate: **King's Carriage House** (251 E 82nd St)

Cake, blackout: **Serendipity 3** (225 E 60th St)

Cake, carrot: **Carrot Top Pastries** (3931 Broadway and 5025 Broadway)

Cake, chocolate: **Cafe Lalo** (201 W 83rd St), **Hard Rock Cafe** (1501 Broadway), **Moishe's Bakery** (115 Second Ave), and **Soutine Bakery** (104 W 70th St)

Cake, chocolate meringue with chocolate mousse: **Soutine Bakery** (104 W 70th St)

Cake, chocolate mud: **Umanoff & Parsons** (467 Greenwich St)

Cake, chocolate raspberry: **Caffe Roma** (385 Broome St)

Cake, white coconut and marshmallow meringue: **Magnolia Bakery** (401 Bleecker St)

Calzone: **Little Italy Gourmet Pizza** (1 E 43rd St)

Candy, Asian: **Aji Ichiban** (167 Hester St)

Candy (bonbons): **Teuscher Chocolates** (620 Fifth Ave and 25 E 61st St)

Candy (butter crunch): **Mondel Chocolates** (2913 Broadway)

Candy (caramels): **Fifth Avenue Chocolatiere** (693 Third Ave)

Candy (chocolate): **A Curious and Original Chocolate Shoppe** (350 Bleecker St) and **Pierre Marcolini, Chocolatier** (485 Park Ave)

Candy (jelly beans): **Myzel Chocolates** (140 W 55th St)

Cannelle: **Payard Patisserie** (1032 Lexington Ave)

Cannelloni: **Giambelli** (46 E 50th St) and **Piemonte Homemade Ravioli Company** (190 Grand St)

Cannoli: **De Robertis Pastry Shop & Caffe** (176 First Ave)

Carpaccio: **Cipriani Downtown** (376 West Broadway)

Cassoulet (seasonally): **Jarnac** (328 W 12th St), **L'Absinthe** (227 E 67th St), and **Savoy** (70 Prince St)

Caviar: **Caviar Russe** (538 Madison Ave), **Firebird** (365 W 46th St), **Petrossian Cafe & Boutique** (911 Seventh Ave), **Petrossian Restaurant** (182 W 58th St), and **Sable's Smoked Fish** (1489 Second Ave)

Caviar (best prices): **Russ & Daughters** (179 E Houston St) and **Zabar's** (2245 Broadway)

Caviar, Urbani: **Cucina & Co.** (Macy's, 151 W 34th St, cellar)

Ceviche (marinated seafood): **Rosa Mexicano** (1063 First Ave and 61 Columbus Ave)

Champagne: **Flute** (40 E 20th St and 205 W 54th St), **Garnet Liquor** (929 Lexington Ave), and **Gotham Wines** (2517 Broadway)

Charcuterie: **Dean & Deluca** (560 Broadway and 1150 Madison Ave)

Cheese, mozzarella: **DiPalo Fine Food** (200 Grand St)

Cheese, ricotta: **Alleva Dairy** (188 Grand St)

Cheese selection: **Dean & Deluca** (560 Broadway and 1150 Madison Ave), **Grace's Marketplace** (1237 Third Ave), **Zabar's** (2245 Broadway), and **Murray's Cheese Shop** (254 Bleecker St)

Cheesecake: **Mitchel London Foods** (22-A E 65th St and 458 Ninth Ave), **New York New York Cheesecake** (405 Eighth Ave), **S&S Cheesecake** (222 W 238th St, The Bronx), **Two Little Red Hens** (1652 Second Ave), and **Yura** (1645 Third Ave)

Cheesecake, combination fruit: **Eileen's Special Cheesecake** (17 Cleveland Pl)

Cheesecake, ricotta: **Primavera** (1578 First Ave)

Chicken, beggar's: **Shun Lee Palace** (155 E 55th St; order in advance) and **Shun Lee West** (43 W 65th St)

Chicken, Dijon: **Zabar's** (2245 Broadway)

Chicken, fried: **Charles' Southern Style Kitchen** (308 Lenox Ave and 2837 Frederick Douglass Blvd), and **M&G Diner** (383 W 125th St)

Chicken, grilled: **Da Nico** (164 Mulberry St)

Chicken, free-roaming, **Murray's**: sold in top-quality meat markets all over the city

Chicken, parmesan: **Il Mulino** (86 W 3rd St)

Chicken, roasted: **davidburke & donatella** (133 E 61st St) and **Mitchel London Foods** (22-A E 65th St and 458 Ninth Ave)

Chicken, tandoori: **Curry in a Hurry** (119 Lexington Ave)

Chicken dishes: **International Poultry** (983 First Ave)

Chicken hash: **21 Club** (21 W 52nd St)

Chicken-in-a-pot: **Fine & Schapiro** (138 W 72nd St)

Chicken Kiev with foie gras sauce: **Picholine** (35 W 64th St)

Chicken salad: **China Grill** (60 W 53rd St)

Chicken salad, curry or walnut: **Petak's** (1246 Madison Ave)

Chicken shish kebab: **Ariana Afghan Kebab** (787 Ninth Ave)

Chicken tikka: **Pakistan Tea House** (176 Church St)

Chili: **Manhattan Chili Company** (Grand Central Terminal, 42nd St at Vanderbilt Ave, lower level)

Chinese vegetables (prepared): **Kam Man** (200 Canal St)

Chocolate Bruno: **Blue Ribbon** (97 Sullivan St)

Chocolate dessert: **ChikaLicious** (203 E 10th St) and **Four Seasons Hotel New York** (57 E 57th St)

Chocolate eclairs: **Patisserie Claude** (187 W 4th St)

Chocolate tasting: **Payard Patisserie & Bistro** (1032 Lexington Ave)

Chocolate truffles: **La Maison du Chocolat** (1018 Madison Ave)

Chops, mutton: **Keens Steakhouse** (72 W 36th St)

Chorizo bocadillo: **Bar Carrera** (175 Second Ave)

Clambake: **Clambakes by Jim Sanford** (205 W 95th St; call 212/865-8976)

Clam chowder: **Aquagrill** (210 Spring St)

Clam chowder, New England: **Pearl Oyster Bar** (18 Cornelia St)

Clams: **Umberto's Clam House** (178 Mulberry St)

Clams, baked: **Frank's Trattoria** (371 First Ave)

Cobbler, strawberry rhubarb (seasonal): **Gramercy Tavern** (42 E 20th St)

Cocas (flatbread pizzas from Catalonia): **Pipa** (38 E 19th St)

Coffee, iced: **Oren's Daily Roast** (1144 Lexington Ave and other locations)

Coffee beans: **Porto Rico Importing Company** (201 Bleecker St, 107 Thompson St, and 40½ St. Marks Pl) and **Zabar's** (2245 Broadway)

Cookies, butter: **CBK** (337 E 81st St, 212/794-3383; by appointment)

Cookies, chocolate chip: **City Bakery** (3 W 18th St), **Hampton Chutney Co.** (68 Prince St), **Jacques Torres Chocolate Haven** (350 Hudson St), **Levain Bakery** (167 W 74th St), and **Ruby et Violette** (457 W 50th St)

Cookies, chocolate chubbie: **Sarabeth's Kitchen** (423 Amsterdam Ave, 1295 Madison Ave, 945 Madison Ave, at Whitney Museum, and 40 Central Park S) and **Sarabeth's Bakery** (75 Ninth Ave)

Cookies, chocolate hazelnut: **De Robertis Pastry Shop & Caffe** (176 First Ave)

Cookies, chocolate turtles: **Yura** (1645 Third Ave and 1292 Madison Ave)

Corn on the cob, cheese-smeared: **Cafe Habana** (17 Prince St)

Cornbread: **Moishe's Bakery** (115 Second Ave) and **107 West** (2787 Broadway)

Corned beef: **Katz's Delicatessen** (205 E Houston St)

Corned beef hash: **Carnegie Delicatessen and Restaurant** (854 Seventh Ave)

Cotton candy: **Four Seasons** (99 E 52nd St)

Crab: **Pisacane Midtown** (940 First Ave)

Crab, soft shell (seasonally): **New York Noodle Town** (28½ Bowery)

Crab cakes: **Acme Bar & Grill** (9 Great Jones St) and **Tropica** (MetLife Building, 200 Park Ave)

Crab claws, stone: **Shelly's Prime Steak, Stone Crab, and Oyster Bar** (104 W 57th St)

Cream puffs: **Choux Factory** (865 First Ave)

Crème brûlée: **Barbetta** (321 W 46th St) and **Tribeca Grill** (375 Greenwich St)

Crepes: **Palacinka** (28 Grand St)

Croissants: **City Bakery** (3 W 18th St) and **Le Pain Quotidien** (100 Grand St and 1131 Madison Ave)

Croissants, almond: **Butterfield Market** (1114 Lexington Ave) and **Marquet Patisserie** (15 E 12th St)

Croquettes: **Tia Pol** (205 Tenth Ave)

Crudo (raw fish, Italian-style): **Cru** (24 Fifth Ave) and **Esca** (402 W 43rd St)

Cupcakes: **Buttercup Bake Shop** (973 Second Ave), **Crumbs** (321½ Amsterdam Ave), **Cupcake Cafe** (545 Ninth Ave and 18 W 18th St), **The Kitchenette** (1272 Amsterdam Ave), **Magnolia Bakery** (401 Bleecker St), **Mitchel London** (22-A E 65th St and 458 Ninth Ave), **Out of the Kitchen** (456 Hudson St), and **William Greenberg Jr. Desserts** (1100 Madison Ave)

Curry: **Baluchis** (193 Spring St), **Brick Lane Curry House** (306-308 E 6th St), and **Tabla Bread Bar** (11 Madison Ave)

Danishes: **Chez le Chef** (127 Lexington Ave)

Dates, piggyback: **Pipa** (ABC Carpet & Home, 38 E 19th St)

Delicatessen assortment: **Dean & Deluca** (560 Broadway), **Grace's Marketplace** (1237 Third Ave), and **Zabar's** (2245 Broadway)

Dessert, chocolate: **ChikaLicious** (203 E 10th St), **Il Laboratorio de**

Gelato (95 Orchard St), **Max Brenner: Chocolate by the Bald Man** (841 Broadway), and **Sugar Sweet Sunshine** (126 Rivington St)

Dessert, frozen low-calorie: **Tasti D-Lite** (1115 Lexington Ave and other locations)

Dessert, Japanese: **Kyotofu** (705 Ninth Ave)

Dessert tasting, chocolate: **Del Posto** (85 Tenth Ave)

Doughnuts: **Krispy Kreme** (1497 Third Ave and other locations)

Doughnuts, whole wheat: **Cupcake Cafe** (545 Ninth Ave and 18 W 18th St)

Duck: **Apple Restaurant** (17 Waverly Pl)

Duck, barbecue: **Big Wong King** (67 Mott St)

Duck, Beijing: **Shun Lee Palace** (155 E 55th St)

Duck, braised: **Quatorze Bis** (323 E 79th St) and **Tang Pavilion** (65 W 55th St; order in advance)

Duck, corned (appetizer): **wd-50** (50 Clinton St)

Duck, Peking: **Home's Kitchen** (22 E 21st St), **Our Place** (1444 Third Ave), **Peking Duck House Restaurant** (28 Mott St), **Shun Lee Palace** (155 E 55th St), and **Shun Lee West** (43 W 65th St)

Duck, roasted: **Four Seasons** (99 E 52nd St)

Duck, tea-smoked: **Grand Sichuan** (227 Lexington Ave and other locations)

Dumplings: **Chin Chin** (216 E 49th St), **Excellent Dumpling House** (111 Lafayette St), **Joe's Shanghai** (9 Pell St), and **Peking Duck House Restaurant** (28 Mott St)

Dumplings, chicken: **Chiam** (160 E 48th St)

Dumplings, crispy fried: **New Green Bo** (66 Bayard St)

Dumplings, Shanghai: **Goody's** (1 East Broadway)

Egg cream: **Carnegie Delicatessen and Restaurant** (854 Seventh Ave), **EJ's Luncheonette** (447 Amsterdam Ave and 1271 Third Ave), and **The Soda Shop** (125 Chambers St)

Eggs, Alsatian *en cocotte*: **August** (359 Bleecker St)

Eggs, coddled: **Telepan** (72 W 69th St)

Eggs, fresh Jersey: stands at 72 E 7th St (Thurs only: 7 a.m.-5:30 p.m.) and 1750 Second Ave

Eggs, Scotch: **Myers of Keswick** (634 Hudson St)

Eggs, soft-boiled: **Le Pain Quotidien** (100 Grand St and 1131 Madison Ave)

Empanadas: **Ruben's** (64 Fulton St, 505 Broome St, and 122 First Ave) and **Il Buco** (47 Bond St)

Escargots: **Artisanal** (2 Park Ave) and **Town** (15 W 56th St)

Espresso: **Caffe Dante** (79-81 MacDougal St) and **Caffe Reggio** (119 MacDougal St)

Espresso, purist: **Ninth Street Espresso** (700 E 9th St)

Falafel: **Alfanoose** (8 Maiden Lane), **Horus Cafe** (93 Ave B), **Sahara East** (184 First Ave), and **Taïm** (222 Waverly Pl)

Fish vendor: **Tan My My** (249 Grand St)

Fish, Chilean sea bass (when available): **Cellini** (65 E 54th St)

Fish, cod (battered): **A Salt & Battery** (112 Greenwich Ave)

Fish, fresh: **Citarella** (1313 Third Ave and 2135 Broadway)

Fish, grilled: **Estiatorio Milos** (125 W 55th St)

Fish, pickled herring: **Sable's Smoked Fish** (1489 Second Ave)

Fish, smoked: **Russ & Daughters** (179 E Houston St) and **Barney Greengrass** (541 Amsterdam Ave)

Fish, sturgeon: **Barney Greengrass** (541 Amsterdam Ave) and **Sable's Smoked Fish** (1489 Second Ave)

Fish, tuna steak: **Gotham Bar & Grill** (12 E 12th St) and **Union Square Cafe** (21 E 16th St)

Fish, tuna tartare: **Tropica** (MetLife Building, 200 Park Ave)

Fish, turbot (seasonally): **Jean Georges** (1 Central Park W)

Fish and chips: **A Salt & Battery** (112 Greenwich Ave), **BLT Fish** (21 W 17th St), **Finnegan's Wake** (1361 First Ave), and **Telephone Bar & Grill** (149 Second Ave)

Flatbreads: **Kalustyan's** (123 Lexington Ave)

Foie gras: **Balthazar** (80 Spring St), **Daniel** (60 E 65th St), **Gascogne** (158 Eighth Ave), **Le Bernardin** (155 W 51st St), **Le Périgord** (405 E 52nd St), and **Veritas** (43 E 20th St)

Foie gras, Shabu Shabu (occasionally): **Masa** (10 Columbus Circle)

Fondue: **La Bonne Soupe** (48 W 55th St)

Food and kitchen equipment (best all-around store): **Zabar's** (2245 Broadway)

French fries: **Atomic Wings** (528 Ninth Ave), **Cafe de Bruxelles** (118 Greenwich Ave), **Cafe Loup** (105 W 13th St), **Grand Saloon** (158 E 23rd St), **The Harrison** (355 Greenwich St), **Les Halles** (411 Park Ave S and 15 John St), **Market Cafe** (496 Ninth Ave), **Michael's** (24 W 55th St), **Pampa** (768 Amsterdam Ave), **Pastis** (9 Ninth Ave), **Petite Abeille** (466 Hudson St), and **Steak Frites** (9 E 16th St)

Fries, steak: **Balthazar** (80 Spring St) and **Montparnasse** (230 E 51st St)

Fries, sweet potato: **F&B Güdtfood** (150 E 52nd St and 269 W 23rd St)

Frites (French fries with mayonnaise): **Pommes Frites** (123 Second Ave)

Fruits and grains: **Nature's Gifts** (1297 Lexington Ave and 320 E 86th St)

Fruits and vegetables: **Balducci's** (155-A W 66th St) and **Fairway Market** (2127 Broadway)

Fruit dessert plate: **Primavera** (1578 First Ave)

Game: **Ottomanelli's Meat Market** (285 Bleecker St) and **Da Umberto** (107 W 17th St)

Gelati: **Caffe Dante** (81 MacDougal St)

Gelato, homemade: **Da Enzo** (494 Ninth Ave) and **Fiamma Osteria** (206 Spring St)

Gingerbread house (with one week notice during Christmas season): **Chez le Chef** (127 Lexington Ave)

Gnocchi, potato: **Hearth** (403 E 12th St)

Goat, roasted baby (by request): **Primavera** (1578 First Ave)

Gourmet food: **Grace's Marketplace** (1237 Third Ave)

Groceries, specialty: **Gourmet Garage** (453 Broome St, 301 E 64th St, 2567 Broadway, and 117 Seventh Ave S)

Guacamole: **Manhattan Chili Company** (Grand Central Terminal, 42nd St at Vanderbilt Ave) and **Rosa Mexicano** (1063 First Ave and other locations)

Haggis (Scottish pudding made of sheep innards): **St. Andrew's** (120 W 44th St)

Halibut, steamed: **Le Bernardin** (155 W 51st St)

Hamburgers: **burger joint at Le Parker Meridien** (118 W 57th St), **Corner Bistro** (331 W 4th St), **DB Bistro Moderne** (55 W 44th

St), **Jackson Hole Burgers** (232 E 64th St and other locations), and **Shake Shack** (Madison Square Park at 23rd St)

Hamburgers, Roquefort: **Burger Heaven** (9 E 53rd St)

Hen, Cornish: **Lorenzo and Maria's Kitchen** (1418 Third Ave)

Heros: **Hero Boy** (492 Ninth Ave) and **Italian Food Center** (186 Grand St)

Heros, sausage: **Manganaro Grosseria Italiana** (488 Ninth Ave)

Hominy, fried spiced: **Cookshop** (156 Tenth Ave)

Horseradish, kosher: **The Pickle Guys** (49 Essex St)

Hot chocolate: **City Bakery** (3 W 18th St), **Jacques Torres Chocolate Haven** (350 Hudson St and 66 Water St), **Lunettes et Chocolat** (25 Prince St), **Payard Patisserie** (1032 Lexington Ave), and **Vosges Haut-Chocolat** (132 Spring St)

Hot dogs: **Brooklyn Diner USA** (212 W 57th St), **Crif Dogs** (113 St. Marks Pl), **Dash Dogs** (127 Rivington St), **Dawgs on Park** (178 E 7th St), **F&B Güdtfood** (269 W 23rd St), **Gray's Papaya** (402 Ave of the Americas, 539 Eighth Ave, and 2090 Broadway), **Old Town Bar** (45 E 18th St), and **Papaya King** (179 E 86th St and other locations)

Huitlacoche (Mexican specialty): **Rosa Mexicano** (1063 First Ave and 61 Columbus Ave)

Hummus: **Hoomoos Asli** (100 Kenmare St)

Ice cream: **Ciao Bella Cafe** (27 E 92nd St), **Petrossian Cafe and Boutique** (911 Seventh Ave), **Petrossian Restaurant** (182 W 58th St), and **Serendipity 3** (225 E 60th St)

Ice cream, caramel (occasionally): **Gramercy Tavern** (42 E 20th St)

Ice cream sundae: **Brooklyn Diner USA** (212 W 57th St)

Ice cream sundae ("Forbidden Broadway"—awesome!): **Serendipity 3** (225 E 60th St)

Ice cream sundae, sesame: **Bôi** (246 E 44th St)

Indian snacks: **Lassi** (28 Greenwich Ave)

Jambalaya: **107 West** (2787 Broadway)

Juice, fresh-squeezed: **Candle Cafe** (1307 Third Ave)

Kebabs: **Turkish Cuisine** (631 Ninth Ave) and **Turkish Kitchen** (386 Third Ave)

Knishes: **Murray's Sturgeon Shop** (2429 Broadway)

Kobe beef: **L'Atelier de Joël Robuchon** (57 E 57th St) and **Riingo** (205 E 45th St)

Lamb, rack of: **Gotham Bar & Grill** (12 E 12th St) and **Shun Lee Palace** (155 E 55th St)

Lamb shank: **Bolo** (23 E 22nd St) and **Molyvos** (871 Seventh Ave)

Lamb stew: **Bouterin** (420 E 59th St)

Lasagna: **Via Emilia** (472 E 21st St)

Latkes: **Just Like Mother's** (110-60 Queens Blvd, Forest Hills, Queens)

Lemonade: **Lexington Candy Shop** (1226 Lexington Ave) and **Pyramida** (401 E 78th St)

Liver, chopped: **Fischer Brothers** (230 W 72nd St)

Liverwurst: **The Modern** (Museum of Modern Art, 9 W 53rd St)

Lobster: **Blue Ribbon Sushi** (119 Sullivan St) and **Docks Oyster Bar and Seafood Grill** (2427 Broadway and 633 Third Ave)

Lobster, poached: **per se** (10 Columbus Circle)

Lobster roll: **BLT Fish** (21 W 17th St) and **Pearl Oyster Bar** (18 Cornelia St)

Lollipops, cheesecake: **davidburke & donatella** (133 E 61st St)
Macaroni and cheese: **S'mac** (345 E 12th St)
Marinara sauce: **Patsy's** (236 W 56th St)
Meat (best service): **Oppenheimer Meats** (2606 Broadway) and **Jefferson Market** (450 Ave of the Americas)
Meat (German deli-style cold-cut selection): **Schaller & Weber** (1654 Second Ave)
Meat and poultry (best prices): **Empire Purveyors** (883 First Ave)
Meatballs: **Il Gattopardo** (33 W 54th St) and **Kefi** (222 W 79th St)
Meatballs, duck and foie gras: **A Voce** (41 Madison Ave)
Meatloaf (Sunday special): **Ouest** (2315 Broadway)
Meatloaf, bison: **Ted's Montana Grill** (110 W 51st St)
Mexican foodstuffs: **Kitchen/Market** (218 Eighth Ave)
Meze (Turkish tapas-like appetizer): **Beyoglu** (1431 Third Ave)
Milkshakes: **Comfort Diner** (214 E 45th St) and **Brgr** (287 Seventh Ave)
Moussaka: **Kefi** (222 W 79th St) and **Periyali** (35 W 20th St)
Mozzarella, smoked: **Joe's Dairy** (156 Sullivan St)
Mozzarella and ricotta: **Russo and Son** (344 E 11th St)
Mücver (zucchini pancakes): **Turkuaz Restaurant** (2637 Broadway)
Muffins: **Between the Bread** (145 W 55th St) and **The Muffins Shop** (222 Columbus Ave)
Muffins, corn: **107 West** (2787 Broadway)
Muffins, pear-walnut: **Soutine Bakery** (104 W 70th St)
Mushrooms, grilled portobello: **Giovanni Venti Cinque** (25 E 83rd St)
Mushrooms, wild: **Grace's Marketplace** (1237 Third Ave)
Mussels: **Jubilee** (347 E 54th St)
Nachos: **Benny's Burritos** (113 Greenwich Ave)
Napoleon: **Ecco** (124 Chambers St)
Natural foods: **Whole Foods Market** (2421 Broadway and other locations)
Noodle bar: **Kampuchea Noodle Bar** (78 Rivington St) and **Momofuku Noodle Bar** (163 First Ave)
Noodles: **Golden Bridge** (50 Bowery St), **Kelley and Ping** (127 Greene St and 325 Bowery St), **Mei Lai Wah Coffee House** (64 Bayard St), **Sammy's Noodle Shop & Grill** (453 Ave of the Americas), and **Yuen Yuen Restaurant** (61 Bayard St)
Noodles, Asian: **Republic** (37 Union Sq W)
Noodles, Chinese: **Je'Bon Noodle House** (15 St. Mark's Pl)
Noodles, cold with hot sesame sauce: **Sung Chu Mei** (615 Hudson St)
Noodles, green tea: **Ten Ren's Tea Time** (79 Mott St)
Noodles, Shanghai-style: **Shun Lee Palace** (155 E 55th St)
Noodles, soba: **Soba Nippon** (19 W 52nd St)
Noodles (mainly non-vegetarian): **Momofuku Noodle Bar** (163 First Ave)
Nuts: **A. L. Bazzini Co.** (339 Greenwich St)
Oatmeal: **Sarabeth's Kitchen** (1295 Madison Ave, 423 Amsterdam Ave, 40 Central Park S, and 945 Madison Ave, at Whitney Museum)
Olive oils: **Oliviers & Co.** (249 Bleecker St and 412 Lexington Ave)
Olives: **International Grocery** (543 Ninth Ave)
Onion rings: **Cornerstone Grill** (187 Duane St), **Home Restaurant** (20 Cornelia St), **Palm One** (837 Second Ave), **Palm Too** (840 Second Ave), and **Palm West Side** (250 W 50th St)

Oyster stew: **Grand Central Oyster Bar Restaurant** (Grand Central Terminal, 42nd St at Vanderbilt Ave, lower level)

Oysters Rockefeller (occasionally): **City Hall** (131 Duane St)

Oysters, wood-roasted: **Beacon** (25 W 56th St)

Paella: **Bolo** (23 E 22nd St), **Boqueria** (53 W 19th St), and **Sevilla** (62 Charles St)

Pajun: **Han Bat** (53 W 35th St)

Pancakes: **Friend of a Farmer** (77 Irving Pl) and **Vinegar Factory** (431 E 91st St; weekend brunch)

Pancakes, blue corn: **Mesa Grill** (102 Fifth Ave)

Pancakes, kimchi: **Dok Suni's** (119 First Ave)

Pancakes, potato: **Rolf's** (281 Third Ave)

Pancakes, raspberry: **Veselka** (144 Second Ave)

Panini: **'ino** (21 Bedford St) and **'inoteca** (98 Rivington St)

Panna cotta (dessert, occasionally): **Gramercy Tavern** (42 E 20th St)

Pasta: **Arqua** (281 Church St), **Bottino** (246 Tenth Ave), **Cafe Pertutti** (2888 Broadway), **Caffe Buon Gusto** (236 E 77th St), **Cinque Terre** (22 E 38th St), **Col Legno** (231 E 9th St), **Fresco by Scotto** (34 E 52nd St), **Gabriel's** (11 W 60th St), **Il Valentino** (330 E 56th St), **Paola's** (245 E 84th St), **Piano Due** (151 W 51st St), **Pinocchio** (1748 First Ave), **Roberto Passon** (741 Ninth Ave), **Teodora** (141 E 57th St), and **Todaro Bros.** (555 Second Ave)

Pasta, angel hair: **Piemonte Homemade Ravioli Company** (190 Grand St) and **Nanni** (146 E 46th St)

Pasta, handmade egg: **Balducci's** (155-A W 66th St)

Pasta (inexpensive): **LaMarca** (161 E 22nd St)

Pasta, Venetian: **Remi** (145 W 53rd St)

Pastrami: **Artie's Delicatessen** (2290 Broadway), **Carnegie Delicatessen and Restaurant** (854 Seventh Ave), and **Katz's Delicatessen** (205 E Houston St)

Pastries: **Financier Patisserie** (3-4 World Financial Center and 62 Stone St)

Pastries, French: **La Bergamote** (169 Ninth Ave)

Pastries, Hungarian: **Hungarian Pastry Shop** (1030 Amsterdam Ave)

Pastries, Italian: **LaBella Ferrara Pastry** (108-110 Mulberry St) and **Rocco Pastry Shop** (243 Bleecker St)

Pastries, Japanese (traditional): **Minamoto Kitchoan** (608 Fifth Ave)

Paté: **Zabar's** (2245 Broadway)

Peanut butter: **Peanut Butter & Co.** (240 Sullivan St)

Pickle plate (seasonally): **Momofuku Noodle Bar** (163 First Ave)

Pickled-herring sampler: **Smörgas Chef** (53 Stone St)

Pickles, kosher: **The Pickle Guys** (49 Essex St)

Pickles, sour or half-sour: **Russ & Daughters** (179 E Houston St)

Pie, apple: **William Greenberg Jr. Desserts** (1100 Madison Ave) and **Yura** (1645 Third Ave and 1292 Madison Ave)

Pie, apple crumb: **Cupcake Cafe** (545 Ninth Ave) and **Wimp's Southern Style Bakery** (29 W 125th St)

Pie, banana cream: **Sarabeth's Kitchen** (423 Amsterdam Ave, 1295 Madison Ave, 40 Central Park S, and 945 Madison Ave, at Whitney Museum)

Pie, cheddar-crust apple (autumn only): **Little Pie Company** (424 W 43rd St)

Pie, cherry crumb (summer only): **Magnolia Bakery** (401 Bleecker St)

Pie, clam: **Lombardi's** (32 Spring St)

Pie, duck shepherd's: **Balthazar** (80 Spring St)

Pie, key lime: **Little Pie Company** (424 W 43rd St) and **Union Square Cafe** (21 E 16th St)

Pie, pecan: **Magnolia Bakery** (401 Bleecker St)

Pie, sweet potato: **Wimp's Southern Style Bakery** (29 W 125th St)

Pie, walnut sour-cream apple: **Little Pie Company** (424 W 43rd St)

Pies: **E.A.T.** (1064 Madison Ave)

Pig, roast suckling: **Eleven Madison Park** (11 Madison Ave)

Pig's feet (occasionally): **Daniel** (60 E 65th St)

Pistachios: **A.L. Bazzini Co.** (339 Greenwich St)

Pizza (by the slice): **Pizza 33** (489 Third Ave)

Pizza, designer: **Paper Moon Milano** (39 E 58th St)

Pizza, gourmet: **apizz** (217 Eldridge St)

Pizza, grilled: **Gonzo** (140 W 13th St)

Pizza, Neapolitan: **Sal's & Carmine's Pizza** (2671 Broadway) and **Stromboli Pizzeria** (112 University Pl)

Polenta, mushroom: **La Focaccia** (51 Bank St)

Popcorn: **Dale & Thomas Popcorn** (1592 Broadway and 2170 Broadway)

Popovers: **Popover Cafe** (551 Amsterdam Ave)

Pork: **Oppenheimer Meats** (2606 Broadway)

Pork, barbecue: **Big Wong King** (67 Mott St)

Pork, braised: **Daniel** (60 E 65th St)

Pork buns: **Mei Lai Wah Coffee House** (64 Bayard St)

Pork, European-style cured: **Salumeria Biellese** (376 Eighth Ave)

Pork and chicken buns: **Lung Moon Bakery** (83 Mulberry St)

Pork chops, smoked: **Yorkville Packing House** (1560 Second Ave)

Pork shank: **Maloney & Porcelli** (37 E 50th St)

Potato chips: **Vinegar Factory** (431 E 91st St)

Potatoes, mashed: **Mama's Food Shop** (200 E 3rd St) and **Union Square Cafe** (21 E 16th St)

Pretzels and cookies, hand-dipped chocolate: **Evelyn's Chocolates** (4 John St)

Prime rib: **Smith & Wollensky** (797 Third Ave)

Produce, fresh: **Fairway Market** (2127 Broadway)

Profiteroles: **Cafe Cluny** (284 W 12th St)

Pudding, rice: **Rice to Riches** (37 Spring St)

Ravioli: **Bruno Ravioli** (2204 Broadway and other locations), **Di Palo Fine Food** (200 Grand St), **Osteria del Circo** (120 W 55th St), **Piemonte Homemade Ravioli Company** (190 Grand St), and **Ravioli Store** (75 Sullivan St)

Ravioli, steamed Vietnamese: **Indochine** (430 Lafayette St)

Ribs: **Brother Jimmy's BBQ** (1485 Second Ave), **Hog Pit** (22 Ninth Ave), **RUB BBQ** (208 W 23rd St), and **Sylvia's** (328 Lenox Ave)

Ribs, baby back: **Baby Buddha** (753 Washington St) and **Ruby Foo's** (1626 Broadway and 2182 Broadway)

Ribs, braised short beef: **Daniel** (60 E 65th St) and **Deborah** (43 Carmine St)

Rice: **Rice** (227 Mott St)
Rice, fried: **Ollie's** (1991 Broadway and other locations)
Rice, sticky, with mango: **Vong** (200 E 54th St)
Risotto: **Four Seasons** (99 E 52nd St) and **Risotteria** (270 Bleecker St)
Rugelach: **Margaret Palca Bakes** (191 Columbia St, Brooklyn) and **Ruthy's Cheesecake and Rugelach Bakery** (75 Ninth Ave)
Sake: **Sakagura** (211 E 43rd St)
Salad, Caesar: **Pearl Oyster Bar** (18 Cornelia St) and **Post House** (28 E 63rd St)
Salad, egg: **Murray's Sturgeon Shop** (2429 Broadway)
Salad, lobster: **Sable's Smoked Fish** (1489 Second Ave)
Salad, red beet: **Roberto Passon** (741 Ninth Ave)
Salad, seafood: **Gotham Bar & Grill** (12 E 12th St)
Salad, tuna: **Cosi Sandwich Bar** (504 Ave of the Americas and other locations), **Murray's Sturgeon Shop** (2429 Broadway), and **Todaro Bros.** (555 Second Ave)
Salad, warm white bean: **Caffe Grazie** (26 E 84th St)
Salad, whitefish: **Barney Greengrass** (541 Amsterdam Ave)
Salad bar: **Azure** (830 Third Ave) and **City Bakery** (3 W 18th St)
Salmon fillets, Norwegian: **Sea Breeze** (541 Ninth Ave)
Salmon, smoked: **Aquavit** (65 E 55th St), **Murray's Sturgeon Shop** (2429 Broadway), and **Sable's Smoked Fish** (1489 Second Ave)
Sandwich, avocado (Thursday special): **Olives** (120 Prince St)
Sandwich, bacon, lettuce and tomato (BLT): **Eisenberg's Sandwich Shop** (174 Fifth Ave), **Good** (89 Greenwich Ave), **Marquet** (15 E 12th St), and **Sullivan Street Bakery** (533 W 47th St)
Sandwich, *banh mi* (Vietnamese hoagie): **Nicky's Vietnamese Sandwiches** (150 E 2nd St)
Sandwich, beef brisket: **Smith's Bar & Restaurant** (701 Eighth Ave)
Sandwich, cheesesteak: **BB Sandwich Bar** (120 W 3rd St) and **Wogie's Bar & Grill** (39 Greenwich Ave)
Sandwich, chicken: **Ranch 1** (315 Seventh Ave and other locations)
Sandwich, *croque monsieur:* **Payard Patisserie** (1032 Lexington Ave)
Sandwich, Cuban: **Margon Restaurant** (136 W 46th St)
Sandwich, flatbread: **Cosi Sandwich Bar** (504 Ave of the Americas and other locations)
Sandwich, French dip: **Sandwich Planet** (534 Ninth Ave)
Sandwich, green: **Shorty's** (576 Ninth Ave)
Sandwich, grilled cheese: **Say Cheese** (649 Ninth Ave)
Sandwich, grilled portobello: **Zoë** (90 Prince St)
Sandwich, loin of pork: **Bottino** (246 Tenth Ave)
Sandwich, pastrami on rye: **Katz's Delicatessen** (205 E Houston St)
Sandwich, Philly cheesesteak: **Carl's Steaks** (507 Third Ave and 79 Chambers St) and **99 Miles to Philly** (94 Third Ave)
Sandwich, pig (pulled pork): **Hard Rock Cafe** (1501 Broadway)
Sandwich, po' boy: **Two Boots** (42 Ave A)
Sandwich, *poulet roti* (roast chicken): **Chez Brigitte** (77 Greenwich Ave)
Sandwich, turkey: **Viand Coffee Shop** (2130 Broadway, 300 E 86th St, 673 Madison Ave, and 1011 Madison Ave)
Sandwiches (many varieties): **Call Cuisine** (1032 First Ave)
Sashimi: **Sakagura** (211 E 43rd St)

Sauerkraut: **Katz's Delicatessen** (205 E Houston St) and **Wallsé** (344 W 11th St)

Sausage, blood: **Buenos Aires** (513 E 6th St)

Sausage, European-style: **Kurowycky Meat** (124 First Ave) and **Mandler's** (26 E 17th St)

Sausage, freshly made (over 40 kinds; selection varies daily): **Salumeria Biellese** (376 Eighth Ave)

Sausage, *morcilla* (Spanish-style blood sausage): **Bar Carrera** (175 Second Ave)

Scallops: **Le Bernardin** (155 W 51st St)

Schnecken (cinnamon yeast pastry rollups): **William Greenberg Jr. Desserts** (1100 Madison Ave)

Schnitzel (occasionally): **Café Gray** (10 Columbus Circle)

Scones: **Mangia** (50 W 57th St), **The Muffins Shop** (222 Columbus Ave), and **Tea & Sympathy** (108 Greenwich Ave)

Seafood dinners: **Le Bernardin** (155 W 51st St)

Shabu-shabu (Japanese hot pot): **Swish Cafe & Shabu Shabu** (88 W 3rd St)

Shrimp, grilled: **Periyali** (35 W 20th St)

Sliders (mini burgers): **Sassy's Sliders** (1530 Third Ave)

Snacks, soups, and sandwiches: **Serendipity 3** (225 E 60th St)

Sorbet: **La Boite en Bois** (75 W 68th St) and **La Maison du Chocolat** (1018 Madison Ave; summer only)

Soufflé: **Capsouto Frères** (451 Washington St)

Soufflé, apricot: **Gordon Ramsay at the London** (151 W 54th St)

Soufflé, Grand Marnier: **La Grenouille** (3 E 52nd St)

Soup: **Sheng Wang** (27 Eldridge St)

Soup, black bean: **Union Square Cafe** (21 E 16th St)

Soup, chestnut and fennel (seasonally): **Picholine** (35 W 64th St)

Soup, chicken: **Brooklyn Diner USA** (212 W 57th St), **Bubby's** (120 Hudson St), **craftbar** (900 Broadway), **Fred's** (Barneys New York, 660 Madison Ave), **Teresa's** (103 First Ave), and **Via Emilia** (47 E 21st St)

Soup, Chinese: **New Chao Chow** (111 Mott St)

Soup, dill broth: **Perry Street** (176 Perry St)

Soup, duck: **Kelley and Ping** (127 Greene St)

Soup, French onion: **Casanis** (81 Ludlow St), **La Bonne Soupe** (48 W 55th St), and **Le Singe Vert** (160 Seventh Ave)

Soup, hot and sour: **Shun Lee Cafe** (43 W 65th St)

Soup, hot yogurt: **Beyoglu** (1431 Third Ave)

Soup, *kimchi chigae* (spicy stew with beef, tofu, and pork): **Do Hwa** (55 Carmine St)

Soup, matzoh ball: **Blue Ribbon Bakery** (33 Downing St)

Soup, minestrone: **Il Vagabondo** (351 E 62nd St) and **Trattoria Spaghetto** (232 Bleecker St)

Soup, noodle: **New Chao Chow** (111 Mott St)

Soup, pumpkin (seasonally): **Mesa Grill** (102 Fifth Ave)

Soup, split pea: **Cafe Edison** (228 W 47th St) and **Joe Jr.** (482 E 6th St and 167 Third Ave)

Soup, tapioca noodle: **Bao Noodles** (391 Second Ave)

Soup, tomato: **Sarabeth's Kitchen** (423 Amsterdam Ave, 1295 Madison Ave, 40 Central Park S, and 945 Madison Ave, at Whitney Museum)

Soup, white borscht (weekends): **Teresa's** (80 Montague St, Brooklyn)

Soup, wonton: **New Chao Chow** (111 Mott St)

Southwestern fare: **Lonesome Dove Western Bistro** (29 W 21st St)

Soybeans: **Soy** (102 Suffolk St)

Spaghetti, homemade: **L'Impero** (45 Tudor City Place)

Spareribs, Chinese: **Fu's House** (972 Second Ave)

Spices: **Aphrodisia** (264 Bleecker St), **International Grocery** (543 Ninth Ave), and **Kalustyan's** (123 Lexington Ave)

Spinach pies, Greek: **Poseidon Bakery** (629 Ninth Ave)

Spring rolls, crab: **Vong** (200 E 54th St)

Squab, roasted stuffed (seasonally): **Daniel** (60 E 65th St)

Steak, Black Angus and French fries: **Steak Frites** (9 E 16th St)

Steak, Cajun rib: **Morton's of Chicago** (551 Fifth Ave) and **Post House** (28 E 63rd St)

Steak, pepper: **Chez Josephine** (414 W 42nd St)

Steak, Porterhouse: **Morton's of Chicago** (551 Fifth Ave) and **Porters New York** (216 Seventh Ave)

Steak tartare: **Brasserie Ruhlmann** (45 Rockefeller Plaza), **Cafe at Country** (90 Madison Ave), and **21 Club** (21 W 52nd St)

String beans, Chinese-style: **Tang Tang** (1328 Third Ave)

Strudel: **Cafe Sabarsky** (1048 Fifth Ave, at Neue Galerie), **Del Posto** (85 Tenth Ave), and **The Modern** (9 W 53rd St, at Museum of Modern Art)

Sushi, *omakase* ("astonish me"): **Taka** (61 Grove St)

Sweetbreads: **Casa Mono & Bar Jamone** (52 Irving Place)

Swordfish, charbroiled: **Morton's of Chicago** (551 Fifth Ave)

Tacos: **Gabriela's** (688 Columbus Ave), **Maya** (1191 First Ave), **Mexicana Mama** (525 Hudson St), and **Rosa Mexicano** (1063 First Ave and 61 Columbus Ave)

Tacos, fish: **Mercadito** (179 Ave B)

Tapas: **Azafran** (77 Warren St), **Bar Carrera** (175 Second Ave), **Bolo** (23 E 22nd St), **Boqueria** (53 W 19th St), **Casa Mono & Bar Jamone** (52 Irving Pl), **El Cid** (322 W 15th St), **Flor de Sol** (361 Greenwich St), **Las Ramblas** (170 W 4th St), **Ñ** (33 Crosby St), **Oliva** (161 E Houston St), **Pipa** (38 E 19th St, at ABC Carpet & Home), **Solera** (216 E 53rd St), **Suba** (109 Ludlow St), **Tia Pol** (205 Tenth Ave), and **Xunta** (174 First Ave)

Tart, apple: **Gotham Bar & Grill** (12 E 12th St), **Marquet Patisserie** (15 E 12th St), and **Quatorze Bis** (323 E 79th St)

Tart, chocolate: **Le Bernardin** (155 W 51st St)

Tart, fruit: **Ceci-Cela** (55 Spring St) and **Payard Patisserie** (1032 Lexington Ave)

Tart, fruit and vegetable: **Once Upon a Tart** (135 Sullivan St)

Tart, lemon: **Margot Patisserie** (2109 Broadway)

Tartufo: **Il Corallo Trattoria** (172-176 Prince St), **Il Vagabondo** (351 E 62nd St), and **Sette Mezzo** (969 Lexington Ave)

Tea, green: **Ito En** (822 Madison Ave)

Tea, loose (over 100 kinds!): **Alice's Tea Cup** (102 W 73rd St)

Tempura: **Inagiku** (301 Park Ave, at Waldorf-Astoria Hotel)

Tequila: **Dos Caminos** (373 Park Ave S and other locations)

Tiramisu: **Biricchino** (260 W 29th St), **Caffe Dante** (79 MacDougal St), and **Mezzogiorno** (195 Spring St)

Tonkatsu: **Katsu-Hama** (11 E 47th St)

Torte, sacher (special order): **Duane Park Patisserie** (179 Duane St)
Tortillas, corn: **Pure Food and Wine** (54 Irving Pl)
Tripe *alla parmigiana* (occasionally): **Babbo** (110 Waverly Pl)
Veal rib chop: **Baldoria** (249 W 49th St)
Vegan foods: **Whole Earth Bakery & Kitchen** (130 St. Marks Pl)
Vegetables, raw: **Estiatorio Milos** (125 W 55th St)
Vegetarian combo: **Hudson Falafel** (516 Hudson St)
Vegetarian items: **Vegetarian's Paradise 2** (144 W 4th St)
Vegetarian meals: **Natural Gourmet Institute** (48 W 21st St)
Venison (seasonally): **Chanterelle** (2 Harrison St)
Waffles, Belgian: **Cafe de Bruxelles** (118 Greenwich Ave)**, Le Pain Quotidien** (100 Grand St and other locations), and **Petite Abeille** (107 W 18th St)
Waffles, pumpkin: **Sarabeth's Kitchen** (1295 Madison Ave, 423 Amsterdam Ave, 40 Central Park S, and 945 Madison Ave, at Whitney Museum)
Wagashi (gelatinous sweet confection): **Minimoto Kitchoan** (608 Fifth Ave)
Whiskeys, malt: **Soho Wines & Spirits** (461 West Broadway)
Wine, French: **Park Avenue Liquors** (292 Madison Ave) and **Quality House** (2 Park Ave)
Wine, German: **First Avenue Wines & Spirits** (383 First Ave)

BAGELS

Absolute Bagels (2788 Broadway)
BagelWorks (1229 First Ave)
Bagel Zone (50 Ave A)
Bagels on the Square (7 Carmine St)
Balthazar (80 Spring St)
Ess-a-Bagel (359 First Ave and 831 Third Ave)
H&H Bagels (2239 Broadway and 639 W 46th St)
H&H Midtown Bagels East (1551 Second Ave)
Lenny's (2601 Broadway)
Murray's Bagels (500 Ave of the Americas)
Pick-a-Bagel (200 W 57th St)

BARBECUE

Big Wong King (67 Mott St): Chinese style
Blue Smoke (116 E 27th St)
Bone Lick Park (75 Greenwich Ave): ribs and pork smoked over fruit woods and hickory
Brother Jimmy's BBQ (428 Amsterdam Ave): ribs, sandwiches, good sauce
Copeland's (547 W 145th St): Harlem setting
Daisy May's BBQ USA (623 Eleventh Ave)
Dallas BBQ (1265 Third Ave, 27 W 72nd St, 21 University Pl, and 132 Second Ave): big and busy
Dinosaur Bar-B-Que (646 W 131st St)
Hill Country (30 W 26th St)
Hog Pit (22 Ninth Ave)
Kang Suh (1250 Broadway)
RUB BBQ (208 W 23rd St)
Shun Lee Cafe (43 W 65th St): classy Chinese

Sylvia's (328 Lenox Ave): reputation better than the food
Virgil's Real Barbecue (152 W 44th St): big, brassy, mass production
Woo Chon (8-10 W 36th St): Korean

BARS FOR SENIORS

Bar Room at the Modern (Museum of Modern Art, 9 W 53rd St)
Bemelmans Bar (Carlyle Hotel, 35 E 76th St)
Blue Bar (Algonquin Hotel, 59 W 44th St)
Carnegie Club (156 W 56th St)
King Cole Bar (St. Regis New York, 2 E 55th St)

BREAKFAST

For the real morning-meal power scenes, hotels are the preferred locations. The biggest names:

Four Seasons Hotel New York, 57 (57 E 57th St): excellent pancakes
Loews Regency (540 Park Ave)
Paramount (235 W 46th St)
Peninsula New York Hotel (700 Fifth Ave)
Royalton (44 W 44th St)

Other restaurants serving excellent breakfasts:
Amy Ruth's (113 W 116th St)
Balthazar (80 Spring St)
Bite (211 E 14th St)
Bouley Bakery and Market (130 West Broadway)
Brasserie (100 E 53rd St)
Bright Food Shop (218 Eighth Ave)
Bubby's (120 Hudson St)
Cafe at Country (Carlton on Madison Avenue, 88 Madison Ave)
Cafe Cluny (284 W 12th St)
Carnegie Delicatessen and Restaurant (854 Seventh Ave)
Ceci-Cela (55 Spring St)
City Bakery (3 W 18th St)
Columbus Bakery (474 Columbus Ave): sinful cheese Danishes and
yummy croissants
Comfort Diner (214 E 45th St)
Cucina & Co. (MetLife Building, 200 Park Ave)
David Burke at Bloomingdale's (150 E 59th St): chef David Burke
Dishes (48 Grand Central Terminal, 42nd St at Vanderbilt Ave, lower level)
District (Muse Hotel, 130 W 46th St)
E.A.T. (1064 Madison Ave)
EJ's Luncheonette (447 Amsterdam Ave)
Ellen's Stardust Diner (1650 Broadway)
Fairway Market (2127 Broadway)
Falai Panetteria (79 Clinton St): early-bird crowd
Fitzer's (Fitzpatrick Manhattan Hotel, 687 Lexington Ave)
Florent (69 Gansevoort St)
Friend of a Farmer (77 Irving Pl)
Grey Dog's Coffee (33 Carmine St)
Heartbeat (W New York Hotel, 149 E 49th St)
Katz's Delicatessen (205 E Houston St)

Kitchen/Market (218 Eighth Ave)
Kitchenette (156 Chambers St)
Michael's (24 W 55th St)
Nice Matin (201 W 79th St)
NoHo Star (330 Lafayette St)
Norma's (Le Parker Meridien Hotel, 118 W 57th St)
Once Upon a Tart (135 Sullivan St)
Ouest (2315 Broadway)
Pastis (9 Ninth Ave): haven for weekday breakfasts in the Meatpacking District
Pigalle (790 Eighth Ave)
Pink Tea Cup (42 Grove St): country breakfasts
Popover Cafe (551 Amsterdam Ave)
Restaurant at the Essex House (Jumeirah Essex House, 160 Central Park S)
Rue 57 (60 W 57th St)
Sarabeth's Kitchen (423 Amsterdam Ave, 1295 Madison Ave, 40 Central Park S, and 945 Madison Ave, at Whitney Museum)
Schiller's (131 Rivington St)
Soda Shop (125 Chambers St)
Tramway Coffee Shop (1143 Second Ave)
Veselka (144 Second Ave)
Viand Coffee Shop (300 E 86th St, 673 Madison Ave, 2130 Broadway, and 1011 Madison Ave): crowded, but great value
Viet-Nam Banh Mi So 1 (369 Broome St)
Whole Foods (10 Columbus Circle, 40 E 14th St, 250 Seventh Ave, and 95 E Houston St)
Zucco: Le French Diner (188 Orchard St)

BRUNCH

Alias (76 Clinton St)
Annie's (1381 Third Ave)
Aquagrill (210 Spring St)
Aquavit (65 E 55th St)
Arium (31 Little W 12th St): tea salon/cafe in the Meatpacking District
Balthazar (80 Spring St)
Barney Greengrass (541 Amsterdam Ave)
Beacon (25 W 56th St)
Blue Ribbon Bakery (33 Downing St)
Café Gray (Time Warner Center, 10 Columbus Circle)
Cafe Habana (17 Prince St)
Cafe Lalo (201 W 83rd St)
Cafe Luluc (214 Smith St, Brooklyn)
Calle Ocho (446 Columbus Ave)
Candle 79 (154 E 79th St)
Capsouto Frères (451 Washington St)
Cendrillon (45 Mercer St): Filipino flavors
Church Lounge (2 Ave of the Americas)
Clinton St. Baking Co. & Restaurant (4 Clinton St)
Cookshop (156 Tenth Ave)
Cupping Room Cafe (359 West Broadway)
Danal (90 E 10th St): luscious French toast

davidburke & donatella (133 E 61st St)
Eleven Madison Park (11 Madison Ave)
Employees Only (510 Hudson St)
57 (Four Seasons Hotel New York, 57 E 57th St)
Five Points (31 Great Jones St)
Florent (69 Gansevoort St)
Freeman's (Freeman Alley, off Rivington St bet Bowery and Chrystie St)
Friend of a Farmer (77 Irving Pl)
Goblin Market (199 Prince St)
Good (89 Greenwich Ave)
Good Enough to Eat (483 Amsterdam Ave)
Isabella's (359 Columbus Ave)
Kittichai (60 Thompson St)
Klee Brasserie (200 Ninth Ave)
La Ripaille (605 Hudson St)
Marion's Continental Restaurant & Lounge (354 Bowery)
Nice Matin (201 W 79th St)
Odeon (145 West Broadway)
Olives New York (W New York Hotel, 201 Park Ave S)
Parea (36 E 20th St)
Paris Commune (99 Bank St): Bohemian West Village bistro
Park Avenue Cafe (100 E 63rd St)
Pig 'n Whistle (922 Third Ave): traditional Irish breakfast
Popover Cafe (551 Amsterdam Ave)
Prune (54 E 1st St): inspired weekend brunch
Rainbow Room (General Electric Building, 30 Rockefeller Plaza, 65th floor)
Restaurant at the Essex House (Jumeirah Essex House, 160 Central Park S)
River Cafe (1 Water Street, Brooklyn)
Sarabeth's Kitchen (1295 Madison Ave, 423 Amsterdam Ave, 40 Central Park S, and 945 Madison Ave, at Whitney Museum)
Spring Street Natural Restaurant (62 Spring St)
Sylvia's (328 Lenox Ave)
Tartine (253 W 11th St)
Tavern on the Green (Central Park W at 67th St): for entertaining out-of-town guests
Town (15 W 56th St)
Tribeca Grill (375 Greenwich St)
202 Cafe (75 Ninth Ave)
Vinegar Factory (431 E 91st St)
Wallsé (344 W 11th St)
Water Club (500 E 30th St)

BURGERS

Bar 89 (89 Mercer St)
Big Nick's (2175 Broadway): You'll love it!
BLT Burger (470 Ave of the Americas)
Blue Ribbon Bakery (33 Downing St)
Blue Smoke (116 E 27th St)
Brasserie 360 (200 E 60th St)
Brgr (287 Seventh Ave)
Burger Heaven (20 E 49th St, 536 Madison Ave, and 9 E 53rd St)

burger joint at Le Parker Meridien Hotel (119 W 56th St)
Burgers and Cupcakes (265 W 23rd St)
Cafe de Bruxelles (118 Greenwich Ave)
Chelsea Grill (675 Ninth Ave)
Chumley's (86 Bedford St)
Corner Bistro (331 W 4th St)
DB Bistro Moderne (City Club Hotel, 55 W 44th St)
DuMont Burger (314 Bedford Ave)
Fanelli's Cafe (94 Prince St)
Flames Steakhouse (5 Gold St)
44 (Royalton Hotel, 44 W 44th St)
Great Jones Cafe (54 Great Jones St)
Hard Rock Cafe (1501 Broadway)
Home Restaurant (20 Cornelia St)
J.G. Melon (1291 Third Ave)
Jackson Hole Burgers (232 E 64th St, 521 Third Ave, 1611 Second Ave, 1270 Madison Ave, and 517 Columbus Ave)
Keens Steakhouse (72 W 36th St)
Knickerbocker Bar and Grill (33 University Pl)
McDonald's (160 Broadway): atypically classy
MetroCafe & Wine Bar (32 E 21st St)
Odeon (145 West Broadway)
Old Town Bar (45 E 18th St)
P.J. Clarke's (915 Third Ave)
Pastis (9 Ninth Ave)
Patroon (160 E 46th St)
Paul's Palace (131 Second Ave)
Popover Cafe (551 Amsterdam Ave)
Prime Burger Cafe (56 Ninth Ave)
Rare Bar & Grill (Shelburne Hotel, 303 Lexington Ave)
Rodeo Bar (375 Third Ave)
Royale (157 Avenue C)
Rue 57 (60 W 57th St)
Shake Shack (Madison Square Park, at 23rd St)
Smith & Wollensky (797 Third Ave)
Soup Burg (1095 Lexington Ave)
Stand (24 E 12th St)
21 Club (21 W 52nd St)
Union Square Cafe (21 E 16th St)
The Waverly Inn (16 Bank St)
White Horse Tavern (567 Hudson St)
Wollensky's Grill (201 E 49th St)
Zip Burger (300 E 52nd St)
Zoë (90 Prince St)

CHEAP EATS

Alias (76 Clinton St)
Alouette (2588 Broadway)
Back Stage Eatery (579 Fifth Ave)
Barocco (42 Union Square E)
Bereket (187 E Houston St)
Beyoglu (1431 Third Ave)
Big Nick's (2175 Broadway)

Bouchon Bakery (10 Columbus Circle, 3rd floor)
burger joint at Le Parker Meridien Hotel (119 W 56th St)
Cafe Cafe (470 Broome St)
Cafe de Bruxelles (118 Greenwich Ave)
Cafe Edison (Hotel Edison, 228 W 47th St)
Cafe Lalo (201 W 83rd St)
Cafe Orlin (41 St. Mark's Pl)
Cafe Riazor (245 W 16th St)
Caffe Vivaldi (32 Jones St)
Carmine's (2450 Broadway)
Casa Adela (66 Ave C)
Chez Brigitte (77 Greenwich Ave)
Chickpea (210 E 14th St)
Chips Mexican Grill & Restaurant (42-15 Queens Blvd, Queens)
City Bakery (3 W 18th St)
Comfort Diner (214 E 45th St)
Corner Bistro (331 W 4th St)
Cosette (163 E 33rd St)
Cucina Stagionale (289 Bleecker St)
Cupcake Cafe (545 Ninth Ave)
Curry & Curry (153 E 33rd St)
Dakshin Indian Bistro (1713 First Ave)
Danal (90 E 10th St)
David Burke at Bloomingdale's (150 E 59th St)
Degustation (239 E 5th St)
Dining Commons (City University of New York Graduate Center, 365
    Fifth Ave, 8th floor)
Dom's (202 Lafayette St)
East Village Cheese (40 Third Ave)
Edgar's Cafe (255 W 84th St)
El Cid (322 W 15th St)
Euzkadi (108 E 4th St)
F&B Güdtfood (269 W 23rd St)
Fatty Crab (643 Hudson St)
First Avenue Coffee Shop (1433 First Ave)
Frank (88 Second Ave)
Golden Unicorn (18 East Broadway)
Go Sushi (3 Greenwich Ave)
Grand Central Oyster Bar Restaurant (Grand Central Terminal,
    42nd St at Vanderbilt Ave, lower level)
Grano Trattoria (21 Greenwich Ave)
Gray's Papaya (402 Ave of the Americas, 539 Eighth Ave, and 2090
    Broadway)
Hallo Berlin (624 Tenth Ave)
Havana Chelsea (190 Eighth Ave)
Havana New York (27 W 38th St)
Hoi An (135 West Broadway)
Home Restaurant (20 Cornelia St)
House of Pita (32 W 48th St)
Hummus Place (109 St. Mark's Pl)
Il Bagatto (192 E Second St)

Ivy's Cafe (154 W 72nd St)
Jasmine (1619 Second Ave)
Jean Claude (137 Sullivan St)
John's Pizzeria (278 Bleecker St and other locations)
Katz's Delicatessen (205 E Houston St)
Kennedy's Restaurant (327 W 57th St)
Kitchenette (156 Chambers St)
Le Gamin (536 E 5th St and other locations)
Le Tableau (511 E 5th St)
Lil' Frankie's Pizza (19 First Ave)
Little Havana (30 Cornelia St)
Luke's Bar & Grill (1394 Third Ave)
McDonald's (160 Broadway and other locations)
Nam (110 Reade St)
Nha Trang (87 Baxter St)
107 West (2787 Broadway)
Pakistan Tea House (176 Church St)
Paul's Palace (131 Second Ave)
Peep (177 Prince St)
Pho Bang (157 Mott St)
Pigalle (790 Eighth Ave)
Pinch, Pizza by the Inch (416 Park Ave S)
Pommes Frites (123 Second Ave)
Popover Cafe (551 Amsterdam Ave)
Pret à Manger (530 Seventh Ave and other locations)
Prime Burger (5 E 51st St)
Room 4 Dessert (17 Cleveland Pl)
Saigon Grill (91-93 University Pl)
Sapporo (152 W 49th St)
Sirtaj (36 W 26th St)
Sosa Borella (460 Greenwich St and 832 Eighth Ave)
Spanky's BBQ (127 W 43rd St)
Spring Street Natural Restaurant (62 Spring St)
Supper (156 E 2nd St)
Suzie's (163 Bleecker St)
Sylvia's (328 Lenox Ave)
Tanti Baci Caffe (163 W 10th St)
Tartine (253 W 11th St)
Tavern on Jane (31 Eighth Ave)
Tea & Sympathy (108 Greenwich Ave)
Tiny's Giant Sandwich Shop (129 Rivington St)
Tossed (295 Park Ave S)
Turkish Cuisine (631 Ninth Ave)
Uncle Moe's (14 W 19th St)
Urban Roots (51 Ave A)
Veselka (144 Second Ave)
Viand Coffee Shop (300 E 86th St, 673 Madison Ave, 2130 Broadway, and 1011 Madison Ave)
'wichcraft (555 Fifth Ave and other locations)
Zum Schneider (107-109 Ave C)

CHEESE PLATES
A.O.C. Bedford (14 Bedford St)
Artisanal (2 Park Ave)
Babbo (110 Waverly Pl)
Chanterelle (2 Harrison St)
craftbar (900 Broadway)
Daniel (60 E 65th St)
Eleven Madison Park (11 Madison Ave)
Gramercy Tavern (42 E 20th St)
Jean Georges (Trump International Hotel and Tower, 1 Central Park W)
La Grenouille (3 E 52nd St)
Le Cirque (1 Beacon Court, 151 E 58th St)
The Morgan Dining Room (Morgan Library & Museum, 225 Madison Ave)
Osteria del Circo (120 W 55th St)
Picholine (35 W 64th St)
Solera (216 E 53rd St)
Tasting Room (72 E 1st St)
Telepan (72 W 69th St)
Wallsé (344 W 11th St)

COFFEEHOUSES
Cafe la Fortuna (69 W 71st St)
Cafe Lalo (201 W 83rd St)
Cafe Mozart (154 W 70th St)
Caffe Dante (79 MacDougal St)
Caffe Roma (385 Broome St)
Caffe Vivaldi (32 Jones St)
City Bakery (3 W 18th St)
Cupcake Cafe (545 Ninth Ave)
Cupping Room Cafe (359 West Broadway)
Dean & Deluca (9 Rockefeller Plaza)
Ferrara Bakery and Cafe (195 Grand St)
French Roast (78 W 11th St and 2340 Broadway)
Hungarian Pastry Shop (1030 Amsterdam Ave)
Jack's Stir Brewed Coffee (138 W 10th St)
Le Figaro Cafe (184 Bleecker St)
Le Pain Quotidien (1131 Madison Ave, 38 E 19th St at ABC Carpet & Home, and other locations)
Once Upon a Tart (135 Sullivan St)
Oren's Daily Roast (1144 Lexington Ave and other locations)
Sarabeth's Kitchen (1295 Madison Ave, 423 Amsterdam Ave, 40 Central Park S, and 945 Madison Ave, at Whitney Museum)
Sensuous Bean (66 W 70th St)
71 Irving Place (71 Irving Pl)
Starbucks (numerous locations)
Veselka (144 Second Ave)

CREPES
Le Gamin (536 E 5th St and other locations)
Mon Petite Cafe (801 Lexington Ave)
Serendipity 3 (225 E 60th St)

DELI/QUICK LUNCH
Artie's Delicatessen (2290 Broadway)
Back Stage III (807 Lexington Ave)
Balthazar (80 Spring St)
Barney Greengrass (541 Amsterdam Ave)
Ben's Kosher Deli (209 W 38th St)
Bread (20 Spring St)
Breadstix Cafe (254 Eighth Ave)
Cafe 55 (914 Third Ave)
Carnegie Delicatessen and Restaurant (854 Seventh Ave)
Charles St. Food (144 Seventh Ave S)
City Market Cafe (551 Madison Ave)
Dil-E Punjab (170 Ninth Ave)
E.A.T. (1064 Madison Ave)
Ess-a-Bagel (831 Third Ave and 359 First Ave)
Fine & Schapiro (138 W 72nd St)
Food Exchange Cafe & Market (120 E 59th St)
Garden of Eden (7 E 14th St, 2780 Broadway, and 162 W 23rd St)
Grace's Marketplace (1237 Third Ave)
Junior's (Grand Central Terminal, 42nd St at Vanderbilt Ave, lower level)
Katz's Delicatessen (205 E Houston St)
Kitchen 82 (461 Columbus Ave)
Likitsakos Market (1174 Lexington Ave)
M&O Market (124 Thompson St)
Out of the Kitchen (456 Hudson St)
Picnic NYC (187 Chrystie St)
RUB BBQ (208 W 23rd St)
Samad's (2867 Broadway)
Sarabeth's Kitchen (40 Central Park S): better with a basket to go than
  eating in
Sarge's Deli (548 Third Ave)
Village Farm & Grocery (146 Second Ave)
Zabar's (2245 Broadway)

DESSERTS
Asiate (Mandarin Oriental New York, 80 Columbus Circle)
Babycakes (248 Broome St)
Bouley (120 West Broadway)
Cafe Lalo (201 W 83rd St)
Cafe Pertutti (2888 Broadway)
Cafe Sabarsky (Neue Galerie, 1048 Fifth Ave)
ChikaLicious (203 E 10th St)
Chocolat Michel Cluizel (ABC Carpet & Home, 888 Broadway)
Cupcake Cafe (545 Ninth Ave)
davidburke & donatella (133 E 61st St)
Egg Custard King Two Cafe (271 Grand St)
Ferrara Bakery and Cafe (195 Grand St)
Gramercy Tavern (42 E 20th St)
Hearth (403 E 12th St)
Il Laboratorio del Gelato (95 Orchard St)
Jacques Torres Chocolate Haven (350 Hudson St and 66 Water St,
  Brooklyn)

Jean Georges (1 Central Park W)
Lady M Cake Boutique (41 E 78th St)
Magnolia Bakery (401 Bleecker St)
Once Upon a Tart (135 Sullivan St)
Payard Patisserie & Bistro (1032 Lexington Ave)
Petrossian (182 W 58th St)
Rocco (181 Thompson St)
Room 4 Dessert (17 Cleveland Pl)
Schiller's Liquor Bar (131 Rivington St)
Serendipity 3 (225 E 60th St)
202 Cafe (75 Ninth Ave)
Veniero's (342 E 11th St)
wd-50 (50 Clinton St)
Zabar's Cafe (2245 Broadway)

DIM SUM

The serving of small tea pastries called "dim sum" originated in Hong Kong and has become a delicious Chinatown institution. Although dim sum is usually eaten for brunch, some restaurants also serve it as an appetizer before dinner. Dim sum items are rolled over to your table on carts, and you simply point at whatever looks good. This eliminates the language barrier and encourages experimentation. When you're finished, the small plates you've accumulated are counted and the bill is drawn up. Some of the most popular dim sum dishes include:

Cha Siu Bow (steamed barbecued pork buns)
Cha Siu So (flaky buns)
Chun Guen (spring rolls)
Dai Tze Gau (steamed scallop and shrimp dumplings)
Don Ta (baked custard tarts)
Dow Sah Bow (sweet bean-paste-filled buns)
Fancy Fans (meat-filled pot-sticker triangles)
Floweret Siu Mai (meat-filled dumplings)
Four-Color Siu Mai (meat-and-vegetable-filled dumplings)
Gau Choi Gau (pan-browned chive and shrimp dumplings)
Gee Cheung Fun (steamed rice-noodle rolls)
Gee Yoke Go (savory pork triangles)
Ha Gau (shrimp dumplings)
Jow Ha Gok (shrimp turnovers)
Pot Sticker Kou The (meat-filled dumplings)
Satay Gai Tran (chicken satay)
Siu Mai (steamed pork dumplings)
Tzay Ha (fried shrimp ball on sugarcane)

For the most authentic and delicious dim sum in New York, try these:

Chinatown Brasserie (380 Lafayette St)
Dim Sum Go Go (5 East Broadway)
Golden Unicorn (18 East Broadway): an especially fine selection
HSF (46 Bowery)
Jing Fong (20 Elizabeth St)
Mandarin Court (61 Mott St)
Nice Restaurant (35 East Broadway)
Oriental Garden (14 Elizabeth St)

Oriental Pearl (103 Mott St)
Our Place (141 E 55th St and 1444 Third Ave)
Ping's Seafood (22 Mott St)
Ruby Foo's (2182 Broadway and 1626 Broadway)
Shun Lee Cafe (43 W 65th St)
Tai-Hong-Lau (70 Mott St)

DINERS

Brooklyn Diner USA (212 W 57th St): outstanding
City Diner (2441 Broadway): retro-elegant
Ellen's Stardust Diner (1650 Broadway)
Empire Diner (210 Tenth Ave)

DINING AND DANCING

Tavern on the Green (Central Park W at 67th St): great setting
World Yacht Cruises (Pier 81, 41st St at Hudson River): nonstop party

DINING SOLO

Some of these restaurants have dining counters, others are tranquil and suitable for single diners:

Aquavit (65 E 55th St)
Babbo (110 Waverly Pl)
Cafe de Bruxelles (118 Greenwich Ave)
Cafe S.F.A. (Saks Fifth Avenue, 611 Fifth Ave)
Carnegie Delicatessen and Restaurant (854 Seventh Ave)
Caviar Russe (538 Madison Ave)
Chez Napoleon (365 W 50th St)
Col Legno (231 E 9th St)
Cupcake Cafe (545 Ninth Ave)
Elephant & Castle (68 Greenwich Ave)
Gotham Bar & Grill (12 E 12th St)
Grand Central Oyster Bar Restaurant (Grand Central Terminal, 42nd St at Vanderbilt Ave, lower level)
J.G. Melon (1291 Third Ave)
Jackson Hole Burgers (232 E 64th St, 521 Third Ave, 1611 Second Ave, and other locations)
Joe's Shanghai (9 Pell St)
Kitchenette (156 Chambers St)
La Bonne Soupe (48 W 55th St)
La Caridad 78 (2199 Broadway)
Mayrose (920 Broadway)
Naples 45 (MetLife Building, 200 Park Ave)
Pepolino (281 West Broadway)
Raoul's (180 Prince St)
Republic (37 Union Square W)
Sarabeth's Kitchen (1295 Madison Ave, 423 Amsterdam Ave, 40 Central Park S, and 945 Madison Ave, at Whitney Museum)
Savoy (70 Prince St)
Stage Deli (834 Seventh Ave)
Trattoria Dell'Arte (900 Seventh Ave)
Tropica (MetLife Building, 200 Park Ave)

Union Square Cafe (21 E 16th St)
Viand Coffee Shop (300 E 86th St, 673 Madison Ave, and 1011 Madison Ave)
Zoë (90 Prince St)

DOG FRIENDLY
Christina's (606 Second Ave)
11th Street Bar (510 E 11th St)
Zum Schneider (107-109 Ave C)

DON'T BOTHER
Too many restaurants spoil the real reason for dining out: to get a good meal in a comfortable setting at a fair price. With so many great choices in Manhattan, why waste time and money on mediocre ones? Some restaurants on the following list are well known and popular, but I feel you can get better value elsewhere.

Angelo's of Mulberry Street: The portrait of former president Reagan is their only claim to fame.

Alto: a cold, impersonal establishment with a location that is hard to find and food that is hard to praise

B-Bar & Grill: The servers are as disinterested as you will be in the food.

Bice: very noisy, very unimpressive

BLT Prime: With its high noise level and mediocre food, it's not up to the standards of its sisters BLT Steak and BLT Fish.

Café des Artistes: The paintings remain appealing, but the beauty of the food has faded.

Chiam: charming in every way except the most important—the food

Cipriani Downtown: expensive journey to Italy

City Crab: The amateurish service and mediocre food are enough to make anyone crabby.

City Grill: big menu, big crowd, not so big taste

Crispo: The anticipation is far better than the reality.

Cru: This room has had its ups and downs, and the present operation is one of the downs.

Cub Room: needs a lot of mothering

Django: The name, the setting, and the platters are different, but different doesn't always mean good.

Foley's Fish House: An exciting view overlooking Times Square is spoiled by unexciting chow.

Giorgio's of Gramercy: utterly unmemorable

Giovanni Venti Cinque: haughty treatment and high prices

Island Burgers and Shakes: overpraised, unattractive hole-in-the wall

La Mirabelle: nice people, but tired menu and surroundings

Les Halles: nothing to excite the taste buds

Le Veau d'Or: Heaven help the stranger.

Lotus: dark, deafening, and disappointing

LUPA: very uneven in both food and service

Maroons: Jamaican and Southern cooking that strays far from its origins

Metrazur: The train left a long time ago!

Mickey Mantle's: a strikeout

No. I Chinese: It's dark, mysterious, and cavernous—that's about all
Old Homestead: *Old* is the best description.
Perry Street: Jean-Georges Vongerichten lives upstairs, but his guests
    downstairs are not treated to his usual greatness in food, atmosphere, or
    service in this disappointingly spare room.
Philippe: expensive Chinese dishes presented poorly with inexcusably bad
    service
Rothmann's Steakhouse & Grill: Why waste bucks at this amateur-
    ish operation when there are so many good alternatives?
Savoy: uncomfortably cute, unappealing plates
Shula's Steak House: A famous name on the door doesn't guarantee a
    great meal. Besides, the prices are ridiculous and the place is dull.
Swifty's: unpleasant greeting, snobby atmosphere
Triomphe: small in size, value, and service
Village: uninspired cooking in an uninspired space
Waikiki Wally's: Hawaii is nothing like this place . . . thank goodness!
    Macadamia nut growers would be aghast at the namesake chicken.
Wolfgang's Steakhouse: Wolfgang Zwiener (formerly of Peter Luger's)
    now has his own place, but I'm sorry to report it doesn't quite make the
    grade.

EATING AT THE BAR OR PUB

Aquagrill (210 Spring St)
Babbo (110 Waverly Pl)
Beacon (25 W 56th St)
Cafe de Bruxelles (118 Greenwich Ave)
China Grill (60 W 53rd St)
Cipriani Dolci (Grand Central Terminal, 42nd St at Vanderbilt Ave)
Delmonico's (56 Beaver St)
Del Posto (85 Tenth Ave)
Emerald Inn (205 Columbus Ave): good choice before an event at Lincoln
    Center
Fanelli's Cafe (94 Prince St)
Five Points (31 Great Jones St)
Gotham Bar & Grill (12 E 12th St)
Grace (114 Franklin St)
Gramercy Tavern (42 E 20th St)
Hallo Berlin (624 Tenth Ave)
Keens Steakhouse (72 W 36th St)
Mesa Grill (102 Fifth Ave)
The Monkey Bar (Elysee Hotel, 60 E 54th St)
Old Town Bar (45 E 18th St)
Patroon (160 E 46th St)
Penang (1596 Second Ave)
Picholine (35 W 64th St)
Rain (100 W 82nd St)
Redeye Grill (890 Seventh Ave)
Tabla (11 Madison Ave)
Union Square Cafe (21 E 16th St)
Wollensky's Grill (201 E 49th St)
Zoë (90 Prince St)

FAMILY-STYLE DINING
Carmine's (2450 Broadway and 200 W 44th St)
China Grill (60 W 53rd St)
Phoenix Garden (242 E 40th St)
Piccolo Angolo (621 Hudson St)
Ruby Foo's (1626 Broadway and 2182 Broadway)
Sambuca (20 W 72nd St)
Tao (42 E 58th St)
Tony's Di Napoli (1606 Second Ave)

FIRESIDE
All-State Cafe (250 W 72nd St)
Beppe (45 E 22nd St)
Chumley's (86 Bedford St)
Cornelia Street Cafe (29 Cornelia St)
Gramercy Tavern (42 E 20th St)
Hunter's (1387 Third Ave)
I Trulli (122 E 27th St)
Keens Steakhouse (72 W 36th St)
March (405 E 58th St)
Molly's Pub and Shebeen (287 Third Ave)
Moran's Chelsea (146 Tenth Ave)
One If By Land, Two If By Sea (17 Barrow St)
per se (10 Columbus Circle)
René Pujol (321 W 51st St)
Savoy (70 Prince St)
Shaffer City Oyster Bar & Grill (5 W 21st St)
Telepan (72 W 69th St)
21 Club (21 W 52nd St)
Vivolo (140 E 74th St)
Water's Edge (44th Dr at East River)

FOREIGN FLAVORS
Some commendable ethnic establishments do not have full write-ups in this chapter. Here are the best of the more exotic eateries, arranged by cuisine:

Afghan: **Afghan Kebab House** (764 Ninth Ave)
African: **Cain** (544 W 27th St)
Argentine: **Chimichurri Grill** (606 Ninth Ave) and **Sosa Borella** (832 Eighth Ave)
Asian: **Lucky Cheng's** (24 First Ave) and **Rain** (100 W 82nd St)
Australian: **Eight Mile Creek** (240 Mulberry St) and **Public** (210 Elizabeth St)
Austrian: **Cafe Sabarsky** (Neue Galerie, 1048 Fifth Ave) and **Wallsé** (344 W 11th St)
Belgian: **Cafe de Bruxelles** (118 Greenwich Ave), **Petite Abeille** (466 Hudson St), and **Resto** (111 E 29th St)
Brazilian: **Churrascaria Plataforma** (221 West Broadway and 316 W 49th St), **Circus** (132 E 61st St), **Emporium Brazil** (15 W 46th St), and **Ipanema** (13 W 46th St)
Canadian: **Inn LW12** (Little West 12th St)

Cantonese: **Tai-Hong-Lau** (70 Mott St)

Caribbean: **Bambou** (243 E 14th St), **Ideya** (349 West Broadway), **Negril Village** (70 W 3rd St), **Sugar Bar** (254 W 72nd St), and **Tropica** (MetLife Building, 200 Park Ave)

Chilean: **Pomaire** (371 W 46th St)

Chinese: **Au Mandarin** (200-250 Vesey St), **Baby Buddha** (753 Washington Ave), **Big Wong** (67 Mott St), **Chin Chin** (216 E 49th St), **China Fun West** (246 Columbus Ave), **Chinatown Brasserie** (380 Lafayette St), **Flor de Mayo** (483 Amsterdam Ave and 2651 Broadway), **Fu's House** (972 Second Ave), **Golden Unicorn** (18 East Broadway), **Grand Sichuan International** (229 Ninth Ave and 745 Ninth Ave), **Hong Kong Station** (128 Hester St), **HSF** (46 Bowery), **Hunan Park** (235 Columbus Ave), **Jing Fong** (20 Elizabeth St), **Joe's Ginger** (25 Pell St), **Joe's Shanghai** (9 Pell St), **Kam Chueh** (40 Bowery), **Mr. K's** (570 Lexington Ave), **New Green Bo** (66 Bayard St), **Oriental Garden** (14 Elizabeth St), **Oriental Pearl** (103 Mott St), **Ping's Seafood** (22 Mott St), **Shanghai Cuisine** (89-91 Bayard St), **Shun Lee Palace** (155 E 55th St), **Shun Lee West** (43 W 65th St), **Tang Pavilion** (65 W 55th St), **Ten Pell Restaurant** (10 Pell St), **Wu Liang Ye** (36 W 48th St), and **Xing** (785 Ninth Ave)

Cuban: **Cabana** (1022 Third Ave), **Cafe Con Leche** (424 Amsterdam Ave), **La Caridad 78** (2199 Broadway), **Little Havana** (30 Cornelia St), and **Victor's Cafe** (236 W 52nd St)

East European: **Danube** (30 Hudson St), **Petrossian** (182 W 58th St), **Sammy's Roumanian** (157 Chrystie St), and **Veselka** (144 Second Ave)

Ethiopian: **Ghenet** (284 Mulberry St), **Meskerem** (468 W 47th St), and **Queen of Sheba** (650 Tenth Ave)

Filipino: **Cendrillon** (45 Mercer St) and **Elvie's Turo-Turo** (214 First Ave)

French: see restaurant write-ups (beginning on page 88)

German: **August** (359 Bleecker St), **Hallo Berlin** (626 Tenth Ave), **Heidelberg Restaurant** (1648 Second Ave), **Loreley** (7 Rivington St), **Rolf's** (281 Third Ave), **Silver Swan** (41 E 20th St), **Spiegel Beer Garden** (South Street Seaport, Pier 17, and **Zum Schneider** (107 Ave C)

Greek: **Anthos** (36 W 52nd St), **Avra** (141 E 48th St), **Estiatorio Milos** (125 W 55th St), **Gus' Place** (192 Bleecker St), **Ithaka** (308 E 86th St), **Kefi** (222 W 79th St), **Kellari Taverna** (19 W 44th St), **Likitsakos Market** (1174 Lexington Ave), **Meltemi** (905 First Ave), **Molyvos** (871 Seventh Ave), **Parea** (36 E 20th St), **Periyali** (35 W 20th St), **Pylos** (128 E 7th St), **Snack** (105 Thompson St), **Thalassa** (179 Franklin St), **Uncle Nick's** (747 Ninth Ave), and **Viand Coffee Shop** (300 E 86th St, 673 Madison Ave, 1011 Madison Ave, and 2130 Broadway)

Indian: **Banjara** (97 First Ave), **Bay Leaf** (49 W 56th St), **Bengal Express** (789 Ninth Ave), **Bombay Talkie** (189 Ninth Ave), **Brick Lane Curry House** (308 E 6th St), **Bukhara Grill** (217 E 49th St), **Chola** (232 E 58th St), **Darbar** (152 E 46th St), **Dawat** (210 E 58th St), **Dévi** (8 E 18th St), **Dimple** (11 W 30th St), **Diwan** (148 E 48th St), **Haveli** (100 Second Ave), **Indian Bread Co.** (194 Bleecker St), **Indus Valley** (2636 Broadway), **Jewel of India** (15 W 44th

St), **Masala Bollywood** (108 Lexington Ave), **Minar** (5 W 31st St), **Salaam Bombay** (317 Greenwich St), **Surya** (302 Bleecker St), **Tabla** (11 Madison Ave), **Taj Mahal** (318 E 6th St), **Tamarind** (41-43 E 22nd St), **Utsav** (1185 Ave of the Americas), and **Yuva** (230 E 58th St)

Healthy diet? Avoid these if you are trying to stay in shape:
Chinese: fried egg rolls, sweet and sour dishes, and spare ribs
French: paté, rich sauces, mousses, and pommes frites (French fries)
Indian: korma (cream sauce dishes), samosas, and chutneys
Italian: lasagna, spaghetti, and calzone and cannelloni stuffed with cheese
Japanese: tempura, teriyaki, and yakitori
Mexican: cheese, deep-fried food, and tortilla chips

Indonesian: **Bali Nusa Indah** (651 Ninth Ave)
Irish: **Neary's** (358 E 57th St)
Italian: see restaurant write-ups (beginning on page 88)
Jamaican: **Maroons** (244 W 16th St)
Japanese: **Benihana** (47 W 56th St), **Bond Street** (6 Bond St), **Chikubu** (12 E 44th St), **Donguri** (309 E 83rd St), **Ebisu** (414 E 9th St), **Hatsuhana** (17 E 48th St), **Inagiku** (Waldorf-Astoria, 301 Park Ave), **Japonica** (100 University Pl), **Jewel Bako** (239 E 5th St), **Kai** (822 Madison Ave), **Kiiroi Hana** (20 W 56th St), **Kuruma Zushi** (7 E 47th St), **Le Miu** (107 Ave A), **Menchanko-Tei** (43 W 55th St), **Minimoto Kitchoan** (608 Fifth Ave), **Nadaman Hakubai** (Kitano Hotel, 66 Park Ave), **Nobu** and **Nobu Next Door** (105 Hudson St), **Omen** (113 Thompson St), **Ono** (18 Ninth Ave), **Ozu** (566 Amsterdam Ave), **Sakagura** (211 E 43rd St), **Seo** (249 E 49th St), **Sugiyama** (251 W 55th St), **Sumile Sushi** (154 W 13th St), **SushiSamba** (245 Park Ave S and 87 Seventh Ave S), and **Sushi Yasuda** (204 E 43rd St)
Korean: **Cho Dang Gol** (55 W 35th St), **Do Hwa** (55 Carmine St), **Dok Suni's** (119 First Ave), **Gahm Mi Oak** (43 W 32nd St), **Hangawi** (12 E 32nd St), **Kang Suh** (1250 Broadway), **Kori** (253 Church St), **Kum Gang San** (49 W 32nd St), **New York Kom Tang** (32 W 32nd St), **Won Jo** (23 W 32nd St), **Woo Chon** (8-10 W 36th St), and **Woo Lae Oak Soho** (148 Mercer St)
Lebanese: **Al Bustan** (827 Third Ave)
Malaysian: **Fatty Crab** (643 Hudson St), **New Malaysia Restaurant** (48 Bowery), and **Penang** (1596 Second Ave)
Mediterranean: **Antique Garage** (41 Mercer St), **L'Orange Bleue** (430 Broome St), **Marseille** (630 Ninth Ave), **Zanzibar** (645 Ninth Ave), and **Zerza Bar** (304 E 6th St)
Mexican: **Centrico** (211 West Broadway), **Dos Caminos Soho** (475 West Broadway), **El Parador Cafe** (325 E 34th St), **El Rey del Sol** (232 W 14th St), **Fresco Tortillas** (766 Ninth Ave), **La Esquina** (106 Kenmare St), **La Hacienda** (219 E 116th St), **Mama Mexico** (2672 Broadway), **Maya** (1191 First Ave), **Mexicana Mama** (525 Hudson St), **Mexican Radio** (19 Cleveland Pl), **Mi Cocina** (57 Jane St), **Miracle Bar and Grill** (415 Bleecker St), **Rinconcito Mexicano**

(307 W 39th St), **Rosa Mexicano** (1063 First Ave and 61 Columbus Ave), **Tortilla Flats** (767 Washington St), **Tulcingo del Valle Restaurant** (665 Tenth Ave), and **Zocalo** (174 E 82nd St)
Middle Eastern: **Bread and Olive** (24 W 45th St), **Cleopatra's Needle** (2485 Broadway), and **Moustache** (265 E 10th St)

Food Tips from Distant Lands

- **Chinese**: The most popular Chinese cuisines are **Cantonese** (heavy on fish, dim sum a specialty); **Chiu Chow** (thick shark's fin soup, sliced goose, China's "Sicilian" cuisine); **Hakka** (salted, use of innards); **Hunan** (spicy, try fried chicken with chili); **Peking** (Peking duck and beggar's chicken are the best known); **Shanghai** (freshwater hairy crab is very popular); and **Szechuan** (spiciest of all, simmering and smoking are common cooking methods).
- **Indian**: Northern Indian food features wheat bread and curries. Fish and chicken are cooked in a tandoor clay oven. Indian food is not necessarily hot and spicy.
- **Indonesian**: Satays of chicken and beef, skewered and served with peanut sauce are the main dishes.
- **Japanese**: Most popular foods are sushi (raw fish atop vinegared rice), sashimi (slices of raw fish), tempura (deep-fried vegetables and fish), and teppanyaki (beef, seafood, garlic, and veggies cooked on a central griddle). Sake (rice wine) and Japanese beers such as Sapporo make good accompanying beverages.
- **Korean**: Table-top griddles are used for barbecuing beef slices for a dish called *bulgogi*.
- **Malaysian**: The best-known dish is laska, a creamy, coconut-based soup with noodles, shrimp, and chicken.
- **Singaporean**: This cross-cultural cuisine favors fried mee (thick yellow noodles) and satays (skewered and barbecued meat). Coconut is featured in sweet rice cakes and laska.
- **Taiwanese**: Fish and other seafoods are cooked in hot pots and enhanced with chili- and sesame-flavored oil condiments.
- **Thai**: Thai food can be very spicy! The national dish is *tom yum gung*, a soup made with chili, lemon grass, and coriander that is topped with shrimp, chicken, or squid.
- **Vietnamese**: You'll find French-inspired dishes like fried frog legs, sausage, and salami cold cuts platter. Spring rolls wrapped in lettuce leaves are traditional.

Pan-Latino: **Calle Ocho** (446 Columbus Ave), **Flor's Kitchen** (149 First Ave and 170 Waverly Pl), **Paladar** (161 Ludlow St), **Pampa** (768 Amsterdam Ave), and **Sucelt Coffee Shop** (200 W 14th St)
Persian: **Persepolis** (1407 Second Ave)
Polish: **Christine's** (208 First Ave) and **Teresa's** (103 First Ave)
Portuguese: **Alfama** (551 Hudson St), **O Lavrador** (138-40 101st Ave, Queens), and **Pao** (322 Spring St)
Puerto Rican: **La Taza de Oro** (96 Eighth Ave)
Russian: **Firebird** (365 W 46th St), **Russian Samovar** (256 W 52nd St), and **Uncle Vanya** (315 W 54th St)
Scottish: **St. Andrew's** (120 W 44th St)

South American: **Cafe Habana** (17 Prince St)
Southwestern: **Agave** (140 Seventh Ave S)
Spanish: **Azafran** (77 Warren St), **Bolo** (23 E 22nd St), **Cafe Español**
 (172 Bleecker St), **Cafe Riazor** (245 W 16th St), **El Cid** (322 W 15th
 St), **El Faro** (823 Greenwich St), **Olé Restaurant** (434 Second Ave),
 Pintxos (510 Greenwich St), **Pipa** (ABC Carpet & Home, 38 E 19th
 St), **Solera** (216 E 53rd St), **Tio Pepe** (168 W 4th St), **Toledo** (6 E
 36th St), and **Ureña** (37 E 28th St)
Swedish: **AQ Cafe** (Scandinavia House, 58 Park Ave) and **Aquavit** (65 E
 55th St)
Thai: **Holy Basil** (149 Second Ave), **Hurapan Kitchen** (19 Seventh Ave
 S), **Peep** (177 Prince St), **Pongsri Thai** (106 Bayard St), **Regional
 Thai Sa-Woy** (1479 First Ave), **Royal Siam Thai** (240 Eighth Ave),
 Siam Grill (592 Ninth Ave), **Thailand Restaurant** (106 Bayard St),
 Topaz (127 W 56th St), and **Vong** (200 E 54th St)
Tibetan: **Tibetan Kitchen** (444 Third Ave) and **Tsampa** (212 E 9th St)
Turkish: **Ali Baba** (212 E 34th St), **Beyoglu** (1431 Third Ave), **Dervish
 Turkish** (146 W 47th St), **Maia** (98 Avenue B), **Pasha** (70 W 71st St),
 Pera Mediterranean Brasserie (303 Madison Ave), **Sip Sak** (928
 Second Ave), **Turkish Cuisine** (631 Ninth Ave), **Turkish Kitchen**
 (386 Third Ave), **Üsküdar** (1405 Second Ave), and **Zeytin** (519 Colum-
 bus Ave)
Vietnamese: **Le Colonial** (149 E 57th St), **Mekong** (18 King St), **Miss
 Saigon** (1492 Second Ave), **Nha Trang** (87 Baxter St), **Pho Viet
 Huong** (73 Mulberry St), and **Rain** (100 W 82nd St)

FRENCH BISTROS

Balthazar (80 Spring St)
Bar Tabac (128 Smith St, Brooklyn)
Cafe Boulud (Surrey Hotel, 20 E 76th St)
Cafe Charbon-Epicerie (170 Orchard St)
Flea Market Cafe (131 Ave A)
Fleur de Sel (5 E 20th St)
Jean Claude (137 Sullivan St)
JoJo (160 E 64th St)
Le Gigot (18 Cornelia St)
Le Jardin Bistro (25 Cleveland Pl)
Pastis (9 Ninth Ave)
Payard Patisserie & Bistro (1032 Lexington Ave)
Raoul's (180 Prince St)
Rue 57 (60 W 57th St)

GAME

Game is generally offered in winter months or by special request.

Aquavit (65 E 55th St)
Aureole (34 E 61st St)
Babbo (110 Waverly Pl)
Barbetta (321 W 46th St)
Blue Hill (75 Washington Pl)
Cafe Boulud (Surrey Hotel, 20 E 76th St)
Chanterelle (2 Harrison St)

Daniel (60 E 65th St)
Danube (30 Hudson St)
Eleven Madison Park (11 Madison Ave)
Felidia (243 E 58th St)
Four Seasons (99 E 52nd St)
Gascogne (158 Eighth Ave)
Il Cantinori (32 E 10th St)
Il Mulino (86 W 3rd St)
Jean Georges (Trump International Hotel and Tower, 1 Central Park W)
La Grenouille (3 E 52nd St)
Le Périgord (405 E 52nd St)
Mesa Grill (102 Fifth Ave)
Nino's (1354 First Ave)
Ouest (2315 Broadway)
Park Bistro (414 Park Ave S)
Picholine (35 W 64th St)
Primavera (1578 First Ave)
Quality Meats (57 W 58th St)
River Cafe (1 Water St, Brooklyn)
Tocqueville (1 E 15th St)
Union Square Cafe (21 E 16th St)

HEALTHY FARE

Angelica Kitchen (300 E 12th St)
Candle 79 (154 E 79th St)
Dine by Design (252 Elizabeth St)
Four Seasons (99 E 52nd St): expensive
Gobo (401 Ave of the Americas and 1426 Third Ave)
Hangawi (12 E 32nd St)
Heartbeat (W New York Hotel, 149 E 49th St)
Josie's Restaurant (300 Amsterdam Ave)
Popover Cafe (551 Amsterdam Ave)
Pure Food and Wine (54 Irving Pl)
Quantum Leap Natural Food (226 Thompson St)
Spring Street Natural Restaurant (62 Spring St): your best bet
Zen Palate (663 Ninth Ave and other locations)

HOTEL DINING

One of the most notable changes on the Manhattan restaurant scene over the last decade has been the resurgence of hotel dining. No longer are on-premises eateries just for the convenience of registered guests. They are destinations for those who desire a less trendy scene with a bit more atmosphere. Here are some of the best:

Algonquin Hotel (59 W 44th St): **Round Table** and **Oak Room** (evening cabaret)
Carlton on Madison Avenue (88 Madison Ave): **Country**
Carlyle Hotel (35 E 76th St): **Restaurant Carlyle** (overpriced)
City Club (55 W 44th St): **DB Bistro Moderne** (Daniel Boulud's urbane bar-restaurant)
Elysee Hotel (60 E 54th St): **The Monkey Bar** (great history and eclectic menu with Asian touches)

Four Seasons Hotel New York (57 E 57th St): **57** (superb dining) and **L'Atelier de Joël Robuchon**

Gansevoort (18 Ninth Ave): **Ono Restaurant**

Giraffe (365 Park Ave S): **Barna**

Hilton New York (1335 Ave of the Americas): **New York Marketplace** (casual, deli-like) and **Etrusca** (Italian, dinner only)

Hilton Times Square (234 W 42nd St): **Restaurant Above and Pinnacle Bar** (breathtaking views, creative American menu with Italian accents

Hotel on Rivington (107 Rivington St): **Thor** (one of downtown's most fashionable scenes)

Inn at Irving Place (56 Irving Pl): **Lady Mendl's Tea Salon** (very proper)

Jumeirah Essex House (160 Central Park S): **Restaurant at the Essex House**

Kimberly Hotel (145 E 50th St): **Ferro's Restaurant** (classic steakhouse)

Kitano (66 Park Ave): **Nadaman Hakubai** (Japanese) and **Garden Cafe**

Le Parker Meridien Hotel (119 W 56th St): **burger joint** (lobby), **Norma's** (breakfast and brunch), and **Seppi's** (classic French bistro)

Library Hotel (299 Madison Ave): **Branzini**

Loews Regency Hotel (540 Park Ave): **540 Park Restaurant** (power scene) and **The Library** (informal)

London NYC (151 W 54th St): **Maze** (dining area of Gordon Ramsay's London Bar)

Lowell Hotel (28 E 63rd St): **Pembroke** and **Post House** (very good meat and potatoes)

Mandarin Oriental New York (80 Columbus Circle): **Asiate**

Millennium Broadway and Premier Tower (145 W 44th St): **Restaurant Charlotte** (American menu)

New York Helmsley (212 E 42nd St): **Mindy's**

New York Marriott Financial Center Hotel (85 West St): **85 West** and **Roy's New York**

New York Marriott Marquis (1535 Broadway): **Encore Restaurant, Katen Sushi Bar** (Japanese cuisine with modern decor), and **The View** (revolving top-floor eatery with New York-centric menu)

New York Palace Hotel (455 Madison Ave): **Istana** (lobby)

Pierre Hotel (2 E 61st St): **Cafe Pierre** (stately and beautiful)

Plaza Athenee (37 E 64th St): **Arabelle** (dignified)

Ritz-Carlton New York, Battery Park (2 West St): **2 West** (New American)

Ritz-Carlton New York, Central Park (50 Central Park S): **BLT Market**

Royalton (44 W 44th St): **44** (chic, favorite of publishing moguls)

St. Regis New York (2 E 55th St): **Adour** and **Astor Court** (you can't do better)

Shelburne Murray Hill (303 Lexington Ave): **Rare Bar & Grill** (elegant burger spot)

Sheraton Manhattan Hotel (790 Seventh Ave): **Russo's Steak & Pasta**

Sheraton New York Hotel and Towers (811 Seventh Ave): **Avenue** (cafe) and **Hudson's Sports Bar & Grill**

Shoreham Hotel (33 W 55th St): **Shoreham Bar and Restaurant**

Soho Grand Hotel (310 West Broadway): **Grand Bar & Lounge** (upscale bar menu) and **The Gallery**

Surrey Hotel (20 E 76th St): **Cafe Boulud** (French-American)

Trump International Hotel and Tower (1 Central Park W): **Jean Georges** (The Donald's personal gem)

Waldorf-Astoria (301 Park Ave): **Bull & Bear** (British atmosphere), **Inagiku** (Japanese), **Oscar's** (cafeteria), and **Peacock Alley Restaurant**

Wales (1295 Madison Ave): **Sarabeth's Kitchen** (delightful)

Warwick (65 W 54th St): **Murals on 54**

W New York (541 Lexington Ave): **Heartbeat** (healthy American)

W New York–Times Square (1567 Broadway): **Blue Fin** (seafood)

KOSHER

Kosher dining experiences in New York City run the gamut from elegant restaurants with celebrity chefs to the falafel stand outside Rockefeller Center and the kosher hot dog stand at Shea Stadium.

Note: *Especially* for kosher dining, call ahead to make sure they are open.

Abigael's on Broadway (1407 Broadway)

Cafe at Makor (35 W 67th St): Makor is designed for interaction. There are programs, lectures, and socials, and if you attend any of them, the cafe is good for a quick pick-me-up.

Cafe K (8 E 48th St): This may be the busiest lunch spot in New York City.

Cafe Roma Pizza (854 Amsterdam Ave)

Cafe Weissman (Jewish Museum, 1109 Fifth Ave): This museum was the old Felix Warburg mansion, and this intimate dining spot in the basement is a kosher oasis on Museum Row.

Caravan of Dreams (405 E 6th St): natural, raw, and vegetarian, East Village kosher restaurant

Circa NY (22 W 33rd St and 5 Dey St): This upscale cafeteria lunch location has everything from sushi to create-your-own salads and hot lasagna—all delicious!

Colbeh (43 W 39th St)

Darna (600 Columbus Ave): Darna's accents are Spanish/Moroccan/Mideastern couscous with a splash of medieval decor

Date Palm Cafe (Center for Jewish History, 15 W 16th St): light but expensive vegetarian and dairy fare within the museum complex

Diamond Dairy (4 W 47th St, mezzanine): Watching the diamond trade is worth the cost of dinner (at affordable old-time prices!), and the Jewish-mother style of cooking will warm your insides and make you nostalgic. Even if it's July, get the soup!

Dimples Indian Fast Food (11 W 30th St): Dimples has been named the cheapest kosher spot in the Tri-State area—and it's filling.

Dougie's Express (74 W 47th St): The ribs are as good as kosher gets, and the original store has spawned a franchise.

Eden Wok (127 W 72nd St): great kosher Chinese restaurant with sushi bar

Essex on Coney Downtown (17 Trinity Pl): Just the wafting aroma is enough to entice you inside.

Estihana (221 W 79th St): closest kosher spot to the Museum of Natural History

Galil (1252 Lexington Ave): a small Israeli meat restaurant with surprisingly large portions of Middle Eastern specialties

Haikara Grill (206 E 63rd St): the first and still the best Japanese kosher steakhouse

Hartley Kosher Deli (Columbia University, 101 Hartley Hall, at 116th St): This kosher dining hall on the Columbia campus is open to the public.

Jerusalem II (1375 Broadway): Crowds keep coming back to one of the first and best pizza, falafel, and salad bar emporiums in town.

Le Marais (150 W 46th St): This French steakhouse, which has a butcher store in the front, sets the kosher standard.

Levana Restaurant (141 W 69th St)

Mendy's Galleria (115 E 57th St): huge portions, fantastic food, and friendly service

Mendy's Rockefeller Plaza (30 Rockefeller Plaza)

My Most Favorite Food (120 W 45th St): Expensive pasta, fish, salads, and desserts are all delectable.

Pizza Cave (218 W 72nd St): Pizza-loving kids say this is the very best.

Tevere (155 E 84th St): old family Italian Jewish recipes and great traditions

Va Bene (1589 Second Ave): superb pastas

Yonah Schimmel's Knishes (137 E Houston St): Schimmel started serving knishes to immigrants 150 years ago, and it's still in business.

LATE HOURS
The city that never sleeps ...

Balthazar (80 Spring St)
Baraonda (1439 Second Ave)
Bereket (187 E Houston St)
Big Arc Chicken (233 First Ave)
Big Nick's (2175 Broadway)
Blue Ribbon (97 Sullivan St)
Blue Ribbon Sushi (119 Sullivan St and 278 Fifth Ave)
Cafeteria (119 Seventh Ave)
Cafe Lalo (201 W 83rd St)
Carnegie Delicatessen and Restaurant (854 Seventh Ave)
Empire Diner (210 Tenth Ave)
Fatty Crab (643 Hudson St)
Florent (69 Gansevoort St)
Frank (88 Second Ave)
French Roast (78 W 11th St)
Fuleen Seafood (11 Division St)
Gam Mee Ok (43 W 32nd St)
Gray's Papaya (2090 Broadway)
Great N.Y. Noodletown (28½ Bowery)
Green Kitchen (1477 First Ave)
Han Bat (53 W 35th St)
Kum Gang San (49 W 32nd St)
Lahore (132 Crosby St)
Landmarc (179 West Broadway)
L'Express (249 Park Ave S)
Mas Farmhouse (39 Downing St)
Momofuku Ssäm Bar (207 Second Ave)
Odessa (119 Ave A)
Pastis (9 Ninth Ave)
P.J. Clarke's (915 Third Ave)
Raoul's (180 Prince St)

Sarge's Deli (548 Third Ave)
Spotted Pig (314 W 11th St)
Veselka (144 Second Ave)
Viand Coffee Shop (2130 75th St)
Wollensky's Grill (201 E 49th St)
Won Jo (23 W 32nd St)

MUNCHING AT THE MUSEUMS

Even the smallest museums often have cafes. They are usually upscale eateries where you can rest your feet and get a surprisingly good meal. Be forewarned that they are usually quite expensive. Some of the best:

American Folk Art Museum (45 W 53rd St): Cafe
Asia Society (Park Ave at 70th St): Garden Court Cafe
Dahesh Museum (580 Madison Ave): Café Opaline
Guggenheim Museum (1071 Fifth Ave): Museum Cafe
Jewish Museum (1109 Fifth Ave): Cafe Weissman
Metropolitan Museum of Art (1000 Fifth Ave): the cafeteria (basement) and Petrie Court Cafe (looks onto Central Park)
Morgan Library and Museum (225 Madison Ave): The Morgan Dining Room
Museum of Modern Art (9 W 53rd St): The Modern
Neue Galerie (1048 Fifth Ave): Cafe Sabarsky
Rubin Museum of Art (150 W 17th St): Cafe at the RMA
Scandinavia House Galleries (58 Park Ave): Cafe AQ
Whitney Museum of American Art (945 Madison Ave): Sarabeth's Kitchen

OLD-TIMERS

1783: **Fraunces Tavern** (54 Pearl St)
1794: **Bridge Cafe** (279 Water St)
1864: **Pete's Tavern** (129 E 18th St)
1868: **Old Homestead** (56 Ninth Ave)
1885: **Keens Steakhouse** (72 W 36th St)
1887: **Peter Luger Steak House** (178 Broadway, Brooklyn)
1888: **Katz's Delicatessen** (205 East Houston St)
1890: **P.J. Clarke's** (915 Third Ave)
1906: **Barbetta** (321 W 46th St)
1913: **Grand Central Oyster Bar Restaurant** (Grand Central Terminal, 42nd St at Vanderbilt Ave, lower level)
1920: **Waverly Inn & Garden** (16 Bank St)
1926: **Palm One** (837 Second Ave)
1927: **Minetta Tavern** (113 MacDougal St)
1929: **21 Club** (21 W 52nd St)

OUTDOOR BARS

Bubby's (120 Hudson St)
Bull McCabe's (29 St. Marks Pl)
Caliente Cab Co. (61 Seventh Ave S)
Casimir (103-105 Ave B)
Chelsea Brewing Company (Pier 59, West St at 18th St)
Finnegan's Wake (1361 First Ave)

Hallo Berlin (624 Tenth Ave)
Iris and B. Gerald Cantor Roof Garden (Metropolitan Museum of Art, 1000 Fifth Ave)
Metro Grill Roof Garden (Hotel Metro, 45 W 35th St)
O'Flaherty's Ale House (334 W 46th St)
Revival (129 E 15th St)
Ryan's Irish Pub (151 Second Ave)
Sweet & Vicious (5 Spring St)
White Horse Tavern (567 Hudson St)

OUTDOOR DINING

Aquagrill (210 Spring St)
August (359 Bleecker St)
Barbetta (321 W 46th St, garden)
Barolo (398 West Broadway)
B Bar & Grill (40 E 4th St)
Bello Giardino (71 W 71st St)
Blue Water Grill (31 Union Sq W)
Bottino (246 Tenth Ave)
Bryant Park Grill (25 W 40th St)
Cafe Centro (200 Park Ave)
Cafe la Fortuna (69 W 71st St)
Cafe St. Bart's (109 E 50th St)
Caffe Dante (79 MacDougal St)
Cascina (647 Ninth Ave)
Cavo (42-18 31st Ave, Queens)
Central Park Boathouse (Central Park at E 72nd St)
Da Nico (164 Mulberry St)
Da Silvano (260 Ave of the Americas)
Druids (736 Tenth Ave)
DuMont (432 Union Ave, Brooklyn)
Empire Diner (210 Tenth Ave)
Financier Patisserie (62 Stone St)
5 Ninth (5 Ninth Ave)
Fragole (394 Court St)
Gascogne (158 Eighth Ave)
Gavroche (212 W 14th St)
Gigino (Wagner Park, 20 Battery Pl)
Grocery (288 Smith St, Brooklyn)
Grotto (100 Forsyth St)
Home Restaurant (20 Cornelia St)
Il Gattopardo (33 W 54th St)
I Trulli (122 E 27th St)
Jackson Hole Burgers (232 E 64th St)
Jean Georges (Trump International Hotel and Tower, 1 Central Park W)
Le Jardin Bistro (25 Cleveland Pl)
Mezzogiorno (195 Spring St)
Moda Restaurant (135 W 52nd St)
New Leaf Cafe (Fort Tryon Park, 1 Margaret Corbin Dr)
Nice Matin (201 W 79th St)
Ono (Hotel Gansevoort, 18 Ninth Ave)
Pampa (768 Amsterdam Ave)

Pampano (209 E 49th St, second floor terrace)
Paradou (8 Little West 12th St)
Pastis (9 Ninth Ave)
Patois (255 Smith St, Brooklyn)
Patroon (160 E 46th St, 3rd floor)
Pete's Tavern (129 E 18th St)
Porters New York (216 Seventh Ave)
Provence (38 MacDougal St)
Pure Food and Wine (54 Irving Pl)
Rialto (265 Elizabeth St)
River Cafe (1 Water St, Brooklyn)
Roc Restaurant (190-A Duane St)
Rock Center Cafe/The Rink Bar (Rockefeller Center, 20 W 50th St)
San Pietro (18 E 54th St)
Sel et Poivre (853 Lexington Ave)
79th Street Boat Basin Cafe (Riverside Park at 79th St; seasonally)
Shake Shack (Madison Square Park at 23rd St; seasonally)
Sheep Meadow Cafe (Sheep Meadow, Central Park; seasonally)
SouthWest NY (225 Liberty St)
Spring Street Natural Restaurant (62 Spring St)
SushiSamba 7 (87 Seventh Ave S)
Tabla (11 Madison Ave)
Tartine (253 W 11th St)
Tavern on the Green (Central Park W at 67th St)
Terrace 5 (Museum of Modern Art, 11 W 53rd St)
Terrace in the Sky (400 W 119th St)
Trattoria Dell'Arte (900 Seventh Ave)
Water Club (East River at 30th St, upstairs)
Waverly Inn & Garden (16 Bank St)
White Horse Tavern (567 Hudson St)
World Yacht Cruises (Pier 81, 41st St at Hudson River)
Yaffa Cafe (97 St. Mark's Pl)

OYSTER BARS

Blue Ribbon (97 Sullivan St)
Docks Oyster Bar and Seafood Grill (2427 Broadway and 633 Third Ave)
Grand Central Oyster Bar Restaurant (Grand Central Terminal, 42nd St at Vanderbilt Ave, lower level)
Pearl Oyster Bar (18 Cornelia St)
Shaffer City Oyster Bar & Grill (5 W 21st St)

PERSONAL FAVORITES

Babbo (110 Waverly Pl): fabulous food
Blue Ribbon (97 Sullivan St): great value
Cucina & Co. (MetLife Building, 200 Park Ave, lobby)
Del Posto (85 Tenth Ave): very classy service
Gotham Bar & Grill (12 E 12th St): Everything is good.
Gramercy Tavern (42 E 20th St): the "in" place
Il Mulino (86 W 3rd St): Italian heaven!
Jackson Hole Burgers (232 E 64th St, 521 Third Ave, 1611 Second Ave, 1270 Madison Ave, and 517 Columbus Ave): best burgers
Kobe Club (68 W 58th St): very expensive, but superb meat

La Grenouille (3 E 52nd St): beautiful
Le Périgord (405 E 52nd St): impeccable
McCormick & Schmick's (1285 Ave of the Americas):
Nobu (105 Hudson St): Japanese food at its best
One If By Land, Two If By Sea (17 Barrow St): romantic
Park Side (107-01 Corona Ave, Queens): Come here to eat!
Piccolo Angolo (621 Hudson St): like family
Post House (Lowell Hotel, 28 E 63rd St): macho meals
Primavera (1578 First Ave): superb service
River Cafe (1 Water St, East River, Brooklyn): Oh, that view!
Sfoglia (1402 Lexington Ave): wonderful bread
Smith & Wollensky (797 Third Ave): old-time flavor
Union Square Cafe (21 E 16th St): justly famous
Wild Salmon (622 Third Ave): amazingly fresh seafood

PIZZA
Adrienne's Pizzabar (86 Pearl St)
Angelo's Pizzeria (117 W 57th St)
apizz (217 Eldridge St)
Arturo's Coal Oven Pizza (106 W Houston St)
Beacon (25 W 56th St)
Bella Vita (211 W 43rd St)
Da Ciro (229 Lexington Ave)
Da Nico (164 Mulberry St)
De Marco's (146 W Houston St)
Denino's (524 Port Richmond Ave, Staten Island)
Fred's at Barneys New York (660 Madison Ave)
Giorgione (307 Spring St)
Grimaldi's (19 Old Fulton St)
Il Corallo Trattoria (176 Prince St)
Joe's (7 Carmine St)
John's of Bleecker Street (278 Bleecker St)
Lazzara's Pizza Cafe (221 W 38th St, upstairs)
Lil' Frankie's Pizza (19 First Ave)
Lombardi's (32 Spring St)
Luca Lounge (220 Ave B)
Luigi's (1701 First Ave)
Mezzogiorno (195 Spring St)
Naples 45 (200 Park Ave)
Nick & Toni's Cafe (100 W 67th St)
Orso (322 W 46th St)
Osteria del Circo (120 W 55th St)
Patsy's (2287 First Ave)
Sal's & Carmine's Pizza (2671 Broadway)
Serafina (29 E 61st St and 38 E 58th St)
Stromboli Pizzeria (112 University Pl)
Sullivan Street Bakery (533 W 47th St)
Totonno Pizzeria Napolitano (1544 Second Ave)
Trattoria Dell'Arte (900 Seventh Ave)
Two Boots (42 Ave A, 74 Bleecker St, and other locations)
Una Pizza Napoletana (349 E 12th St)
Vinny Vincenz's Pizzamobile (231 First Ave)

POWER MEALS
Balthazar (80 Spring St)
Ben Benson's Steak House (123 W 52nd St)
Cafe Boulud (Surrey Hotel, 20 E 76th St)
Cafe Pierre (Pierre Hotel, 2 E 61st St)
Daniel (60 E 65th St)
Da Silvano (260 Ave of the Americas)
Delmonico's (56 Beaver St)
Del Posto (85 Tenth Ave)
540 Park Restaurant (Loews Regency Hotel, 540 Park Ave)
Fives (Peninsula New York Hotel, 700 Fifth Ave)
Four Seasons (99 E 52nd St)
Gabriel's Bar & Restaurant (11 W 60th St)
Gotham Bar & Grill (12 E 12th St)
Il Mulino (86 W 3rd St)
Jean Georges (Trump International Hotel and Tower, 1 Central Park W)
La Grenouille (3 E 52nd St)
Le Bernardin (155 W 51st St)
Maloney & Porcelli (37 E 50th St)
Michael's (24 W 55th St)
The Monkey Bar (Elysee Hotel, 60 E 54th St)
Morton's of Chicago (551 Fifth Ave)
Nobu and **Nobu Next Door** (105 Hudson St)
Palm One (837 Second Ave)
Park Avenue Cafe (100 E 63rd St)
Primavera (1578 First Ave)
Rao's (455 E 114th St)
Restaurant Carlyle (Carlyle Hotel, 35 E 76th St)
Sette Mezzo (969 Lexington Ave)
Smith & Wollensky (797 Third Ave)
21 Club (21 W 52nd St)

PRE-THEATER
Let your waiter know when you sit down that you will be attending the theater so that service can be adjusted accordingly. If it is raining, allow extra time for getting a taxi. Some restaurants have specially priced pre-theater dinners.

Aquavit (65 E 55th St)
Arqua (281 Church St)
Barbetta (321 W 46th St)
Beacon (25 W 56th St)
Becco (355 W 46th St)
Café Gray (10 Columbus Circle)
Cafe Un Deux Trois (123 W 44th St)
Camino Sur (336 W 37th St)
Carmine's (2450 Broadway and 200 W 44th St)
Centolire (1167 Madison Ave)
Chez Josephine (414 W 42nd St)
ChikaLicious (203 E 10th St)
Dawat (210 E 58th St)
Esca (402 W 43rd St)

57 (57 E 57th St)
Firebird (365 W 46th St)
44 (Royalton Hotel, 44 W 44th St)
Four Seasons (99 E 52nd St)
Gino (780 Lexington Ave)
Hearth (403 E 12th St)
Hell's Kitchen (679 Ninth Ave)
Indochine (430 Lafayette St)
La Boite en Bois (75 W 68th St)
Marchi's (251 E 31st St)
Momofuku Noodle Bar (163 First Ave)
Ollie's Noodle Shop and Grill (200 W 44th St, 2315 Broadway, and
    1991 Broadway)
Orso (322 W 46th St)
Picholine (35 W 64th St)
Red Cat (227 Tenth Ave)
Restaurant at the Essex House (Jumeirah Essex House, 160 Central
    Park S)
Sandwich Planet (534 Ninth Ave)
Spice Market (403 W 13th St)
Tavern on the Green (Central Park W at 67th St)
Telepan (72 W 69th St)
Thalia (828 Eighth Ave)
Tropica (MetLife Building, 200 Park Ave)

PUBS AND GOOD BARS

Angel's Share (8 Stuyvesant St)
Anotheroom (249 West Broadway)
APT (419 W 13th St): hidden
Arlene's Grocery (95 Stanton St)
Ava Lounge (Dream Hotel, 210 W 55th St): rooftop
Back Page Sports Bar (1472 Third Ave): football
Balcony Bar (Metropolitan Museum of Art, 1000 Fifth Ave): culture
Baraonda (1439 Second Ave): international
Bar East (1733 First Ave): down-to-earth
Bar 89 (89 Mercer St): renowned for unisex glass bathrooms
Barrow's Pub (463 Hudson St)
Bar Seine (Hotel Plaza Athenee New York, 37 E 64th St)
Bemelmans Bar (Carlyle Hotel, 353 E 76th St): old-school hotel bar
Bill's Gay Nineties (57 E 54th St)
Birdland (315 W 44th St): jazz
Blarney Rock Pub (137 W 33rd St)
Blue Fin (W New York-Times Square, 1567 Broadway): best pre-theater
Blue Note (131 W 3rd St): lots of talent here
Boat Basin Cafe (79th St at Hudson River): view with a bar (seasonally)
Bourbon Street (407 Amsterdam Ave): football
Brandy Library (25 N Moore St): fine liquor
Bull & Bear (Waldorf-Astoria, 301 Park Ave)
Bungalow 8 (515 W 27th St): celeb watering hole
Butterfield 8 (5 E 38th St): unassuming pub and lounge
Campbell Apartment (Grand Central Terminal, 42nd St at Vanderbilt
    Ave, off West Balcony): unique

Cellar Bar (Bryant Park Hotel, 40 W 40th St): good hotel bar
Chelsea Brewing Company (Pier 59, West St at 18th St): big place, big steaks
Chibi's Bar (238 Mott St): Japanese hideaway
Chumley's (86 Bedford St): an old speakeasy in the Village
Corner Bistro (331 W 4th St): eat
Danube (30 Hudson St): Austrian
d.b.a. N.Y.C. (41 First Ave): a relaxed place with the best bar list, including 130 single-malt Scotches and 50 tequilas
The Delancey (168 Delancey St): rooftop
Dempsey's Pub (61 Second Ave)
Dive Bar (732 Amsterdam Ave)
Duvet (45 W 21st St): perfect for an office party
Ear Inn (326 Spring St)
Eleven Madison Park (11 Madison Ave)
Emerald Inn (205 Columbus Ave): friendly Irish pub
ESPN Zone (1472 Broadway): sports
Feinstein's at the Regency Hotel (540 Park Ave): sophisticated cocktail-sipping and people watching
Flatiron Lounge (37 W 19th St): plush banquettes, best Manhattans
Florent (69 Gansevoort St): when you can't sleep
40/40 Club (6 W 25th St): sports
Four Seasons Hotel Bar (57 E 57th St)
Frank's (410 W 16th St)
Ginger Man (11 E 36th St): huge beer selection
Good World Bar & Grill (3 Orchard St)
Gramercy Tavern (42 E 20th St)
Grand Bar (Soho Grand Hotel, 310 West Broadway): recently renovated hotel bar
Heartland Brewery (1285 Ave of the Americas and 35 Union Square W): Try the charcoal stout.
Heights Cafe (84 Montague St, Brooklyn)
Hotel Roger Williams (131 Madison Ave)
Hudson Bar and Books (636 Hudson St): reading
Jeremy's Ale House (228 Front St)
Jimmy's Bait Shack (1644 Third Ave): football
Jimmy's Corner (140 W 44th St)
John Street Bar & Grill (17 John St): spacious rec room
Keens Steakhouse (72 W 36th St)
King Cole Bar (St. Regis New York, 2 E 55th St)
Landmark Tavern (626 Eleventh Ave): 19th-century decor
Lenox Lounge (288 Lenox Ave): Harlem lounge and jazz club
Level V (675 Hudson St): high-energy dance floor
The Library (Loews Regency Hotel, 540 Park Ave): class
Living Room (W New York-Times Square, 1567 Broadway): tourists
Lobby Lounge (Mandarin Oriental New York, 80 Columbus Circle): phenomenal Central Park views
Lollipop (27 E 61st St): Vietnamese-Thai lounge
McCormack's (365 Third Ave): soccer and football
McQuaid's Public House (589 Eleventh Ave)
Mercer Kitchen (99 Prince St): celebrity watching
The Monkey Bar (Elysee Hotel, 60 E 54th St)

Morgan's Bar (237 Madison Ave): great ambience
Mustang Sally's (324 Seventh Ave): basketball
Night Cafe (938 Amsterdam Ave)
No Idea (30 E 20th St)
North Square Lounge (Washington Square Hotel, 103 Waverly Pl)
Oak Room (Algonquin Hotel, 59 W 44th St)
Oasis (W New York, 541 Lexington Ave)
Old Town Bar (45 E 18th St): burgers
The Park (118 Tenth Ave): people watching
Parlour (250 W 86th St)
Peculier Pub (145 Bleecker St): 400 beers!
Pegu Club (77 West Houston St)
Pen Top Bar & Terrace (Peninsula New York Hotel, 700 Fifth Ave):
   rooftop
Peter McManus Cafe (152 Seventh Ave)
Pete's Tavern (129 E 18th St): New York's oldest continuously operating
   pub
Pianos (158 Ludlow St): busy
Pinetree Lodge (326 E 35th St): pleasingly grungy garden
P.J. Clarke's (915 Third Ave)
Play-by-Play (4 Penn Plaza): sports
Proof (239 Third Ave): football and basketball
Pussycat Lounge (96 Greenwich St): dancing
Rao's (455 E 114th St)
Rise (Ritz-Carlton New York, Battery Park, 2 West St, 14th floor): view
Rock Center Cafe (Rockefeller Plaza, 20 W 50th St): watch the ice
   skaters
Rudy's Bar & Grill (627 Ninth Ave)
Sakagura (211 E 43rd St): Japanese restaurant bar
Scruffy Duffy's (743 Eighth Ave): sports
Session 73 (1359 First Ave): live music
Ship of Fools (1590 Second Ave): football
66 Water (66 Water St, Brooklyn): bar, restaurant, club, gallery
Smith's Bar & Restaurant (701 Eighth Ave): drink standing up
Smoke Jazz Club & Lounge (2751 Broadway): best jazz bar
Spotted Pig (314 W 11th St): London-style gastro-pub
Spuyten Duyvil (359 Metropolitan Ave, Brooklyn): Yes, it is in Brooklyn,
   but it is one of the best beer bars around.
Subway Inn (143 E 60th St): cheapo
Swift Hibernian Lounge (34 E 4th St): 26 beers on tap
Tabla Bar (11 Madison Ave): fancy bar menu
Tonic and the Met Lounge (727 Seventh Ave): boxing
Tonic East (411 Third Ave): rooftop
Town Bar (Chambers Hotel, 15 W 56th St): good service
Trailer Park Lounge (271 W 23rd St): turkey burgers
12:31 (Hotel Chandler, 12 E 31st St): cozy
Uncle Ming's (225 Ave B, 2nd floor): mysterious
The View Lounge (New York Marriott Marquis, 1535 Broadway): rotat-
   ing rooftop views
Waterfront Ale House (540 Second Ave): great Belgian beer, good food
Westside Brewing Company (340 Amsterdam Ave)
The Whiskey (1567 Broadway): see and be seen

Wollensky's Grill (201 E 49th St)
Xunta (174 First Ave): tapas bar
Zinc Bar (90 Houston St): good music

ROMANTIC

Aureole (34 E 61st St)
Barbetta (321 W 46th St)
Blue Hill (75 Washington Pl)
Bouley (120 West Broadway)
Bridge Cafe (279 Water St)
Cafe Pierre (Pierre Hotel, 2 E 61st St)
Caffe Reggio (119 MacDougal St)
Caffe Vivaldi (32 Jones St)
Capsouto Frères (451 Washington St)
Chanterelle (2 Harrison St)
Chez Josephine (414 W 42nd St)
Danal (90 E 10th St)
Erminia (250 E 83rd St)
Firebird (365 W 46th St)
Four Seasons (99 E 52nd St)
Il Buco (47 Bond St)
Il Cortile (125 Mulberry St)
I Trulli (122 E 27th St)
Jean Georges (Trump International Hotel and Tower, 1 Central Park W)
King Cole Bar (St. Regis New York, 2 E 55th St)
Lady Mendl's Tea Salon (Inn at Irving Place, 56 Irving Pl)
La Grenouille (3 E 52nd St)
Le Périgord (405 E 52nd St)
Oak Room (Algonquin Hotel, 59 W 44th St)
One If By Land, Two If By Sea (17 Barrow St)
Paola's (245 E 84th St)
Primavera (1578 First Ave)
Rainbow Room (30 Rockefeller Plaza)
River Cafe (1 Water St, Brooklyn)
Scalinatella (201 E 61st St)
Spice Market (403 W 13th St)
Tavern on the Green, Crystal Room (Central Park W and 67th St)
Water Club (East River at 30th St)
Water's Edge (44th Dr at East River, Queens)
Zoë (90 Prince St)

SANDWICHES

Amy's Bread (672 Ninth Ave)
Bread Market & Cafe (1290 Ave of the Americas)
Cafe Gitane (242 Mott St)
Call Cuisine (1032 First Ave)
Carnegie Delicatessen and Restaurant (854 Seventh Ave)
City Bakery (3 W 18th St)
Cosi Sandwich Bar (504 Ave of the Americas and other locations)
Cucina & Co. (MetLife Building, 200 Park Ave)
Deb's (200 Varick St)
E.A.T. (1064 Madison Ave)

Eisenberg's Sandwich Shop (174 Fifth Ave)
Faicco's (260 Bleecker St)
Good and Plenty to Go (410 W 43rd St)
Italian Food Center (186 Grand St)
Manganaro's Hero Boy (492 Ninth Ave)
Mangia (50 W 57th St)
Nicky's Vietnamese Sandwiches (150 E 2nd St): Vietnamese
Once Upon a Tart (135 Sullivan St)
Piada (3 Clinton St): Italian
Popover Cafe (551 Amsterdam Ave)
PressToast (112 MacDougal St): Israeli
Rolls 'n' Curry (101 Lexington Ave): Indian
Salumeria Biellese (376 Eighth Ave)
Sandwich Planet (534 Ninth Ave)
Shorty's (576 Ninth Ave)
Sosa Borella (832 Eighth Ave)
Sullivan Street Bakery (533 W 47th St)
Swich (104 Eighth Ave)
Telephone Bar & Grill (149 Second Ave)
Terramare (22 E 65th St)
Todaro Bros. (555 Second Ave)
Union Square Cafe (21 E 16th St)
'wichcraft (555 Fifth Ave and other locations)

SEAFOOD

Aquagrill (210 Spring St)
Aquavit (65 E 55th St)
BLT Fish (21 W 17th St)
Blue Fin (W New York Times Square, 1567 Broadway)
Blue Ribbon (97 Sullivan St)
Blue Water Grill (31 Union Square W)
Bridge Cafe (279 Water St)
Docks Oyster Bar and Seafood Grill (2427 Broadway and 633 Third Ave)
Ed's Lobster Bar (222 Lafayette St)
Esca (402 W 43rd St)
Estiatorio Milos (125 W 55th St)
Fresh (105 Reade St)
Grand Central Oyster Bar Restaurant (Grand Central Terminal, 42nd St at Vanderbilt Ave, lower level)
Jack's Luxury Oyster Bar (101 Second Ave)
Kuruma Zushi (7 E 47th St)
Le Bernardin (155 W 51st St)
Lure Fishbar (142 Mercer St)
Mary's Fish Camp (64 Charles St)
McCormick & Schmick's (1285 Ave of the Americas)
Mermaid Inn (96 Second Ave)
Oceana (55 E 54th St)
Ocean Grill (384 Columbus Ave)
Oriental Garden (14 Elizabeth St)
Pearl Oyster Bar (18 Cornelia St)
Primola (1226 Second Ave)

Remi (145 W 53rd St)
Sea Grill (19 W 49th St)
Shelly's (41 W 57th St)
Trata Estiatorio (1331 Second Ave)
Tropica (MetLife Building, 200 Park Ave)
Westville (210 W 10th St)
Wild Salmon (622 Third Ave)

SHOPPING BREAKS

To replenish your energy, here are some good places to eat in the major Manhattan stores:

ABC Carpet & Home (888 Broadway, 212/473-3000): **Le Pain Quotidien** (bakery & cafe), **Lucy Mexican Barbecue** (Nuevo Latino), and **Pipa** (South American)

Barneys New York (660 Madison Ave, 212/833-2200): **Fred's** (upscale)

Bergdorf Goodman (men's store, 745 Fifth Ave, 212/753-7300): **Cafe 745**

Bergdorf Goodman (women's store, 754 Fifth Ave, 212/753-7300): **BG Restaurant** (7th floor) and **Goodman** (plaza level)

Bloomingdale's (1000 Third Ave, 212/705-2000): **B Cafe** (6th floor), **59th & Lex** (lower level), **Le Train Bleu** (6th floor), and **Showtime Cafe** (7th floor)

Bodum Cafe & Home Store (413 W 14th St, 212/367-9125)

Lord & Taylor (424 Fifth Ave, 212/391-3344): **An American Place** (5th floor, American) and **Signature Cafe** (6th floor, American)

Macy's (151 W 34th St, 212/695-4400): **Au Bon Pain** (street level and 8th floor), **Cucina Express Marketplace** (cellar level), **Grill Restaurant & Bar** (cellar level), and **Starbucks** (3rd floor)

Saks Fifth Avenue (611 Fifth Ave, 212/753-4000): **Cafe S.F.A.** (8th floor, tasty and classy)

Takashimaya (693 Fifth Ave, 212/350-0100): **Tea Box Cafe** (lower level, Oriental flavor)

Are you feeling under the weather? How about a bowl of chicken soup? Some of the best bowls in the city are served by:

Artie's Delicatessen (2290 Broadway)
Brooklyn Diner USA (212 W 57th St)
Carnegie Delicatessen and Restaurant (854 Seventh Ave)
Fine & Schapiro (138 W 72nd St)
Kitchenette (156 Chambers St)
Second Avenue Kosher Delicatessen and Restaurant (162 E 33rd St)
Zabar's (2245 Broadway): Saul Zabar himself is there to make sure it tastes just like his grandmother's.

SOUPS

Hale and Hearty Soups (849 Lexington Ave and other locations)
Tea Den (689 Ninth Ave)
Veselka (144 Second Ave)

SOUTHERN FLAVORS AND SOUL FOOD

Acme Bar & Grill (9 Great Jones St)
Amy Ruth's (113 W 116th St)
Brother Jimmy's BBQ (1485 Second Ave)
Bubby's (120 Hudson St)
Cafe Con Leche (424 Amsterdam Ave)
Copeland's (547 W 145th St)
Great Jones Cafe (54 Great Jones St)
Londel's Supper Club (2620 Frederick Douglass Blvd)
M&G Diner (383 W 125th St)
Manna's (2331 Frederick Douglass Blvd)
Miss Maude's Spoonbread Too (547 Lenox Ave)
107 West (2787 Broadway)
Pier 2110 (2110 Seventh Ave)
Pink Tea Cup (42 Grove St)
Shark Bar (307 Amsterdam Ave)
Sister's Cuisine (47 E 124th St)
Sylvia's (328 Lenox Ave)

STEAKS

Angelo and Maxie's (233 Park Ave S): reasonable prices
Ben Benson's Steak House (123 W 52nd St)
Bistro le Steak (1309 Third Ave): inexpensive and good
BLT Steak (106 E 57th St)
Bull & Bear (Waldorf-Astoria, 301 Park Ave)
Capital Grille (155 E 42nd St)
Churrascaria Plataforma (Belvedere Hotel, 316 W 49th St)
craftsteak (85 Tenth Ave)
Del Frisco's Double Eagle Steak House (1221 Ave of the Americas)
Frank's (410 W 16th St)
Frankie and Johnnie's (269 W 45th St)
Gallagher's Steak House (228 W 52nd St)
Hacienda de Argentina (339 E 75th St)
Keens Steakhouse (72 W 36th St)
Le Marais (150 W 46th St): kosher
Maloney & Porcelli (37 E 50th St)
MarkJoseph Steakhouse (261 Water St)
Morton's of Chicago (551 Fifth Ave)
Palm One, Palm Too, and Palm West Side (837 Second Ave, 840 Second Ave, and 250 W 50th St)
Patroon (160 E 46th St): outrageously expensive
Peter Luger Steak House (178 Broadway, Brooklyn): a tradition since 1887
Pietro's (232 E 43rd St)
Post House (Lowell Hotel, 28 E 63rd St)
Quality Meats (57 W 58th St)
Ruth's Chris Steak House (148 W 51st St)
Smith & Wollensky (797 Third Ave)
Sparks Steakhouse (210 E 46th St)
Steak Frites (9 E 16th St)
Strip House (13 E 12th St)

SUSHI

In the early 1980s, sushi bars became the fast-food joints of the fashionable set. To this day, New Yorkers love to wrap their chopsticks around succulent slivers of raw or cooked seafood on rice. Although many are content to order assortments concocted by the chef, true aficionados prefer to select by the piece. To tailor your next sushi platter to your own tastes, here's what you need to know:

Amaebi (sweet shrimp)
Anago (sea eel)
California roll (avocado and crab)
Hamachi (yellowtail)
Hirame (halibut)
Ika (squid)
Ikura (salmon roe)
Kappa maki (cucumber roll)
Maguro (tuna)
Nizakana (cooked fish)
Saba (mackerel)
Sake (salmon)
Tekka maki (tuna roll)
Toro (fatty tuna)
Umeshiso maki (plum roll)
Unagi (freshwater eel)
Uni (sea urchin)

Give any of these a try for sushi:

Aki (181 W 4th St)
Avenue A Sushi (103 Ave A)
Blue Ribbon Sushi (119 Sullivan St)
Bond Street (6 Bond St)
Ebisu (414 E 9th St)
Gari (370 Columbus Ave)
Geisha (33 E 61st St)
Hatsuhana (17 E 48th St)
Inagiku (Waldorf-Astoria, 301 Park Ave)
Japonica (100 University Pl)
Jewel Bako (239 E 5th St)
Kai (Ito En, 822 Madison Ave)
Kuruma Zushi (7 E 47th St, 2nd floor)
Le Miu (107 Ave A)
Masa (10 Columbus Circle, 4th floor)
Megu (62 Thomas St)
Nadaman Hakubai (Kitano Hotel, 66 Park Ave)
Nippon (155 E 52nd St)
Nobu and **Nobu Next Door** (105 Hudson St)
Ruby Foo's (1626 Broadway and 2128 Broadway)
Sapporo East (164 First Ave)
Shabu-Tatsu (216 E 10th St)
Sugiyama (251 W 55th St)
Sumile Sushi (154 W 13th St)
Sushi a Go-Go (1900 Broadway)

Sushiden (19 E 49th St and 123 W 49th St)
Sushi Hana (1501 Second Ave)
Sushi of Gari (402 E 78th St)
SushiSamba 7 (87 Seventh Ave)
Sushi Seki (1143 First Ave)
Sushi Yasuda (204 E 43rd St)
Sushi Zen (108 W 44th St)
Taka (61 Grove St)
Takahachi (85 Ave A)
Tomoe Sushi (172 Thompson St)
Tsuki (1410 First Ave)
Ushi Wakamaru (136 W Houston St)
Yama (38 Carmine St and 122 E 17th St)

TAKEOUT

Balthazar (80 Spring St)
Beacon (25 W 56th St)
Bread (20 Spring St)
Cafe Español (172 Bleecker St)
City Market Cafe (551 Madison Ave)
City 75 (75 Rockefeller Plaza)
Cucina Vivolo (138 E 74th St)
Dean & Deluca (560 Broadway and 1150 Madison Ave)
Demarchelier (50 E 86th St)
Diwan Restaurant (148 E 48th St)
Jacques Brasserie (204-206 E 85th St)
Jubilee (347 E 54th St)
L'Absinthe (227 E 67th St)
Lorenzo and Maria's Kitchen (1418 Third Ave)
Maria Pia (319 W 51st St)
Molyvos (871 Seventh Ave)
Murray's Cheese Shop (254 Bleecker St)
Musette (228 Third Ave)
Pepe Verde (559 Hudson St)
RUB BBQ (208 W 23rd St)
Sarabeth's (75 Ninth Ave)
Schiller's (131 Rivington St)
Sushi a Go-Go (1900 Broadway)
Sushi Zen (108 W 44th St)
Tio Pepe (168 W 4th St)
Tossed (295 Park Ave S)
Turkuaz Restaurant (2637 Broadway)
Virgil's Real Barbecue (152 W 44th St)

TEATIME

Alice's Tea Cup (102 W 73rd St and 156 E 64th St)
Astor Court (St. Regis New York, 2 E 55th St)
Bar Seine (Plaza Athenee, 37 E 64th St)
Cafe S.F.A. (Saks Fifth Avenue, 611 Fifth Ave)
Carlyle Hotel Gallery (35 E 76th St)
Cha-an (230 E 9th St, 2nd floor)
Cocktail Terrace (Waldorf-Astoria, 301 Park Ave)
Danal (90 E 10th St)

Gotham Lounge (Peninsula New York Hotel, 700 Fifth Ave)
Harlem Tea Room (1793-A Madison Ave)
Ito En (822 Madison Ave)
King's Carriage House (251 E 82nd St)
Lady Mendl's Tea Salon (56 Irving Pl)
McNally Robinson Book Store and Tea House (50 Prince St)
The Morgan Dining Room (The Morgan Library & Museum, 225 Madison Ave)
Payard Patisserie (1032 Lexington Ave)
Pembroke Room (Lowell Hotel, 28 E 63rd St)
Podunk (231 E 5th St)
Rotunda (Pierre Hotel, 2 E 61st St)
Sant Ambroeus (1000 Madison Ave and 259 W 4th St)
Sarabeth's Kitchen (423 Amsterdam Ave and Hotel Wales, 1295 Madison Ave)
T Salon (Chelsea Market, 75 Ninth Ave)
Tea & Sympathy (108 Greenwich Ave)
Tea Box Cafe (Takashimaya, 693 Fifth Ave)
Teany (90 Rivington St)
Ty Lounge (Four Seasons Hotel New York, 57 E 57th St)
Yaffa's Tea Room (19 Harrison St)

TOP-RATED
Aureole (34 E 61st St)
Babbo (110 Waverly Pl)
Barbetta (321 W 46th St)
Blue Ribbon Sushi (119 Sullivan St and 278 Fifth Ave)
Bouley (120 West Broadway)
Cafe Boulud (Surrey Hotel, 20 E 76th St)
Chanterelle (2 Harrison St)
craft (43 E 19th St)
Daniel (60 E 65th St)
Danube (30 Hudson St)
Del Posto (85 Tenth Ave)
Four Seasons (99 E 52nd St)
Gotham Bar & Grill (12 E 12th St)
Gramercy Tavern (42 E 20th St)
Il Mulino (86 W 3rd St)
Jean Georges (Trump International Hotel and Tower, 1 Central Park W)
La Grenouille (3 E 52nd St)
Le Bernardin (155 W 51st St)
Le Périgord (405 E 52nd St)
Masa (Time Warner Center, 10 Columbus Circle, 4th floor)
Nobu and **Nobu Next Door** (105 Hudson St)
Oceana (55 E 54th St)
Park Avenue Cafe (100 E 63rd St)
per se (Time Warner Center, 10 Columbus Circle, 4th floor)
Peter Luger Steak House (178 Broadway, Brooklyn)
Post House (Lowell Hotel, 28 E 63rd St)
Primavera (1578 First Ave)
River Cafe (1 Water St, Brooklyn)
Sugiyama (251 W 55th St)
Sushi of Gari (402 E 78th St)

Sushi Seki (1143 First Ave)
Sushi Yasuda (204 E 43rd St)
Union Square Cafe (21 E 16th St)
Veritas (43 E 20th St)

VEGETARIAN

Angelica Kitchen (300 E 12th St)
Barbetta (321 W 46th St)
Benny's Burritos (113 Greenwich Ave and 93 Avenue A)
Blossom (187 Ninth Ave)
Cafe Boulud (Surrey Hotel, 20 E 76th St)
Candle Cafe (1307 Third Ave)
Caravan of Dreams (405 E 6th St)
Chennai Garden (129 E 27th St)
Chola Eclectic Indian Cuisine (232 E 58th St)
Counter (105 First Ave)
Gobo (1426 Third Ave)
Green Table (Chelsea Market, 75 Ninth Ave)
Hangawi (12 E 32nd St)
Moda Restaurant (135 W 52nd St)
Monte's Trattoria (97 MacDougal St)
Park Bistro (414 Park Ave S)
Planet One (76 E 7th St)
Pure Food and Wine (54 Irving Pl)
Quantum Leap Natural Foods (226 Thompson St)
Quintessence (263 E 10th St)
Rice (227 Mott St)
Salute! Restaurant and Bar (270 Madison Ave)
Snack (105 Thompson St)
Souen (28 E 13th St and 210 Ave of the Americas)
Spring Street Natural Restaurant (62 Spring St)
Surya (302 Bleecker St)
Two Boots (42 Ave A and other locations)
Vatan (409 Third Ave)
Vegetarian Paradise 2 (144 W 4th St)
Village Natural (46 Greenwich Ave)
Whole Earth Bakery & Kitchen (130 St. Mark's Pl)
Zen Palate (633 Ninth Ave and other locations)

> Watch for the opening of David Bouley and nutritionist Oz Garcia's new vegetarian restaurant in the Lincoln Center area in early 2008.

VIEW

Alma (187 Columbia St, Brooklyn): magical rooftop garden
Asiate (Mandarin Oriental New York, Time Warner Center, 80 Columbus Circle, 35th floor)
Café Gray (Time Warner Center, 10 Columbus Circle, 3rd floor)
Delegates Dining Room (United Nations, First Ave at 45th St, 4th floor)

Metropolitan Museum of Art (1000 Fifth Ave): rooftop bar
Peninsula New York Hotel (700 Fifth Ave): skybar and open-air terrace among lofty midtown skyscrapers
per se (Time Warner Center, 10 Columbus Circle, 4th floor)
Rise (Ritz-Carlton New York, Battery Park, 2 West St): indoor-outdoor lounge on the 14th floor
River Cafe (1 Water St, Brooklyn): A window seat affords that breathtaking view of the downtown skyline you've always seen on postcards and in movies.
Tavern on the Green (Central Park W at 67th St): Magical!
The View Lounge (New York Marriott Marquis, 1535 Broadway): revolves high above Times Square
Top of the Tower (Beekman Tower Hotel, 3 Mitchell Pl): an art deco penthouse delight
Water Club (30th St at East River): Savor the view with Sunday brunch.
World Yacht Cruises (Pier 81, W 41st St at Hudson River): Manhattan from the water

WINE BARS

Ara (24 Ninth Ave)
Artisanal (2 Park Ave)
Bin No. 220 (220 Front St)
Bottega del Vino (7 E 59th St)
Centovini (25 W Houston St)
Eleven Madison Park (11 Madison Ave)
Enoteca I Trulli (122 E 27th St)
Il Posto Accanto (190 E 2nd St)
'inoteca (98 Rivington St)
I Tre Merli (463 West Broadway)
Jadis (42 Rivington St)
MetroCafe & Wine Bar (32 E 21st St)
Monday Room (210 Elizabeth St)
Morrell Wine Bar & Cafe (1 Rockefeller Plaza)
Paradou (8 Little West 12th St)
Proseccheria (447 Third Ave)
Pudding Stones (1457 Third Ave)
Punch & Judy (26 Clinton St)
Ten Degrees (121 St. Mark's Pl)
Tintol (155 W 46th St)
Turks and Frogs (323 W 11th St)
Veritas (43 E 20th St)
Wined Up (913 Broadway, 2nd floor)
Xicala Wine & Tapas Bar (151-B Elizabeth St)

A visit to **Shopsin's General Store** (120 Essex St, 212/388-0449) is an experience! To say that it is a different sort of place is an understatement.

New York Restaurants: The Best in Every Price Category

ABBOCCATO
136 W 55th St (bet Ave of the Americas and Seventh Ave)
Breakfast, Lunch, Dinner: Mon-Sat; Sun: Early Dinner (4 p.m.)
Expensive   212/265-4000
                                                    www.abboccato.com

The Livanos family is known and respected on the New York restaurant scene. They own this elegant Italian dining spot, which serves some traditional (as if you are really in Italy) plates, so expect big things—especially if you like rather fussy Italian dishes. Personally, I like a simple approach, so I found some items a bit overwhelming, but nonetheless very good. Most of the appetizers, especially the pastas, are excellent, and the breadsticks are fabulous! Try the suckling pig, the signature rack of lamb, or roasted veal shank—all of them are delicious! The dessert menu is a dream, with ten choices, including homemade gelati. However dreamy the dining experience, the sizable tab will wake you up.

ACAPPELLA
1 Hudson St (bet West Broadway and Chambers St)   212/240-0163
Lunch: Mon-Fri; Dinner: Mon-Sat   www.acappella-restaurant.com
Moderately expensive

Acappella is a classy, upscale—in atmosphere, food, and pricing—Tribeca dining room with a highly professional staff that provides a very special dining experience. It's a good place for a romantic interlude, for an important business lunch, or to experiment with some unique Northern Italian dishes. You'll find homemade pastas, risotto, calamari, fish, veal scaloppine, veal chops, Kobe beef, breaded breast of chicken, and prime steak on the menu. For dessert, splurge on the homemade Italian cheesecake or chocolate truffle torte.

Hungry for a good lunch in midtown? Try **Amalia** (204 W 55th St, 212/245-1234). Recommended: Greek Island salad, stuffed crispy chicken, and one of the best burgers in the city.

ALOUETTE
2588 Broadway (bet 97th and 98th St)   212/222-6808
Dinner: Daily   www.alouettenyc.com
Moderate

Looking for a bustling eatery on the Upper West Side with reasonable prices and good food? Alouette meets all these criteria and is made even more desirable by a friendly and helpful staff. Seating is provided in smallish quarters on the street floor, and more tables are available on the mezzanine. You'll find many French specialities to start: paté de foie gras de canard, onion soup gratinee, escargots, and a delicious warm goat cheese tartelette. Seafood dishes are available, but Alouette really shines in the steak category. Hanger steak and sirloin are excellent choices, with superb pommes frites (as you would expect) and a coconut-infused spinach side dish. Pretend you are in Paris and enjoy the cheese plate for dessert.

ANGELS RISTORANTE
1135 First Ave (bet 62nd and 63rd St)   212/980-3131
Daily: 11:30 a.m.-11:30 p.m.   www.angelsnyc.com
Moderate

For years Angels has been one of the most popular East Side Italian restaurants. They bring consistency to the preparation of homemade pastas, breads, cheeses, salads, and exotic appetizers. Entree offerings include a variety of fish and meat dishes. Known for huge portions and good service, Angels is an experience not to be missed. Stroll around the corner and find a variety of home-baked goodies, ready-to-eat pastas, and sandwiches for takeout or delivery from **Wings on Angels** (212/371-8484).

ANNIE'S
1381 Third Ave (bet 78th and 79th St)   212/327-4853
Breakfast: Mon-Fri; Lunch, Dinner: Daily; Brunch: Sat, Sun
Inexpensive to moderate   www.anniesrestaurant.com

Doesn't anyone in Manhattan go out for breakfast or lunch on Saturday? It would seem that way, with most restaurants pulling the shades down until dinner time. Not Annie's. This place hops at brunch with neighborhood regulars who know they can get a good meal at a sensible price. On the brunch menu are tasty eggs, omelets, frittatas, cereals, and homemade baked items. Lunch and dinner menus feature tasty soups and salads, sandwiches, pastas, steaks, chicken, burgers, and seafood. Don't pass up the delicious beef short ribs for dinner! Can you imagine desserts under $7 in inflated New York? Annie's offers affordable homemade apple pie, tarts, gelati, and sorbet. No wonder this is such a popular place. Even standing in line is worth the trouble when you get value like this! Delivery is free from 57th to 96th streets between East End and Fifth avenues.

The restaurant scene on the Lower East Side these days is no less than amazing. One of the cleanest and best—so good it's worth a trip from uptown—is **Falai** (68 Clinton St, 212/253-1960). The cuisine is Italian, the outdoor patio is highly inviting, the chicken-in-a-pot is fabulous, the homemade breads are among the best I have ever tasted, and the profiteroles are to die for. The sorbets are also first-class. **Falai Panetteria**, a tiny satellite operation just across the street (79 Clinton St, 212/777-8956), is a good spot for quick takeout or eat-in soups, pastas, salads, and paninis.

A.O.C. BEDFORD
14 Bedford St (at Ave of the Americas and Houston St)
Dinner: Daily   212/414-4764
Moderate to moderately expensive   www.aocbedford.com

If you would like to spend some quality time with a special date in a cozy setting, consider A.O.C. Bedford. In France, the letters "A.O.C." designate products that exhibit the finest qualities and characteristics of a given geographical area. A.O.C. Bedford is a warm, quaint room in an area where you would not expect to find a classy operation. The menu changes seasonally. Order lamb if it is offered. A nice touch is the cheese course, presenting some unusual soft cheeses from all over the world. The Spanish blue cheese is especially good. The dessert selection is small but adequate, with crepes Suzette the best choice.

AQUAVIT
65 E 55th St (bet Park and Madison Ave)   212/307-7311
Lunch: Mon-Fri (Sat in cafe only); Dinner: Daily; Brunch: Sun
Moderately expensive   www.aquavit.org

If you are looking for a true Scandinavian experience, you can't do better than Aquavit. Owner Hakan Swahn and chef Marcus Samuelsson have put together a first-class establishment. The tab will likely be sizable, but you can reduce it somewhat by dining in the more informal cafe, which serves the same wonderful food. The atmosphere is conducive to classy dining; they prefer that gentlemen wear jackets. The raw shell plate, lobster roll, or foie gras *ganache* will get the meal off to a great start. The seafood offerings—salmon, halibut, trout, and more—are the pride of the house. You'll find typical Scandinavian dishes, like gravlax and Swedish meatballs, served in the cafe. Hearty appetites will enjoy the seafood stew. My dessert suggestion is mint chocolate mousse with blood orange sauce.

> Reasonably priced dim sum is available almost any hour at **Ollie's** (1991 Broadway, 212/595-8181). A selection of steamed "Chinese healthy" dishes is offered. This is a good family restaurant.

ARABELLE
Hotel Plaza Athenee
37 E 64th St (bet Madison and Park Ave)   212/606-4647
Breakfast: Daily; Lunch, Dinner: Tues-Sat; Brunch: Sun
Moderately expensive to expensive   www.arabellerestaurant.com

Dining in this attractive room is a civilized experience. It is elegant and charming, and the adjacent lounge is one of the classiest places in Manhattan. For starters, try real French onion soup (in the lounge), sauteed Hudson Valley foie gras, or sashimi ahi tuna. If you still have room, entree winners include pan-roasted Atlantic halibut, pork and shrimp dumplings, beef tenderloin, and a tasty Maine lobster salad. By all means try the warm valrhona chocolate soufflé for dessert. Order it at the start of your meal. The wait staff is unusually attentive and professional.

ARTISANAL
2 Park Ave (at 32nd St)   212/725-8585
Lunch: Mon-Fri; Dinner: Daily; Brunch: Sat, Sun
Moderate to moderately expensive   www.artisanalcheese.com

Imagine a combination bistro, brasserie, and *fromagerie*, and you'll have a clear picture of this exciting operation. Being a cheese lover, I found the menu and attractive in-house takeout cheese counter first-rate. There is much more! The crab and avocado salad is a wonderful way to start. Pricey seafood platters include lobster, clams, scallops, oysters, shrimp, sea urchin, and more. Several fondues are offered, including a classic Swiss and a wonderful Stilton and Sauterne. Seafood specialties include soft-shell crabs (in summer), cod, and Dover sole. Heartier appetites will be sated by grilled lamb chops, several steak items, and daily offerings. For dessert, cruise the cheese counter and load your plate from a selection of 250 of the world's finest. Seating is comfortable in the spacious room, service is highly informed and refined, and the energy level is high. Great wine selection, too!

ASIATE
Mandarin Oriental New York
80 Columbus Circle (at 60th St)   212/805-8881
Breakfast, Dinner: Daily; Lunch: Mon-Fri
Expensive   www.mandarinoriental.com

I greatly admire the Mandarin Oriental hotel group, whose original hotel in Hong Kong has been my favorite resting place for decades. So when the news came that they were coming to New York, I lit up. As far as the restaurant is concerned, that light faded quickly. In the first place, they may claim "there are no reservations for six weeks," but that is baloney. I have walked in several times to see a multitude of empty tables. And the much-trumpeted French-Japanese cuisine of chef Noriyuki Sugie is nothing you will remember for long. On the plus side, the 35th-floor view is absolutely fabulous! But that, unfortunately, is the only reason I would visit Asiate.

Manhattan's Chinatown is a fascinating place to visit. It's fun just wandering in and out of the neighborhood shops, restaurants, and unique amusements of this busy place. Here are some of the best for eating:
Big Wong King (67 Mott St, 212/964-0540): barbecue
New Green Bo (66 Bayard St, 212/625-2359): Shanghai cuisine
Oriental Garden (14 Elizabeth St, 212/619-0085): fresh fish
Ping's Seafood (22 Mott St, 212/602-9988): great meal
Tan My My (249 Grand St, 212/966-7878): fresh fish

AUREOLE
34 E 61st St (bet Madison and Park Ave)   212/319-1660
Lunch: Mon-Fri; Dinner: Mon-Sat   www.charliepalmer.com
Expensive

Owner-chef Charlie Palmer usually does a fine job with the preparation of his dishes, which are beautifully served by personnel who are more than a little impressed that they work here. If you manage to get seated without a questionable wait at the bar and are lucky enough to sit on the first floor, with its seasonal garden views, consider yourself fortunate. Best bets are the game dishes. Desserts look better than they taste. Personally, I would rather spend my hard-earned money where the staff appreciates the business. On the plus side, the four-course tasting luncheon is a good value.

A VOCE
41 Madison Ave (at 26th St)   212/545-8555
Lunch: Mon-Fri; Dinner: Daily   www.cerestaurant.com
Moderate to moderately expensive

The name means "word of mouth," and the word got out quickly! A Voce is a busy place, with talented (and highly experienced) chef Andrew Carmellini taking well-deserved bows. The setting is rather cold, but the vast windows opening up on a terrace, great in the nice weather, does soften the place. Like so many of the hot restaurants, this one is overbearingly noisy, but the good food makes up for any discomfort. The changing menu tends toward grilled octopus and Maine scallop saltimbocca. Even lowly dishes like spaghetti and potato gnocchi (delicious) are available. The slim and attractive wait staff is well rehearsed on how to sell. I was impressed with the mature greeting by the restaurant manager, so different than the snotty and unschooled persons one encounters so many times these days at the door in Manhattan eateries. By all means, finish your meal with the vanilla custard doughnuts (*bombolino*) served with hot fudge.

Someone always has a great new idea! Here is one for those who find it difficult to get reservations at some of Manhattan's best restaurants. **Prime Time Tables** (www.primetimetables.com) is a web-based outfit that handles reservations. Several types of membership are available, including a pay by reservation or an "unlimited" annual membership. Another helpful website (www.weekendepicurenyc.com) also books tables for a reservation fee. Just contact these folks online and they will do their best to get you that "hot table."

BABBO
110 Waverly Pl (at Washington Square)   212/777-0303
Dinner: Daily   www.babbonyc.com
Moderate to moderately expensive

Surely you have heard about Babbo! For many years 110 Waverly Place has been one of my favorite dining addresses. First it was the legendary Coach House, and now it is the magnificent Italian watering spot Babbo, which means "daddy" in the native tongue. It has become one of the most respected houses of fine Italian dining in New York, and a reservation here is one of the toughest in Manhattan. The townhouse setting is warm and comfortable, the service is highly professional, and an evening at Babbo is one you will savor for a long time! Most everything is good, but I especially recommend sweetbreads, grilled ribeye steak for two, and beef cheek ravioli. Wonderful desserts include chocolate hazelnut cake, saffron panna cotta, pistachio and chocolate *semifreddo*, and the ever-popular cheese plate. Best of all is the assortment of homemade gelati and sorbetti.

BALDORIA
249 W 49th St (bet Eighth Ave and Broadway)   212/582-0460
Lunch: Mon-Fri; Dinner: Daily   www.baldoriamo.com
Moderately expensive

New Yorkers in the know head *way* uptown to Rao's on 114th Street. This midtown offshoot of that famous Italian eatery is a definite winner. The seasonings and sauces at Baldoria make almost every dish memorable. There are mussels and clams to start, wonderfully fresh seasonal salads, a good selection of pastas, and especially delectable spaghetti dishes. The meatballs are sensational! Their lemon chicken is one of the best I have ever tasted. If fresh peach *semifreddo* is on the menu, try it for dessert; otherwise I recommend Italian cream puffs with espresso cream and chocolate caramel sauce. The place is busy, but an abundance of personnel will make sure you are well taken care of.

BALTHAZAR
80 Spring St (at Crosby St)   212/965-1414
Breakfast, Lunch, Dinner: Daily; Brunch: Sat, Sun
Moderate   www.balthazarny.com

Balthazar is a popular destination at any time of the day (or night, as they serve late). The setting—with old mirrors, ceiling fans, and a yellow tin roof—is unique, and the food is quite good, considering the size of the operation. The personnel are harried but well-trained, and you will not wait for your water glass to be filled. Excellent bakery items shine at breakfast; be sure to pick up some tasty bread next door at their bakery on your way out. At lunch and dinner you can enjoy delicious seasonal salads, sandwiches, cheeses, panini, fabulous French onion soup, *brandade*, escargots, steak *frites*, and an abundant seafood selection (including a seafood bar). For dessert the *tarte tatin* is a must. This brasserie is fun and different, and its takeout menu is a plus.

The **Time Warner Center** (10 Columbus Circle) presents a mixed bag of restaurant opportunities. There is no question about the quality of some of the operations, but prices can be sky high.
Bar Masa (212/823-9800): good sushi
Bouchon Bakery (212/823-9366): casual dining
Café Gray (212/823-6338): dramatic setting, excellent chef
Landmarc (212/823-6123): big, brassy, busy
Masa (212/823-9800): superb Japanese dishes, very expensive
per se (212/823-9335): chef-owner Thomas Keller's small, elegant, pricey jewel

---

BAR AMERICAIN
152 W 52nd St (bet Ave of the Americas and Seventh Ave)
Lunch: Mon-Fri; Dinner: Daily; Brunch: Sat, Sun   212/265-9700
Moderately expensive to expensive   www.baramericain.com

Bar Americain is indeed almost purely American. It can perhaps best be described as an American brasserie. The setting is large, occupying a space that was once the Judson Grill. The decor is a bit offbeat; however, chef David Rockwell has made the room come alive. The food quality and attentive, professional service make this a good bet. The cocktails are numerous and interesting. To start, an eye-catching raw bar is stocked with oysters, clams, lobsters, and more. One could make a meal on the appetizers. The Vidalia onion soup, with its blistered Vermont cheddar cheese, is superb. The same holds true for the crawfish and Dungeness crab griddle cakes. For entrees: cioppino, duck (with dirty wild rice), and rack of pork are worth a try. Five steak dishes are offered. Don't pass up a side of hot potato chips with a blue cheese sauce. I took extra time studying the dessert menu! Would it be carrot pineapple layer cake, caramel whiskey éclairs, or blackberry soufflé? All turned out first-class.

BARBETTA

321 W 46th St (bet Eighth and Ninth Ave)   212/246-9171
Lunch, Dinner, Supper: Tues-Sun   www.barbettarestaurant.com
Moderate to moderately expensive

Barbetta is one of those special places you'll find only in New York, and owner Laura Maioglio is a very special person, as well. It is an elegant restaurant serving *Piemontese* cuisine. Piemonte is located in northern Italy, and the cuisine reflects that charming part of the country. You can dine here in European elegance. One of New York's oldest restaurants, Barbetta celebrated its 100th anniversary in 2006. Amazingly, it is still owned by the family that founded it. One of the special attractions is dining alfresco in the garden during the summer. The main dining room and private party rooms are magnificent! They offer an a la carte luncheon menu as well as a four-course pre-theater dinner menu. Eight choices are offered at each course, and service is expeditious so that you can make opening curtain. After 8 p.m. you can enjoy a leisurely dinner with *crespelle* (almost a meal in itself), handmade ravioli, or the fabulous quail's nest of *fonduta* with white truffles. Barbetta specializes in fish and game dishes, which vary daily. Try squab prepared with hazelnuts and chestnuts. Other selections include rabbit, beef braised in red wine with polenta, and delicious rack of venison. Sixteen desserts are prepared daily, including several chocolate offerings; an assortment of cakes, tarts, and fruits; and panna cotta that's among the best in the city. Barbetta's extraordinary wine list features some 1,650 wines.

Don't miss a visit to **Café Borgia** (161 Prince St, 212/677-1850), where the coffees, lattes, teas, and sandwiches are legendary. It is always packed with a high-energy crowd of all ages. The prices are modest and the place is really fun!

BARMARCHE

14 Spring St (at Elizabeth St)   212/219-2399
Lunch: Mon-Fri; Dinner: Daily; Brunch: Sat, Sun   www.barmarche.com
Moderate

Spring Street is full of small, cozy, and interesting places to dine. The area is called Nolita (shortland for "north of Little Italy"). One of the best stops hereabouts is Barmarche, where the folks are very friendly, the food is excellent, the price is right, and the atmosphere is appealing. You'll find a number of small plates, like a small pizza or chilled oysters, along with fresh salads, sandwiches, taquitos, and one of the best burgers in the city. The garlic fries served alongside the burgers are crisp, non-greasy, and delicious. Barmarche also does catering and is available for parties.

BEACON

25 W 56th St (bet Fifth Ave and Ave of the Americas)
Lunch: Mon-Fri; Dinner: Daily; Brunch: Sun   212/332-0500
Moderately expensive   www.beaconnyc.com

In a huge space divided into intimate sections, Beacon serves tasty dishes cooked over an open fire. If you can get seated near the open kitchen ("the pit"), it is a fascinating show. With over 200 seats and an expansive menu for lunch and dinner, the staff have been well trained to provide superior service. Over a dozen appetizers (from grilled quail to oysters on the half shell), sandwiches, salads, steaks, chops, seafood, and pasta are available at noon. Menu offerings increase at night. The wood-roasted chops and veal dishes are special. Several game dishes are listed on the dinner menu. Dessert soufflés add a festive ending to a great meal. All breads and rolls are made in-house and available for purchase.

Bianca (5 Bleecker St, 212/260-4666), a small Italian neighborhood restaurant, has gotten a lot of attention. The lasagna is great, the mashed potatoes are sinful, and the *tartufo is* almost the real thing. The tab is modest. Take cash, as credit cards are not accepted.

BEN BENSON'S STEAK HOUSE
123 W 52nd St (bet Ave of the Americas and Seventh Ave)
Lunch: Mon-Fri; Dinner: Daily   212/581-8888
Moderately expensive   www.benbensons.com

For years Ben Benson's has been a favorite of the meat-and-potato set, and with justification. The atmosphere is macho-clubby, and the food is uniformly good. Unlike some other steakhouses, service is courteous and efficient. The menu is what you would expect: sirloin steak, filet mignon, T-bone, prime rib, chops, and the like. But Ben Benson's also offers seafood, chicken, calves liver, and chopped steak. A special steak-style veal chop offers 22 ounces of delicious indulgence. The soups are outstanding! Wonderful potatoes, onion rings, or healthy spinach will complete the stomach-filling experience. Daily lunch specials include lobster cakes, grilled chicken breast, roast beef hash, and chicken pot pie. Just don't come looking for bargains. Ben treats you well, and you pay well in return!

BIG NICK'S
2175 Broadway (at 77th St)   212/362-9238
Daily: 24 hours   www.bignicksnyc.com
Cash only
Inexpensive

This unfancy, inexpensive place offers good food at low prices. Breakfasts are super, and they serve lots of salads and sandwiches for lunch. The burgers are sensational. There is a special selection for diet-watchers. Filo pastries and meat, cheese, and spinach pies are all specialties. There are pizzas, baked potatoes served any way you want, delicious cakes and pies, homemade baklava, and Greek yogurt. The service is friendly, and they offer free delivery. Big Nick's has been at it since 1962 with virtually no publicity.

BISTRO LES AMIS
180 Spring St (at Thompson St)   212/226-8645
Lunch, Dinner: Daily   www.bistrolesamis.com
Moderate

Bistro les Amis is a delightful bistro worth stopping by in the middle of a Soho shopping trip or gallery excursion. In the warmer months, doors open onto the sidewalk, and the passing parade is almost as inviting as the varied menu. French onion soup with gruyere is a must, and salmon marinated with fresh dill and herbs is just as good. Lunch entrees include sandwiches and fresh salads. In the evening, seafood and steak dishes are available. The steak *frites* with herb butter are first-class. There's nothing very fancy about this bistro—just good food with an extra touch of friendly service.

BLAUE GANS
139 Duane St (bet Church St and West Broadway)
Daily: 8 a.m.-midnight (bar stays open to 1 a.m.)   212/571-8880
Moderate to moderately expensive   www.wallse.com

The space may be familiar to you, as it used to house Le Zinc. However, the food at Blaue Gans ("Blue Goose") is very different! Chef Kurt Gutenbrunner lives up to his heritage with an Austro-German bistro that offers delicious platters like red cabbage and good salad, smoked trout, goulash, vegetable strudel, wiener schnitzel, *burenwurst* (with sauerkraut), blood sausage, and *Kavalierspitz* (boiled beef shoulder) served with fabulous creamed spinach. *Tafelspitz* (boiled beef) is Austria's national dish, and it, too, is available. I am a great lover of Vienna, especially the fabulous Sacher Torte, which is a tradition in this great city. Unfortunately, Blaue Gans' Sacher Torte falls far short of fabulous. Instead, go for the Salzburger Nockerl, a warm dessert soufflé that's jazzed up with tart huckleberries. The folks here are delightful, which makes the meal even more memorable.

Colors (417 Lafayette St, 212/777-8443) is a worker-owned restaurant with a staff from more than 30 countries. Many of the employees are survivors of the terrorist attack of 9/11 who were off-duty or otherwise not at the World Trade Center at the time. Many of the global dishes are prepared using recipes from the countries represented by the friendly and accommodating staff.

BLT STEAK
106 E 57th St (bet Park and Lexington Ave)   212/752-7470
Lunch: Mon-Fri; Dinner: Mon-Sat   www.bltsteak.com
Moderately expensive to expensive

No, BLT does not stand for the popular bacon, lettuce, and tomato sandwich. It stands for Bistro Laurent Tourondel, and chef Tourondel's considerable talents in the kitchen have made this French/American steakhouse one of the best in Manhattan. The delicious popovers served at the start absolutely melt in your mouth! Most of the pricey salads are big and healthy, and the soups are filling and hearty. Save room for the main show: hanger steak, Kobe flat-iron steak, filets, New York strip steak, and more. You have your choice of seven great sauces to accompany the meat entree. Also on the menu: fish, shellfish, and potatoes done eight different ways. (I could make an entire meal of BLT's potato choices!) The rack of lamb is superb. Chocolate tart smothered with almond milk ice cream is one of the best desserts in Manhattan.

BLUE HILL
75 Washington Pl (bet Ave of the Americas and MacDougal St)
Dinner: Daily   212/539-1776
Moderate to moderately expensive   www.bluehillfarm.com

Dramatic it is not. Comfortable it is—barely. Solid it is—in spades. Blue Hill is named for a farm in the Berkshires (see below) inhabited by a member of the owner's family. The restaurant reflects the chef's solid upbringing with David Bouley. The smallish menu, with only a half dozen appetizers and entrees, includes some spectacular standouts and changes periodically. Poached duck is a specialty. The crabmeat salad, if available, is top rate. If your evening plans involve intimate conversation, forget Blue Hill, as eavesdropping is inevitable and rampant. The chocolate bread pudding ("chocolate silk") is really the only dessert worth the calories. This is one of those spots that older relations may especially enjoy, as it is very civilized.

Did you ever imagine that you might be able to dine at the Rockefeller family mansion in Pocantico Hills, New York? Well, now you can. For a really superb experience, make reservations up to two months in advance for **Blue Hill at Stone Barns** (914/366-9600, www.blue hillstonebarns.com). Only 80 guests are accommodated nightly in what was once a cow barn. Executive chef Dan Barber presides over a kitchen that serves a *prix fixe* dinner from about $65 to $110. Brunch is served on Sundays. Many of the ingredients are grown on the estate.

BLUE RIBBON
97 Sullivan St (bet Spring and Prince St)   212/274-0404
Daily: 4 p.m.-4 a.m.   www.blueribbonrestaurants.com
Moderate

Blue Ribbon is one of the most popular spots in Soho, with a bustling bar scene and people lining up for its limited number of tables. Regulars appreciate the exceptional food in this unpretentious restaurant. There is a raw bar to attract seafood lovers, along with clams, lobster, crab, boiled crawfish, and the house special "Blue Ribbon Royale." One can choose from two dozen appetizers, including barbequed ribs, smoked trout, caviar, and chicken wings. Entrees are just as wide-ranging: sweetbreads, catfish, tofu ravioli, fried chicken and mashed potatoes, burgers, and more. How the smallish kitchen can turn out so many dishes is amazing, but they certainly do it well. Don't come for a relaxed evening; this is strictly an all-American culinary experience. Those who experience hunger pangs after midnight will appreciate the late hours. Try the excellent sushi at their nearby **Blue Ribbon Sushi** (119 Sullivan St, 212/343-0404).

BLUE RIBBON BAKERY
35 Downing St (at Bedford St)   212/337-0404
Lunch, Dinner: Daily; Brunch: Sat, Sun
Moderate   www.blueribbonrestaurants.com

Another Blue Ribbon operation! The rustic breads at this cafe and bakery are excellent, and there is so much more. Downstairs, customers may dine in a fantastic grotto-like atmosphere, complete with two small dining rooms, a wine cellar, and wonderful fresh-bread aroma. The upstairs and downstairs menus feature sandwiches, steaks, seafood, cheeses, grilled items, veggies, and yummy desserts (including profiteroles).

BLUE SMOKE

116 E 27th St (bet Lexington Ave and Park Ave S)   212/447-7733
Lunch, Dinner: Daily   www.bluesmoke.com
Moderate

With Blue Smoke, Danny Meyer filled a real void in the Manhattan dining scene, satisfying legions of barbecue lovers who found it difficult to get real down-home ribs in the Big Apple. In addition to ribs, you'll find chili, smoked beef brisket, tasty sandwiches, pit-baked beans, and more. Blue Smoke is not just a barbecue place; it is a scene, with an ultra-busy bar attracting fun-loving trendsetters.

BLUE WATER GRILL

31 Union Square W (at 16th St)   212/675-9500
Lunch, Dinner: Daily; Brunch: Sun   www.brguestrestaurants.com
Moderate

This seafood restaurant really knows the ocean and all the edible creatures that inhabit it! The Blue Water Grill is a highly professional operation (except for their phone system). Superbly trained personnel operate in a building that once served as a bank and is now a very bustling restaurant. Wonderful appetizers include lobster bisque, grilled baby octopus, and Maryland crab cakes. Tuna, salmon, and swordfish are prepared several ways. Lobsters and oysters (several dozen varieties) are fresh and tasty. For those who want to stick to shore foods, there are pastas, chicken dishes, and grilled filet mignon. A half dozen sensibly priced desserts include a seasonal fruit plate and warm valrhona chocolate cake with vanilla ice cream.

The story of the **Campbell Apartment**, located off the West Balcony of Grand Central Terminal (42nd St at Vanderbilt Ave, 212/953-0409), is a fascinating one. The space was once the private office of John Campbell, a very wealthy financier. In its heyday, these classy digs had a butler and some of the most expensive furnishings available. Well, the Campbell Apartment—which is both an unusual attraction and a thriving bar—has recently undergone renovations and is more attractive than ever. Even jaded New Yorkers like to tell stores about this fellow and that room. It is surely worth a visit!

BOLO

23 E 22nd St (bet Broadway and Park Ave S)   212/228-2200
Lunch: Mon-Fri; Dinner: Daily   www.bolorestaurant.com
Moderate to moderately expensive

The menu at Bolo doesn't copy that of the namesake restaurant at the Ritz Hotel in Madrid, but it does encompass contemporary Spanish as well as Southwestern flavors in an attractive and comfortable setting. The atmosphere and personnel are upbeat, as the folks here want your meal to be both tasty and fun. The dozen or so tapas are delicious. Try the chicken and shellfish paella. The logistics are a miracle, with the tiny kitchen turning out a bevy of wonderful and sometimes seasonal dishes.

BOND 45
154 W 45th St (bet Ave of the Americas and Seventh Ave)
Lunch, Dinner: Daily 212/869-4545
Moderate to moderately expensive www.bond45.com

In the middle of the Theater District, busy restaurateur Shelly Fireman has created another huge dining hall. Billed as an Italian steak and seafood room, Bond 45 is named for the old Bond men's store that used to occupy this site. If it's Italian, Bond 45 has it! The antipasto bar at the entrance makes a mouth-watering beginning. Beyond that there are salads, mozzarella, carpaccio dishes, oysters, clams, cured meats, pastas, steaks, and so on. An overabundance of wait personnel ensures prompt service. Be advised that the dessert selection doesn't live up to the rest of the fare.

Camaje (85 MacDougal St, 212/673-8184) is a great bistro for a quick meal. Ask owner Abigail Hitchcock about her cooking classes.

BOTTEGA DEL VINO
7 E 59th St (bet Fifth and Madison Ave)
Breakfast, Lunch, Dinner: Daily 212/223-3028, 212/223-2724
Moderately expensive www.bottegadelvinonyc.com

This is a serious restaurant that serves serious food. Translated: don't come expecting bargains or typical Italian fare. The location is handy for those visiting or living on the Upper East Side. Service is very professional. All the dishes I tried were good, especially the steaks. If risotto with shrimp and asparagus tips is on the menu, go for it! The signature dish, risotto Amarone (as in Amarone wine), lives up to its reputation. Desserts are tasty and filing, and the cheese selection is excellent.

BOULEY
Mohawk Atelier Building
162 Duane St (at Hudson St) 212/964-2525
Lunch, Dinner: Daily www.davidbouley.com
Expensive

UPSTAIRS AT BOULEY
130 West Broadway (at Duane St) 212/608-5829
Breakfast, Lunch, Dinner: Daily www.davidbouley.com
Moderate

BOULEY BAKERY
120 West Broadway (at Duane St) 212/219-1011
Daily: 7 a.m.-11 p.m. www.davidbouley.com

If I could ask just one person in Manhattan to visit my kitchen and prepare the best of everything, it would be David Bouley. He is an intensely inventive and hard-working chef who enjoys giving his guests a food and dining experience second to none.

His empire has changed considerably in recent years. His **Bouley** restaurant, the epitome of dining with class, has moved into a space that provides more intimate dining with a working fireplace and a fabulous wine cellar. Its French/American menu, superbly professional service, and many seasonal treats make dining here a rare and special experience. **Upstairs at Bouley,** a more casual cafe venue, now serves breakfast, lunch, and dinner upstairs, downstairs, and outside. David is around quite a bit, and the vibes and food are great. **Bouley Bakery** will move into the former restaurant space, offering breads and pastries, cakes, and the like, along with fish, meat, and sauces that David calls *mise en place* (i.e., you can take the items home with you). A wine bar and grill will also be on the premises. Finally, David's long anticipated **Test Kitchen** (88 West Broadway) is now in full operation; call 212/964-2525 for more information.

Ever heard of *BelDel?* Well, it's another "new" Manhattan neighborhood, and it means <u>Bel</u>ow <u>Del</u>aney. It sure is changing—from a rundown area to a brighter place to shop or dine. For now you can feast at **Casanis** (81 Ludlow St), a French bistro, or have a drink at **Koca Lounge** (76 Orchard St).

BRASSERIE
100 E 53rd St (bet Park and Lexington Ave)   212/751-4840
Breakfast, Lunch: Mon-Fri; Dinner: Daily; Brunch: Sat, Sun
Moderate   www.patinagroup.com

For those who like big, brassy, fun dining spots that serve very good food, Brasserie is a New York tradition. What was once a round-the-clock operation now keeps handy late hours (Mon-Thurs till midnight; Fri, Sat till 1 a.m.; Sun till 10 p.m.) in very attractive quarters—a grand staircase fit for a fashion show with sexy lighting—and a bar that offers all manner of goodies. Much of the food has a French flair, but there is more: well-prepared grill dishes, short ribs, grilled bass, scallops, crab cakes, *pot-au-feu*, steamed mussels with *frites*, and daily specials. Big favorites include good old-fashioned onion soup, burgers, and salad niçoise. For dessert, try the chocolate *beignets*.

BRASSERIE 8½
9 W 57th St (bet Fifth Ave and Ave of the Americas)   212/829-0812
Lunch: Mon-Sat; Dinner: Daily; Brunch: Sun (summer hours vary)
Moderately expensive   www.patinagroup.com

The interior and the dining are both dramatic at Brasserie 8½. Descending a long spiral staircase, you enter a spectacular room filled with comfy chairs, an attractive bar, a wall of Léger stained glass, and a collection of signed Matisse prints. Even the tableware is pleasing. Main-course winners include crab cakes, roast chicken, grilled sea scallops, grilled veggie salad, and Maine lobster salad. Specials are offered daily. Friday's seafood bouillabaisse and Sunday brunch are both worth a visit. Great desserts include chocolate soufflé with malt ice cream. On top of everything, these folks seem genuinely happy to greet their diners. Three private rooms are available for special events.

BRASSERIE RUHLMANN
45 Rockefeller Plaza (enter on 50th St, bet Fifth Ave
    and Ave of the Americas)   212/974-2020
Lunch, Dinner: Mon-Sat: Brunch: Sun
Moderate to moderately expensive   www.brasserieruhlmann.com

This is *the* place for steak tartare! The attraction here is the location: in the heart of the midtown shopping area. The large room (232 seats) is bold and classy, the service highly professional, and the door greeting exceptional. They seem really glad to see you. Some signature dishes: for brunch, scrambled eggs with caviar; for lunch, mallard duck confit; for dinner, Dover sole; and for dessert, coffee and chocolate trifle. Of course, Oysters Rockefeller are on the menu! You will also appreciate designer Emile-Jacques Ruhlmann's art-deco interior. Brasserie Ruhlmann opens early and closes late.

No other place on earth has bigger restaurants! New York's top chefs and restaurateurs keep pumping up the square footage of their newest outposts. Bigger is not necessarily better, but for most of these operations, size and quality coexist just fine.

Buddakan (75 Ninth Ave, 212/989-6699): 368 seats
Country (90 Madison Ave, 212/889-7100): 200 seats
Del Posto (85 Tenth Ave, 212/497-8090): very good indeed; 548 seats
Morimoto (80 Tenth Ave, 212/989-8883): you'll like it; 168 seats
Nobu 57 (40 W 57th St, 212/757-3000): done with style and grace; 500 seats
Rosa Mexicano (9 E 18th St, 212/533-3350): tasty South of the Border treats; 335 seats
Tao (42 E 58th St, 212/888-2288): like no other; 300 seats

BRAVO GIANNI
230 E 63rd St (bet Second and Third Ave)   212/752-7272
Lunch: Mon-Fri; Dinner: Mon-Sun
Moderately expensive

Fans of Bravo Gianni—and there are many—may be upset that I've spoiled their secret by including it in this book. It's so comfortable and the food so good that they don't want it to become overcrowded and spoiled. But it doesn't look like there's any real danger of that happening as long as Gianni himself is on the job. The not-too-large room is pleasantly appointed, with beautiful plants on every table. The atmosphere is intimate. And what tastes await you! You can't go wrong with any of the antipasto selections or soups. They have the best ravioli in town. No one does *tortellini alla panna*, *fettuccine con ricotta*, or roast baby lamb better, either. I can recommend every dish on the menu, with top billing going to the fish dishes and rack of lamb. Marvelous desserts, many of them made in-house, will surely tempt you. Legions of loyal customers come back again and again, and it's easy to see why.

BRIDGE CAFE
279 Water St (beneath Brooklyn Bridge)   212/227-3344
Lunch: Mon-Fri: Dinner: Daily; Brunch: Sun   www.eatgoodinny.com
Moderate

The Bridge Cafe—located north of South Street Seaport, beneath the Brooklyn Bridge—has been in operation since 1794, making it the oldest business establishment in the city. Over the decades—nay, over the centuries!—it has housed its share of brothels and saloons. Start with famous Bridge Cafe salad. Other great dishes include buffalo steak, lobster pot pie, and vegetable strata. There is nothing fancy about this place—just good food and especially pleasant personnel. Don't leave without trying the old-fashioned butterscotch pudding. On Sunday, the French toast will get you off to a great start!

New Yorkers are lining up to fill their lunch plates with items from a growing number of attractive and well-stocked delis and buffets. They offer eat-in or takeout sandwiches, soups, drinks (including smoothies), huge salad bars, hot entrees, and a good selection of desserts. The advantages are obvious: quick service, reasonable prices, and tasty food. Here are several I recommend:

Amy's Bread (75 Ninth Ave, 212/462-4338)
Azure (830 Third Ave, 212/486-8080)
Balthazar (80 Spring St, 212/965-1785)
Ben's Kosher Deli (209 W 38th St, 212/398-2367)
Bonsignour Cafe (35 Jane St, 212/229-9700)
Breadstix Cafe (254 Eighth Ave, 212/243-8444)
Cafe 55 (914 Third Ave, 212/935-5100)
Churrascaria Plataforma (behind Belvedere Hotel, 316 W 49th St, 212/245-0505)
City Bakery (3 W 18th St, 212/366-1414)
City Market Cafe (551 Madison Ave, 212/572-9800)
Clinton St. Baking Company (4 Clinton St, 646/602-6263)
Dimple (11 W 30th St, 212/643-9464)
Food Exchange (120 E 59th St, 212/759-0656)
Garden of Eden (162 W 23rd St, 212/675-6300; 7 E 14th St, 212/255-4200; and 2780 Broadway, 212/222-7300)
Mangia (50 W 57th St, 212/582-5882; 16 E 48th St, 212/754-7600; 22 W 23rd St, 212/647-0200; and 40 Wall St, 212/425-4040)
North Village Deli Emporium (78 Eighth Ave, 212/229-0887)
Todai (6 E 32nd St, 212/725-1333)

BROOKLYN DINER USA
212 W 57th St (bet Broadway and Seventh Ave)   212/977-1957
Breakfast, Lunch, Dinner, Late Supper: Daily   www.brooklyndiner.com
Moderate

Brooklyn Diner USA (which is located in Manhattan) is worth a visit. With all-day dining, an expansive menu, pleasant personnel, better-than-average diner food, and reasonable prices, this place is a winner. You can find just about anything your heart desires: breakfast fare, sandwiches (the cheeseburger is a must), salads, hearty lunch and dinner plates, homemade desserts, and good drinks. Their muffins are moist, flavorful, and outrageously good. A tile floor and comfortable booths add to the authentic diner ambience.

BRYANT PARK GRILL
25 W 40th St (bet Fifth Ave and Ave of the Americas)
Lunch: Mon-Fri; Dinner: Daily; Brunch: Sat, Sun   212/840-6500
Moderate   www.arkrestaurants.com
This place is one of Manhattan's most charming American grills. A handy

location in midtown, a refreshing view of Bryant Park, and a sensible, family-friendly menu make this a popular destination. Although the menu changes with the seasons, one can count on a good selection of soups, salads, steak, and seafood items at lunch and dinner. A $30 *prix fixe* pre-theater menu is available from 5 to 7 daily with three courses—handy for those going to shows nearby. The $27 *prix fixe* weekend brunch is popular, too. Personnel are friendly and child-oriented. The four kiosks in the park offer different seasonal dishes.

BUTTER
415 Lafayette St (bet 4th St and Astor Pl)   212/253-2828
Dinner: Mon-Sat   www.butterrestaurant.com
Moderately expensive

Noisy and fun, Butter prides itself on turning out exceptional dishes. The appetizer menu includes lobster rolls, delicious foie gras, and fresh salads. For entrees, any of the seafood dishes and the outstanding grilled organic ribeye are good. They do braised beef shanks well, too! The upside-down apple crisp will appeal to your sweet tooth, and the warm banana bread is a good choice, if it's on the menu. A tasting menu is also offered. Informal downstairs dining is available, as well.

> A very satisfying Saturday or Sunday brunch can be enjoyed at **Cafe de Bruxelles** (118 Greenwich Ave, 212/206-1830). What to order? Belgian waffles, of course, which come with delicious Belgian fries and a green salad.

BUTTERFIELD 8
5 E 38th St (bet Fifth and Madison Ave)   212/679-0646
Lunch, Dinner: Daily   www.butterfield8nyc.com
Moderate

Old-time New Yorkers will remember Butterfield 8 as a classy telephone prefix. This nostalgic phrase was revived as an attractive, busy retreat serving American fare. The atmosphere is strictly old-time New York, and so is the food: nachos; Caesar and Cobb salads; cheesesteak sandwiches, Angus burgers, oysters, and seared ahi tuna steaks. There's even mac and cheese. What's for dessert? New York-style cheesecake, of course! A young, attractive wait staff makes visiting here a pleasure.

CAFE BOULUD
20 E 76th St   212/772-2600
Lunch: Tues-Sat; Dinner: Daily   www.danielnyc.com
Moderately expensive

Boulud is a famous name in Manhattan food circles. If you are one of the "ladies who lunch" or like to look at those who do, then this is the place for you. The food is quite good, though the room is rather drab and I sometimes find the attitude haughty. Once seated, however, you'll enjoy the innovative menu. There are always vegetarian selections, world cuisines (every season highlights a different area), traditional French classics and country cooking, and menu items inspired by the "rhythm of the seasons." A two- or three-course *prix fixe* menu is available at lunch. Dinner prices are higher, but remember this place belongs to *the* Daniel Boulud, one of the nation's best chefs. Unfortunately he isn't in the kitchen here, because he is busy doing great things at Daniel.

CAFE CENTRO
MetLife Building
200 Park Ave (45th St at Vanderbilt Ave)   212/818-1222
Lunch: Mon-Fri; Dinner: Mon-Sat   wwwpatinagroup.com
Moderate

A grand cafe reminiscent of Paris in the 1930s, New York's Cafe Centro offers a classic Parisian brasserie menu. Guests are greeted by a gas-fired rotisserie and a beautiful open kitchen that's spotlessly clean and efficient. For starters, crusty French bread is laid out in front of you. A raw bar is featured. One can always find such entree favorites as light and tasty chicken pie *bisteeya* (with almonds, raisins, and orange-flower essence). Other specialties include a hefty seafood platter, excellent steaks and French fries, sea bass, penne pasta, and a moist, flavorful roast chicken. The pastry chef obviously has a chocolate bias (good for him!). *La marquise au chocolat*, bittersweet chocolate mousse, *soufflé chaud au chocolat*, valrhona bittersweet chocolate ice cream, and crème brûlée with caramel sauce are just a sampling. Adjoining the dining room is a busy beer bar that serves light sandwiches and appetizers.

> It's no wonder that **Cafe Lalo** (201 W 83rd St, 212/496-6031) is a madhouse at all hours. For delicious, reasonably priced sandwiches and other light meals, this room is first-rate. The dessert selection can only be described as awesome!

CAFE D'ALSACE
1695 Second Ave (at 88th St)   212/722-5133
Lunch: Mon-Fri; Dinner: Daily; Brunch: Sat, Sun www.cafedalsace.com
Moderate

When dress and noise level are not important and perhaps kids are involved, Cafe d'Alsace is a good choice for dining on the Upper East Side. The menu is large and varied: quiches (excellent!), sandwiches, sausages served with sauerkraut, salads, steaks, charcroute, and a full brunch selection. Their burger includes onions braised in Riesling. Young helpers provide informed service. The chef features Alsatian specialties, including Alsatian sugar cookies for dessert. If bistro life appeals to you, so will this charmer. Adults, this place stocks over 110 varieties of beer!

CAFÉ GRAY
Time Warner Center
10 Columbus Circle, 3rd floor   212/823-6338
Dinner: Daily   www.cafegray.com
Moderately expensive

Celebrity chef Gray Kunz, who once was the head man at Lespinasse,

has another winner on his hands. In a dramatic setting at the new Time Warner Center, he has created a room that is warm and interesting (the open kitchen is between diners and the park view), with memorable food and friendly, solicitous service. All of this comes without the outrageous prices charged at other Time Warner restaurants. The menu changes periodically, so confer with your server about the specials.

CAFE INDULGE
561 Second Ave (at 31st St)   212/252-9750
Breakfast, Lunch, Dinner: Daily; Brunch: Sat, Sun
Inexpensive to moderate

The fresh-baked goods are tasty, reasonably priced, and attractive. I particularly recommend the flourless chocolate cake and the devil's food cake with chocolate frosting. But there is much more at this cozy, unpretentious hideaway! The three-egg omelets are excellent, and nearly three dozen varieties are offered. Breakfast pastries, especially scones, are also terrific. For light meals you'll find wraps, salads, sandwiches, and pastas. Burgers are a specialty, as are smoothies and a variety of cafe drinks. For a special treat, try the grilled portobello mushroom sandwich. Comfortably priced dinners include steaks, grilled chicken, baked meatloaf, lasagna, and filet of sole.

Beware of Restaurant Pricing Ripoffs!
- Check your bill to verify the price of wine you selected. Also make sure the correct vintage is delivered to the table.
- Bottled water is grossly overpriced.
- See if gratuities have been added to the bill, and double-check the math.
- Daily specials are usually more expensive than regular menu items, so proceed with caution.
- Ask to make sure an offered birthday cake or slice is complimentary.
- Add up the items on your bill to ensure that the total charge is correct.
- Be sure to read the fine print about surcharges.

CAFE SABARSKY
Neue Galerie
1048 Fifth Ave (at 86th St)   212/288-0665
Breakfast, Lunch: Wed-Mon; Dinner: Thurs-Sun
Moderate   www.cafesabarsky.com

The setting is quaint, the personnel gracious, the prices right, and the German-Austrian food delicious. For breakfast, try Sabarsky *Frühstück* (Viennese mélange, orange juice, soft-boiled eggs, and Bavarian ham). Lunch and dinner selections include pea soup with mint, paprika sausage salad, crepes with smoked trout, Bavarian sausage, späetzle with mushrooms and peas, and Hungarian beef goulash. Cafe Sabarsky also serves sandwiches, sensational sweets (like Viennese dark chocolate cake and apple strudel), Viennese coffees, and much more. Cafe Sabarsky is crowded, so come early and expect a wait! Music is offered Wednesday through Friday.

CAMAJE

85 MacDougal St (bet Bleecker and Houston St)   212/673-8184
Daily: noon-midnight; Brunch: Sat, Sun   www.camaje.com
Inexpensive

Abigail Hitchcock knows how to cook a great meal. In tiny quarters (capacity 20 or so), this cozy French bistro can evoke memories of some wonderful little place you may have discovered in Paris. Camaje is one of those New York restaurants relatively few know about, yet those who do return often. From the moment delicious crusty bread arrives through the serving of excellent homemade desserts, everything is wholesome and tasty. I don't think I've ever had a better sandwich than their shrimp salad and avocado. There's three-onion soup *gratinee*, smoked trout salad, a half-dozen sandwiches, crostini, small plates, meat and fish entrees, and veggie side dishes. You can create your own three-ingredient crepe. Try one of their crepes *sucrées* for dessert; my favorite is a chocolate ice cream crepe with caramel sauce. Another plus is the large selection of quality teas. Cooking classes are offered three times a week.

Some Pocketbook Concerns

The latest trend in New York restaurants is fine dining (sometimes with well-known chef names, too) at prices that the average person simply cannot afford. The owners will tell you that they must charge those prices to pay for all the special ingredients, superior service, and astronomical real estate. I cannot argue with this, but it is a shame that a lot of diners are priced out of the market.

To save on the tab, eat at the bar where smaller portions and lower prices are offered. Granted, the surroundings are not as intimate or glamorous as the main dining rooms, but the food is just as good.

In this regard I recommend **Gordon Ramsay at the London** (London NYC Hotel, 151 W 54th St, 212/468-8888; lunch and dinner daily). The London Bar is the place to be seated here. You'll find tasty delights from across the pond that are new to NYC, superbly prepared with polished service to match.

Picholine (35 W 64th St, 212/724-8585; dinner daily) is another great place to experience the food by taking advantage of bar seating. At Picholine, Terrance Brennan has refined his culinary talents with goodies like paella spring rolls, tomato bread with cheese and bacon, eggs polenta, and a great sherry-flavored sorbet. Don't miss the Picholine cheese carts! By the way, Eric, the bartender, has to be one of the friendliest and most accommodating individuals in the business. Finally, the desserts at both Picholine and the London Bar are worth a visit in themselves.

CAPITAL GRILLE

Chrysler Center, Trylon Towers
155 E 42nd St (bet Lexington and Third Ave)   212/953-2000
Lunch: Mon-Fri; Dinner: Mon-Sun   www.thecapitalgrille.com
Moderately expensive

Hungry for lobster bisque? Start here! With all the top-drawer steakhouses in Manhattan, it's amazing they are all so busy. This one is stunningly decorated with Philip Johnson's glass-and-steel pyramids. The room exudes comfort and congeniality, and this is underscored by a welcoming, pleasant, efficient, and informed wait staff. Some say this is a Republican establishment, but no one asks for political affiliation and I found them to be super-nice to everyone. The midtown location is handy, the menu is full of the usual appetizers, soups, and salads (a good bet for lunch), and the steaks and chops are fabulous. There are five potato dishes, all first-class. Desserts are good—I liked the flourless chocolate espresso cake—but not overly memorable.

CAPSOUTO FRÈRES
451 Washington St (south of Canal St; entrance at 135 Watts St)
Lunch: Tues-Fri; Dinner: Daily; Brunch: Sat, Sun   212/966-4900
Moderate   www.capsoutofreres.com

In 1891, when the Landmark Building was constructed, this was an "in" area. Now it is hot all over again, the building is still a beauty, and Capsouto Frères (which is housed within) just gets better and better. Serving contemporary French cuisine, three brothers operate this classic establishment, complete with ceiling fans, wooden tables, good cheer, and tasty plates. An assortment of savory soufflés is very popular. At noon a special *prix fixe* lunch is offered, or you can order from an a la carte menu laden with salads, fish, meat, and pasta dishes. In the evening they serve more of the same, along with quail, duckling, and first-rate sirloin steak. They are known for their signature dessert soufflés. This bistro is a great setting for a casual evening with good friends who like to live it up!

You'll find a place like this only in New York City. For a bit of nostalgia and perhaps a taste of caviar, venison, borscht, chicken Kiev or beef Stroganoff (order in advance), head to the newer version of the famous **Russian Tea Room** (150 W 57th St, 212/581-7100). They are open weekdays for breakfast and lunch, brunch on the weekend, and dinner every night. It's colorful and expensive, but the food is not great and the service leaves a lot to be desired.

CARMINE'S
2450 Broadway (bet 90th and 91st St)   212/362-2200
Lunch, Dinner: Daily
200 W 44th St (bet Seventh and Eighth Ave)   212/221-3800
Lunch, Dinner: Daily   www.carminesnyc.com
Moderate

Time to treat the gang or the whole family? Call Carmine's for reservations and show up famished. You will be treated to Southern Italian-style family dining with huge portions and zesty seasonings. The platters are delicious and filling. Show up early if your party numbers less than six, as they will not reserve tables for smaller parties after 7 p.m. Menu choices run the gamut of pastas, chicken, veal, seafood, and tasty Italian appetizers such as calamari. Wall signs explain the offerings. There is also a delivery menu.

CARNEGIE DELICATESSEN AND RESTAURANT

854 Seventh Ave (at 55th St)   212/757-2245, 800/334-5606
Breakfast, Lunch, Dinner: Daily (6:30 a.m.-4 a.m.)
No credit cards
Moderate   www.carnegiedeli.com

There's no city on earth with delis like New York's, and Carnegie is one of the best. Its location in the middle of the hotel district makes it perfect for midnight snacks. Everything is made on the premises, and free delivery is offered between 7 a.m. and 2 a.m. within a five-block radius. Where to start? Your favorite Jewish mother didn't make chicken soup better than Carnegie's homemade variety. You can order it with matzo balls, golden noodles, rice, kreplach, or kasha. There's more: Great blintzes. Open-faced sandwiches, hot and delicious. Ten different deli and egg sandwiches. A very juicy burger with all the trimmings. Lots of fish dishes. Corned beef, pastrami, and rare roast beef. An unequaled choice of egg dishes. Salads. Side orders of everything from hot baked potatoes to potato pancakes. Outrageous cheesecake served plain or topped with strawberries, blueberries, or cherries. Desserts from A to Z—even Jell-O.

CERCLE ROUGE

241 West Broadway (bet Walker and White St)   212/226-6174
Lunch: Mon-Fri; Dinner: Daily; Brunch: Sat, Sun
Moderate   www.cerclerougeresto.com

Classic bistro dishes are available in a true French setting at Cercle Rouge. Other features include a kid-friendly Saturday and Sunday brunch with clowns and magicians, a spacious outdoor terrace, and private party facilities. A grand shellfish platter, an oyster bar, a number of mussel entrees, and a large cheese selection are among the specialties.

'CESCA

164 W 75th St (at Amsterdam Ave)   212/787-6300
Dinner: Daily   www.cescanyc.com
Moderate to moderately expensive

You'll love 'Cesca's atmosphere, as it's situated in a former hotel lobby that is both intimate and attractive. The wait staff is highly skilled and accommodating, and the food is deliciously Italian from start to finish. The menu changes often, but the dishes are uniformly well done. Superb Italian bread adds to the meal. One of the most pleasant and economical ways to enjoy a place like 'Cesca is to build your dinner around their cheese plate. The regional cheeses of Italy are all spectacular.

CHANTERELLE

2 Harrison St (at Hudson St)   212/966-6960
Lunch: Thurs-Sat; Dinner: Daily   www.chanterellenyc.com
Expensive

For over 25 years I have been a great admirer of Chanterelle. Karen and David Waltuck have created something unique and special for Manhattan diners. All the ingredients are here: magnificent decor, extremely professional service, wonderful food, and owners who look after every detail. Of course, nothing this good comes cheaply, and Chanterelle's dinners can be tough on the pocketbook. However, the *prix fixe* lunch is a real deal. As the

menu changes often, there are many featured items. Ask Karen (who is out front) or David (in the kitchen) to suggest a menu. The seafood dishes are especially tasty. Their grilled seafood sausage is rightly famous. If you have any room after this, then you might try the superb cheese selection. A mousse, soufflé, or an unusual flavor of ice cream are great dessert choices, and Chanterelle's petit fours (served with coffee) make all others seem mundane.

CHEZ JACQUELINE
72 MacDougal St (bet Bleecker and Houston St)   212/505-0727
Dinner: Daily; Brunch: Sat, Sun   www.chezjacqueline.com
Moderate

Chez Jacqueline is a very popular neighborhood French bistro, and no wonder. The atmosphere and service are appealingly relaxed. All ages seem to be happy here: young lovers hold hands, and seniors have just as good a time on a special evening out. Popular appetizers are fish soup, escargots, and goat cheese salad. As you might expect from a French house, the loin dishes are excellent. My favorite is the hearty beef stew in red wine, tomato, and carrot sauce. For dessert, try the caramelized apple tart.

It is not too often that your author gets really excited about a Japanese restaurant, but **Megu** (62 Thomas St, 212/964-7777, www.megunyc.com) absolutely deserves top billing. The theme is pricey modern Japanese. The selection of dinner dishes, the adept service, and the romantic and compelling atmosphere add up to a truly superb dining experience. Of course there is sushi in abundance, but the star of the menu is thin slices of Kobe beef that one can cook over a hot rock. The Japanese version of a Caesar salad is delicious. Even the desserts (yes, in a Japanese restaurant) are plentiful and fanciful. Try Megu for lunch or dinner Monday through Friday.

CHINATOWN BRASSERIE
380 Lafayette St (at Great Jones St)   212/533-7000
Lunch (dim sum): Daily; Dinner: Daily
Moderate   www.chinatownbrasserie.com

Here's a welcome addition to New York's Chinese restaurant scene! This place is big, attractive, energetic, and well-organized. Moreover, it serves really delicious food, mostly with an Oriental accent. You'll find wraps, salads, soups, crispy rolls, fish, meat, and chicken dishes. Their dim sum is truly first-rate and cooked to order. Peking duck with Mandarin pancakes is a specialty. Of course there are plenty of rice and noodle dishes, along with General Tsao's chicken. There is even a good dessert: peanut parfait with candied bananas. A sexy downstairs bar space is available in the late hours. Service is quick and efficient.

CHIN CHIN
216 E 49th St (bet Second and Third Ave)   212/888-4555
Lunch: Mon-Fri; Dinner: Daily   www.chinchinny.com
Moderate to moderately expensive

Chin Chin is a very classy Chinese restaurant whose ambience and price reflect a superior cooking style. There are two rooms and a garden in back. The soups and barbecued spareribs are terrific starters. Chin Chin house specialties include Grand Marnier prawns and orange beef. I'd concentrate on the seafood dishes, though you might also try the wonderful Peking duck dinner, with choice of soup, crispy duck skin with pancakes, fried rice, poached spinach, and homemade sorbet and ice cream. The menu is much the same for lunch or dinner. A reasonable *prix fixe* lunch is available.

CITY BAKERY
3 W 18th St (at Fifth Ave)   212/366-1414
Breakfast, Lunch: Daily   www.thecitybakery.com
Moderate

Your taste buds will tingle the moment you walk into the bustling City Bakery—which is really not a bakery but a buffet operation. Your eyes and stomach will savor the fresh-looking salad bar, tempting hot entrees, hearty sandwiches, yummy pastries, chocolate room, and much more. I am impressed with the well-trained personnel, who keep displays well stocked, tables clean, and checkout counters running efficiently. For a casual, moderately priced meal in unfancy surroundings, this is a good deal. Catering is available.

> For those who yearn for a taste of their Scottish ancestry, I have several suggestions: **Brandy Library** (25 N Moore St, 212/226-5545) and **St. Andrews Pub** (120 W 44th St, 212/840-8413). You might even find haggis on the menu!

CLINTON ST. BAKING CO. & RESTAURANT
4 Clinton St (at Houston St)   646/602-6263
Breakfast, Lunch, Dinner: Mon-Sat; Brunch: Sat, Sun
Moderate   www.greatbiscuits.com

This is where you'll find New York's best pancakes! Their hot buttered cider is famous, too! Clinton Street may be a bit out of the way—it's on the Lower East Side—but the trip is worth it if you want wholesome food at very reasonable prices. At breakfast you will find homemade granola, French toast, biscuit sandwiches, omelets, and more. For lunch, homemade soups, salads, eggs, and sandwiches are featured. The evening menu includes delicious homemade potato chips, oysters, butcher's salad, halibut, macaroni and cheese, rib steak, and garlic chicken. Homemade cakes and pastries are available all day. Extra thick shakes, sundaes, and sodas are a feature of their fountain. The atmosphere may be a bit dull, but the food certainly isn't. A large takeout menu is available.

COMPASS
208 W 70th St (at Amsterdam Ave)   212/875-8600
Dinner: Daily; Brunch: Sun   www.compassrestaurant.com
Moderately expensive

The setting is warm, the service excellent, and the new listings—including *prix fixe* and tasting menus—are worthwhile. Pastry chef Vera Tong does a good job making sure your desserts are as tasty as the rest of the meal.

COUNTRY CAFE
69 Thompson St (bet Spring and Broome St)   212/966-5417
Lunch, Dinner: Daily; Brunch: Sat, Sun
Moderate

You have to know what you're looking for to find this tiny Soho establishment. Once inside, you'll appreciate the no-nonsense approach to Moroccan country dining. The service and atmosphere could easily be transplanted to any small village in Europe. The menu would fit right in as well, with items like homemade country paté with onion and fruit chutney, vegetable couscous, snails in garlic butter, sea bass, and one of the city's best steaks *au poivre* with real homemade French fries. The pressed chicken dish is fabulous. I love the informality of the place, the sizable portions, and the obvious delight the young staff takes in showing guests what it is like to be treated by some real homebodies. *Bon appetit!*

A dessert bar? That is what **ChikaLicious** (203 E 10th St, 212/995-9511) calls itself. It is a tiny room, with bar stools and several tables, with *prix fixe* dessert for $12 and a wine pairing for $7 more. Choices include cheesecake, chocolate dishes, cheeses, and more. Portions are miserly, the tastes leave a lot to be desired, and the plates look too fussy to be truly inviting.

COWGIRL
519 Hudson St (at 10th St)   212/633-1133
Lunch: Daily; Dinner: Daily; Brunch: Sat, Sun   www.cowgirlnyc.com
Inexpensive to moderate

Colorful and busy, Cowgirl is Manhattan's version of famous Texas chuckwagon cuisine. The menu is varied, with something for everyone: burgers, fajitas, enchiladas, chilis, chicken, steak, sausages, catfish, and macaroni and cheese. Kids love the place! Portions are large and quite tasty, the wait staff enters into the fun, and the tab is friendly, too. The smoked BBQ ribs are a specialty. They are bathed in a delicious sauce and served with really tasty BBQ beans and slaw. Ask for the ice cream "baked potato" for dessert: vanilla ice cream shaped like a spud, with heaps of hot fudge, chopped pecans, and a pat of butter (which is really frosting). If that sounds like a bit much, you can opt for a slice of pecan or key lime pie.

CRAFT
43 E 19th St (bet Park Ave S and Broadway)   212/780-0880
Dinner: Daily; Brunch: Sat, Sun   www.craftrestaurant.com
Expensive

It is fun to create your own menu here. Craft is utterly unique and worth visiting for a number of reasons. The atmosphere is conducive to good eating, and the help is particularly friendly. Most of all, the way you order is unique. Everything is a la carte. The menu is divided into sections: fish and shellfish, meats, vegetables, mushrooms, potatoes, grains, and beans. You can put together any combination you find appealing, and the plates won't overwhelm your appetite. Chef-owner Tom Colicchio came from the Gramercy Tavern, and his expertise shows. Even the dessert selection is great: wonderful cheeses, pastries, custards, fruits, ice creams, and sorbets (with many sauces available). If you're not terribly hungry or there are picky eaters in the group, head to craft. **Craftbar** (900 Broadway, 212/461-4300), its sister operation, is more casual, with a contemporary New American menu and composed dishes.

CUCINA & CO.
MetLife Building
200 Park Ave (45th St at Vanderbilt Ave), lobby   212/682-2700
Breakfast, Lunch, Dinner: Mon-Fri
Takeout: Mon-Fri (7 a.m.-9 p.m.); Sat (8-4)   www.patinagroup.com
Moderate

Hidden among three hyped restaurants (Tropica, Naples 45, and Cafe Centro) in the bowels of the huge MetLife Building, Cucina & Co. is a treasure. The takeout counter is one of the best in mid-Manhattan, displaying all sorts of prepared foods, sandwiches, salads, great cookies and cakes, breads, and whatever else you might want to take home or to the office. Adjoining is a bustling, crowded cafe that serves first-class food at reasonable prices for such a prime location. You will find delicious burgers (served on sesame brioche rolls), baked pastas, quiches, seafood, health food dishes, and a good selection of dessert items. The service is fast and the personnel highly professional. They have to be in order to serve so many people during rush hours! I heartily recommend this place, especially for lunch. Two other locations for **Cucina & Co.** (30 Rockefeller Center, 212/332-7630 and Macy's Cellar, 212/868-2388) occupy similarly prime Manhattan locales and offer the same quality of food and service.

Daisy May's BBQ USA (623 Eleventh Ave, 212/977-1500) offers takeout and catering. The best bet is Kansas City sweet and sticky ribs, which are tender and delicious. And there is much more: beef short ribs, bourbon half chicken, beef and pork sandwiches, baked beans, creamy cole slaw, peaches in bourbon, and superb mashed sweet potatoes with brown sugar. Prices are easy on the pocketbook.

CUCINA STAGIONALE
289 Bleecker St (at Seventh Ave)   212/924-2707
Lunch, Dinner: Daily
Inexpensive

When you serve good food at low prices, word gets around. So it's no wonder there's a line in front of this small Greenwich Village cafe almost any time of day. Its name translates as "seasonal kitchen," and the seasonal specialties are real values. It's a bare-bones setup, with seating for only a few dozen hungry folks. Service is impersonal and nonprofessional, but who cares at these prices? Innovative Italian cuisine—tasty, attractive, and filling —is served, and you can do well on a slim budget. Recommended appetizers include smoked salmon with endive and radicchio, and sauteed wild mushrooms. For a few pennies more, you can get a large dish of linguine or ravioli. They now have a full bar. One word of warning: don't go if it's raining, because you'll probably have to wait outside to get seated.

Burke and owner Donatella Arpaia really shines with its desserts. Butterscotch panna cotta, coconut layer cake, and a dollhouse stove full of yummy candy are all created by an excellent pastry chef. Of course there are other attractions at this popular spot, which is more of a ladies' dining choice. If I had to choose one word to describe the place, it would be *fussy*. Their chef's salad is absolutely the best I have ever tasted. I also like the way bread is served: warm, in a small pan, like a muffin. The menu changes periodically. A white limousine is parked outside for smokers!

DAWAT
210 E 58th St (bet Second and Third Ave)   212/355-7555
Lunch: Mon-Sat; Dinner: Daily
Moderate

Ms. Madhur Jaffrey, a highly respected cookbook author, creates innovative Indian dishes that set Dawat apart as one of the best Indian restaurants in the city. There are numerous good seafood choices, including a sensational entree called Shrimp Konju Pappaas. Chicken, goat, and lamb dishes are other favorites, as is an attractive choice of vegetarian dishes. Different varieties of excellent breads are available. Don't pass up Jaffrey's desserts, which are unusually good for an Indian restaurant.

DB BISTRO MODERNE
55 W 44th St (bet Fifth Ave and Ave of the Americas)   212/391-2400
Lunch: Mon-Sat; Dinner: Daily   www.danielnyc.com
Moderate to moderately expensive

Renowned restaurant impressario Daniel Boulud's venture is, for him, a more casual dining experience. Even burgers are served, and they are very good. (At $32, they should be!) Of course, this is no ordinary hamburger. It is ground sirloin filled with short ribs, foie gras and black truffles, served on a parmesan bun and accompanied by delicious, light *pommes soufflés* in a silver cup. Diners have their choice of two rooms with a communal table that is comfortable for singles between them. The stylish menu is divided into sections like *thon* (tuna), *saumon* (salmon), *canard* (poultry), and *boeuf* (beef), offering several items in each category. For dessert, the cheese selection is a real winner, as are any of Daniel's specialties that use berries and other fresh fruit.

DELEGATES DINING ROOM
United Nations
First Ave at 45th St, 4th floor
Lunch: Mon-Fri   212/963-7626
Moderate   www.aramark-un.com

Don't let the name or security measures keep you away! The public can enjoy the international food and special atmosphere at the U.N's Delegates Dining Room. Conversations at adjoining tables are conducted in almost every language. The setting is charming, overlooking the East River. The room is large and airy, the service polite and informed. There is a large selection of appetizers, soups, salads, entrees, and desserts on the daily "Delegates Buffet." All of the dishes are attractively presented and very tasty. A huge table of salads, baked specialties, seafoods, meats, vegetables, cheeses, desserts, and fruits await the hungry noontime diner. Some rules apply: jackets are required, jeans and sneakers are prohibited, and a photo ID is needed. There isn't a more appetizing complete daily buffet available in New York.

DEL FRISCO'S DOUBLE EAGLE STEAK HOUSE

McGraw-Hill Building
1221 Ave of the Americas (at 49th St)   212/575-5129
Lunch: Mon-Fri; Dinner: Daily   www.delfriscos.com
Expensive

Del Frisco's provides a good meal with accommodating service in a setting where both the ceiling and prices are high. Fresh, warm bread is brought to the table as you enjoy a seafood appetizer or great beefsteak tomato and sliced onion salad. Steaks, chops, veal dishes, and lobster are all first-rate, while accompanying side dishes are large and uneven. In-house desserts include bread pudding with Jack Daniel's sauce, crisp chocolate soufflé cake with raspberries, and strawberries Romanoff with vanilla ice cream. All are winners. This establishment is inviting, except when it comes to price. Isn't $18.95 for a shrimp cocktail a bit steep? To be frank, I've also found myself wondering whether every dish is freshly cooked for each diner.

Folks wait even in cold, wet weather to get into **EJ's Luncheonette** (1271 Third Ave, 212/472-0600), where breakfast, lunch, and dinner are served daily. You'll find great flapjacks, waffles, omelets, sandwiches, burgers, baked items, salads, and everything in between. In addition to a huge menu, especially at breakfast, you'll enjoy the very reasonable prices. Free delivery, too!

DEL POSTO

85 Tenth Ave (bet 15th and 16th St)   212/497-8090
Lunch: Wed, Fri; Dinner: Daily   www.delposto.com
Expensive

It's big and bold! No question about it, Del Posto is an "occasion" restaurant. Mario Batali has shown what can be done with good taste. Afterward, diners may feel their wallet has become a bit thinner, but they will long remember the experience of dining here. In a warm room with enough space between tables, a huge staff, informed service, and beautiful china, this is surely among the best of Manhattan's newer restaurants. Some dishes are prepared tableside. The wine steward dutifully tastes from each bottle before it is presented to the guest. Bread baskets are superb. Soothing piano music will calm those who arrive after a harried day. All of these touches speak to the classiness of the operation. What to order? *Carciofi alla Romana* (artichokes) are fabulous. Ravioli with brown butter and thyme is the best I have ever tasted. Any one of the ten dessert choices (strudel, crepes, gelati, and more) is exceptional. Leave room for the fine selection of complimentary after-dinner cookies. Private party spaces on the balcony level provide an enchanting view of the professional proceedings below. (Note: You can save a few bucks by eating at the bar!)

DEMARCHELIER
50 E 86th St (at Madison Ave)   212/249-6300
Lunch, Dinner: Daily   www.demarchelierrestaurant.com
Moderate

Drop in on Fridays for delicious bouillabaisse! For years diners have come to this French bistro for two reasons: good food and no pretense. If you like solid French fare like artichokes and asparagus in season, crusty bread, *paté de campagne*, and salad niçoise, you will love Demarchelier. Steak dishes are also a specialty. Service is extremely efficient and prompt—ideal if you are in a lunch rush. Takeout dishes are available, too.

DEVIN TAVERN
363 Greenwich St (bet Franklin and Harrison St)   212/334-7337
Lunch: Mon-Fri; Dinner: Daily; Brunch: Sun   www.devintavern.com
Moderate to moderately expensive

With a distinctly masculine atmosphere, wood and fireplaces throughout, and a spacious interior, this place is for hearty diners. The emphasis is on basics like rack of lamb and beef short ribs, but the fish is also quite good. The lobster club sandwich and Devin Tavern cheeseburger with crispy fries are terrific, if not exactly bargain priced. (The cheeseburger is $16.) The cast-iron potatoes are great. This would be ideal for a big party. A trip here is worthwhile for the dessert of chocolate-covered waffle-cut potato chips, with chocolate pistols and other goodies thrown in.

DINING COMMONS
City University of New York Graduate Center
365 Fifth Ave (at 34th St)   212/817-7953
Breakfast (1st floor), Lunch (8th floor): Mon-Fri
Inexpensive

The Dining Commons offers excellent food in comfortable surroundings at affordable prices. Continental breakfasts—featuring muffins, Danishes, croissants, bagels, and more—are available. Lunches feature deli sandwiches, salads, and some hot entrees. It is possible to eat heartily for under $10, and both eat-in and takeout are available. The facility is open to faculty, students, and the general public. This is no run-of-the-mill fast-food operation. Restaurant Associates does a particularly good job of offering tasty, adequate portions without fancy touches.

DOCKS OYSTER BAR AND SEAFOOD GRILL
2427 Broadway (bet 89th and 90th St)   212/724-5588
Lunch: Mon-Sat; Dinner: Daily; Brunch: Sun

633 Third Ave (at 40th St)   212/986-8080
Lunch: Mon-Fri; Dinner: Daily; Brunch: Sat, Sun
Moderate   www.docksoysterbar.com

If you appreciate a great raw bar, sail up Broadway to the original Docks or to the larger operation on Third Avenue. At both lunch and dinner you'll find fresh swordfish, lobster, tuna, Norwegian salmon, red snapper, and other seafood specials that change with the season. Crab cakes are outstanding. At dinner the raw bar offers four oyster and two clam selections. For a lighter meal, try steamers in beer broth or mussels in tomato and garlic.

Delicious smoked sturgeon and whitefish are available. Docks has a special New England clambake on Sunday and Monday nights. The atmosphere is congenial, and so are the professional waiters.

ELEVEN MADISON PARK
11 Madison Ave (at 24th St)   212/889-0905
Lunch: Mon-Fri; Dinner: Daily; Brunch: Sat, Sun
Expensive   www.elevenmadisonpark.com

Another fine Danny Meyer operation! In a soaring space previously used for business meetings, he's crafted an attractive dining room with an intimate bar and several private rooms. Swiss chef Daniel Humm offers a very special, intensely flavored, contemporary French menu that changes frequently. The food is delicious! Try pecan praline pancakes for brunch. When you visit, be sure to tour the building and study the archival photos throughout.

Good dining is available downtown on Stone Street. The area located between Broad and Whitehall streets is particularly pleasant in nice weather, so you can eat outdoors. My top suggestions:
Adrienne's Pizzabar (54 Stone St, 212/248-3838)
Brouwers of Stone Street (45 Stone St, 212/785-5400)
Stone Street Tavern (52 Stone St, 212/785-5658)
Ulysses (58 Stone St, 212/482-0400)

ELIO'S
1621 Second Ave (at 84th St)   212/772-2242
Dinner: Daily
Moderate to moderately expensive

For years Elio's has been *the* classic clubby Upper East Side dining room for those who are recognizable, as well as those who aspire to be! In not so fancy surroundings, with waiters who greet regulars as if they are part of the family, tasty platters of beef carpaccio, clams, mussels, stuffed mushrooms, and minestrone are offered as starters. Lots of spaghetti and risotto dishes follow, along with seafood (their specialty), liver, scaloppine, and the usual Italian assortment. They are going organic. For dessert, try the delicious sorbets. Although half the fun is watching the not-so-subtle eye contact among diners, the food is excellent, and it is easy to see why Elio's remains a neighborhood favorite.

ELLEN'S STARDUST DINER
1650 Broadway (at 51st St)   212/956-5151
Breakfast, Lunch, Dinner: Daily   www.ellensstardustdiner.com
Inexpensive to moderate

Come here for good food and a singing wait staff! Ellen's fits right into the theater neighborhood. A casual, fun, and noisy spot, it serves satisfying food the traditional American way. Trains are the theme of the decor. A track circles the balcony, with a locomotive and cars that would thrill any railroad buff. The breakfast menu includes bagels and muffins, along with tasty buttermilk pancakes, Belgian waffles, French toast, and omelets. For the rest of the day, comfort foods are the order: salads and sandwiches, burgers, chicken pot pie, meatloaf, barbecue baby back ribs, turkey, and steak. There is more: egg creams, shakes, malts, and a nice selection of caloric desserts. Be sure to ask that your shake be made "thick"! Delivery is available.

EL PARADOR CAFE

325 E 34th St (bet First and Second Ave)   212/679-6812
Lunch, Dinner: Daily   www.elparadorcafe.com
Moderate

Having been in business for six decades, El Parador is the granddaddy of New York's Mexican restaurants. Delicious Mexican food is served in a fun atmosphere at down-to-earth prices. Moreover, they are some of the nicest folks in the city. Warm nachos are put on the table when you arrive. From there, you have a choice of specialties. There are quesadillas, Spanish sausages, and black bean soup to start. Delicious shrimp and chicken dishes follow. Create your own tacos and tostaditas, or try stuffed jalapenos. El Parador has over 50 brands of premium tequila, and they make what many consider the best margaritas in New York.

ETATS-UNIS

242 E 81st St (bet Second and Third Ave)   212/517-8826
Dinner: Daily   www.etatsunisrestaurant.com
Moderate to moderately expensive

Etats-Unis is like a large family dining room. There are only 14 tables and a busy kitchen where owner Luca Pecora works to produce some of the best food this side of your grandmother's! Appetizers, entrees, and desserts (usually about five of each) change every evening and are always delicious. It's very wholesome food, not cute or fancy, and served professionally in portions that are substantial but not overwhelming. Fresh homemade bread is an attraction. Try date pudding or chocolate soufflé for dessert. The tab is not cheap, but in order to support an operation with limited hours and few tables, the folks at Etats-Unis must make every meal count. A bar/cafe across the street by the same name is open for lunch (except Sunday). The entire room is available for private parties.

F&B GÜDTFOOD

150 E 52nd St (bet Lexington and Third Ave)   212/421-8600
269 W 23rd St (bet Seventh and Eighth Ave)   646/486-4441
Lunch, Dinner: Daily   www.gudtfood.com
Inexpensive

Güdtfood means "good food," of course. This place is unlike any other. There are tables at the 52nd Street location, but you eat counter style at the 23rd Street one. And what do they prepare? European street food such as British fish and chips, steak, French *frites*, Belgian *pommes*, Swedish meatballs . . . you get the idea. Kids' menus and healthy vegetarian items are also available. For dessert there are apple *beignets* and Belgian waffles. The people-watching is pretty good, and the prices are even better! It's a great place for kids' parties, and catering is available.

FAIRWAY CAFE & STEAKHOUSE

2127 Broadway (at 74th St), upstairs   212/595-1888
Breakfast and Lunch: Daily (as Fairway Cafe);
Dinner: Daily (after 5:30 p.m., as Fairway Steakhouse)
Moderate   www.fairwaymarket.com

Most folks know of Fairway as a busy market, but there is more. Take the stairway by the entrance, and you'll find a rather bare-bones room that serves unbelievably good food—much of it of the comfort variety—at comfortable prices. Breakfasts include eggs, pancakes, omelets, smoked salmon, and the like. The luncheon soups, salads, and sandwiches are extremely good values for the quality offered. In the evening the place turns into a modestly priced steakhouse, with complete steak dinners—your choice of cut, plus salad, soup, vegetables—for $40. There are chops, rack of lamb, short ribs, fish, chicken, even spaghetti. All desserts are only $5. An extensive catering menu is available.

FIAMMA OSTERIA

206 Spring St (bet Ave of the Americas and Sullivan St)   212/653-0100
Lunch: Mon-Fri; Dinner: Daily   www.brguestrestaurants.com
Moderate to moderately expensive

Some restaurants just make you feel good when you enter. Located on a busy Soho street, Fiamma is one of them. They have a flair for tasty Italian dishes that include fresh seafood, excellent chicken, tender meat, and wonderful pastas like ricotta cheese tortelloni and handmade pasta quills (when available). The duck breast is tender and appealing. As for desserts, imagine savoring dark chocolate praline cake, caramel *zabaglione* with a milk-chocolate rum center, or homemade gelati and sorbets. A delicious selection of Italian cheeses is also available.

57

Four Seasons Hotel New York
57 E 57th St (bet Park and Madison Ave), lobby level   212/758-5757
Breakfast, Lunch, Dinner: Daily; Brunch: Sun   www.fourseasons.com
Moderate to moderately expensive

When the name Four Seasons is on the door, you can be assured that the service inside is something special. So it is at 57, one of Manhattan's star hotel dining rooms. The room is highlighted by handsome cherry floors with mahogany inlays, ceilings of Danish beechwood, and bronze chandeliers. The tabletops match the floor in material and design. Served in an informal yet elegant atmosphere, the food has the authority of classic American cooking. The menu changes by season, featuring some exceptionally well-thought-out pasta entrees. Salads and fish are good lunch choices. Taste and personal attention, not the ego of a famous chef, are what makes this room tick. A thoughtful touch is the offer of rapid service for "power breakfast" guests.

FLAMES STEAKHOUSE

5 Gold St (at Maiden Lane)   212/514-6400
Lunch, Dinner: Mon-Fri   www.flamessteakhouse.com
Moderate to moderately expensive

Gold Street is hardly a locale for gourmets, but those who frequent or work in this area know that Flames is one of the best. With a rather old-time masculine feel, this house features top-grade meats and superior service. Prices aren't cheap, but they are fair for the value. Their half-pound lean chopped sirloin burger is one of the best in the city. At lunch you'll find salads, sandwiches, pasta, chicken dishes, salmon, grilled New York sirloin, and more. In the evening, prime dry-aged beef is served in a number of ways. For a party of four or more big eaters, a mammoth porterhouse is available at a hefty price. Chops, lobster, and rack of lamb are available, too. The Italian desserts are not very exciting, however.

Biergartens (beer gardens; seasonal):
Hallo Berlin (626 Tenth Ave, 212/977-1944)
Zum Schneider (107 Ave C, 212/598-1098)

FLEUR DE SEL
5 E 20th St (bet Fifth Ave and Broadway)   212/460-9100
Lunch: Mon-Sat; Dinner: Daily   www.fleurdeselnyc.com
Moderately expensive (lunch), expensive (dinner)

Chef-owner Cyril Renaud does interesting and exciting things with a constantly changing menu at Fleur de Sel. The plates are all well presented. The charming exposed-brick room features some of Renaud's own oil paintings. Lobster salad with avocado is different and delicious. Entrees tend to be on the rich, exotic side, so your meat-and-potato husband may prefer to go elsewhere. However, those with more adventurous palates will find marinated beef cheeks to be tender and delicious. To be honest, I found Fleur de Sel worthy of a visit but not the unabashed raves it has received. By the way, the chocolate tart soufflé with vanilla ice cream and white chocolate caramel ganache are both magnificent. Dinner is *prix fixe*. A luncheon tasting menu is available, too.

44 & X HELL'S KITCHEN
622 Tenth Ave (at 44th St)   212/977-1170
Dinner: Daily; Brunch: Sat, Sun
Moderate to moderately expensive

The Hell's Kitchen area may seem an unlikely place for a first-rate restaurant, but this one qualifies in spades! A menu of "reinvented American classics" is served in a rather sterile white-on-white atmosphere. This spot literally sparkles with tasty dishes presented in a most professional manner. There is an abundance of polite, well-trained servers and helpers. Your every desire seems to be their uppermost concern as they parade their clever *Heaven* (on the front) and *Hell* (on the back) T-shirts. The bisque of butternut squash was so good I just about licked the bowl. Other classy starters: Mediterranean chopped salad, pan-seared scallops, and crab fritters. Don't miss buttermilk fried chicken, a super burger with outstanding fries, a hefty casserole of Maine lobster, comfortable tomato meatloaf, or melt-in-your-mouth barbecued salmon. Delicious apple crisp and white chocolate bread pudding are stars on the dessert menu.

FOUR SEASONS
99 E 52nd St (bet Park and Lexington Ave)   212/754-9494
Lunch: Mon-Fri; Dinner: Mon-Sat   www.fourseasonsrestaurant.com
Expensive

Four Seasons is elegant and awe-inspiring in its simplicity and charm. Two separate dining areas—the Grill Room and the Pool Room—are different in menu and appeal. *Prix fixe* and a la carte menus are available in both rooms. The dark suits (translation: business and media heavy hitters) congregate at noon in the Grill Room, where the waiters know them by name and menu preference (great salads, a wonderful duck entree, steak tartare, or burgers). The Pool Room, set beside an actual marble pool, is more romantic and feminine. Ladies who lunch and couples who want to dine with the stars are made to feel right at home with superb service. The dessert menu can only be described as obscene. Individual soufflés in coffee cups are a splendid treat.

If a sexy atmosphere and intimate seating is more important than gourmet food, you might try **Frederick's** (8 W 58th St, 212/752-6200). The bar is very busy, the dining areas are strictly informal, and the food is really quite passable. For aging yuppies, this may be a desirable destination.

FRANK'S
410 W 16th St (bet Ninth and Tenth Ave)   212/243-1349
Lunch, Dinner: Daily   www.franksnyc.com
Moderate

The Molinari family—the third generation in a business that started in 1912—has kept up the quality and appeal of this popular spot. Customers are usually folks with large appetites! Reservations are suggested, as the place is very popular. There are great pastas, huge steaks, superb prime rib, fresh fish, veal, lamb, and really good French fries. New York cheesecake is the preferable dessert choice.

FRANK'S TRATTORIA
371 First Ave (bet 21st and 22nd St)   212/677-2991
Lunch, Dinner: Daily
Inexpensive

It's true in New York, just as it is elsewhere in the country, that no one knows great, cheap places to eat better than the boys in blue. Manhattan's finest are some of the best customers of this modest trattoria, and it is easy to see why. The menu runs the gamut of Florentine dishes. Each is prepared to order and served piping hot (as is the bread, which is always a good sign). There is a large seafood selection, plus steaks, lobster, chops, and chicken. You can choose from over 20 pizzas, served whole or by the piece. Everyone here is informal and friendly, and Frank is delighted that the good word about his place has spread beyond the neighborhood regulars.

FRED'S AT BARNEYS NEW YORK
660 Madison Ave (at 60th St), 9th floor   212/833-2200
Lunch, Dinner: Daily; Brunch: Sat, Sun
Moderate to moderately expensive

It would be a tossup as to which is better at Fred's—the food or the people watching. The "beautiful people" definitely like to see and be seen here. You'll find the dishes ample and delicious (and they should be at the prices charged). Selections include seafood dishes, pastas, salads, comfort food (like excellent Tuscan pot roast), pizzas, and sandwiches. Tasty French fries are served Belgian-style. There's no shortage of selections or calories on the dessert menu. I just wonder if all those skinny model types really finish their meals! I find it hard to say good things about Barneys these days, but their restaurant is first-class.

FREEMAN'S

Freeman Alley (at Rivington St)
Dinner: Daily; Brunch: Sat, Sun   212/420-0012
Moderate   www.freemansrestaurant.com

Unique is the word here! You don't want to miss Freeman's—even though it is almost impossible to locate. It used to be a halfway house. Freeman's is crowded, noisy, and unpretentious. It has extra-friendly service personnel, clean restrooms, a great bar and bartender, and a nice kitchen. But most of all, it has really delicious food. You must start with "Devils on Horseback": Stilton-stuffed prunes wrapped in bacon and served piping hot. Then there is a delicious hot artichoke dip with crisp bread. (All the breads are excellent.) Organic poached chicken with carrots and celery in parsley broth is outstanding, as are the roasted pork loin and seared filet mignon. A dish of marinated beets with dill is special. Desserts are just okay, but a visit here is so unique you can overlook your sweet tooth! Reservations can only be made for parties of six or more.

> On the Lower East Side you'll love **Frankie's Spuntino** (17 Clinton St, 212/253-2303), which is crowded, inexpensive, cozy, and delicious.

FRESCO BY SCOTTO

34 E 52nd St (bet Madison and Park Ave)   212/935-3434
Lunch: Mon-Fri; Dinner: Mon-Sat   www.frescobyscotto.com
Moderate to moderately expensive

Fresco by Scotto has become a Manhattan tradition for lunch and dinner. Dining here has been made even more interesting with the addition of several new items: potato and zucchini chips with gorgonzola cheese, and eggplant and zucchini pie. Executive chef Steven Santoro is producing dishes in line with his Tuscan training. Fresco by Scotto always offers at least four fresh fish dishes daily, along with tender steaks and veal and lamb chops. Crispy polenta fries are a popular side. The bombolonis are filled with raspberry preserves and served with vanilla cream. **Fresco on the Go** (40 E 52nd St, 212/635-5000) offers homemade muffins and pancakes, sticky buns, eggs to order, and much more for breakfast. At noon, delicious sandwiches, pizzas, soups, salads, and homemade desserts are available at this next-door facility. Private parties from 20 to 150 are welcome all day long.

FRESH

105 Reade St (bet Church St and West Broadway)   212/406-1900
Lunch: Mon-Fri; Dinner: Mon-Sat   www.freshrestaurantnyc.com
Moderate

Wow! The minute you walk into Fresh, your taste buds will begin buzzing. The place is attractive, friendly, and inviting. All of this is a reflection of the charming personality of executive chef Kento Komoto. This is a top-notch seafood house with very fresh items. Appetizers include lobster tartare, crispy Florida shrimp, salads, soup, fried clams, and raw bar items (oysters, sashimi, ceviche, and crab claws). You'll find wild salmon, grilled striped bass, haddock, and sunflower seed-crusted halibut among the dozen entrees. Flourless chocolate cake completes a great meal. If you're really hungry, try the seven-course tasting menu.

GABRIEL'S BAR & RESTAURANT
11 W 60th St (bet Broadway and Columbus Ave)　　212/956-4600
Lunch: Mon-Fri; Dinner: Mon-Sat　　www.gabrielsbarandrest.com
Moderate

Gabriel's is a winner for dining in the Lincoln Center area. You are greeted by Gabriel Aiello, an extremely friendly host, as "Gabriel ... Gabriel" plays in the background. And what good food and drink! Delicious bread. Fresh peach or blueberry *bellinis*. A fine assortment of Italian appetizers. Then on to first-class pastas (like tagliatelle with peppers), chicken, steaks, and wood-grilled seafood dishes. The in-house gelati creations are among New York's best, as is the flourless chocolate torte. To cap it all off, Gabriel's offers more than a dozen unusual teas (like peach melba, raspberry, and French vanilla). Gabriel doesn't have to blow his own horn; his satisfied customers are happy to do it for him! Private party facilities are available.

Everyone loves "pigs-in-a-blanket" at cocktail hour! The best place to get them:
Eli's Manhattan (1411 Third Ave, 212/717-8100)
Eli's Vinegar Factory (431 E 91st St, 212/987-0885)

GABY
Sofitel New York
44 W 45th St (bet Fifth Ave and Ave of the Americas)　　212/782-3040
Breakfast, Lunch, Dinner: Daily
Moderate

Gaby is a convenient stop in busy midtown Manhattan, open from early morning until late in the evening. The theme is French, and they do well with a full menu of French favorites. Foie gras and snails are popular starters. The French onion soup has a double cheese crust. For a delicious and filling lunch item, I recommend the Maine lobster club sandwich. Crisp open-faced sandwiches topped with salmon, tuna, or buffalo mozzarella are available. However, the real star is their traditional crème brûlée—just about the best in the city.

GASCOGNE
158 Eighth Ave (at 18th St)　　212/675-6564
Lunch: Tues-Fri; Dinner: Daily; Brunch: Sat, Sun
Moderate　　www.gascognenyc.com

Hearty appetites will delight in the southwestern French cooking at this intimate, unaffected Chelsea bistro. The capable and friendly waiters will happily explain the fine points of the rather limited menu. Salads are popular. Foie gras lovers will be in heaven. The main-course menu features duck, cassoulet, quail, and roasted rabbit. Seafood dishes are especially tasty. All desserts are made in-house and show imagination. There are sorbets, fruit tarts, soufflés, and some unusual ice cream flavors (prune, Armagnac, and chocolate mint). A small dining area is available downstairs, but it is rather claustrophobic. The garden is charming. If you are longing for an extensive French dining experience, look at the pre-theater *prix fixe* menu. By the way, Gascony is the only region in the world where Armagnac, a brandy distilled from wine, is produced.

GAVROCHE
212 W 14th St (bet Seventh and Eighth Ave)   212/647-8553
Lunch: Tues-Fri; Dinner: Daily; Brunch: Sun   www.gavroche-ny.com
Moderate

This unpretentious establishment, hidden on West 14th Street, serves some of the tastiest French country food in the city. There is no pretense, just good, solid French cuisine prepared by individuals who were brought up across the ocean. The bread is served warm, the salads served cold, and the bountiful entrees will satisfy the most exacting palate. By the way, this is a really good place to go if you are by yourself and need some time to think while enjoying a reasonably priced meal.

Try **Chat Noir** (22 E 66th St, 212/794-2428) for a very pleasant light lunch or good dinner, especially if you are a wine lover. The wine selection is large and prices are reasonable. They also offer brunch on Saturday and Sunday.

GEISHA
33 E 61st St (bet Park and Madison Ave)   212/813-1113
Lunch: Mon-Fri; Dinner: Mon-Sat   www.geisharestaurant.com
Moderately expensive to expensive

Sushi is the star here, but Geisha also does well with other offerings. You can choose from an assortment of menu items, including a regular one and a sushi one. The excellent sushi rolls include caterpillar roll (saltwater eel, cucumber, and avocado) and the signature Geisha roll (served with lobster honey miso dressing and *shiso* vinagrette). The house is divided into a downstairs bar and upstairs dining room, plus an adjacent *tatami* (family) room decorated with rich kimono fabrics. Main courses run the gamut from skate, salmon, halibut, and cod to filet mignon and rack of lamb. A number of tasty salads are just right for lunch. Unlike the desserts, the collection of green teas is special. A private party room is available.

GINO
780 Lexington Ave (at 61st St)   212/758-4466
Lunch, Dinner: Daily
Cash only (checks accepted from regular guests)
Moderate

This is a New York institution; the ubiquitous crowd will immediately clue you into the fact that the food is great. Why? Because this Italian restaurant is filled with native New Yorkers. You'll see no tourist buses out front. The menu has been the same for years: a large selection of popular dishes (over 30 entrees!) from antipasto to soup, and pasta to fish. There are daily specials, but you only have to taste such regulars as chicken *alla* Capri, Italian sausages with peppers, or scampis a la Gino to get hooked. Gino's staff has been here forever, taking care of patrons in an informed, fatherly manner. The best part comes when the tab is presented. East Side rents are always climbing, but Gino has resisted price hikes by taking cash only and serving delicious food that keeps the tables full. No reservations are accepted, so come early.

Those tasty Spanish appetizers known as tapas are popular these days. People like to order three or four plates to share, and some can make complete meals. Sangria is the favorite liquid accompaniment. The best tapas in Manhattan can be found at the following:

Casa Mono (52 Irving Pl, 212/253-2773): very good
Ñ (33 Crosby St, 212/219-8856)
Pipa (ABC Carpet & Home, 38 E 19th St, 212/677-2233)
Xunta (174 First Ave, 212/614-0620): outstanding

GIORGIONE
307 Spring St (bet Greenwich and Hudson St)   212/352-2269
Lunch: Mon-Fri; Dinner: Daily; Brunch: Sun
Moderate

When the name Deluca (as in Dean & Deluca) is involved, you know it is a quality operation. Giorgio Deluca is one of the partners in this attractive, high-tech establishment, which features shiny metal-top tables and an inviting pizza oven that turns out some of the best pies in the area. This is a very personal restaurant, with Italian dishes like you'd find in mother's kitchen in the Old Country: carpaccio, prosciutto, ravioli, risotto, and linguine. The minestrone is as good as I have tasted anywhere. Pizzas come in eight presentations. Finish with a platter of tasty Italian cheeses or pick from the appealing dessert trolley. A raw bar is also available.

GOBLIN MARKET
199 Prince St (bet MacDougal and Sullivan St)   212/375-8275
Dinner: Daily; Brunch: Sat, Sun   www.goblinmarket.com
Moderate

Despite the unusual name, there's nothing scary here—just excellent tasting and comfortably priced egg dishes and omelets, melt-in-your-mouth lemon buttermilk pancakes, and Irish steel-cut oatmeal for weekend brunch! For dinner, the lamb, steak, and sea bass platters are excellent. However, the real winners are macaroni and cheese and Angus burgers with non-greasy French fries.

GOLDEN UNICORN
18 East Broadway (at Catherine St)   212/941-0911
Breakfast, Lunch, Dinner, Dim Sum: Daily
Inexpensive

Golden Unicorn prepares the best dim sum outside of Peking! This bustling, two-floor, Hong Kong-style Chinese restaurant serves delicious dim sum every day of the week. Besides delicacies from the rolling carts, diners may choose from a wide variety of Cantonese dishes off the regular menu. Pan-fried noodle dishes, rice noodles, and noodles in soup are house specialties. Despite the size of the establishment (they can accommodate over 500 diners), you will be amazed at the fast service, cleanliness, and prices. This is one of the best values in Chinatown.

One of the best and most popular places to pick up a quick takeout lunch downtown is **Olives** (120 Prince St, 212/941-0111). The soups, salads, and sandwiches are all delicious and reasonably priced. Sample sandwiches include Olives' hero (copa, salami, marinated onions, and more), mozzarella, smoked turkey, ancho chili-rubbed steak, and grilled chicken breast. This place is a winner!

GONZO
140 W 13th St (bet Ave of the Americas and Seventh Ave)
Dinner: Daily   212/645-4606
Moderate

In today's world, service is the number one consideration! It is a wonder that more restaurants don't understand that what diners really want is tasty food, decent atmosphere, and competent service. All of this is available at Gonzo, a popular spot in Manhattan. Seating is available at the bar, and in the smallish, attractive back room. Grilled pizzas are big and modestly priced. There are also chopped salads, sliced meat and cheese plates, real Italian pastas, and a nice selection of meat and fish entrees. My choices: braised short ribs of beef (the meat literally falls off the bone) and grilled whole fish (which varies each day). A dozen or more side-dish offerings, a number of them grilled, will satisfy veggie lovers. Chef-owner Vincent Scotto knows what the younger crowd likes and caters to them.

GOOD
89 Greenwich Ave (bet Bank and 12th St)   212/691-8080
Lunch: Tues-Fri; Dinner: Daily; Brunch: Sat, Sun
Moderate   www.goodrestaurantnyc.com

Good is a casual, friendly, take-your-time establishment. It is a popular destination for locals, especially for brunch. The solid, contemporary American fare is served by very friendly personnel. The brunch menu highlight is the "Good Breakfast": a heaping plate of eggs with a choice of pancakes, home fries, and bacon or sausage. Burgers are tasty, and pork tenderloin and house-smoked pulled pork are good bets for dinner.

GOOD ENOUGH TO EAT
483 Amsterdam Ave (at 83rd St)   212/496-0163
Breakfast, Lunch: Mon-Fri; Dinner: Daily; Brunch: Sat, Sun
Inexpensive   www.goodenoughtoeat.com

New York is a weekend breakfast and brunch town, and you cannot do better than Good Enough to Eat in both categories. Savor the apple pancakes, four-grain pancakes with walnuts and fresh bananas, and chocolate chip and coconut pancakes. There is more: French toast, waffles, six kinds of omelets, four scrambled egg dishes, corned beef hash, homemade Irish oatmeal, fresh-squeezed orange juice, and homemade sausage. The lunches in this homey and noisy room—with a tile floor and wooden tables and bar —feature inexpensive and delicious salads, burgers (juicy and delicious), pizzas, and sandwiches. More of the same is served for dinner, plus meatloaf, turkey, pork chops, fish, and roast chicken plates. A children's menu is available, and an outdoor cafe is popular during nice weather. This is comfort food at its best, all the way through wonderful homemade pies, cakes, and ice creams.

GOTHAM BAR & GRILL
12 E 12th St (bet Fifth Ave and University Pl)   212/620-4020
Lunch: Mon-Fri; Dinner: Daily   www.gothambarandgrill.com
Moderately expensive

The Gotham is a must! For over two decades it has been recognized as one of New York's best. Dining here can be summed up in one word: *exciting*! It is not inexpensive, but every meal I have had has been worth the tab—and there is a really good *prix fixe* lunch deal. You may also eat at the bar. Alfred Portale is one of the most talented chefs in the city. The modern, spacious, high-ceilinged space is broken by direct spot lighting on the tables. Fresh plants lend a bit of color. There are great salads (try the seafood), excellent free-range chicken, and superior grilled salmon and roast cod. Each entree is well seasoned, attractively presented, and delicious. The rack of lamb is one of the tastiest in town. Desserts are all made in-house; try the carrot cake or unique ice cream flavors.

With more Americans visiting Cuba, there is renewed interest in the cuisine of this country. One of the best places in Manhattan for creating your own paella or tasting delicious Havana-style barbecued ribs with mango ginger sauce is **Havana Central** (22 E 17th St, 212/414-4999). Jeremy Merrin, a hands-on partner, welcomes diners with counter service at lunch and tables at dinner. The price is right, and vegetarians will feel right at home.

GRAMERCY TAVERN
42 E 20th St (bet Park Ave S and Broadway)   212/477-0777
Lunch: Mon-Fri (main dining room), Daily (tavern); Dinner: Daily
Expensive   www.gramercytavern.com

Every detail has been honed to perfection at Gramercy Tavern, and the public has responded. This is a *very* busy place. The space is unusually attractive, the servers are highly trained, and the food is excellent. The ceiling is a work of art, the private party room is magnificent, and there is not a bad seat in the house. A new chef, Michael Anthony, has created his own American menu. Both a regular and a vegetarian tasting menu are available. You'll enjoy a superior offering of cheeses, sorbets, and ice creams for dessert. This is a truly great place for a party!

GRAND CENTRAL OYSTER BAR RESTAURANT

Grand Central Terminal (42nd St at Vanderbilt Ave), lower level
Mon-Fri: 11:30-9:30; Sat: 12-9:30   212/490-6650
Moderate   www.oysterbarny.com

Native New Yorkers know about the nearly century-old institution that
is the Oyster Bar at Grand Central. This midtown destination has been
restored and is once again popular with commuters and residents. (They
serve over 2,000 folks a day!) The young help are accommodating, and
the drain on the pocketbook is minimal. The menu boasts more than 72
seafood items (with special daily entrees), 20 to 30 varieties of oysters, a
superb oyster stew, clam chowder (Manhattan and New England styles),
oyster pan roast, bouillabaisse, *coquille St. Jacques*, Maryland crab cakes
(Wednesday special), Maine lobsters, 75 wines by the glass, and marvelous
homemade desserts.

GYU-KAKU

34 Cooper Square (bet Astor Pl and 4th St)   212/475-2989
Lunch: Mon-Sat; Dinner: Daily   www.gyu-kaku.com
Moderate to moderately expensive

A fun experience and very tasty food is the best way to describe this
Japanese barbecue restaurant. After a gracious greeting, you are seated at
tables with a burner in the center. Then you carefully examine a lengthy
menu of appetizers, salads, soups, beef tongue, *kalbi* (short rib), *harami* (outside skirt), *yaki shabu* (belly), ribeye, filet mignon, intestine, vegetables, rice,
noodles, and more. Accommodating servers will help with your choices and
give instructions on how to cook the various items. The Kobe beef slices are
marvelous, as are the lamb and seafood dishes. Tender pieces of lobster tail
are a treat. If you order fresh orange juice, they will squeeze it right at the
table! Japanese restaurants are generally not great for desserts, but getting
your hands and face gooey with the S'mores dish at Gyu-Kaku is worth the
trouble.

HATSUHANA

17 E 48th St (bet Fifth and Madison Ave)   212/355-3345
237 Park Ave (at 46th St)   212/661-3400
Lunch, Dinner: Mon-Fri (Dinner on Sat at 48th St location)
Moderate   www.hatsuhana.com

Hatsuhana has a longstanding reputation as one of the best sushi houses
in Manhattan. One can sit at a table or the sushi bar and get equal attention
from the informed help. There are several dozen appetizers, including broiled
eel in cucumber wrap and chopped fatty tuna with aged soybeans. Next try
salmon teriyaki or any number of tuna or sushi dishes. Forget about desserts
and concentrate on the exotic appetizer and main dish offerings.

HEARTH

403 E 12th St (at First Ave)   646/602-1300
Dinner: Daily   www.restauranthearth.com
Moderately expensive

In a cozy atmosphere in the East Village, with an open kitchen and
pleasant personnel, Hearth is one of those places where the clientele seem

more focused on their dining companion than the food. Nevertheless, the New American/Tuscan dishes are done well, even if the prices are a bit inflated. The black sea bass, guinea hen, and sirloin steak are very popular. The menu changes every season. All in all, it's a good place for that must-talk-to-date evening—but avoid the back room, as it is unattractive.

HOUSTON'S
Citicorp Center
153 E 53rd St (entrance is at 54th St and Third Ave)   212/888-3828
378 Park Ave S (bet 26th and 27th St)   212/689-1090
Lunch, Dinner: Daily   www.houstons.com
Moderate to moderately expensive

It's not glamorous, but Houston's is reliable. If you are meeting someone for a business lunch, the two Houston's locations are very handy. Houston's serves really good burgers, sandwiches, and salads. For heartier appetites, the barbecued ribs, seared tuna steak, and prime rib roast can't be beat. I could make a meal out of their giant baked potato with all the trimmings. Apple walnut cobbler will finish off a meal that's certain to expedite any deal you're trying to make. Best of all, you will be served in attractive surroundings by pleasantly enthusiastic personnel.

Many old-time New York natives and visitors fondly remember Horn and Hardart's Automats, where you inserted coins, opened a door, and grabbed your goodies. Now there is a new automat: **Bamn!** (37 St. Mark's Pl, 212/358-7685). The selection may not be gourmet, but try it for a snack.

I COPPI
432 E 9th St (bet First Ave and Ave A)   212/254-2263
Lunch: Sat, Sun; Dinner: Daily   www.icoppinyc.com
Moderate

The husband and wife team of Lorella Innocenti and John Brennan have created a charming Tuscan restaurant where tasty food matches the appealing East Village atmosphere. They have imported talent from the Old Country to ensure that the breads are authentic. A brick pizza oven adds a special touch. The menu changes seasonally. Outstanding luncheon dishes may include Tuscan-style omelets and thin egg noodles with *bolognese* sauce. Pastas, grilled striped bass, roasted rabbit, and grilled sirloin steak make excellent dinner choices. Save room for gelati, sorbet, or Tuscan cheese for dessert. The heated and canopied outdoor garden is especially inviting. There's no need to rush uptown to fancier and pricier Tuscan restaurants, as I Coppi is as professional as I have found anywhere in the city.

IL BAGATTO
192 E 2nd St (bet Ave A and B)   212/228-0977
Dinner: Tues-Sun (closed Aug)   212/228-3710 (delivery)
Inexpensive

One of Manhattan's best bargains, Il Bagatto is the place to come if you're feeling adventurous. Housed in tiny digs in an area you would hardly call compelling, this is an extremely popular Italian trattoria. The owners have discovered the rules of success: being on the job and ensuring that every dish tastes just like it came out of mama's kitchen. About a dozen tables upstairs and in the lounge are always filled, so it's best to call ahead for reservations. There's delicious spaghetti, homemade gnocchi with spinach, tortellini with meat sauce (made from a secret recipe), and wonderful tagliolini with seafood in a light tomato sauce. Other menu offerings include chicken, carpaccio, and salads, and there are always a few specials. They deliver, too. The adjacent wine bar serves both food and drink.

> Yes, it is big. Yes, the setting is quite dramatic. Yes, you can find a place like this only in New York. **Buddakan** (75 Ninth Ave, 212/989-6699), in the Chelsea district, fits right into the local atmosphere. The menu is mostly modern Asian with some additions and subtractions. One nice and novel feature is a huge communal table at the bottom of the grand staircase; it is an attraction for single diners or large groups. Remember, though, bigger is not always better. The food here is just so-so.

IL CORTILE
125 Mulberry St (bet Canal St and Hester St)   212/226-6060
Lunch, Dinner: Daily   www.ilcortile.com
Moderate

Here is a reason for visiting Little Italy! Little Italy is more for tourists than serious diners, but there are some exceptions. Il Cortile is an oasis of tasty Italian fare in an attractive and romantic setting. A bright and airy garden area in the rear is the most pleasant part of the restaurant. The menu is typically Italian, with just about anything you could possibly want. Entree listings include fish, chicken, and veal dishes, plus excellent spaghetti, fettuccine, and ravioli. Sauteed vegetables like bitter broccoli, hot peppers, mushrooms, spinach, and green beans are specialties of the house. One thing is for certain: the waiters zip around like they are on roller skates. Service is excellent and expeditious. If you can fight through the gawking visitors, you will find Il Cortile worth the effort!

IL GATTOPARDO
33 W 54th St (bet Fifth Ave and Ave of the Americas)   212/246-0412
Lunch, Dinner: Daily   www.ilgattopardonyc.com
Expensive

This is the kind of place that appeals to serious gourmets, as food and service leave little to be desired. The room is not fancy; it is, in fact, rather claustrophobic. In nice weather, the outdoor patio is charming. The interesting and varying appetizers may include beef and veal meatballs wrapped in cabbage, scallops, and shrimp salad. Among the many pastas, homemade *scialatielli* is delicious. Main-course highlights include Neapolitan meatloaf, herb-crusted rack of lamb, fish and shellfish stew, and much more. For dessert, warm chocolate cake with ice cream is sinfully good.

IL MULINO
86 W 3rd St (bet Sullivan and Thompson St)   212/673-3783
Lunch: Mon-Fri; Dinner: Mon-Sat   www.ilmulinonewyork.com
Moderately expensive

Il Mulino is a New York experience not to be missed! Never mind that reservations usually must be made a month or so in advance. Never mind that it's always crowded, the noise level is intolerable, and the waiters nearly knock you down as you wait to be seated. It's all part of the ambience at Il Mulino, one of New York's best Italian restaurants. Your greeting is usually "Hi, boss," which gives you the distinct impression that the staff is accustomed to catering to members of the, uh, "family." When your waiter finally comes around, he'll reel off a lengthy list of evening specials with glazed eyes. A beautiful, mouth-watering display of these specials is arrayed on a huge entrance table. After you're seated, the waiter delivers one antipasto after another while he talks you into ordering one of the fabulous veal dishes with portions bountiful enough to feed King Kong. Osso buco is a favorite dish. By the time you finish one of the luscious desserts, you'll know why every seat in the small, simple dining room is kept warm all evening.

IL POSTINO
337 E 49th St (bet First and Second Ave)   212/688-0033
Lunch: Mon-Sat; Dinner: Daily
Expensive

It is nice to splurge on occasion, if what you get is worth the extra bucks. Il Postino does have rather hefty prices, but the offerings rival the best in Manhattan! The setting is comfortable and not showy. You'll be impressed by the captains, who can recite a lengthy list of specials without hesitation. You have your choice of ground-level tables or a slightly raised balcony; I have found the latter to be more comfortable. An extraordinarily tasty bread dish and assorted small appetizer plates get things off to a good start. Sensational pastas like linguine with three kinds of clams or tagliolini with mushrooms should not be missed. Chicken in a baked crust is very satisfying, and roasted loin of veal for two is also top-grade. The authentically Italian sorbets finish a memorable gourmet experience. Incidentally, lunch is equally tasty and easier on the wallet.

IL RICCIO
152 E 79th St (bet Third and Lexington Ave)   212/639-9111
Lunch, Dinner: Daily
Moderate

There's nothing fancy here—just good Italian fare. Il Riccio is consistent, so you can count on leaving satisfied and well fed. Spaghetti with crabmeat and fresh tomato is one of my favorites. So is thinly sliced beef with truffled pecorino cheese and breaded rack of veal. Also offered are Dover sole and grilled sardines with broccoli, along with seasonal specials. The patio is a small, comfortable place to dine in nice weather. Service is unfailingly pleasant. Fruit tarts are homemade and delicious, and marinated peaches (when available) are the signature dessert.

IL VAGABONDO
351 E 62nd St (bet First and Second Ave)   212/832-9221
Lunch: Mon-Fri; Dinner: Daily
Inexpensive

Il Vagabondo is a good spot to recommend to your visiting friends, and many folks consider it their favorite restaurant! This bustling restaurant has been popular with New Yorkers in the know since 1965. The atmosphere is strictly old-time, complete with white tablecloths, four busy rooms, and an even busier bar. You may have spaghetti, ravioli, and absolutely marvelous veal or chicken *parmigiana*. There is no pretense at this place, which is a terrific spot for office parties. You will see happy faces, compliments of a delicious meal and reasonable bill. Save room for the Bocce Ball Dessert (*tartufo*). Il Vagabondo, you see, is the only restaurant in New York with an indoor bocce court!

JACK'S LUXURY OYSTER BAR
101 Second Ave (bet 5th and 6th St)   212/253-7848
Dinner: Mon-Sat
Moderate to moderately expensive

Jack and Grace Lamb have moved their tiny operation to a one-floor facility, but their tasty food hasn't changed a bit. With another tiny kitchen and another tiny bar that's fun to eat at, you can enjoy fresh oysters (done six ways), excellent barbecued lobster, littleneck clams, glazed quail, and more. In some cases, smaller *is* better.

Egg Cream

A New York invention, the egg cream is generally credited to Louis Auster, a Jewish immigrant who owned a candy store at Stanton and Cannon streets during the early part of the 20th century. Mostly to amuse himself, he started mixing carbonated water, sugar, and cocoa until he concocted a drink he liked. It was such a hit that the famous fountain operation of Schraft's reportedly offered him $20,000 for the recipe. Auster wouldn't sell and secretly continued making his own syrup in the back room of his store. When he died, his recipe went with him. Some years later, Herman Fox created another chocolate syrup, which he called Fox's U-Bet. Fox's brand is regarded as the definitive egg cream syrup to this day.

JACKSON HOLE BURGERS
232 E 64th St (bet Second and Third Ave)   212/371-7187
521 Third Ave (at 35th St)   212/679-3264
1611 Second Ave (at 84th St)   212/737-8788
1270 Madison Ave (at 91st St)   212/427-2820
517 Columbus Ave (at 85th St)   212/362-5177
69-35 Astoria Blvd, Jackson Heights, Queens   718/204-7070
35-01 Bell Blvd, Bayside, Queens   718/281-0330
Lunch, Dinner: Daily   www.jacksonholeburgers.com
Inexpensive

Jackson Hole is my favorite burger destination! You might think that a burger is a burger. But having done hamburger taste tests all over the city, I can attest that this is the best. Each one weighs at least seven juicy, delicious ounces. You can get all kinds: pizza burger, Swiss burger, English burger, or a Baldouni burger (mushrooms, fried onions, and American cheese). Or try an omelet, a Mexican item, a salad, or grilled chicken breast. The atmosphere isn't fancy, but once you sink your teeth into a Jackson Hole burger, accompanied by great onion rings or French fries and a homemade dessert, you'll see why I'm so enthusiastic (as is former President Bill Clinton). Free delivery and catering are available.

JACQUES BRASSERIE
204 E 85th St (bet Second and Third Ave)   212/327-2272
Lunch, Dinner: Daily; Brunch: Sat, Sun   www.jacquesnyc.com
Moderate

It is easy to understand why this bistro is so popular with folks in the neighborhood. It is cozy, friendly, moderately priced, and serves great food. In addition, Jacques himself is one of the friendliest proprietors in town. All of the classic French dishes are available: onion soup, steak *au poivre*, crème brûlée, cheeses, and a wonderful chocolate soufflé with Tahitian vanilla ice cream. There are also outstanding seafood dishes, including mussels prepared six ways. Moreover, this bistro is intimate, making it a great place for private parties.

An affordable place to eat at the Time Warner Center is **Bouchon Bakery** (10 Columbus Circle, 3rd floor, 212/823-9366). The setting is attractive and inviting, but the personnel need schooling in Customer Relations 101. Salads, sandwiches, soups, quiches, and pastries are available. People-watching is the most fun.

JARNAC
328 W 12th St (at Greenwich St)   212/924-3413
Dinner: Tues-Sun; Brunch: Sun   www.jarnacny.com
Moderate

Owner Tony Powe grew up in Jarnac, France, and that locale is the inspiration for his tiny and charming West Village bistro. With talented chef Maryann Terillo at Tony's side, his plain, no-hype establishment makes the diner concentrate on the ever-changing menu. For such a small place, the selection is sizable: hearty soups, fresh salads, great beef short ribs, top-notch cassoulet, and other choices. A well-chosen cheese course is an extra attraction. The dozen or so tables are filled with Village regulars. Because there is such a variety of dishes, every one seems fresh and innovative, and clean-cut, informed servers add to the pleasure of the meal. The desserts, however, don't measure up to the rest of the menu.

JEAN GEORGES
Trump International Hotel and Tower
1 Central Park West (bet 60th and 61st St)   212/299-3900
Breakfast: Daily (in cafe); Lunch: Mon-Fri;   www.jean-georges.com
Dinner: Mon-Sat; Brunch: Sun
Very expensive

A treat for the senses! Jean Georges Vongerichten has created a French dining experience in a setting that can only be described as cool, calm, and calculating. I mean *calculating* in the sense that one is put into a frame of mind to sample *haute cuisine* at its best in a very formal dining room that's awash with personnel. The New French menu changes regularly. Come ready to be educated! In keeping with any operation bearing the Trump name, the hype at Jean Georges continues. But to be honest, if price is unimportant, you can't do better. The cafe, **Nougatine**, is a bit less intimidating.

JOHN'S PIZZERIA
278 Bleecker St (bet Ave of the Americas and Seventh Ave)
212/243-1680
260 W 44th St (bet Eighth Ave and Broadway) 212/391-7560
408 E 64th St (bet First and York Ave) 212/935-2895
Daily: 11:30 a.m. to 11:30 p.m.
Moderate www.johnspizzerianyc.com

These are not ordinary pizzas! Pete Castelotti (there is no John) is known as the "Baron of Bleecker Street." However, he also brought his John's Pizzerias to the Upper West Side and the Upper East Side so that more New Yorkers could taste some of the best brick-oven pizzas in the city. John's offers 54 (count 'em) varieties, from cheese and tomatoes to a gut-busting extravaganza of cheese, tomatoes, anchovies, sausage, peppers, meatballs, onions, and mushrooms. John's does homemade spaghetti, cheese ravioli, and manicotti well, too. Things are higher-class uptown; in fact, the enormous 44th Street location occupies a renovated former church.

KATZ'S DELICATESSEN
205 E Houston St (at Ludlow St) 212/254-2246
Mon, Tues: 8 a.m.-9:45 p.m.; Wed, Thurs: 8 a.m.-10:45 p.m.;
Fri, Sat: 8 a.m.-2:45 a.m.; Sun: 8.a.m.-10:45 p.m. www.katzdeli.com
Inexpensive

If you're experiencing hunger pangs on the Lower East Side, try Katz's Delicatessen. It is a super place with hand-carved and overstuffed sandwiches that are among the best in town. Mainstays include pastrami, hot dogs, corned beef, and potato pancakes. Prices are reasonable. Go right up to the counter and order—it is fun watching the no-nonsense operators slicing and fixing—or sit at a table where a seasoned waiter will take care of you. Try dill pickles and sauerkraut with your sandwich. Incidentally, Katz's is a perfect place to sample the unique (and disappearing) "charm" of the Lower East Side. While you wait for a table or discover that the salt and pepper containers are empty and the catsup is missing, you'll know what I mean. Catering (at attractive rates) and private party facilities are available.

KEENS STEAKHOUSE
72 W 36th St (bet Fifth Ave and Ave of the Americas)
Lunch: Mon-Fri; Dinner: Daily 212/947-3636
Moderate www.keens.com

One of the most reliable long-time Manhattan restaurants is Keens Steakhouse, a unique New York institution. I can remember coming here decades ago, when those in the garment trade made Keens their lunch headquarters. This has not changed. Keens still has the same attractions: the bar reeks of atmosphere, and there are great party facilities and fine food to match. Keens has been a fixture in the Herald Square area since 1885. For some time it was for "gentlemen only," and although it still has a masculine atmosphere, ladies feel comfortable and welcome. The famous mutton chop with mint is the house specialty, but other delicious dishes include steak, lamb, and fish. For the light eater, especially at lunch, there are some great salads. Lobster has been added to the menu. They do single-malt Scotch tastings from fall to spring and stock one of the largest collections in New York. If you have a meat-and-potato lover in your party, this is the place to come. Make sure to save a little room for the deep-dish apple pie.

KING'S CARRIAGE HOUSE
251 E 82nd St (bet Second and Third Ave)   212/734-5490
Lunch: Mon-Sat; Dinner: Daily; Tea: Daily (at 3)
Moderately expensive

Even some folks in the immediate neighborhood are unaware of this sleeper. King's is indeed an old carriage house, remade into a charming two-story dining salon that your mother-in-law will love. The ambience is Irish manor house, and the menu changes every evening. In a quaint setting with real wooden floors, you dine by candlelight in a very civilized atmosphere. The luncheon menu stays the same: salads, sandwiches, and lighter fare. Afternoon tea is a treat. The continental menu changes nightly and may feature grilled items (like loin of lamb). On Sundays, it is a roast dinner (leg of lamb, loin of pork, chicken, or tenderloin of beef). The $49 prix fixe menu is a really good value. I found the Stilton cheese with a nightcap of ruby port absolutely perfect for dessert. Chocolate truffle cake and rhubarb tart are excellent, too.

> The **Hungarian Pastry Shop** (1030 Amsterdam Ave, 212/866-4230) is a cafe *and* bakery! The wonderful cakes are only part of the appeal. The cafe serves all sorts of waist-expanding items, along with delicious Viennese coffee.

KITTICHAI
60 Thompson St (at Broome St)   212/219-2000
Lunch: Mon-Fri: Dinner: Daily   www.kittichairestaurant.com
Moderately expensive

Kittichai serves real Thai food! One's eyes rest as much on the tableware, the black-draped service personnel, and the fish tank as on the food. As is true in most Thai restaurants, seafood is high on the list. Marinated monkfish is a splendid starter, and the seafood soup is a must on a cold evening. The salad of banana blossoms, artichokes, and roasted chili was a pleaser at my table. Don't overlook the chocolate (cocoa powder) baby back ribs marinated in Thai spices. For entrees, Chilean sea bass and wok-fried chicken with roasted cashew nuts are winners. Kittichai's curries are exceptional. Honestly, I found this place a bit much, both in attitude and dishes, but you do get a peek at the mystique of Thailand.

KLEE BRASSERIE
200 Ninth Ave (at 22nd St)   212/633-8033
Lunch: Thurs-Sun: Dinner: Daily; Brunch: Thurs-Sun
Moderate   www.kleebrasserie.com
Enjoy a bit of Austrian atmosphere in a sparklingly clean room. At noon-

time the homemade warm potato chips are addictive. You can also enjoy a well-selected cheese platter, some thin-crust pizzas, Tyrolean macaroni and cheese pasta, Kobe beef hot dog, or traditional weiner schnitzel. In the evening, duckling from the stone wood-fired oven, steaks from the mesquite grill, a good choice of pastas that change daily, and many of the lunch items are available. For dessert? Sacher torte, of course!

Italian Specialties

Bruschetta: slices of crispy garlic bread, usually topped with toma-toes and basil

Carpaccio: thin shavings of raw beef topped with olive oil and lemon juice or mayonnaise

Risotto: creamy, rice-like pasta, often mixed with shellfish and/or vegetables

Saltimbocca: Thinly sliced veal topped with prosciutto and sage is sauteed in butter and slow-simmered in white wine. The name means "jumps in your mouth."

Zabaglione: dessert sauce or custard made with egg yolks, marsala, and sugar; also known as *sabayon* in France

---

KOBE CLUB
68 W 58th St (bet Fifth Ave and Ave of the Americas) 212/644-5623
Lunch: Mon-Fri; Dinner: Mon-Sat www.chinagrillmgt.com
Very expensive

This club has its lovers and its detractors. I happen to like it! Sexy, dark, dramatic, and delicious—Kobe Club is all of the above. The menu offers main-course selections of Kobe and Kobe-style beef, fillet, strip and loin, ribeye from America, Australia, or Japan, priced from $35 to $160 (steaks range in size from four to ten ounces). By all means, go for the beef from Japan; you will never taste anything better! About a dozen different sauces, butters, and toppings are available. Side dishes include hash browns, creamed spinach, creamed corn, and wild mushrooms. There is much more on the menu, like beef tartare, sake-cured salmon, and salads (for starters). Additional entrees include wild salmon, Dover sole, chicken, and pasta. The servers are attired all in black to match the atmosphere and are highly professional. Desserts are just as delicious as the meats. This is a one-of-a-kind place, so start saving up for a very special occasion!

LA BOITE EN BOIS
75 W 68th St (at Columbus Ave) 212/874-2705
Lunch: Tues-Sat; Dinner: Daily; Brunch: Sun www.laboitenyc.com
Moderate

You don't have to pronounce the name of this French restaurant properly to have a good time! It packs them in every evening for obvious reasons: delicious food, personal service, and moderate prices. Salads are unusual, and the country paté is a great beginner. For an entree, I recom-mend filet of snapper, roast chicken with herbs, or *pot-au-feu*. The atmo-sphere is intimate, and all the niceties of service are operative from start to finish. The French toast at brunch is a treat. Desserts are made in-house;

try one of their sorbets. Call for reservations, since La Boite en Bois is small and popular.

LA BOTTEGA
Maritime Hotel   212/243-8400
88 Ninth Ave (at 17th St)   www.themaritimehotel.com
Breakfast, Lunch, Dinner: Daily; Brunch: Sat, Sun
Moderate

In nice weather, outside dining at La Bottega is very pleasant. At other times, the inside seating at this downtown hotel offers a relaxing venue for business meetings. The food is basic Italian, moderately priced, with no surprises. Pizzas, pastas, and salads are the main offerings. Sliced prosciutto with seasonal fruit is one of the best light dishes. Several flavors of gelato are on the dessert menu.

Worth a try is **Hudson River Cafe** (697 W 133rd St, 212/491-9111). The patio dining is pleasant and, the seafood plates are delicious.

LA GRENOUILLE
3 E 52nd St (bet Fifth and Madison Ave)   212/752-1495
Lunch: Tues-Fri; Dinner: Mon-Sat   www.la-grenouille.com
Expensive

Put on your finest clothes if you're going to dine here! La Grenouille remains a special place that must be seen to be believed. Beautiful, fresh-cut flowers herald a unique, not-to-be-forgotten dining experience. The food is as great as the atmosphere, and although prices are high, La Grenouille is worth every penny. Celebrity-watching adds to the fun. You'll see most of the famous faces at the front of the room. The professional staff serves a complete French menu. Be sure to try the cold hors d'oeuvres, which are a specialty of the house. So are the lobster dishes, sea bass, and poached chicken. Nowhere in New York are sauces any better. Don't miss the superb dessert soufflés. The tables are close together, but what difference does it make when the people at your elbows are so interesting?

LA LUNCHONETTE
130 Tenth Ave (at 18th St)   212/675-0342
Lunch, Dinner: Daily
Inexpensive to moderate

La Lunchonette proves that you don't have to be fancy to succeed, as long as you serve good food. In an unlikely location, this popular spot offers some of the tastiest French dishes around: snails, sauteed portobello mushrooms, and lobster bisque to start, and omelets, grilled lamb sausage, sauteed calves liver, and more for entrees. On Sunday evenings, live music is a feature. You'll be pleasantly surprised when the bill comes!

LANDMARC
Time Warner Center
10 Columbus Circle, 2nd floor   212/823-6123
Breakfast, Lunch, Dinner: Daily

179 West Broadway
Lunch, Dinner: Daily
Moderate

212/343-3883
www.landmarc-restaurant.com

Big menu, very tasty food, accommodating staff—what more could you ask for? Seafood entrees include grilled salmon, tuna, and monkfish. Pork chops and roasted chicken are excellent. Daily pasta specials are available, and steaks with French fries are a specialty. Delicious fresh salads are a lunch favorite. Looking for a novel entree? Try the crispy sweetbreads or the popular mussels and littleneck clams with a selection of sauces. Both locations are crowded and offer high-energy dining.

> I am a big fan of **Sarabeth's**, but I am doubly disappointed with the newest addition to the franchise at 40 Central Park South. Not only is the food not up to Sarabeth's standards, but the room—the scene of numerous restaurant funerals—is cold and the personnel are inattentive and poorly trained.

LA PETITE AUBERGE
116 Lexington Ave (at 28th St)
Lunch: Mon-Fri: Dinner: Daily
Moderate

212/689-5003
www.lapetiteaubergeny.com

Genuine French cooking in this area is not easily found, but this smallish, unpretentious restaurant is worth a casual lunch or dinner visit. Friendly personnel will lead you through the usual French favorites: onion soup, escargots, frog legs, roast duck, filet mignon, rack of lamb, and filet of sole. Delicious soufflés are the best way to finish a satisfying meal.

LA RIPAILLE
605 Hudson St (at 12th St)
Lunch, Dinner: Daily; Brunch: Sun
Moderate

212/255-4406

This small, bright, Parisian-style bistro in the West Village (complete with fireplace) makes a cozy spot for an informal meal. You might want to enjoy a cocktail on the lovely outdoor terrace. The chef puts his heart into every dish. Entrees are done to perfection; the seafood is always fresh, and they do an excellent job with rack of lamb and duck *magret*. White chocolate is a house favorite; at least half of the dessert offerings use it as an ingredient. Proudly displayed at the front of the room are rave notices from a number of New York gourmets.

L'ATELIER DE JOËL ROBUCHON
Four Seasons Hotel New York
57 E 57th St (bet Madison and Park Ave)
Lunch, Dinner: Daily
Very expensive

212/350-6658
www.fourseasons.com

This one falls in the "if it is expensive, it must be great" category. Well, it *is* very expensive, and I would classify it as very good—but certainly not worth the price. If the occasion is something highly special, give it a try. I'd recommend sitting at the counter, as the service is much better than at the tables and the personnel seem more anxious to please. The greeting, like that at so many New York restaurants, is haughty. However, if you do get a chance to meet the manager, she is a gem and very gracious. The menu is full of delicacies like caviar and foie gras—spendy, but done with great class and eye appeal. Flavors abound here, and you may never have experienced some of them before. Frog legs, lobster, and sea bass are all memorable dishes. Even the burger—actually, two small ones, complete with foie gras and all the trimmings—is delicious. Desserts are varied, outrageously expensive, and rather ordinary. The molten chocolate cake is probably the best. Is L'Atelier de Joël Robuchon excessive? Yes. Is dining here an event? Definitely.

> If you have ever fantasized about a lobster frittata with ten ounces of sevruga caviar, rush over to **Norma's** (Le Parker Meridien Hotel, 118 W 57th St, 212/708-7460). The price: $1,000. The budget version, with one ounce of caviar, goes for a mere $100.

LE BERNARDIN
155 W 51st St (at Seventh Ave)   212/489-1515
Lunch: Mon-Fri; Dinner: Mon-Sat   www.le-bernardin.com
Expensive

You surely have heard of this seafood palace! There has to be one restaurant that tops every list, and for seafood Le Bernardin holds that spot. Co-owner Maguy LeCoze and executive chef Eric Ripert make this house extremely attractive to the eye and very satisfying to the stomach. Wonderfully fresh oysters and clams make a great start. Whatever your heart desires from the ocean is represented on the entree menu. What distinguishes La Bernardin is presentation. Signature dishes change nightly and might include yellowfish tuna (appetizer), monkfish, halibut, and skate. *Prix fixe* lunch is $59; dinner is $107. The dessert menu usually includes a cheese assortment, superb chocolate dishes, and unusual ice creams. A tasting menu is also available.

LE BIARRITZ
325 W 57th St (bet Eighth and Ninth Ave)   212/245-9467
Lunch: Mon-Fri; Dinner: Mon-Sat   212/757-2390 (reservations)
Moderate   www.lebiarritz.com

New York is full of neighborhood restaurants, and Le Biarritz is one of the best. Happily, nothing changes here. It seems like home every evening as regulars claim most of the seats in this warm, smallish eatery. The place has been at the same location and in the same hands for four decades. Gleaming copper makes any eating establishment look inviting, and you'll see a first-rate collection of beautiful French copper cooking and serving pieces. The chef prepares escargots well. You might also try French onion soup or crepes a la Biarritz (stuffed with crabmeat). Entrees include frog legs *provençale*, duck in cherry sauce with wild rice, and all kinds of chicken, lamb, beef, veal, and fish dishes, each served with fresh vegetables. Desserts are homemade and very good. The reasonably priced dinners include soup, salad, and choice of dessert. If you are going to a Broadway show or an event at Lincoln Center, try Le Biarritz.

LE BOEUF À LA MODE
539 E 81st St (bet York and East End Ave)   212/249-1473
Dinner: Daily
Moderately expensive

My idea of a perfect restaurant is Le Boeuf à La Mode. This Upper East Side French bistro has been pleasing New Yorkers for decades, and rightfully so. The owners know the recipe for success: warm, comfortable surroundings; pleasant and informed service; outstanding and reliable food; and prices that will not decimate one's pocketbook. The classic French fare includes snails in garlic butter, sauteed shrimp, onion soup, outstanding grilled baby lamb chops, and filet mignon. To top it off, the dessert cart is so appetizing you'll want to order one of each item! Visit Le Boeuf à La Mode and you'll feel as if you've taken a trip to Paris.

LE CIRQUE
One Beacon Court
151 E 58th St (bet Lexington and Third Ave)   212/644-0202
Lunch: Mon-Fri; Dinner: Mon-Sat   www.lecirque.com
Expensive

It's all about Sirio Maccioni! Probably no one on the Manhattan restaurant scene has more devoted followers than this charming gentleman. Now he has a difficult-to-find retreat that's frequented by fans looking for *quenelles de brochet*, honey-glazed duck breast, or pig's feet. Most of all they want to be seen by the "swells" and get a kiss from Sirio himself. The food, under the direction of chef Pierre Schaedelin, is absolutely superb. The atmosphere is what you would expect (classy, subdued, coat-and-tie) as are the prices (expensive). If you want the same great food in a more relaxed setting, head to the wine lounge. Private facilities are also available. I love watching Sirio, who is the epitome of what a restaurant owner should be. And he sure knows how to pick the chefs.

LE GIGOT
18 Cornelia St (bet Bleecker and 4th St)   212/627-3737
Lunch, Dinner: Tues-Sun; Brunch: Sat, Sun
Moderate   www.legigotrestaurant.com

This is a charming, romantic 28-seat bistro in the bowels of the Village. Most taxi drivers have never heard of Cornelia Street, so allow extra time if you come by cab. Once you're here, the cozy atmosphere and warm hospitality of the ladies who greet and serve combine with hearty dishes that will please the most discerning diner. My suggestion for a memorable meal: *bouillabaisse* or, in winter, *le boeuf Bourguignon* (beef stew in red wine with shallots, bacon, carrots, mushrooms, and potatoes). Snails and patés make delicious starters. Tasty desserts like upside-down apple tarts and flambéed bananas with cognac are offered. Brunches are a specialty. Le Gigot is a lot less expensive than its counterpart in Paris, but just as appealing. Note: pay by cash or American Express only.

LE JARDIN BISTRO
25 Cleveland Place (bet Kenmare and Spring St)   212/343-9599
Lunch, Dinner: Daily; Brunch: Sat, Sun   www.lejardinbistro.com
Moderate

This charming downtown restaurant has thrived over the years because it is an excellent operation in every way. The setting, particularly by the garden, is homey and pleasant. The service is unobtrusive and friendly. The menu prices offer good value. You'll find many French favorites: onion soup, tuna tartare, niçoise salad, and more to start. For the main course, I'd suggest *bouillabaisse*, breast of duck, or rack of lamb. For dessert, Le Jardin's profiteroles (vanilla ice cream in puff pastry) are New York's best, mainly because of the fabulous chocolate sauce.

French Specialties

Bouillabaisse: French seafood stew

Confit: goose, duck, or pork that has been salted, cooked, and preserved in its own fat

Coulis: a thick, smooth sauce, usually made from vegetables but sometimes from fruit

En croute: anything baked in a buttery pastry crust or hollowed-out slice of toast

Foie gras: duck or goose liver, usually made into paté

Tartare: finely chopped and seasoned raw beef, often served as an appetizer

---

LE PÉRIGORD
405 E 52nd St (bet First Ave and East River)   212/755-6244
Lunch: Mon-Fri; Dinner: Daily   www.leperigord.com
Expensive

I love this place! *Civilized* is the word to describe Le Périgord. It is like dining in one of the great rooms of Manhattan in the "good old days," but with a distinctively modern presence. From gracious host Georges Briguet to the talented chef, everything is class personified. Gentlemen should wear jackets. Every captain and waiter has been trained to perfection. Fresh roses and Limoges dinner plates adorn each table. But this is just half the pleasure of the experience. Every dish—from the magnificent cold appetizer buffet that greets guests to the spectacular dessert cart—is tasty and memorable. You may order a la carte, of course. Soups are outstanding. Dover sole melts in your mouth. A fine selection of game is available in winter. Roasted free-range chicken, served with the best potato dish I have ever tasted (*bleu de gex* potato gratin), should not be missed. The chocolate mousse is without equal in Manhattan. The luxurious setting of Le Périgord makes one appreciate what gracious dining on a special night out is all about.

LE REFUGE
166 E 82nd St (bet Third and Lexington Ave)   212/861-4505
Dinner: Daily   www.lerefuge.com
Moderate

In any other city, Le Refuge would be one of the hottest restaurants in town. But aside from folks in the neighborhood, few seem to have heard of it. This charming, three-room French country restaurant offers excellent food, professional service, and delightful surroundings. The front room is cozy and comfortable, and the rear sections provide nice views and pleasant accommodations. A back garden is open in the summer. This is another house where the owner is the chef, and as usual, it shows in the professionalism of the presentations. Specialties of the house: duck with fresh fruit, *bouillabaisse de crustaces*, and couscous Mediterranean with shrimp. Finish off your meal with crème brûlée, profiteroles, or chocolate truffle cake.

LE RIVAGE
340 W 46th St (bet Eighth and Ninth Ave)　　212/765-7374
Lunch, Dinner: Daily　　www.lerivagenyc.com
Moderate

Le Rivage is one of the survivors along the highly competitive "restaurant row" of 46th Street. They endure by serving French food that's well prepared and reasonably priced. Escargots, onion soup, *coq au vin rouge*, and peach melba are all delectable and well-presented. Besides, the atmosphere and the pleasant attitude of the servers puts one in the proper frame of mind to enjoy a Broadway show.

Insieme (777 Seventh Ave, 212/582-1310) is a classic Italian restaurant featuring tasty food, prompt service, and a comfortable atmosphere. The name means "together" in Italian. You'll find the veal tartare to be superb!

LES HALLES
411 Park Ave S (bet 28th and 29th St)　　212/679-4111
Daily: 7:30 a.m. to midnight　　www.leshalles.net
Moderate

Come here anytime you are hungry! Les Halles has struck a responsive chord on the New York restaurant stage. No doubt that is because the establishment provides the necessary ingredients for success in today's restaurant sweepstakes: tasty food in an appealing atmosphere at reasonable prices. Specialties like blood sausage with apples, lamb stew, and fillet of beef are served in hefty portions with fresh salad and delicious French fries. Harried waiters try their best to be polite and helpful, but they are not always successful, as tables turn over rapidly. If a week in Paris is more of a dream than a reality, then you might settle for mussels (ten ways), snails, onion soup, and classic cassoulet at this busy establishment. The dessert selection is a disappointment, except for the crepes Suzette, prepared tableside. (Note: Their butcher shop, by the front door, is open daily.) The quieter **Les Halles Downtown** (15 John St, 212/285-8585) has much the same menu.

L'IMPERO
45 Tudor City Pl (bet 41st and 43rd St)　　212/599-5045
Lunch: Mon-Fri; Dinner: Mon-Sat　　www.limpero.com
Expensive

Tucked away in Tudor City Place, this 1928 landmark room in the United Nations area is for serious diners. The theme at L'Impero is rustic Italian, but the menu will appeal to diverse tastes. Chef Scott Conant changes the menu seasonally. The pastas are uniformly delicious, with homemade spaghetti especially recommended. Tuna poached in olive oil is superb, as is baby goat.

I particularly enjoyed designing a cheese plate from a mouth-watering selection of nearly a dozen varieties. The gelati is authentic. For a different dessert, try sesame cannoli with orange mascarpone mousse and blood orange sorbet. Get a rich relative to pick up the check, especially if you succumb to the magnificent tasting menu.

LITTLE OWL

90 Bedford St (at Grove St)   212/741-4695
Dinner: Daily; Brunch: Sat, Sun   www.thelittleowlnyc.com
Moderate

There's not much to look at but a lot to be satisfied with in the food category at Little Owl. With tiny tables for only 40 diners, this corner establishment is a very personal place with a wait staff that is warm and eager to please. Every dish I tasted was excellent and reasonably priced. The mixed green salad was as delicious as any I have had in the city. Some outstanding entrees: potato gnocchi, crispy chicken, and grilled pork chops. Beans are a top side dish. The brunch menu is particularly attractive, with dishes like blueberry corn pancakes, grilled New York steak, yellowfin tuna, and bacon cheeseburger with spiced fries. If they have them, baked strawberry custard and brownie with praline coffee sauce are wonderful desserts. At an Italian house, you would expect the pizzas and pastas to be good—and they are. Just one drawback: Little Owl is very popular, so reservations are a must.

If it is atmosphere you are looking for in a dining experience and the size of the check makes no difference, then go for dinner at **Bruno Jamais** (24 E 81st St, 212/396-3444). In the magnificent townhouse that once housed the famed Parioli Romanissimo restaurant, a room has been created that brings visions of dining in a European palace! Wine glasses hang from the ceiling, the service is hushed, many full-suited functionairies walk the floor, and the platters presented are attractive and tasty (if not particularly memorable). Music and dancing are available after dining. You'll see all ages here. Just hold on tight to your wallet!

MAI HOUSE

186 Franklin St (bet Hudson and Greenwich St)   212/431-0606
Dinner: Mon-Sat   www.myriadrestaurantgroup.com
Moderate

This is not one of the small, family-operated Vietnamese restaurants that are so popular these days because of the cheap prices. Mai House is definitely an upscale house, with many exotic Vietnamese specialties. Yes, there are spring rolls, but also frog leg lollipops, barbecued quail, and wild boar *nem* sausage for appetizers. Thinly sliced lemongrass short ribs are delicious, as are sweet and sour spicy red snapper and nuggets of cuttlefish. Traditionalists will find many kinds of noodles and rice. A glass of sake will finish off a tasty meal in Mai House's rather sophisticated atmosphere.

MALONEY & PORCELLI

37 E 50th St (bet Park and Madison Ave)   212/750-2233
Lunch, Dinner: Daily   www.maloneyandporcelli.com
Expensive

If your accountant wrangles you a nice tax refund, take him or her to Maloney & Porcelli! Most everything is expensive: the ambience, the platters, and (yes) the check. But the meat dishes—fabulous sirloin steaks and crackling pork shank—are wonderful. It is tempting to fill up on the great bread basket; instead, try first-rate appetizers like oven-fired pizzas, crab cakes, and pastrami salmon. Lobster dishes are a specialty, particularly the "Angry Lobster." An intriguing dessert selection is available. Their private dining room is a great facility for an office party or wedding reception.

MANGIA È BEVI
800 Ninth Ave (at 53rd St)   212/956-3976
Lunch, Dinner: Daily; Brunch: Sat, Sun
Inexpensive to moderate   www.mangiaebevirestaurant.com

Dining on Ninth Avenue? Mangia È Bevi is a top choice for delicious food at unbelievably low prices (for Manhattan). The noise level is almost unbearable, the tables allow you to instantly become friendly with strangers, and the waiters are very casual yet surprisingly helpful. The abundant antipasto platter, overflowing with nearly a dozen choices, is a house specialty. This rustic trattoria also features a large selection of pastas, fish, meat dishes, salads and a bevy of in-season veggies. Brick-oven pizza lovers will be in heaven with pleasing combinations and equally pleasing prices. There's nothing special about desserts, except for the homemade tiramisu. It is easy to see why this colorful spot is one of the most popular destinations along Ninth Avenue.

MARCHI'S
251 E 31st St (near Second Ave)   212/679-2494
Dinner: Mon-Sat (special hours for private parties)
Moderate   www.marchirestaurant.com

Marchi's has been a New York fixture since 1930 when it was established by the Marchi family in an attractive brownstone townhouse. Three sons are on hand, lending a homey flavor to the restaurant's three dining rooms and garden patio (a great spot for a private dinner). It's almost like eating at your favorite Italian family's home, especially since there are no menus. Bring a hearty appetite to take full advantage of a superb feast. The first course is a platter of antipasto—including radishes, *finocchio,* and Genoa salami—plus a salad of tuna, olives, and red cabbage. The second is an absolutely delicious homemade lasagna. The third is crispy deep-fried fish, light and tempting, served with beets and string beans. The entree is delicious roast chicken and veal served with fresh mushrooms and tossed salad. Dessert consists of fresh fruit, cheese, lemon fritter, and sensational *crostoli* (crisp fried twists sprinkled with powdered sugar). The tab is reasonable. Come to Marchi's for a unique, leisurely meal and an evening you will long remember. In the summer, dining alfresco with a full view of the Empire State Building is a memorable option.

MARKJOSEPH STEAKHOUSE
261 Water St (off Peck Slip)   212/277-0020
Lunch: Mon-Fri; Dinner: Mon-Sat www.markjosephsteakhouse.com
Moderately expensive

A fun visit! If the trendy uptown steakhouses turn you off, then head downtown—with good directions, as Water Street turns into Pearl Street near this location—to a comfortable, homey neighborhood room that is high on quality meat and low on attitude. The room is filled with folks in casual garb, more interested in delving into a huge, juicy steak than wondering who's sitting at the next table. Some of the personnel (including a few who came over from Peter Luger) are all business. If you're dining with a group or family, the seafood combination platter (lobster, shrimp, clams, calamari, and mussels) is a great place to start. Porterhouse steak and filet mignon are highly recommended. Baked or hash brown potatoes are great side dishes. At lunch, the half-pound burgers are wonderful, as is the signature steak sandwich. If there's still room for dessert, opt for tartufo or the MarkJoseph special. You'll be surprised at its contents!

> At **BLT Fish** (21 W 17th St, 212/691-8888), outstanding features include daily oyster selections, a raw bar, wonderful garlic bread, a large selection of fish, fresh Maine lobsters, homemade pies, and other yummy desserts.

MCCORMICK & SCHMICK'S
1285 Ave of the Americas (at 52nd St)   212/459-1222
Lunch: Mon-Sat; Dinner: Daily   www.mccormickandschmick.com
Moderate to moderately expensive

Since I live on the Pacific coast, I can recognize a great seafood house. Oregon-based McCormick & Schmick's seafood restaurant chain has landed an operation in Manhattan, and it is a dandy. The fresh seafood sheet lists over 30 treats from the world's waterways, all prepared with imagination and care. And the prices, unlike those at some of the so-called class seafood houses in Manhattan, are very much within reach of the average pocketbook. What's good and special: pan-fried Willapa Bay oysters, oysters on the half-shell, Massachusetts steamer clams, Atlantic salmon, and Dungeness crab legs sauteed with mushrooms, artichoke hearts, and sherry. Two dozen seafood specialty entrees run the gamut from cashew-crusted red tilapia from Ecuador to Nantucket Bay scallops and mahi-mahi from Costa Rica. There are also ample choices for non-seafood diners. Don't miss the dessert tray, which will complete a memorable meal!

MÉTISSE
239 W 105th St (bet Amsterdam Ave and Broadway)   212/666-8825
Dinner: Daily; Brunch: Sat, Sun   ww.metisserestaurant.com
Moderate

This Upper West Side French bistro does all the good things you would expect, but it is the atmosphere that adds so much to a dinner at Métisse. The place is quiet and restful, the waiters unobtrusive, the cuisine satisfying, and the check reasonable. Imagine a $14.95 *prix fixe* luncheon, a $15.95 *prix fixe* brunch, and a $21 *prix fixe* dinner. Salads are fresh, the varied entree selection includes seafood, steaks, and chops. For dessert, chocolate mousse will top off a fine meal. Live jazz adds to the experience on Wednesday evening.

METROCAFE & WINE BAR
32 E 21st St (bet Park Ave S and Broadway) 212/353-0800
Lunch: Mon-Fri; Dinner: Daily www.metrocafenyc.com
Moderate

Reasonable pricing is the draw at MetroCafe. In addition to a complete menu, wine lovers will delight in 125 wines by the glass and 21 wine flights. Other attractions: a good selection of Kobe burgers and steaks and dim sum. You can dine on fresh salads, thin-crust pizzas, filling sandwiches, pastas, excellent chargrilled burgers, and a selection of comfort foods that include meatloaf, fish and chips, grilled chicken *paillard*, and grilled filet of salmon. Desserts are tasty, and the atmosphere is family-friendly. Takeout is also available.

Shopping at Bloomingale's when hunger pangs strike? Dart across the street to **Brasserie 360** (200 E 60th St, 212/688-8688). It's not fancy or gourmet, but the food is well-prepared, the price is right, and the place is always jumping.

MEZZOGIORNO
195 Spring St (near Ave of the Americas) 212/334-2112
Lunch, Dinner: Daily www.mezzogiorno.com
Moderate

Florence, Italy, is one of the world's most charming cities, not only because of its abundance of great art, but also for the wonderful small restaurants on every street corner. At Mezzogiorno, a Florence-style trattoria in New York, the food is comparably good (though some of the art is questionable). The place is busy and noisy, and tables are so close together that conversation is almost impossible. The decor is best described as "modern Florence." Check out the unusual writing on the ceiling, done by master fresco artist Pontormo. Better yet, keep your eyes on the food. The salad selection is outstanding, and their lasagna is one of the best. Mezzogiorno is also famous for pizza. You'll find all the ingredients for a wonderful make-believe evening in Florence.

MICHAEL JORDAN'S THE STEAK HOUSE N.Y.C.
23 Vanderbilt Ave (at Grand Central Terminal) 212/655-2300
Lunch, Dinner: Daily www.theglaziergroup.com
Moderately expensive

Grand Central Terminal has come back to life, and Michael Jordan's establishment is one more reason to visit this historic building, even if you are not catching a train. Service and food quality is spotty. The menu is very much what you would expect: steaks, chops, lobster, and salmon. You'll fill up on the sizable portions, but if you feel especially hungry, try the sliced tomatoes and sweet onion appetizer. Forget about calories and order the special French fries as a side dish. For a change, desserts are reasonably priced. They include brownie ice cream sundae and a fabulous 12-layer chocolate cake.

MICHAEL'S
24 W 55th St (bet Fifth Ave and Ave of the Americas) 212/767-0555
Breakfast, Lunch: Mon-Fri; Dinner: Mon-Sat
Moderately expensive to expensive   www.michaelsnewyork.com

"A midtown scene" would best describe this very attractive restaurant, located conveniently for shoppers, business types, hotel visitors, and the like. The several rooms are airy and pleasant, especially in nice weather. Service is professional and attentive. You'll see some familiar media faces, society types, important-looking business execs, and ordinary fat-walleted gawkers. The food is expensive: Michael's burger is tabbed around $30, and seafood dishes are even more. While it is a bit overpriced, there is no question about the quality or presentation. Appetizers like clams, oysters, ravioli, and foie gras terrine are quite special. Perhaps the real treat is the fabulous Cobb salad, probably the best in New York. Prepare to splurge!

Looking for a quick bite in midtown? Try **Certe** (20 W 55th St, 212/397-2020). You'll find breakfast items, fresh baked goods, sandwiches, health foods, good soups and burgers, pizzas, and more. I especially like the selection of jumbo muffins.

MINETTA TAVERN
113 MacDougal St (near Bleecker St)   212/475-3850
Lunch, Dinner: Daily
Moderate

Established in 1937, Minetta Tavern has been serving excellent Northern Italian food for generations in Greenwich Village. Located on the spot where Minetta Brook wandered through Manhattan in the early days, this tavern was made famous by Eddie "Minetta" Sieveri, a friend of many sports and stage stars of yesteryear. Dozens of old pictures adorn the walls of this intimate, scrupulously clean tavern, where professional personnel serve no-nonsense Italian food at attractive prices. Grilled mushrooms, steamed clams, or homemade *tortellacci* are good ways to get the juices flowing. If you'd like something a bit heftier, veal and various chicken dishes are available. Chocolate mousse cake, profiteroles, and other pastries cap off a satisfying meal. Everyone is made to feel comfortable here.

MORAN'S CHELSEA
146 Tenth Ave (at 19th St)   212/627-3030
Lunch, Dinner: Daily   www.moranschelsea.com
Moderate

In a building that's nearly 200 years old, Moran's has seen a lot of history, including time as a speakeasy and as a Jewish lodging house during Prohibition days. The years have been kind to this exceptionally charming tavern, complete with fireplaces in every room, hardwood paneling, large and attractive party facilities, and a cozy bar. There is copper everywhere you look. The old tin ceiling adds a special dimension. Fresh seafood, aged chops, lobster, crab cakes, prime rib, and shepherd's pie are just a few of the specialties. You'll also find excellent burgers, fresh salads, and a few pastas. If you are looking for a unique venue for a group of up to 250, I strongly suggest checking out Moran's. The personnel are friendly and accommodating.

THE MORGAN DINING ROOM
225 Madison Ave (bet 36th and 37th St)   212/683-2130
Lunch: Tues-Fri; Dinner: Fri; Brunch: Sat, Sun   www.themorgan.org
Moderate

The Morgan Library & Museum is a grand place to visit, and you can extend the experience by dining in the cozy room where J.P. Morgan himself broke bread. It is a great place to meet friends, and the tab itself is surprisingly friendly. First courses include house-cured salmon, salads, and tarts. Among the tasty entrees are large salads, chicken fricassee, and pastas. Director Paul Huyck has assembled a friendly wait staff.

Mama's Food Shop (200 E 3rd St, 212/777-4425) is an inexpensive and tasty destination for homemade dishes like meatloaf, grilled salmon, and fried, roasted, and grilled chicken. Sides include mashed potatoes, macaroni and cheese, honey-glazed sweet potatoes, green beans, Swiss chard, and turnips. Don't miss the banana cream pie! Takeout, delivery, and catering are available.

MORTON'S OF CHICAGO
551 Fifth Ave (at 45th St)   212/972-3315
Lunch: Mon-Fri; Dinner: Daily   www.mortons.com
Moderately expensive to expensive

Every member of the highly efficient staff at this franchised, high-end steakhouse has been trained in the Morton's manner. At the start of your meal, you are shown a cart with sample entree items: various cuts of beef, lobster, and whatever else happens to be featured. Every dish is fully explained. Appetizers are heavy in the seafood department. Shrimp, oysters, smoked salmon, sea scallops, and salads are attractive and appetizing. The steaks and chops are so tender you can cut them with a fork. They arrive promptly, too, which is not the case in many steakhouses. There are several potato choices, including wonderful hash browns. Sauteed spinach with mushrooms and steamed broccoli and asparagus are fresh and tasty. Top it all off with a delicious soufflé—chocolate, Grand Marnier, lemon, or raspberry—that's large enough for two hungry diners. A busy bar (which serves bar bites) and function rooms are added attraction at Morton's.

MR. K'S
570 Lexington Ave (at 51st St)   212/583-1668
Lunch, Dinner: Daily   www.mrksnyc.com
Moderately expensive to expensive

Mr. K's is a very classy Chinese dining room where high-powered politicos and famous celebrities come to dine. All manner of goodies will whet the appetite: Shanghai spring rolls, dumplings, and a delicious seafood dish of sauteed crab, shrimp, and scallops. Of course, there is chicken and corn chowder; in my opinion, no Chinese dinner is complete without it. What else? Share an assortment of plates with your table partners: lemon chicken, Peking duck, honey-braised pork ribs, sesame beef, crispy sea bass, and sesame prawns with shiitake mushrooms. If you like hot dishes, go for the firecracker prawns with Szechuan sauce!

MUSEUM OF MODERN ART
9 W 53rd St (bet Fifth Ave and Ave of the Americas)   212/333-1220
The Modern (dining room)   www.themodernnyc.com
Lunch: Mon-Fri; Dinner: Mon-Sat
Bar Room
Lunch, Dinner: Daily
Cafe 2 and Terrace 5: museum hours
Moderate to moderately expensive (Bar Room and The Modern)

Both the Museum of Modern Art and its dining venues are special New York-only treats. Under the expert eye of top restaurateur Danny Meyer, the museum features four unique dining venues. **The Modern** dining room is top-drawer and formal (gentlemen are asked to wear coats), with a grand view of the sculpture garden. The menu features creative multi-course *prix fixe* French cuisine. Next door is the **Bar Room**, where food is a bit less expensive but equally tasty and not quite so fancy. The *tarte flambé* is worth a visit in itself. You'll find over 30 menu items here. **Cafe 2** and **Terrace 5** are on the upper floors and appeal mainly to families visiting the museum, with some dishes aimed at quick service and kids.

Fish lovers, take note: **Esca** (402 W 43rd St, 212/564-7272) is one of Manhattan's best seafood restaurants. The emphasis is on Southern Italian seafood and pastas. This attractive establishment in the Theater District is always crowded—and deservedly so.

NAPLES 45
MetLife Building, 200 Park Ave   212/972-7001
Breakfast, Lunch, Dinner: Mon-Fri   www.patinagroup.com
Moderate

This may well be the best pizza house in Manhattan! Absolutely delicious, authentic Neapolitan pizzas are made with *caputo* flour, imported from Southern Italy, and other tasty ingredients. Cooked in a wood-burning (oak) oven, they are a sight to behold and taste! You have your choice of individual ten-inch plates or their "Mezzo Metro," large enough to feed three or four persons. But there is more: small dishes (like veal meatballs or fried calamari), pizza bread sandwiches, soups, seafood, pastas, and salads. Takeout and delivery are available, as is patio dining in nice weather. The place is jammed!

NICOLA'S
146 E 84th St (bet Lexington and Third Ave)   212/249-9850
Dinner: Daily
Moderately expensive

Upper-crust New Yorkers who like a clubby atmosphere and good food —which are not often found together—love this place! At times the noise level rivals that of a Broadway opening. In a setting of rich wood with familiar framed faces on the walls, no-nonsense waiters serve delicious platters of pasta, veal, chicken, fish, and steak. The emphasis is Italian, and there are inviting daily specials in every category. Concentrate on the main part of your meal, as desserts show little imagination.

Asian Specialties

Dim sum: a whole meal of succulent nibblers, such as steamed dumplings, shrimp balls, and savory pastries

Egg foo yung: thick, savory pancakes made of eggs, vegetables, and meat, often slathered with a rich, broth-based sauce

General Tso's chicken: breaded, deep-fried chicken chunks tossed in a spicy-sweet sauce

Moo shu: stir-fried shredded meat, vegetables, and seasonings, scrambled with eggs and rolled (usually by the diner) inside thin pancakes

Peking duck: Air is pumped between a duck's skin and flesh, then the bird is coated with honey and hung up until the skin dries and hardens. The duck is roasted, cut into pieces, and served with scallions and pancakes or steamed buns.

Sashimi: sliced raw fish served with *daikon* (Japanese radish), wasabi (Japanese horseradish), pickled ginger, and soy sauce

Sukiyaki: stir-fried pieces of meat (and sometimes vegetables, noodles, or tofu) flavored with soy sauce, *dashi* (Japanese fish stock), and *mirin* (sweet rice wine)

Sushi: raw fish or vegetables served atop vinegared rice or inside rolls wrapped in *nori* (sheets of dried seaweed)

Tempura: fried, battered seafood and vegetables

Teriyaki: a sauce of rice wine, soy sauce, sugar, and seasonings that is used to marinate beef or chicken, which is then grilled or stir-fried

---

NOBU 57
40 W 57th St (bet Fifth Ave and Ave of the Americas) 212/757-3000
Lunch: Mon-Fri; Dinner: Daily www.myriadrestaurantgroup.com

NOBU NEW YORK
105 Hudson St (at Franklin St) 212/219-0500
Lunch: Mon-Fri; Dinner: Daily

NOBU NEXT DOOR
105 Hudson St (bet Franklin and N Moore St) 212/334-4445
Dinner: Daily
Expensive

Yes, these places are busy and expensive, but they are worth every penny and any frustrating wait for reservations. Nobu Matsuhisa has put together spectacular venues for those who love sushi and great Japanese food that's not too complex but unfailingly tasty. Because I like salty dishes, this menu appeals to me. I like the feel: at once classy and crowded, with an unmistakable party atmosphere. Sitting at the sushi bar allows you to watch the large, superbly trained staff perform like a symphony orchestra. A wood-burning oven adds to the splendid array of dishes. The black cod is a standout. Dozens of sushi, sashimi, and sushi roll selections are available. Fresh, delicious salads abound. Leave room for the Bento Box dessert: warm chocolate fondant cake with green tea ice cream. You're going to pay well for all these treats—especially if you have the Kobe beef—but you'll go away relishing a very special dining experience.

OCEAN GRILL
384 Columbus Ave (bet 78th and 79th Ave)   212/579-2300
Lunch, Dinner: Daily; Brunch: Sun   www.brguestrestaurants.com
Moderate

Ocean Grill is one of the few good seafood restaurants on the Upper West Side. In nice weather, watching the passing parade from an outside table is fun. Quite popular with young professionals, the place is noisy, too. The food is good (not great), with littleneck clams topping the list. For a party, chilled shellfish platters—offering a selection of lobster, clams, oysters, shrimp, and more—are appropriate. A wood-burning grill turns out Scottish salmon, big-eye tuna, mahi-mahi, and wild striped bass. Other attractions include crab cakes, lobster bisque, and seafood Cobb salad. For brunch, sesonal quiche and blueberry, banana, and buttermilk pancakes are good bets.

I don't know quite what they are trying to do with the revitalized restaurant **Peacock Alley** (Waldorf-Astoria, 301 Park Ave, 212/355-3000). There are few more dramatic settings than the fabulous lobby of the historic Waldorf, and those who choose to have a drink at the front part of Peacock Alley can see and be seen by the passing parade. But the back is a small, dull area that offers fair-to-middling dishes at sky-high prices with little atmosphere and pretentious service. Have a martini and be on your way.

OCEANA
55 E 54th St (bet Park and Madison Ave)   212/759-5941
Lunch: Mon-Fri; Dinner: Mon-Sat   www.oceanarestaurant.com
Expensive

When you finally save enough money to afford a cruise, you want to do it right and book passage on a really fabulous ship. Well, the same holds true if you want a really first-rate seafood meal. Oceana is just that kind of place. This midtown townhouse offers several floors of classy dining, with relatively new chef Ben Pollinger turning out terrific three-course *prix fixe* dinners ($78). The menu changes frequently, and the seafood catches are so fresh they practically swim to the table. For entrees I suggest striped bass, Icelandic cod, or crispy Maine skate. The gnocchi is a blue-ribbon winner! The sticky toffee pudding and pumpkin strudel with ice cream are delectable desserts.

OLIVES NEW YORK
W New York Union Square
201 Park Ave S (at 17th St)   212/353-8345
Breakfast: Daily; Lunch: Mon-Fri; Dinner: Daily; Brunch: Sat, Sun
Moderate   www.toddenglish.com

For yuppies, this is *the* place! The trendy crowd seems to like the New

England influence of Todd English's open-kitchen charmer. A spirited and jazzy atmosphere combines with superbly trained personnel and great food to make a pleasant dining experience. Portions are big, with delicious pastas high on the list. If your tastes are not too fancy, the burgers are very good and the peanut butter pancakes at brunch are "to die for."

ONE IF BY LAND, TWO IF BY SEA
17 Barrow St (bet Seventh Ave and 4th St)   212/228-0822
Dinner: Daily   www.oneifbyland.com
Expensive

The candlelight, fireplace, flowers, and background piano music all add to the ambience of this romantic room. One If By Land, Two If By Sea is housed in an 18th-century carriage house once owned by Aaron Burr. Allow extra time to find this place, as Barrow Street (one of the West Village's most charming) is generally unknown to taxi drivers. Besides, there's no sign out front! Tables at the front of the balcony are particularly appealing. You can't go wrong with rack of lamb or breast of duck. Individual beef Wellington is usually excellent, as is the spice-roasted lobster. A *prix fixe* five-course tasting menu is available. Their classic crème brûlée is a favorite dessert.

Norma's (Le Parker Meridien Hotel, 118 W 57th St, 212/708-7460) is rightfully praised as having the best breakfast menu in Manhattan. Here is a sample of the offerings: blueberry and buttermilk pancakes, Johnny applecakes, crispy Belgian waffles with fresh fruit, crunchy pecan and macadamia-nut granola, a melted, gooey, four-cheese omelet, an overstuffed croissant of smoked salmon and scrambled eggs, and much more. First-class!

ONIEAL'S GRAND STREET
174 Grand St (bet Lafayette and Mulberry St)   212/941-9119
Lunch, Dinner: Daily; Late Night Menu: Thurs-Sat;
Brunch: Sat, Sun   www.onieals.com
Moderate

This legendary and historic speakeasy, with its secret tunnel to the old police headquarters, evokes memories of days long past. Housed beneath a 150-year-old hand-carved mahogany ceiling, this bar, lounge, and restaurant is reminiscent of another time. Onieal's achieved additional celebrity as a backdrop on HBO's *Sex and the City*. They serve one of the best burgers in town. You'll find marinated grilled yellowfin tuna, Cobb salad, hanger steak *au poivre*, risotto, and more. For dessert, try the Four Devils chocolate soufflé cake (named after the four devils intricately carved on the ceiling). Service at Onieal's is friendly and efficient.

ORSO
322 W 46th St (bet Eighth and Ninth Ave)   212/489-7212
Lunch, Dinner: Daily; Brunch: Sun   www.orsorestaurant.com
Moderate

This restaurant features the same menu all day long, which is great for those with unusual dining hours and handy for theatergoers. Orso is one of the most popular places on midtown's "restaurant row," so if you're planning a six o'clock dinner, be sure to make reservations. The smallish room is cozy and comfortable. It's watched over by a portrait of Orso, a Venetian dog who is the mascot for this Italian bistro. The kitchen is open in the back, allowing diners to see the experienced staff at work. The changing menu offers many good appetizers, including cold roast veal and grilled eggplant salad. A variety of pizzas and some excellent pasta dishes are also offered. For an entree, you can't go wrong with the popular sauteed calves liver. The strawberry tiramisu, one of many homemade desserts, will finish off a great meal. A special Sunday brunch menu is available.

OSTERIA DEL CIRCO

120 W 55th St (bet Ave of the Americas and Seventh Ave)
Lunch: Mon-Fri; Dinner: Daily   212/265-3636
Moderately expensive   www.osteriadelcirco.com

Were it not for the fact that the owners are the sons of Sirio Maccioni (the legendary restaurateur of Le Cirque fame), this establishment might just be written off as another Italian restaurant. But here we have three brothers—Mario, Marco, and Mauro (and mother Egidiana)—operating a classy establishment with a friendly, circus-themed ambience, atypical Italian menu, and a bit of Le Cirque's magic. The tastiest items include great pizzas and salads, satisfying soups, and unusual pastas. A unique dessert is an Italian favorite called *bomboloncini:* small vanilla-, chocolate- and marmalade-filled doughnuts.

Dishes has it all: breakfasts, baked items, sandwiches, salads, soups, and smoothies to eat in or take out. Catering is a specialty. Dishes has three locations: 6 E 45th St, 212/687-5511; Grand Central Terminal, 42nd St at Vanderbilt Ave, 212/808-5511; and 399 Park Ave, 212/421-5511.

OUEST

2315 Broadway (at 84th St)   212/580-8700
Dinner: Daily; Brunch: Sun   www.ouestny.com
Moderate

Ouest is overflowing with happy locals enjoying one of the best rooms in the city. The comfortable booths, open kitchen, cozy (if dark and noisy) balcony, and pleasant serving staff combine to make Thomas Valenti's jewel first-class. This is not surprising, as Valenti gained experience at Alison on Dominick St. and Butterfield 81 on the Upper East Side. The bistro menu is just as inviting as the semicircular tables, with appetizer choices like smoked duck breast with crispy eggs and bitter greens, goat cheese ravioli, and several fresh salads. The braised short ribs melt in your mouth. Nightly specials include braised lamb shanks on Thursday and meatloaf on Sunday. From delicious warm bread to rich chocolate cake for dessert, the whole experience is pure pleasure.

OUR PLACE

1444 Third Ave (at 82nd St)   212/288-4888
Lunch: Mon-Sat; Dinner: Daily; Brunch: Sat, Sun
Moderate   www.ourplaceuptown.com

Our Place is not a typical Chinese restaurant. Classy service, moderate prices, and delicious food have been its trademarks for many years. Appreciative Upper East Siders have kept its two spotlessly clean dining rooms filled for nearly every meal. Single diners obviously enjoy the atmosphere and feel comfortable here. You'll find many of your favorite Chinese dishes on the menu. I've enjoyed wonton soup, moo shu pork, tangerine beef, Szechuan chicken, duck-wrapped lettuce with pine nuts, and home-style chicken casserole. Free delivery is offered in a wide area. Prices are as comfortable as the chairs.

OUR PLACE SHANGHAI TEA GARDEN
141 E 55th St (bet Lexington and Third Ave)   212/753-3900
Lunch: Mon-Sat; Dinner: Daily   www.ourplace-teagarden.com
Moderate

Shanghai flavors are a bit more complex than other Chinese dishes, and that holds true at this clean, first-rate Oriental room. Shanghai specialties include "Lion's Head" (giant meatballs and vegetable hearts in brown sauce), sauteed squid, and Shanghai-style braised pork shoulder. Besides the Shanghai specialties, there are more typical Chinese dishes, with an excellent assortment of dumplings, soups, chicken, and duck. Their barbecued honey spare ribs are the best in the city. Service is highly efficient and professional. If you want to take the family out for a tasty meal at a reasonable price, I suggest coming here.

PALM ONE
837 Second Ave (at 44th St)   212/687-2953

PALM TOO
840 Second Ave (at 44th St)   212/697-5198

PALM WEST SIDE
250 W 50th St (bet Eighth Ave and Broadway)   212/333-7256
Lunch: Mon-Fri; Dinner: Daily   www.thepalm.com
Expensive

Even with the glut of new steakhouses in Manhattan, steak and lobster lovers still have a special place in their hearts for the Palm (a.k.a. Palm One), which started as a speakeasy in 1926. All three locations have much the same atmosphere. They're noted for huge, delicious steaks, chops, and lobsters. Don't miss the terrific Palm fries (homemade potato chips) or onion rings. These are earthy spots, so don't get too dressed up. Indolent waiters are part of the scene.

PAOLA'S
245 E 84th St (bet Second and Third Ave)   212/794-1890
Lunch, Dinner: Daily; Brunch: Sat, Sun   www.paolasrestaurant.com
Moderate

A wonderful place for a romantic evening! The Italian home cooking is first-class, with Paola herself in the kitchen. Great filled pastas, superb veal dishes, and tasty hot vegetables (like baby artichoke hearts) are house specialties. Be advised that they don't spare on the garlic! Mirrors reflect the warmth and flicker of candles, and the lady of the house will charm any guest. Top off your reasonably priced meal with a rich chocolate mousse.

PARIS COMMUNE
99 Bank St (at Greenwich St)   212/929-0509
Lunch, Dinner: Daily; Brunch: Sat, Sun   www.pariscommune.net
Moderate

There is a new attraction at Paris Commune: the Rouge Wine Bar. This restaurant is a popular gathering spot in the West Village, where regulars outnumber visitors every night. The French/Continental menu includes pastas, salads, steaks, and seafood. The staff is prompt and efficient. Dining by candlelight is a big attraction. The weekend brunch features spectacular French toast, along with the usual fare. Delicious dishes include vegetable frittata and their famous gingerbread. Their homemade cheesecakes are good and rich.

PARK AVENUE CAFE
100 E 63rd St (at Park Ave)   212/644-1900
Lunch: Mon-Fri; Dinner: Daily; Brunch: Sat, Sun
Moderately expensive   www.parkavenuecafe.com

Park Avenue Cafe is a showpiece for Alan Stillman. Its windows face Park Avenue, and walls favor a folk-art look. Chefs Kevin Lasko and Lucas Billheimer prepare innovative American cuisine with offerings like crispy Chatham cod and Maine lobster *tagine*. Highly professional waiters make dining here an experience in classy customer care. The people-watching is great, and conversations at adjacent tables can be fascinating. (It's not eavesdropping when you can't help it.) Desserts are sensational!

If you want to eat, play, and dance *big*, then head to **Slate** (54 W 21st St, 212/989-0096). Check out these plus-sized eats: 14-inch pie-cut burgers, 54 oz. porterhouse steaks, hearty sausage rolls, chocolate fondue with vanilla sponge cake, and assorted fruits. The noise level is big, too, as deafening music plays while you eat and dance on weekends. You can also play ping-pong and billiards. I'm happy to say that the food is quite good, especially considering the many distractions!

PARK BISTRO
414 Park Ave S (bet 28th and 29th St)   212/689-1360
Lunch: Mon-Fri; Dinner: Mon-Sat
Moderate

A cheery meal! The Park Bistro is full of smiling faces and more. This small, homey jewel specializes in authentic French cuisine from the Provence region. From the start, when warm and tasty bread is placed before you, to the finishing touch of rich and luscious homemade desserts (like chocolate napoleon), you are surrounded by attentive service and magnificent food. Don't miss the hanger steak or lamb stew. A professional team runs this place, and it shows.

PARK SIDE
107-01 Corona Ave (51st Ave at 108th St, Corona, Queens)
Lunch, Dinner: Daily   718/271-9274
Moderate   www.parksiderestaurant.com

Talk about fun! Do you want to show someone who claims to know everything about New York a place he or she likely hasn't heard about? Would you like to eat on your way to or from LaGuardia or Kennedy Airport? Do you want a special meal in an unusual setting? Well, all of the above are excellent reasons to visit Park Side, in Queens. I've included a restaurant that isn't in Manhattan because it *is* exceptional. Joseph Oliva runs a first-class, spotlessly clean restaurant that serves wonderful Italian food at very affordable prices. Start with garlic bread and then choose from two dozen kinds of pasta and an opulent array of fish, steak, veal, and poultry dishes. The meat is all prime-cut and fresh—nothing frozen. You'll also find polite, knowledgeable waiters in an informal atmosphere. Get a table in the garden room or the Marilyn Monroe room upstairs. Eat to your heart's content, and then be pleasantly surprised at the tab.

Don't miss a visit to **Pop Burger** (58-60 Ninth Ave, 212/414-8686), where thick, creamy milkshakes, tasty burgers (large and small), and non-greasy French fries are the attractions. In the evening, the backroom pool hall and lounge offer a heartier menu.

PASTIS
9 Ninth Ave (at Little West 12th St)   212/929-4844
Breakfast, Dinner: Daily; Lunch: Mon-Fri; Brunch: Sat, Sun
Moderate   www.pastisny.com

In what was once a garage, a large area has been gutted and converted into a bar and dining space with touches that make it look as though it has been around for a long time. Keith McNally, who knows how to hype a restaurant, has turned this Meatpacking District warehouse into one of the most high-energy rooms in Manhattan. The huge bar is awash with hundreds of young Turks—and some not so young—who come to see and be seen. The dining room, if you can get in, serves reasonably good food to hordes who love the unbelievable noise level and classic bistro fare. A nice touch is a long table in the center of the dining space for singles and others who do not want to wait in the reservation line. The menu includes oysters on the half shell, omelets, shellfish stew, roast lobster, sauteed chicken, braised beef, patés, good French fries, and their "Floating Island" dessert. The first question you will ask is "How did they cram all these people into this place?" After a few minutes, you'll understand that the crowd is part of the attraction. Pastis offers delivery, too.

PATSY'S
236 W 56th St (bet Broadway and Eighth Ave)   212/247-3491
Lunch, Dinner: Daily   www.patsys.com
Moderate

For over half a century, the Scognamillo family has operated this popular eatery, specializing in Neapolitan cuisine. At present, the son and a grandson are taking care of the front of the house, while another grandson is following the family tradition in the kitchen. "Patsy" was an immigrant gentleman chef whose nickname graces this bi-level restaurant. Each floor has its own cozy atmosphere and convenient kitchen. The family makes sure that every party is treated with courtesy and concern, as if they are in a private home.

A full Italian menu includes a special soup and seafood entree each day. If you can't find what you like among the two dozen pasta choices, you are in deep trouble! There are *prix fixe* lunch and dinner (pre-theater) menus as well.

PAYARD PATISSERIE & BISTRO
1032 Lexington Ave (bet 73rd and 74th St)   212/717-5252
Lunch, Tea, Dinner: Mon-Sat   www.payard.com
Moderate

Francois Payard has created a winner! Everything about this place is appealing: the look of the bakery cases as you enter, the attractively presented appetizers and entrees, and informed service by a well-trained staff. Payard is a combination French bistro and pastry shop that works to perfection. When you pair experts like pastry chef Francois and executive chef Philippe Bertineau, you're going to get the very best. The bakery opens at 7 a.m., offering croissants, muffins, tea cakes, seasonal tarts, individual pastries, *gateaux*, petit fours, biscuits, handmade candies, and superb chocolates. Classic and seasonal ice creams and sherbets are offered. Prepared soups, salads, sandwiches, and other goodies are also available for takeout. But don't miss the opportunity to dine here, as Payard offers terrific appetizers, superb salads, homemade foie gras, seafood dishes, traditional *bouillabaisse*, steaks, and more.

> The setting is magnificent. The history of the room is awesome. **Gilt** (455 Madison Ave, 212/891-8100) got off to a rather rocky start. Located in the 19th century Villard Mansion, once the home of the legendary Le Cirque, diners expected something very special; they were disappointed. However, a different team has been brought in by chef Christopher Lee. They now serve dinner Tuesday through Saturday, with prices in the very expensive category. The signature dish is tuna Wellington, with a number of other equally tasty fish entrees. An extensive wine list (some pricey, some reasonable) is offered. *Bombolini* (filled doughnuts) is a good dessert choice. At last the food matches the setting!

PERSHING SQUARE
90 E 42nd St (at Park Ave)   212/286-9600
Breakfast, Lunch, Dinner: Daily; Brunch: Sat, Sun
Moderate   www.pershingsquare.com

In a space opposite Grand Central Station, Pershing Square serves throngs of hungry local and traveling New Yorkers. The odd-shaped room is full of energy and conversation, much of it relating to the broad variety of menu offerings. For those who missed breakfast before boarding their train, Pershing Square offers Irish oatmeal, eggs Benedict, vanilla-bean brioche French toast, and great buttermilk pancakes. Omelets are a specialty. Lunch and dinner items include seafood dishes, boneless beef short ribs, roast chicken, steaks, and pastas. The grilled hamburger with a selection of cheeses and crisp steak fries is a winner any time of day. Seafood dishes—like seared sea scallops with saffron orzo and tomato cream sauce, and pan-seared

Atlantic salmon—are popular for dinner. Try chocolate mousse cake for dessert. A friendly wait staff and an attractive bar are pluses.

PETER LUGER STEAK HOUSE
178 Broadway (at Driggs Ave), Brooklyn   718/387-7400
Lunch, Dinner: Daily   www.peterluger.com
Expensive

Peter Luger's reputation is sometimes larger than the restaurant itself! Folks don't go here for the ambience or service, but if it's steak you want, you simply can't do better. The menu makes it simple: your choices are steak for one, two, three, or four. The creamed spinach and steak sauce are out of this world. Tell your waiter to go easy on the whipped cream if you order dessert. Peter Luger is only a stone's throw from Manhattan (take the very first right off the Williamsburg Bridge), and the staff is accustomed to ordering cabs. Making reservations well in advance is suggested.

At almost any hour there is a crowd at **Bread** (20 Spring St, 212/334-1015). Some are eating in; some avoid the mobs by taking advantage of the free local delivery (from 10 a.m. to midnight and to 1 a.m. on Friday and Saturday). No wonder! The salads, pastas, hot plates, and sandwiches are big and delicious. Besides, the prices are right!

PICHOLINE
35 W 64th St (bet Broadway and Central Park West)   212/724-8585
Lunch: Tues-Sat; Dinner: Daily   www.picholinenyc.com
Moderately expensive to expensive

Terrance Brennan is a workhorse, and it shows in his attractive restaurant. The warm atmosphere is a perfect backdrop for the seasonal, Mediterranean-inspired plates. The many positives include outstanding service, perfectly done fish dishes, superbly prepared game, and daily classic cuisine specials. For lunch, a "sea" menu and an "earth" menu are offered. The wine room and small private party room are fabulous settings for a memorable evening. I always look forward to the magnificent cheese cart for dessert. Jackets are recommended for gentlemen.

PIETRO'S
232 E 43rd St (bet Second and Third Ave)   212/682-9760
Lunch: Mon-Fri; Dinner: Mon-Sat (closed Sat in summer)
Expensive   www.pietros.com

Pietro's is a steakhouse featuring Northern Italian cuisine. Everything is cooked to order. The menu includes great salads (they claim to make New York's best Caesar salad), steaks, chops, seafood, chicken, and an enormous selection of veal dishes. Tell your companions not to bother dressing up. Bring an appetite, however, because portions are huge. Although they're best known for steaks, you will also find abundant chicken and veal selections (marsala, cacciatore, scaloppine, piccata, *francaise,* etc.) and nine potato dishes. Prices border on expensive and the place is boisterous, but you'll certainly get your money's worth. By the way, Pietro's is very child-friendly.

PINOCCHIO
1748 First Ave (bet 90th and 91st St)   212/828-5810
Dinner: Tues-Sun
Moderate

Come here for serious Italian dining. Mark Petrillo presides over this
unpretentious 12-table etablishment on the Upper East Side, where wonderful home-style Italian food is served. There are numerous specials every
night, and I'd suggest letting the boss order for you. You'll always find great
pastas, like cheese-filled ravioli, tortellini Pinocchio (meat-filled tortellini
with cream, peas, and prosciutto), several spaghetti dishes, and fettuccine
alfredo.

Mexican Specialties
Ceviche: citrus-marinated raw fish
Chilis rellenos: mild to spicy chili peppers stuffed with cheese and fried
  in egg batter
Chorizo: spicy pork sausage
Empanadas: meat-filled pastries surrounded by a fat-laden crust
Enchiladas: soft corn tortillas filled with meat, beans, vegetables, or
  cheese and topped with salsa and cheese
Fajitas: marinated beef, shrimp, chicken, and/or vegetables served with
  warm tortillas for wrapping by the diner
Paella: an elaborate saffron-flavored rice casserole with a variety of
  seafood and meats
Tamales: chopped meat and vegetables encased in cornmeal dough

---

P.J. CLARKE'S
915 Third Ave (at 55th St)   212/317-1616

P.J. CLARKE'S ON THE HUDSON
4 World Financial Center (at Vesey St)   212/285-1500
Lunch, Dinner: Daily; Brunch: Sun

P.J. CLARKE'S AT LINCOLN CENTER
44 W 63rd St   212/957-9700
Lunch, Dinner: Daily; Brunch: Sat, Sun   www.pjclarkes.com
Moderate

P.J. Clarke's can rightfully be called a Manhattan institution. Every day at
lunch and dinner the regulars are joined by hordes of visitors guzzling at
the bar, eyeing the raw bar, or fighting for a table. No one is disappointed
with the sizable platters, great burgers, and fresh seafood. Service is highly
professional, and the price is right. Upstairs at the Third Avenue location,
you'll be taken with the decor at **The Sidecar**, which has its own kitchen
and entrance. All patrons at P.J. Clarke's on the Hudson have a stunning view
of New York Harbor and the Statue of Liberty. A seasonal cafe alongside the
marina is great for leisurely dining. The 63rd Street locale is a stellar venue
for munchies after a performance at Lincoln Center.

PÓ
31 Cornelia St (bet Bleecker and 4th St)   212/645-2189
Lunch: Wed-Sun; Dinner: Daily   www.porestaurant.com
Moderate

Steve Crane has found the formula for a successful eating establishment. The space is crowded, but tables are not on top of each other. The service is family-friendly, informed, and quick. The food is hearty, imaginative and exceptionally tasty. The prices are right. No wonder the place is always busy! As I have noted before, if the bread is good, chances are what follows will be also. Pó has hearty, crusty, fresh Italian bread. The pastas—tagliatelle, tortellini, linguine, and a special or two—are huge. The tasting menus offer great value, with a six-course meal going for just $50. Pastas and some heavier entrees (like grilled salmon) are available for lunch, along with inventive sandwiches like marinated portobello with roasted peppers. *Affogato*, an unusual and satisfying dessert, consists of coffee gelato in chilled cappuccino with chocolate and caramel sauces.

> Tribeca residents and visitors shouldn't miss a visit to **Bubby's** (120 Hudson St, 212/219-0666). First of all, the regular menu items are tasty and reasonably priced. The Sunday brunch is delicious and a real scene for the locals! Then there are the great pies: mile-high apple, sour cherry, key lime, and chocolate peanut butter. Homemade cakes, too! Delivery in the Tribeca area is free.

PORTERS NEW YORK
216 Seventh Ave (bet 22nd and 23rd St)   212/229-2878
Lunch: Mon-Fri; Dinner: Daily; Brunch: Sat, Sun
Moderate   www.portersnyc.com

No big name or trendy buzz at Porters, just good food in a clean and modest Chelsea location. It is very satisfying if you are looking for sensible, well-prepared food at affordable prices. At dinnertime, popular appetizers (such as filet mignon carpaccio), salads, shellfish stew, great burgers, and coconut-crusted salmon are available. They also offer a nice selection of steak and chicken dishes. Yukon mashed potatoes are a smash.

PORTOFINO GRILLE
1162 First Ave (bet 63rd and 64th St)   212/832-4141
Lunch: Mon-Fri; Dinner: Daily; Brunch: Sat, Sun
Moderate   www.portofinogrille.com

The decor at Portofino evokes the ambience of a small fishing village in Italy, with color and music designed to augment a very pleasant dining experience. The menu is complete, from soups and salads to pastas, chicken platters, fish, meat, and a number of side dishes. The julienne fried zucchini is excellent. The charm here is the rustic and pleasant atmosphere, friendly waiters, and a price structure that will accommodate family budgets. I found the various spaghetti dishes particularly appealing. The desserts are not memorable. Delivery service is offered from 59th to 72nd streets and Third Avenue to the river.

POST HOUSE
Lowell Hotel
28 E 63rd St   212/935-2888
Lunch: Mon-Fri; Dinner: Daily   www.theposthouse.com
Moderately expensive

This Manhattan steakhouse is an "in" social and political hangout that serves excellent food in comfortable surroundings. The guest list usually includes many well-known names and recognizable faces. They are attracted by the good food and warm ambience. Hors d'oeuvres like crabmeat cocktail, lobster cocktail, and stone crabs are available in season, but the major draws are steak and lobster. Prices for the latter are definitely not in the moderate category; ditto for lamb chops. However, the quality is excellent, and the cottage fries, fried zucchini, hash browns, and onion rings are superb. Save room for the chocolate box (white and dark chocolate mousse with raspberry sauce). If you can walk out under your own steam after all this, you're doing well!

At **Pure Food and Wine** (54 Irving Pl, 212/477-1010), the food is not quite raw—but nothing is cooked over 117 degrees, so as not to destroy the food's enzymes. You will find a tasty selection of soups, salads, lasagna, ravioli, pizzas, and other choices. There's a juice bar, and takeout is available. Reservations are suggested.

PRIMAVERA
1578 First Ave (at 82nd St)   212/861-8608
Dinner: Daily   www.primaveranyc.com
Expensive

Rave reviews on this one! Primavera is one of my favorite places, and it keeps getting better. Owner Nicola Civetta is the epitome of class, and his wife, Peggy, is equally charming. They know how to make you feel at home and present a superb Italian meal. Don't come if you're in a hurry, as Primavera is geared toward relaxed dining. I could wax eloquently with descriptions of the dishes, but you can't go wrong no matter what you order. All the veal dishes are spectacular. Let Nicola choose for you, as there are specials every day. To top it all off, they have one of the most beautiful desserts anywhere: a gorgeous platter of seasonal fruit that looks too good to eat. Primavera is always busy, so reservations are a must. A beautiful private party room is available.

PUMP ENERGY FOOD
40 W 55th St (bet Fifth Ave and Ave of the Americas)   212/246-6844
112 W 38th St (bet Broadway and Ave of the Americas) 212/764-2100
Crystal Pavilion, 805 Third Ave (at 50th St)   212/421-3055
113 E 31st St (bet Park and Lexington Ave)   212/213-5733
31 E 21st St (bet Park Ave and Broadway)   212/253-7676
Breakfast: Mon-Fri; Lunch, Dinner: Daily; Brunch: Sat, Sun
Moderate   www.thepumpenergyfood.com

No, these are not gourmet restaurants! But with so many readers into health and fitness, I thought I would mention these healthy retreats, which feature good, tasty, and nutritious food at reasonable prices. The dozens of super-charged dishes are appropriately given names like Hercules (grilled chicken roast and lentil soup) and Hard Core (grilled turkey breast with soy sauce). Also on the menu are salads and toasted sandwiches, healthy sweet treats (no butter, oil, sugar, or salt), soups, chili, and healthy sides like hummus, brown rice, steamed spinach, and baked falafel. Free delivery is offered.

QUALITY MEATS
57 W 58th St (bet Fifth Ave and Ave of the Americas)   212/371-7777
Lunch: Mon-Fri; Dinner: Daily   www.qualitymeatsnyc.com
Moderately expensive to expensive

On the site of the former Manhattan Ocean Club, Michael Stillman—son of Smith & Wollensky boss Alan Stillman—has opened a "somewhat" steakhouse that's become popular with younger meat lovers. With a butcher-shop look on several levels, outstanding chef Craig Koketsu in the kitchen, and a wait staff who really know what they are doing, Quality Meats has all of the basics soundly covered. They have lots of oyster selections, stone crab claws in season, ample salads, and tasty appetizers (like steak tartare and smoked corn chowder). Entrees include a number of steaks (the filet is fantastic), roasted pork, rack of lamb, and fish. Don't pass up the pan-roasted crispy potatoes, gnocchi and cheese, sautéed spinach, and grilled asparagus. For dessert, the homemade ice creams are a treat (try the "coffee and doughnuts"). As if all of this weren't enough, the pie and tart selection is outstanding. (P.S. Check out the restrooms!)

Cigarette smokers will be pleased to learn about **Circa Tabac** (32 Watts St, 212/941-1781). This place is one of the few locations where you can still smoke, drink, and eat in Manhattan. Cocktails, appetizers, and desserts are available. Nonsmokers in your party will be pleased that this retreat features a state-of-the-art air filtration system.

RAO'S
455 E 114th St (at First Ave)   212/722-6709
Dinner: Mon-Fri   www.raos.com
No credit cards
Inexpensive

Don't be put off by rumors, such as a two-month wait for reservations. If you want to go to Rao's—an intimate, old-time (1896) Italian restaurant—you should plan a bit in advance, however. The place is crowded all the time for two reasons: the food is great, and prices are ridiculously low. Don't walk or take a car; hail a taxi and get out in front of the restaurant, which is in Spanish Harlem. When you're ready to leave, they'll call a taxi. Frankie Pellegrino is a gregarious and charming host who makes guests feel right at home and will even sit at your table while you order. Be prepared for leisurely dining. While you're waiting, enjoy the excellent bread and warm atmosphere. Believe it or not, the Southern fried chicken (Rao's style) is absolutely superb and would be my number-one choice. (Hint: Try appearing unannounced at the door or call the same day, as tables are often available on the spur of the moment.)

RAOUL'S
180 Prince St (bet Sullivan and Thompson St)   212/966-3518
Dinner: Daily   www.raoulsrestaurant.com
Moderate

Old World touches here! There are dozens of good places to eat in Soho, and Raoul's is one of the best. This long, narrow restaurant used to be an old saloon. There are paper tablecloths and funky walls covered with a mish-mash of posters, pictures, and calendars of every description. The bistro atmosphere is neighborly, friendly, and intimate; the prices are moderate; and the service is attentive. The trendy clientele runs the gamut from jeans to fur coats. The house favorites are steak *au poivre* and paté *maison*. Raoul's is a natural for those whose days begin when the rest of us are ready to hit the sack.

There are things both old and new at **Provence** (38 MacDougal St, 212/475-7500). New management has retained the style of cooking and rustic atmosphere of the south of France. However, there is a new look to the menu, with an emphasis on seafood. Lunch and dinner are served daily, prices are moderate, and the food is tasty.

RARE BAR & GRILL
Shelburne Murray Hill   212/481-1999
303 Lexington Ave (at 37th St)   www.rarebarandgrill.com
Breakfast, Lunch, Dinner: Daily; Brunch: Sat, Sun
Moderate

If noise is your thing, you will be right at home at Rare. Inhabited by tables filled with yuppies and button-down business types, this restaurant literally vibrates with energy. The food is almost secondary to the scene, but the burgers are fabulous. You can get a classic burger or order one of their more exotic types: Mexican, foie gras, Kobe beef, barbecued pork, turkey scallion, crab, shrimp, and vegetable. They also serve a French fry tasting basket (cottage, shoestring, and sweet potato fries with three dipping sauces), salads, soups, fried Oreos, and a huge banana split.

(THE FAMOUS) RAY'S PIZZA OF GREENWICH VILLAGE
465 Ave of the Americas (at 11th St)   212/243-2253
Sun-Thurs: 11 a.m.-2 a.m.; Fri, Sat: 11 a.m.-3 a.m.
Inexpensive

In Manhattan, the name "Ray" is synonymous with pizza! Ray's is so popular that guests have had pizzas shipped to Midwestern relatives. No pizzeria in the Big Apple is better than this one, supposedly featuring the *real* Ray. The pizza is gourmet at its best, and you can create your own from the many toppings offered. You can have a fresh slice, whole pizza, or Sicilian square. You won't leave hungry, as pizzas are a generous 18 inches. Take-and-bake personal pizzas—ten-inch pies that are all natural and handmade—cook in your oven in just 12 minutes. Free delivery is available.

REDEYE GRILL
890 Seventh Ave (at 56th St)   212/541-9000
Lunch: Mon-Sat; Dinner: Daily; Brunch: Sun   www.redeyegrill.com
Moderately expensive

From the day it opened, the Redeye Grill has been a busy place! Owner Sheldon Fireman knows how to appeal to the eye, taking a cue from his successful Trattoria dell'Arte. Specialties include all shapes and sizes of shrimp (this is "the home of the dancing shrimp bar"), a huge seafood appetizer platter (at a huge price), grilled fish, and pastas. There's more: burgers, egg dishes, and sushi. The personnel are hip and helpful, but the scene is the major attraction. There is DJ music in the evenings and live jazz during Sunday brunch.

REMI
145 W 53rd St (bet Ave of the Americas and Seventh Ave)
Lunch, Dinner: Daily   212/581-4242
Moderate

Come here for the best seafood risotto in town! Remi operates in a spectacular space in midtown, handy to hotels and theaters. In an unsually long room dominated by a dramatic 120-foot Venetian wall painting by Paulin Paris, the food soars as high as the setting. In warm weather, the doors open up and diners can enjoy sitting at tables in the adjoining atrium. Waiters, chairs, and wall fabrics all match in attractive stripes. Antipasto like roasted quail wrapped in bacon (available seasonally) will get you off to a delicious start. Main dishes are not of the usual variety. The spaghetti, linguine, and ravioli (stuffed with such items as shrimp, ricotta, and vegetables) can match any house in Venice. Of course, there are fish and meat dishes for more mainstream appetites. The chocolate-raspberry mousse cake is superb. Paddle on down (Remi means "oars") for a first-class experience! Takeout and delivery are available.

You can satisfy your eyes and ears, as well as your tummy, at several eateries that provide both food and entertainment:
Spotlight Live (1604 Broadway, 212/262-1111): karaoke
Zipper Factory Theater and Tavern (336 W 37th St, 212/695-4600): musicals, comedy, burlesque

---

RENÉ PUJOL
321 W 51st St (bet Eighth and Ninth Ave)   212/246-3023
Lunch, Dinner: Tues-Sun   www.renepujol.com
Moderate

First, order a chocolate soufflé for dessert! René Pujol is a very attractive French restaurant that makes an ideal spot for a pre-theater dinner or private party. It's always busy, and a large number of customers are regulars (which always speaks well of a restaurant). One reason for René Pujol's success is that it's a family enterprise. The owners—the daughter and son-in-law of the retired René Pujol—are on the job, and the waiters are superb. Housed in an old brownstone, the restaurant has two warmly decorated, cozy, and comfortable dining rooms, complete with a working fireplace. There are attractive private party rooms upstairs, too. The menu is vintage French, with filet mignon, grilled Atlantic salmon, and tasty tarts being the specialties of the house. An award-winning wine list, too!

RISTORANTE GRIFONE
244 E 46th St (bet Second and Third Ave)   212/490-7275
Lunch: Mon-Fri; Dinner: Mon-Sat   www.grifonenyc.com
Moderate to moderately expensive

New Yorkers get so hyped up about trendy new places that they tend to forget about old-timers that quietly continue to do a good job. Grifone is one of those. If you are looking for an attractive, comfortable, and cozy place to dine—one with impeccable service and great food—then try Grifone. The menu is Northern Italian, and the many daily specials include a good selection of pasta, chicken, veal, fish, and beef dishes. A takeout menu is available as well. Quality never goes out of style; just ask the neighborhood regulars who flock here year after year.

RIVER CAFE
1 Water St (Brooklyn Bridge), Brooklyn   718/522-5200
Lunch: Mon-Sat; Dinner: Daily; Brunch: Sun   www.rivercafe.com
Moderately expensive

The River Cafe isn't in Manhattan, but it *overlooks* Manhattan, and that's the main reason to come. The view from the window tables is fantastic, awesome, romantic—you name it. There's no other skyline like it in the world. And so the River Cafe—just across the East River in the shadow of the Brooklyn Bridge—remains an extremely popular and sophisticated place. Call at least a week in advance to make reservations, and be sure to ask for a window table. This is a flag-waving special-occasion restaurant that's proud of its American cuisine. The seafood, lamb, and steak entrees are particularly good, and desserts are rich and fresh. The "Brooklyn Bridge" dessert, done in dark chocolate, is unforgettable.

ROLF'S
281 Third Ave (at 22nd St)   212/477-4750
Lunch, Dinner: Daily
Moderate

In a city with few good German restaurants, Rolf's is worth remembering. It's a colorful destination where several dozen tables and wooden benches perfectly complement the eclectic decor. Faux Tiffany lampshades, old pictures, tiny lights, strings of beads, and what-have-you add up to a charming and comfortable setting for tasty German dishes. The schnitzels, goulash, sauerbraten, boiled beef, veal shanks, and bratwurst are served in ample portions with delicious potato pancakes and sauerkraut. German, apple, and potato pancakes come with applesauce on the side. For dessert, save room for homemade apple strudel or Black Forest cake.

ROSA MEXICANO
1063 First Ave (at 58th St)   212/753-7407
61 Columbus Ave (at 62nd St)   212/977-7700
9 E 18th St (bet Fifth Ave and Broadway)   212/533-3350
Lunch: Mon-Fri; Dinner: Daily; Brunch: Sat, Sun
Moderate to moderately expensive   www.rosamexicano.com

This is, quite simply, classic Mexican cuisine. Start with the guacamole *en molcajete*; prepared fresh at the table, it is the best in town. There are also great appetizers, like small tortillas filled with sauteed shredded pork, small shrimp marinated in mustard and chili vinaigrette, and raviolis filled with sauteed chicken, tomato, and onion. Main-course entrees include huge, tasty crepes filled with shrimp and a multi-layered tortilla pie. Grilled specialties like beef short ribs and skewered marinated shrimp are tempting. Even the desserts are first-class. Choose from a traditional flan, Mexican spongecake, or mango with ice cream. The atmosphere at these three locations is friendly, the energy level high, and the dining top-drawer.

A quick snack or meal at any time of day is a routine for many of us. New York eating establishments have come to recognize this trend. You can now find excellent comfort-food stops all over Manhattan:

- **Danny Meyer's Shake Shack** (Madison Square Park, 23rd St bet Madison Ave and Broadway), is a popular seasonal place, with long lines in nice weather. And no wonder! Wonderful burgers, hot dogs, frozen custards, shakes, floats, and more are served.
- **Westville** (210 W 10th St and 173 Ave A) is a tiny stop with big flavors, serving salads, soups, burgers, hot dogs, sandwiches, complete platters, and yummy desserts. Brunch is served on weekends and holidays, with the usual bagel, egg, and breakfast dishes.
- Fast counter service is offered at **New York Burger Co.** (303 Park Ave and 678 Ave of the Americas). Choices include excellent burgers and fries, fresh salads, smoothies, and other good choices. The crowds are a good indication that this is a tasty spot!
- **Mary's Dairy** (171 W 4th St and 158 First Ave) is perfect for delicious homemade ice cream, sorbets, fancy dessert dishes, and more.
- For European street food, try **F&B Güdtfood** (269 W 23rd St and 150 E 52nd St). You'll find soups and salads, vegetable dogs and *haute* dogs (a specialty), sweets, and more.

ROUND TABLE
Algonquin Hotel   212/840-6800
59 W 44th St (bet Fifth Ave and Ave of the Americas), lobby level
Breakfast: Daily; Lunch: Sun-Fri; Dinner: Daily; Brunch: Sat
Moderate to moderately expensive   www.algonquinhotel.com

The dishes here have seen a lot of history! At the Algonquin's famous Round Table, all manner of famous personalities in the arts, business, and politics would meet to exchange stories and repartee. And it is still alive and kicking! You can even reserve the famous table if your party numbers seven or more. The Round Table reeks of days past, but the food is very good and the servers will shower you with loving care. Don't expect anything fancy; just relax in the manner of the good old days (if that is what they really were!).

ROY'S NEW YORK
New York Marriott Financial Center Hotel
130 Washington St (bet Carlisle and Albany St)   212/266-6262
Breakfast: Daily; Lunch: Mon-Fri; Dinner: Mon-Sat; Brunch: Sat, Sun
Moderate to moderately expensive   www.roysrestaurant.com

I have never seen operations run as efficiently as Roy's. This large one in Manhattan's Financial District brings to 31 the number Roy Yamaguchi oversees all around the globe. The menu blends ideas from Europe (where Roy was trained) with popular ingredients from Asia and the Pacific. The changing menu includes wonderful coconut shrimp on a stick, grilled Szechuan baby back pork ribs, and Macadamia nut-crusted mahi-mahi with lobster butter sauce. Top it off with hot chocolate soufflé or cherry *crostada*. Seats at the counter overlooking the kitchen will provide an extra dimension to your meal.

If you are looking for adventure on a far East Village street that once was a drug haven, you might explore Avenue C. While Avenues A and B are still rather tough, Avenue C has a bewildering mix of Australian, Brazilian, Latin, Middle Eastern, and Vietnamese joints along with some others that are a bit more conventional, including **Bao III** (111 Avenue C, 212/254-7773). P.S. For heaven's sake, don't dress up for a visit to this neighborhood.

RUBY FOO'S

2182 Broadway (at 77th St)	212/724-6700
1626 Broadway (at 49th St)	212/489-5600
Lunch, Dinner: Daily	www.brguestrestaurants.com
Moderate	

What a scene this is! The three-level Ruby Foo's on the Upper West Side seats about 500 people and is packed. You'd better call for reservations or be prepared to spend an eternity at the bar. The same is true at the Times Square location. Ruby Foo's is billed as a dim sum and sushi palace, with the best dishes being in the latter category. However, if you and your tablemates share glazed baby back ribs with Asian pear napa slaw, you will go home happy. There is a large selection of maki rolls: spicy tuna, fresh crabmeat, tempura shrimp, California crab, and many more. The seven different sushi platters are well-selected and great for a party. Hand rolls, soups, salads, and rice dishes are also featured. The crowd is hip, the noise level high, the food very good, and the value outstanding.

RUE 57

60 W 57th St (at Ave of the Americas)	212/307-5656
Lunch: Mon-Fri; Dinner: Daily; Brunch: Sat, Sun	www.rue57.com
Moderate (lunch) to moderately expensive (dinner)	

With an extremely convenient location, friendly service, and pleasant atmosphere, this Parisian-style brasserie is one busy place. The menu encompasses soups and salads, oysters and clams, steaks, varied other entrees (like salmon, chicken, risotto, and ravioli), and daily specials. The young ones will enjoy the great burgers. Lovers of Japanese cuisine will find sushi, sashimi, maki, and temaki. Don't pass up the beefsteak tomato salad with onions and Roquefort!

SAN PIETRO

18 E 54th St (bet Fifth and Madison Ave)	212/753-9015
Lunch, Dinner: Mon-Sat	www.sanpietro.net
Moderately expensive	

The Bruno brothers have brought the joys of Southern Italy to their upscale restaurant, which is popular with society mavens and the well-to-do. Fresh fruit and veggies are legendary, as is linguine with anchovy juice. Spaghetti dishes and *scialatelli* are special, too. Fish, veal, and chicken dishes are very well crafted. On the downside, waiters can be offhand and even snooty if they think you're not a big tipper, and desserts leave a lot to be desired. However, if you want to enjoy tasty Italian dishes while seeing how the other half lives, San Pietro might be the ticket!

SARABETH'S KITCHEN
423 Amsterdam Ave (at 80th St)   212/496-6280
1295 Madison Ave (at 92nd St)   212/410-7335
Breakfast, Lunch, Dinner: Daily
40 Central Park S (bet Fifth Ave and Ave of the Americas)
Breakfast, Lunch, Dinner: Daily; Brunch: Sat, Sun   212/826-5959
Moderate

SARABETH'S AT THE WHITNEY
Whitney Museum of American Art
945 Madison Ave (bet 74th and 75th St)   212/570-3670
Lunch: Tues-Fri; Brunch: Sat, Sun   www.sarabeth.com
Moderate

I am reminded of the better English tearooms when visiting one of Sarabeth's locations. Swinging it is not. Reliable it is. The big draw is the homemade quality of the dishes, including the baked items and excellent desserts. They also make gourmet preserves and sell them nationally. Menu choices include excellent omelets, porridge, and fresh fruit for breakfast; a fine assortment of light items for lunch; and fish, game, or meat dishes for dinner. The chocolate mousse cake, chocolate soufflé, warm berry bread pudding, and homemade ice cream are splendid desserts. Service is rapid and courteous. Look in on Sarabeth's bakery and cafe at the Chelsea Market (75 Ninth Ave, 212/989-2424), too.

SAVORE
200 Spring St (at Sullivan St)   212/431-1212
Lunch, Dinner: Daily; Brunch: Sat, Sun   www.savoreny.com
Moderate

Soho has no shortage of restaurants, some of them with a snooty attitude that's in keeping with the area. Savore has none of this. You come here for good, fresh food served in a casual and friendly atmosphere. It is a particularly attractive destination in nice weather when tables are placed outside. The menu offers a large selection of pastas, like hand-cut spaghetti with basil and roasted tomato. In true Tuscan fashion, salads are served after the main course. I am partial to their crème brûlée, which features a wonderful coffee flavor.

SCALINI FEDELI
165 Duane St (bet Greenwich and Hudson St)   212/528-0400
Lunch: Tues-Fri; Dinner: Mon-Sat   www.scalinifedeli.com
Expensive

This very upscale Italian restaurant is for those who want a truly classy and classic meal. The offerings are exotic: seared foie gras and roasted apples, soft egg-yolk ravioli with ricotta and spinach . . . and that's just to start! Then it's on to delicious braised short ribs of beef, breast of Muscovy duck, and wonderful tuna. Desserts are equally fabulous, like a flourless chocolate cake (cooked to order) with a trio of gelati or a warm caramelized apple tart in a baked fillo crust. Luncheons are a bit lighter. *Prix fixe* dinner menus are the order of the day. As you look around this sedate establishment, note the relative youth of some of the gourmet diners. A private room in the wine cellar is available for parties.

Restaurant Tipping Guide	
Coat check	$1 per item
Maitre d'	$10 to $100 (depending on the occasion, restaurant, and level of service you wish to receive; given prior to seating)
Wait staff	15% to 20% of the bill before taxes; 25% is appropriate for truly outstanding service
Sommelier	15% of the wine bill
Restroom attendant	50¢ to $1 for handing you a towel or if you use any products or cosmetics

SCHILLER'S

131 Rivington St (at Norfolk St)   212/260-4555
Lunch: Mon-Fri; Dinner: Daily (open late); Brunch: Sat, Sun
Moderate   www.schillersny.com

There is no place quite like Schiller's in Manhattan. Leave your pinstripes at home and bring the gang downtown. Keith McNally has created an unusual, fun, and deservedly popular munching and drinking spot in an area not renowned for exciting places. Schiller's Liquor Bar (that's the full name) joins a group of busy brasseries run by McNally, including his very "in" Balthazar. The atmosphere is rather Parisian and the service informal, with much emphasis on the wine selection. Cheap, decent, and good vintages are offered and priced accordingly. They serve good Bibb lettuce salads, excellent burgers, Welsh rarebit, modestly priced steaks, rotisserie chicken, and daily specials. For those who lament the lack of good German food in Manhattan, call Schiller's to see what specials are on the menu. Sticky toffee pudding and chocolate cream pie are two of the better desserts. Takeout and delivery are also offered.

THE SEA GRILL

19 W 49th St (bet Fifth Ave and Ave of the Americas)   212/332-7610
Lunch: Mon-Fri; Dinner: Mon-Sat   www.theseagrillnyc.com
Moderately expensive

You'll pay for the setting as well as the food at this Rockefeller Center seafood house, which overlooks the ice-skating rink in winter and features open-air dining in nice weather. Take advantage of the seafood bar (clams, oysters, shrimp, mussels, crab, and lobster) to start. Well-prepared but somewhat pricey main courses include tasty crab cakes, salmon, and Nantucket bay scallops. I love the desserts! Offerings might include such delights as warm chocolate steamed pudding, warm apple tart, key lime pie, and "Palette of Sorbets." Rockefeller Center has been spruced up, and the Sea Grill is one of its gems. Now if they could just lighten up on the prices!

SERENDIPITY 3
225 E 60th St (bet Second and Third Ave)   212/838-3531
Daily: 11:30 a.m.-midnight (Fri till 1 a.m., Sat till 2 a.m.)
Moderate   www.serendipity3.com

How does a "Golden Opulence Sundae" sound? It costs $1,000 and must be ordered a week in advance, but it actually contains edible gold leaf! The young and young-at-heart rate Serenpidity 3 *numero uno* on their list of "in" places, as it has been for a half century. In an atmosphere of nostalgia set in a quaint, two-floor brownstone, this full-service restaurant offers a complete selection of delicious entrees, sandwiches, soups, salads, and pastas. The real treats are the fabulous desserts, including favorites like hot fudge sundaes and frozen hot chocolate (which can also be purchased in mix form to take home). An added pleasure is the opportunity to browse a shop loaded with trendy gifts, books, clothing, and accessories. If you are planning a special gathering for the teens in your clan, make Serendipity 3 the destination!

A number of Manhattan restaurants have superior wine lists, including:

A Voce (41 Madison Ave, 212/545-8555)
Babbo (110 Waverly Pl, 212/777-0303)
Balthazar (80 Spring St, 212/965-1414)
Compass (208 W 70th St, 212/875-8600)
Daniel (60 E 65th St, 212/288-0033)
Le Périgord (405 E 52nd St, 212/755-6244)
Primavera (1578 First Ave, 212/861-8608)
Union Square Cafe (21 E 16th St, 212/243-4020)
Veritas (43 E 20th St, 212/353-3700)

SETTE MEZZO
969 Lexington Ave (at 70th St)   212/472-0400
Lunch, Dinner: Daily
Cash only
Moderate

Sette Mezzo is small, professional, and busy, and it makes a great place for people-watching! There are no affectations in decor, service, or food preparation. This is strictly a business operation, with the emphasis on serving good food at reasonable prices. Don't worry about dressing up, as most diners come casually attired to enjoy a variety of Italian dishes done to perfection. In the evening, all of the grilled items are excellent. Fresh seafood is a specialty. Ask about the special pasta dishes; some of the combinations are marvelous. For more traditional Italian plates, try veal chops, veal cutlets, stuffed baked chicken, or fried calamari and shrimp. All desserts are made in-house. They include several caloric cakes, tasty lemon tarts, sherbet, and ice cream.

✦ SFOGLIA

1402 Lexington Ave (at 92nd St)   212/831-1402
Breakfast, Lunch, Dinner: Mon-Sat   www.sfogliarestaurant.com
Moderate

Rustic Italian at its best! Most folks would probably never notice this unassuming little trattoria on the Upper East Side, but believe me when I say you don't want to miss it! Of course, I was delighted right from the start, when delicious warm bread arrived. I could make a whole meal of this homemade, crusty treat. The place is rather bare bones, with several large tables where you might be seated with folks unknown. No problem! The food is so good you will quickly become best friends with the strangers at your elbows as you exchange bites. Proprietors Ron and Colleen Marnell-Suhanosky and their staff couldn't be friendlier. The menu changes every few weeks, but you will always find something good: fish, *papperdella*, meat, ravioli, chicken, *orata*, etc. You'll feel healthier just gazing upon the bowls of fruit or vegetables on the tables. Don't miss the cheese platter.

SHUN LEE CAFE

Lunch: Sat, Sun; Dinner: Daily

SHUN LEE WEST

Lunch: Mon-Fri; Dinner: Daily; Brunch: Sat, Sun
43 W 65th St (bet Columbus Ave and Central Park West)
Moderate   212/769-3888, 212/595-8895
                                         www.shunleewest.com

Dim sum and street-food combinations are served in an informal setting at Shun Lee Cafe. It's a fun place where you can try some unusual and delicious Chinese dishes. A waiter comes to your table with a rolling cart and describes the various goodies. The offerings vary, but don't miss stuffed crab claws if they are available. Go on to the street-food items: delicious roast pork, barbecued spare ribs, a large selection of noodle and rice dishes and soups, and a menu full of mild and spicy entrees. Sauteed prawns with ginger and boneless duckling with walnut sauce are great choices. A vegetarian dish of shredded Chinese vegetables is cooked with rice noodles and served with a pancake (like moo shu pork, but without the meat). For heartier appetites, Shun Lee West—the excellent old Chinese restaurant that adjoins Shun Lee Cafe—is equally good. Some of the best Chinese food in Manhattan is served here. If you come with a crowd, family-style dining is available. Prices are a bit higher at the restaurant than in the cafe.

SHUN LEE PALACE

155 E 55th St (bet Lexington and Third Ave)   212/371-8844
Lunch, Dinner: Daily   www.shunleepalace.com
Moderate to moderately expensive

There are all manner of Chinese restaurants in Manhattan: The colorful Chinatown variety. The mom-and-pop corner operations. The overly Americanized establishments. The grand Chinese dining rooms. Shun Lee Palace belongs in the latter category, possessing a very classy and refined look. You are offered a delicious journey into the best of this historic cuisine. You can dine rather reasonably at lunch; a three-course *prix fixe* experience is available. Ordering from the menu (or through your captain) can be a bit pricier, but the platters are worth it. Specialties include beggar's chicken (24 hours advance notice required), curried prawns, and Beijing duck. There's much more, including casserole specials and spa cuisine. Yes, this is just about the nearest thing Manhattan has to a real Chinese palace.

SISTINA
1555 Second Ave (at 80th St)   212/861-7660
Lunch: Mon-Sat; Dinner: Daily
Moderate

The philosophy of this family operation is that the joy is in the eating, not the surroundings, and for that they get top marks. Because the atmosphere is pretty plain, one comes to Sistina for the food, and it can't be beat for classy Italian cooking. The specialty of the house is seafood; the Mediterranean red snapper and salmon are excellent dishes. There are also the usual choices of pasta, veal, and chicken, as well as daily specials.

SMITH & WOLLENSKY
797 Third Ave (at 49th St)   212/753-1530
Lunch, Dinner: Daily   www.smithandwollensky.com
Moderate to moderately expensive

When visitors to the Big Apple want a taste of what this great city is all about, there is no better spot than Smith & Wollensky. There is an abundance of space (two floors) and talented, helpful personnel. I always grade a place on the quality of their bread, and Smith & Wollensky's is excellent. There is no better lobster cocktail anywhere in the city. Featured entrees include wonderful steaks (USDA prime, dry-aged and hand-butchered), prime rib, and lamb chops. Every man in the family will love the place, and the ladies will appreciate the special attention paid to them. Come here when you and your guests are really hungry.

For those who like really intimate dining, try **Table d'Hote** (44 E 92nd St, 212/348-8125). The place is so tiny and the mix-and-match tables and chairs so tightly squeezed together that you'll find it difficult to leave after a full meal! By the way, this French bistro's food isn't bad.

SPARKS STEAKHOUSE
210 E 46th St (bet Second and Third Ave)   212/687-4855
Lunch: Mon-Fri; Dinner: Mon-Sat   www.sparkssteakhouse.com
Moderately expensive

You come here to eat, period. This is a well-seasoned and popular beef restaurant with little ambience. For years, businessmen have made an evening at Sparks a must, and the house has not let time erode its reputation. You can choose from veal and lamb chops, beef scaloppine, and medallions of beef. There are a half-dozen steak items, like steak *fromage* (with Roquefort), prime sirloin, sliced steak with sauteed onions and peppers, and top-of-the-line filet mignon. Seafood dishes are another specialty. Rainbow trout, filet of tuna, and halibut steak are as good as you'll find in most seafood houses. The lobsters are enormous, delicious, and expensive. Skip the appetizers and desserts, and concentrate on the main dish. Private party rooms are available.

SPICE MARKET

403 W 13th St (at Ninth Ave)   212/675-2322
Lunch, Dinner: Daily   www.jean-georges.com
Moderate

For atmosphere and mostly tasty Asian street food, this is one of the city's hot dining spots. Located in the trendy Meatpacking District, Spice Market is a charming space with tables surrounding an open area that leads to an inviting downstairs bar. The decor is tasteful, while the food is different and exciting. The Vietnamese spring rolls are yummy, the salads unusual and tasty, and the chicken skewer with peanut sauce outstanding. Other wonderful dishes: striped bass or cod with Malaysian chili sauce; onion-and-chili-crusted short ribs that melt in your mouth; and a large selection of vegetables, noodles, and rice. Desserts are even better. Thai jewels and fruits with fresh coconut snow—one of the most famous street desserts in Thailand—is a must. Other sweet selections: Ovaltine *kulfi* and a really fabulous chocolate and Vietnamese coffee tart served with ice cream.

Dining in Harlem is now quite fashionable for New York visitors. Here are some favorites:

Amy Ruth's (113 W 116th St, 212/280-8779): good breakfasts

Copeland's (549 W 145th St, 212/234-2357): Try the Sunday gospel brunch.

Londel's Supper Club (2620 Frederick Douglass Blvd, 212/234-6114): jazz entertainment on weekends

Miss Maude's Spoonbread Too (547 Lenox Ave, 212/690-3100): pork chops and spoonbread, of course

Native (161 Lenox Ave, 212/665-2525): French-Caribbean

Rao's (455 E 114th St, 212/722-6709): famous Italian landmark

Revival (2367 Frederick Douglass Blvd, 212/222-8338): soul food

Settepani (196 Lenox Ave, 917/492-4806): deli and bakery specialties

Sylvia's (328 Lenox Ave, 212/996-0660): now larger, with soul food and entertainment

Yvonne (301 W 135th St, 212/862-1223): Southern specialties

SPIGOLO

1561 Second Ave (at 81st St)   212/744-1100
Dinner: Daily
Moderately expensive

Some Upper East Siders swear by this Italian house, perhaps because it is tiny and reservations are not easy to come by. I really don't know what all the raves are about. I found Spigolo to be good but not great. Seafood dishes at the start are quite flavorful, including clams, oysters, and salmon tartare. Braised lamb shank makes for a hearty and satisfying main dish, as does breast of veal served with delicious butternut squash puree. If a somewhat out-of-the-way location appeals to you and you don't mind waiting days for a reservation, then go right ahead. Otherwise, I could name and have written about numerous Italian eateries that do just as well—and many of them much better—for a far more reasonable price.

SPRING STREET NATURAL RESTAURANT

62 Spring St (at Lafayette St)   212/966-0290
Daily: 9 a.m.-11:30 p.m.; Fri, Sat until 12:30 a.m.; Brunch: Sat, Sun
Moderate   www.springstreetnatural.com

Before eating "naturally" became a big thing, Spring Street Natural Restaurant was a leader in the field. That tradition continues after 30 years. In attractive surroundings, the kitchen provides meals prepared with fresh, unprocessed foods, and most everything is cooked to order. Neighborhood residents are regular customers, so you know the food is top-quality. Specials are offered every day, with a wide variety of organic salads, pastas, vegetarian meals, free-range poultry, and fresh fish and seafood. Try wonderful roasted salmon with creamy risotto and baby asparagus stalks. Spring Street also believes in great desserts, like chocolate walnut pie, honey raspberry blueberry pie, and honey pear pie. The last two are made without sugar and dairy products.

STRIP HOUSE

13 E 12th St (bet Fifth Ave and University Pl)   212/328-0000
Dinner: Daily   www.theglaziergroup.com
Moderately expensive

The Strip House is a classy steakhouse with a sexy red ambience. If anything separates it from others in this macho business, it is the attitude of the personnel. Everyone is friendly, helpful, and informed. Besides, the food is quite good. On the broiled side, there are New York strips, filet mignon, rib chops, Colorado lamb rack, and lobster. And there is seafood, chicken, and linguine. There are many daily specials, and a side of crisp goose-fat potatoes is tasty. I even liked the black truffle creamed spinach! The toughest part of dining here is choosing between chocolate profiteroles and chocolate fondue for dessert.

TABLA

11 Madison Ave (at 25th St)   212/889-0667
Dining Room (upstairs)   www.tablany.com
Lunch: Mon-Fri; Dinner: Daily

Bread Bar (downstairs)
Lunch: Mon-Sat: Dinner: Daily
Moderate (downstairs) to expensive (upstairs)

Another of Danny Meyer's unique restaurants! Upstairs you will find American food with Indian spices. Dinner is *prix fixe* only, while lunch is both a la carte and *prix fixe*. Downstairs features homestyle Indian cooking with an a la carte menu. For those who like a taste of India without going overboard, I assure you that this is a first-class operation in every way.

TAO

42 E 58th St (bet Madison and Park Ave)   212/888-2288
Lunch: Mon-Fri; Dinner: Daily   www.taorestaurant.com
Moderate

You'll love this place! Tao is billed as an Asian bistro, but it is much more than that. In a huge space that once served as a theater, a dramatic dining setting has been created with a huge Buddha looking down as you enjoy wonderful food at reasonable prices. Hordes of diners can be accommodated on two levels; a sushi bar and several regular bars are also available. Reservations are strongly recommended, as thirty-somethings make Tao their headquarters. A number of small plates are available to start, including Thai stuffed shrimp and squab lettuce wraps. Save room for a delicious Kobe beef steak or filet mignon cooked at your table in a hot pot, or a marvelous wok-seared New York sirloin with shiitake mushrooms that melts in your mouth. A $24 *prix fixe* lunch is offered daily. For dessert, try the molten chocolate cake with coconut ice cream.

What is Momofuku? It translates into "lucky peach," but in the dining arena it is the domain of chef David Chang. His original location, **Momofuku Noodle Bar** (163 First Ave, 212/475-7899), is open daily for lunch (noon to 4) and dinner (5:30 to 11 or 12). You'll find noodles, small dishes, and a large variety of small plates, with items changing by the season, plus heritage pork and shellfish offerings. Chang's other operation, **Momofuku Ssäm Bar** (207 Second Ave, 212/254-3500), is open daily for lunch (11 to 6) and dinner (6 p.m. to 2 a.m.). This place first offers a choice of *ssäm* (like a Korean wrap) or bowl, and then a protein (pork, chicken, beef, or tofu), followed by extras like beans or roasted onions. You won't go away hungry. Best description: earthy, Asian-accented meathead cuisine—whatever that means!

TARTINE
253 W 11th St (at 4th St)   212/229-2611
Lunch: Mon-Fri; Dinner: Daily; Brunch: Sat, Sun
Cash only
Moderate

Read carefully! Tartine will be your kind of place if you don't mind: (1) waiting outside in the rain, cold, or heat, (2) bringing your own drinks, (3) paying cash, and (4) having your used fork laid back down in front of you for the next course. All of this, of course, is secondary to the fact that this tiny place (about 30 chairs) serves some of the tastiest dishes in the Village. There are soups, salads, quiches, and omelets, plus chicken, meat, and fish entrees at pleasing prices. French fries are a treat. Desserts and pastries are baked on-premises. For about half the price of what you would pay uptown, you can finish your meal with splendid custard-filled tarts, a fabulous hazelnut-covered chocolate ganache, strawberry shortcake, or thinly sliced warm apples with cinnamon on puff pastry with ice cream. There is always a wait at dinner—a good sign, since neighborhood folks know what's best! If you want wine, you are encouraged to bring your own.

TASTE
1413 Third Ave (at 80th St)   *above zabars*   212/717-9798
Dinner: Daily   www.elismanhattan.com/taste
Moderate (Taste Cafe) to moderately expensive (Taste)

When it comes to quality food (with prices to match), there is no equal in Manhattan to Eli Zabar. Taste has all the pluses and minuses you've come to expect from this gentleman. Dinners change nightly and feature such winners as sauteed duck livers, roasted artichoke hearts, wild Pacific salmon, pork chops, and quail. A wine bar serves good wines that aren't *too* expensive by the glass. With Zabar's market just below, it looks like Taste is getting really fresh food. And the breads, as you would expect, are superb. The more informal, self-service **Taste Cafe** serves breakfast, lunch, and a weekend brunch.

New York's Top Chefs

Anthony, Michael: Gramercy Tavern

Batali, Mario: Babbo, Casa Mono, Del Posto, Esca, Lupa, Otto

Benno, Jonathan: per se

Bouley, David: Bouley, Bouley Bakery, Bouley Market, Danube, Upstairs

Boulud, Daniel: Cafe Boulud, Daniel, Daniel Boulud Brasserie, DB Bistro Moderne

Burke, David: davidburke & donatella, David Burke at Bloomingdale's

Chang, David: Momofuku Noodle Bar, Momofuku Ssäm Bar

Colicchio, Tom: craft, craftbar, craftsteak, 'wichbar

Conant, Scott: Alto, L'Impero

Dufresne, Wylie: wd-50

English, Todd: English Is Italian, Olives New York

Goldfarb, Will: Room 4 Dessert

Gutenbrunner, Kurt: Blaue Gans, Cafe Sabarsky/Fledermaus, Wallsë

Humm, Daniel: Eleven Madison Park

Keller, Thomas: Bouchon Bakery, per se

Kunz, Gray: Café Gray

Martinez, Zarela: Zarela

Matsuhisa, Nobu: Nobu 57, Nobu New York, Nobu Next Door

McNally, Keith: Balthazar, Morandi, Pastis, Schillers Liquor Bar

Meyer, Danny: Eleven Madison Park, Gramercy Tavern, Tabla, Union Square Cafe

Nieporent, Drew: Centrico, Crush Wine & Spirits, Mai House, Nobu 57, Nobu New York, Nobu Next Door, Rubicon, Tribeca Grill

Palmer, Charlie: Aureole, Metrazur

Portalo Alfred: Gotham Bar & Grill

Torres, Jacques: Jacques Torres Chocolate Haven

Valenti, Tom: Ouest

Vongerichten, Jean Georges: Jean Georges, JoJo, Mercer Kitchen, Perry Street, Spice Market, Vong

Waxman, Jonathan: Barbuto

TASTING ROOM
264 Elizabeth St (bet Houston and Prince St)   212/358-7831
Dinner: Tues-Sun   www.thetastingroomnyc.com

TASTING ROOM WINE BAR AND CAFE
72 E 1st St (bet First and Second Ave)
Mon-Fri: 7 a.m.-12 a.m.; Sat, Sun: 9 a.m.-12 a.m.
Inexpensive to moderate

The Tasting Room restaurant, recently spruced up, features two dining rooms, space for private parties, an extensive wine list, and a menu that changes daily. Renee (in front) and chef-husband Colin Alevras offer tasting plates and larger share plates, if you like. The Tasting Room Wine Bar and Cafe serves good coffee, a large wine list, and homemade goodies in a relaxed atmosphere. A light menu is featured, and you can eat at the bar or on benches.

TAVERN ON THE GREEN
Central Park West at 67th St   212/873-3200
Lunch: Mon-Fri; Dinner: Daily; Brunch: Sat, Sun
Moderate to moderately expensive   www.tavernonthegreen.com

There's no place like this back home! Tavern on the Green is a destination attraction. The setting in Central Park, with lights twinkling in nearby trees and glamorous indoor fixtures, makes for dining experiences that residents and visitors alike never forget. Even though the operation is big and busy, the food and service are usually first-rate. Chef Brian Young has a big job keeping this place hopping. If you are planning an evening that must be extra special, make reservations in the **Crystal Room**. Your out-of-town relatives will love it! Seasonal menus can be viewed online.

Pick up a quick bite from **Zeytinz Fine Food Market Place** (24 W 40th St, 212/575-8080), which offers gourmet sandwiches, wraps, paninis, pizzas, soups, and salads. You can also try something from the cold buffet, sushi bar, or grill. Zeytinz offers specialty drinks like lattes and smoothies, a large selection of breakfast items, and custom-made cakes, tarts, and cookies. Catering, gift baskets, and delivery are available.

TELEPAN
72 W 69th St (at Columbus Ave)   212/580-4300
Lunch: Wed-Fri; Dinner: Daily; Brunch: Sat, Sun   www.telepanny.com
Moderate to moderately expensive

When you are overloaded on flash, step back and be Bill Telepan's humble guest. Everything about this place—surroundings, menu, and service—reflects the laid-back personality of chef/owner Telepan. It is a quiet and reliable restaurant enhancing the Upper West Side dining scene for more mature sorts. Local ingredients are featured on the changing menu. Order the spring vegetables bread soup, if it's on the menu; it could make an entire meal. There is more: a number of egg dishes, soft shell crab, organic chicken, and braised short ribs with garlic potato puree. Steamed chocolate cake with caramel ice cream and chocolate sauce is properly sinful.

THOR

Hotel on Rivington
107 Rivington St (bet Essex and Ludlow St)   212/475-2600
Breakfast, Lunch, Dinner: Daily; Brunch: Sat, Sun
Moderate to moderately expensive   www.hotelonrivington.com

Would you believe a first-class hotel and restaurant on Rivington Street on the Lower East Side? Thor is proof that you never know what you are going to find when exploring New York City. With a Central European flavor, dramatic atmosphere, and one of the nicest wait staffs in the city, Thor is worth a special evening. Tastings of a number of cold and hot plates are encouraged. You'll find specialties like homemade yogurt with black mission figs and Lower East Side rooftop honey! Plenty of fish and meat dishes are available, and the poached half lobster is delicious. Parsley-crusted venison with brussel sprouts and lingonberries is another specialty. Be sure to save room for the one-bite chocolate lollipops and malted shake for dessert!

JAMES BEARD HOUSE

167 W 12th St (bet Ave of the Americas and Seventh Ave)
212/675-4984
www.jamesbeard.org

This is a real chefs' place! The legendary James Beard had roots in Oregon, so anything to do with his life is of special interest to this author. He was a familiar personality on the Oregon coast, where he delighted in serving the superb seafood for which the region is famous. When Beard died in 1985, his Greenwich Village brownstone was put on the market and purchased by a group headed by Julia Child. Now the home is run by the nonprofit James Beard Foundation as a food and wine archive, research facility, and gathering place. It is the nation's only such culinary center. There are nightly dinners anyone can attend at which some of our country's best regional chefs show off their talents. For foodies, this is a great opportunity to have a one-on-one with some really interesting folks. Call for scheduled dinners.

TINI'S

1562 Second Ave (at 81st St)   212/628-3131
Dinner: Daily   www.tinirestaurant.com
Moderately expensive

Welcome to Italy! The atmosphere at Tini's is conducive to pleasant conversation, and staff members are incredibly well-trained and -mannered. Tini's prices are not out-of-line with the quality of food served, and every dish can be counted on for quality and attractive presentation. Brothers Giuseppe (executive chef) and Vincenzo Lentini are to be congratulated for a menu that reflects the best of Italy, whether it is a superb pasta, choice broiled veal chop, or breaded fried calamari. Try the homemade gelati for dessert.

TOCQUEVILLE

1 E 15th St (bet Union Square W and Fifth Ave)   212/647-1515
Lunch: Mon-Sat; Dinner: Daily; Brunch: Sun
Moderately expensive   www.tocquevillerestaurant.com

Marco Moreira and wife Jo-Ann Makovitzky have moved their pride-and-joy restaurant into a larger, more elegant location. Innovative dishes are featured on a constantly changing menu. At lunchtime, a *prix-fixe* menu is offered. Your entree might be 60-second seared dry-aged sirloin, followed by a wonderful apple tart dessert. You will enjoy an absolutely fabulous meal made all the more pleasant by a well-trained and accommodating staff. Homemade brioche, rosemary, and French rolls are so good you must be careful not to ruin your appetite. The new locale affords room for private dining (up to 25 people) and a bar area where you can enjoy drinks and snacks or order from the full menu. This talented pair also operates **Catering by Tocqueville**, a catering service accessible via the restaurant's phone number. Personal food delivery is a given, but they can also take care of rental items, flowers, photographers, and professional service staff.

Young and old alike line up at the Times Square location of the **Hard Rock Cafe** (1501 Broadway, 212/343-3355; Sun-Thurs: 11 a.m.-12:30 a.m.; Fri, Sat: 11 a.m.-1:30 a.m.). Upstairs you'll find Hard Rock merch: clothing and souvenirs. Downstairs a 700-seat restaurant serves burgers, salads, and pastas. A unique outdoor space above the Hard Rock marquee offers a space for private parties.

TONY'S DI NAPOLI
1606 Second Ave (at 83rd St)   212/861-8686
Dinner: Daily (open at 2 p.m. on Sat, Sun)
147 W 43rd St (bet Broadway and Ave of the Americas)
Lunch, Dinner: Daily   212/221-0100
Moderate   www.tonysnyc.com

Tony's is not to be missed for great family-style dining. The kids will love it, as will your hungry husband or wife. The place is colorful, noisy, and busy. The Times Square location is a bit more subdued. Huge platters of appetizers, delicious salads, pastas, chicken and veal dishes, broiled items, and seafood come piping hot and ready for the whole crew to dig into. Most everyone finds that they can't eat it all; you'll see lots of take-home boxes exiting these locations. Even the dessert menu is gigantic: cheesecakes, strawberry shortcake, sundaes, sorbets, and *tartufo* (almost the real thing). Sheer fun, believe me!

TRATTORIA DELL'ARTE
900 Seventh Ave (at 57th St)   212/245-9800
Lunch, Dinner: Daily; Brunch: Sun
Moderate   www.trattoriadellarte.com

The natives already know about Trattoria Dell'Arte, as the place is bursting at the seams every evening. A casual cafe is at the front, seats are available at the antipasto bar in the center, and the dining room is in the rear. One would be hard-pressed to name a place at any price with tastier Italian food. The antipasto selection is large, fresh, and inviting; you can choose a platter with various accompaniments. There are daily specials, superb pasta dishes, grilled fish and meats, and salads. Wonderful pizzas are available every day. The atmosphere and personnel are warm and pleasant. I recommend this place without reservation—although you'd better have one if you want to sit in the dining room.

TRESTLE ON TENTH
242 Tenth Ave (at 24th St)   212/645-5659
Lunch: Tues-Fri; Dinner: Daily (closed Mon in winter)
Moderate   www.trestleontenth.com

Employing a restrained Swiss accent, this house does well with a limited menu of chicken, lamb saddle, veal kidneys, pork loin, braised beef short ribs, and superb *crépinette* (pulled pork shoulder). I always enjoy a light and tasty butter lettuce salad to start. Here it is done with crispy bacon and a delicious buttermilk dressing. Cured meats and aged cheeses are also featured. A *nusstorte* (pie) with walnuts and caramel is a reliable dessert. The folks are down-to-earth and the atmosphere unpretentious.

TRIBECA GRILL
375 Greenwich St (at Franklin St)   212/941-3900
Lunch: Mon-Fri; Dinner: Daily; Brunch: Sun
Moderate   www.myriadrestaurantgroup.com/tribecagrill

It hardly seems possible this place is several decades old! Please note the address is Greenwich *Street*, not Avenue. The setting is a huge old coffee-roasting house in Tribeca. The inspiration is Robert DeNiro. The bar comes from the old Maxwell's Plum restaurant. The kitchen is first-class. The genius is savvy Drew Nieporent. Put it all together, and you have a winner. No wonder the people-watching is so good here! Guests enjoy a spacious bar and dining area, a fabulous private screening room upstairs, a collection of paintings by Robert DeNiro, Sr., and banquet facilities for private parties. The food is stylish and wholesome. Excellent salads, seafood, veal, steak, and first-rate pastas are house favorites. One of the top dishes is seared tuna with sesame noodles. The tarts, tortes, and mousses also rate with the best. Their wine list (1,500 selections!) is world-class.

Here is a name and address you won't want to forget: **Cafeteria** (119 Seventh Ave, 212/414-1717). Not only is good food served at attractive prices, but also they are open 24 hours a day, seven days a week. The place is always humming with customers.

TROPICA
MetLife Building
200 Park Ave (45th St at Vanderbilt Ave), lobby   212/867-6767
Lunch, Dinner: Mon-Fri   www.tropicany.com
Moderate

Realizing that most New Yorkers have limited time to spend over lunch, Tropica provides speedy and efficient service in addition to very tasty food. Dinner hours are a bit more relaxed in this bright, charming, tropical seafood house, which is hidden away on the concourse of the MetLife Building in midtown. Featured entrees include excellent tuna (in the sushi and sashimi assortment), seafood salads, and a variety of chicken, beef, and seafood preparations. Stick to the fish and shellfish, and you'll be more than satisfied. The molten chocolate cake easily wins best dessert honors.

T SALON

Chelsea Market
75 Ninth Ave (bet 15th and 16th St)   212/243-2259
Moderate   www.tsalon.com

Given renewed interest in tea, the unusual and enchanting T Salon is sure to captivate tea addicts, as well as those who just want to experiment on an occasional basis. You will find green teas (light colored Oriental tea with a delicate taste), oolong teas (distinctively peach flavor), black teas (heavy, deep flavor and rich amber color), as well as white and red teas. Tea blending is a specialty. Miriam Novalle, the T Salon's guru, has brewed up some changes. Look for a full bar, foods to go, and reasonably priced tea-making accessories, in addition to over 200 varieties of tea. This is a place for afternoon tea as well as a unique destination for special events and private parties. A satellite T Salon with about 15 tea selections is located inside **Te Casen** (382 West Broadway, bet Spring and Broome St), providing respite for shoe shoppers weary of seeking the perfect footwear from three floors of one-of-a-kind shoes. T Salon is one of the more unusual operations in Manhattan, again proving that no other city in the world is quite like the Big Apple.

---

wd-50 (50 Clinton St, 212/477-2900) has a lot going for it. Owner Wylie Dufresne is a talented chef. His room is attractive, with good lighting, unique restrooms, and a dramatic semi-open kitchen. Much of the fare is delicious. However, unless you are one of those contemporary gourmets who enjoys unusual dishes served with equally unusual accompaniments—like pork belly with black soybeans and turnips—I would suggest heading elsewhere.

TURKISH KITCHEN

386 Third Ave (bet 27th and 28th St)   212/679-6633
Lunch: Mon-Fri; Dinner: Daily; Brunch: Sun
Moderate   www.turkishkitchen.com

Turkey is in! I mean both the country and the food. This Turkish delight has great food and is absolutely spotless. Moreover, the staff exudes charm! There are all kinds of Turkish specialties, like zucchini pancakes, *istim kebab* (baked lamb shanks wrapped with eggplant slices), hummus, and tasty baked and grilled fish dishes. You can wash it all down with sour cherry juice from Turkey or *cacik*, a homemade yogurt. This family-run Gramercy-area operation is one of the best.

21 CLUB

21 W 52nd St (bet Fifth Ave and Ave of the Americas)   212/582-7200
Lunch: Mon-Fri; Dinner: Mon-Sat (closed Sat in summer)
Expensive to very expensive   www.21club.com

You know about 21! It has been around for a long time, with a reputation as a place to see and be seen. I can remember fascinating lunches there with my uncle, who was a daily diner. Alas, things have changed. Yes, there is still a gentleman at the door to give you the once over. Jackets and ties are required (no jeans or sneakers). There are still 21 classics on the menu, even a not-so-lowly burger at $30. And the atmosphere is still quite special. But there the tradition ends, as far as I am concerned. The service is haughty, and the food is just okay. If your out-of-town guests simply *must* see this place and you're feeling flush, then go; otherwise, the memories are better!

202
Chelsea Market
75 Ninth Ave (bet 15th and 16th St)   646/638-1173
Breakfast: Mon-Fri; Dinner: Tues-Sun; Brunch: Daily
Moderate

This unique operation in the busy Chelsea Market—a cafe and a store all in one—is a good place to rest weary feet. You'll find full English breakfasts (bacon, sausage, mushrooms, and poached eggs), buttermilk pancakes, bagels, salads, tuna burgers, steaks, and more. The young personnel are very accommodating, and the platters are more than adequate. Adjoining is a rather sparse clothing and gift store that's worth browsing but not much more. The expensive duds are by designer Nicole Farhi.

Here's one the kids will love! Dark tunnels, Martian men and women, interactive games, plus good food and drink—all can be found at **Mars 2112** (1633 Broadway, 212/582-2112). Menu offerings include out-of-this-world Interstellar Shrimp, Meteor Talapia, Pavonis Mons Chinese Chicken Salad, and others.

---

2 WEST
Ritz-Carlton New York, Battery Park
2 West St (at Battery Pl)   917/790-2525
Breakfast, Lunch, Dinner: Daily; Brunch: Sun
Moderately expensive

The view is the thing here! Not that the food isn't very good, but the edibles are outclassed by the visual sights. The park and water view combines with the gorgeous indoor glass pieces and artwork to make a memorable feast for the eyes. The serving pieces are just as attractive, too. When you combine all of this with extremely fast, informed service and good food, I have no complaints. This room is just one of the hotel's dining choices, all of them done to Ritz-Carlton's standards of perfection. You'll find a rich selection of plates carefully designed and presented with local ingredients. I like the dessert plate; the chocolate tart is exceptional. If you're looking for a special place for afternoon tea, the adjoining Lobby Lounge is perfect.

UNCLE JACK'S STEAKHOUSE
440 Ninth Ave (at 34th St)   212/244-0005
44 W 56th St (bet Fifth Ave and Ave of the Americas) 212/245-1550
Lunch: Mon-Fri; Dinner: Daily   www.unclejacks.com
Moderate (lunch) to expensive (dinner)

Entering this atmospheric steakhouse is like going back decades in time. The hand-carved mahogany bar, the antique light fixtures, the blackboard menu, and the private Library Room make the place comfortable and colorful. You will be well taken care of, as the wait staff and captains are right on the job. Uncle Jack's is one of the few steakhouses in Manhattan that specialize in Kobe beef, which is famous for its tenderness and flavor. The beef is aged for 21 days and cooked to perfection, and you can expect an equally grand price tag. Other menu items are what you would expect from a first-class steakhouse, and all are tasty and more comfortably priced. A Sommelier's Dinner, a feast of food and wine, is available for $99.95. For a gentlemen's evening out, a bachelor party, or office celebration, I can't imagine a more pleasant place. The bottled steak sauce is a must purchase for taking home!

UNION SQUARE CAFE

21 E 16th St (bet Fifth Ave and Union Square W)   212/243-4020
Lunch, Dinner: Daily   www.unionsquarecafe.com
Moderate

The Stars and Stripes fly high here, as Union Square Cafe is a very popular American restaurant (albeit with an Italian soul). The clientele is as varied as the food. Conversations are often oriented toward the publishing world, as well-known authors and editors are in attendance at lunch. The menu is creative, the staff unusually down-to-earth, and the prices very much within reason. Owner Danny Meyer offers such specialties as oysters Union Square, hot garlic potato chips, and wonderful black bean soup. For lunch, try the yellowfin tuna burger served on a homemade poppyseed roll or the great pastas. Dinner entrees from the grill are always delicious (tuna, shell steak, and veal). I go here just for the warm banana tart with honey-vanilla ice cream and macadamia nut brittle! Try a light afternoon cheese plate at the bar.

> Do the words "Rainbow Room" bring back nostalgic memories of old New York? Well, you can still enjoy dinner from 5 to 11 daily at the **Rainbow Room Grill** (30 Rockefeller Plaza, 212/632-5100), high atop the city. This should be an "occasion" venue, as prices will put a dent in the pocketbook.

VALBELLA

421 W 13th St (bet Ninth Ave and Washington St)   212/645-7777
Lunch: Mon-Fri; Dinner: Mon-Sat   www.valbellany.com
Moderate

In my opinion, service is the name of the game in today's highly competitive marketplace. Patronizing so many restaurants every month, I can immediately assess the quality of the service. At Valbella, the service is top-notch. Wait staff don't stand around and talk—they are in constant motion and obviously well-trained. The Italian fare is also first-rate, featuring a decent selection of typical dishes. The pastas caught my eye: penne *alla* vodka, *cavatelli, trenette* (sautéed jumbo shrimp), fettuccine, risotto with wild mushrooms, and more. The pecan-crusted lamb chops in champagne and maple butter on hashbrown potatoes is an especially delicious dish. Like most Italian houses, veal is also a specialty.

VERITAS
43 E 20th St (near Park Ave S)   212/353-3700
Dinner: Daily   www.veritas-nyc.com
Moderately expensive

There are only 55 seats at Veritas, and all of them are kept warm every meal. Getting to enjoy chef Scott Bryan's refreshingly simple dishes is definitely worth the wait. The world-class wine cellar stocks 1,300 bottles, ranging from $18 to $100,000. Like the food, the room is done in superb taste; every color and surface spells quality. Top dishes include seared foie gras, crisp sweetbreads, pepper-crusted venison, and roasted organic chicken that melts in your mouth. Chocolate soufflé is a must for dessert. Finally, someone has gotten the word that complex food combinations just don't work most of the time.

Vegetarian diners who like classy Indian dishes should visit **Dévi** (8 E 18th St, 212/691-1300). A main course vegetarian lunch is reasonably priced. In the evening a six-course tasting menu is $60.

VINEGAR FACTORY   *Brunch*
431 E 91st St (bet York and First Ave)   212/987-0885
Cafe: Daily (6 a.m.-6 p.m.); Brunch: Sat, Sun (upstairs)
Moderate   www.elizabar.com

Savvy Upper East Siders quickly learned that weekend brunch at Eli Zabar's Vinegar Factory is delicious. Taste buds spring to alertness as you wander the packed aisles of the Vinegar Factory (a great gourmet store) on your way upstairs to the Cafe for Saturday or Sunday brunch. Don't expect bargain prices; after all, this is an Eli Zabar operation. But the quality is substantial. Wonderful breads (Eli is famous for them), a fresh salad bar, omelets, pizzas, pancakes, blintzes, and huge sandwiches are the order of the day; many are available self-serve. Your hungry teens will love the massive portions, and you'll appreciate the fast, friendly service.

VIVOLO
140 E 74th St (bet Park and Lexington Ave)   212/737-3533
Lunch: Mon-Fri; Dinner: Mon-Sat   www.vivolonyc.com
Moderate

Angelo Vivolo has created a neighborhood classic in an old townhouse converted into a charming two-story restaurant with cozy fireplaces and professional service. His empire also includes **Cucina Vivolo** (138 E 74th St, 212/717-4700), a specialty food shop, and the sensual **bar.vetro** (222 E 58th St, 212/308-0222, www.barvetro.com). There are great things to eat at all three places. You can sit down and be pampered, have goodies ready for takeout, or place an order for delivery. The cucina menu offers wonderful Italian specialty sandwiches made with all kinds of breads, as well as soups, cheeses, sweets, espresso, and cappuccino. A box lunch is also available. In the restaurants proper, there are pastas, stuffed veal chops, and daily specials. Vivolo serves over 60 scaloppine preparations. Bar.vetro features small plates served in curved, interlocking dishes for sharing or as a tasting menu. Whichever Vivolo eatery you choose, save room for the cannoli *alla* Vivolo, a tasty version of the Italian classic.

VONG

200 E 54th St (bet Second and Third Ave)   212/486-9592
Lunch: Mon-Fri; Dinner: Daily   www.jean-georges.com
Moderate to moderately expensive

The atmosphere is Thai-inspired, with romantic and appetizing overtones. The ladies will love the colors and lighting, and the gentlemen will remember the great things Vong does with peanut and coconut sauces. I could make a meal of appetizers like chicken and coconut milk soup, prawn satay with oyster sauce, and raw tuna wrapped in rice paper. Order crispy squab or venison medallions, if available. A vegetarian menu is offered. For dessert I suggest passionfruit sorbet or warm chocolate cake. Dining here is a lot cheaper than a week at Bangkok's Oriental Hotel and just as delicious!

The attractive and busy **Hawaiian Tropic Zone** (729 Seventh Ave, at Times Square, 212/626-7312) is themed "the hottest spot on earth," and the staff attire, designed by Nicole Miller, makes that a reality. Everyone in the family will like the menu—salad of prosciutto and melon, honey-glazed salmon, chicken and penne pasta, and much more. The gentlemen will love the waitresses' scanty outfits.

WALKER'S

16 N Moore St (at Varick St)   212/941-0142
Lunch: Mon-Fri; Dinner: Daily; Brunch: Sat, Sun
Inexpensive

If you are looking for a glimpse of old Manhattan, you'll love Walker's. In three crowded rooms, at tables covered with plain white paper so that diners can doodle with crayons, you will be served hearty food at agreeable prices. The regular menu includes homemade soups, salads, omelets (create your own), sandwiches, and quiches. Their burgers are big and satisfying. A dozen or so daily specials include fish and pasta dishes. For those coming from uptown, it is a bit of an undertaking to get here. For those in the neighborhood, it is easy to see why Walker's is a community favorite, especially on Sunday jazz nights.

WALLSÉ

344 W 11th St (at Washington St)   212/352-2300
Dinner: Daily; Brunch: Sat, Sun   www.wallserestaurant.com
Moderate to moderately expensive

Ready for crispy cod strudel? Vienna it is not, but Kurt Gutenbrunner has brought a somewhat Austrian flavor to the West Village. The two dining rooms are sparse but comfortable. The staff is pleasant and helpful, adding to the dining experience. Appetizers like foie gras terrine and chestnut soup with Armagnac prunes are seasonal favorites. Yes, there is wiener schnitzel with potato-cucumber salad. Great pastries for dessert: apple strudel, cheesecake, and Salzburger *nockerl*. The cheese selection is first-rate. Of couse, I'd rather be at Hotel Sacher in Vienna.

WATER CLUB

500 E 30th St (at East River)   212/683-3333
Lunch: Mon-Sat; Dinner: Daily; Buffet Brunch: Sun
Moderately expensive   www.thewaterclub.com

Warning! Do not fill up on the marvelous small scones that are made fresh and served warm. They are the best things you have ever tasted, but they will diminish your appetite for the excellent meal to follow. The Water Club presents a magnificent setting on the river. The place is large and noisy, with a fun atmosphere that is ideal for special occasions. (They also have excellent private party facilities.) There is nightly piano music, as well as accommodations for a drink or light meal on the roof (weather permitting). A large selection of seafood appetizers is available. Entrees include numerous fish dishes, plus meat and poultry items. Homemade fruit sorbet and fresh-baked apple crisp (served at Sunday brunch) will round off a special meal. Be advised that getting here from the north can be confusing. (Directions: Exit FDR Drive at 23rd Street and make two left turns.)

Blue Ribbon Downing St. (34 Downing St, 212/691-0404, Tues-Sat: 6 p.m.-2 a.m.) is right across the street from Blue Ribbon Bakery. With the Blue Ribbon name attached, you know the food will be first-class. Small plates, smoked meats, fish, and a good selection of wines and cognacs are featured. Chalk up another winner for the Bromberg brothers!

WAVERLY INN & GARDEN

16 Bank St (bet 4th and Waverly St)   212/243-7900
Lunch, Dinner: Daily
Moderately expensive to expensive

The Waverly Inn is owned by Graydon Carter, publisher and editor of *Vanity Fair*. Because it is his personal establishment, the average diner will find it difficult, if not impossible, to enjoy the tastes of a truly good restaurant in a most attractive space. That is because it is nearly impossible to reach Waverly Inn by phone to make a reservation. My best advice is to drop in early for dinner (they open at 6 p.m.), and you might be lucky enough to snare a table. You won't be disappointed. Small plates include oysters on the half shell, salads, salmon tartare, crab cakes, and more. Braised short ribs are a sensational entree. You might also choose a Waverly burger, several fish dishes, or grilled mussels. The surroundings are charming. In the garden room a working fireplace adds to the ambience. Once seated, you'll find the service to be very professional, and they really seem happy to serve you.

WILD SALMON

622 Third Ave (at 40th St)   212/404-1700
Lunch: Mon-Fri; Dinner: Mon-Sat; Brunch: Sun
Moderate to moderately expensive   www.chinagrillmgt.com

In a large, attractive, and soaring space, chef Charles Ramseyer has created a fabulous new venue featuring products from his native Nothwest. What is most appealing is the freshness of the seafood. Delicious tiny Oregon Bay shrimp, Olympia oysters, and Manita clams make superb appetizers from the raw bar. Large seafood platters of shrimp, oysters, clams, mussels, and scallops are available. Other starters include crab and corn chowder, glazed Oregon quail, and famous Washington Wagyu beef carpaccio. Accompanying these is fresh-baked flat bread. Salmon dishes are the house specialty, but tender beef entrees with a large selection of sauces are also very good. There is more: rockfish, Dungeness crab, Northwest seafood cioppino, and short ribs. How about sweet stuffed baked Walla Walla onions with pepper bacon as a side? The Scharfenbeger (a chocolate extravaganza dessert) is worth a visit in itself! This is one of the best of the new dining houses in Manhattan. On top of it all, you'll find the service informed and professional.

Manhattan has always been known as a place where speakeasies once flourished. Well, today there are a few places that still have the flavor of past decades:

Bill's Gay Nineties (57 E 54th St, 212/355-0243, www.billsnyc.com)
Fanelli's Cafe (94 Prince St, 212/226-9412, www.fanellicafe.com)
Onieal's Grand Street (174 Grand St, 212/941-9119, www.onieals.com)
21 Club (21 W 52nd St, 212/582-7200, www.21club.com)

WOO CHON
10 W 36th St (off Fifth Ave)   212/695-0676
Daily: 11 a.m.-2 a.m.   www.woochonnyc.com
Moderate

Look at the hours they keep at Woo Chon! This Korean restaurant is sparkling clean, friendly, and inviting. For a group dinner, order a variety of beef, pork, or shrimp dishes and have fun broiling them at your table. The sizzling seafood pancake is a winner! Accompanying dishes add a special touch to your meal. In addition to marinated barbecue items, there are such tasty delights as Oriental noodles and vegetables, traditional Korean herbs and rice served in beef broth, a variety of noodle dishes, and dozens of other treats from the Far East. If you are unfamiliar with Korean food, the helpful personnel will explain the dishes and how to eat them.

Hungry for a really good salad? Try **Nicole's at Nicole Fahri** (10 E 60th St, 212/223-2288).

WOO LAE OAK SOHO
148 Mercer St (bet Prince and Houston St)   212/925-8200
Lunch, Dinner: Daily   www.woolaeoaksoho.com
Moderate to moderately expensive

In attractive Soho surroundings, one can choose from a large selection of hot and cold appetizers, as well as traditional Korean specialties. The best include Dungeness crab wrapped in spinach crepes and tuna tartare served over sliced Asian pears. Rice and side dishes such as seasoned seaweed, radish *kimchi,* and raw garlic are also available. The big draws are the barbecued items, cooked right at the table. Available for barbecuing are slices of beef, short ribs, chicken, lamb, pork, scallops, shrimp, tuna, veggies, and much more. The personnel are very helpful to beginners and seem genuinely pleased when diners show interest in their unusual menu.

ZOË
90 Prince St (bet Broadway and Mercer St)   212/966-6722
Lunch: Mon-Fri; Dinner: Tues-Sun; Brunch: Sat, Sun
Moderate   www.zoerest.com

Once inventive and now at times routine, Zoë is still worth a visit. Zoë occupies an old building, and the original tiles and columns still show. The setting is attractive and particularly enjoyable for younger diners who like to sit at the chef's counter and watch the interactive kitchen. There is a wood-burning grill, a wood-fueled pizza oven (used for lunch), and a rotisserie. The grill features delicious steaks. The menu is contemporary American and changes seasonally. Save room for the chocolate desserts!

Look for the **Treats Truck** (212/691-5226, www.treatstruck.com), which wanders the streets of Manhattan pureying delicious goodies.

III. Where to Find It: Museums, Tours, Tickets, and More

A Week in New York

"I'm going to be in New York for a week. What do you recommend that I do?" I've been asked that question a thousand times in the last 50 years, and I'm always torn about how to answer. You could spend an entire lifetime in New York and still never see and do everything this fabulous city has to offer. If you're here for a week, the first two things you need to do are gather information and make some choices.

My advice is to pick one or two places you really want to visit each day and build your itinerary around them. Because New York is so big, I suggest limiting your daily itinerary to just one or two neighborhoods. Also check to be sure that places you want to visit will be open on that day before you get too far along in your planning. You'll need to know that the Metropolitan Museum of Art, for instance, is closed on Mondays and the Museum of Modern Art is closed on Tuesdays. Many museums and other tourist spots have reduced hours in the winter months. Of course, some activities are seasonal: ice skating in Rockefeller Plaza can be done only in winter, while Shakespeare in the Park is offered only in summer.

Every trip to New York is different, and each person will have a different list of favorites. If you have friends who know New York, by all means ask for their recommendations. The following itinerary for a week in New York combines my own favorites with some of the absolute "don't miss" classics. Whether you follow this outline, take a friend's suggestions, or make up your own, remember that part of the pleasure of New York is simply taking it all in at your leisure. Whatever else you do, spend a little time just walking around!

MONDAY: Getting Oriented
- Buy the current edition of *Time Out New York*, and read the various "This Week in New York" sections over coffee.
- Go for a walk in the neighborhood around your hotel.
- Stop by **NYC & Company** (810 Seventh Ave, near 53rd St), the city's main tourist information center, to pick up maps and brochures and ask any questions you may have.
- Take a **Circle Line** tour of Manhattan (Pier 83, 42nd St at 12th Ave)

- Lunch at **Smith & Wollensky** (797 Third Ave)
- Walk along Madison Avenue in the 60s and 70s, checking out all the big-name boutiques.
- Take a walk through Central Park.
- Dinner at **Trattoria Dell'Arte** (900 Seventh Ave)

TUESDAY: Museum Mile
- Breakfast at **Sarabeth's Kitchen** (1295 Madison Ave)
- **Cooper-Hewitt National Design Museum** (2 E 91st St)
- **Solomon R. Guggenheim Museum** (1071 Fifth Ave)
- Lunch in the cafeteria at the **Metropolitan Museum of Art** (Fifth Ave bet 80th and 84th St)
- **Metropolitan Museum of Art** (see above)
- **Whitney Museum of American Art** (945 Madison Ave)
- **Frick Collection** (1 E 70th St)
- Dinner at **Tao** (42 E 58th St)
- Take in a comedy show at **Caroline's on Broadway** (Broadway at 50th St).

WEDNESDAY: Midtown
- Stroll through **Rockefeller Plaza** (Fifth Ave bet 49th and 51st St).
- Stop by **St. Patrick's Cathedral** (Fifth Ave at 51st St).
- Lunch at **Grand Central Oyster Bar Restaurant** (Grand Central Terminal)
- Take the 12:30 p.m. tour of **Grand Central Terminal** offered only on Wednesday by the Municipal Art Society.
- Visit the **New York Public Library** (Fifth Ave bet 40th and 42nd St).
- Spend the afternoon touring the **Museum of Modern Art** (11 W 53rd St)
- Dinner at **The Modern** (in the Museum of Modern Art)

THURSDAY: Upper West Side
- Start the day with a nosh at **Zabar's** (2245 Broadway).
- Stop by the **Cathedral Church of St. John the Divine** (Amsterdam Ave at 112th St).
- Stock up on sweets at **Mondel Chocolates** (2913 Broadway).
- Lunch at **Cafe Lalo** (201 W 83rd St)
- Spend the afternoon at **The Cloisters** (Fort Tryon Park).
- Dinner at **McCormick & Schmick's** (1285 Ave of the Americas)
- Go see a Broadway show. Get tickets well in advance from Americana Tickets, or try your luck at a TKTS booth.

FRIDAY: Lower Manhattan
- Take the first ferry from Battery Park to the **Statue of Liberty** and **Ellis Island**.
- Walk up the **Battery Park Esplanade**.
- Late lunch at **Spice Market** (403 W 13th St)
- Stop by **St. Paul's Chapel** (211 Broadway).
- Take a leisurely late afternoon stroll on the **Brooklyn Bridge**.
- Dinner at **River Cafe** (1 Water St, Brooklyn)
- Go see a performance at **Lincoln Center**.

SATURDAY: Chelsea and Soho
- Go shopping at **ABC Carpet & Home** (888 Broadway).

- Go gallery hopping on and around West 22nd Street in Chelsea.
- Have a late morning brunch at **Blue Ribbon** (97 Sullivan St).
- Go gallery hopping and shopping on and around West Broadway in Soho.
- Dinner at **Balthazar** (80 Spring St)
- Take a late evening elevator ride up the observation deck of the **Empire State Building** (Fifth Ave bet 33rd and 34th St).

SUNDAY: Lower East Side
- Lunch at **Katz's Delicatessen** (205 E Houston St)
- Take the noon tour at the **Lower East Side Tenement Museum** (108 Orchard St).
- Take the 1 p.m. walking tour of the Lower East Side sponsored by the Lower East Side Tenement Museum (see above).
- Visit the remarkable **Eldridge Street Synagogue** (12 Eldridge St).
- Dinner in Chinatown at **Golden Unicorn** (18 East Broadway)

Information on all places I've included in these itineraries can be found in other sections of this book. Whatever else you do during your visit, I have two final pieces of advice:

- Get to know the subway system. It is generally safe, reliable, convenient, inexpensive (particularly if you get a seven-day pass), and by far the most efficient way to travel in New York, unless you have mobility issues. If you take cabs everywhere you go, you'll burn both money and time.
- Slow down and enjoy yourself. New Yorkers move very fast. It is fun to get into the flow of things, but it is also good to slow down and take a look around. Don't get so focused on your destination that you fail to enjoy the journey. It's a remarkable city! Enjoy!

Top 10 Places to Visit in New York

There are certain places in New York that everyone has on their "must visit" list. I've listed mine here, in alphabetical order, for easy reference.

AMERICAN MUSEUM OF NATURAL HISTORY
Central Park West (bet 77th and 81st St)   212/769-5100
www.amnh.org

Founded in 1869, this remarkable museum has taught generations of New York children and out-of-town visitors alike about the remarkable diversity of our planet and the natural world around us. It is hard to overstate the size of this sprawling place: the museum, the Hayden Planetarium, and the Rose Center for Earth and Space have 45 permanent exhibition halls in 25 interconnected buildings covering almost 20 acres. The museum alone has more than 30 million artifacts and specimens.

Like several other museums of its size in New York, the American Museum of Natural History can seem overwhelming. My advice is to go to the information desk when you first arrive, get a floor plan, and then sit down and think about where you would like to go. If you're planning to see an IMAX movie or the Space Show at the Rose Center, be sure to note the time on your ticket and plan the other parts of your visit accordingly. While the constantly changing special exhibits are often fascinating, be forewarned that they are also often very crowded. So, too, are some of the permanent exhibits, including the Hall of Biodiversity, the Akeley Hall of African Mammals, the Milstein Hall of Ocean Life, and the Hall of Human Origins. Exhibits on the Northwest Coast and other Native Americans, as well Asian, African, and Central and South American cultures, however, are often entirely empty even on busy days and yet full of fascinating items. Between all of the fossils, minerals, skeletons, and insects, there's really something for everyone. Plan to stay for at least a couple hours.

Guided tours are available, as are two restaurants and more gifts shops than you can count. **Hours**: daily from 10 to 5:45 (the adjacent Rose Center for Earth and Space stays open until 8:45 on the first Friday of every month). **Admission**: $14 for adults, $10.50 for seniors and students with ID, and $8 for children between 2 and 12 are suggested *but not required*. Prices are higher if you want to see an IMAX movie or go to the Space Show at Rose Center.

If you're a garden lover and are willing to venture out of the more traveled parts of Manhattan or into the outer boroughs, try these gems:

- **Brooklyn Botanic Gardens**: 1000 Washington Avenue, Brooklyn (718/623-7200, www.bbg.org)
- **Heather Garden**: Fort Tryon Park at Fort Washington Avenue in northern Manhattan (www.nycgovparks.org)
- **New York Botanical Garden**: Bronx River Parkway at Fordham Road, The Bronx (718/817-8700, www.nybg.org)
- **Wave Hill**: 675 W 252nd Street, The Bronx (718/549-3200, www.wavehill.org)

CENTRAL PARK
Fifth Ave to Central Park West from 59th to 110th St

This urban gem was designed in 1858 by Frederick Law Olmsted, the same landscape architect who designed the U.S. Capitol grounds in Washington, D.C. A rectangle running between Fifth Avenue on the East Side to Central Park West on the West Side, Central Park's 843 acres of grass, rocky outcroppings, ponds, trees, and paths stretch from 59th Street to 110th Street in the heart of Manhattan. Tennis courts, baseball diamonds, playgrounds, a couple restaurants, ice-skating (in winter), miniature golf (in summer), and even a castle are all here! Thanks to the Central Park Conservancy, a nonprofit organization that began managing the park in 1980, it is all clean, safe, and wonderfully accessible to the 25 million people who use it every year.

Regardless of season, the best way to experience Central Park is just to walk in it. (If you ever get lost, it helps to know that the first digits of the number plate on the lampposts correspond to the nearest cross streets.) There's so much to see and do in the park that it's almost like a city within the city. Just about every New Yorker has a favorite spot. Some of my favorites include **Conservancy Gardens** (just off Fifth Avenue and 105th Street), **The Boathouse** (near 72nd Street on the east side), **Central Park Zoo** (just off Fifth Avenue at 64th Street), **Belvedere Castle** (mid-park near 79th Street), and **Strawberry Fields** (near Central Park West, between 71st and 74th streets). You can get one of those quintessential

New York photos standing on the rock outcroppings just inside the park off 59th Street and Avenue of the Americas.

Another great way to experience Central Park is to attend an event in it. Particularly in the summer, it's home to everything from free concerts by the New York Philharmonic and the Metropolitan Opera, Shakespeare in the Park performances, and all sorts of other cultural events. For a compete listing of what's going on in the park, walking tours, and other information, go to www.centralparknyc.org.

On a Clear Day

When I first started writing this book, the observation deck atop the 70-story RCA Building at 30 Rockefeller Plaza was one of my favorite New York viewing spots. For a variety of reasons, it closed in 1986 and stayed closed two decades. But the **"Top of the Rock"** is open again! From 8 a.m. to midnight every day, you can ride to what seems like the top of the world. The entrance and ticket offices are on 50th Street between Fifth Avenue and Avenue of the Americas. Be forewarned: like almost everything, it's going to cost you! For more information, go to www.topoftherocknyc.com or call 212/698-2000. **Admission**: $17.50 for adults, $16 for seniors, and $11.25 for children.

EMPIRE STATE BUILDING
350 Fifth Ave (bet 33rd and 34th St)   212/736-3100
                                                        www.esbnyc.org

When people think of New York, this 102-story building is often the first image that comes to mind. Soaring above its neighbors just south of downtown, this skyscraper was built in 1931 and has defined the New York City skyline ever since. Sometimes confused with its shorter uptown neighbor, the Chrysler Building, the Empire State Building is the tallest building in the city. (In case you're wondering, there are 1,860 steps from bottom to top!)

Lots of tourists from all over the world and fans of movies like *King Kong*, *An Affair to Remember*, and *Sleepless in Seattle* simply can't come to New York without visiting this landmark and its observation deck on the 86th floor. (For an extra $15 each, you can go to the very top.) On a clear day, you can almost see forever. But be forewarned: the lines are long, the lobby is crowded, and the staff is alternately bored and rude. It's also worth noting that the ticket desk and line to go through security are actually on the second floor. The lobby on the first floor is kept clear for all the office workers who actually work in the Empire State Building. If you really have your heart set on a visit here, consider coming early in the morning or late at night, or buying advance tickets online. (Note that tickets to the 102nd floor observatory can only be purchased on-site.) **Hours**: daily from 8 a.m. to 2 a.m. (the last elevator goes up at 1:15 a.m.). **Admission**: $18 for adults, $16 for seniors and youth between 12 and 17, $12 for children between 6 and 11, and free for active duty military in full uniform and children under 6. Tickets to the 102nd floor observatory or for Skyride (a simulated helicopter ride over New York) cost extra.

You can tell a real New Yorker from a wanna-be if he or she:
- Refuses to refer to Sixth Avenue as Avenue of the Americas.
- Refers to the MetLife Building as the PanAm Building.
- Has never been to either the Empire State Building or the Statue of Liberty.
- Has never bought a bagel at a grocery store.
- Doesn't flinch when the dinner bill exceeds $300 for two people but also knows where to get a perfectly good meal for under $20.
- Doesn't own a car but rents one on weekends to go to Ikea and Home Depot—or doesn't have a driver's license at all.
- Never eats dinner before 8 p.m.
- Thinks Ohio is "out west."
- Knows the differences between Lombardi's and John's and has a strong opinion about which one's pizza is better.
- Buys the Sunday *New York Times* on Saturday night.
- Keeps a bike in the living room.
- Gives directions to cab drivers.
- Never rides a bus—but if he or she did, would exit via the back door.

FIFTH AVENUE

London. Paris. Tokyo. They all have fashionable streets with out-of-sight rents. But nowhere in the world is quite as fashionable or quite as expensive as New York's Fifth Avenue. Fifth Avenue starts down in Greenwich Village at **Washington Square Park**, and the **Empire State Building** is on Fifth Avenue between 33rd and 34th Street. However, when tourists say they want to visit Fifth Avenue, they mean midtown and the Upper East Side.

The stretch of Fifth Avenue between 42nd Street and 59th Street is the heart of New York. It was once lined with mansions and is still home to some of the grandest and most recognizable buildings in the city. They include the mid-Manhattan branch of the **New York Public Library** (at 42nd Street), **Rockefeller Center** (between 48th and 50th St), **Saks Fifth Avenue** (at 50th St), **St. Patrick's Cathedral** (at 51st St), **Tiffany & Company** (at 57th St), and the **Plaza Hotel** (at 59th St). Newcomers like **Apple Store** (between 58th and 59th St), **Niketown** (at 57th St), the **NBA Store** (at 52nd St), **American Girl Place** (at 49th St), and the **Build-a-Bear Workshop** (at 46th St) suggest what a tourist mecca Fifth Avenue has become.

The stretch of Fifth Avenue between 59th Street and 110th Street runs along the east side of Central Park. This area is one of the city's most prestigious residential neighborhoods and home to the famed Museum Mile, which is perhaps the single greatest concentration of art in all the world. In addition to various foreign consulates, elite private schools, and luxury apartment buildings, you'll find the **Frick Collection** (at 70th St), the **Metropolitan Museum of Art** (bet 80th and 84th St), the **Neue Galerie** (at 86th St), the **Guggenheim Museum** (at 89th St), the **National Academy of Design** (bet 89th and 90th St), the **Cooper-Hewitt National Design Museum** (at 91st St), the **Jewish Museum** (at 92nd St), the **Museum of the City of New York** (bet 103rd and 104th St), and **El Museo del Barrio** (at 104th St). When it is completed in a few years, the **Museum of African Art** will extend Museum Mile all the way to the top of Central Park at 110th Street.

Like much of New York, the best way to see Fifth Avenue is on foot. The sidewalks running along Central Park are a particular pleasure. There's no subway line running on Fifth Avenue, although there are lots of buses and cabs. Traffic on Fifth Avenue is one-way heading south. One more tip: under no circumstances should you go into a store on Fifth Avenue in midtown with "going out of business" signs in the windows! They have a habit of going out of business regularly!

GUGGENHEIM MUSEUM
1071 Fifth Ave (at 89th St)   212/423-3500
                                                        www.guggenheim.org

The Solomon R. Guggenheim Museum began in 1939 as the Museum of Non-Objective Painting, created to house the growing art collection of American industrialist Solomon Guggenheim. His collection included the work of such contemporaries as Vasily Kandinsky, Paul Klee, and Marc Chagall, and many of those original pieces form the backbone of this remarkable museum today. Of course the collection has grown tremendously since then and now incorporates work from artists ranging from late-19th-century impressionists to contemporary artists.

Although Guggenheim museums in Berlin, Venice, and Balbao, Spain— and even Las Vegas—showcase parts of the collection, the museum on Fifth Avenue is still the Guggenheim. In addition to the work displayed inside, people put this world-famous museum at the top of their itineraries because of its instantly recognizable building. It's an inverted ziggurat that looks a bit like a snail from the outside and allows visitors on the inside to wind their way through the collection rather than roaming in and out of rooms. The Guggenheim was designed by Frank Lloyd Wright and sits at the north end of Museum Mile, right across Fifth Avenue from Central Park. It opened in 1959 and recently underwent an extensive renovation in preparation for its 50th anniversary. Stand across the street to get the best architectural view.

In some ways, the breadth of the Guggenheim's collection rivals those of the Museum of Modern Art (in midtown) and the Metropolitan Museum of Art (a few blocks south on Fifth Avenue). But the great pleasure of the Guggenheim is that it's a bit smaller and more intimate than its famous cousins, giving art lovers time to linger. If 20th-century art is your passion, then there's no place you'll rather spend a day! **Hours**: daily except Thursday from 10 to 5:45 (Friday till 7:45). **Admission**: $18 for adults, $15 for seniors and students with ID, and free for children under 12. "Pay-as-you-wish" on Friday between 5:45 and 7:45.

LINCOLN CENTER
Columbus Ave bet 62nd and 65th St   www.lincolncenter.org

Just as Museum Mile along Fifth Avenue is the most stunning concentration of art anywhere in the world, the 16-acre Lincoln Center campus may be the most stunning concentration of performing arts institutions anywhere in the world. The **Julliard School of Music** is housed here, as are the **New York City Ballet**, the **New York City Opera**, the **Chamber Music Society of New York**, the **New York Philharmonic**, and the **Metropolitan Opera**. There is also a branch of the New York Public Library devoted entirely to the performing arts.

Lincoln Center will celebrate its 50th anniversary in 2009, and a major renovation is underway. If you want to peek inside some of the concert halls and other spaces here, daily tours are available (212/875-5350). You're also welcome to just wander around, enjoying the fountains, open terraces, and other public spaces. Each of the several stops here are well worth your time. And if you're interested in seeing one of the hundreds of performances that take place here every year, call the **Lincoln Center Events Hotline** (212/546-2656) for current information. Seeing a production at Lincoln Center is a special only-in-New-York treat!

Plan Ahead

Nobody wants to spend time waiting in lines. Because millions of tourists come to New York each year and many of them want to go to the same high-profile places, the lines can sometimes be pretty long for things like the Empire State Building, the Statue of Liberty, and even the Metropolitan Museum of Art.

That's why it helps to plan ahead. Most museums and attractions offer advance tickets through their websites, allowing you to bypass lines and shorten your wait. It usually pays to show up early in the morning, before most people get going. And if you know you want to visit certain places—the Guggenheim, the Empire State Building, the Museum of Modern Art, the Statue of Liberty, and the American Museum of Natural History—you'll bypass the lines and save a bundle with a nine-day **New York CityPass**. It costs $53 for adults and $44 for children—prices that will seem very reasonable when you look at the admission prices at places like the Metropolitan Museum of Art and the Statue of Liberty.

Go to any participating museum or www.citypass.com for more information.

METROPOLITAN MUSEUM OF ART
1000 Fifth Avenue (bet 80th and 84th St) 212/535-7710
www.metmuseum.org

Five thousand years of art. That's how the Metropolitan Museum of Art ("the Met," as its known to New Yorkers and art fans) describes its holdings. Egyptian tombs? Greek sculpture? African masks? Armor from the Crusades? Vases from China? Early American furniture? Tiffany windows? Nineteenth-century costumes? Twentieth-century photography? Twenty-first-century videography? It's all here. And no matter how many times you visit or how much time you spend here, there's just no way you'll ever see it all. The depth and breadth of the Met's collection is unparalleled.

There are several ways to approach touring the Met. I suggest coming early on a weekday morning, getting a copy of the floor plan at the information desk, and figuring out a couple areas of the museum you want to visit over the course of a day. You can always break for lunch at one of the museum's several restaurants or end your day with a drink at The Balcony bar. Another alternative is taking a "Museum Highlights" tour, offered daily in various languages. My favorite strategy is simply going where everyone else isn't. Crowds can be overwhelming on weekends (which is why strollers are banned on Saturday and Sunday) and whenever there's a special exhibit. Buying advance tickets ("guest passes") at the Met is a good way to avoid long lines.

A favorite part of any Met visit for many people is a trip to one of the museum's many gift stores. Although you can now visit Met gift stores at LaGuardia and Kennedy airports, as well as at Rockefeller Plaza, it's more fun browsing the gift shops inside the Met itself. **Hours**: Tuesday through Friday from 9:30 to 5:30, Saturday and Sunday from 9:30 to 9. **Admission**: Donations of $20 for adults, $15 for seniors with ID, $10 for students with ID, and free for children under 12 are strongly suggested. Same-day admission to The Cloisters—the amazing branch of the Met in northern Manhattan's Fort Tryon Park, featuring medieval art and architecture—is included.

MUSEUM OF MODERN ART
11 W 53rd St (bet Fifth Ave and Ave of the Americas) 212/708-9400
www.moma.org

This recently expanded museum is itself a masterpiece, filled with glass and soaring spaces. On West 53rd Street just off Fifth Avenue in midtown, MoMA (pronounced MO'ma) is the leading museum in the world dedicated to modern art. Well over 100,000 pieces of art—paintings, prints, photography, sculpture—are housed here, along with a remarkable archive and film library. From Cezanne, van Gogh, Matisse, and Picasso to Jasper Johns, Jeff Koons, Georgia O'Keefe and Jackson Pollack, just about any artist you can imagine is represented. Indeed, MoMA's sleek galleries are a Who's Who of modern art history.

MoMA's curatorial departments include Architecture and Design; Drawings, Painting and Sculpture; Photography, Prints and Illustrated Books; and Film and Media. Pieces from each department are always on display in various collection galleries. In addition, MoMA has changing exhibitions and often hosts special traveling exhibitions. If you have time, I suggest starting on the sixth floor and working your way down. If you want a quick tour of some of the museum's most famous holdings (Van Gogh's *Starry Night*, Picasso's *Guitar*, Matisse's *Dance (1)*, and Andy Warhol's *Campbell's Soup Cans* are just a few examples), stop by the information desk and get a map.

A visit to this amazing place is not complete without a stop at the MoMA Bookstore (just off the foyer on the first floor) and the MoMA Design Store (across the street). Although there is some overlap between the two stores, there are enough differences to make it well worth your time to peruse both, as well as lunch at either of the two cafes at MoMA or dinner at The Modern, a high-end restaurant. **Hours**: daily except Tuesday from 10:30 to 5:30 (Friday until 8:30). **Admission**: $20 for adults, $16 for seniors with ID, $12 for students with ID, and free for children under 16 and everybody between 4 and 8 on Friday. Some films carry an additional charge. Admission to PS 1, an affiliated museum in Long Island City, is free if you show your MoMA ticket stub within 30 days.

STATUE OF LIBERTY
New York Harbor (south of Battery Park) 212/363-3200
www.nps.gov/stli

They call her Lady Liberty. This 151-foot bronze statue of a woman holding a torch was created by Frederic-Auguste Bartholdi and given to the

United States as a gift from France in 1886. Standing on Liberty Island in New York Harbor, it's probably the single most iconic sight in all of New York. For generations of immigrants who came through the nearby Ellis Island, it was also the first real sight they had of this new land. The words from "The New Colossus," a poem written by Emma Lazarus to help raise money for the completion of the pedestal for this powerful monument, still expresses the most noble instincts of our country and the symbolism of the Statue of Liberty: "Give me your tired, your poor/Your huddled masses yearning to breathe free."

A trip out to Liberty Island and the Statue of Liberty will take the better part of a morning or afternoon, so plan accordingly. Both the Statue of Liberty and Ellis Island are run by the National Park Service. Visiting either or both requires a trip by boat from Battery Park. Head to Castle Clinton in Battery Park for tickets and detailed information, or buy your tickets in advance from www.statuereservations.com. Even if you have tickets, you'll need to wait in line for the next available boat. My advice: Go early on a weekday and bring along lots of patience. **Hours**: daily from 9 to 5 (longer in summer). **Admission**: free, but a ferry ticket costs $11.50 for adults, $9.50 for seniors, and $4.50 for children between 4 and 12.

Long considered off-limits, even during daylight hours, the 66-acre **Fort Tryon Park** at the northern tip of Manhattan is fast becoming a real jewel in the crown of the city's parks. Named for William Tryon, the last British governor of colonial New York, the park occupies the highest spot in all of Manhattan, with commanding views of the Hudson River and New Jersey beyond. The park sits between the Hudson and Broadway from West 192nd Street to Dyckman Street.

Most people familiar with Fort Tryon Park know it only as home to The Cloisters, and of course that terrific branch of the Metropolitan Museum of Art is reason enough to visit. But a stroll through the park's gorgeous grounds in the fall or spring is now a great treat as well, as is a stop at the **New Leaf Cafe**. The cafe, opened in 2001 in a restored 1930s building, offers lunch and dinner Tuesday through Saturday, with brunch on Sunday. All profits go to the continued restoration of the park. For information on hours and menu, go to their website (www.nyrp.org/newleaf).

TIMES SQUARE
42nd St at Broadway and surrounding area   www.timessquarenyc.org

When I first starting writing this book, Times Square was synonymous with petty crime, prostitution, and filth. Not anymore. In fact, I find it hard to believe that the Times Square of yesteryear and the Times Square of the 21st century are the same place. Named for the original New York Times building and incorporating the neighborhood around 42nd Street and Broadway, Times Square is now a center of New York's burgeoning tourist industry. It's full of family-friendly restaurants, hotels, and entertainment venues. **Madame Toussaud's** wax museum; a **Toys 'R Us**, complete with a real ferris wheel; and **ESPN Zone** are just a few of the hundreds of family-oriented attractions that have sprouted up here. There's even a terrific tourist information center in the Embassy Theater (on Seventh Avenue between 46th and 47th streets), and a long-awaited TKTS booth will be unveiled soon after this book goes to press.

All of those changes do not, however, put Times Square at the top of my list of places I recommend to visitors. In fact, I would avoid it all together unless you particularly want to see three-story billboards and lots of neon. The whole area is wildly crowded with out-of-towners, the food is almost uniformly bad, prices are sky-high, and service tends to run from surly to incompetent. The whole area is loud and in-your-face. In fact, it's a bit like going to a big mall somewhere in the nondescript suburbs around the winter holidays, except that you have to deal with traffic and there are few bargains to be had. Yuck.

The Best of the Rest

The previous "Top Ten" list includes the museums and sights everyone wants to see when they come to New York. Although many of the museums and sights on that list are definite "must sees," they are by no means all there is to New York. In fact, some of *my* "must sees" are less well known, smaller, or a bit off the beaten path. The following list includes what I consider to be the crown jewels of this remarkable city.

Up-to-Date Information

If you want to find out about current exhibits, look in the front of the *New Yorker*, the back of *New York* magazine, the "Museums" section of *Time Out New York*, or *Where New York* magazine (distributed free in most hotels).

AMERICAN FOLK ART MUSEUM
45 W 53rd St (at Ave of the Americas)   212/265-1040
www.folkartmuseum.org

The American Folk Art Museum's award-winning building is half the reason to visit this gem. A sleek and beautiful addition to midtown, it is filled with light and interesting spaces. The museum's collection of American paintings, textiles, and other folk art spans several centuries and is thoughtfully displayed in galleries and public spaces throughout the eight-story building. The museum's cafe and gift shop are excellent. **Hours**: Tuesday through Sunday from 10:30 to 5:30 (Friday till 7:30). **Admission**: $9 for adults, $7 for seniors and students, and free for children under 12 and everyone after 5:30 on Friday.

BROOKLYN BRIDGE
foot of bridge is just east of City Hall in Lower Manhattan

Spanning the East River, this spectacular suspension bridge links Lower Manhattan to Brooklyn. It took 15 years and two generations to build. After its designer, John Roebling, was killed in an accident, his son Washington and wife Emily took over the project. Pedestrians and bicyclists share the bridge's historic promenade; bicyclists have the north lane, pedestrians the south. To reach the bridge, go to the east side of City Hall Park, just off Broadway, and follow the signs. Sunset and sunrise are particularly beautiful times to take a stroll on the bridge, although it's open 24 hours a day.

CATHEDRAL CHURCH OF ST. JOHN THE DIVINE
1047 Amsterdam Ave (at 112th St)   212/316-7490
www.stjohndivine.org

Gracing Amsterdam Avenue on the east side of Columbia University, the Cathedral Church of St. John the Divine is one of the largest Christian houses of worship in the world. And it isn't even finished! Part Gothic, part Romanesque, and part Byzantine, this magnificent Episcopal cathedral is so big that the Statue of Liberty could easily fit inside the main sanctuary. For information about daily tours, call 212/932-7347. **Hours**: Daily from 7 to 6 (Sunday till 7). **Admission**: free, although donations are accepted and a minimal fee is charged for tours.

Ground Zero

Just the words *Ground Zero* evoke graphic pictures in our collective memory of the terrorist attacks on the twin towers of the World Trade Center on September 11, 2001. Tens of thousands of people worked here every day and more than 3,000 people from over a hundred countries lost their lives here on that fateful day. It's not a museum, and it feels odd to call it an attraction. In fact, despite groundbreaking in 2004 for a new Freedom Tower on the site, there's not much to see except the retaining wall that continues to hold back the Hudson River and a vast amount of empty space. But hundreds of thousands of people visiting New York every year stop to pay their respects. Church, Liberty, Barclay, and West streets form the boundaries of the site. Most visitors make a stop at the Wall of Heroes along Church Street. The glass-enclosed back wall of the **World Financial Center**, directly across West Street from Ground Zero, also offers a good view of the site.

The September 11 Families Association has created a **WTC Tribute Center** (120 Liberty St, bet Greenwich and Church St). Family members, neighbors, and others directly affected by the events of September 11 lead tours of the site, and galleries display various items relating to the World Trade Center and those who died there. (For more information, go to www.tributewtc.org or call 212/393-9160.) A $10 donation is requested.

Perhaps the most moving of the many other memorials is an exhibit inside **St. Paul's Chapel** called "Unwavering Spirit: Hope and Healing at Ground Zero." A gathering place for thousands fleeing the destruction on September 11, the chapel is located on Broadway between Fulton and Vesey streets. The exhibit is open Monday through Saturday from 10 to 6 and Sunday from 9 to 4. Admission is free.

THE CLOISTERS
Fort Tryon Park   212/923-3700

Perhaps the finest medieval art museum in the world, this branch of the Metropolitan Museum of Art is also one of the quietest and most beautiful places in all of New York. Built at the far north end of the island on land donated by John D. Rockefeller, Jr. in the late 1930s, the museum incorporates large sections of cloisters and other medieval buildings brought from Europe. Tapestries, ivories, paintings, sculpture, and other decorative items are part of the spectacular collection on display here. From the outdoor terrace, you can look out at the medieval gardens, the Hudson River, and the Palisades beyond, easily forgetting that you're in a 21st century city. **Hours:** Tuesday through Sunday from 9:30 to 5:15 (till 4:45 from November through February). **Admission:** $20 for adults, $15 for seniors with ID, $10 for students with ID, and free for children under 12 is "suggested." Same-day admission to the Metropolitan Museum of Art is part of the price.

New York-ese

Many places in America have their own special words and phrases that people from elsewhere don't understand. Here are some terms commonly heard in New York:

Bridge and tunnel crowd: a disparaging term for visitors from New Jersey; also "B&T crowd"

The City: shorthand for New York City

Coffee regular: coffee with milk and sugar

The FDR: Franklin Roosevelt Drive, an expressway running the length of Manhattan's East Side along the East River

Fuhgeddaboudit: "Forget about it," as in "Don't mention it." It can also mean "No way."

The Garden: Madison Square Garden

The Island: Long Island

Houston: a street in lower Manhattan, pronounced *HOUSE-ton*

The Met: the Metropolitan Opera or Metropolitan Museum of Art

Schlep: as a verb, to drag or haul something; as a noun, a jerk

Shmeer: a smear of cream cheese, usually on a bagel

Slice: a piece of pizza

Soda: any sweet carbonated beverage; short for "soda pop"

COOPER-HEWITT NATIONAL DESIGN MUSEUM
2 E 91st St (at Fifth Ave)   212/849-8400
                                                             www.ndm.si.edu

Founded as the Cooper Union Museum for the Arts of Decoration in 1997, this remarkable institution became part of the Smithsonian Institution in 1967. Its exhibitions, covering 24 centuries of every facet of design, are consistently well conceived and interesting. But what I really love about the Cooper-Hewitt is that it's housed in Andrew Carnegie's 64-room mansion. The Great Hall and the gardens are particular pleasures! If you're interested in seeing how New York's wealthiest citizens lived a hundred years ago you might want to take a trip to the Rockefeller Rooms, on the fifth floor of the Museum of the City of New York, and Mr. Morgan's Library and Study, at the Morgan Library and Museum. **Hours:** Monday through Thursday from 10 to 5, Friday from 10 to 9, Saturday from 10 to 6, and Sunday from noon to 6. **Admission:** $12 for adults, $9 for seniors and students, and free for children under 12 and Smithsonian Associates.

FRICK COLLECTION
1 E 70th St (at Fifth Ave)

212/288-0700
www.frick.org

This elegant mansion takes my breath away! Built by industrialist Henry Clay Frick almost a century ago to house his growing art collection, the Frick Collection is one of the last great mansions on Fifth Avenue and on the very top of my "must see" list in New York. Gilbert Stuart's portrait of George Washington is here, as are works by Rembrandt, El Greco, Goya, and masters ranging from the Italian Renaissance to the 19th century. But it isn't just the paintings that dazzle. Frick's collection also includes stunning Oriental rugs, Chinese porcelain, Limoge enamels, and a wide range of decorative arts that must be seen to be believed. Take time to wander here, looking at everything from the paintings to the light fixtures to the rugs. Be forewarned: Children under 10 are not allowed into the Frick and children under 16 must be accompanied by an adult. **Hours:** Tuesday through Saturday from 10 to 6, Sunday from 11 to 5. **Admission:** $15 for adults, $10 for seniors, and $5 for students with ID. "Artphone," an audio tour that you can use at your own pace, is provided free with admission. Pay-what-you-wish on Sunday from 11 to 1.

GRAND CENTRAL TERMINAL
42nd St bet Vanderbilt and Lexington Ave

www.grandcentralterminal.com

New York's past, present, and future come together in this marble palace. Opened in 1913, Grand Central is first and foremost a train station, home to hundreds of commuter trains that take commuters between Manhattan and points north in Westchester County and Connecticut. But thanks to a renovation and cleaning undertaken a decade ago, it now also plays host to an upscale food market, dozens of shops featuring everything from toys to lingerie, and a great food court downstairs. You'll even find safe public bathrooms! Come in the Vanderbilt Avenue entrance and watch the action from the balcony, or come on Wednesday at 12:30 for a fascinating tour offered by the Municipal Art Society ($10 per person is the suggested donation). **Hours:** 5:30 a.m. to 1:30 a.m. (stores and restaurants keep shorter hours). **Admission:** free.

JEWISH MUSEUM
1109 Fifth Ave (at 92nd St)   212/423-3200

www.thejewishmuseum.org

Operated by the Jewish Theological Seminary of America and housed in yet another grand Fifth Avenue mansion—this one donated by Felix Warburg's widow in 1947 (Warburg was a Jewish philanthropist)—the Jewish Museum is home to the largest collection of Jewish art and Judaica in the United States. Art and artifacts from 4,000 years of Jewish history are on display here, as is the work of contemporary artists. Some pieces were rescued from European synagogues and Jewish communities before and during World War II. The heart of the museum is "Culture and Continuity: The Jewish Journey," a two-floor exhibit featuring 800 works from around the world. A visit to the museum's excellent gift shop or Celebrations, a smaller design shop in an adjacent brownstone, is well worth an extra half-hour. The Jewish Museum recently opened its doors on Saturday; admission is free, but the restaurant and museum stores are closed in honor of the Sabbath. **Hours:** Saturday through Thursday from 11 to 5:45 (Thursday till 8). **Admission:** $12 for adults, $10 for seniors, $7.50 for students, free to children under 12 and free to everyone on Saturday.

LOWER EAST SIDE TENEMENT MUSEUM
108 Orchard St (bet Delancey and Broome St)   212/431-0233
www.tenement.org

Whether or not you're one of the hundreds of thousands of people in this country whose family traces its arrival in this country to the Lower East Side, a visit to this living history museum is another one of my "must sees" in New York. Every tour starts at the visitors center and then crosses the street to the tenement building at 97 Orchard Street, where various apartments are frozen in time. Home to as many as 7,000 people from more than 20 nations between 1863 and 1935, this building is a living memorial to the tens of thousands of people who passed through the Lower East Side as new immigrants to this country. Depending on the tour, you'll encounter various immigrant families modeled on real people who lived in this building between the 1870s and the 1930s. A walking tour of the Lower East Side is also available on weekends in warmer months. Take time for the excellent 25-minute film about the history of immigration on the Lower East Side, which runs continuously at the visitors center. Take time for browsing in the excellent gift shop, too. **Hours:** The visitors center is open weekdays from 11 to 6 (Monday till 5:30) and weekends from 10:45 to 6. Tour times vary, so call ahead or check the website for details. **Admission:** The visitors center is free but most tours cost in the range of $15; reservations are strongly suggested.

Because of ongoing security concerns, the **New York Stock Exchange** is no longer open to the public.

MORGAN LIBRARY AND MUSEUM
225 Madison Ave (at 36th St)   212/685-0008
www.themorgan.org

Two rooms make a visit to this out-of-the-way museum well warranted: Mr. Morgan's Library and Study. Designed by famed architect Charles McKim in the very beginning of the 20th century to house the astonishing collection amassed by Pierpont Morgan (an industrialist and financier). These two elegant rooms and their contents will transport you to another time and place. Just imagine yourself surrounded by these paintings, sculptures, furniture, books, architectural details, and textiles spanning many centuries and several continents! It's hard to believe anyone ever lived like this. Morgan's collection includes everything from musical scores by Mozart to drawings by Rembrandt to seals and tablets from Babylon. The spaces in the rest of the museum, including a new atrium and other galleries, are often crowded and feel a bit disjointed. However, this is a good place to eat. **Hours:** Tuesday through Thursday from 10:30 to 5, Friday from 10:30 to 9, Saturday from 10 to 6, and Sunday from 11 to 6. **Admission:** $12 for adults, $8 for seniors, students with ID, and children under 16, and free for children under 12 and everyone from 7 to 9 on Friday. Admission to Mr. Morgan's Library and Study is also free on Tuesday from 3 to 5 and Sunday from 4 to 6.

MUSEUM OF THE CITY OF NEW YORK
1220 Fifth Ave (bet 103rd and 104th St)   212/534-1672
www.mcny.org

Why this museum and the New-York Historical Society don't merge their massive holdings and consolidate their operations is beyond me. Both are dedicated to preserving the history of New York from the earliest European settlement, and both have remarkable collections. For the casual visitor, Museum of the City of New York is probably the more accessible of the two. It's certainly the most family-friendly. With four floors of changing and permanent exhibits, there's something for everyone, from Broadway costumes to fine silver to the bedroom and dressing room from the home of John D. Rockefeller, Sr.—high on my "don't miss" list—up on the fifth floor. That said, the whole place is a bit dowdy and most of the staff seemed quite disinterested during a recent visit. The museum also offers an exceptional array of children's programs, lectures, classes, and other events. **Hours:** Tuesday through Sunday from 10 to 5. **Admission:** $9 for adults, $5 for seniors, free for children under 12, and free for everyone from 10 to noon on Sunday. Families with no more than two adults can pay $20.

Historic Churches and Synagogues

Because New York was a British colony for much of its early history, the city's lower half is full of historic Episcopal churches. They include **Trinity Church** (Broadway at Wall St); **St. Paul's Chapel**, the oldest church building in the city, dating from 1764 (Broadway between Fulton and Vesey St); **St. Mark's in the Bowery**, constructed on the site of Peter Stuyvesant's personal chapel in 1799 (10th St at Second Ave); **Grace Church** (Broadway between 10th and 11th St); and the **Church of the Transfiguration**, also known as "the Little Church Around the Corner" (Fifth Ave at 29th St).

Other historic houses of worship in Manhattan include **Abyssinian Baptist Church** (132 W 138th St), **Central Synagogue** (Lexington Ave at 55th St), **Marble Collegiate Church** (1 W 29th St), **Riverside Church** (490 Riverside Dr), the **Spanish and Portuguese Synagogue** (8 W 70th St), the **Bialystoker Synagogue** (7-11 Willet St), and **Temple Emanu-El** (1 E 65th St).

Separate entries for the **Cathedral Church of St. John the Divine**, **Eldridge Street Synagogue**, and **St. Patrick's Cathedral** can be found in this section. A complete listing of churches, synagogues, mosques, and other houses of worship can be found in the Manhattan Yellow Pages.

MUSEUM OF JEWISH HERITAGE: A LIVING MEMORIAL TO THE HOLOCAUST
36 Battery Place   646/437-4202
                                                www.mjhnyc.org

This remarkable and sometimes overlooked museum just north of Battery Park in lower Manhattan manages to be not only a memorial to those who perished in the Holocaust but also a vibrant, life-affirming celebration of Jewish culture and its endurance. Using first-person narrative and a remarkably diverse collection, the museum's three-part permanent display tells the unfolding story of Jewish life a century ago, the persecution of Jews and the Holocaust, and modern Jewish life and renewal in the decades since. The recent addition of a new wing has made changing exhibitions possible, and the first few have been exceptional. Both the cafe, which has amazing views of the Statue of Liberty and New York Harbor, and the museum's gift shop are worthy of a visit. Andy Goldsworthy's *Garden of Stone* outside the museum is a terrific spot to sit and think. Because of the sobering subject matter, this may not be a place to take very young children, and all visitors here should be prepared to take their time. **Hours**: Sunday through Tuesday and Thursday from 10 to 5:45, Wednesday from 10 to 8, and Friday from 10 to 5 (till 3 during Daylight Savings Time). **Admission**: $10 for adults, $7 for seniors, $5 for students, free for children under 12, and free for everyone from 4 to 8 on Wednesday.

NEW YORK PUBLIC LIBRARY
455 Fifth Ave (bet 40th and 42nd St) 212/ 340-0833
www.nypl.org

This mid-Manhattan branch of the New York Public Library is a working library and has the largest collection of circulating and reference works in the entire system. It's also home to a wide range of public programs. But this isn't just any library! Located along Fifth Avenue, it's a "must see" if you're in midtown. Standing guard out front are two stately lions, named Patience and Fortitude by New York Mayor Fiorello LaGuardia. Inside you'll find marble staircases, an excellent gift shop, the beautifully renovated Rose Main Reading Room on the third floor, an amazing map room on the first floor, and various gallery spaces. Stop by the information desk in the breathtaking lobby to find out about the frequent tours offered by the Friends of the New York Public Library. **Hours**: Monday through Wednesday from 9 to 9, Thursday through Saturday from 10 to 6. **Admission**: free.

ROOSEVELT ISLAND
In the East River, between Manhattan and Queens

If you're a photographer looking for that perfect shot of the Manhattan skyline, a trip to Roosevelt Island should be at the top of your itinerary. At various times in its history, Roosevelt Island was known as Blackwell's Island and Welfare Island, and it's been home to various prisons, hospitals, and asylums. Today the two-mile island in the middle of the East River is home to 9,000 residents, many of whom commute into Manhattan each day. Visitors come for the view, particularly from the tram and from the northwest tip of the Lighthouse Park. The four-minute tram ride from Manhattan leaves from a small station at Second Avenue and 59th Street. **Hours**: The tram to Roosevelt Island runs from 6 a.m. to 2:30 a.m. (till 3:30 a.m. on weekends). **Admission**: $2 each way ($2 round trip for seniors).

ST. PATRICK'S CATHEDRAL
Fifth Ave bet 50th and 51st St 212/753-2261
www.saintpatrickscathedral.org

Designed in the middle of the 19th century by famed architect James Renwick, Jr., this Gothic cathedral is a much-loved Fifth Avenue landmark and the largest Roman Catholic church in the United States. The main organ has 9,000 pipes, and the sanctuary can seemingly seat half of Manhattan.

Whether you're here for a service or just peeking inside, it's hard to over-state the beauty and elegance of St. Patrick's. Please remember that this is an active church. Mass is said several times each day, eight times on Sunday, and even more on Holy Days. You are welcome to come in and light a candle or just sit in silence. Here's a tip: the cathedral's steps along Fifth Avenue are one of the best places in New York for resting your feet and watching the world go by! **Hours**: daily from 6:30 a.m. to 8:45 p.m. **Admission**: free.

STATEN ISLAND FERRY
Whitehall Ferry Terminal (at the foot of Whitehall St)

www.siferry.com

Five different ferries make 104 trips every day between Staten Island and the Whitehall Ferry Terminal on Manhattan's southern tip. The trip takes 25 minutes and covers five miles. And what a trip it is! Like the ferries that ply Puget Sound near Seattle, the Staten Island ferries offer some of the very best views and a comfortable place to sit and take them in. Best of all: it's free. Just show up anytime of day or night and there will be a sailing again soon.

Outside Manhattan

Just because I've limited myself to museums and sights in Manhattan doesn't mean that there aren't places in other boroughs worth ex-ploring. The **New York Transit Museum** in Brooklyn (718/243-8601, www.meta.nyc.ny.us/museum) should be at the top of the list for anyone interested in trains and subways. The **Brooklyn Art Museum** (718/638-5000, www.brooklynart.org) is one of the coun-try's most prestigious museums and has one of the best Egyptian col-lections in the world. The recently renovated and expanded **Bronx Museum of the Arts** (718/681-6000, www.bronxmuseum.org) offers wonderful opportunities to see new and emerging artists through its Arts in the Marketplace program. The **New York Hall of Science** in Queens (718/699-0005, www.nyhallsci.org), the **Bronx Zoo** (718/367-1010, www.bronxzoo.org), and the **Liberty Science Center**, just across the Hudson in New Jersey (201/200-1000, www. lsc.org), are all world-class destinations.

TRINITY CHURCH
74 Trinity Place (Broadway at Wall St)   212/602-0800

www.trinitywallstreet.org

In the heart of lower Manhattan's Financial District, this is the third Epis-copal church to occupy a site on land donated by King William III of England in 1698. This building was completed in 1846, although the headstones in the 2.5 acre graveyard date back to the late 17th century. Believe it or not, Trinity Church was the tallest building in Manhattan for most of the 19th century. Today it offers a small museum, guided tours and concerts, in addi-tion to daily worship services. Tours are offered daily at 2. **Hours**: Although the church itself is open longer hours, the museum is open Monday through Friday from 9 to 11:45 and 1 to 3:45, Saturday from 10 to 3:45, and Sunday from 1 to 3:45. **Admission**: free (although donations are happily accepted).

UNITED NATIONS

First Ave bet 42nd and 47th St   212/963-8687
www.un.org/tours

New York is a great American city, but it is also a great *international* city and the headquarters of the United Nations. The flags of 192 member nations fly along First Avenue in front of the General Assembly building, and many languages are spoken on the streets in this area as delegates come and go. You can visit the beautiful and peaceful grounds of the UN, wander through the changing exhibits in the large lobby, or go inside the main building for a tour. Whatever else you do, be sure to visit the stores in the basement, as well as the UN's very own post office. **Hours**: daily from 9 to 5 (closed weekends in Jan and Feb). **Admission**: free, although tours cost $13 for adults, $9 for senior citizens, $8.50 for students under 30 with ID, and $7 for children between 5 and 14. Children under 5 are not allowed on tours.

The Third Time's the Charm

The gallery space on the corner of Madison Avenue and 57th Street has been home to the IBM Gallery and the Freedom Forum's Newseum. Now it is home to the **Dahesh Museum of Art**, a wonderful little museum dedicated to show-casing work by classically trained European artists of the 19th and 20th centuries. In addition to beautiful art and the respite it offers in the midst of the bustle of midtown, a window seat in the second-floor **Café Opaline** makes for some pretty great people-watching! For information about hours and exhibits, go to www.daheshmuseum.org or call 212/759-0606.

WHITNEY MUSEUM OF AMERICAN ART

945 Madison Ave (at 75th St)   212/570-3676
www.whitney.org

The artist and art collector Gertrude Vanderbilt Whitney started this museum in 1931 with her personal collection of 20th-century art. It has grown in the years since (and moved twice) but remained true to its mission: collecting and displaying modern American art. Of course that mission means the Whitney's remarkable collection now spans more than a century and continues to expand. It includes the world's largest collections of Edward Hopper, Reginald Marsh, and Alexander Calder, as well as sculpture, paintings, drawings, media installations, and other work by established and emerging artists. A branch of **Sarabeth's Kitchen**, long a popular East Side restaurant, is located on the museum's lower level. **Hours**: Wednesday and Thursday from 11 to 6, Friday from 1 to 9, and Saturday and Sunday from 11 to 6. **Admission**: $15 for adults, $10 for seniors and students, and free for children under 12 and New York public high school students. Visitors are invited to pay-what-you-wish on Friday from 6 to 9.

Smaller Museums and Special Spots

AMERICAN NUMISMATIC SOCIETY

33 Liberty St (bet Nassau and William St)   www.numismatics.org

The Federal Reserve Bank of New York, in the heart of Wall Street, is the perfect place for the American Numismatic Society's fascinating permanent display of some of the highlights of its collection, entitled "Drachmas, Doubloons, and Dollars: The History of Money." **Hours**: weekdays from 10 to 4. **Admission**: free.

AMERICAS SOCIETY GALLERY
680 Park Ave (at 68th St)   212/249-9850
www.americas-society.org

The Americas Society was founded in 1965 by David Rockefeller with the simple but important goal of furthering understanding between the Americas. The changing exhibitions in its small but elegant gallery space showcase the diverse work of artists from throughout the Americas. **Hours**: Wednesday through Saturday from noon to 6. **Admission**: free.

ASIA SOCIETY AND MUSEUM
725 Park Ave (at 70th St)   212/288-6400

Using both private collections and its own extensive holdings of art from the more than 30 countries that make up the Asia-Pacific region, the Asia Society mounts changing exhibits in its recently renovated headquarters. The lovely restaurant and gift shop are well worth a visit. **Hours**: Tuesday through Sunday from 11 to 6 (Friday till 9). **Admission**: $10 for adults, $7 for seniors, $5 for students with ID, and free to everyone from 6 to 9 on Friday.

BARD GRADUATE CENTER
18 W 86th St (at Central Park West)   212/501-3000
www.bgc.bard.edu/exhibit

The Bard Graduate School is known around the world for its passionate commitment to the decorative arts, design, and culture. Its beautiful townhouse on the Upper West Side hosts several changing exhibits each year. **Hours**: Tuesday through Sunday, 11 to 5 (Thursday till 8). **Admission**: $3 for adults, $2 for seniors and students.

BRYANT PARK
Ave of the Americas bet 40th and 42nd St   www.bryantpark.org

More than almost anywhere else in all of New York, this park symbolizes for me the remarkable transformation that has occurred throughout the city in the past 30 years. Long a place to be avoided, Bryant Park is now a thriving part of the city's life. Home to a wonderful carousel, an ice rink in the winter, free movies in the summer, and chess and backgammon games throughout the year, this urban jewel sits behind the New York Public Library. Have lunch, go to an event, or just wander through: this is what all urban parks should aspire to be!

CHELSEA ART MUSEUM
556 W 22nd St (at Eleventh Ave)   212/255-0719
www.chelseaartmuseum.org

A great stop if you're gallery hopping in Chelsea, this museum is dedicated to showcasing the work of artists from the 20th and 21st centuries whose work is not as well known in the United States as it is in their home countries. It is also the home of the Jean Miotte Foundation. **Hours**: Tuesday through Saturday, noon to 6 (Thursday till 8). **Admission**: $6 for adults and $3 for seniors and students.

CHINA INSTITUTE
125 E 65th St (bet Madison and Park Ave)   212/744-8181
www.chinainstitute.org

This is the only not-for-profit gallery in New York (other than the Metropolitan Museum of Art) dedicated to showcasing the traditional art of China. Changing exhibits in this beautiful East Side townhouse are of consistently high quality. **Hours**: Monday through Saturday from 10 to 5 (Tuesday and Thursday till 8). **Admission**: $5 for adults, $3 for students and seniors, free for children under 12, and free for everyone on Tuesday and Thursday from 6 to 8.

Call Before Going!

If you have your heart set on visiting a small museum or a particular gallery inside a larger one, my advice is to call before going. Many museums now rent out space for parties, movie shoots, and other events, sometimes closing altogether or closing off certain areas—even during regularly posted hours. I've seen this happen repeatedly at the American Museum of Natural History, and I know it happens at other places as well. It's really frustrating, but don't say I didn't warn you! It's also worth noting that some of the smaller museums and galleries host only a few exhibitions each year and so sometimes are closed between shows.

DRAWING CENTER
35 Wooster St (bet Grand and Broome St)   212/219-2166
www.drawingcenter.org

Dedicated exclusively to showcasing contemporary and historical drawings, this Soho institution mounts highly regarded changing exhibitions. **Hours**: Tuesday through Friday from 10 to 6, Saturday from 11 to 6. **Admission**: free.

DYCKMAN FARMHOUSE MUSEUM
4881 Broadway (at 204th St)   212/304-9422
www.dyckmanfarmhouse.org

The last surviving example of the sort of farmhouse built all over New York well into the 19th Century, this is a little time machine sitting on what was once Kingsbridge Road (now known as Broadway). Look here for particularly good family programs. **Hours**: Wednesday through Saturday from 11 to 4, Sunday from noon to 4. **Admission**: $1 for adults and free for children under 10, although additional donations are appreciated.

EL MUSEO DEL BARRIO
1230 Fifth Ave (at 104th St)   212/831-7272
www.elmuseo.org

El Museo del Barrio means "Museum of the Neighborhood" in Spanish, and it was founded almost 40 years ago by neighborhood artists and community activists as a place to showcase the diverse art of Puerto Rico and Latin America. An extensive renovation is underway as this book goes to press, promising to make this small but vibrant museum a full-fledged member of Museum Mile. **Hours**: Wednesday through Sunday from 11 to 5. **Admission**: $6 for adults, $4 for seniors and students, and free for children under 12.

ELDRIDGE STREET SYNAGOGUE
12 Eldridge Street (bet Canal and Division St)   212/219-0888
www.eldridgestreet.org

For decades after it opened in 1887, the Eldridge Street Synagogue on the Lower East Side was a central part of the life of thousands of Eastern European Jewish immigrants. After it fell on hard times and was literally falling apart, a nonprofit organization was formed to restore its original grandeur and tell some of the stories that passed through these doors. Call or visit the website for details about public programs and tours.

FEDERAL HALL NATIONAL MEMORIAL
26 Wall St (bet Broad and William St)   212/825-6888
www.nps.gov/feha

Everyone knows that Washington, D.C. is the nation's capital, but it didn't start out that way. In fact, George Washington was inaugurated on this spot in the first Federal Hall (it was torn down in 1812 and the current building was built in 1842), which served briefly as the U.S. Capitol. After extensive renovations, this National Park Service site hosts a small gallery and an information center largely focused on lower Manhattan. **Hours**: weekdays (except Federal holidays) from 9 to 5. **Admission**: free.

FORBES MAGAZINE GALLERIES
62 Fifth Ave (at 12th St)   212/206-5548
www.forbesgalleries.com

Tucked beside the lobby of the Forbes Magazine building, these little galleries showcase some of the diverse collections of the late Malcolm Forbes and his sons. You can see 10,000 toy soldiers and related figurines, 500 toy boats, and even a 1920 edition of the Landlord's Game—the forerunner to today's Monopoly. Gone are the eggs and other pieces from the House of Fabergé, but these galleries now also host all sorts of small, changing exhibits as well. **Hours**: Tuesday, Wednesday, Friday, and Saturday from 10 to 4 (group tours are held on Thursday). **Admission**: free (although children under 16 are not allowed without an adult and no more than four children per adult are allowed).

FRAUNCES TAVERN MUSEUM
54 Pearl St (at Broad St)   212/425-1778
www.frauncestavernmuseum.org

Fraunces Tavern was a meeting place for the Sons of Liberty before the Revolutionary War and the site of General George Washington's farewell address to his troops after the war. It actually traces its history back to 1719 and is one of the oldest buildings in New York. The first floor still operates as a restaurant (call 212/968-1776 for reservations), while the second floor is dedicated to a museum focused largely on the Revolutionary War period. **Hours:** Tuesday through Friday from noon to 5 and Saturday from 10 to 5. **Admission:** $4 for adults, $3 for seniors and students, and free for children under 6.

HISPANIC SOCIETY OF AMERICA
Audubon Terrace (Broadway bet 155th and 156th St)

212/926-2234
www.hispanicsociety.org

The former farm of naturalist John James Audubon seems like an unlikely place for the Hispanic Society of America, and a man named Archer Milton Huntington sounds like an unlikely benefactor. But the most significant collection of paintings, textiles, ceramics, photographs, and other items from the Iberian Peninsula and Latin America in North America indeed sits atop Audubon's farm and was largely assembled by Huntington. If you're interested in the subject, a trek up to this out-of-the-way spot will be well worth your time. An exceptional reference library is also housed here. **Hours:** Tuesday through Saturday from 10 to 4:30 and Sunday from 1 to 4. **Admission:** free.

A New Museum on Museum Mile

In late 2009, the **Museum for African Art** will take up residence in its new home on Duke Ellington Circle, adjacent to the northeast corner of Central Park at Fifth Avenue and 110th Street. The museum will feature contemporary and historic African art. As a big fan of the museum's old home in Soho, I can't wait for this expansive new space!

INTERNATIONAL CENTER FOR PHOTOGRAPHY
1133 Ave of the Americas (at 43rd St)

212/857-0000
www.icp.org

If you like photography, this center for the study, preservation, and exhibition of photographic art is a "must see." Beautiful gallery spaces and exceptionally well-conceived shows combine to make a visit here a real treat. **Hours:** Tuesday through Sunday from 10 to 6 (Friday till 8). **Admission:** $12 for adults, $8 for seniors and students, and free for children under 12. Admission is "pay what you wish" on Friday from 5 to 8.

JAPAN SOCIETY GALLERY
333 E 47th St (bet First and Second Ave)

212/832-1155
www.japansociety.org

Celebrating its centennial in 2007, the Japan Society is a remarkable institution dedicated to furthering understanding between the United States and Japan. In addition to language classes, lecture series, films, and other programs, the society has a small but elegant gallery space that often houses changing exhibitions. **Hours:** Tuesday through Thursday from 11 to 6, Friday from 11 to 9, and Saturday and Sunday from 11 to 5 during exhibitions. **Admission:** $10 for adults, $5 for seniors and students, and free for children under 16 and for everyone on Friday.

MERCHANT'S HOUSE MUSEUM
29 East 4th St (bet Lafayette St and Bowery) 212/777-1089
www.merchantshouse.com

Step back in time to an era when this part of town was considered the suburbs and New York was the country's leading port city. Built in 1832, this townhouse is a real time capsule, full of the furniture, clothes, and other items used by one of New York's wealthy merchant families. The servant call bells, the elegant four-poster beds, and the gas chandeliers are just a few of the many little period details you'll find as you wander through this beautifully preserved home—the only one from this period left in New York and a National Historic Landmark. **Hours**: Thursday through Monday from noon to 5. **Admission**: $8 for adults, $5 for seniors and students, and free for children under 12.

MORRIS-JUMEL MANSION
65 Jumel Terrace (bet 160th and 162nd St) 212/923-8008
www.morrisjumel.org

I'm not sure if George Washington actually slept here but he did use this mansion on a hill overlooking the Harlem River, Long Island Sound, the Hudson River, and the Palisades as his headquarters at the beginning of the Revolutionary War. Built in 1765, its commanding views offered an important strategic position first to Washington and later to the British. When the British finally left, General Washington returned in 1790 for a dinner with a range of the country's founding fathers, including John Adams, Thomas Jefferson, and Alexander Hamilton. Several owners and lots more history passed through these rooms in the intervening years, and most of the furniture—including a bed said to have belonged to Napoleon—dates from the 19th Century. A guided tour is offered on Saturday at noon, but visitors can wander through the mansion anytime. **Hours**: Wednesday through Sunday from 10 to 4. **Admission**: $4 for adults ($5 for the Saturday tour), $3 for seniors and students, and free for children under 12.

MOUNT VERNON HOTEL MUSEUM AND GARDEN
421 E 61st St (between First and York Ave) 212/838-6878
www.mvhm.org

Another time machine tucked into the 21st century, this amazing little spot started life as a carriage house for a large estate that burned in 1826. It served as a day hotel in the early 19th century and eventually became a private home. Now owned and lovingly preserved by the Colonial Dames of America and full of period pieces reflecting its years as a destination for day-trippers coming out to the country by boat or by carriage from lower Manhattan, the Mount Vernon Hotel Museum and Garden (a relatively new name for what was once known as the Abigail Adams Smith Museum) will transport you back 200 years. Tours are provided on request by wonderfully knowledgeable docents. **Hours**: Tuesday through Sunday from 11 to 4 (Tuesday till 9 in June and July). **Admission**: $5 for adults, $4 for seniors and students, and free for children under 12.

MUSEUM OF AMERICAN ILLUSTRATION
128 E 63rd St (bet Park and Lexington Ave) 212/838-2560
www.societyillustrators.org

Changing exhibitions from the Society of Illustrators' permanent collection are housed in the elegant 1853 carriage house that today serves as the society's headquarters. **Hours**: Tuesday from 10 to 8, Wednesday through Friday from 10 to 5, and Saturday from noon to 4. **Admission**: free.

MUSEUM OF BIBLICAL ART
1865 Broadway (at 61st St)   212/408-1500
                                                    www.mobia.org

This remodeled and expanded museum is the only one in the world dedicated to preserving and understanding art inspired and influenced by the Hebrew Scriptures and the Christian Testament. From ecclesiastical art to contemporary, secular work, this fascinating museum offers a unique perspective on how the symbols and narratives of the Bible influence art and are often incorporated into it. **Hours**: Tuesday through Sunday from 10 to 6 (Thursday till 8). **Admission**: $7 for adults, $4 for seniors and students, and free for children under 12.

Most galleries are open Tuesday through Saturday from 10 or 11 a.m. to 5 or 6 p.m. Some close for a few weeks in summer.

MUSEUM OF CHINESE IN THE AMERICAS
70 Mulberry St (at Bayard St)   212/619-4785
                                                    www.moca-nyc.org

I can't say enough good things about this thriving little museum. Housed on the second floor of an old elementary school, it is dedicated to telling and preserving the stories of Chinese immigrants to this country. In addition to its fascinating and well-conceived exhibits, the Museum of Chinese in the Americas is obviously an active participant in the life of this neighborhood and a partner in Lower Manhattan's recovery from the trauma of September 11, 2001. An expansion is in the works. **Hours**: Tuesday through Sunday from noon to 6. **Admission**: $2 for adults, $1 for seniors and students, and free for children under 12 and for everyone on Friday.

MUSEUM AT FIT
Seventh Ave at 27th St   212/217-7999
                                                    www.fitnyc.edu/museum

The Fashion Institute of Technology is one of the world's leading fashion schools and a branch of the State University of New York. This little museum is dedicated to the art of fashion. Color, texture, design are front and center in this museum's changing exhibitions. Its collection includes over a million articles of clothing! **Hours**: Tuesday through Friday from noon to 8, Saturday from 10 to 5. **Admission**: free.

MUSEUM OF SEX
233 Fifth Ave (at 27th St)   212/689-6337
                                                    www.museumofsex.com

Opened in 2002, this entire affair (excuse the pun) is a bit tawdry, appearing to run on a shoestring budget despite the exorbitant admission fee. However, if you're not shy about what can only be described as soft-core pornography, there's a lot to be learned about the history of sex and its influence on our culture. The free audiophone is definitely worth using. **Hours**: daily from 11 to 6:30 (Saturday till 8). **Admission**: $14.50 plus tax for adults, $13.50 plus tax for seniors and students with ID. No one under 18 is allowed in the museum.

MUSEUM OF TELEVISION AND RADIO
25 W 52nd St (bet Fifth Ave and Ave of the Americas)   212/621-6800
www.mtr.org

Is there an episode of *The Brady Bunch* you've always wanted to show your kids? A segment of *The Ed Sullivan Show* you've always wanted to see again? What about the Nixon-Kennedy debates? Or that Mean Joe Greene Coca-Cola commercial? For folks who love television, this place is Nirvana. In addition to scheduled screenings, you can select from the library's more than 120,000 programs—spanning the history of radio and television—for your own viewing. There's no memorabilia here, just thousands of hours of programming. **Hours**: Tuesday through Sunday from noon to 6. **Admission**: $10 for adults, $8 for seniors and students, and $5 for children under 14.

Oregon Connections

Many New Yorkers likely couldn't find my home state of Oregon on a map, but like every other state in the nation, Oregon has made numerous contributions to this great city. Legendary chef James Beard had Oregon roots and brought our Pacific seafood to many of his menus. The 10,000-year-old Willamette meteor—on display in the Hall of the Universe at the Rose Center for Earth and Space—came from Oregon and remains sacred to the Confederated Tribes of the Grande Ronde. An Oregon architect—Brad Cloepfil, of Allied Works Architecture in Portland—is working on the redesign of the Huntington Hartford Building on Columbus Circle as a new home for the Museum of Arts and Design, sometime in 2008.

NATIONAL ACADEMY OF DESIGN
1083 Fifth Ave (bet 89th and 90th St)   212/369-4880
www.nationalacademy.org

The National Academy, New York's first art school, opened its doors in 1826. Modeled after the Royal Academy of London, it has been among the city's leading art institutions ever since. Smaller than some of the other museums along Museum Mile, the National Academy nonetheless is worth a stop if you're interested in 19th- and 20th-century American art. Winslow Homer, Thomas Eakins, John Singer Sargent, Federic Church, and Jasper Johns are just a few members of the National Academy whose work is in its permanent collection. **Hours**: Wednesday and Thursday from noon to 5, Friday and Sunday from 11 to 6. **Admission**: $10 for adults and $5 for seniors and students with ID.

NATIONAL MUSEUM OF THE AMERICAN INDIAN
1 Bowling Green (at the foot of Broadway)   212/514-3700
www.nmai.si.edu

The George Gustav Heye Center (formerly the Alexander Hamilton Customs House) houses one of three branches of the National Museum of the American Indian. Opened in 1994, this branch in Lower Manhattan offers changing exhibitions featuring items and work both old and new. (The largest branch is now open on the National Mall in Washington, D.C.) Its two terrific gift shops are well worth a visit, as is the building itself. Take time to look up at the intricate details in the ceilings, especially in the rotunda and the library, and to descend the exquisite (if a bit worn) staircase. **Hours**: daily from 10 to 5 (Thursday till 8). **Admission**: free.

Not Your Father's New York

A city in constant motion, change is the name of the game in New York. When I first started writing this book almost three decades ago, I never imagined that:

- Columbus Circle and Times Square would become tourist destinations
- Bryant Park would have ice skating in winter and a carousel ride in summer
- subway tokens would become collectors' items, having been replaced entirely with the remarkably efficient and easy-to-use MetroCard
- the Plaza Hotel would be turned into condominiums
- so many young children would be attending Broadway shows, eating in fine restaurants, and visiting New York with their parents
- the Lower East Side would be transformed into a neighborhood of hipsters

---

NEUE GALERIE
1048 Fifth Ave (at 86th St)
212/628-6200
www.neuegalerie.org

Ronald Lauder and his longtime friend, the late Serge Sabarsky, loved German and Austrian art and design from the early 20th century and dreamed of opening a museum to showcase it. Lauder purchased this amazing building, once home to Mrs. Cornelius Vanderbilt III, in 1994 and transformed his dream into this first-class museum. Public tours are offered at 2 p.m. on Saturday and Sunday. Children under 12 are not welcome, and children from 13 to 16 must be accompanied by an adult. **Hours**: Monday and Thursday through Sunday from 11 to 6 (Friday till 9). **Admission**: $15 for adults and $10 for seniors and students.

NEW-YORK HISTORICAL SOCIETY
170 Central Park West (bet 76th and 77th St)
212/873-3400
www.nyhistory.org

John James Audubon's watercolors for *Birds of America*, Thomas Cole's *The Course of Empire* and more Tiffany lamps than you can imagine are just a few highlights of the New-York Historical Society. A visit to this *grande dame*—located just south of the American Museum of Natural History—is a great way to glimpse the city's past. The best part of this museum is the Henry Luce III Center for the Study of American Culture, on the fourth floor. Brimming with thousands of pieces from the museum's vast permanent

RADIO CITY MUSIC HALL
1260 Ave of the Americas (at 50th St)

212/307-7171 (tour information)
www.radiocity.com

Part of Rockefeller Center, this Art Deco wonder was built in 1932 and seats more than 6,000 people. It's home to a world famous Christmas show, complete with live animals; an equally fabulous Easter show; and varied productions throughout the year. Countless entertainers have performed here over the years, and you can soak up some of its storied history by looking up at the giant marquee. **Hours:** Tours are offered daily from 10 to 5 (Sunday from 11). **Admission:** Tours cost $17 ($10 for children under 12). The cost of attending individual shows varies dramatically.

The Lower East Side has become a fascinating mix of new and old, trendy, and decidedly old-fashioned. While you're in the area, be sure to visit some of my favorite places! **Yonah Schimmel's Knishes** (137 E Houston St), **Sammy's Roumanian Steakhouse** (157 Chrystie St), and **Russ & Daughters** (179 E Houston St) offer some only-in-New-York taste treats. Go to **Harris Levy** (278 Grand St) for excellent linens and service. These places have rich histories that go back several generations. Enjoy!

ROCKEFELLER CENTER
Bounded by Fifth Ave, Ave of the Americas, 49th St, and 50th St

212/632-3875
www.rockefellercenter.com

A 30-building complex built as the Depression raged in the 1930s, Rockefeller Center is in some ways the anchor of midtown Manhattan. Technologies have come and gone, as radio gave way to television and now to all sorts of new media. Tenants and owners have come and gone, too, but this amazing complex is one of the few constants in this ever-changing city. Rockefeller Center includes Radio City Music Hall, NBC Studios, Channel Gardens, the world-famous ice-skating rink, a two-floor Metropolitan Museum of Art store, a post office (on the lower level, near the skating rink), and subway stop. You can shop on the lower level, wave to the folks back home outside the *Today Show*'s windows, have dinner while watching the ice skaters, or take a trip up to the "Top of the Rock" (212/698-2000, www.topoftherocknyc.com), towering 60 floors above the street. You can even tour NBC Studios and Rockefeller Center. Go to the **NBC Experience Store** (on 49th St bet Fifth Ave and Ave of the Americas) for schedules and prices. What I mostly like to do at Rockefeller Center, however, is simply walk around. It's like visiting an old friend! The concourse is open from 7 a.m. to midnight.

ROSE MUSEUM AT CARNEGIE HALL
154 W 57th St (at Seventh Ave)   212/903-9629

If you're interested in the history of music in New York, this little upstairs museum—adjacent to Carnegie Hall and across and down the street just a bit from the Steinway piano store—is a fun place to stop. Its permanent exhibit traces the history of Carnegie Hall from 1891. It's open to the public during the day and to evening concertgoers during intermission. **Hours**: daily from 11 to 4:30. **Admission**: free.

SCANDINAVIA HOUSE GALLERIES
58 Park Ave (bet 37th and 38th St)   212/879-9779
www.scandinaviahouse.org

This sleek building, just south of Grand Central Terminal, is home to the American-Scandinavian Foundation. Dedicated to building ties and improving understanding between the United States and the Nordic countries of Sweden, Denmark, Iceland, Norway, and Finland, the foundation offers films, children's programs, lectures, and more. Its galleries host changing art, design, and historical exhibitions. A small cafe, a beautiful store, and well-designed public spaces make a visit here a real pleasure. **Hours**: Tuesday through Saturday from noon to 6. **Admission**: $3 for adults and $2 for seniors and students.

SKYSCRAPER MUSEUM
39 Battery Place   212/968-1961
www.skyscraper.org

Where better to have a museum dedicated to the history and future of skyscrapers than New York City? Founded in 1996, this ironically small museum shares a building with the Ritz-Carlton New York, Battery Park, at the southern end of Battery Park City. After four homes in six years, it seems to have settled into a permanent space. **Hours**: Wednesday through Sunday from noon to 6. **Admission**: $5 for adults and $2.50 for seniors and students.

SOUTH STREET SEAPORT
209 Water St (at Fulton St)   212/748-8600
www.southstseaport.org

Two centuries ago, New York was one of the world's most active ports. Even as recently as 1967—when the South Street Seaport Museum was founded—Fulton Street was synonymous with its Fulton Fish Market (which finally moved to The Bronx a couple years ago). Little is left today except the history, and that's what you'll find as you explore the galleries and ships while wandering around this area. With its cobblestone streets, beautiful old boats, and salty breezes, it's easy to imagine that you've been transported to a different era. If you're here in warmer months, consider touring the harbor aboard the 1885 schooner *Pioneer*. It will cost extra, but the views are fabulous and the boat is absolutely beautiful. (Call 212/748-8786 for ticket prices, sailing times, and reservations.) If you're interested in archeology, be sure to visit **New York Unearthed**, a special archeology exhibit at 17 State Street. (Call 212/748-8753 for reservations.) While you're down here, look for a TKTS reduced-price theater ticket booth at the intersection of John and Front Streets. **Hours**: 10 to 6 daily (reduced hours in winter). **Admission**: You can walk around for free, but admission to the galleries and ships is $8 for adults, $6 for seniors and students, $4 for children from 5 to 12, and free for children under 5.

STUDIO MUSEUM IN HARLEM
144 W 125th St (bet Malcolm X and Adam Clayton Powell, Jr. Blvd)
212/864-4500
www.studiomuseuminharlem.org

Like the Museum of Chinese in the Americas, this wonderful place is both a museum and a vibrant part of the community. Recently expanded to include more gallery space and an auditorium, the Studio Museum displays the work of black artists from around the block and around the world. An Artist in Residence program, a wide range of programs for families and children, and film screenings are just a few ways the Studio Museum engages its audience and reaches into the community. **Hours:** Wednesday through Friday from 11 to 6, Saturday from 10 to 6, and Sunday from noon to 6. **Admission**: $7 for adults, $3 for seniors and students, and free for children under 12.

TIBET HOUSE
22 W 15th St (bet Fifth Ave and Ave of the Americas)   212/807-0563
www.tibethouse.org

Tibet House is the center of efforts in the United States to preserve Tibetan culture. It has a small gallery space and offers changing exhibits showcasing work by Tibetan artists. **Hours**: Weekdays from noon to 6. **Admission**: free (although donations are welcome).

The Sports Museum of America, a comprehensive display space associated with over 60 single-sport museums, has plans to open in Lower Manhattan in April 2008.

THEODORE ROOSEVELT BIRTHPLACE
28 E 20th St (bet Broadway and Park Ave)   212/260-1616
www.nps.gov/thrb

This wonderful brownstone is a reconstruction of Theodore Roosevelt's childhood home. Operated by the National Park Service, it houses a small museum and various period rooms in the living quarters. Guided tours of the rooms begin on the hour between 10 and 4 and last about half an hour. **Hours:** Tuesday through Saturday from 9 to 5 (closed on Federal holidays). **Admission**: $3.

UKRAINIAN MUSEUM
222 E 6th St (between Second and Third Ave)   212/228-0110
www.ukrainianmuseum.org

This recently expanded museum in the heart of the East Village invites visitors to "discover the wonderful heritage of your parents and grandparents." Displaying folk art, costumes, paintings, and an amazing collection of *pysanky* (Ukrainian Easter eggs), this museum is a terrific cultural resource for anyone who wants to learn more about Ukrainian heritage—yours or otherwise. **Hours:** Wednesday through Sunday from 11:30 to 5. **Admission**: $8 for adults, $6 for seniors and students, and free for children under 12.

UNION SQUARE PARK
Bounded by Broadway, Park Ave S, 14th St, and 17th St

Like several other city parks, Union Square Park has undergone a remarkable transformation in the last ten years. Now home to the city's best known and largest Greenmarket (which is open on Monday, Wednesday, Friday, and Saturday), it's full of New Yorkers and tourists alike enjoying the beautifully renovated and surprisingly clean public spaces. The famous Union Square Cafe is just one of dozens of restaurants in the area.

Sailing Up, Sailing Down

The Hudson and East rivers, which have long been engines of commerce of this region, became very polluted in the second half of the 20th century and were little used when I first began writing this book almost 30 years ago. No longer! Whether it's basic transportation or a nostalgic sail on a hundred-year-old schooner, there are many options for getting out on the water. They include:

The Adirondack—This 80-foot schooner is docked at the Chelsea Piers complex and is available for both public cruises and charters (646/336-5270, www.sail-nyc.com).

Bateaux New York—Also moored at the Chelsea Piers, this company's elegant glass boat has regularly scheduled lunch and dinner cruises, as well as sightseeing cruises (866/211-3806, www.bateauxnew york.com).

Circle Line—In addition to the three-hour cruise around the island of Manhattan mentioned earlier, this company runs the boats that go to and from the Statue of Liberty and Ellis Island, as well as a variety of other sightseeing and adventure cruises from several ports in the city. Thrill-seekers will like the *Shark Speedboat* (866/925-4631, www.circle linedowntown.com).

New York Water Taxi—Based at South Street Seaport, this company's boats are all painted to look like old-fashioned taxis. Commuter boats, sightseeing tours, and even an eco-friendly Audubon tour are available (212/742-1969, www.nywatertaxi.org).

New York Waterway—This company runs water taxis for commuters as well as sightseeing boats for tourists in New York Harbor and around the island of Manhattan (800/533-3779, www.nywaterway. com).

The Pioneer—This wonderful 1885 schooner is docked at the South Street Seaport (212/748-8786, www.southstseaport.org). It takes regularly scheduled tours around New York Harbor.

The Ventura—This classic old yacht is docked at North Cove, near the World Financial Center in Battery Park City, as is the 1950 speedboat *Petrel* (212/786-1204, www.sailnewyork.com). The *Ventura* takes folks out for regularly scheduled cruises in the summer; the *Petrel* is available for private charters for up to four people.

YANKEE STADIUM
161st St at River Ave (in The Bronx)   718/293-6000, 718/579-4531
www.yankees.com

Every baseball fan knows about "the House that Ruth Built" (Babe Ruth, that is). Home of the New York Yankees, Yankee Stadium is probably the most famous sports stadium in North America, if not the world. But it's also a required stop, even in the off-season, for those who grew up either loving the Yankees or hating them. And you don't have much longer; plans for a new Yankee Stadium are in the works. Advance tickets can be purchased through the team's website. Tours of the stadium, including the dugouts, the press box, and Monument Park, are offered daily throughout the year, except on weekends or prior to game day during any Yankee home stand. **Hours**: daily at noon. **Admission**: $15 for adults, $6 for seniors 60 and older and children 14 and under.

YESHIVA UNIVERSITY MUSEUM
15 W 16th St (at Fifth Ave)   212/294-8330
www.yumuseum.org

Part of the Center for Jewish History, this surprisingly large and vibrant museum houses an exceptional collection of paintings, books, artifacts, and other items relating to Jewish life, history, and culture. A trip here can be wonderfully rewarding, but be sure to check the hours, as the museum seems closed as often as its open. **Hours**: Sunday, Tuesday, Wednesday, and Thursday from 11 to 5. The museum is closed on major Jewish holidays. **Admission**: $8 for adults, $6 for seniors and students with ID, and free for children under 5.

Isn't That Where . . .

New York is full of backdrops for movies and television shows. If you are a fan of shows like the *Sopranos* or *Sex in the City*, one of the many tours offered by **On Location Tours** (www.sceneontv.com) may be the highlight of your trip. Particularly popular with young people, these tours will take you to see where scenes from various movies and television shows were filmed. Tours take you to different places and focus on various topics, but all of them are by bus. Children under 15 must be accompanied by an adult. Go to the website to learn more about specific tours and prices. Advance reservations are required.

Galleries

When people think of art, they sometimes think only of museums. While the art museums in New York are exceptional, anyone interested in art ought to visit some commercial galleries, too. Galleries are places where potential buyers and admirers alike can look at the work of contemporary and 20th-century artists (a few galleries specialize in older works) at their own pace and without charge. Let me stress "admirers alike." A lot of people are afraid to go into galleries because they think they'll be expected to buy something or be treated poorly if they don't know everything there is to know about art. That just isn't true, and an afternoon of gallery hopping can be fun.

First decide what kind of art you want to see. New York has long been considered the center of the contemporary art world, and it follows that the city is home to literally hundreds of galleries of all sizes and styles. In general, the more formal and conventional galleries are on or close to Madison Avenue on the Upper East Side and along 57th Street. (You'll need to look up to find a lot of them, particularly on 57th Street.) Some of the less formal, avant-garde galleries tend to be in Soho on West Broadway, between Broome and Houston streets; on Greene Street between Prince and Houston streets; and on Prince Street, between Greene Street and West Broadway. Some of the latter are also in Tribeca.

As a general rule, artists who have yet to be discovered go where the rents are lower, and then more established artists and galleries follow. Gallery hot spots include the west end of Chelsea, the northwest corner of the West Village (on and around West 14th Street), the Lower East Side (particularly on and around Rivington Street), and several parts of Brooklyn.

If you want to experience the diversity of the New York gallery scene, sample a couple of galleries in each neighborhood. The Art Dealers Association of America (212/940-8590, www.artdealers.org) is a terrific resource if you have particular artists or areas of interest in mind.

Galleries are typically known for the artists they showcase. If you are interested in the work of just one artist, the *New Yorker* and *New York* magazine contain listings of gallery shows arranged by artists' names. Be sure to look at the dates, as shows sometimes change quickly. *Time Out New York* has a list of galleries by neighborhood in its "Arts" section, complete with descriptions of current shows. The Friday and Sunday editions of the *New York Times* are also good resources.

The **New York Landmarks Conservancy** has published several books detailing self-guided walking tours in Lower Manhattan, the Upper East Side, Harlem, and the Flatiron District. Call 212/995-5260 or go to www.nylandmarks.org for more information. If you specifically want to visit Harlem, I highly recommend **Harlem Spirituals** (212/391-0900, www.harlemspirituals.com)

Tours and Tour Operators

Whether you like to walk or ride, be part of a small group or with a whole herd, New York has a tour for you. While I definitely advocate getting out and exploring on your own at least part of the time you're in New York, there are lots of interesting tours that will take you places you either won't go or can't go by yourself.

If you're interested in having a tour organized for your group, **Doorway to Design** (212/221-1111, www.doorwaytodesign.com), **Manhattan Passport** (212/861-2746, www.manhattanpassport.com), and **Viewpoint International** (212/246-6000, www.viewpointinternational.com) are all reputable companies that have been around for a long time. If you want a particular kind of tour or a guide with special skills or areas of expertise, contact the **Guides Association of New York** (212/969-0666, www.newyorkcitytourguides.com). The website has information about the city's licensed guides and their specialties, as well as practical details about the tours they offer. And if you're looking for a really personalized introduction to New York, get in touch with **Big Apple Greeter** (212/669-8159, www.bigapplegreeter.org). A nonprofit volunteer service designed to hook visitors up with real New Yorkers, this is a great way to get an insider's view of the city.

If you're feeling a little overwhelmed by New York and want to see the sights from the safety and anonymity of a tour bus, **Gray Line** (212/445-0848, www.graylinenewyork.com) is your best bet. The company offers all sorts of different packages on its double-decker buses, including a three-day tour that includes trips to the Statue of Liberty and the Empire State Building, as well as a two-day hop-on and hop-off tour of over 50 stops all around New York. Prices vary, as do the lengths of the various tours. Another great way to get a quick and basic orientation is **Circle Line**'s three-hour cruise all the way around the island of Manhattan. The narration tends toward the corny, but you'll learn a ton, get some great photo opportunities, and really get a sense of New York as an island. Tickets cost $29 for adults, $24 for seniors, and $16 for kids. Call 212/563-3200 or go to www.circleline42.com for more information.

If you want a personal orientation tour, try **My Kind of Town New York** (212/754-4500, www.mykindoftownny.com). These private tours are undertaken in the comfort of a Mercedes Benz sedan and tailored just for you.

Many of the museums and sights listed previously offer tours of their own collections or of surrounding neighborhoods. The Municipal Art Society's tour of **Grand Central Terminal** (every Wednesday at 12:30), the **Lower East Side Tenement Museum**'s walking tour of its surrounding neighborhood (weekends at 1 and 3 in warmer months), and just about any tour offered by the Central Park Conservancy are personal favorites.

Following are places not mentioned in other parts of this book that offer particularly interesting or popular tours:

How many Yankees caps can we lose?

The lost-and-found department at **Grand Central Terminal** receives an average of 4,000 items every day. Laptop computers, cell phones, glasses, keys, and suit jackets turn up by the hundreds. Among the more unusual items in recent years: a movie script with the director's notes, an urn with human ashes, and Pete Seeger's banjo.

CARNEGIE HALL
153 W 57th St (at Seventh Ave)   212/903-9765
                                                   www.carnegiehall.org

Perhaps you've heard the old joke: How do you get to Carnegie Hall? Practice, practice, practice. Or you could take a tour of this musical mecca, including the 2,800 seat Isaac Stern Auditorium and its two smaller performance spaces. **Hours:** Tours are offered at 11:30, 2, and 3 during the season. The box office is open between 11 and 3. **Admission:** $9 for adults, $6 for seniors, and $3 for children under 12.

CITY HALL
Chambers St at Park Row   212/639-9675 or 311 (in New York)
                                                   www.nyc.gov

Built in the early 19th century and still used as the City Hall for all five New York boroughs, this grand building is open for public tours by appointment. In addition to grand staircases, beautiful art, and a soaring rotunda, you'll get to visit the historic Governors Room. Combined tours of City Hall and the nearby Tweed Courthouse are also available. Find out about availability and make tour reservations online. **Hours**: weekdays by appointment. **Admission**: free.

FEDERAL RESERVE BANK
33 Liberty St (bet Nassau and William St)   212/720-6130
www.newyorkfed.org

More than 20 countries keep their gold buried in the bedrock of Manhattan at the Federal Reserve Bank. Daily tours of this incredible institution are free, but reservations must be made at least a week in advance and children under 16 are not allowed. Be sure to look for the American Numismatic Society's display on the history of money. **Hours**: weekdays (except bank holidays) at 9:30, 10:30, 11:30, 1:30 and 2:30 (advance reservation required. **Admission**: free.

GRACIE MANSION
88th St at East End Ave   212/639-9675 or 311 (in New York)
www.nyc.gov

Thanks to Fiorello LaGuardia, New York is one of the few cities in the U.S. with an official mayoral residence. Built in 1799, this historic mansion is one of the oldest continuously occupied homes in New York (well, sort of—current mayor Michael Bloomberg actually lives in an East Side townhouse). It's located in Carl Schurz Park, overlooking the East River. **Hours**: Wednesday at 10, 11, 1, and 2 (advance reservation required). **Admission**: $7 for adults, $4 for seniors, and free for students.

MADISON SQUARE GARDEN
33rd St at Seventh Ave   212/465-6741
www.thegarden.com

If you've always wanted to see the New York Knicks' locker room, here's your chance. This historic arena in the heart of Manhattan is a little worn around the edges, but it still holds lots of great memories. Be forewarned that tour schedules are often abbreviated and access to certain areas may be limited because of events at "The Garden." **Hours**: Tours are offered daily between 11 and 3. **Admission**: $17 for adults and $12 for children.

METROPOLITAN OPERA
Lincoln Center (Columbus Ave at 64th St)   212/769-7020
www.metoperafamily.org/edcation

Even folks who don't care for opera will be wowed by this behind-the-scenes look at this country's most famous opera company. Visit the stage and get an up-close look at some of the costumes and sets. These popular 90-minute tours are offered by the Metropolitan Opera Guild on most weekday afternoons and Saturday mornings during the season —which runs from late September to early June—but times can change, so check the calendar on the guild's website. Plan well in advance, as tours often sell out. **Hours**: Variable (advance reservation required). **Admission**: $15 for adults and $5 for full-time students.

NBC STUDIOS
30 Rockefeller Plaza (49th St bet Fifth Ave and Ave
  of the Americas)   212/664-7174
                                          www.nbcuniversalstore.com

NBC's studios are located in Rockefeller Center, right in the heart of midtown. If you want to take a look around the sets of the *Today Show*, *Saturday Night Live*, and other NBC television shows, here's your chance. Be forewarned: the studios are often crowded, overhyped, and a bit chaotic, and children under 6 are not allowed on the tour. **Hours**: Monday through Thursday from 8:30 to 4:30, Friday and Saturday from 9:30 to 5:30, and Sunday from 9:30 to 4:30. **Admission**: $18.75 for adults and $15.50 for seniors and children from 6 to 12.

NEW AMSTERDAM THEATER
214 W 42nd St (bet Seventh and Eighth Ave)   212/282-2952
                  www.disney.go.com/disneytheatrical/newamsterdam

Tours of this beautifully restored theater—once home to the Ziegfeld Follies and now to *The Lion King*—offer a glimpse into Broadway's past and present. **Hours**: Daily except Wednesday at 10 and 11. **Admission**: $14 for adults and $7 for children under 12.

Walking Tours

Walking tours are another great way to get to know parts of New York you otherwise might overlook. *Time Out New York* lists scheduled walking tours in its "Around Town" section each week. Here are some tour guides.

BIG ONION WALKING TOURS
                                          212/439-1090
                                          www.bigonion.com

Seth Kamil and his band of guides—most of them graduate students in American history from Columbia University and New York University —share their vast knowledge of New York through a wide array of walking tours. Governor's Island, George Washington's New York, Historic Catholic New York, and the Civil War and Draft Riots are just a few of the many topics. You can even take a wildly popular tour of the Lower East Side on Christmas Day. Most tours cost $15 for adults, $12 for senior citizens, and $10 for students. Reservations are required for the popular Multiethnic Noshing Tour (which costs another $5 per person), but you can just show up for most other tours.

JOYCE GOLD'S HISTORY TOURS OF NEW YORK
                                          212/242-5762
                                          www.nyctours.com

Nowhere in the United States are past and present so closely quartered as in New York, and few people are better able to convey that simultaneous sense of timelessness and modernity than historian Joyce Gold. Her scheduled tours—which include such topics as the American Revolution, the Gilded Age of J. P. Morgan, and Gangs of New York—are usually given on weekends and cost $15 per person ($12 for senior citizens). Joyce personally leads all her tours and is available for private tours as well. Reservations for her scheduled tours are not required.

MUNICIPAL ART SOCIETY

212/439-1049
www.mas.org

This terrific advocacy group offers a wide array of thematic and area-specific walking tours for people interested in the city's architecture and history. Most tours are led by historians. The diverse topics include architectural oddities, immigrant New York, downtown skyscrapers, and subway art and design. Most tours last 90 minutes and cost $15 per person. As mentioned elsewhere, the society's excellent tour of **Grand Central Terminal** is offered Wednesday at 12:30 and costs $10 per person.

Seth Kamil, Eric Wakin, and Kenneth Jackson—founders of Big Onion Walking Tours—have written a wonderful book outlining self-guided walking tours of New York. It's loaded with interesting details about this wonderful city. **The Big Onion Guide to New York City: The Historic Tours** is sold in bookstores. You can also call 212/439-1090 to order copies.

URBAN PARK RANGERS

212/360-2774
www.nycgovparks.org

The city's Department of Parks and Recreation employs Urban Park Rangers, who give wonderful weekend walking tours of Central Park and other parks throughout Manhattan and the outer boroughs. Tours are free, and many are designed for children or families. Go to the department's website and click "Divisions" and "Urban Park Rangers" to get a full schedule of upcoming tours and other events.

IV. Where to Find It: New York's Best Food Shops

> **"Gerry Says"**
> It's hard to go a block in New York without being tempted by a bakery, deli, candy shop, or just a corner store brimming with fresh produce and great baked goods. Street vendors have all sorts of delicious food to offer, sometimes from the far corners of the globe. And then there are the food markets, including the huge Greenmarkets in Union Square, the Essex Street Market, and Chelsea Market, as well as every foodie's favorite stores: **Zabars**, **Grace's Marketplace**, and **Dean & Deluca**. Here's my advice—stop and sample. The word in New York is "nosh" (Yiddish for snack). You just haven't lived until you've eaten a fresh bagel in New York, savored some high-quality chocolates, and noshed on thin-cut pastrami or lox.

Asian

ASIA MARKET
71½ Mulberry St (bet Canal and Bayard St)   212/962-2020
Daily: 8-7

Fresh fruit and vegetables, plus exotic herbs and spices from all over Asia, are the main attractions at Asia Market. You'll find items from Thailand, Indonesia, Malaysia, the Philippines, Japan, and China, plus a staff ready to explain how to prepare dishes from these countries. Asia Market provides produce to some of New York's best restaurants.

Bakery Goods

AMY'S BREAD
672 Ninth Ave (Hell's Kitchen, bet 46th and 47th St)   212/977-2670
75 Ninth Ave (Chelsea Market, bet 15th and 16th St)   212/462-4338
250 Bleecker St (bet Carmine and Leroy St)   212/675-7802
Hours vary by store   www.amysbread.com

As the aroma of freshly baked bread and sweets drifts onto Ninth Avenue, locals and tourists line up outside of Amy's Hell's Kitchen location to sample the many treats for sale. An oasis in the heart of midtown, Amy's Bread is a cross between a Parisian *boulangerie* and a cozy Midwestern kitchen. Of course, you should come for the bread—Amy's signature semolina with golden raisins and fennel, the green olive *picholine*, or just a simple French baguette. Among the goodies are grilled sandwiches, sticky buns, old-fashioned double layer cakes, and decadent brownies. The staff provides consistent, friendly service.

Glossary for Bread Lovers

Bakers use these terms loosely:

Boule: round, domed bread

Baguette: long, thin loaf with soft interior and a crackly crust

Batard: short, slightly flattened baguette

Ciabatta: flat, rectangular Northern Italian bread with an airy interior and chewy crust

Ficelle: extra-thin baguette

Focaccia: flat, dense, and tender bread flavored with olive oil; from Liguria

Fougasse: chewy-crusted, rather flat sourdough wheat bread from Provence

Integrale: Italian term for "whole wheat"

Miche: round sourdough French bread

Pain au levain: dense, whole-wheat French sourdough bread with a very chewy crust

Pugliese: big, round bread with a very dark crust and light, airy interior

Sourdough: bread made from cultured dough ("starter") that is saved to use for leavening many bread batches

---

A. ORWASHER BAKERY

308 E 78th St (bet First and Second Ave)   212/288-6569
Mon-Sat: 7-7; Sun: 9-4   www.orwashers.com

Orwasher has occupied the same location and been run by the same family for nearly a century. Many of its breads are made from recipes handed down from father to son. You'll find Old World breads that once were commonly made in the local immigrant bakeries but are now extremely rare. Over 30 varieties are always available. Hearth-baked in brick ovens, they're made with natural ingredients and come in a marvelous array of shapes and sizes—triple twists, cornucopias, and hearts, just to name a few. Be sure to sample the onion boards, rye, cinnamon raisin bread, and challah. It's almost as good as the home-baked variety. Best of all is the raisin pumpernickel, which comes in small rolls or loaves and is sensational when warm. The Irish soda bread is also special!

BANGKOK CENTER GROCERY

104 Mosco St (bet Mott and Mulberry St)   212/732-8916
Daily: 10-8 (Tues to 6)   www.thai-grocery.com

You'll find a complete selection of Thai foods in this amazing store, including teas, sticky rice, rice noodles, Thai herbs and spices, frozen foods, and prepared foods you can take home for dinner. They also offer snacks, candles, beverages, magazines, and Asian cookware.

BILLY'S BAKERY
184 Ninth Ave (bet 21st and 22nd St)   212/647-9956
Mon-Thurs: 9 a.m.-11 p.m.; Fri, Sat: 9 a.m.-midnight;
Sun: 10 a.m.-11 p.m.   www.billysbakerynyc.com

You simply cannot leave this place without some of the delicacies offered: wonderful layer cakes (like Aunt Flossy's chocolate cherry cake), cheesecakes, icebox pies, cupcakes, bars, cookies, muffins, and much more. Items are made right on the premises, and it is a very clean and professional operation. Special cake designs and inscriptions are available. By the way, the Waldorf-Astoria cake (a.k.a. red velvet cake) is available.

CAFE LALO
201 W 83rd St (at Amsterdam Ave)   212/496-6031
Mon-Thurs: 8 a.m.-2 a.m.; Fri: 8 a.m.-4 a.m.; Sat: 9 a.m.-4 a.m.;
Sun: 9 a.m-2 a.m.   www.cafelalo.com

In my opinion, this is the best dessert shop in town. You will be reminded of a fine European pastry shop as you enjoy cappuccino, espresso, cordials, and a large selection of delicious desserts. Cafe Lalo offers more than a hundred choices, including cakes, cheesecakes, tarts, pies, and connoisseur cheese platters. Yogurt and ice cream are also available, and soothing music makes every calorie go down sweetly. Breakfasts and brunches are a treat. Delivery is offered throughout Manhattan.

COLUMBUS BAKERY
474 Columbus Ave (at 83rd St)   212/724-6880
Daily: 7:30 a.m.-10 p.m.; Brunch: Sat, Sun   www.arkrestaurants.com

This top-quality bakery on the Upper West Side sells great rosemary rolls, delicious onion rolls (terrific for burgers), multigrain breads, really crusty sourdoughs, wonderful cakes, and pastries. You can eat in or take out, but what a pleasure just to sit and smell those fresh loaves. Catering is available.

CREATIVE CAKES
400 E 74th St (at First Ave)   212/794-9811
Mon-Fri: 8-4:30; Sat: 9 a.m.-11 a.m.   www.creativecakesny.com

Being in the "creative cake" business myself, I know all about making special concoctions. Creative Cakes knows how to have fun using fine ingredients and ingenious patterns. Cake lovers are fans of the fudgy chocolate cake with buttercream icing and sensational designs. Among other things, Bill Schutz has replicated the U.S. Customs House in cake form for a Fourth of July celebration. Prices are reasonable, and the results are sure to be a conversation piece at any party.

DESSERT DELIVERY
360 E 55th St (bet First and Second Ave)   212/838-5411
Mon-Fri: 8:30-7; Sat: 10-6   www.dessertdeliveryny.com

An unusual concept: Dessert Delivery sells only what they consider to be the best pastry items made in the city. Created by different chefs, there are chocolate-chip cookies, strawberry shortcake, cakes and cupcakes, and much more. Delivery service—they say within two hours—is offered without advance notification. For office parties or home celebrations, this is a very good bet. Bill Clinton and Donald Trump think so, too!

Looking for really good baguettes? Here are some suggestions:
Balthazar Bakery (80 Spring St)
Pain d'Avignon (Corrado Bread & Pastry, Grand Central Market, Grand Central Terminal, 42nd St at Vanderbilt Ave)
Sullivan Street Bakery (533 W 47th St)
Zabar's (2245 Broadway)

D'AIUTO
405 Eighth Ave (bet 30th and 31st St)   212/564-7136
Daily: 4 a.m.-8 p.m.   www.newyorknewyorkcheesecake.com

If it is baked, you'll find it here, made fresh every day. You'll find the famous Baby Watson cheesecakes, plus 25 other cakes and pies, all from three generations of bakers. Also featured are banana bread, cornbread, crumb cakes, cupcakes, cannoli lobster tails, Mississippi mud cakes, pecan pies, banana cream pies, apple strudel, cookies, scones, napoleon eclairs, opera pastries, chocolate doughnuts, and much more. Just thinking about D'Aiuto makes me hungry!

DOUGHNUT PLANT
379 Grand St (bet Essex and Norfolk St)   212/505-3700
Tues-Sun: 6:30 a.m.-7 p.m. (or until doughnuts are gone)
          www.doughnutplant.com

Mark Isreal has come a long way since delivering doughnuts on his bicycle. Now he presides over an establishment that is truly unique, concocting fluffy, fresh organic doughnuts made with spring water. The last time I counted there were 26 flavors, including orange, banana with pecans, "Yankee" (blueberry pin stripes), and rosewater (yes, with fresh rose petals!). Cake and jelly doughnuts are available, too. Doughnuts are hand-cut, yeast-raised, and very large. They also serve cinnamon buns, sticky buns, and such beverages as hot chocolate, chai tea, and organic coffee.

DUFOUR PASTRY KITCHENS
25 Ninth Ave (at 13th St)   212/929-2800
Mon-Fri: 9-5   www.dufourpastrykitchens.com

The air at Dufour is full of pastry flour, so don't wear your best black outfit. All items are frozen, so you'll have to bake them yourself (instructions included). These are the only drawbacks. You'll find delicious and sensibly priced pastry items of high quality at Dufour, which counts many fancy uptown restaurants among its customers. Chocolate and regular puff-pastry dough are available in sheets and in bulk. Wonderful hors d'oeuvres include bite-size, hand-filled "party lites" in flavors like fresh mushroom paté, Swiss cheese, and spinach.

EUROPAN BAKERY CAFE

2503 Broadway (bet 93rd and 94th St)	212/222-5110
135 Columbus Ave	212/799-4100
Daily: 24 hours	

Hunger pangs in the wee hours? This is the place! This bakery features delicious cakes, pastries, and cookies. And there is more: pizzas, wraps, salads, sandwiches, deli goods, breakfast items (pancakes, eggs, French toast, Danishes, and jumbo bagels), paninis, and ice cream. Their selection of international wraps is outstanding.

New York is famous for good cheesecakes. Here are the best:

Eileen's Special Cheesecake (17 Cleveland Pl, 212/966-5585, 800/521-CAKE, www.eileenscheesecake.com)

Junior's (1515 Broadway, 212/302-2000 and Grand Central Terminal (42nd St bet Vanderbilt and Lexington Ave, 212/586-4677): The restaurant is on the lower level, and the bakery is on the main concourse, near Track 36.

New York New York Cheesecake (405 Eighth Ave, 212/564-7136)

Two Little Red Hens (1652 Second Ave, 212/452-0476, www.two littleredhens.com

---

FERRARA CAFE

195 Grand St (bet Mulberry and Mott St)	212/226-6150
Daily: 8 a.m.-midnight (Fri, Sat till 1 a.m.)	www.ferraracafe.com

This store in Little Italy is one of the biggest little *pasticcerias* in the world. The business deals in wholesale imports and other ventures, but their edible goodies could support the whole business. Certainly, the atmosphere would never suggest that this is anything but a very efficiently run Italian bakery.

GLASER'S BAKE SHOP

1670 First Ave (bet 87th and 88th St)	212/289-2562
Tues-Fri: 7-7; Sat: 8-7; Sun: 8-3	
Closed July and part of Aug	

If it's Sunday, it won't be hard to find Glaser's. The line frequently spills outside as people queue up to buy the Glaser family's fresh cakes and baked goods. One isn't enough of anything here. Customers typically walk out with arms bulging. The Glasers have run their shop as a family business since 1902 at this same location, and they're justifiably proud of their breads, brownies, cakes, cookies (try the chocolate chip!), and wedding cakes.

H&H BAGELS

2239 Broadway (at 80th St)	212/595-8000
639 W 46th St (bet Eleventh and Twelfth Ave)	212/765-7200
Daily: 24 hours	www.hhbagels.com

If you find yourself out and about in the middle of the night, you can get a fresh hot bagel without having to wait in H&H's long daytime line. Regardless of the hour, you can satisfy your hot bagel craving day or night at H&H, which bakes the best bagels in Manhattan. They ship worldwide; call 800/NY-BAGEL for mail order.

Bagels on the Square (7 Carmine St, 212/691-3041) is a bagel lover's paradise! Just about every kind of bagel and cream cheese you might imagine can be found.

KOSSAR'S BIALYS
367 Grand St (at Essex St)   212/473-4810
Sun-Thurs: 6 a.m.-8 p.m.; Fri: 6-3:30   877-4-BIALYS
                                                  www.kossarsbialys.com

Tradition has it that the bialy derives its name from Bialystoker, where they were first made. Kossar's brought the recipe over from Europe almost a century ago, and their bialys, bagels, horns, and onion boards are fresh from the oven. The taste is Old World and authentic.

LADY M CAKE BOUTIQUE
41 E 78th St (at Madison Ave)   212/452-2222
Mon-Fri: 9-7; Sat: 10-7; Sun: 11-6   www.ladymconfections.com

For some of the area's most outstanding cakes—and they *should* be, at the prices charged—a visit to this house is a must. You'll find a dazzling selection of over 20 handmade cakes, which can be enjoyed in the small cafe (where they stop serving at 3 p.m.) or taken home. Special packaging for gifts is also available. Customers can enjoy tea while sampling goodies by the slice.

LE PAIN QUOTIDIEN
1131 Madison Ave (bet 84th and 85th St)   212/327-4900
833 Lexington Ave (bet 63rd and 64th St)   212/755-5810
100 Grand St (at Mercer St)   212/625-9009
38 E 19th St (bet Park Ave and Broadway)   212/673-7900
1270 First Ave (bet 68th and 69th St)   212/988-5001
50 W 72nd St (bet Columbus Ave and Central Park West)
                                                        212/712-9700
922 Seventh Ave (at 58th St)   212/757-0775
10 Fifth Ave (at 8th St)   212/253-2324
Hours vary by store   www.painquotidien.com

Le Pain Quotidien traces its roots to Brussels, Belgium. It is a country-style bakery with long communal tables that serve customers breakfast, lunch, and light afternoon meals. European breads and pastries are sold at the counter. The meals offered are simple and the service very refined. You'll find delicious croissants, *pain au chocolate,* brioche, heaping bread baskets, Belgian sugar waffles, an unusual Tuscan platter, crisp salads, and a splendid board of French cheeses. They also make wonderful sandwiches, like Scottish smoked salmon with dill and Parisian ham with three mustards. Don't pass up the Belgian chocolate brownies!

LITTLE PIE COMPANY

424 W 43rd St (at Ninth Ave)   212/736-4780
Mon-Sat: 8-8; Sun: 10-7   www.littlepiecompany.com

Former actor Arnold Wilkerson started baking apple pastries for private orders in his own kitchen. Now he and educator Michael Deraney operate a unique shop that makes handmade pies and cakes using fresh seasonal fruits. Although they specialize in apple pie, they also make fresh peach, cherry, blueberry, and other all-American fruit pie favorites, along with cream, meringue, and crumb pies. Stop by for a hot slice of pie a la mode and a cup of cider. Also available are delicious brownies, bars, muffins, fruit Danish, applesauce carrot cake, white coconut cake, chocolate cream pies, and cheescakes with wild blueberry, cherry, and orange toppings. No preservatives are used! Other offerings include croissants (ham, cheese, and turkey), and homemade "little" quiches. Little Pie Company has two other locations: a large eat-in American bakery at 407 West 14th Street (212/414-2324) and a spot in Grand Central Terminal (212/983-3538).

MAGNOLIA BAKERY

401 Bleecker St (at 11th St)   212/462-2572
Mon: noon-11:30; Tues-Thurs: 9 a.m.-11:30 p.m.; Fri: 9 a.m.-
12:30 a.m.; Sat: 10 a.m.-12:30 a.m.; Sun: 10 a.m.-11:30 p.m.

What a charming place! Everything is made right on the premises: layer cakes, pies, cupcakes, brownies, cookies, icebox desserts, and banana pudding. Birthday cakes are a specialty that come in various types and sizes. You won't go away hungry!

The United Nations of Doughnuts

Greece: **Parea** (36 E 20th St, 212/777-8448)
Italy: **A Voce** (41 Madison Ave, 212/545-8555)
Japan: **Riingo** (205 E 45th St, 212/867-4200)
Spain: **Suba** (109 Ludlow St, 212/982-5714)

MOISHE'S HOMEMADE KOSHER BAKERY

115 Second Ave (bet 6th and 7th St)   212/505-8555
Sun-Thurs: 7 a.m.-9 p.m.; Fri: 7-6

Jewish bakery specialties are legendary, and they are done to perfection at Moishe's. The cornbread is prepared exactly as it was in the Old Country (and as it should be now); the pumpernickel is dark and moist; and the ryes are simply scrumptious. Black Russian pumpernickel bread is the house feature; it cannot be bested in any old-fashioned Russian bakery. The cakes and pies are special, too! The owners are charming and eager to please, and they run one of the best bakeries in the city, with the usual complement of bagels, bialys, cakes, and pastries. By all means try the challah; Moishe's produces the best in town. The chocolate layer cakes are also superb. (Note: They make no cornbread or white bread on Friday.)

MURRAY'S BAGELS
500 Ave of the Americas (bet 12th and 13th St) 212/462-2830
242 Eighth Ave (bet 22nd and 23rd St) 646/638-1335
Hours vary by store www.murraysbagels.com

Delicious hand-rolled, kettle-boiled and baked bagels—18 kinds of them!
—are featured, but there is much more. You'll also find smoked fish, spreads
and schmears, deli items for sandwiches, plus soups and pastries. It's all
available for eat-in, catering platters, and free home delivery (within limits).

Attention all bakers! **New York Cake & Baking Supply** (56
W 22nd St, 212/675-CAKE) is a treasure house of cake and chocolate
supplies. You'll find everything in the baking world for sale here at
reasonable prices. You can browse conveniently at www.nycake.com
and then phone, fax, or order online.

POSEIDON BAKERY
629 Ninth Ave (bet 44th and 45th St) 212/757-6173
Tues-Sat: 9-7 www.poseidonbakery.com

Poseidon was founded in 1922 by Greek baker Demetrios Anagnostou.
Today it is run by his great grandson, Paul, to the same exacting standards.
Tremendous pride is evident here. When a customer peers over the counter
and asks about something, the response is usually a long description and
sometimes an invitation to taste. There is homemade baklava, strudel, *katalf*,
trigona, *tiropita* (cheese pie), spanakopita, and *saragli*. Poseidon's handmade
phyllo is world-renowned. They have cocktail-size frozen spinach, cheese,
vegetable, and meat pies for home consumption or for parties.

ROCCO'S PASTRY SHOP & ESPRESSO CAFE
243 Bleecker St (bet Ave of the Americas and Seventh Ave)
Daily: 7:30 a.m.-midnight 212/242-6031
www.roccospastry.com

Family-owned and -operated, this establishment has long been satisfying
throngs who love fresh-Italian baked goods. Their cannolis are famous!

SILVER MOON BAKERY
2740 Broadway (at 105th St) 212/866-4717
Mon-Fri: 7:30 a.m.-8 p.m.; Sat, Sun: 8:30-7
www.silvermoonbakery.com

Silver Moon presents delicious French, German, and Italian breads,. They
also offer French pastries and cakes, tarts, French macaroons, challah,
brioche (fresh fruit, raspberry, raisin, and chocolate chip), muffins, scones, and
more. You can also enjoy a sandwich or quiche and watch the passing parade.

STREIT'S MATZOS
150 Rivington St (bet Clinton and Suffolk St) 212/475-7000
Mon-Thurs: 9-4:30 www.streitsmatzos.com

Matzo is a thin, wafer-like unleavened bread. According to tradition, it came out of Egypt with Moses and the children of Israel when they had to flee so quickly there was no time to let the bread rise. Through the years, matzo was restricted to the time around Passover, and even when matzo production became automated, business shut down for a good deal of the year. But not today and not in New York. Streit produces matzo throughout the year, pausing only on Saturday and Jewish holidays to clean the machines. Streit allows a peek at the production process, which is both mechanized and extremely primitive. Matzo is baked in enormous thin sheets that are later broken up. If you ask for a fresh batch, they might break it right off the production line. They also offer noodles, wafers, ready-to-serve canned soups, potato products, Hanukkah products, and specialty dishes.

SULLIVAN STREET BAKERY
533 W 47th St (bet Tenth and Eleventh Ave)   212/265-5580
Mon-Sat: 7-7; Sun: 8-4   www.sullivanstreetbakery.com

Fresh, crusty, warm French loaves is why you come here! If you savor really fresh authentic Italian country bread, this is also *the* place to go. Their sourdough is served in a number of restaurants, so you know it is first-rate. Sullivan Street Bakery carries the only flatbread *pizza bianca romana* (Roman-style white pizza) in Manhattan. Raisin-walnut bread is another specialty. You'll find great sandwiches at the 47th Street store.

For a real hit at your next party or event, order some personalized cookies from **Eleni's Cookies** (Chelsea Market, 75 Ninth Ave, 212/255-7990, www.elenis.com).

SYLVIA WEINSTOCK CAKES
273 Church St (bet Franklin and White St)   212/925-6698
Mon-Fri: 9-4 (by appointment)   www.sylviaweinstock.com

Sylvia Weinstock has been in the cake business for over two decades, so she knows how to satisfy customers who want the very best. Lifelike floral decorations are her trademark. Although weddings are a specialty (two months notice is required), she will produce masterpieces—including hand-molded sugar figures—for any occasion.

VESUVIO BAKERY
160 Prince St (bet West Broadway and Thompson St)   212/925-8248
Sun-Thurs: 8-7; Fri, Sat: 8 a.m.-11 p.m.

You'll love the look of this oldtime favorite! Since 1920, Vesuvio Bakery has been a popular place to buy good bread. You will also find bagels, eggs, and other breakfast items; special paninis and sandwiches; various wraps, including vegetable; bruschettas; salads; and desserts.

WHOLE EARTH BAKERY & KITCHEN
130 St. Mark's Pl (bet First Ave and Ave A)   212/677-7597
Daily: 10-10

This is a completely vegan establishment. It's the only Manhattan bakery that uses organic flours and organic, unprocessed sweeteners. They feature great pizza, lasagna, and soup, plus daily selections of savory foods. Catering is available.

YONAH SCHIMMEL'S KNISHES
137 E Houston St (bet First and Second Ave)   212/477-2858
Sun-Thurs: 9-7; Fri, Sat: 9 a.m.-10 p.m.   www.knishery.com

Yonah Schimmel has been selling knishes for so long that his name is legendary. He started out dispensing knishes among the pushcarts of the Lower East Side. A Yonah Schimmel knish is a unique experience. It doesn't look or taste anything like the mass-produced things sold at supermarkets, lunch stands, and New York ballgames. Yonah's knishes have a thin, flaky crust—almost like strudel dough—surrounding a hot, moist filling, and they are kosher. The best-selling filling is potato, but kasha (buckwheat), spinach, and a half-dozen others are also terrific. No two knishes come out exactly alike, since each is handmade. You can order by fax (212/477-2858) for delivery anywhere in the continental U.S.

> Yes, there is such a thing as Indian fast food! Come try some at **Indian Bread Co.** (194 Bleecker St, 212/228-1909, www.indianbreadco.com). Hours are Mon-Thurs: noon-11; Fri, Sat: noon-1 a.m.; and Sun: noon-10.

Beverages

NEW YORK BEVERAGE WHOLESALERS
515 Bruckner Blvd (bet 149th and Austin Pl), The Bronx
Mon-Fri: 8:30-6; Sat: 8:30-5   212/831-4000, 718/401-7700
                                      www.nybeverage.com

The *buy*-words here are tremendous variety and great prices. This outfit has one of the largest retail beer selections in New York City, with over 500 brands available, plus soda, mineral and natural waters, iced teas, and seltzers. They will deliver to your door, supply specialty imports, and work with you on any quantities needed. Call to place a delivery order. Don't forget the ice!

RIVERSIDE BEER AND SODA DISTRIBUTORS
2331 Twelfth Ave (at 133rd St)   212/234-3884
Mon-Sat: 9-6

This place mainly supplies wholesalers and large retail orders, but they are not averse to serving retail customers. Once you've made the trek up here, you might as well take advantage of the discount and buy in quantity.

British

MYERS OF KESWICK
634 Hudson St (bet Horatio and Jane St)   212/691-4194
Mon-Fri: 10-7; Sat: 10-6; Sun: noon-5   www.myersofkeswick.com

Peter and Irene Myers are to English food what Burberry, Church, and Laura Ashley are to English clothing. They've made it possible for you to visit "the village grocer" for imported staples and fresh, home-baked items you'd swear came from a kitchen in Soho—the London neighborhood, that is. Among the tins, a shopper can find Heinz treacle sponge pudding, trifle mix, ribena, mushy peas, steak and kidney pie, Smarties, lemon barley water, chutneys, jams and preserves, and all the major English teas. Fresh goods include sausage rolls, Myers' pork pie, Scotch eggs, British bangers, and Cumberland sausages, all made fresh daily. There are also cheeses—the double Gloucester is outstanding!—and chocolates. For Anglophiles and expatriates alike, Myers of Keswick is a *luverly* treat.

Candy

DYLAN'S CANDY BAR
1011 Third Ave (at 60th St)   646/735-0078
Mon-Fri: 10-10; Sat: 10 a.m.-11 p.m.; Sun: 11-8
www.dylanscandybar.com

Ralph Lauren's daughter, Dylan, is in the candy business in a big way. Dylan's is a huge candy emporium, delighting kids and grown-ups alike. You'll find an old-fashioned soda fountain with custom-made ice cream flavors, a candy spa (for goodies like chocolate bath salts), the world's largest lollipop, 21 colors of M&Ms, Pez dispensers, and much more. This is a two-level operation, with stairs that look like gummies! A private party room with all kinds of candy activities—like designing your own candy picture frame—is available. The candy selection includes 5,000 varieties of sweets from all over the world, and there are Dylan candy-themed housewares, apparel, and parties!

Is your sweet tooth aching? Since 1894, **Veniero's** (342 E 11th St, 212/674-7070, www.venierospastry.com) has been serving Italian pastries, cakes, and gelati to satisfied customers. The quarters still have many of the original details, including hand-stamped metal ceilings and etched glass doors.

ECONOMY CANDY
108 Rivington St (bet Essex and Ludlow St)   212/254-1531
Sun-Fri: 9-6; Sat: 10-5   800/352-4544 (outside New York)
www.economycandy.com

The same family has been selling everything from penny candies to beautiful gourmet gift baskets at Economy Candy since 1937. What a selection of dried fruits, candies, teas, cookies, crackers, nuts, and chocolates—even sugar-free goodies! The best part is the price. You'll find much for your baking needs: almond paste, cocoas, baking chocolate, and glazed fruits. Old-time favorites include Pixie Sticks, candy buttons, wax lips, and ice cubes. Mail orders are filled efficiently and promptly; an online catalog is available.

JACQUES TORRES CHOCOLATE HAVEN
350 Hudson St (at King St)   212/414-2462
Mon-Sat: 9-7; Sun: 10-6   www.mrchocolate.com

You can see those delicious Jacques Torres bars and other creations being made right in front of you! In a hefty space that houses a factory, retail counter, and cafe, Jacques Torres will send the chocoholic in you to heaven.

LA MAISON DU CHOCOLAT
1018 Madison Ave (bet 78th and 79th St)   212/744-7117
Mon-Sat: 10-7; Sun: noon-6

30 Rockefeller Plaza (49th St bet Fifth Ave and Ave of the Americas)
Mon-Fri: 9:30-7; Sat: 10-7; Sun: noon-6   212/265-9404
www.lamaisonduchocolat.com

What a place! Over 40 delicious variations of light and dark chocolates are available under one roof. They carry French truffles, plain and fancy champagnes, orangettes, coffee beans, chocolate-covered almonds, caramels, candied chestnuts, and fruit paste. There's even a tea salon that serves pastries and drinks. Everything is made in Paris, and La Maison du Chocolat is the first branch of the store outside of France. Prices are a cut above the candy-counter norm, but then so are exotic flavors like September raspberries, freshly grated ginger root, raisins flamed in rum, marzipan with pistachio and kirsh, and caramel butter.

> One of my favorite snacks is a fresh, juicy strawberry dipped in chocolate. You can watch them being made at **Godiva** (745 Seventh Ave, 212/921-2193). Your taste buds will insist you leave with at least a few of these magnificent morsels for afternoon tea or a special dessert!

LEONIDAS
485 Madison Ave (bet 51st and 52nd St)   212/980-2608
Mon-Fri: 9-7; Sat: 10-7; Sun: noon-6   www.leonidas-chocolate.com

This is a U.S. importer of the famous Belgian confectionary company and a haven for those who appreciate exquisite sweets. Over 80 varieties of confections—milk, white, and bittersweet chocolate pieces, chocolate orange peels, solid chocolate medallions, fabulous fresh cream fillings, truffle fillings, and marzipan—are flown in fresh every week. Leonidas' pralines are particularly sumptuous. Jacques Bergier, the genial general manager, can make the mouth water just describing this treasure trove. Best of all, prices are reasonable. Speaking of Leonidas, three retail locations of **Manon Cafe** (120 Broadway, 212/766-6100; 3 Hanover Square, 212/422-9600; and 74 Trinity Pl, 212/233-1111) serve Leonidas' Belgian chocolates, as well as coffee, espresso, cappuccino, sandwiches and salads.

LI-LAC CANDY SHOP
40 Eighth Ave (at Jane St)   212/242-7374
Mon-Fri: 10-8; Sat: noon-8; Sun: noon-6

Grand Central Terminal (42nd St at Vanderbilt Ave)   212/370-4866
Mon-Fri: 7 a.m.-9 p.m.; Sat: 10-7; Sun: 11-6
www.li-lacchocolates.com

Since 1923, Li-Lac has been *the* source for fine chocolate in Greenwich Village. Li-Lac's delicious chocolate fudge is made fresh every day, and maple walnut fudge is every bit as good. Then there are pralines, mousses, French rolls, nuts, glacé fruits, and hand-dipped chocolates. All are handmade.

MARIEBELLE FINE TREATS & CHOCOLATES
484 Broome St (bet West Broadway and Wooster St)   212/925-6999
762 Madison Ave (at 65th St)   212/249-4587
Mon-Sat: 11-7; Sun: noon-7   www.mariebelle.com

Forget the diets and rush down to this delicious location! What awaits you is thick European hot chocolate, homemade cookies and biscuits, a cocoa bar, and wines. The exotic chocolate flavors are packed with class. What a great gift for chocoholics! Crepes and fondues are available at the Cocoa Bar. Small private events are a specialty.

How about a chocolate tour? **New York Chocolate Tour** (917/292-0680, www.sweetwalks.com) will take you to delicious places that will excite the heart (and taste buds) of every chocoholic! Several different tours are available; contact them for details of time and place. Private tours are available upon request.

MONDEL CHOCOLATES
2913 Broadway (at 114th St)   212/864-2111
Mon-Sat: 11-7; Sun: noon-6

Mondel has been a tasty gem in the neighborhood for over a half-century. Owner Florence Mondel's father founded the store. The aroma is fantastic! The chocolate-covered ginger, orange peel, nut barks, and turtles are especially good. I routinely order their nonpareils. A dietetic chocolate line is offered.

I still like to go to real old-time places! Established in 1925, **Lexington Candy Shop** (1226 Lexington Ave, 212/288-0057) continues to provide great breakfasts, burgers, ice cream, and candy.

TEUSCHER CHOCOLATES OF SWITZERLAND
25 E 61st St (at Madison Ave)   212/751-8482
Mon-Sat: 10-5:45; Sun: 11-5   www.teuschermadison.com

620 Fifth Ave (Rockefeller Center)   212/246-4416
Mon-Sat: 10-6; Thurs: 10-7:30; Sun: 11-5 www.teuschernewyork.com

If there was an award for "most elegant chocolate shop," it would have to go to Teuscher. These are not just chocolates; they're imported works of art. Chocolates are shipped weekly from Switzerland. They are packed into stunning handmade boxes that add to the decor of many a customer's home. The truffles are almost obscenely good. The superb champagne truffle has a tiny dot of champagne cream in the center. The cocoa, nougat, butter-crunch, muscat, orange, and almond truffles all have their own little surprises. Truffles are the stars, but Teuscher's marzipan, praline chocolates, and mints (shaped like sea creatures) are of similar high quality.

Catering, Delis, Food to Go
ABIGAIL KIRSCH
Chelsea Piers, Pier 60 (23rd St at Hudson River)   212/336-6060
Daily: 9-5 (by appointment)

Abigail Kirsch's food, service, decor, and tableware are of the very highest quality, and so is her pricing. But you will get your money's worth if it's a class event that you are looking for. You will not have to worry about any detail from this organization, since you are relying on over three decades of experience.

Favorite Chocolate Shops of a Serious Chocoholic (Me!)

Burdick Chocolates (800/299-2419): mail order or delivery

Charbonnel et Walker (Saks Fifth Avenue, 611 Fifth Ave, 8th floor, 212/588-0546)

Chocolate Michel Cluizel (ABC Carpet & Home, 888 Broadway, 212/477-7335)

Chocolate Bar (48 Eighth Ave, 212/366-1541 and at Henri Bendel, 712 Fifth Ave)

Christopher Norman Chocolates (60 New St, 212/402-1243; also carried at Dean & Deluca and Whole Foods Market)

Eric Girerd (www.chocosphere.com)

Fifth Avenue Chocolatiere (693 Third Ave, 212/935-5454)

Francois Payard (1032 Lexington Ave, 212/717-5252)

Jacques Torres Chocolate Haven (350 Hudson St, 212/414-2462 and 285 Amsterdam Ave)

Kee's Chocolates (80 Thompson St, 212/334-3284)

La Bergamote (169 Ninth Ave, 212/627-9010)

Laderach Chocolatier Suisse (800/231-8154)

La Maison du Chocolat (1018 Madison Ave, 212/744-7117 and 30 Rockefeller Center, 212/265-9404)

Leonidas (485 Madison Ave, 212/980-2608 and at Manon Cafe locations)

Manhattan Fruitier (105 E 29th St, 212/686-0404)

MarieBelle Fine Treats & Chocolates (484 Broome St, 212/925-6999 and 762 Madison Avenue, 212/249-4587)

Martine's (400 E 82nd St, 212/744-6289 and at Bloomingdale's, 1000 Third Ave).

Max Brenner, Chocolate by the Bald Man (841 Broadway and 141 Second Ave, 212/388-0030)

Neuchatel Chocolates (55 E 52nd St, 212/759-1388)

Richart Design et Chocolat (7 E 55th St, 212/371-9369)

Scharffen Berger (473 Amsterdam Ave, 212/362-9734)

Teuscher Chocolates of Switzerland (25 E 61st St, 212/751-8482 and 620 Fifth Ave, 212/246-4416

Vosges Haut-Chocolat (132 Spring St, 212/625-2929 and 1100 Madison Ave, 212/717-2929)

Best Restaurants for Chocolate Desserts

Bar Room at the Modern (9 W 53rd St, 212/333-1220): hazelnut *dacquoise*

craft (43 E 19th St, 212/780-0880): chocolate soufflé

Jean Georges (1 Central Park W, 212/299-3900): warm, soft chocolate cake

The Spotted Pig (314 W 11th St, 212/620-0393): flourless chocolate cake

AGATA & VALENTINA
1505 First Ave (at 79th St)   212/452-0690
Daily: 8 a.m.-8:30 p.m.   www.agatavalentina.com

This is a very classy expanded gourmet shop with an ambience that will make you think you're in Sicily. There are good things to eat at every counter, with each one more tempting than the next. In summer they have a sidewalk cafe. You'll love the great selection of gourmet dishes, bakery items, seafood, magnificent fresh vegetables, meats, cheeses, appetizers, candies, and gelati. Extra virgin olive oil is a house specialty. There is a cappuccino bar and their restaurant across the street, at 1513 First Avenue, serves lunch and dinner daily and brunch on weekends.

AZURE
830 Third Ave (at 51st St)   212/486-8080
Daily: 24 hours

Azure's 125 feet of hot and cold offerings is quite a sight. What a salad bar! Of course, there is more: homemade soups, hot Italian sandwiches, stuffed baked potatoes, pizzas, sushi, and great muffins. Azure also offers healthy Mongolian grill fare.

If you would like to shop where chefs stock up, consider visiting **Trufette** (a.k.a. **S.O.S. Chefs**, 104 Ave B, 212/505-5813). There are some interesting finds here: many kinds of preserves, glazes, chocolates, truffles, mushrooms, foie gras, spices, flavored salts, nuts, vanilla beans, saffron, fennel pollen, and more It is a discovery center, for sure!

BALDUCCI'S
155-A W 66th St (bet Broadway and Amsterdam Ave) 212/653-8320
Daily: 7 a.m.-9 p.m.   212/741-3700
81 Eighth Ave (at 14th St)
Daily: 7 a.m.-9 p.m.   www.balduccis.com

Balducci is synonymous with food in Manhattan, especially fresh fruits and vegetables. The Balduccis started their empire in 1946, offering fabulous selections of cakes and pastries, coffees, breads, meats, seafood, prepared entrees, and domestic and imported cheeses. You'll find a huge selection of Italian foodstuffs: focaccia, fresh-cut pastas and ravioli, sauces, and *taralli*. There are spectacular displays in the produce area, and it all looks so inviting! This uptown store carries on the family's quality tradition, with attractive presentation and decor. Local delivery is available.

BARNEY GREENGRASS
541 Amsterdam Ave (bet 86th and 87th St)   212/724-4707
Tues-Sun: 8-6 (takeout)
Tues-Fri: 8:30-4; Sat, Sun: 8:30-5 (restaurant)
                                    www.barneygreengrass.com

Those who like sturgeon love Barney Greengrass! This family business has occupied the same locale since 1929. Barney has been succeeded by his grandson Gary, but the same quality gourmet smoked fish is still sold over the counter, just as it was in Barney's day. Greengrass lays claim to the title of "Sturgeon King," and few would dispute it. While sturgeon is indeed king, Greengrass also has other smoked-fish delicacies: Nova Scotia salmon, belly lox, and whitefish. There is more: caviar, pickled herring, and kippered salmon salad. The dairy and deli line—including vegetable cream cheese, great homemade cheese blintzes, homemade salads and borscht, and a smashing Nova Scotia salmon with scrambled eggs and onions—is world-renowned. In fact, because so many customers couldn't wait to get home to unwrap their packages, Greengrass started a restaurant next door.

Bazzini (339 Greenwich St, 212/334-1280, www.bazzininuts.com) is Tribeca's gourmet food emporium. You'll find a great showing of fine foods: meats, fish, produce, deli items, prepared foods to go, charcuterie, and more. There is an on-premises cafe; kids are welcome; kitchenware (dishes, flatware, linens, candles) is stocked; and nuts and dried fruits are a specialty. Delivery is available.

BARRAUD CATERERS
405 Broome St (at Centre St)   212/925-1334
Mon-Fri. 10-6   www.barraudcaterers.com

Owner Rosemary Howe has an interesting background. She was born in India and grew up British, and is therefore familiar with Indian and Anglo-Indian food. Her training in developing recipes is on the French side. Because she was raised in the tradition of afternoon tea, she knows finger sandwiches and all that goes with them. Her menus are unique. All breads are menu-specific, every meal is customized from a lengthy list, a wine consultant is available, and consultations on table etiquette are given. Dinners focused on cheese and wine are a specialty. This is a real hands-on operation, with Rosemary taking care of every detail of your brunch, tea, lunch, or dinner. She now features degustation (tasting) menus, paired with appropriate wines for each course.

BUTTERFIELD MARKET
1114 Lexington Ave (bet 77th and 78th St)   212/288-7800
Mon-Fri: 7 a.m.-8 p.m.; Sat: 7:30-5:30; Sun: 8-5
                                www.butterfieldmarket.com

Upper East Siders have enjoyed the goodies at Butterfield for nearly a century. Highlights of this popular market include an excellent prepared foods section, produce, a good selection of quality specialty items, tasty pastries, charcuterie, attractive gift baskets, a terrific cheese selection, and a diet-busting candy and sweets section. Catering is a feature, and service is personal and informed.

CHARLOTTE'S CATERING
328 E 117th St (bet First and Second Ave)   212/732-7939
Mon-Fri: 10-6   www.charlottescateringny.com

Quality is Number One! Charlotte's has developed an outstanding reputation for catering, with no detail too small for their careful attention. Their client list reads like a who's who. Charlotte's is a full-service catering establishment, from menus and music to flowers and waiters' outfits. Come here when you want real experts to handle wedding receptions, dinner dances, teas, luncheons, business meetings or dinners, and so forth. Specialties include wonderful tapas, a spa buffet menu, and outrageous desserts. They'll work parties outside of Manhattan as well.

CHELSEA MARKET
75 Ninth Ave (bet 15th and 16th St)   212/243-6005
Mon-Sat: 8 a.m.-9 p.m.; Sun: 10-8   www.chelseamarket.com

In a complex of 18 former industrial buildings, including the old Nabisco Cookie Factory of the late 1800s, an 800-foot-long concourse houses one of the most unusual marketplaces in the city. The space is innovative, including a waterfall fed by an underground spring. Among the nearly two dozen shops, you'll find **Amy's Bread** (big choice, plus a cafe); **Bowery Kitchen Supplies** (kitchen buffs will go wild!); **Chelsea Wholesale Flower Market** (really fresh cut flowers); **Chelsea Wine Vault** (climate-controlled); **Cleaver Company** (catering and event planning); **Ronnybrook Farm Dairy** (fresh milk and eggs); **buonItalia** (great Italian basics); **Hale & Hearty Soups** (dozens of varieties); **The Lobster Place** (takeout seafood); **Sarabeth's Bakery**; **Frank's Butcher**; **Manhattan Fruit Exchange** (for buying in bulk); **Goupil & DeCarlo Patisserie**; **Chelsea Thai** (wholesale and takeout); **Fat Witch Bakery** (brownies, goodies, gifts); and **Eleni's Cookies** (artfully iced sugar cookies, bagels, ice cream, and more). **Ruthy's Cheesecake and Rugelach Bakery** is outstanding!

Be sure to stop at **Blue Ribbon Bakery Market** (14 Bedford St, 212/647-0408). You'll find a yummy selection of famous Blue Ribbon breads—even toast with scrumptious toppings!

DEAN & DELUCA
560 Broadway (at Prince St)   212/431-1691
Daily: 10-8
1150 Madison Ave (at 85th St)   212/717-0800
Daily: 8-8   www.deananddeluca.com

Dean & Deluca is one of the icons of the American epicurean experience. The flagship store in Soho offers an extraordinary array of local, national, and international culinary selections. Among the many temptations are fresh produce and flowers, fresh-baked breads and pastries, prepared dishes, a good showing of cheeses and charcuterie, and a selection of meats, poultry, and seafood. A bustling espresso bar serves coffee and cappuccino, as well as sweets and savories. This part of the business has been expanded into smaller cafes throughout the city, including **The Shack**, located on Prince Street. To complete a gourmet adventure, Dean & Deluca offers an assortment of housewares. They can also cater intimate gatherings and corporate events.

DELMONICO GOURMET FOOD MARKET

320 Park Ave (at 50th St)	212/317-8777
55 E 59th St (bet Madison and Park Ave)	212/751-5559
375 Lexington Ave (at 42nd St)	212/661-0150
24 hours	

Each of these markets has gourmet groceries, fresh produce, pastries, bakery, a huge selection of cheeses, and much more. This is a good choice if you are planning a catered event for your office or home. I like the ultra-clean surroundings and accommodating help. Don't miss the charcuterie selection and salad bars.

ELI'S MANHATTAN

1411 Third Ave (bet 80th and 81st St)	212/717-8100
Daily: 7 a.m.-9 p.m.	www.elismanhattan.com

You know quality is foremost when the name Eli Zabar is attached. This is true at Eli's Manhattan, which carries dairy items, pastries, flowers, prepared foods, appetizers, smoked fish, coffee, wine and spirits, and gift baskets. Prices can be high; this is not a cut-rate store. Other features include catering, a self-service cafe, and the neighboring restaurant **Taste** (1413 Third Ave, 212/717-9798).

The Lower East Side's **Essex Street Market** (120 Essex Street, at Delancey St) has been a historic shopping destination since 1947. You'll find vendors of seafood, meats, ethnic groceries, baked goods, produce, and bulk-food items. The market also features specialty stores dispensing clothing, electronics, household goods, hardware, and religious items. No matter what you are looking for, Essex Street Market promises a unique shopping experience.

FAIRWAY

2127 Broadway (at 74th St)	212/595-1888
Daily: 6 a.m.-1 a.m.	
2328 Twelfth Ave (at 133rd St)	212/234-3883
Daily: 8 a.m.-11 p.m.	www.fairwaymarket.com

The popular institution known as Fairway made its name with an incredible selection of fruits and vegetables. They offer produce in huge quantities at very reasonable prices. The uptown store is newer and larger, stocking a wonderful array of cheeses, meats, bakery items, and more. Additions to the Broadway store include an on-premises bakery, a cafe, organically grown produce, expanded fish and meat departments, and a catering service. Fairway operates its own farm on Long Island and has developed a good relationship with area produce dealers. Both stores offer a full line of organic and natural grocery, health, and beauty items. There is an all-kosher bakery at the Twelfth Avenue location, in Harlem. As you make your rounds on the Upper West Side, you can't go wrong by carrying a Fairway bag on one arm and a Zabar's bag on the other!

FINE & SCHAPIRO
138 W 72nd St (bet Broadway and Columbus Ave)
Daily: 10-10   212/877-2874, 212/877-2721
www.fineandschapiro. com

Ostensibly a kosher delicatessen and restaurant, Fine & Schapiro also offers great dinners for home consumption. Because of the high quality, they term themselves "the Rolls-Royce of delicatessens." That description is apt. Fine & Schapiro dispenses a complete line of cold cuts, hot and cold hors d'oeuvres, catering platters, and magnificent sandwiches—try the pastrami! Everything that issues from Fine & Schapiro is perfectly cooked and artistically arranged. The sandwiches are masterpieces; the aroma and taste are irresistible. Chicken in the pot and stuffed cabbage are among their best items.

GARDEN OF EDEN
162 W 23rd St (bet Ave of the Americas and
   Seventh Ave)   212/675-6300
7 E 14th St (bet University Pl and Fifth Ave)   212/255-4200
Mon-Sat: 7 a.m.-10 p.m.; Sun: 7 a.m.-9:30 p.m.
www.edengourmet.com

These stores are both farmers markets and gourmet shops! The food items are fresh, appetizing, and priced to please. Moreover, the stores are immaculate and well organized, and the personnel are exceptionally helpful. You'll find breads and bakery items, cheeses, veggies, meats, seafood, pastas, desserts and more. All manner of catering services are available. Platters of cheese, meats, fruit, vegetables, fish, patés, and breakfast items are offered.

Soups, salads, and sandwiches are available at an excellent *patisserie* called **Financier** (35 Cedar St, 212/952-3838; World Financial Center, 212/786-3220; and 62 Stone St, 212/344-5600).

GLORIOUS FOOD
504 E 74th St (bet East River and York Ave)   212/628-2320
Mon-Fri: 9-5 (by appointment)   www.gloriousfood.com

Glorious Food is at the top of many New Yorkers' lists when it comes to catering. They are a full-service outfit, expertly taking care of every small detail of any event. They have met most every challenge for over a quarter of a century. Give 'em a try!

GOURMET GARAGE
453 Broome St (at Mercer St)   212/941-5850
1245 Park Ave (at 96th St)   212/348-5850
301 E 64th St (at Second Ave)   212/535-6271
2567 Broadway (at 96th St)   212/663-0656
117 Seventh Ave S (at 10th St)   212/699-5980
Hours vary by store   www.gourmetgarage.com

A working-class gourmet food shop is the best way to describe Gourmet Garage. These stores carry a good selection of in-demand items—including fruits and veggies, cheeses, breads, pastries, coffees, meats, and olive oils—at low prices. Organic foods are a specialty. Catering and gift baskets are available, and delivery is offered for a nominal fee.

GRACE'S MARKETPLACE
1237 Third Ave (at 71st St)   212/737-0600
Mon-Sat: 7 a.m.-8:30 p.m.; Sun: 8-7   www.gracesmarketplace.com

I come from a multi-generational family business where being available to customers was the key to success for over two decades. I am therefore well aware of operations that still exhibit those values. Grace's Marketplace is a prime example. Founded by Grace Balducci Doria and the late Joe Doria, Sr., Grace's is one of the city's finest and most popular food emporiums. The Doria family presides over this operation, and they can be seen helping customers on the floor. Products, service, and ambience are all top of the line. You'll find smoked meats and fish, cheeses, fresh pastas, homemade sauces, produce, a full range of baked goods, candy, coffees, teas, dried fruit, pastries, gourmet groceries, prepared foods, prime meats, produce, and seafood. Quality gift baskets and catering are specialties. Try their adjoining restaurant, **Grace's Trattoria** (201 E 71st St, 212/452-2323, www.graces tratoria.com), for great Italian fare. This place is a must visit!

GREAT PERFORMANCES
287 Spring St (bet Hudson and Varick St)   212/727-2424
Mon-Fri: 8:30-5:30 (by appointment)   www.greatperformances.com

Great Performances has been creating spectacular events in the New York area for 26 years with the help of folks from the city's artistic community. Each division of this full-service catering company has a team of expert staff. They take pride in recruiting the best and brightest the industry has to offer. Their people bring creativity, personality, and technical expertise to each event. From intimate dinner parties to gala dinners for thousands, Great Performances is a complete event-planning resource.

H&H MIDTOWN BAGELS EAST
1551 Second Ave (bet 80th and 81st St)   212/734-7441
Daily: 24 hours   www.hhmidtownbagelseast.com

Delicious bagels are made fresh right on the premises, and if you're lucky, you'll get 'em warm! But there is more: homemade croissants, assorted Italian cookies, soups, cold cuts, sandwiches, salads, salmon, lox, sturgeon, and pickled herring. The emphasis is on carryout, but tables are available for those who can't wait to dive in.

HAN AH REUM
25 W 32nd St (bet Broadway and Fifth Ave)   212/695-3283
Daily: 9 a.m.-midnight

Note the late hours! Do you need prepared foods for an 11 p.m. party perhaps? Korean, Chinese, and Japanese food items are the specialties here. How do pre-packed sashimi and Korean pears sound?

INTERNATIONAL GROCERY
543 Ninth Ave (at 40th St)   212/279-1000
Mon-Sat: 8-6

Ninth Avenue is one great wholesale market of international cookery. Accordingly, International Grocery is both a spice emporium and an excellent source for rudiments on which to sprinkle the spices. You will sacrifice frills for some of the best prices and freshest foodstuffs in town. Lamb can be special-ordered.

KELLEY & PING
127 Greene St (bet Houston and Prince St)   212/228-1212
325 Bowery (at Second Ave)   212/475-8600
Lunch: Mon-Fri (11:30-5); Dinner: Daily (5:30-11)   www.eatrice.com

The exotic cuisines of Asia—Thai, Chinese, Vietnamese, Japanese, Malaysian, and Korean—are popular in restaurants and at home. Kelley & Ping specializes in groceries and housewares from this part of the world. A restaurant is now a major part of the operation, and they do catering, too. If you have questions about how to prepare Asian dishes, these are the folks to ask.

Located in the heart of midtown Manhattan, **Grand Central Market** (Grand Central Terminal, 42nd Street at Park Ave) has some of Manhattan's finest quality food retailers, including Bella Cucina, Ceriello Fine Foods, Corrado Bread & Pastry, Dishes at Home, Greenwich Produce, Koglin German Hams, Li-Lac Chocolates, Murray's Cheese, Oren's Daily Roast, Penzeys Spices, Pescatore Seafood Company, Wild Edibles, and Zaro's Bread Basket.

MANGIA
50 W 57th St (bet Fifth Ave and Ave of the Americas) 212/582-5882
16 E 48th St (bet Fifth and Madison Ave)   212/754-7600
22 W 23rd St (bet Fifth Ave and Ave of the Americas) 212/647-0200
40 Wall St (bet Broad and William St)   212/425-4040
Hours vary by store   www.mangiatogo.com

At Mangia, the old European reverence for ripe tomatoes and brick-oven bread endures. This outfit offers four distinct services: corporate catering, with everything that's needed for an office breakfast or luncheon; a juice bar; a carryout shop with an antipasti bar, soups, salads, sandwiches, entrees, sweets, and cappuccino; and a restaurant with a full menu and made-to-order pastas. Prices are competitive, and delivery is offered.

NEWMAN & LEVENTHAL
45 W 81st St (bet Central Park West and Columbus Ave)
By appointment   212/362-9400

Having been a kosher caterer for nearly a century, this firm is known for unique menus and top quality. Be prepared to pay well for outstanding food.

PETAK'S
1246 Madison Ave (bet 89th and 90th St)   212/722-7711
Mon-Thurs: 7:30 a.m.-8 p.m.; Fri, Sat: 7:30-7; Sun: 9-7

Ellen Petak is a third-generation member of a family that has owned appetizer businesses in the South Bronx and New Jersey. He made the leap to Manhattan. This "appy shop" was the first in the Carnegie Hill neighborhood in a long time. No neighborhood has truly arrived until it has a gourmet shop, and Petak's filled that void. There are all the appy standbys, such as salads (60 of them!), corned beef, pastrami, smoked fish, and all sorts of takeout foods. The store offers full corporate catering, a sushi chef, picnic hampers, and a full-service cafe/restaurant.

PUFF & PAO
105 Christopher St (bet Hudson and Bleecker St)   212/633-7833
Mon-Fri: 7 a.m.-10 p.m.; Sat, Sun: 8 a.m.-10 p.m. www.puffandpao.com

There's nothing artificial here! Owner Stephen Elliot makes sure all ingredients for his large line of products are natural, and everything is made fresh in the store. You'll find first-class baked goods, sandwiches, lattes, specialty salads, and fine espresso. You may become addicted to their cream puffs and cupcakes! Also available are *paolitos*, a Brazilian-style cheese bread. Free local delivery (with purchase of $10 or more) is offered.

For those New Yorkers who don't find grocery shopping a pleasant pastime, there is hope. **Fresh Direct** (212/796-8002, www.fresh direct.com) sells over 3,000 organic and prepared food items. They also provide useful information like calorie counts, recipes, and cooking information. Prices are competitive, as they do not have a storefront or deal with middle men. Delivery charges are reasonable.

RUSS & DAUGHTERS
179 E Houston St (bet Allen and Orchard St)
Mon-Sat: 9-7; Sun: 8-5:30   212/475-4880, 800/RUSS-229
www.russanddaughters.com

One of my favorite places! A family business in its fourth generation, Russ & Daughters has been a renowned New York shop since it first opened its doors. They carry nuts, dried fruits, lake sturgeon, salmon, sable, and herring. Russ & Daughters has a reputation for serving only the very best. Six varieties of caviar are sold at low prices. Their chocolates are premium quality. They sell wholesale and over the counter, and ship anywhere. Many a Lower East Side shopping trip ends with a stop at Russ & Daughters. It is clean, first-rate, friendly—what more could you ask?

SABLE'S SMOKED FISH
1489 Second Ave (bet 77th and 78th St)   212/249-6177
Mon-Fri: 8:30-7:30; Sat: 8-7:30; Sun: 8-5   www.sablesnyc.com

Kenny Sze was the appetizers manager at Zabar's for many years, and he learned the trade well. He's brought that knowledge to the Upper East Side, where he offers wonderful smoked salmon, lobster salad, Alaskan crab salad, sturgeon, caviar (good prices), cold cuts, cheeses, coffees, salads, fresh breads, and prepared foods. Sable's catering service can provide platters (smoked fish, cold cuts, and cheese), jumbo sandwiches, whole hams, cured meats, and more. Free delivery is offered in the immediate area, and they'll ship anywhere in the U.S. Cold cuts and chicken dishes are specialties. Tables for eat-in are available.

SALUMERIA BIELLESE
378 Eighth Ave (at 29th St)   212/736-7376
Mon-Fri: 7-6; Sat: 9-5   www.salumeriabiellese.com

This Italian-owned grocery store is also the only French charcuterie in the city. If that isn't contradiction enough, consider that the loyal lunchtime crowd thinks it's dining at a hero shop when it's really enjoying the fruits of a kitchen that serves many fine restaurants in the city. To understand how all this came about, a lesson in New York City geography is necessary. In 1945, when Ugo Buzzio and Joseph Nello came to this country from the Piedmontese city of Biella, they opened a shop a block away from the current one in the immigrant neighborhood known as Hell's Kitchen. (Today, this gentrified area is called Clinton.) The two partners almost immediately began producing French charcuterie. Word spread among the chefs of the city's restaurants that Salumeria Biellese was producing a quality product that could not be duplicated. Buzzio's son, Marc, is one of three partners who run the business today. Offerings include sausages (pork, game, veal, lamb, and poultry), cured meats, and specialty patés. **Biricchino** (260 W 29th St, 212/ 695-6690), a restaurant offering Northern Italian cuisine, is located in back.

> There are any number of great delicatessens in Manhattan, but the **Stage Deli** (834 Seventh Ave) is definitely not one of them. Not only is the place rather unattractive, but also the food is, in many cases, quite unacceptable, and the smell is unappealing. You can do better.

SARGE'S
548 Third Ave (bet 36th and 37th St)   212/679-0442
Daily: 24 hours   www.sargesdeli.com

Sarge's isn't fancy, but it could feed an army, and there's much to be said for the taste, quality, and price. Sarge's will cater everything from hot dogs to hot or cold buffets for almost any size crowd, and there are remarkably reasonable package deals. Sarge's also caters deli items and has an excellent selection of cold hors d'oeuvre platters, offering everything from canapes of caviar, sturgeon, and Nova Scotia salmon to shrimp cocktail. To make the party complete, Sarge's can supply utensils, condiments, and staff. Delivery is available.

SONNIER & CASTLE FOOD
532 W 46th St (bet Tenth and Eleventh Ave)   212/957-6481
By appointment   www.sonnier-castle.com

A new chef here is doing great things! This full-service caterer will help with locations, flowers, entertainment, and anything else a customer might need for a special gathering. Russ Sonnier and David Castle are young enough to be inventive, yet mature enough to do a first-class job.

TODARO BROS.
555 Second Ave (bet 30th and 31st St)   212/532-0633
Mon-Sat: 6:30 a.m.-10 p.m.; Sun: 6:30 a.m.-9 p.m.
                                                    www.todarobros.com

This is food heaven! An icon in the Kips Bay/Murray Hill area since 1917, Todaro Bros. carries the very best in specialty foods. Great lunch sandwiches, fresh mozzarella, sausages, and prepared foods are offered daily. The fresh fish and meats are of the highest quality. The cheese department offers a huge variety of imported varieties. The shelves are stocked with artisanal oil, vinegar, pasta, condiments, coffee, fresh produce, and exquisite pastries.

VINEGAR FACTORY
431 E 91st St (near York Ave)   212/987-0885
Daily: 7 a.m.-9 p.m.; Brunch: Sat, Sun: 7-4   www.elizabar.com

Located on the site of what used to be a working vinegar factory, this operation of Eli Zabar's has bearable prices on fresh produce, pizzas, fish, flowers, meats, desserts, seafood, cheeses, baked goods (including Eli's great breads), coffee, deli items, paper goods, books, and housewares. Breakfast and brunch (on weekends) are available on the balcony. This is one of the most intriguing food factories around! Catering is also offered.

Old-time New Yorkers were disappointed when Second Avenue Kosher Delicatessen and Restaurant closed its doors some time ago. But there is good news: this famed institution is back in business! So come check out the famed matzo ball soup at the new **Second Avenue Kosher Delicatessen and Restaurant** (162 E 33rd St, 212/677-0606).

WHOLE FOODS MARKET
Time Warner Center
10 Columbus Circle   212/823-9600
4 Union Square S   212/673-5388
250 Seventh Ave (at 24th St)   212/924-5969
95 East Houston (at Bowery)   212/420-1320
Hours vary by store   www.wholefoods.com

Whole Foods is big, beautiful, and busy! If you can't find a particular food item here, it probably doesn't exist. In addition to all the usual things, this grocery superstore has a huge deli, a seafood selection, bakery, flowers, sushi, fresh juices, and all kinds of carry-out items. Forty check-out stands are on hand at the Bowery location to ring up purchases.

ZABAR'S
2245 Broadway (at 80th St)   212/787-2000
Mon-Fri: 8-7:30; Sat: 8-8; Sun: 9-6   www.zabars.com
Mezzanine (housewares): Mon-Sat: 9-7:30; Sun: 9-6

No trip to Manhattan is complete without a visit to this fabulous store. You will find enormous selections of breads, smoked fish, coffees, prepared foods, cheeses, deli items, gift baskets, candy, and much more. Moreover, all are of the very highest quality and affordably priced. A cafe next door provides snacks all day at bargain prices. Upstairs you will find the best housewares department in America, with a varied selection and good prices. Saul Zabar comes from a legendary food family in Manhattan; you will often see him wandering the aisles to make sure everything is top-notch. Assistants Scott Goldshine and David Tait provide that extra-special service for which Zabar's is renowned.

I love hot dogs! In my restaurant (Gerry Frank's Konditorei, 310 Kearney St, Salem, OR, 503/585-7070), we call them "Gerry's Franks!" For the best in Manhattan try:

Artie's Delicatessen (2290 Broadway, 212/579-5959)
Brooklyn Diner USA (212 W 57th St, 212/977-2280)
Crif Dogs (113 St. Mark's Pl, 212/614-2728)
Dawgs on Park (178 E 7th St, 212/598-0667)
Gray's Papaya (2090 Broadway, 212/799-0243; 539 Eighth Ave, 212/904-1588; and 402 Ave of the Americas, 212/260-3532): inexpensive
Hallo Berlin (626 Tenth Ave, 212/977-1944 and a stand at 54th St and Fifth Ave)
Katz's Delicatessen (205 E Houston St, 212/254-2246)
Mandler's (26 E 17th St, 212/255-8999)
Nathan's Famous Hot Dogs (stands all over Manhattan)
Second Avenue Kosher Delicatessen and Restaurant (162 E 33rd St, 212/677-0606)
Shake Shack (Madison Square Park, Madison Ave at 23rd St, 212/889-6600): seasonal

---

Cheese

ALLEVA DAIRY
188 Grand St (at Mulberry St)   212/226-7990, 800/4-ALLEVA
Mon-Sat: 8:30-6; Sun: 8:30-3   www.allevadairy.com

Alleva, founded in 1892, is the oldest Italian cheese store in America. The Alleva family has operated the business from the start, always maintaining meticulous standards. Robert Alleva oversees the production of over 4,000 pounds of fresh cheese a week, including *parmigiano*, *fraschi*, *manteche*, *scamoize*, and *provole affumicale*. The ricotta is superb, and the mozzarella tastes like it was made on a side street in Florence. Quality Italian meats, olives, and gift baskets are offered. A mail-order catalog is available.

DIPALO FINE FOODS
200 Grand St (at Mott St)   212/226-1033
Mon-Sat: 9-6:30; Sun: 9-4

One word describes the cheeses and pastas offered at DiPalo: *superb*. If it's Italian, they carry it: olive oils, meats, and more. It's worth a trip to the Lower East Side for the goodies, not to mention the friendly greetings.

EAST VILLAGE CHEESE
40 Third Ave (bet 9th and 10th St)   212/477-2601
Daily: 8:30-6:30

Value is the name of the game. For years this store has prided itself on selling cheese at some of the lowest prices in town. They claim similar savings for whole-bean coffees, fresh pastas, extra-virgin olive oil, quiches, patés, and a wide selection of fresh bread. Good service is another reason to shop here. Cash only.

IDEAL CHEESE SHOP
942 First Ave (at 52nd St)   212/688-7579
Mon-Sat: 8:30-6 (till 5 on Sat in summer)   800/382-0109
                                                            www.idealcheese.com

Hundreds of cheeses from all over the world are sold here, and the owners are constantly looking for new items, just as is done in the fashion business. Ideal Cheese Shop has been in operation since 1954, and many Upper East Siders swear by its quality and service. They carry gourmet items: olive oils, vinegars, mustards, gourmet coffees, biscuits, preserves, specialty meats, and olives. A catalog is available, and they will ship anywhere in the U.S.

If you believe that nutritional products can keep you looking younger, then visit **Dr. Nicholas Perricone** (791 Madison Ave, 866/791-7911, www.nvperriconemd.com). His store is filled with healthy foods, books, and advice.

JOE'S DAIRY
156 Sullivan St (bet Houston and Prince St)   212/677-8780
Tues-Sat: 9-6

This is the best spot in town for fresh mozzarella. Anthony Campanelli makes it smoked, with prosciutto, and more.

MURRAY'S CHEESE SHOP
254 Bleecker St (bet Ave of Americas and Seventh Ave) 212/243-3289
Mon-Sat: 8-8; Sun: 9-6   www.murrayscheese.com

Boy, does this place smell good! This is one of the best cheese shops in Manhattan. Founded in 1940, Murray's offers wholesale and retail international and domestic cheeses of every description. Frank Meilak is the man to talk to behind the counter. There is also a fine selection of cold cuts, prepared foods, cheesecakes, pastas, antipasti, breads, sandwiches, and specialty items. Owner Rob Kaufelt has built on the traditions of the city's oldest cheese shop. Special attractions include great party platters, gift baskets, and wholesale charge accounts for local residents. There is also a smaller outlet at Grand Central Market (in Grand Central Terminal). Ask to tour the underground cheese-curing caves!

Chinese

GOLDEN FUNG WONG BAKERY
41 Mott St (at Pell St)   212/267-4037
Daily: 7:30 a.m.-8:30 p.m.

Golden Fung Wong is the real thing. Everyone from Chinatown residents to the city's gourmands extol its virtues. The pastries, cookies, and baked goods are traditional, and delicious. Flavor is not compromised in order to appeal to Western tastes. The bakery features a tremendous variety of baked goods, and it has the distinction of being New York's oldest and largest authentic Chinese bakery.

KAM MAN FOOD PRODUCTS
200 Canal St (bet Mott and Mulberry St)   212/571-0330
Daily: 9-8:30

Kam Man is the largest Oriental grocery store on the East Coast. In addition to Chinese foodstuffs, they carry Japanese, Thai, Vietnamese, Malaysian, and Filipino products. Native Asians should feel right at home in this store, where all types of traditional condiments are available. All of the necessities for the preparation and presentation of Asian foods can be found, from sauces and spices to utensils, cookware, and tableware. For the health-conscious, Kam Man stocks teas and Chinese herbal medicines. Prices are reasonable, and you needn't speak Chinese to shop here.

Would you believe that New York's largest and newest **Whole Foods Market** (95 E Houston St, 212/420-1320) is on the Lower East Side? This Whole Foods location features a large cafe and even a *fromagerie*. Its arrival is a further sign of transformation in the neighborhood.

TONGIN MART
91 Mulberry St (at Canal St)   212/962-6622
Daily: 9-8

Planning a home-cooked Chinese dinner? There's no better source than this store in Chinatown. Tongin Mart boasts that 95% of its business is conducted with the Chinese community. They have an open and friendly attitude, and great care is taken to introduce customers to the wide variety of imported Oriental foods, including Japanese, Thai, and Filipino products.

Coffee, Tea

BELL BATES NATURAL FOOD MARKET
97 Reade St (bet Church St and West Broadway)   212/267-4300
Mon-Fri: 9-7; Sat: 10-6   www.bellbates.com

Bell Bates is a hot-beverage emporium specializing in organic and natural foods and all manner of teas and coffees. The selection is extensive and prices are competitive. Bell Bates considers itself a complete food source, stocking health foods, vitamins, nuts, dried fruit, spices, herbs, and gourmet items. Ask for the marvelous Mrs. Sayage.

EMPIRE COFFEE AND TEA COMPANY
568 Ninth Ave (bet 41st and 42nd St)   212/268-1220
Mon-Fri: 8-7; Sat: 9-6:30; Sun: 11-5   www.empirecoffeetea.com

Midtown java lovers have all wandered in here at one time or another. Empire carries an enormous selection of coffee (75 types of beans!), tea, and herbs. Because of the aroma and array of the bins, choosing is almost impossible. Empire's personnel are very helpful, but a perusal of their free catalog before visiting the shop might save you some time. Fresh coffee beans and tea leaves are available in bulk; everything is sold loose and can be ground. Empire also carries a wide selection of teapots and coffee machines. Gourmet gift baskets, too!

ITO EN
822 Madison Ave (bet 68th and 69th St)   212/988-7111
Mon-Sat: 10-7; Sun: noon-6 (closed Sat, Sun in summer)
www.itoen.com

Ito En is the world's leading supplier of green tea, which has won much attention for its healthy, antioxidant properties. Their very gracious Japanese lunches, dinners, and teas will be a soothing interlude in your day.

JAVA GIRL
348 E 66th St (bet First and Second Ave)   212/737-3490
Mon-Fri: 6:30 a.m.-7 p.m.; Sat, Sun: 8:30-6

The aroma of fresh-ground coffee that greets you upon entering this tiny place is overwhelming! For fine coffees, teas, pastries, sandwiches, and spring rolls, look no further. Java Girl has creative gift boxes as well.

When you do your market shopping, don't overlook **Westside Markets** (77 Seventh Ave, 212/807-7771 and 2171 Broadway, 212/595-2536). These are first-class operations—immaculately clean and well-priced, with a large stock. Catering, free delivery in a ten-block radius, and food items to eat on premises are additional features. You will be very pleasantly surprised!

JOE—THE ART OF COFFEE
141 Waverly Pl (bet Ave of the Americas and Seventh Ave)
9 E 13th St (at Fifth Ave)   212/924-7400
130 Greene St (at Houston St)   212/941-7330
Mon-Fri: 7 a.m.-8 p.m.; Sat, Sun: 8-8   212/924-6750
www.joetheartofcoffee.com

Jonathan Rubinstein, an ex-talent agent, always wanted to share his passion for espresso, and he has done it at one of the city's most unique spots. Espresso drinks, coffees, whole beans, and brewing equipment make a visit to Joe a great stop for espresso fanatics.

McNULTY'S TEA AND COFFEE COMPANY
109 Christopher St (bet Bleecker and Hudson St)
Mon-Sat: 10-9 (closed Tues in July and Aug); Sun: 1-7
212/242-5351, 800/356-5200
www.mcnultys.com

McNulty's has been supplying choosy New Yorkers with coffee and tea since 1895. Over the years they have developed a complete line that includes spiced and herbal teas, coffee blends ground to order, and coffee and tea accessories. They have a reputation for personalized gourmet coffee blends and work hard to maintain it. The blends are unique, and the personal service is highly valued. McNulty's maintains an extensive file of customers' special blend choices.

M. ROHRS' HOUSE OF FINE TEAS AND COFFEES
310 E 86th St (at Second Ave)   212/396-4456
Mon-Thurs: 6 a.m.-9:30 p.m.; Fri, Sat: 6 a.m.-10 p.m.;
Sun: 6 a.m.-9 p.m.   www.rohrs.com

M. Rohrs' turned a century old in 1996. Owner Donald Wright carries expanded lines of tea and coffee, plus a wide variety of honey, jam, cookies, and chocolates. Rohrs' has a bar for espresso and an assortment of daily brewed coffees and teas, and they offer easy Internet access. It truly is a village store with Old World charm in the big city. Wright, who is himself a great lover of coffee, claims to drink seven cups a day!

Latte Lingo and Other Coffee Terminology

A *tall* is any 12-ounce espresso drink, while a *grande* is 16 ounces, and a *venti* is 20 ounces. A *double* is any espresso drink with a second shot added. Finally, a *skinny* is any drink made with nonfat milk.

Americano: A one- or two-ounce shot of espresso is mixed with as much as seven ounces of hot water. This alternative to drip brewing yields a rich cup of gourmet coffee.

Cafe au Lait: equal portions of drip coffee and steamed milk

Cafe Breve: a latte made with half-and-half instead of milk

Cafe Coretto: espresso to which liquor, typically brandy or coffee liqueur, has been added

Caffe Latte: A two-ounce shot of espresso is combined with steamed milk and topped with a spoonful of milk froth.

Caffe Mocha: a latte with an ounce of chocolate flavoring (powder or syrup)

Cappuccino: This unique coffee drink consists of equal parts steamed milk, coffee, and foamed milk. It may be topped with cinnamon, nutmeg, chocolate sprinkles, or cocoa powder.

Cappuccino (dry): a cappuccino with foam but very little or no steamed milk

Cappuccino (wet): a cappuccino with less foam and more steamed milk

Con Panna: espresso topped with whipped cream

Espresso: This well-known coffee beverage is produced by using pressure to rapidly infuse finely ground coffee with boiling water.

Flavored Caffe Latte: a latte with an ounce of Italian syrup (such as almond, hazelnut, and vanilla) or liqueur

Granita: This frozen Italian drink is prepared with a granita machine (or *granitore*) and can be made with espresso and milk or fresh fruits and juices.

Shot, Straight Shot, Single Shot, Double Shot: espresso served straight up without milk or flavorings

---

NESPRESSO
759 Madison Ave (at 65th St)   800/562-1465
Mon-Fri: 8-8; Sat, Sun: 9-7

Espresso lovers will not want to miss this classy boutique bar and store.

In the front you can enjoy some first-rate espresso drinks, while all manner of machines and accessories are available in the back, along with coffee beans. The bar also serves salads, hot and cold sandwiches, pastries, and much more.

PORTO RICO IMPORTING COMPANY

201 Bleecker St (main store)	212/477-5421, 800/453-5908
40½ St. Mark's Pl (coffee bar)	212/533-1982
107 Thompson St (coffee bar)	212/966-5758
Hours vary by store	www.portorico.com

In 1907, Peter Longo's family started a small coffee business in the Village. Primarily importers and wholesalers, they were soon pressured to serve the local community, so they opened a small storefront as well. That operation gained a reputation for the best and freshest coffee available, developing a loyal corps of customers. Since much of the surrounding neighborhood consists of Italians, the Longo family reciprocated their loyalty by specializing in Italian espressos and cappuccinos, as well as health and medicinal teas. Dispensed along with such teas are folk remedies and advice to mend whatever ails you. Today, the store remains true to its tradition. Peter has added coffee bars, making it possible to sit and sip from a selection of 150 coffees and 225 loose teas while listening to folklore or trying to select the best from the bins. All coffees are roasted daily at Porto Rico's own facility. (Hint: The inexpensive house blends are every bit as good as some of the more expensive coffees.)

No question about it: The best frozen yogurt in Manhattan is the coffee flavor at **40 Carrots**, on the metro level at **Bloomingdale's** (1000 Third Ave).

SENSUOUS BEAN OF COLUMBUS AVENUE

66 W 70th St (at Columbus Ave)   212/724-7725, 800/238-6845
Mon-Wed: 8:30-6; Thurs, Fri: 8:30-7; Sat: 8-6; Sun: 9:30-6
www.sensuousbean.com

The Sensuous Bean was in business long before the latest coffee craze started. This legendary coffee and teahouse carries 72 varieties of coffee and 52 teas. A coffee-of-the-month club is offered; after purchasing ten pounds, customers receive one pound free. The bulk bean coffees and loose teas come from all around the world. Teas from England, France, Germany, Ireland, and Taiwan are featured. They carry a large variety of green, white, chai, herbal, rooibos and blended loose teas, along with many organic and fair-trade coffees. They make lattes, cappuccinos, and espressos; steep teas; and offer many sweets, biscottis, and chocolates to accompany these beverages. They specialize in gift packaging and signature presentations.

TEN REN TEA & GINSENG CO.

75-79 Mott St (at Canal St)	212/349-2286
Daily: 10-8	www.tenrenusa.com

This company was founded in 1953 and is the largest tea grower and manufacturer in East Asia. They sell green, oolong, jasmine, and black teas, plus tea sets and all manner of accessories. Various kinds of ginseng are also available. A delicious and chewy "bubble tea" contains tapioca pearls. Ten Ren means "heavenly love," and you will likely fall in love with one of their flavors. Some can set you back $100 a pound!

> Smoothies can be very healthy and low-calorie, too. If you're in the mood for a really good one, try **Health King** (642-A Lexington Ave, 212/593-1020), where you can create your own combination. They provide a list of remedies for almost every ailment (i.e., carrot, beet, and cucumber for headaches, and carrot, celery, and parsley for diabetes).

Foreign Foodstuffs (The Best)

Chinese, Thai, Malaysian, Philippine, Vietnamese
Asia Market* (71½ Mulberry St)
Bangkok Center Grocery (104 Mosco St, at Mott St)
Chinese American Trading Company (91 Mulberry St)
Fong Inn Too (46 Mott St)
Hong Keung Seafood & Meat Market (75 Mulberry St)
Hung Chong Imports (14 Bowery)
Kam Kuo Foods (7 Mott St)
Kam Man Food Products* (200 Canal St)
Tea & Tea (157 2nd St)
Ten Ren Tea & Ginseng Co.* (75-79 Mott St)
Thuan-Nguyen Market (84 Mulberry St)
United Noodles (349 E 12th St)

English
Myers of Keswick* (634 Hudson St)

German
Schaller & Weber* (1654 Second Ave)

Greek
Zeytuna (59 Maiden Lane and 161 Maiden Lane)

Indian
Foods of India (121 Lexington Ave)
Kati Roll (99 MacDougal St)
Kalustyan's* (123 Lexington Ave)

Italian
DiPalo Fine Foods* (200 Grand St)
Todaro Bros.* (555 Second Ave)

Japanese
Han Ah Reum (25 W 32nd St)
JAS Mart (2847 Broadway)
Katagiri & Company* (224 E 59th St)

Polish
East Village Meat Market (139 Second Ave)

West African
West African Grocery (535 Ninth Ave)

*Detailed write-ups of these shops can be found in this chapter.

The Best Places to Buy Caviar

Caviar Russe (538 Madison Ave, 212/980-5908): a luxury spot

Caviarteria (212/759-7410, www.caviarteria.com): I like everything about this shop, which is acquiring a new location

Dean & Deluca (1150 Madison Ave, 212/717-0800 and 560 Broadway, 212/431-1691)

Firebird (365 W 46th St, 212/586-0244): housed in a re-creation of a pre-revolutionary Russian mansion

Petrossian (182 W 58th St, 212/245-2214): Providing ambience befitting the caviar set, this is also a spectacular place to dine.

Russ & Daughters (179 East Houston St, 212/475-4880)

Sable's Smoked Fish (1489 Second Ave, 212/249-6177)

Zabar's (2245 Broadway, 212/787-2000): If good prices are important, then make this your first stop.

Types of Caviar

Beluga: Roe are large, firm, and well-defined, with a smooth, creamy texture.

Osetra: strong, with a sweet, fruity flavor

Sevruga: subtle, clean taste with a crunchy texture

Caviar, which is the roe of sturgeon from the Caspian and Black seas, is surely a delicacy, and a pricey one. But beware! Buy only from a recognized purveyor. Choices include Royal Osetra ($100 an ounce), Caspian Sevruga ($80 an ounce), Iranian Gold ($200 an ounce), Black Pearl ($55 an ounce), and American Spoonbill ($20 an ounce—from Tennessee and Mississippi). All prices are approximate.

Fruits, Vegetables

GREENMARKET
51 Chambers St (bet Broadway and Centre St), Suite 1231 (office)
212/788-7900

Note: These markets are arranged from uptown to downtown.

Inwood (Isham St bet Seaman & Cooper St)
175th St (175th St at Broadway)
Harlem Hospital (Lenox Ave bet 136th and 137th St)
Columbia (Broadway bet 114th and 115th St)
Stranger's Gate (106th St at Central Park W)
Mt. Sinai Hospital (99th St bet Madison and Park Ave)
97th St (97th St at Columbus Ave)
92nd St (First Ave bet 92nd and 93rd St)
82nd St/St. Stephens (82nd St bet First and York Ave)
77th St (77th St at Columbus Ave)
Tucker Square (66th St at Columbus Ave)
57th St (57th St at Ninth Ave)
Rockefeller Center (Rockefeller Plaza at 50th St)
Dag Hammarskjöld Plaza (47th St at Second Ave)
43rd St/Hell's Kitchen (43rd St bet Ninth and Tenth Ave)
Murray Hill (Second Ave at 33rd St)
26th St/Phipps Houses (26th St bet Second Ave and Mt. Carmel Pl)

collection, it's like wandering through the city's attic. A special exhibit on the history of slavery in New York is a recent addition as well. Hours: Tuesday through Sunday from 10 to 6 (Friday till 8). Admission: $10 for adults, $7 for seniors and teachers, $6 for students, free for children under 12, and free for everyone from 6 to 8 on Friday.

NEW YORK CITY FIRE MUSEUM
278 Spring St (bet Hudson and Varick St)   212/691-1303
www.nycfiremuseum.org

In a renovated 1904 firehouse, this fun museum is a "must see" for anyone interested in firefighting. With hundreds of artifacts dating from the late 18th century, the collection is among the most extensive of its kind in the country. Highlights include leather fire buckets, hand-pumped fire engines, and a horse-drawn ladder wagon. Call ahead to make sure your visit won't coincide with one by a large school group. **Hours:** Tuesday through Saturday from 10 to 5, Sunday from 10 to 4. **Admission:** $5 for adults, $2 for seniors and students, and $1 for children under 12.

NEW YORK CITY POLICE MUSEUM
100 Old Slip (bet Water and South St)   212/480-3100
www.nycpolicemuseum.org

Located in New York's first precinct house, this museum is dedicated to preserving the long history of the New York City Police Department. Displays include a jail cell, famous criminals, women in police work, and a special memorial to the officers who died on September 11, 2001. A large gift shop is a hit with kids and adults alike. **Hours:** Monday through Saturday from 10 to 5. **Admission:** $5 for adults, $3 for seniors, $2 for children from 6 to 18, and free for children under 6.

The More Things Change . . .

The last peep shows have moved out of Times Square and even the seafood merchants have moved out of the old Fulton Fish Market, but some things in New York haven't changed. If it's nostalgia you want, try **The Waldorf-Astoria** (301 Park Ave), **Radio City Music Hall** (Ave of the Americas at 50th St), the overpriced **21 Club** (21 W 52nd St), the **Grand Central Oyster Bar Restaurant** (Grand Central Terminal), or **McSorley's Old Ale House** (15 E 7th St). You might also check out some of the old-time shops on the Lower East Side, like **Katz's Delicatessen** (205 E Houston St).

NICHOLAS ROERICH MUSEUM
319 W 107th St (bet Broadway and Central Park West)
212/864-7752
www.roerich.org

The late Nicholas Roerich was Russian, but in many ways he was a citizen of the world. He dedicated much of his life to convincing governments to protect art even in times of conflict. His own paintings, many done in (and of) the Himalayas, are on display at this unassuming townhouse near Columbia University. **Hours:** Tuesday through Sunday from 2 to 5. **Admission:** $5.

Union Square (17th St at Broadway)
Abingdon Square (12th St at Hudson St)
St. Mark's Church (10th St at Second Ave)
Tompkins Square (7th St at Ave A)
Orchard St (Orchard St bet Broome and Delancey St)
Tribeca (Greenwich St bet Chambers and Duane St)
City Hall Park (Broadway bet Chambers and Warren St)
Downtown PATH (Vesey St at Church St)
Bowling Green (Broadway at Battery Pl)

Starting in 1976 with just one location, these unique open-air markets have sprung up in various neighborhoods. They are sponsored and overseen by a nonprofit organization. Bypassing the middle man means prices are significantly less than at supermarkets, and Greenmarket provides small family farms in the region with a profitable outlet for their produce. All produce (over 600 varieties), baked goods, flowers, and fish come straight from the sources. (Hint: Come early for the best selection.) Call the listed office number to find out the hours and address of the Greenmarket nearest you. Most are seasonal, operating from 8 to 3, although hours, days, and months of operation may vary.

The Best Natural Foods Emporiums

Bell Bates Natural Food Market (97 Reade St, 212/267-4300): herbs, coffees
Commodities Natural Market (165 First Ave, 212/260-2600): cheeses, good prices
Health Nuts (2611 Broadway, 212/678-0054): juice bar
Integral Yoga Natural Foods (229 W 13th St, 212/243-2642): organic produce, baked items, yoga classes in same building
Lifethyme Natural Market (408-410 Ave of the Americas, 212/420-9099): salad bar, produce
Uptown Whole Foods (2421 Broadway, 212/874-4000): one of Manhattan's best; juice bar and kosher items
Whole Foods Market (Time Warner Center, 10 Columbus Circle, 212/823-9600; 4 Union Square S, 212/673-5388; 250 Seventh Ave, 212/924-5969; and 95 E Houston St, 212/420-1320): salad bar, flowers, large selection

---

Gift and Picnic Baskets

MANHATTAN FRUITIER
105 E 29th St (bet Park and Lexington Ave)
Mon-Fri: 9-5; Sat: deliveries only   212/686-0404, 800/841-5718
www.mfruit.com

Most fruit baskets are pretty bad, but this outfit makes tasty, great-looking ones using fresh seasonal and exotic fruits. You can add such comestibles as hand-rolled cheddar cheese sticks, biscotti, and individually wrapped chocolates. Locally handmade truffles, fine food hampers, and fresh flowers are also available. Delivery charges in Manhattan are reasonable, and gifts may be shipped nationwide.

SANDLER'S
530 Cherry Lane   212/279-9779, 800/75-FRUIT
Floral Park, NY 11001   www.sandlers.com
Mon-Fri: 9-5

Though they are not located in Manhattan, Sandler's is a key source for scrumptious candies, delicacies, and some of the best chocolate chip cookies. They are even better known for gift baskets filled with fancy fresh fruits, natural cheeses, and gourmet delicacies. No one does it better!

The Best Ice Cream in Manhattan

Bussola (65 Fourth Ave, 212/254-1940)

Chinatown Ice Cream Factory (65 Bayard St, 212/608-4170)

Ciao Bella (27 E 92nd St, 212/831-5555; 285 Mott St, 212/431-3591; and 2 World Financial Center, 212/786-4707): gelati and sorbets

City Bakery (3 W 18th St, 212/366-1414): elegant flavors

Cones, Ice Cream Artisans (272 Bleecker St, 212/414-1795): 36 flavors of ice cream and sorbet

E.A.T. (1064 Madison Ave, 212/772-0022)

Emack & Bolio's (389 Amsterdam Ave, 212/362-2747; 73 W Houston St, 212/533-5610; and 1564-A First Ave, 212/734-0105): vanilla bean ice cream (Amsterdam Ave location open only in summer)

Il Laboratorio del Gelato (95 Orchard St, 212/343-9922): gelati, sorbets

La Maison du Chocolat (1018 Madison Ave, 212/744-7117 and 30 Rockefeller Center, 212/265-9404)

Payard Patisserie & Bistro (1032 Lexington Ave, 212/717-5252): top-grade gelati

Pinkberry (7 W 32nd St, 212/695-9631; 170 Eighth Ave, 212/861-0574; and 41 Spring St, 212/274-8883)

Ronnybrook Farm Dairy (75 Ninth Ave, 212/741-6455): great flavors

Sant Ambroeus (1000 Madison Ave, 212/570-2211)

Greek

LIKITSAKOS
1174 Lexington Ave (bet 80th and 81st St)   212/535-4300
Mon-Fri: 7 a.m.-9 p.m.; Sat, Sun: 8-8

Likitsakos is one of the better places in New York for Greek and international specialties, including salads, fruits, vegetables, grains, dips, and appetizers.

Health Foods

GARY NULL'S UPTOWN WHOLE FOODS
2421 Broadway (at 89th St)   212/874-4000
Daily: 8 a.m.-11 p.m.

This is Manhattan's premier health food supermarket. Organic produce, fresh juices, discounted vitamins, and a full line of healthy supermarket products are featured. They will deliver in Manhattan and ship anywhere in the world. A takeout deli offers rotisserie chicken, vegetarian entrees, and even popcorn. The deli and salad bar are organic and kosher.

HEALTH & HARMONY
470 Hudson St (bet Barrow and Grove St)   212/691-3036
Mon-Fri: 8 a.m.-8:30 p.m.; Sat: 9-7:30; Sun: 10-7

A great find for the health-conscious! Health & Harmony stocks plenty of good things to eat, organic produce, vitamins and herbs, and herbal remedies. They will also deliver.

Kids have a supermarket of their own! (Well, just about.) Brightly colored **Kidfresh** (1628 Second Ave, 800/365-4337) sells quality health-oriented food for young ones at breakfast, lunch, and dinner. Kids can choose from about 35 prepared favorites, such as sandwiches, chicken, macaroni and cheese, cereals, crackers, ice cream, and more. Much of it is organic. Additional attractions include a special kids' entrance and kid shopping carts, along with toys and books. You can eat in (after microwaving the items that need it) or take out.

INTEGRAL YOGA NATURAL FOODS
229 W 13th St (bet Seventh and Eighth Ave)   212/243-2642
Mon-Fri: 8 a.m.-9:30 p.m.; Sat: 8 a.m.-8:30 p.m.; Sun: 9-8:30
www.integralyoganaturalfoods.com

Selection and quality abound in this clean, attractive shop, which features a complete assortment of healthy, natural foods. Vegetarian items, packaged groceries, organic produce, bulk foods, and baked items are available at reasonable prices. A juice bar, salad bar, and deli are on-premises. They occupy the same building as a center that offers classes in yoga, meditation, and philosophy. Across the street is **Integral Apothecary** (234 W 13th St, 212/645-3051), a vegetarian, vitamin, and herb shop with a nutritional consultant on staff.

LIFETHYME NATURAL MARKET
408-410 Ave of the Americas (bet 8th and 9th St)   212/420-9099
Mon-Fri: 8 a.m.-10 p.m.; Sat, Sun: 9 a.m.-10 p.m.
www.lifethymemarket.com

You'll find one of the area's largest selections of organic produce at this natural supermarket. In addition, there is an organic salad table, over 5,000 health-related books, a deli serving natural foods, a "natural cosmetics" boutique, a complete vegan bakery, and an organic juice bar. Occupying two renovated 1839 brownstones in the heart of the Village, this busy shop also sells discounted vitamins, does catering, and offers custom-baked goods for dietary needs.

Ice Cream and Other Goodies

CONES, ICE CREAM ARTISANS
272 Bleecker St (at Seventh Ave)   212/414-1795
Mon-Thurs, Sun: 1-11; Fri, Sat: 1-1

The D'Aloisio family brought their original Italian ice-cream recipes to Manhattan . . . and boy, are they good! Cones specializes in creamy gelati made with all-natural ingredients. Thirty-two flavors (try the coffee mocha chocolate chip) and fat-free fruit flavors are available every day. All are made on the premises, ensuring creamy goodness, and can be packed for takeout. Made-to-order ice cream cakes are available, too.

> Even if you have a favorite neighborhood market, pay a visit to the following unique large marketplaces in Manhattan. All are first-rate and feature a number of fine purveyors:
>
> **Bridgemarket** (415 E 59th St, under the 59th Street Bridge at First Ave, 212/758-1126)
>
> **Chelsea Market** (75 Ninth Ave, www.chelseamarket.com)
>
> **Essex Street Market** (120 Essex St, 212/388-0449, www.essexstreet market.com): Lower East Side
>
> **Grand Central Market** (Grand Central Terminal, 42nd St at Park Ave, www.grandcentralterminal.com)

Indian

FOODS OF INDIA
121 Lexington Ave (at 28th St)   212/683-4419
Mon-Sat: 10-8; Sun: 11-6

This is the place to stock up on curry leaves, rice, lentils, dried limes, mango chutney, and all kinds of fresh and dried imported Indian foods. Homemade breads and vegetarian items are also available.

KALUSTYAN'S
123 Lexington Ave (bet 28th and 29th St)
                                           212/685-3451, 800/352-3451
Mon-Sat: 10-8; Sun: 11-7   www.kalustyans.com

In 1944, Kalustyan's opened as an Indian spice store at its present location. After all this time, it is still a great spot. Many items are sold in bins or bales rather than prepackaged containers. The difference in cost, flavor, and freshness is extraordinary. The best indication of freshness and flavor is the store's aroma! Kalustyan's is both an Indian store and an export trading corporation with a specialty in Middle Eastern and Indian items. There is a large selection of dried fruit, nuts, mixes, coffee and tea, and accessories.

Italian

RAFFETTO'S CORPORATION
144 W Houston St (bet Sullivan and MacDougal St)   212/777-1261
Tues-Fri: 9-6:30; Sat: 9-6

You can go to a gourmet market for pasta, but why not go straight to the source? Raffetto's has been producing fresh-cut noodles and stuffed pastas since 1906. Though most of the business is wholesale, Raffetto's will sell their noodles, ravioli, mini-ravioli, tortellini, manicotti, gnocchi, and fettuccine to anyone. Variations include Genoa-style ravioli with meat and spinach, and Naples-style ravioli with cheese. More than ten homemade sauces are personally prepared by Mrs. Raffetto. Daily bread, dry pasta, and bargain-priced olive oils and vinegars are also featured.

RAVIOLI STORE
75 Sullivan St (bet Spring and Broome St)
Mon-Fri: 10-7; Sat, Sun: 11-7   212/925-1737, 877/727-8269
www.raviolistore.com

Since 1989, this factory has been producing some of New York's most unique ravioli and gourmet pasta products. Goat cheese ravioli in black peppercorn pasta is one of about a dozen unusual raviolis at this factory outlet. Various fresh pastas are available daily, along with sauces and cheeses.

Japanese
KATAGIRI & COMPANY
224 E 59th St (bet Second and Third Ave)   212/755-3566
Daily: 10-8 (gift shop open till 7)   www.katagiri.com

Are you planning a Japanese dinner? Do you have some important clients you would like to impress with a sushi party? Katagiri features all kinds of Japanese food, sushi ingredients, and utensils. You can get some great party ideas from the helpful personnel. Delivery in Manhattan is available.

SUNRISE MART
4 Stuyvesant St (at Third Ave), 2nd floor   212/598-3040
Sun-Thurs: 10 a.m.-11 p.m.; Fri, Sat: 10 a.m.-12 a.m.

494 Broome St (bet West Broadway and Wooster St)   212/219-0033
Daily: 10-10

In a part of the East Village that is home to growing numbers of young Japanese and stores that cater to them, these all-purpose grocery stores do a bustling business. Japanese is spoken more often than English, and many packages bear nothing but Japanese calligraphy. In addition to snack foods and candy, they sell fruits, vegetables, meats, fish, and other grocery items. They also carry bowls, chopsticks, and items for the home. The Broome Street location stocks hard-to-find Japanese beauty products. Sunrise Mart rents Japanese-language videos, too. A Japanese bake shop, **Panya Bakery** (10 Stuyvesant St, 212/777-1930), adjoins the Stuyvesant Street location.

Kosher
Note: see Chapter 3 ("Restaurants") for additional Kosher listings.

SIEGEL'S KOSHER DELI AND RESTAURANT
Will soon have a new Upper East Side location   212/288-3632

Siegel's, a top kosher deli and gourmet appetizer store for 28 years, is currently seeking to acquire a new location on the Upper East Side. Check their phone number for updates.

Latin American
KITCHEN MARKET
218 Eighth Ave (bet 21st and 22nd St)   212/243-4433
Daily: 9 a.m.-11 p.m.   www.kitchenmarket.com

This store features an extensive selection of Latin American food items. They also operate a Mexican/Asian restaurant next door, **Bright Food Shop** (216 Eighth Ave, 212/243-4433), and offer bulk prices online. If you want to know anything about Mexican foods, ask chef/owner Dona Abramson. Catering is available.

Holyland Market (122 St. Mark's Pl, 212/477-4440, www.israeli market.com) is an excellent place for kosher meats, cheeses, and hard-to-find Israeli grocery imports.

Liquor, Wine

ACKER, MERRALL & CONDIT
160 W 72nd St (bet Amsterdam and Columbus Ave)   212/787-1700
Mon-Sat: 9 a.m.-10 p.m.; Sun: noon-8   www.ackerstore.com

What a place! Acker, Merrall & Condit (AMC, for short) is the oldest operating wine and liquor store in America, having opened its doors in 1820. There are in-store wine tastings Friday and Saturday afternoons. Wine seminars are offered to companies by the Wine Workshop. Wine parties can be arranged in private residences for special occasions. Free delivery is available in Manhattan. This service-oriented firm stocks a good inventory of American wines and also specializes in French vintages from Bordeaux and the Rhine. The Wine Workshop—Acker, Merrall & Condit's special-events affiliate—offers wine-tasting classes and dinners that range in price from $40 to $1,295. AMC is the largest independent fine-wine auction company in the United States; they even have monthly online auctions.

ASTOR WINES & SPIRITS
399 Lafayette St (at 4th St)   212/674-7500
Mon-Sat: 9-9; Sun: noon-5   www.astorwines.com

One of the city's largest selections of French and Italian wines is available at Astor, along with numerous sakes and sparkling wines. These folks claim to stock 10,000 labels. That's a lot of vino!

BEST CELLARS
1291 Lexington Ave (at 87th St)   212/426-4200
Mon-Thurs: 9:30-9; Fri, Sat: 9:30 a.m.-10 p.m.; Sun: noon-8
www.bestcellars.com

Are those expensive wines really worth the price? If you're shopping for great-tasting wines at low prices, come to Best Cellars, which offers over 150 values. Most are under $15, and the friendly personnel are very knowledgeable.

BURGUNDY WINE COMPANY
143 W 26th St (bet Ave of the Americas and Seventh Ave)
Mon-Sat: 10-7   212/691-9092
www.burgundywinecompany.com

In New York, there is a store for just about every specialty. The customer is the winner because the selection is huge and the price range is broad. Such is the case with Burgundy Wine Company, a compact and attractive store in Chelsea. These folks are specialists in fine Burgundies, Rhones, and Oregon wines, with over 2,000 labels to choose from. There are some great treasures in their cellars; ask the expert personnel. Tastings are offered all day Saturday, and Monday through Friday from 5 to 7. "Wine Wednesdays" include jazz from 5 to 7.

CROSSROADS WINES AND LIQUORS
55 W 14th St (at Ave of the Americas)   212/924-3060
Mon-Sat: 9-8:30   www.crossroadswines.com

Crossroads carries 4,000 wines from all the great wine-producing countries. They stock rare, unique, and exotic liquors as well. Crossroads will special-order items, deliver, and help with party and menu planning. Their experienced staff has a passion for matching wines and foods, and their prices are as low as their attitude is low-key.

De-Vino Wines (30 Clinton St, 212/228-0073, www.de-vino.com) is the personal achievement of personable Italian-born Gabrio Tosti di Valminuta. This man is a walking encyclopedia of the wine industry, besides being a wonderful salesman and teacher. You could consider him your "personal sommelier." Talk about service! He will even deliver a bottle to a BYOB restaurant. It's no surprise that Italian wines are his specialty.

CRUSH WINE & SPIRITS
153 E 57th St (bet Third Ave and Lexington Ave)   212/980-9463
Mon-Sat: 10-9; Sun: noon-4   www.crushwineco.com

What's different about Crush Wine & Spirits is their focus on small artisanal producers, elegant space, daily free tastings, personal wine consultations, and a stock of rare and collectible bottles at reasonable prices.

GARNET LIQUORS
929 Lexington Ave (bet 68th and 69th St)   212/772-3211
Mon-Sat: 9-9; Sun: noon-6   800/USA-VINO (out of state)
                                          www.garnetwine.com

You'll love Garnet's prices, which are among the most competitive in the city for specialty wines. If you're in the market for Champagne, Bordeaux, Burgundy, Italian, or other imported wines, check here first, as selections are impressive. They stock virtually everything except New York wines. Prices are good on other wines and liquors, too.

IS-WINE
24 W 8th St (bet Fifth Ave and Ave of the Americas)   212/254-7800
Mon-Wed: noon-9; Thurs-Sat: noon-10; Sun: noon-7 www.is-wine.com

Everything is first-class here—the wines, the service, and the information available to customers. Specialties include informative seminars available with wine tastings and food.

ITALIAN WINE MERCHANTS

108 E 16th St (bet Union Square E and Irving Pl)   212/473-2323
Mon-Fri: 10-7; Sat: 11-7   www.italianwinemerchant.com

If Italian wines are your passion, then Italian Wine Merchants should be your destination. You will find Italian wines exclusively, with specialties in cult and tightly allocated wines, many from undiscovered producers. Just wait until you see the place—it is class personified!

K&D FINE WINES AND SPIRITS

1366 Madison Ave (bet 95th and 96th St)   212/289-1818
Mon-Sat: 9-9   www.kdwine.com

K&D is an excellent wine and spirits market on the Upper East Side. Hundreds of top wines and liquors are sold at competitive prices. Occasional newspaper ads in local newspapers highlight special bargains.

Looking for attractive fresh fruit arrangements to use as centerpieces, for desserts, or whatever? Try **Edible Arrangements** (62 W 38th St, 212/221-8330 and other locations). All of their stores are independently owned and operated.

MISTER WRIGHT

1593 Third Ave (bet 89th and 90th St)   212/722-4564
Mon-Sat: 9 a.m.-9:30 p.m.; Sun: 1-6:45

Meet Mr. Wright! If you are interested in Australian wines, this shop has a nice selection. A neighborhood store for over three decades, Mister Wright has a reputation for fine stock at comfortable prices and extra-friendly Aussie service. They also stock many wines from other countries.

MORRELL & COMPANY

1 Rockefeller Plaza (49th St bet Fifth Ave and Ave of the Americas)
Mon-Sat: 10-7   212/688-9370
www.morrellwine.com

Charming and well informed, Peter Morrell is the wine expert at this small, jam-packed store, which carries all kinds of wine and liquor. The stock is overwhelming, and a good portion of it must be kept in the wine cellar. However, it is all easily accessible, and the Morrell staff is amenable to helping you find the right bottle. The stock consists of spirits, including brandy, liqueurs, and wine vintages ranging from old and valuable to young and inexpensive. While you are here, check out the inviting menu at **Morrell Wine Bar Cafe**.

NANCY'S WINES FOR FOOD

313 Columbus Ave (at 75th St)   212/877-4040
Mon-Sat: 10-9; Sun: noon-6   www.nancyswines.com

These folks are pros at matching wines with food. Prices are reasonable, the selection is excellent, and they offer a "wine of the month" program. German white wines, "grower" champagnes, and boutique wines are specialties.

QUALITY HOUSE
2 Park Ave (on 33rd St,)   212/532-2944
Mon-Fri: 9-6:15; Sat: 10-3; closed Sat in July, Aug
                                    www.qualityhousewines.com

Quality House boasts one of the most extensive stocks of French wine in the city, equally fine offerings of domestic and Italian wines, and selections from Germany, Spain, and Portugal. True to their name, this is a quality house, not a bargain spot; however, delivery is available and usually free.

SHERRY-LEHMANN
505 Park Ave (at 59th St)   212/838-7500
Mon-Sat: 9-7   www.sherry-lehmann.com

Sherry-Lehmann is one of New York's best-known wine shops, boasting an inventory of over 7,000 wines from all over the world. Prices run the gamut from $5 to $10,000 a bottle. This firm has been in business since 1932, and it offers many special services for their customers.

SOHO WINES AND SPIRITS
461 West Broadway (bet Prince and Houston St)   212/777-4332
Mon-Sat: 10-8   www.sohowines.com

Stephen Masullo's father ran a liquor store on Spring Street for over 25 years. When the neighborhood evolved into the Soho of today, sons Stephen, Victor, and Paul expanded the business and opened a stylish Soho establishment for wine on West Broadway. The shop is lofty. In fact, it looks more like an art gallery than a wine shop. Bottles are tastefully displayed, and classical music plays in the background. Soho Wines also has one of the largest selections of single-malt Scotch whiskeys in New York. Services include party planning and advice on setting up and maintaining a wine cellar.

VINO
121 E 27th St (bet Lexington Ave and Park Ave S)   212/725-6516
Mon-Sat: noon-9; Sun: noon-8   www.vinosite.com

If you love Italian wine, then come to Vino. You will find over 500 labels, many of them reasonably priced. The staff is extra friendly, and you might even get a sample tasting.

VINTAGE NEW YORK
482 Broome St (at Wooster St)   212/226-9463
Mon-Sat: 11-9; Sun: noon-9

2492 Broadway (at 93rd St)   212/721-9999
Daily: noon-10 (wine bar till midnight)   www.vintagenewyork.com

Vintage New York offers wines from dozens of New York wineries, along with local artisanal cheeses, patés, and other foods. Sampling is available daily in the tasting room or wine bar. You'll also find wine-lifestyle accessories and can even create your own custom gift baskets of food and wine. Attached to the Soho location on Broome Street is **Vintage New York Winebar Restaurant**, which offers over 200 wines by the glass. Susan Wine insures that all menu items have a New York "element"—all paired with wines.

WAREHOUSE WINES & SPIRITS
735 Broadway (bet 8th St and Waverly Pl)   212/982-7770
Mon-Thurs: 9-8:45; Fri, Sat: 9 a.m.-9:45 p.m.; Sun: noon-6:45

If you are looking to save a few bucks on wine and liquor, especially for a party, Warehouse Wines & Spirits is a good place to try. Their selections and prices are appealing, and free delivery is available with a minimum purchase.

Meat, Poultry

FAICCO'S ITALIAN SPECIALTIES
260 Bleecker St (at Ave of the Americas)   212/243-1974
Tues-Thurs: 8:30-6; Fri: 8:30-7; Sat: 8-6; Sun: 9-2

An Italian institution, Faicco's carries delectable dried sausage, cuts of pork, and sweet and hot sausage. They also sell equally good meat cuts for barbecue and an oven-ready rolled leg of stuffed pork. Pork loin, a house specialty, is locally famous. They carry veal cutlets, veal chops, ground veal, veal for stew, olive oils, and every ingredient needed to make an antipasto. If you're into Italian-style deli, try Faicco's first. And if you're pressed for time, take home their heat-and-eat chicken rollettes: boneless breast of chicken rolled around cheese and dipped in a crunchy coating. Prepared hot foods to take home—including lasagna, baby back ribs, and eggplant parmesan—are also available.

FLORENCE MEAT MARKET
5 Jones St (bet Bleecker and 4th St)   212/242-6531
Tues-Fri: 8:30-6:30; Sat: 8-6

A distinct advantage at Florence Meat Market is that everything is cut-to-order by hand. Owner Benny Pizzuco has had long relationships with his suppliers, ensuring high-quality meats. Their "Newport steak" is so delicious that many folks have it shipped to them overnight!

> Don't miss the sausage sandwiches at **Mandler's: The Original Sausage Co.** (26 E 17th St, 212/255-8999, www.mandlers.com). They're served on crusty, fresh-baked rolls with your choice of toppings and corn fritters. Mandler's makes poultry, seafood, and vegetable sandwiches, too!

GIOVANNI ESPOSITO & SONS MEAT MARKET
500 Ninth Ave (at 38th St)   212/279-3298
Mon-Sat: 8-6:30

Family members still preside over an operation that has been at the same location since 1932. Whatever you need in the way of meats, you'll find them here at good prices. Their homemade Italian sausages are a specialty. Every kind you can imagine—breakfast, sage, garlic, smoked, hot dogs—is available. The cold cuts selection is awesome: bologna, liverwurst, pepperoni, salami, ham, turkey breast, American and Muenster cheese, and much more. Hosting a dinner? You'll find pork roasts, crown roasts, pork chops, spare ribs, slab bacon, tenderloins, sirloin steaks, short ribs, filet mignon, London broil, corned beef brisket, leg of lamb, pheasant, quail, and venison. Free home delivery is available in midtown for "modestly minimum orders."

JEFFERSON MARKET
450 Ave of the Americas (at 10th St)   212/533-3377
Mon-Sat: 7:30 a.m-9 p.m.; Sun: 8-8

Quality and personal service are the bywords at Jefferson Market. Originally a prime meat and poultry market, Jefferson has grown into an outstanding full-line store. Second-generation family management ensures hands-on attention to service. Prime meats, fresh seafood, select produce, gourmet coffee, fancy groceries, Bell and Evans chicken, and fresh salads are all tempting. There are bakery, deli, cheese, produce, and fish sections. Delivery service is available. If you don't feel like cooking dinner, let Louis Monturri send you home with some delicious hot or cold prepared foods.

KUROWYCKY MEAT PRODUCTS
124 First Ave (bet 7th and 8th St)   212/477-0344
Mon-Sat: 8-6; closed Mon in July, Aug   www.sausagenyc.com

Erast Kurowycky came to New York from Ukraine in 1954 and opened this tiny shop. Almost immediately it became a mecca and bargain spot for the city's Poles, Germans, Hungarians, Russians, Lithuanians, and Ukrainians. Many of these East European nationalities still harbor centuries-old grudges, but they all come to Kurowycky, where they agree on at least two things: the meats are the finest and prices are the best. A third-generation family member, Jaroslaw Kurowycky, Jr., runs the shop. Hams, sausages, meat loaves, and breads are sold. There are also condiments, including homemade Polish mustard, honey from Poland, sauerkraut, and a half-dozen other Ukrainian specialties.

LOBEL'S PRIME MEATS
1096 Madison Ave (bet 82nd and 83rd St)   212/737-1373
Mon-Sat: 9-6: closed Sat in July, Aug   www.lobels.com

Lobel's runs periodic sales on some of the best cuts of meat (poultry, lamb, and veal, too). Because of their excellent service and reasonable prices, few carnivores in Manhattan *haven't* heard of the shop. The staff has published eight cookbooks, and they are always willing to explain the best uses for each cut. It's hard to go wrong, since Lobel's carries *only* the best. They will ship all over the country. Great ready-to-cook hamburgers, too!

L. SIMCHICK
944 First Ave (at 52nd St)   212/888-2299
Mon-Fri: 8-7; Sat: 8-6

One and a half centuries in business have made these folks famous! You'll find wild game, prime meats, poultry products, wonderful homemade sausage, and a good selection of prepared foods. Delivery is provided on the East Side with a $25 minimum order.

OPPENHEIMER PRIME MEATS
2606 Broadway (bet 98th and 99th St)   212/662-0246
Mon-Fri: 8-7; Sat: 8-6   www.oppenheimermeats.com

Reliable and trustworthy, Oppenheimer is a first-rate source for prime meats in New York. Under the ownership of Robert Pence, an experienced butcher and chef, the traditions of Harry Oppenheimer have been carried forward. It's an old-fashioned butcher shop, offering the kind of service and quality you won't find at any supermarket. Prime dry-aged beef, milk-fed veal, free-range poultry, game, and fresh seafood are all sold at competitive prices. Delivery is available throughout Manhattan.

> **Guss' Pickles** is a New York legend. Dipping into their barrels was one of the treats of a Lower East Side visit. Alas, they are no longer in Manhattan, but you can find them on Long Island (504A Central Ave, Cedarhurst, 516/569-0909). You'll find sour, half-sour, sour tomato, and sauerkraut. If you can't make the trip, order by fax (516/569-0901) or e-mail (GussPicklePower@aol.com).

OTTOMANELLI'S MEAT MARKET
285 Bleecker St (bet Seventh Ave and Jones St)   212/675-4217
Mon-Sat: 8-6   www.wildgamemeatsrus.com

Looking for something unusual? Ottomanelli's stock-in-trade is rare gourmet fare. Among the weekly offerings are boar's head, whole baby lambs, game, rabbits, and pheasant. They also stock buffalo, ostrich, rattlesnake, alligator meat, suckling pig, and quail. Quality is good, but service from the right person can make the difference between a serviceable cut and an excellent one. This four-brother operation gained its reputation by offering full butcher services and a top-notch selection of prime meats, game, prime-aged steaks, and milk-fed veal. The latter is cut into Italian roasts, chops, and steaks, and their preparation by Ottomanelli's is unique. Best of all, they will sell it by the piece for a quick meal at home.

PARK EAST KOSHER BUTCHER & FINE FOODS
1623 Second Ave (bet 84th and 85th St)   212/737-9800
Mon-Wed: 7:30-7:30; Thurs: 7 a.m.-9 p.m.; Fri: 5 a.m. till two hours before sunset; Sun: 9-6   www.parkeastkosher.com

This is one-stop kosher shopping: butcher items, cooked foods, packaged meats, bakery goods, candy, sauces and dressings, pickled products, salads and dips, frozen food, vegetables, fruits, cheeses, and sushi. Park East carries over 700 items in all! They promise delivery within three hours throughout Manhattan. **Park East Grill** (1564 Second Ave, 212/717-8400) is their restaurant, offering fine kosher items.

SCHALLER & WEBER
1654 Second Ave (bet 85th and 86th St)   212/879-3047
Mon-Sat: 8-6   www.schallerweber.com

Once you've been in this store, the image will linger because of the sheer magnitude of cold cuts on display. Schaller & Weber is *Babes in Toyland* for delicatessen lovers. There is nary a wall or nook that is not covered with deli meats. Besides offering a complete line of deli items, Schaller & Weber stocks game and poultry. Try their sausage and pork items, which they will prepare, bake, smoke, or roll.

YORKVILLE PACKING HOUSE
1560 Second Ave (at 81st St)   212/628-5147
Mon-Sat: 8-6; Sun: 9-5   www.hungarianmeatmarket.com

Yorkville used to be a bastion of Eastern European ethnicity and culture before becoming the Upper East Side's swinging singles playground. Here and there, remnants of Old World society remain. Yorkville Packing House is patronized by Hungarian-speaking old ladies in black, as well as some of the city's greatest gourmands. The reason is simple: these prepared meats are available nowhere else in the city and possibly on the continent. The shop offers a vast variety of sausages and salami. Smoked meats include pork shoulder and tenderloin. Goose is a mainstay of Hungarian cuisine, so goose liverwurst, smoked goose, and goose liver are staples here. Fried bacon bits and bacon fried with paprika (a favorite Hungarian spice) are other popular offerings. And there's more: preserves, jams, spices, ground nuts, jellies, prepared delicacies, head cheese, breads, and takeout meals—all of it authentic!

If you are looking for good prices on an excellent selection of fresh seafood at just about any hour, try **Downeast Seafood** (311 Manida St, The Bronx, 212/243-5639, www.downeastseafoodnyc.com). They are open daily (except Sunday) from midnight to 4 p.m., and delivery to Manhattan is available.

Seafood

CATALANO'S FRESH FISH MARKET
Vinegar Factory
431 E 91st St (bet York and First Ave)   212/987-0885
Mon-Sun: 7 a.m.-9 p.m.

Joe Catalano is that rare blend of knowledge and helpfulness. Catalano's customers, including many local restaurants, rely on him to select the best items for their dinner menus. He does so with a careful eye toward health, price, and preparation. Catalano's at the Vinegar Factory also has a good selection of poached fish, plus crawfish and soft-shell crabs in season. On cold winter days, don't miss the Manhattan clam chowder.

GRAMERCY FISH CO.
383 Second Ave (at 23rd St)   212/213-5557
Mon-Sat: 9-7; Sun: 10-6

Quality fresh seafood is the name of the game here. You'll find oysters, clams, crawfish, salmon, and more, plus both hot and refrigerated chowders and bisques. Prices are competitive and usually better than at the chain markets.

LEONARD'S SEAFOOD AND PRIME MEATS
1385 Third Ave (bet 78th and 79th St)   212/744-2600
Mon-Fri: 8-7; Sat: 8-6; Sun: 11-6

A family-owned business since 1910, Leonard's has expanded its inventory. You'll find oysters, crabs, striped bass, halibut, salmon, live lobsters, and squid. In addition, there are farm-fresh vegetables and organic dairy products. Their takeout seafood department sells codfish cakes and crab cakes; hand-sliced Norwegian, Scottish, and Irish smoked salmon; lobsters; and some of the best Manhattan clam chowder in Manhattan. Barbecued poultry, cooked and prepared foods, and aged prime meats (beef, lamb, and veal) round out Leonard's selection. Their homemade seafood chili, turkey chili, and beef stew are customer favorites. They also make beautiful platters of boiled shrimp, crabmeat, and smoked salmon for parties. This service-oriented establishment provides fast, free delivery.

LOBSTER PLACE
75 Ninth Ave (bet 15th and 16th St)   212/255-5672
Mon-Fri: 9:30-8; Sat: 9:30-7; Sun: 10-6
252 Bleecker St (bet Ave of the Americas and Seventh Ave)
Mon-Sat: 10-8; Sun: 10-7   212/352-8063
                                                  www.lobsterplace.com

Imagine distributing one million pounds of lobster every year! The Lobster Place does just that, and they have a full line of fish, shrimp, and shellfish, too. Top hotels and restaurants take advantage of their buying power, so you are assured of quality, freshness, and value.

> If you can put up with periodic poor service at **Pisacane Midtown Seafood** (940 First Ave, 212/752-7560), this wholesale and retail seafood operation is worth a visit.

MURRAY'S STURGEON SHOP
2429 Broadway (bet 89th and 90th St)   212/724-2650
Sun-Fri; 8-7; Sat: 8-8   www.murraysturgeon.com

Murray's is the stop for fancy smoked fish, fine appetizers, and caviar. Choose from sturgeon, Eastern and Norwegian salmon, whitefish, kippered salmon, sable, pickled herring, and schmaltz. The quality is excellent, and prices are fair. Murray's also offers kosher cold cuts, dried fruits, and nuts.

WILD EDIBLES
535 Third Ave (bet 35th and 36th St)   212/213-8552
Mon-Fri: 11-9; Sat: 1-8; Sun: 11-7   www.wildedibles.com

You can't beat these folks for fresh, high-quality seafood, some of it unique and imported. Many of the same foods served at Manhattan's top restaurants are sold here. A catering menu boasts that seafood caught anywhere in the world can be put on your home or office table! Kosher (uncertified) and health foods are stocked. The market also offers an oyster bar with wine and beer. You'll find another Wild Edibles location at the Grand Central Market (Grand Central Terminal, 212/213-8552). Delivery is available throughout the city.

Spanish

DESPAÑA BRAND FOODS
408 Broome St (bet Lafayette and Centre St)   212/219-5050
Mon-Sat: 11-8; Sun: 11-5   www.despananyc.com

Tasty and authentic Spanish foods are available here. Try their *bocadillos* or warm *caldo gallego*. Fresh bread is available during the day. More specialties: serrano ham, blood sausage, chestnuts in syrup, and pickled cardoons.

Spices

APHRODISIA
264 Bleecker St (bet Ave of the Americas and Seventh Ave)
Mon-Sat: 11-7:30; Sun: noon-5:30   212/989-6440

Aphrodisia is stocked from floor to ceiling with nearly every herb and spice imaginable—800 of them, which are neatly displayed in glass jars. Some of the teas, potpourri, dried flowers, and oils (200 of them!) are really not what one might expect. The general accent is on folk remedies, but most ingredients for ethnic cooking can be found as well. Aphrodisia also conducts a mail-order business.

SPICE CORNER
135 Lexington Ave (at 29th St)   212/689-5182
Daily: 10-8   www.spicecorner29.com

Indian cooking specialties can be found here in abundance. Shelves are packed with beans, grains, chutneys, and spices, plus a good selection of reasonably priced specialty foods and cookware items.

For some of the best oyster selections in Manhattan, head to these shops at Grand Central Terminal: **Pescatore Market** (212/557-4466) and **Wild Edibles** (212/213-8552). See write-up on page 273.

V. Where to Find It: New York's Best Services

Do you need to get an antique doll repaired? Are you looking to replace a missing button for a sweater? Are you wondering where to buy a ribbon for your grandfather's old typewriter? You really can find just about everything in Manhattan, if you just know where to go. This chapter is a great place to start!

Air Conditioning

AIR-WAVE AIR CONDITIONING COMPANY

2421 Jerome Ave (at Fordham Road), The Bronx   212/545-1122
Mon-Sat: 8:30-5:30 (closed Sat in fall and winter) www.airwaveac.com

If the dog days of summer are getting you down or you want to plan ahead to make sure that they don't, give these folks a call. Air-Wave has been in business for half a century and sold tens of thousands of units over the years: top brands like Friedrich, Carrier, Westinghouse, and Panasonic. They offer same-day delivery and installation.

Animal Adoptions

AMERICAN SOCIETY FOR THE PREVENTION OF CRUELTY TO ANIMALS

424 E 92nd St (bet First and York Ave)   212/876-7700, ext. 4120
Mon-Sat: 11-7; Sun: 11-5   www.aspca.org

This is one of the oldest animal protection organizations in the world, and these folks take pet adoptions very seriously. You'll need to fill out an application, go through an interview, bring two pieces of identification (at least one with a photograph), provide two references that the ASPCA staff can call, and offer proof of income. The whole process sometimes takes longer than you might wish—but then *they're* sure that *you're* serious, and you can go home with a good pet that needs a loving home. Adoption fees for dogs and cats start at $75; puppies and kittens are higher. The fee includes a veterinarian's exam, vaccinations, and spaying or neutering. ASPCA also enforces animal cruelty laws and has an on-site animal hospital.

Animal Services

ANIMAL MEDICAL CENTER
510 E 62nd St (bet FDR Dr and York Ave)   212/838-8100
Daily: 24 hours   www.amcny.org

If your pet becomes ill, try the Animal Medical Center first. This nonprofit organization does all kinds of veterinary work reasonably and competently. They handle over 60,000 cases a year and have more than 80 veterinarians on staff. The care is among the best in the city. They suggest calling for an appointment first; emergency care costs more.

BISCUITS & BATH
1535 First Ave (at 80th St)   212/419-2500
701 Second Ave (at 38th St)
41 W 13th St (at Fifth Ave)
469 Columbus Ave (at 82nd St)
160 Riverside Dr (at 68th St)
Mon-Fri: 7 a.m.-10 p.m.; Sat, Sun: 8 a.m.-10 p.m.
                                            www.biscuitsandbath.com

One could refer to any of these places as Doggy City! They offer grooming, training, workshops and seminars, vet care, dog walking, day and overnight care, adoption, a retail boutique, transportation services, and even Sunday brunches. The place is pocketbook-friendly.

CAROLE WILBOURN
299 W 12th St (bet Eighth and Ninth Ave)   212/741-0397
Mon-Sat: 9-6   www.thecattherapist.com

Would you like to talk to the author of *Total Cat*, *Cats on the Couch*, and *Cat Talk*? Perhaps you need a fascinating speaker? Carole Wilbourn is an internationally known cat therapist who has the answers to most cat problems. Carole makes house calls from coast to coast and can take care of many feline issues with just one session and a follow-up phone call. She does international consultations, takes on-site appointments at Westside Veterinary Center, and is available for speaking engagements.

EAST VILLAGE VETERINARIAN
241 Eldridge St (at Houston St), Room 241   212/674-8640
Daily: 9-3:30 (Wed, Sat till noon)

This is the only practicing homeopathic veterinary clinic in New York City. It features a complete homeopathic dispensary, with over a thousand remedies in stock. It is also a full-service animal hospital with an emphasis on prevention.

FIELDSTON PETS   718/796-4541
Mon-Sat: 9-7   www.pawsacrossamerica.com

Bash Dibra is a warm, friendly man who speaks dog language. Known as the "dog trainer to the stars," Bash is an animal behaviorist. If your dog has bad manners, Bash will teach it to behave. He believes in "tandem training"—training owners to train their dogs—because it's the owner who'll be in charge. Bash's experience in training a pet wolf gave him unique insight into canine minds, and his success in bringing the most difficult pets to heel has made him a regular on the talk show circuit. In addition to training sessions, dog and cat grooming is available.

LE CHIEN
Trump Plaza
1044 Third Ave (bet 61st and 62nd St)   212/752-2120, 800/LECHIEN
Mon-Sat: 8:30-6:30   www.lechiennyc.com

Occupying two floors of Trump Plaza, Le Chien is a luxurious pet day spa offering grooming and attentive boarding services. A boutique carries a fabulous selection of custom and imported accessories, as well as Le Chien's own fragrance lines. They sell puppies directly from show breeders.

NEW YORK DOG SPA & HOTEL
32 W 25th St (bet Ave of the Americas and Broadway)   212/243-1199
www.dogspa.com

This is a full-service hotel for dogs, offering boarding, day care, massage, training, vet services, and more.

PETS CARE NETWORK
Daily: 9-6 and by appointment   212/580-6004, 646/256-1642
www.petscarenetwork.com

Pets Care Network, a kennel alternative established in 1985, offers all the comforts of home to pets (dogs, cats, and birds) in 35 separate New York apartments. Your pet will receive individual attention from caring "dog people" or "cat people." There are no cages. One or two weeks notice is preferred. These folks are bonded and insured.

> Sometimes it is handy or even necessary to have a vet make a house call. One of the best is **Dr. Amy Attas** (212/581-7387).

SUTTON DOG PARLOUR
311 E 60th St (bet First and Second Ave)   212/355-2850
Mon-Fri: 7-7; Sat, Sun: 9-6   www.suttonpets.com

Sutton Dog Parlour has been around for over four decades, so you know it is a responsible establishment. You will find dog grooming, boarding and day care, and supplies for dogs, cats, and birds. There's even a private outdoor park for your beloved pooch to enjoy. Sutton also boards birds, with each housed in its own large cage. A radio in the bird room keeps them up-to-date on world affairs—a necessity, of course!

Antique Repair and Restoration

CENTER ART STUDIO
307 W 38th St (bet Eighth and Ninth Ave), Suite 1315
212/847-3550, 800/242-3535
Mon-Thurs: 9-6; Fri: 9-5 (by appointment)   www.centerart.com

"Fine art restoration and display design since 1919" is the motto here. The word *fine* should really be emphasized, as owners of fine paintings, sculpture, and ceramics have made Center Art Studio the place to go for restoration. The house specialty is art conservation. They will clean and restore paintings, lacquer, terra cotta, scagliola, and plaster. Their craftsmen will also restore antique furniture and decorative objects. They will even design and install display bases and mounts for sculpture. Among the oldest and most diverse restoration studios in the city, Center Art offers a multitude of special services for the art collector, dealer, or designer.

MICHAEL J. DOTZEL AND SON
402 E 63rd St (at York Ave)   212/838-2890
Mon-Fri: 8-4:30

Dotzel specializes in the repair and maintenance of antiques and precious heirlooms. They won't touch modern pieces or inferior antiques, but if your older piece is made out of metal and needs repair, this is the place for the job. They pay close attention to detail and will hand-forge or hammer metal work, including brass. If an antique has lost a part or if you want a duplication, it can be re-created. Dotzel also does stripping and replating, but since it isn't always good for an antique, they may try to talk you out of it.

SANO STUDIO
767 Lexington Ave (at 60th St), Room 403   212/759-6131
Mon-Fri: 10-5 (by appointment; closed Aug)

Jadwiga Baran presides over this fourth-floor antique repair shop with an eye for excellence. That eye is focused on the quality of the workmanship and goods to be repaired. Both must be the best. Baran is a specialist who limits herself to repairing porcelain, pottery, ivory, and tortoise-shell works and antiques. She has many loyal customers.

> Did someone break a prized piece of glassware? Don't worry—just call **Gus Jochec** (1597 York Ave, 212/517-3287).

Appliance Repair
AUDIOVISION
1386 Second Ave (bet 71st and 72nd St)   212/639-1733
Mon-Fri: 9:30-6:30; Sat: 9:30-4:30

Audiovision has been in business for two decades, providing top-quality radio and TV repairs (guaranteed for three months) on all major brands. Pickup and delivery, installation, and hookup are also offered.

Art Appraisals
ABIGAIL HARTMANN ASSOCIATES
415 Central Park W (at 101st St)   212/316-5406
Mon-Fri: 9-6 (by appointment; also available on weekends)

This firm specializes in fine and decorative art appraisals for insurance, donation, or other reasons. Their highly principled and experienced staff does not buy, sell, or receive kickbacks. (This is a common practice with some auction houses, insurance companies, and galleries.) Fees are by the hour, and consultations are available. The friendly personnel can also provide restoration, framing, shipping, and storage contacts.

Art Services

A.I. FRIEDMAN
44 W 18th St (bet Fifth Ave and Ave of the Americas) 212/243-9000
Mon-Fri: 9-7; Sat: 10-7; Sun: 11-6 www.aifriedman.com

Those who want to frame it themselves can take advantage of one of the largest stocks of ready-made frames in the city at A.I. Friedman. Nearly all are sold at discount. In addition to fully assembled frames, they sell do-it-yourself frames that come equipped with glass and/or mats. Custom framing is also available. They are really a department store for creative individuals, providing a large assortment of tools, furniture, paints, easels, books, and other supplies and materials for the graphic artist.

ELI WILNER & COMPANY
1525 York Ave (bet 80th and 81st St) 212/744-6521
Mon-Fri: 9:30-5:30 www.eliwilner.com

Eli Wilner's primary business is period frames and mirrors. He keeps over 3,300 19th- and early 20th-century American and European frames in stock and can locate any size or style. Wilner can create an exact replica of a frame to your specifications. His staff of over 25 skilled craftsmen also does expert restoration of frames. Boasting such clients as the Metropolitan Museum of Art and the White House, Wilner's expertise speaks for itself.

GUTTMANN PICTURE FRAME ASSOCIATES
180 E 73rd St (bet Lexington and Third Ave) 212/744-8600
Mon-Thurs: 10-4:30 (by appointment)

Though the Guttmanns have worked on frames for some of the nation's finest museums, including the Metropolitan, they stand apart from other first-class artisans in that they are not snobby or picky about the work they will accept. They will restore, regild, or replace any type of picture frame. They work with masterpieces but are equally at home framing a snapshot. Even better, they are among the few experts who don't price themselves out of the market. Bring a broken or worn-out frame, and they will graciously tell you exactly what it will cost to fix it.

J. POCKER & SON
135 E 63rd St (bet Park and Lexington Ave)
212/838-5488, 800/443-3116
Mon-Fri: 9-5:30; Sat: 10-5:30 (closed Sat in summer)
www.jpocker.com

Three generations of this family have been in the custom framing business, so rest assured that you will receive expert advice from a superbly trained staff. As a sidelight, Pocker offers a gallery specializing in English sporting and botanical prints. Pickup and delivery are offered.

JINPRA NEW YORK PICTURE FRAMING
1208 Lexington Ave (at 82nd St)   212/988-3903
Mon: 11-4; Tues-Sat: 10:30-6:30

The proprietor of Jinpra is Wellington Chiang, and his service is as unique as his name. Jinpra provides art services (cleaning and gilding) in general and picture framing in particular. Chiang makes the high-quality frames himself; his artistry is evident in every piece he creates, including his murals.

JULIUS LOWY FRAME AND RESTORING COMPANY
223 E 80th St (bet Second and Third Ave)   212/861-8585
Mon-Fri: 9-5:30   www.lowyonline.com

Serving New York City since 1907, Lowy is the nation's oldest, largest, and most highly regarded firm for the conservation and framing of fine art. Lowy's services include painting and paper conservation, professional photography, conservation framing, and curatorial work. They sell antique frames (the largest inventory in the U.S.) and authentic reproduction frames (the best selection anywhere). In addition, Lowy provides complete conservation work, mat-making, and fitting services. Their client base includes art dealers, private collectors, auction houses, corporate collections, institutions, and museums.

KING DAVID GALLERY
124 W 23rd St (bet Ave of the Americas and Seventh Ave)
Mon-Thurs: 10-9; Fri, Sat: 10-8; Sun: 11-6   212/727-7184
                                                   www.kingdavidgallery.com

These people provide very professional service in a number of areas: design consulting and custom framing for fine art and mirrors, canvas stretching, glass cutting, 24K gold-leaf framing, shadow boxes, glass panels for shower doors, and designing and building framed TV mirrors to cover your LCD or plasma TV. Custom glass work is really their specialty, but they can do almost anything in this field beginning, with designer sketches and measurements.

LEITH RUTHERFURD TALAMO
By appointment   212/396-0399

Did movers mishandle a treasured painting? Has the masterpiece that hung over the fireplace darkened with age? Do you need help hanging or lighting a collection? All of these services—plus cleaning, relining, gilding, and polishing frames—are done with expertise and class by Leith Rutherfurd Talamo.

Nannies (all highly recommended)
Basic Trust (212/222-6602): day care
Fox Agency (212/753-2686): good record
Pavillion Agency (212/889-6609): very reliable

Babysitters

BABY SITTERS' GUILD
60 E 42nd St (bet Madison and Park Ave), Suite 912   212/682-0227
Daily: 9-9   www.babysittersguild.com

Established in 1940, the Baby Sitters' Guild charges high rates, but their professional reputation commands them. All guild sitters have passed rigorous scrutiny, and only the most capable are sent out on jobs. Believe it or not, the sitters can speak 16 languages among them. They enforce a four-hour minimum and add on any travel expenses.

> Plans can change quickly in New York. If you need a nanny at the last minute, this is the number to call: **A Choice Nanny** (850 Seventh Ave, Suite 706, 212/246-5437, www.achoicenanny.com; Mon-Thurs: 9-4; Fri: 9-3). Alan and Joan Friedman make sure the nannies they send have been carefully screened. You are charged a one-time registration fee of $350, and then rates run from $12 to $16 an hour.

BARNARD BABYSITTING AGENCY
49 Claremont Ave (at 119th St), 2nd floor   212/854-2035
Call for hours   www.barnard.edu/babysitting

Barnard Babysitting Agency is a nonprofit organization run by students at the undergraduate women's college affiliated with Columbia University. The service provides affordable child care in the New York metropolitan area. At the same time, it allows students to seek convenient employment. Live-in help is also available. A minimum registration fee is required.

Beauty Services

DASHING DIVA SALON & NAIL BOUTIQUE
41 E 8th St (bet University Pl and Broadway)   212/673-9000
590 Columbus Ave (bet 88th and 9th St)   212/877-9052
1341 Second Ave (bet 70th and 71st St)   212/570-0770
Hours vary by location   www.dashingdiva.com

The owner of Dashing Diva is said to be the largest manufacturer of artificial nails in the world. These folks claim that Virtual Nails are quicker and healthier than regular wraps or tips. These also have the first eyelash bars in Manhattan.

NINA'S EUROPEAN DAY SPA & LASER CENTER
5 W 35th St (bet Fifth Ave and Ave of the Americas)   212/594-9610
Mon-Fri: 10-8; Sat, Sun: 10-7 (Sun by appointment)
                                                    www.ninasskincare.com

Nina has been in the skin-care field for 20 years, so you can be assured that she and her staff know the business inside out. You will find just about everything at this spa: facial treatments, body treatments, body-fat reduction, body wraps, microdermabrasion, electrolysis, massages, waxing, nail care, tanning, exfoliation, reflexology, and more. It's a worldly place, too: the expertise is Russian, the atmosphere French, and the technology American. I'm intrigued by their "chocolate treatments"!

Botox Treatment
Verve Laser and Medical Spa (216 E 50th St, 212/888-3003)

Cellulite Treatment
Wellpath (1100 Madison Ave, 212/737-9604): up-to-date equipment

Cosmetic Surgeons and Consultants
Dr. Amiya Prasad (61 E 66th St, 212/265-8877): plastic surgeon, eyelids
Dr. Neil Sadick (911 Park Ave, 212/772-7242): Polaris anti-aging treatment

---

Need a quick rest in midtown Manhattan? **Yelo** (315 W 57th St, 212/245-8235, www.yelonyc.com) offers private treatment cabins, where you can rest and relax with your own lighting and sounds. Options include blankets and scents to suit your mood. "YeloNaps" are available in five-minute increments from 20 to 40 minutes, priced from $12 to $24. Yelo reflexology treatments are also available. Eventually Yelo plans to expand to as many as 30 storefront centers in New York.

Day Spas (by neighborhood)

Chelsea

Azure Day Spa and Laser Center (26 W 20th St, 212/563-5365): Their ear-candling therapy relieves allergies, migraines and sinus infections.
Graceful Spa (205 W 14th St, 2nd floor, 212/675-5145): budget friendly
Nickel Spa (77 Eighth Ave, 212/242-3203): males-only retreat
Spa at Chelsea Piers (Sports Center, Chelsea Piers, 2nd floor, 212/336-6780): spa parties

East Village

Great Jones Spa (29 Great Jones St, 212/505-3185)
Mezzanine Spa at Soho Integrative Health (62 Crosby St, 212/431-1600): medical spa
Priti Organic Spa (35 E 1st St, 212/254-3628): organic skin products

Flatiron District

Completely Bare (103 Fifth Ave, 212/366-6060): one of the best laser treaments in town; dewrinkling
Just Calm Down (32 W 22nd St, 212/337-0032): "Peelin' Groovy" facial and chocolate treatments
Longevity Health (12 W 27th St, 9th floor, 212/675-9355)

Gramercy

Aerospa (Gramercy Park Hotel, 2 Lexington Ave, 212/920-3300)
Gloria Cabrera Salon and Spa (309 E 23rd St, 212/689-6815)

Greenwich Village

Acqua Beauty Bar (7 E 14th St, 212/620-4329): Indonesian flavor; pedicures
Silk Day Spa (47 W 13th St, 212/255-6457): "Silk Supreme Eastern Indulgence Body Scrub and Polish"

SPArty (39 E 20th St, 646/736-1777): They bring the spa to you!

Harlem

Turning Heads Beauty Salon and Day Spa (218 Lenox Ave, 212/828-4600): specials on Tuesdays and Wednesdays

Kips Bay

Oasis Day Spa (1 Park Ave, 212/254-7722)

Essential Therapy (122 E 25th St, 212/777-2325): spa services with a healing bent

Meatpacking District

G Spa (Hotel Gansevoort, 18 Ninth Ave, 212/206-6700): spa by day, lounge at night

---

Gentlemen, if your beard is tough, try the pre-shave oil available at **The Art of Shaving** (141 E 62nd St, 212/317-8436).

Midtown

Avalon Day Spa (40-A E 33rd St, 212/213-2000): honey almond pedicure

Bliss 57 (19 E 57th St, 212/219-8970)

Cornelia Day Resort (663 Fifth Ave, 212/871-3050)

Elizabeth Arden Red Door Salon (691 Fifth Ave, 212/546-0200)

Exhale Spa (150 Central Park S, 212/561-7400): deep flow massage

Faina European Skin Care Center and Day Spa (330 W 58th St, Suite 402, 212/245-6557)

Frederic Fekkai Fifth Avenue (Henri Bendel, 712 Fifth Ave, 4th floor, 212/753-9500): the ultimate

Ido Holistic Center (9 E 45th St, 8th floor, 212/599-5300): immune-system boost

Jurlique (477 Madison Ave, 212/752-1980): Australian herbal treatment

Juva Skin and Laser Center (60 E 56th St, Suite 2, 212/688-5882): "Clarisonic" brush facial

Juvenex (25 W 32nd St, 646/733-1330): 24-hour Korean oasis, body scrub

La Prairie at the Ritz-Carlton Spa (50 Central Park S, 212/521-6135): top-drawer

La Beauté Salon & Spa (805 Third Ave, 212/752-9664): hair removal

Le Petit Spa (140 E 34th St, 212/685-0773): chocolate spa pedicure

Lia Schorr (686 Lexington Ave, 4th floor, 212/486-9670): efficient and reasonably priced

Metamorphosis (127 E 56th St, 212/751-6051): small but good, men and women

Okeanos (211 E 51st St, 212/223-6773): coed sauna, "*Platza*" (ancient Russian technique using bundled birch leaves)

Peninsula New York Spa (Peninsula New York Hotel, 700 Fifth Ave, 212/903-3910)

Remede Spa (St. Regis New York, 2 E 55th St, 212/339-6715)

Repéchage (115 E 57th St, 212/751-2500): European; men, too

Salon and Spa at Saks Fifth Avenue (611 Fifth Avenue, 212/940-4000)

Salon de Tokyo (200 W 57th St, Room 1308, 212/757-2187): Shiatsu parlor, open till midnight

Smooth Synergy (686 Lexington Ave, 3rd floor, 212/397-0111): "Medspa" with a resident physician

Spa at the Four Seasons Hotel New York (57 E 57th St, 212/350-6420)

Susan Ciminelli Day Spa (Bergdorf Goodman, 754 Fifth Ave, 9th floor, 212/872-2650): highly recommended ultra spa package for men ... but if you have to ask the price ...

Townhouse Spa (39 W 56th St, 212/245-8006)

Warren Tricomi (Sports Club LA, 45 Rockefeller Plaza, 212/218-8650): chair massage

Yi Pak (10 W 32nd St, 2nd floor, 212/594-1025)

Murray Hill

Oasis Day Spa (Affinia Dumont, 150 E 34th St, 212/254-7722): Ask about the weekend package

Murray Hill Skin Care (567 Third Ave, 212/661-0777): "backcial" (a facial for the back)

Queens

Oasis Day Spa (Jet Blue Terminal 6 at JFK Airport, 212/254-7722)

Soho

Aveda Institute (233 Spring St, 212/807-1492)

Bunya CitiSPA (474 West Broadway, 212/388-1288)

Bliss Spa (568 Broadway, 2nd floor, 212/219-8970): oxygen facial

Erbe (196 Prince St, 212/966-1445)

Haven (150 Mercer St, 212/343-3515): calm and refreshing; try the facial for the feet; open weekends

SkinCareLab (568 Broadway, Suite 403, 212/334-3142): body treatments, facials

Soho Sanctuary (119 Mercer St, 212/334-5550): pomegranate-infused scrub

Thai Privilege Spa (155 Spring St, 212/274-8121): massage

Tribeca

Euphoria (18 Harrison St, 2nd floor, 212/925-5925): "Fresh Air Facial"

TriBeCa MedSpa (114 Hudson St, 212/925-9500): exfoliation

Ula (8 Harrison St, 212/343-2376)

Upper East Side

Ajune (1294 Third Ave, 212/628-0044): full-service, Botox, superb facials

Bliss 49 (W New York Hotel, 541 Lexington Ave, 212/755-1200)

Casa Spa and Fitness (The Regency, 540 Park Ave, 212/223-9280): nutritional counseling

Chantecaille Energy Spa at Barneys (600 Madison Ave, 212/833-2700): facials to detoxify and decrease puffiness

Completely Bare (764 Madison Ave, 212/717-9300): sunspot removal

Dr. Howard Sobel Skin and Spa (960-A Park Ave, 212/288-0060): medical personnel on the premises

Equinox Wellness Spa (140 E 63rd St, 212/750-4671): facials, sport massage

Gloss Day Spa (51 E 73rd St, Suite 2B, 212/249-2100): customized facials

Institute Beauté (885 Park Ave, 212/535-0229): foot facial

InSPArations (at 92nd Street YMHA/YWHA, 1395 Lexington Ave, 212/415-5795

Paul Labrecque Salon and Spa (171 E 65th St, 212/595-0099): facials

Skin N.Y. (655 Park Ave, 212/794-3900): Dr. Wells' anti-aging procedure

Yasmine Djerradine (30 E 60th St, 212/588-1771): remodeling facial

Yin Beauty and Arts (22 E 66th St, 212/879-5040): detoxifying body treatment

Upper West Side

Dorit Baxter Skin Care, Beauty & Health Spa (47 W 57th St, 3rd floor, 212/371-4542): salt scrub

Ettia Holistic Day Spa (239 W 72nd, 212/362-7109)

Paul Labrecque Salon and Spa (Reebok Sports Center, 160 Columbus Ave, 212/595-0099): Thai massages, facials

Prenatal Massage Center of Manhattan (123 W 79th St, 212/330-6846): new spa

Spa at Mandarin Oriental (Time Warner Center, 80 Columbus Circle, 35th floor, 212/805-8880): Lomi Lomia deep tissue massage and holistic foot ritual

Spa Ja (300 W 56th St, 212/245-7566): Brazilian body sculpting

Le Spa Naturale (269 W 72nd St, 212/873-5891)

Eyebrow Styling

Shobha Threading (594 Broadway, Suite 403, 212/931-8363): shaping

Robin Narvaez at Borja Color Studio (118 E 57th St, 212/308-3232)

Hairstyling

Discount Haircuts

Mingle Salon (10 W 55th St, 2nd floor, 212/459-3320): $10 cuts on Wednesday, 7 p.m.-9 p.m.

Parlor (102 Ave B, 212/673-5520): Check out "Apprentice Monday"— prices start at nothing!

Family Haircuts

Feature Trim (1108 Lexington Ave, 212/652-9746)

Hair Blowout

Salon A.K.S. (694 Madison Ave, 212/888-0707): Mika Rummo; also does house calls

Jean Louis David (locations throughout Manhattan, 212/779-3555): good work at reasonable prices

Warren Tricomi (16 W 57th St, 4th floor, 212/262-8899): for work that lasts

Blow Styling Salon (342 W 14th St, 212/989-6282): for the budget-conscious

Hair Care   (best in Manhattan, by area)

Chelsea

Antonio Prieto (127 W 20th St, 212/255-3741): popular styling for the average woman

MESS Studios (224 W 30th St, 212/643-3191): makeup and hairstyling parties; photography studio, too.

East Village

Astor Place Hair Stylists (2 Astor Pl, at Broadway, 212/475-9854): one of the world's largest barber shops; inexpensive

Salon Zoia (448 E 13th St, 212/614-1898)

Flatiron District

Sacha and Oliver (6 W 18th St, 212/255-1100): very French

Salon 02 (20 W 22nd St, 212/675-7274)

Inexpensive prices on grooming are available if you are willing to try training schools. Here are some of the better ones.

Dentistry: **New York University College of Dentistry** (345 E 24th St, 212/998-9800)—initial visit, X-rays, and all, for $90!

Facials and manicures: **Christine Valmy International School** (437 Fifth Ave, 2nd floor, 212/779-7800)—facials for $27

Haircut (blow dry): **Jean Louis David** (10 E 41st St, 212/779-3555)—$36

Haircut: **Mark Garrison Salon** (108 E 60th St, 212/570-2455)—training price: $50-$65!

Hairstyling and manicures: **LIBS** (22 W 34th St, 212/695-4555)—an old-fashioned learning institute; perms for $25, color rinse for $20, and manicure for $5

Hairstyling: **Bumble & Bumble** (146 E 56th St and 415 W 13th St, 212/521-6500)—good deals

Massage: **Swedish Institute** (226 W 26th St, 212/924-5900):—twelve one-hour Swedish-shiatsu massages for $250

Men's haircuts: **Atlas Barber School** (34 Third Ave, 212/475-1360)—haircuts for $5; women are welcome, too

---

Greenwich Village

Gemini Salon and Spa (547 Hudson St, 212/675-4546): "opti-smooth" (straightening treatment)

Lower East Side

Laicale Salon (129 Grand St, 212/219-2424): no attitude

Snip 'n Sip (204 Waverly Pl, 212/242-3880)

Tease Salon (137 Rivington St, 212/979-8327): extensions and relaxers

Midtown

Bumble & Bumble (146 E 56th St, 212/521-6500): no-nonsense establishment

Kenneth's (Waldorf-Astoria, 301 Park Ave, lobby floor, 212/752-1800): full service with an able staff, but a long wait for Kenneth himself

Nardi Salon (111 E 56th St, 212/421-4810): long-hair specialists
Ouidad Hair Salon (37 W 57th St, 4th floor, 212/888-3288): curly- and frizzy-hair specialists
Pierre Michel (131 E 57th St, 212/593-1460): J.F. Lazartigue treatment products, eyelash extensions
Salon Ishi (70 E 55th St, 212/888-4744): scalp massages for men and women
Salon Mai (10 W 55th St, 212/956-3001): Japanese hair straightening
Stephen Knoll (625 Madison Ave, 212/421-0100): highly recommended

Soho

Frederic Fekkai Salon (394 West Broadway, 212/888-2600): Wi-Fi, food from Barolo, and espresso
John Masters (77 Sullivan St, 212/343-9590): all-organic
Oscar Bond Salon (42 Wooster St, 212/334-3777)
Privé (310 West Broadway, 212/274-8888): all hair services, shampoos a specialty, trendy, open Sunday

---

Close shave? One of the few places left where a fellow can get a straight-edged razor shave is **Paul Mole** (1031 Lexington Ave, 212/535-8461). Cost? A whopping $35!

Upper East Side

Frederic Fekkai (Henri Bendel, 712 Fifth Ave, 212/753-9500): elegant
Garren New York (Sherry Netherland Hotel, 781 Fifth Ave, 212/841-9400): personally customized services
John Barrett Salon (Bergdorf Goodman, 754 Fifth Ave, penthouse, 212/872-2700): top cut
John Frieda (797 Madison Ave, 212/879-1000): very "in"
Julian Farel Salon (605 Madison Ave, 2nd floor, 212/888-8988): upscale, computers available, private hair parties
Mark Garrison Salon (108 E 60th St, 212/570-2455): popular
Oscar Blandi (746 Madison Ave, 212/988-9404): reliable
Salon A.K.S. (694 Madison Ave, 212/888-0707)
Salon and Spa at Saks Fifth Avenue (Saks Fifth Avenue, 611 Fifth Ave, concourse level, 212/940-4000): top grade, full service
Vidal Sassoon (730 Fifth Ave, 212/535-9200): popular with men and women
Yves Durif (130 E 65th St, 212/452-0954): reliable

Upper West Side
Salon Above (2641 Broadway, 212/665-7149): salon and spa

Hair Coloring
Borja Color Studio (118 E 57th St, 212/308-3232)
Louis Licari Salon (693 Fifth Ave, 212/758-2090)
Q Hair (19 Bleecker St, 212/614-8729): brunettes
Salon AKS (694 Madison Ave, 212/888-0707)
Warren Tricomi (16 W 57th St, 4th floor, 212/262-8899)

Hair Loss Treatment

Le Metric Hair Center for Women (124 E 40th St, Suite 601, 212/986-5620)

Hair Removal

J. Sisters Salon (35 W 57th St, 212/750-2485): waxing
Verve Laser and Medical Spa (216 E 50th St, 212/888-3003)

Home Services

Eastside Massage Therapy Center (351 E 78th St, 212/249-2927)
Joseph Martin (717 Madison Ave, 2nd floor, 212/838-3150): hair coloring, manicure, and pedicure
Lady Barber (Kathleen Giordano, 212/826-8616): will come to offices
Paul Podlucky (25 E 67th St, 212/717-6622): his place or yours
Trish McEvoy (800-A Fifth Ave, 212/758-7790): makeup, large artistic staff

Integrative Medicine

Beth Israel Continuum Center for Health & Healing (245 Fifth Ave, 646/935-2231): Gua Sha Chinese healing process

Liposuction

Taranow Plastic Surgery (169 E 69th St, 212/772-2100)

Makeup

Kimara Ahnert Makeup Studio (1113 Madison Ave, 212/452-4252)
Makeup Center (150 W 55th St, 212/977-9494): good value
Makeup Shop (131 W 21st St, 212/807-0447): by appointment

Massage

Relax (716 Greenwich St, 212/206-9714)

Men's Grooming

Frank's Chop Shop (19 Essex St, 212/228-7442): antique barber chairs
Frederic Fekkai Fifth Avenue (Henri Bendel, 712 Fifth Ave, 4th floor, 212/753-9500): men's lounge, L'Atelier de Frederic
Greenhouse Spa (127 E 57th St, 212/644-4449): manicure, pedicure
John Allan's Men's Club (95 Trinity Pl, 212/406-3000): full-service
Kiehl's (109 Third Ave, 212/677-3171): toiletries
La Boîte à Coupe (38 E 57th St, 212/246-2097)
Neighborhood Barbers (439 E 9th St, 212/777-0798): bargain haircuts at $14
Paul Labrecque (171 E 65th St, 212/595-0099): straight razor shave with Martial Vivot
Pierre Michel (131 E 57th St, 212/593-1460): manicure
SkinCareLab (568 Broadway, Suite 403, 212/334-3142): manicure
Salon A.K.S. (694 Madison Ave, 212/888-0707): hair coloring
Soho Integrative Health (62 Crosby St, 212/431-1600): pedicure
Patrick Melville (Sports Club LA, 45 Rockefeller Plaza, 212/218-8650): pedicure

Truman's Gentlemen's Groomers (120 E 56th St, 212/759-5015): upscale men's spa
Yasmine Djerradine (30 E 60th St, 212/588-1771): men's facials

Men's Hairstylist

Chelsea Barber (465 W 23rd St, 212/741-2254): inexpensive
York Barber Shop (981 Lexington Ave, 212/988-6136)

Nails and Pedicures

Angel Nails (151 E 71st St, 212/535-5333): nail-wrapping, massage, body-waxing
Christine Valmy International School (437 Fifth Ave, 2nd floor, 212/779-7800): inexpensive
Jin Soon Natural Hand & Foot Spa (56 E 4th St, 212/473-2047 and 23 Jones St, 212/229-1070)
Karen Wu (1377 Third Ave, 212/585-2044)
Paul Labrecque Salon & Spa (160 Columbus Ave, 212/595-0099)
Pierre Michel (131 E 57th St, 212/593-1460): old-school
Rescue Beauty Lounge (34 Gansevoort St, 212/206-6409)
Sweet Lily (222 West Broadway, 212/925-5441): "natural" nail spa and boutique

Sauna

Russian and Turkish Baths (268 E 10th St, 212/473-8806): since 1892; sauna, steam, and pool

Skin Care

Advanced Skin Care Day Spa (532 Madison Ave, 3rd floor, 212/758-8867)
Aida Bicaj (629 Park Ave, 212/772-6968): Dr. Kressell, lifting facial
Alla Katkov (Miano Viel, 16 E 52nd St, 2nd floor, 212/980-3222): great facials
Georgette Klinger Advanced Aesthetics (501 Madison Ave, 212/838-3200)
Glow Skin Spa (30 E 60th St, Suite 808, 212/319-6654): skin transformation
Joean Skin Care (163 Hester St, 212/966-3668): Chinese style
Lia Schorr (686 Lexington Ave, 4th floor, 212/486-9541)
Ling Skin Care Salons (105 W 77th St, 212/877-2883; 12 E 16th St, 212/989-8833; and 191 Prince St, 212/982-8833): great skin care
Oasis Day Spa (1 Park Ave, 212/254-7722): facials a specialty
Paul Labrecque East (171 E 65th St, 212/595-0099): Regina Viotto is a great facialist.
Shizuka New York (7 W 51st St, 6th floor, 212/644-7400): anti-aging facial with intense pulsed light
Tracie Martyn (59 Fifth Ave, 212/206-9333): resculpting facial

Teeth Whitening

Dr. Jan Linhart (230 Park Ave, 212/682-5180)
Dr. Frederick Solomon (Tribeca Smiles, 44 Lispenard St, 212/473-4444)

SmileOasis Spa (128 E 71st St, 212/288-4455)

Tanning

Brazil Bronze (580 Broadway, Suite 501, 212/431-0077): bronzing formula spray

City Sun Tanning (50 E 13th St, 212/353-9700): spray

Paul Labrecque East (Chatham Hotel, 171 E 65th St, 212/595-0099): air bronzing with exfoliation

Spa at Equinox (205 E 85th St, 212/396-9611): body bronzing

Tattoos and Cosmetology

Dr. Roy Geronemus (317 E 34th St, 212/686-7306): tattoo removal

LiteTouch Medical Cosmetology (1775 Broadway, Suite 433, 866/837-1390): tattoo removal

Timeless Image Aesthetics (580 Broadway, Suite 905, 212/226-8399): permanent makeup by a registered nurse

Toupees

Bob Kelly (151 W 46th St, 212/819-0030)

Bookbinding

TALAS
20 W 20th St (bet Fifth Ave and Ave of the Americas), 5th floor
Mon-Fri: 9-5:30   212/219-0770
www.talasonline.com

Jake and Marjorie Salik preside over this outlet which offers tools, supplies, and books for artists, restorers, collectors, bookbinders, museums, archives, libraries, calligraphers, and retail customers. Expanded inventories feature custom boxes and portfolios, a wide variety of photo storage and display items, and archival papers. They are also distributors of conservation supplies.

We all know about those unfortunate spills on the carpet. No worry, just call **ID Carpet Cleaners** (212/645-8027, www.idcleaners.com). They will even treat floor coverings with flame retardant.

Cabinetry

HARMONY WOODWORKING
153 W 27th St (bet Ave of the Americas and Seventh Ave), Room 902
By appointment   212/366-7221

Expert woodworker Ron Rubin devotes his time to custom projects, especially bookcases, wall units, entertainment centers, desks, and tables.

JIM NICKEL
By appointment   718/963-2138

Jim Nickel, who lives in Brooklyn, is an expert in projects that use wood:

cabinets, bookcases, wall sculptures, and much more. He prefers small- to medium-sized jobs and can do an entire project—from consultation and design to installation—all by himself. He has decades of experience and is budget conscious. Call in the afternoon or evening for an appointment.

Good sliding doors can be helpful in home or office. Try the **Sliding Door Company** (230 Fifth Ave, Room 1804, 212/213-9350, www.slidingdoorco.com).

Carpentry

Finding a reliable carpenter is not easy. In my opinion, the best outfit to call is **R&N Construction** (914/699-0292). These folks do quality work, and they are reasonably priced and nice to deal with. Ask for Nick Alpino.

If you are interested in cabinetry, call Joe Lonigro at **European Woodworking** (914/969-5724). His custom millwork is outstanding, and believe it or not, some folks have actually claimed that he "tends to undercharge"!

Carriages

CHATEAU STABLES/CHATEAU THEATRICAL ANIMALS/CHATEAU WEDDING CARRIAGES

Call for reservations   212/246-0520
Mon-Fri: 8:30-6:30   www.chateaustables.net
                                    www.chateauweddingcarriages.com

There is nothing quite as romantic as a ride in an authentic Hansom cab. If you would like to arrive at your next dinner party in a horse-drawn carriage, Chateau is the place to call. They have the largest working collection of horse-drawn vehicles in the U.S. and have been a family business for over 40 years. Although they prefer advance notice, requests for weddings, group rides, tours, funerals, movies, and overseas visitors can be handled at any time.

If you are having a cocktail party and want specialized bar catering, try **Cuff & Buttons** (212/625-2090, www.cuffandbuttons.com).

Cars for Hire

AAMCAR CAR RENTALS

315 W 96th St (bet West End Ave and Riverside Dr)
Mon-Fri: 7:30-7:30; Sat, Sun: 9-5   212/222-8500, 800/722-6923

506 W 181st St (at Amsterdam Ave)   212/927-7000
Mon-Fri: 9-7; Sat: 9-1   www.aamcar.com

This independent car rental company has a full line of cars, vans, and sport utility vehicles. AAMCAR has been around for several decades and offers over 200 cars.

CAREY LIMOUSINE NY
24 hours   212/599-1122 (reservations), 800/336-4646
www.ecarey.com

Carey is the grandfather of car-for-hire services. They provide chauffeur-driven limousines and sedans and will take clients anywhere, at any time, in almost any kind of weather. Last-minute reservations are accepted on an as-available basis. Discuss rates before making a commitment.

CARMEL CAR SERVICE
2642 Broadway (at 100th St)   212/666-6666, 800/9CARMEL
24 hours   www.carmellimo.com

These people are highly commended for good service and fair prices. Full-size and luxury sedans, minivans, passenger vans, and limos are available. Prices for limos begin at $74 per hour.

COMPANY II LIMOUSINE SERVICE
24 hours   718/430-6482

A good choice! Steve Betancourt provides responsible, efficient service at reasonable prices. I can personally vouch that his reputation for reliability is well earned.

Casting

SCULPTURE HOUSE CASTING
155 W 26th St (bet Ave of the Americas and Seventh Ave)
Mon-Fri: 8-5 (Sat by appointment)   212/645-9430, 888/374-8665
www.sculptshop.com

Sculpture House has been a family-owned business since 1918, making it one of the city's oldest casting firms. It is a full-service casting foundry, specializing in classical plaster reproductions, mold-making, and casting in all mediums and sizes. Ornamental plastering is available, and sculpting tools and supplies are sold here.

Chair Caning

VETERAN'S CHAIR CANING AND REPAIR SHOP
442 Tenth Ave (bet 34th and 35th St)   212/564-4560
Mon-Thurs: 7:30-4:30; Fri: 7:30-4; Sat: 8-1 www.veteranscaning.com

John Bausert, a third-generation chair caner, has written a book about his craft. His prices and craftsmanship are among the best in town. Bausert believes in passing along his knowledge and encourages customers to repair their own chairs. The procedure is outlined in Bausert's book, and necessary materials are sold in the shop. If you don't want to try it yourself, Veteran's will repair your chair. For a charge, they'll even pick it up from your home. In addition to caning, Veteran's stocks materials for fixing chairs and furniture, repairs, wicker, and repairs and reglues wooden chairs.

China and Glassware Repair

GLASS RESTORATIONS
1597 York Ave (bet 84th and 85th St)　　　　　212/517-3287
Mon-Fri: 9:30-5

Did you chip your prize Lalique glass treasure? These folks can restore all manner of crystal, including pieces by Steuben, Baccarat, Daum, and Waterford, as well as antique art glass. Glass Restoration is a find, as too few quality restorers are left in the country. Ask for Gus Jochec!

Vance (33 E 33rd St, 4th floor, 212/935-4040, www.vanceglobal. com) is a name you may want to jot down. These reliable folks do a number of important jobs: investigations, security consulting, crisis management, personal and property safety, security for all kinds of events, labor unrest protection, litigation strategy, travel risk planning, and much more.

Clock and Watch Repair

FANELLI ANTIQUE TIMEPIECES
790 Madison Ave (bet 66th and 67th St), Suite 202　　212/517-2300
Mon-Fri: 10-6; Sat: 11-5

In a beautiful clock gallery, Cindy Fanelli specializes in the care of high-quality "investment-type" timepieces, especially carriage clocks. Her store has one of the nation's largest collections of rare and unusual Early American grandfather clocks and vintage wristwatches. They do sales and restoration, make house calls, give free estimates, rent timepieces, and purchase single pieces or entire collections.

J&P TIMEPIECES
1057 Second Ave (at 56th St)　　　　　　　　212/980-1099
Mon-Fri: 10-5; Sat: 11-4　　　　　　　　　www.jptimepieces.com

In Europe, fine-watch repairing is a family tradition, but this craft is slowly being forgotten in our country. Fortunately for Manhattan, the Fossners have passed along this talent from father to son for four generations. You can be confident in their work on any kind of mechanical watch. They guarantee repairs for six months and will generally turn around jobs within ten days.

SUTTON CLOCK SHOP
139 E 61st St (at Lexington Ave)　　　　　　　212/758-2260
Tues-Fri: 11-4 (call ahead)

Sutton's forte is selling and acquiring unusual timepieces, but they are equally interested in the maintenance and repair of antique clocks. Some of the timepieces they sell—even the contemporary ones—are truly outstanding, and numerous satisfied customers endorse their repair work. They sell and repair barometers as well. Sutton's will even make house calls.

TIME PIECES REPAIRED
115 Greenwich Ave (at 13th St)   212/929-8011
Tues-Fri: 10:30-6:30; Sat: 9-5; Mon: by appointment
www.timepiecesrepaired.com

Grace Szuwala services, restores, repairs, and sells antique timepieces. Her European training has made her a recognized expert on antique watches and clocks. She has a strong sensitivity for pieces that have more sentimental than real value. She has been doing business on Greenwich Avenue since 1978.

Clothing Repair

FRENCH-AMERICAN REWEAVING COMPANY
119 W 57th St (bet Ave of the Americas and Seventh Ave), Room 1406
Mon-Fri: 10:30-5:30; Sat: 11-2   212/765-4670

Has a tear, burn, or stain ruined your favorite outfit? These folks will work on almost any garment for men or women in nearly every fabric. Often a damaged item will look just like new!

Computer Service and Instruction

ABC COMPUTER SERVICES
375 Fifth Ave (bet 35th and 36th St), 2nd floor   212/725-3511
Mon-Fri: 9-5   www.abccomputerservices.com

ABC Computer provides sales, service, and supplies for desktop and notebook computers, as well as all kinds of printers. They'll work on Apple, Microsoft, and Novell-based systems, and they are an authorized Hewlett-Packard service center. Computer instruction is offered in your home or office. They have been around for well over a decade, which is a good recommendation in itself.

For computer rentals, try **Business Equipment Rental** (250 W 49th St, 212/582-2020). Prices are reasonable; pickup and delivery are available. These are the best shops in town for computer repair:
Data Vision (445 Fifth Ave, 212/689-1111)
Machattan (175 Fifth Ave, 212/242-9393): Macs only
RCS Computer Experience (575 Madison Ave, 212/949-6935)

ONSITEIN60.COM
990 Ave of the Americas, (bet 36th and 37th St), Suite 8G
Mon-Fri: 7 a.m.-11 p.m.; Sun: 11-5   646/827-9578
www.onsitein60.com

This organization provides special information technology (IT) services for the dental, financial, health care, legal, media, design, and nonprofit sectors. It is staffed with several dozen highly talented computer geeks. Call and they will arrive in short order and do good work. They speak Spanish, Korean, Hebrew, Russian, and Polish, not to mention English!

TEKSERVE
119 W 23rd St (bet Ave of the Americas and Seventh Ave)
Mon-Fri: 9-7; Sat: 10-6; Sun: noon-6   212/929-3645
www.tekserve.com

For Apple Computer sales and service, you can't do better than this outfit. Tekserve carries a huge inventory of computers and peripherals, and the firm is noted for excellent customer care. A full range of services, including data recovery, is available. They also sell iPods and accessories and will replace batteries while you wait.

WEB2ZONE: CYBER CENTER
54 Cooper Square (at Astor Place)   212/614-7300
Mon-Fri: 9 a.m.–midnight; Sat: 10 a.m.–midnight;
Sun: noon-10 (hours may vary)   www.web2zone.com

Web2Zone has been named one of the best cyber centers in the nation, and with good reason. You'll find high-speed Internet access; a laptop area; PC and iMac stations; faxing, copying, and CD burning; a tech-repair component; scanning facilities; and game-zone PCs and consoles (xBox and PS3). Prices are reasonable, the personnel are knowledgeable, and the atmosphere is clean and pleasant. Located in the East Village, this popular cyber center is owned by Samsung. Birthday parties are big in the game-zone area!

Delivery, Courier, Messenger Services

AVANT BUSINESS SERVICES
60 E 42nd St (bet Park and Madison Ave)   212/687-5145
Daily: 24 hours   www.avantservices.com

Even before the big guys got in the business, this outfit was doing round-the-clock local and long-distance deliveries. If you have time-sensitive material, give them a call. They'll promptly pick up your item, even in the middle of the night or during a snowstorm. There are several branches throughout the city.

KANGAROO COURIER
153 W 27th St (bet Ave of the Americas and Seventh Ave), 1st floor
Daily: 24 hours   212/989-1919
                                          www.needitnowcourier.com

Kangaroo is set up to provide any and all courier services. They can handle everything from a crosstown rush letter (delivery completed within an hour) to delivering nearly anything worldwide.

Doll Repair

NEW YORK DOLL HOSPITAL
787 Lexington Ave (bet 61st and 62nd St), 2nd floor   212/838-7527
Mon-Sat: 10-6

New York Doll Hospital has been restoring dolls to health since 1900. Owner Irving Chais has operated in this cramped two-room "hospital" since 1947. That was the year he took over from his father, who had begun fixing dolls for his clients' children in his hair salon. Chais has replaced antique fingers, reconstructed china heads and German rag dolls, and authentically restored antique dolls. Additional services include appraisals, made-to-order dolls, and buying and selling antique dolls and toys. Chais will also work on teddy bears and other stuffed animals. He can even fix talking dolls that have computer chips!

Dry Cleaners, Laundries

CLEANTEX
2335 Twelfth Ave (at 133rd St)   212/283-1200
Mon-Fri: 8-4

In business since 1928, Cleantex specializes in cleaning draperies, furniture, balloon and Roman shades, vertical blinds, and Oriental and area rugs. They provide free estimates, pickup, and delivery. Museums, churches, and rug dealers are among their satisfied clients.

> For years I searched Manhattan for a dry cleaner and tailor shop that are open on Sunday. In emergencies, these two services may be necessary before facing a new week. Finally, I ran across **Reliable Laundromat** (47 Clinton St, 212/598-0381) and **Orchard Tailor Services** (145 Orchard St, at Rivington St, 212/228-0429). Both are open seven days a week from 9 a.m. to 7 p.m.

HALLAK CLEANERS
1232 Second Ave (at 65th St)   212/879-4694
Mon-Fri: 7-6:30; Sat: 8-3   www.hallak.com

Hallak has been a family business for four decades. Joseph Hallak, Sr., a native of France, instilled his work ethic and dedication to detail into sons John-Claude and Joseph, Jr. This no doubt accounts for the pride and personal service they offer customers. Much of their work comes from referrals by such famed boutiques as Armani and Ferragamo. Hallak does all work in their state-of-the-art plant. They will clean shirts, linens, suede, leather, and draperies. Their specialties are museum-quality cleaning and preservation of wedding gowns and a unique couture handbag cleaning service. For those (like your author) who have trouble with stains on ties, Hallak is the place to go. Their skilled work takes time, though rush service is available at no additional cost, and they serve clients throughout the U.S. via FedEx and UPS.

> It is not necessary to pay big bucks for good alterations. Try Hong Kong-trained Angela Gong at **G-G Cleaners** (30 Grand St, 212/966-9813). Her work is professional, and the price is right! This specialty tailor is legendary among fashion editors and boutique owners.

LEATHERCRAFT PROCESS OF AMERICA
Cameo Cleaners (dropoff site)
284 Third Ave (at 22nd St)   212/564-8980, 800/845-6155
Mon-Fri: 8-5   www.leathercraftprocess.com

Leathercraft will clean, re-dye, re-line, repair, and lengthen or shorten any suede or leather garment. That includes boots, gloves, clothing, and handbags, as well as odd leather items. Because leather is extremely difficult to clean, the process can be painfully expensive. However, Leathercraft has a reputation dating back to 1938, and their prices remain competitive. You can drop off items at Cameo Cleaners or call to arrange shipping to Leathercraft's facility in New Jersey.

MADAME PAULETTE CUSTOM COUTURE CLEANERS
1255 Second Ave (bet 65th and 66th St)
Mon-Fri: 7:30-7; Sat: 8-5   212/838-6827, 877/COUTURE

Reebok Sports Club NY, 160 Columbus Ave (at 67th St)
Mon-Fri: 8-8; Sat, Sun: 8-5   212/501-1408
www.madamepaulette.com

What a clientele: Christian Dior, Vera Wang, Chanel, Givenchy, Saks, Burberry, and Henri Bendel. This full-service establishment has been in business for nearly 50 years. They do dry cleaning (including knits, suedes, and leathers), tailoring (including reweaving and alterations), laundry, and household and rug cleaning. They provide seasonal storage of furs. Taking care of wedding dresses is a specialty, and they do superior hand-cleaning of cashmere, making sure that each item's shape is maintained. Their experts can repair garments damaged by water, bleach, and fire; do wet cleaning; and hand-clean upholstery and tapestry. Madame Paulette offers free pickup and delivery throughout Manhattan, and will set up charge accounts. One-day service is available upon request.

> When you need a really good dry cleaner, try **Chris French Cleaners** (57 Fourth Ave, 212/475-5444) in the East Village. There is none better!

MEURICE GARMENT CARE
31 University Pl (bet 8th and 9th St)   212/475-2778
Mon-Fri: 7:30-6 (Wed till 7); Sat: 9-6; Sun: 10-3

245 E 57th St (bet Second and Third Ave)   212/759-9057
Mon-Fri: 7:30-6; Sat: 9-6   www.garmentcare.com

Meurice specializes in cleaning and restoring fine garments. They handle each piece individually, taking care of details like loose buttons and tears. Special services include exquisite hand-finishing; expert stain removal; museum-quality preservation; cleaning and restoration of wedding gowns; careful handling of ultra fragile and chemically sensitive garments; on-site leather cleaning and repairs; and smoke, fire, and water restoration. Delivery and shipping are available.

MIDNIGHT EXPRESS CLEANERS
Mon-Fri: 5 a.m.-8 p.m.; Sat: 7-1   718/392-9200
www.midnightexpressny.com

Midnight Express does dry cleaning, shirt laundering, leather and suede cleaning and repair, and bulk laundering. Best of all, they will pick up and deliver. Prompt return is assured. They specialize in dry-cleaning restoration of smoke, fire, and water-damaged goods. This is Manhattan's only OSHA-compliant laundry service for bloodborne pathogen and hazard communication standards. Be sure to keep their number handy!

NEW YORK'S FINEST FRENCH CLEANERS & TAILORS
154 Reade St (bet Hudson and Greenwich St)   212/431-4010
Mon-Fri: 7-7; Sat: 8-5

There are new owners at this quality business, which features pickup, delivery, and one-day service. Tailoring and storage are available, as is care for fine silks and leathers.

TIECRAFTERS
252 W 29th St (bet Seventh and Eighth Ave)   212/629-5800
Mon-Fri: 9-5   www.tiecrafters.com

Old ties never fade away at Tiecrafters. Instead, they're dyed, widened, narrowed, straightened, and cleaned. They believe that a well-made tie can live forever, and they provide services to make longevity possible. In addition to converting tie widths, they restore soiled or stained ties and clean and repair all kinds of neckwear. Owner Andy Tarshis will give pointers on tie maintenance. (Hint: if you hang a tie at night, wrinkles will be gone by morning.) Tiecrafters offers several pamphlets on the subject, including one that tells how to remove spots at home. Their cleaning charge is reasonable, and they also make custom neckwear, bow ties, braces, scarves, vests, and cummerbunds.

> At **Knit New York** (307 E 14th St, 212/387-0707, www.knitnewyork.com), you can enjoy stitching, chatting, and first-rate instruction.

VILLAGE TAILOR & CLEANERS
125 Sullivan St (at Prince St)   212/925-9667
Mon-Fri: 7-7; Sat: 8-6   www.villagetailor.com

They have been in business since the early 1930s! Located in the heart of Soho, Village Tailor specializes in custom-making men's and ladies apparel, including leather and suede garments, and performing alterations. Wash-and-fold shirt service is also available, as is same-day turnaround,

> No one likes garments that reek of smoke. **Fashion Award Cleaners** (2205 Broadway, 212/289-5623, www.fashionaward.com) will leave your clothes smelling like new! (Hours: Mon-Fri: 7:30-6:30; Sat: 8-4)

Electricians

ALTMAN ELECTRIC
283 W 11th St (at Bleecker St)   212/924-0400, 800/287-7774
Daily: 24 hours   www.altmanelectric.com

The licensed crew at this reliable outfit is available day and night. They will do small or large jobs at home or office, and rates are reasonable. Altman has been in business for over half a century.

Electronics Repair

PORTATRONICS
385 Fifth Ave (bet 35th and 36th St)   646/797-2838
Mon-Sat: 11-7   www.portatronics.com

Portatronics provides on-the-spot repair of iPods, PSP, Creative labs, Dell, Archos, and more. Their work on portable electronics (not including laptops) is done while the customer waits. You'll find replacement hard drives, LDS screens, motherboards, headphone jacks, and scroll wheels.

Embroidery

JONATHAN EMBROIDERY PLUS

256 W 38th St (bet Seventh and Eighth Ave) 212/398-3538
Mon-Fri: 8:30-6:30 www.jeplus.com

Any kind of custom embroidery work can be done at this classy workshop. Bring a photo or sketch, or just give them an idea, and they will produce a design that you can then amend or approve.

Where to Get Things Fixed
Ceramics: **Ceramic Restorations** (224 W 29th St, 12th floor, 212/564-8669; by appointment)
Clocks: **Sid Shapiro** (212/925-1994)
Furniture: **Joseph Biunno** (129 W 29th St, 212/629-5630)
Glassware: **Glass Restorations** (1597 York Ave, 212/517-3287)
Jewelry: **Murrey's Jewelers** (1395 Third Ave, 212/879-3690)
Leather: **Falotico Studio** (315 E 91st St, 212/369-1217)
Silver: **Thome Silversmiths** (49 W 37th St, 212/764-5426; by appointment)

Exterminators

ACME EXTERMINATING

460 Ninth Ave (bet 35th and 36th St) 212/594-9230
Mon-Fri: 9-5 www.acmeexterminating.com

Acme is expert at debugging homes, offices, stores, museums, and hospitals. They employ state-of-the-art integrated pest-management technology.

Fashion Schools

FASHION INSTITUTE OF TECHNOLOGY

Seventh Ave at 27th St 212/217-7675 (admissions)
212/217-7999 (general information)
www.fitnyc.edu

The Fashion Institute of Technology (FIT), a branch of the State University of New York, is the fashion industry's premier educational institution. The school was founded more than 60 years ago. Its graduate roster reads like a "who's who" of the fashion world, including Jhane Barnes, Calvin Klein, and Norma Kamali. The school offers associate's, bachelor's, and master's degrees in a multitude of majors including advertising and marketing, illustration, photography, fine arts, fashion merchandising, management, direct marketing, production management, patternmaking, jewelry, textile, and toy design. FIT maintains a student placement service; all students are top-caliber. The **Museum at FIT** is the world's largest repository of fashion, with over a million articles of clothing. Call 212/217-5800 for information about exhibits and shows.

Formal Wear

A.T. HARRIS FORMALWEAR
11 E 44th St (bet Madison and Fifth Ave), 2nd floor   212/682-6325
Mon-Fri: 9-6 (Thurs till 7)   www.atharris.com
Sat: 10-5 (by appointment)

Ten U.S. presidents have been fitted for formal attire at this store! A.T. Harris has been in business since 1892, selling and renting formal wear of the highest quality. You will find cutaways, tails, tuxedos, shoes, top hats, stud and cuff-link sets, and kid and suede gloves.

BALDWIN FORMALS
1156 Ave of the Americas (at 45th St), 2nd floor
Mon-Fri: 9-7; Sat: 10-5   212/245-8190, 800/427-0072
                     www.nyctuxedos.com

If you are invited to some upscale function, Baldwin can take care of the dressing details. They rent and sell all types of formal attire: suits, overcoats, top hats, shoes, and more. They will pick up and deliver for free in midtown and for a slight charge to other addresses. Same-day service is guaranteed for rental orders received by early afternoon. Rapid alteration service (from two hours to several days) is available for an additional charge.

Funeral Service

FRANK E. CAMPBELL FUNERAL CHAPEL
1076 Madison Ave (at 81st St)   212/288-3500
Daily: 24 hours   www.frankecampbell.com

In time of need, it is good to know of a highly professional funeral home. These folks have been providing superior service since 1898.

Furniture Rental

CHURCHILL CORPORATE SERVICES
245 W 17th St (bet Seventh and Eighth Ave)
Mon-Thurs: 9-6; Fri: 9-5; Sun: 11-5   212/686-0444, 800/658-7366
                   www.furnishedhousing.com

Churchill carries both traditional and starkly contemporary furniture. They can furnish any size business or residence, and they offer free interior-decorating advice. A customer can select what is needed from stock or borrow from the loaner program until special orders are processed. Churchill also offers a comprehensive package, including housewares and appliances. They specialize in executive relocations and will rent anything from a single chair to furnishings for an entire home. Churchill offers corporate apartments and housing on short- or long-term bases. Their clients include sports managers, executives on temporary assignment, and actors on short-term contracts.

CORT FURNITURE RENTAL
711 Third Ave (bet 44th and 45th St)   212/867-2800
Mon-Fri: 9-6; Sat: 10-5   www.cort.com

Cort rents furnishings for a single room, entire apartment, or office. They show accessories as well. All furnishings (including electronics and housewares) are available for rental with an option to purchase. An apartment

The personnel inside of what was once a modest neighborhood barbershop give some of New York's trendiest and most far-out haircuts. It all started when the Vezza brothers inherited a barbershop from their father in the East Village at a time when "not even cops were getting haircuts." Enrico took note of the newly gentrified neighborhood's young trendies and their sleek haircuts and changed the name of the shop to "Astor Place Hair Stylists." Now, the shop is staffed with a resident manager, a doorman, and 50 barbers.

ATLAS BARBER SCHOOL
34 Third Ave (bet 9th and 10th St)   212/475-1360
Mon-Fri: 9-7:45; Sat: 9-5:45

Atlas Barber School teaches general barbering and shaving techniques. They've been at it since 1949. High style it isn't; great value it is!

FEATURE TRIM
1108 Lexington Ave (bet 77th and 78th St)   212/650-9746
Mon-Fri: 10-7; Sat: 10-6

This neighborhood establishment maintains its standard of basic hair care for men, women, and children. Low maintenance is the key to Feature Trim's haircuts. Easy care, reasonable prices, friendly faces, and more than 50 years of experience keep an impressive clientele. Appointments are encouraged, but walk-ins are welcome.

PAUL MOLE FAMILY BARBERSHOP
1031 Lexington Ave (at 74th St)   212/535-8461
Mon-Fri: 7:30-6:30; Sat: 7:30-5:30; Sun: 9-3:30   www.paulmole.com

As the name says, this is a family business. They will trim the heads of both dad and the kids, with customer-friendly hours and pocketbook-friendly prices. The place is packed after school and on weekends, so appointments are suggested.

Kevin Coulthard (917/515-8039) is a top massage therapist and personal trainer.

Health and Fitness Clubs

I have listed the most popular and esablished health clubs in Manhattan. Note that special membership offers appear regularly in local newspapers. For out-of-town visitors, reciprocal memberships are available at some clubs, and one- or two-day passes may be obtained. Most Manhattan hotels have some kind of fitness equipment. Don't be afraid to check out a location to see if staff, cleanliness, and equipment meet your needs.

New York's Best Health and Fitness Clubs

Bally Sports Club and **Bally Total Fitness** (multiple locations, 800/515-2582, www.ballyfitness.com)
Clay (25 W 14th St, bet Fifth Ave and Ave of the Americas, 212/206-9200): concierge service

Crunch (multiple locations, 888/310-6011, www.crunch.com)
David Barton (215 W 23rd St, at Seventh Ave, 212/414-2022 and 30 E 85th St, bet Fifth and Madison Ave, 212/517-7577)
Dolphin Fitness (18 Ave B, 212/777-1001 and 94 E 4th St, 212/387-9500)
Equinox Fitness Clubs (multiple locations, 212/799-1818, www.equinox fitness.com)
Hanson Fitness (multiple locations, 212/431-7682, www.hansonfitness. com)
Manhattan Plaza Health Club (482 W 43rd St, at Tenth Ave, 212/563-7001)
New York Health & Racquet Club (multiple locations, 800/472-2378, www.nyhrc.com)
New York Sports Club (multiple locations, 800/666-0808, www.ny sportsclubs.com)
Paris Health Club (752 West End Ave, bet 96th and 97th St, 212/749-3500)
Printing House Fitness & Racquet Club (421 Hudson St, at Leroy St, 212/243-7600)
Reebok Sports Club NY (160 Columbus Ave, at 67th St, 212/362-6800)
Sports Center at Chelsea Piers (Pier 60, 12th Ave at Hudson River, 212/336-6000)
Sports Club LA (330 E 61st St, bet First and Second Ave, 212/355-5100 and 45 Rockefeller Plaza, bet 50th and 51st St, 212/218-8600)

Clubs with Child Care

Crunch (some locations, www.crunch.com)
Equinox Fitness Clubs: (all locations, www.equinoxfitness.com)
New York Health & Racquet Club (all locations, www.nyhrc.com)
Paris Health Club (752 West End Ave bet 96th and 97th St, 212/749-3500)
Sports Club LA (330 E 61st St, 212/355-5100)

Health and Fitness Specialties

Personal Trainers
Bodysmith (212/249-1824): women only
Casa Specialized Private Fitness (Loews Regency, 212/223-9280)
Christa Bache (646/279-5926)
Jean Pierre Cusin (917/539-7813)
Joe Massiello (212/319-3816)
La Palestra Center for Preventative Medicine (212/799-8900)
Madison Square Club (212/683-1836)
Mike Creamer (Anatomically Correct, 212/353-8834)
Nathaniel Oliver (917/867-0606)
Sal Anthony's Movement Salon (190 Third Ave, bet 17th and 18th St, 212/420-7242, www.movementsalon.com): a real exercise salon; pay by the class or service for training, Pilates, massage, yoga
Salvatore Fichera (212/687-1646, www.forzafitness.com): consultant-trainer with two decades of experience; one of the very best
Shelby Grayson (212/362-3543): clinical exercise
Sitaras Fitness (212/702-9700)

Pilates
Alycea Ungaro (Real Pilates, 177 Duane St, 212/625-0777)
RE:AB (33 Bleecker St, Suite 2C, 212/420-9111)
Power Pilates (multiple locations, 212/627-5852)
Soho Sanctuary (119 Mercer St, 212/334-5550)

Prenatal
Maternal Massage and More (73 Spring St, 212/533-3188): pre- and post-natal, labor, and with baby, too !
Patricia Durbin-Ruiz (646/643-8369): pre- and post-natal
Physique 57 (24 W 57th St, Suite 805, 212/399-0570): prenatal workout system

Registered male nurse and masseur
John Percik (212/924-7684)

Spinning
SoulCycle (117 W 72nd St, 212/787-1300): studio for spinning only

Yoga
Ashtanga Yoga Research Institute (430 Broome St, 212/431-3738, www.ayny.org)
Bikram Yoga (multiple locations, 212/245-2525)
Centerpoint Yoga Studio (324 Lafayette St, 212/925-4789)
Chopra Center and Spa (Dream Hotel, 1710 Broadway, 212/246-7600)
Integral Yoga Institute (227 W 13th St, 212/929-0585)
Integral Yoga Uptown Center (200 W 72nd St, 212/721-4000)
Jivamukti Yoga Center (841 Broadway, 2nd floor, 212/353-0214 and 853 Lexington Ave, 2nd floor, 646/290-8106)
Laughing Lotus (59 W 19th St, 3rd floor, 212/414-2903)
Om Yoga (826 Broadway, 6th floor, 212/254-9642)

Hotels

The hotel scene in Manhattan has changed drastically in the past several years. Fewer rooms are available because of high building costs and the conversion of properties to condos and apartments. With greater demand due to increased foreign and domestic travel, room prices have rapidly increased. The average nightly room is now around $250, and occupancy rates range from 80% to 90%—even higher in peak holiday periods.

Legendary larger hotels like the Plaza and St. Regis New York have converted hotel rooms to pricey private suites that are selling for as much as $5 to $8 million. Less expensive rooms are in great demand, and a number of older buildings have been converted. Branded chain hotels have sprung up all around town, providing comfortable (but not luxury) accommodations. Fitness centers, business accommodations, and spas are the norm for newer and more modernized properties. Some of the pricier hotels still have their top-name chefs and restaurants, many with sky-high pricing.

The Lower Manhattan area is the fastest-growing market for new rooms, with at least a dozen properties in one stage or another of development. Luxury developments include a new **W Hotel** (123 Washington Street) and a boutique hotel at 75 Wall Street. If all present plans proceed, the area will increase by about a thousand rooms to nearly 3,500. With more young people traveling on business and more women seeking accommodations on their own, livelier venues and modern amenities are very much in demand.

The good news is that you still have lots of choices when you're looking for a place to stay. There are family-friendly suites, great little boutique hotels in neighborhoods both uptown and downtown, and a couple "only in New York" grande dames like The Waldorf-Astoria. What you won't find are a lot of bargains (although I've included the few that do exist in these pages!).

My advice is to think about what part of town you want to stay in, look through this section to get some ideas, and then go to www.tripadvisor.com or similar sites to see what people are saying about various hotels. I also suggest making your plans early, particularly for summer travel or between Thanksgiving and New Year's.

Don't say I didn't warn you about outrageous phone costs when you use hotel-room phones! Here is a sampling from one of the better New York hotels.

Local calls: $1.50, plus 15 cents per minute after the first 5 minutes

Interstate (USA) long distance calls: Operator assisted-day rates, plus $4 hotel surcharge, plus 12.5%

International calls: Operator-assisted day rates, plus $8.70 hotel surcharge, plus 60%

Directory assistance: $2.50 per call

See what I mean? Remember to bring your cell phone or use a calling card.

Special Hotel Classifications

Extended Stays

If you are planning to be in Manhattan for awhile, check out these extended-stay facilities. Some require a 30-day minimum stay. Amenities may include kitchens, daily maid service, fitness facilities, laundry facilities, business centers, and planned activities.

Bristol Plaza (210 E 65th St, 212/753-7900)

59th Street Bridge Apartments (351 E 60th St, 212/754-9388)

Phillips Club (155 W 66th St, 212/835-8800)

Residence Inn New York Manhattan (Times Square, 1033 Ave of the Amercas, 212/938-0180)

Webster Apartments (419 W 34th St, 212/267-9000): women only

Hostels

Big Apple Hostel (119 W 45th St, 212/302-2603, www.bigapplehostel. com): midtown location, dorms and private rooms, reservations made online

Central Park Hostel (19 W 103rd St, 212/678-0491): dorm-style rooms with shared baths ($26 and up), lockers, private rooms ($85 and up)

Chelsea International Hostel (251 W 20th St, 212/647-0010): dormitory rooms ($30 and up) and private rooms ($70 and up)

Chelsea Star Hostel (300 W 30th St, 212/244-7827): hotel ($89 and up) and hostel ($35 and up)

Hostelling International New York (891 Amsterdam Ave, 212/932-2300, www.hinewyork.org): one of the world's largest; prices start at $30

Times Square Beds and Rooms (356 W 40th St, 2nd floor, 212/216-0642): dorms and private rooms with shared baths and lockers

---

New York Hotels with Exceptional Swimming Pools

Crowne Plaza Times Square Manhattan (1605 Broadway, 212/977-4000): 15th-floor pool open to guests and non-guests

Hotel Gansevoort (18 Ninth Ave, 212/206-6700): in the Meatpacking District, with a heated outdoor glass-enclosed pool and great views

Hotel QT (125 W 45th St, 212/354-2323): in Times Square, a lobby pool with underwater music

Le Parker Meridien (118 W 57th St, 212/245-5000): penthouse pool with sundeck; non-guests may purchase user passes

Mandarin Oriental (80 Columbus Circle, 212/805-8800): an indoor 75-foot lap pool in a dramatic setting on the 35th floor with floor-to-ceiling windows

Melrose Hotel (140 E 63rd St, 212/838-5700): access to on-site Equinox Fitness Center pool

Millennium U.N. Plaza Hotel (1 United Nations Plaza, 212/758-1234): heated indoor pool, plus an indoor tennis court

Peninsula New York (700 Fifth Ave, 212/956-2888): luxurious facility with poolside lunch; non-guests may purchase user passes

Skyline Hotel (725 Tenth Ave, 212/586-3400): heated indoor pool

Trump International Hotel & Tower (1 Central Park W, 888/448-7867): 55-foot lap pool

---

Inexpensive

Affinia Dumont (150 E 34th St, 212/481-7600)
Bedford Hotel (118 E 40th St, 212/697-4800)
Belvedere (319 W 48th St, 212/245-7000)
Best Western Seaport Inn Downtown (33 Peck Slip, 212/766-6600)
Carlton Arms (160 E 25th St, 212/679-0680)
Chelsea Hotel (222 West 23rd St, 212/243-3700)
Doubletree Metropolitan (569 Lexington Ave, 212/752-7000)
Eastgate Tower (222 E 39th St, 212/687-8000)
Excelsior Hotel (45 W 81st St, 212/362-9200)
414 Hotel (414 W 46th St, 212/399-0006)
Gershwin Hotel (7 E 27th St, 212/545-8000)
Holiday Inn Express (232 W 29th St, 212/695-7200)
Holiday Inn Soho (138 Lafayette St, 212/966-8898)
Hotel Edison (228 W 47th St, 212/840-5000)
Hotel 57 (130 E 57th St, 212/753-8841)
Hotel Grand Union (34 E 32nd St, 212/683-5890)
Hotel Metro (45 W 35th St, 212/947-2500)
Hotel Newton (2528 Broadway, 212/678-6500)
Hotel QT (125 W 45th St, 212/354-2323)
Hotel Roger Williams (131 Madison Ave, 212/448-7000)
Hotel Stanford (43 W 32nd St, 212/563-1500)

Hotel 31 (120 E 31st St, 212/685-3060)
Hotel Thirty-Thirty (30 E 30th St, 212/689-1900)
Hudson Hotel (356 W 58th St, 212/554-6000)
LaQuinta Manhattan Midtown (17 W 32nd St, 212/736-1600)
Larchmont (27 W 11th St, 212/989-9333)
Manhattan Broadway Hotel (273 W 38th St, 212/921-9791)
Milburn Hotel (242 W 76th St, 212/362-1006)
Milford Plaza (270 W 45th St, 212/869-3600)
Millennium UN Plaza Hotel (1 United Nations Plaza, 212/758-1234)
Murray Hill Inn (143 E 30th St, 212/545-0879)
New Yorker, a Ramada Inn Hotel (481 Eighth Ave, 212/971-0101)
Off Soho Suites (11 Rivington St, 212/353-0860)
On the Avenue Hotel (2178 Broadway, 212/362-1100)
Park Central New York (870 Seventh Ave, 212/247-8000)
Park South Hotel (122 E 28th St, 212/448-0888)
Portland Square Hotel (132 W 47th St, 212/382-0600)
Ramada Inn Eastside (161 Lexington Ave, 212/545-1800)
Super 8 Times Square (59 W 46th St, 212/719-2300)
The Time (224 W 49th St, 212/246-5252)
Union Square Inn (209 E 14th St, 212/614-0500)
Washington Jefferson Hotel (318 W 51st St, 212/246-7550)
Washington Square Hotel (103 Waverly Pl, 212/777-9515)
Westside Inn (237 W 107th St, 212/866-0061)
Wolcott Hotel (4 W 31st St, 212/268-2900)

Chic on the Lower East Side!
The **Blue Moon Hotel** (100 Orchard St, 212/533-9080, www.bluemoon-nyc.com) offers unusual artifacts, wet bars, whirlpools, 22 large rooms (320 sq. ft), complimentary breakfast, kosher restaurant, classy bathroom amenities, and in-room refrigerators. Prices are moderate, considering current Manhattan rates.

Hotels Near Airports

The following are conveniently located, provide airport transportation, have restaurants, and are reasonably priced (ask for corporate rates). Some have recreational facilities, such as fitness rooms and pools.

John F. Kennedy International: **Anchor Motor Inn** (66 rooms, Bayside, Queens, 718/428-8000), **Courtyard by Marriott** (166 rooms, Jamaica, Queens, 718/848-2121), **Crowne Plaza JFK** (184 rooms, Jamaica, Queens, 718/489-1000), **Doubletree** (386 rooms, Jamaica, Queens, 718/322-2300), **Golden Gate Motor Inn** (150 rooms, Brooklyn, 718/743-4000), **Hampton Inn** (216 Rooms, Jamaica, Queens, 718/322-7500), **Holiday Inn** (360 rooms, Jamaica, Queens, 718/659-0200), and **Ramada Plaza Hotel-JFK** (478 rooms, Jamaica, Queens, 718/995-9000)

LaGuardia: **Best Western City View Inn** (71 rooms, Long Island City, 718/392-8400), **Clarion Hotel at LaGuardia** (170 rooms, East Elmhurst, Queens, 718/335-1200), **Comfort Inn** (50 rooms, Flushing,

Queens, 718/939-5000), **Courtyard by Marriott** (288 rooms, East Elmhurst, Queens, 718/446-4800), **Crowne Plaza New York-LaGuardia** (358 rooms, East Elmhurst, Queens, 718/457-6300), **Marriott LaGuardia Airport** (437 rooms, East Elmhurst, Queens, 718/565-8900), **Sheraton LaGuardia East** (173 rooms, Flushing, Queens, 718/460-6666), and **Wyndham Garden Hotel** (229 rooms, East Elmhurst, Queens, 718/426-1500)

Newark International: **Four Points by Sheraton** (260 rooms, Elizabeth, NJ, 908/527-1600), **Hilton Newark Airport** (327 rooms, Elizabeth, NJ, 908/351-3900), **Hilton Newark Penn Station** (253 rooms, Newark, NJ, 973/622-5000), **Holiday Inn** (412 rooms, Newark, NJ, 973/589-1000), **Marriott Newark Liberty Airport** (591 rooms, Newark, NJ, 973/623-0006), **Ramada Newark Airport** (347 rooms, Newark, NJ, 973/824-4000), and **Sheraton Newark Airport** (504 rooms, Newark, NJ, 973/690-5500)

New Hotels in Manhattan
Bowery Hotel (212/505-1300): near Soho and the East Village
Duane Street Hotel (Luxe Hotel Group, 212/964-4600): Tribeca
Hotel Mela (212/710-7000): Times Square
Hotel 373 Fifth Avenue (888/261-3268): across from the Empire State Building
6 Columbus Circle (212/431-0400): Upper West Side

New York's Finest Hotels

Bearing in mind that this *is* New York, I have categorized hotels by nightly room tariff (without taxes) as follows:

- Inexpensive: $199 and under
- Moderate: $200 to $299
- Moderately Expensive: $300 to $399
- Expensive: $400 to $499
- Very Expensive: $500 and up

AFFINIA HOTELS

Affinia Dumont, 150 E 34th St (bet Third and Lexington Ave)	
	212/481-7600
Affinity Gardens, 215 E 64th St (bet Second and Third Ave)	
	212/355-1230
Affinia 50, 155 E 50th St (at Third Ave)	212/751-5710
Affinity Manhattan, 371 Seventh Ave (at 31st St)	212/563-1800
Beekman Tower, 3 Mitchell Pl (at 49th St)	212/355-7300
The Benjamin, 125 E 50th St (at Lexington Ave)	212/715-2500
Eastgate Tower, 222 E 39th St (bet Second and Third Ave)	
	212/687-8000
Shelburne Murray Hill, 303 Lexington Ave (at 37th St)	
	212/689-5200
Surrey Hotel, 20 E 76th St (bet Madison and Fifth Ave)	
	212/288-3700
Moderate to moderately expensive	www.affinia.com

These all-suites hotels are among the most reasonably priced and conveniently located in New York. Each features 24-hour attendants and modern kitchens. Over 2,000 suites in all—studio, junior, and one- or two-bedroom suites—are available at attractive daily, weekly, or monthly rates. These are particularly convenient for long-term corporate visitors and traveling families who can economize by having the kids sleep on pull-out couches and by using the fully equipped kitchens. Fitness centers are available at most properties. Food facilities vary. The famous **Cafe Boulud** is located at the Surrey. Women especially like these accommodations when traveling and dining alone.

ALEX HOTEL
205 E 45th St (at Third Ave)   212/867-5100
Moderately expensive to expensive   www.thealexhotel.com

The Alex is housed in a newly constructed 33-story tower, providing classy rooms and suites, plus all of the amenities you would expect from a member of the Leading Hotels of the World. Conveniences include flat-screen TVs, luxurious linens, a business center, DVD players, 24-hour room service, fully equipped kitchens in the suites, and spa availability. The on-site restaurant, **Riingo**, offers Japanese/American food; sushi is a specialty.

ALGONQUIN HOTEL
59 W 44th St (bet Fifth Ave and Ave of the Americas)
Moderately expensive   212/840-6800, 888/304-2047
                                                         www.algonquinhotel.com

The legendary Algonquin was designated a historic landmark by the city of New York in 1987. This home of the famous Roundtable—where Dorothy Parker, Alexander Woollcott, Harpo Marx, Tallulah Bankhead, Robert Benchley, and other literary wits sparred and dined regularly—now exudes the same charm and character as it did in the Roaring Twenties! There are 174 rooms, including 26 suites (some named after well-known personalities), and the atmosphere is intimate and friendly. The remodeled lobby is the best place in the city for people-watching, and the **Oak Room** is arguably the finest cabaret venue in New York.

✳CARLTON ON MADISON AVENUE *nice*
88 Madison Ave (at 29th St)   212/532-4100
Moderate to moderately expensive   www.carltonhotelnyc.com

Built in 1904 as the Seville Hotel, the Carlton has undergone a complete facelift to the tune of over $60 million. Its 316 rooms and suites—along with a dramatic three-story lobby, a lobby bar, and fine meeting facilities—blend modern comfort with historic preservation. For those doing business in the Madison Park, Gramercy Park, or Murray Hill neighborhoods, the Carlton is very conveniently located.

CASABLANCA
147 W 43rd St (bet Broadway and Ave of the Americas)
Moderate   212/869-1212, 888/922-7225
                                                         www.casablancahotel.com

Now that the Times Square area has been cleaned up, you might consider staying at Casablanca, an attractive, safe, and clean boutique hotel with a

Moroccan flavor. It's small (48 rooms and suites), newly renovated, and family-owned. It offers complimentary amenities and comfortable rates, and the atmosphere is friendly. Special attractions: free continental breakfast, passes to the New York Sports Club, free browsing on the lounge computer, and bottled water, iced tea, and chocolates in the rooms. High-speed wireless Internet access is available in all guest rooms. Best of all, you are right in the center of the action!

DREAM HOTEL
210 W 55th St (bet Broadway and Seventh Ave)   212/247-2000
Moderate   www.dreamny.com

If you're dreaming of a trendy, modern boutique hotel, then the Dream Hotel is for you. They offer pre-loaded iPods, luxurious sheets and bathrobes, and two restaurants (one Italian and one Mediterranean). The on-premises **Chopra Center and Spa** (1710 Broadway, 212/246-7600) is available for those who need relaxation and moments of meditation.

> For young folks, bargain hunters, and groups, **Broadway Hotel & Hostel** (230 W 101st St, 212/865-7710, www.broadwayhotelnyc.com) is a winner. Rates start at about $30 a night for dormitory-style rooms. The location on the Upper West Side is convenient. They have 300 beds (some private rooms, which are a bit more expensive), no curfews or lockouts, 24-hour security, high-speed Internet access, elevator, and daily housekeeping service. The rooms are comfortable and have been recently renovated.

FOUR SEASONS HOTEL NEW YORK
57 E 57th St (bet Madison and Park Ave)   212/758-5700
Expensive   www.fourseasons.com

In the hotel world, fewer names elicit higher praise or win more awards than Four Seasons. Upscale visitors to the Big Apple have an elegant, 52-story Four Seasons to make their home away from home. Designed by I. M. Pei and Frank Williams, the Four Seasons provides 364 oversized rooms and suites (some with terraces), and several fine eating places, including the top-notch **L'Atelier de Joël Robuchon** and a lobby lounge for light snacks and tea. There's also a fully equipped business center, complete with free-standing computer terminals and modem hookups; a $3.5 million, 6,000-square-foot fitness center and spa with all the latest equipment; and numerous meeting rooms. The principal appeal, however, is the size of certain guest rooms, which run to 600 square feet, offer spectacular views of the city, and feature luxurious marble bathrooms with separate dressing areas. A classy staff makes this another award-winning Four Seasons property. The penthouse suite (3,000 square feet) can be had for a whopping $35,000 a night, making it the most expensive hotel room in Manhattan.

GRAMERCY PARK HOTEL
2 Lexington Ave (bet 21st and 22nd St)   212/920-3300
Expensive   www.gramercyparkhotel.com

A key that will allow you to enter Gramercy Park is part of the package here! Ian Schrager has created a one-of-a-kind resting place that can best be described as anti-establishment. The Jazz Age look and many Jazz Age guests combine to make a stay here more fun than restful, although Old World luxury abounds. The Gramercy Park Hotel's 185 rooms are served by a capable, willing, and attractive staff. Artist-designer Julian Schnabel has provided a classy lobby, several watering holes, a spa, and a restaurant. This place is eclectic and eccentric—quite a combination!

HILTON NEW YORK
1335 Ave of the Americas (bet 53rd and 54th St)   212/586-7000
Moderate to moderately expensive www.newyorktowers.hilton.com

A popular business and convention hotel, the Hilton outfits its rooms with the most up-to-date communications equipment. Special features include an outstanding art collection, upscale executive floors with private lounge and large luxury suites, dozens of rooms equipped for the disabled, a highly trained international staff, and an 8,000-square-foot state-of-the-art fitness club and spa. For those leisure travelers interested in shopping, theater, Radio City Music Hall, and other midtown attractions, this location is highly desirable. The Hilton New York features two restaurants: **New York Marketplace**, an all-day dining facility, and **Etrusca**, an intimate Italian room featuring Tuscan foods and wines.

HOTEL GANSEVOORT
18 Ninth Ave (bet 13th and Gansevoort St)   212/206-6700
Moderate to moderately expensive   www.hotelgansevoort.com

A classy hotel in the Meatpacking District? Yes, Hotel Gansevoort is a 12-story beauty with dramatic outdoor lighting. Its 187 rooms offer many creature comforts but are not overdone. Ceilings are high, beds and linens are first-class, and many rooms have good views of the Hudson River. A top-floor lounge with a retractable glass roof is an exciting place to gather—and you'll find a swimming pool there, as well! A large Japanese restaurant, **Ono**, is an additional attraction, as is a new spa. Their G-Spa attracts many celebrities, some of whom arrive in a free luxury SUV available in the morning.

HOTEL QT
125 W 45th St (bet Ave of the Americas and Seventh Ave)
Moderate   212/380-2700
www.tablehotels.com

With 140 rooms and a handy location, this hotel is popular for those who don't want to spend a fortune yet enjoy chic surroundings and a full slate of amenities. This is a good bet for young people with a somewhat limited budget, as some rooms for four are available. You'll find DVDs, flat-screen TVs, a swimming pool with underwater music, a busy lobby lounge, sauna, and a complimentary breakfast (but no restaurant). You can say you stayed in a Manhattan penthouse at a really comfortable price!

HOTEL 17
225 E 17th St (bet Second and Third Ave)   212/475-2845
Inexpensive   www.hotel17ny.com

There's no luxury here, except for the luxury of low prices. Though the decor is haphazard, Hotel 17 is clean and comfortable enough to pass for an old-school tourist-class hotel. The area is relatively safe, and for those who don't care much about where they spend the night, this is a good place. The biggest drawback is shared bathrooms.

HOTEL WOLCOTT
4 W 31st St (bet Fifth Ave and Broadway)   212/268-2900
Inexpensive   www.wolcott.com

One of Manhattan's better hotel bargains, Hotel Wolcott offers a good location (just south of midtown), refurbished rooms with private baths, good security, direct-dial phones, TVs with in-room movies and videogames, and fitness and business centers. No wonder students, foreign travelers, and savvy business people are regular patrons!

HUDSON HOTEL
356 W 58th St (bet Eighth and Ninth Ave)   212/554-6000
Inexpensive to moderate   www.hudsonhotel.com

Hudson Hotel is an affordable hotel in an often unaffordable area. A lushly landscaped courtyard garden is open to the sky. You will find abundant amenities plus a reasonably priced restaurant and busy bars. There are 800 guest rooms with minimal decor and furniture, but given the reasonable prices you won't worry too much about that. There are some nice decorative touches, such as attractive wood paneling. The scene is the big thing here, especially the fabulous **Library Bar**.

JUMEIRAH ESSEX HOUSE
160 Central Park S (bet Ave of the Americas and Seventh Ave)
Moderately expensive to expensive   212/247-0300
                                   www.jumeirahessexhouse.com

With a superb location right on Central Park, a gracious and welcoming staff, and a recent $90 million renovation, the Jumeirah Essex House remains one of the prize resting places in Manhattan. The tastefully decorated rooms and suites are equipped with every modern facility. All-marble bathrooms add a classy flavor. The Lobby Lounge is a convenient place for cocktails or traditional afternoon tea. A health spa and a fully equipped club lounge with business center add to the attractions. The $10 million world class **Restaurant at the Essex House**, designed by Tony Chi, serves contemporary international cuisine, overlooks Central Park, and can be entered from the hotel lobby or from Central Park South. You'll love this place!

KIMBERLY HOTEL
145 E 50th St (bet Lexington and Third Ave)   212/755-0400
Moderate   www.kimberlyhotel.com

If big hotels turn you off, then the Kimberly may be just what you are looking for. This charming and hospitable boutique hotel in the center of Manhattan offers guests the kind of personal attention that is a rarity in today's commercial world. There are 192 luxury guest rooms, marble bathrooms, in-room safes, one- and two-bedroom suites with fully equipped kitchens, and private terraces with most suites. There is eating at **Ferro's** or enjoy the scene at **Nikki Midtown**. Access to the New York Health and Racquet Club is complimentary, and room service is available.

LE PARKER MERIDIEN HOTEL
118 W 57th St (bet Ave of the Americas and Seventh Ave)
Moderate to moderately expensive   212/245-5000
www.parkermeridien.com

This large midtown hotel has a lot going for it: great location, ergonomically designed rooms, good eateries, excellent health club, penthouse pool, high-speed Internet access, CD and DVD players, junior suites with separate sitting areas, and more! They even boast of having baths and showers big enough for two. **Norma's** is one of New York's top breakfast rooms. You won't find better burgers in town than at Le Parker's well-hidden, street-level **burger joint**, or if you prefer French, try the classic bistro **Seppi's**. This hotel can even help plan your visit through their "New York Smart Aleck" program. It's a lot less expensive than going to Paris! (Note: The entrance to Le Parker Meridien for those driving a car is on 56th Street.)

> If you are looking for a noisy and fun spot for a meal or snack after the show, I'd suggest **Seppi's** (123 W 56th St, 212/708-7444). This bit of Paris in midtown Manhattan adjoins Le Parker Meridien Hotel and is just right for late dining (till 2 a.m.!). You'll find a raw bar, typical French appetizers, omelets, pastas, fish, meat, and sandwiches. Saturday and Sunday brunches are a specialty.

LIBRARY HOTEL
299 Madison Ave (at 41st St)   212/983-4500
Moderate   www.libraryhotel.com

For the avid reader, check out the Library! Rooms are individually appointed with artwork and books relating to a specific theme. Guests can also enjoy the 14th-floor Poetry Terrace, which houses volumes of verse by assorted authors. Breakfast and an afternoon wine-and-cheese reception are included in the rate. The 60 rooms are wired for high-speed Internet access. A unique feature: room numbers are based on the Dewey decimal system of book classification.

LOEWS REGENCY HOTEL
540 Park Ave (at 61st St)   212/759-4100
Moderately expensive to expensive   www.loewshotels.com

With an outstanding location on Park Avenue, this contemporary and relaxed Loews hotel offers 351 spacious rooms and 86 outstanding suites. These include 12 grand suites that have housed many of the entertainment world's greats. The one-bedroom suites feature two bathrooms. Room phones have two lines and data ports; fax machines and printers are provided on request. Use of the fitness center and overnight shoeshine service are complimentary. Two excellent restaurants—the classy **540 Park** and

The Library, an intimate, residential-style lounge—offer daily meal service. **Feinstein's at Loews Regency** is a classy nightclub. Power breakfasts at the Regency are legendary. More than 70% of the hotel's guests are repeat visitors!

LONDON NYC
151 W 54th St (bet Ave of the Americas and Seventh Ave)
Expensive   212/307-5000
                                                         www.thelondon.com

This completely redone hotel has beautiful new suites and an outstanding restaurant! Furnishings are first-class and the service is very personal. The hotel offers a 24-hour business center, fitness facility, and complimentary newspapers. The **London Bar** and **Gordon Ramsay at the London NYC** provide excellent eating facilities and room service.

> The Lower East Side is changing at a rapid pace, and that includes new hotel accommodations. The **Bowery Hotel** (335 Bowery, 212/505-9100) is overpriced. The lobby is attractive, while rooms and bathrooms reek of tradition—not modernity. For those who like to party, there are plenty of on-site venues. This place also appeals to those who like unique Manhattan views. **Gemma** is the on-premises restaurant.

LOWELL HOTEL
28 E 63rd St (bet Park and Madison Ave)   212/838-1400
Moderately expensive   www.lowellhotel.com

Like an attractive English townhouse, this classy, well-located hotel features 47 suites and 21 deluxe rooms. Amenities include a 24-hour multilingual concierge service, at least two phones per room, fax machine with a dedicated line, VCRs, outlets for personal computers, marble bathrooms, complimentary shoeshines, and a fitness center. Most suites have wood-burning fireplaces, and ten of them have private terraces. The "Hollywood Suite" has all the latest entertainment amenities, plus a fully equipped kitchen.

MANDARIN ORIENTAL NEW YORK
80 Columbus Circle (at 60th St)   212/805-8800
Expensive to very expensive   www.mandarinoriental.com

Boasting a superior location at the Time Warner Center, the Mandarin Oriental offers great views of Central Park from the 38th floor up. In its usual classy (and pricey) style, the Mandarin Oriental offers New York visitors 203 deluxe rooms (not large for the price) and 48 suites, all beautifully furnished and equipped with the latest entertainment technology. Magnificent art pieces dot the public spaces. **Asiate** (see restaurant reviews) features French-Japanese fare, the 35th-floor **Mobar** is a popular spot for drinks, a beautiful ballroom is available, and a two-story spa features "holistic rejuvenation." A 75-foot lap pool has a spectacular setting.

MARITIME HOTEL
363 W 16th St (at Ninth Ave)   212/242-4300
Moderate   www.themaritimehotel.com

The Maritime is located in an area with few modern hotels, making it convenient for those doing business in Chelsea. Amenities include Italian and Japanese restaurants (**La Bottega** and **Matsuri**), a fitness center, flat-screen TVs, and wireless Internet service. In good weather, you can dine and drink alfresco. Rooms and bathrooms are small.

MARMARA-MANHATTAN
301 E 94th St (at Second Ave)   212/427-3100, 800/621-9029
Moderate   www.marmara-manhattan.com

The conveniently located Marmara-Manhattan is an extended-stay hotel that provides turn-key living for folks who need temporary quarters. They offer flexible lease terms for stays beyond 30 days. Suites with up to three bedrooms, as well as studio apartments, are available. Choose from sleek and sophisticated to more traditional, "comfy" rooms. Amenities include modern kitchens with cooking and serving utensils, daily housekeeping, 24-hour concierge and doorman services, spacious bathrooms, terraces, and laundry and exercise rooms. There are over a hundred custom-decorated suites, many with sensational views.

There is much to be said for finding great hotel rates online. Try a hotel consolidator like **Quikbook** (800/789-9887, www.quikbook.com), **Hotels.com** (800/964-6835, www.hotels.com), or **Priceline** (www.priceline.com). They buy excess rooms and pass on the savings. Perhaps the best rates for Manhattan hotel rooms can be obtained at www.nycvisit.com (click on "Book Your Hotel"). Remember that prices change from day to day and even hour to hour.

MILFORD PLAZA
270 W 45th St (at Eighth Ave)   212/869-3600, 800/221-2690
Moderate   www.milfordplaza.com

Value is the key word here. The Milford Plaza, located at the edge of the Theater District, offers reasonable rates that are partially offset by its location. Rest assured the hotel has extremely tight security. The 1,300 guest rooms are small but clean, late-night dining is available, and there is a state-of-the-art fitness center. Very attractive rates are available on weekends and for groups.

MUSE HOTEL
130 W 46th St (bet Ave of the Americas and Seventh Ave)
Moderate   212/485-2400
                                            www.themusehotel.com

Guests at the Muse appreciate the large rooms (181 "dream rooms," 19 suites), the excellent restaurant **District**, and the busy lounge. Rates are very comfortable. A free newspaper is delivered daily, and wireless 'net access is available in public areas. Feather beds and duvets help ensure a restful stay.

NEW YORK MARRIOTT FINANCIAL CENTER
85 West St (at Battery Park)   212/385-4900
Moderate   www.nymarriottfinancialcenter.com

For those doing business in the Wall Street area, this 497-room hotel is ideal. It has two restaurants, including a branch of the famous **Roy's** chain, a popular lobby lounge (**85 West**), restful beds with down comforters, good Internet connections, and a great fitness center and swimming pool.

NEW YORK MARRIOTT MARQUIS
1535 Broadway (bet 45th and 46th St)   212/398-1900
Moderate to moderately expensive   www.nymarriottmarquis.com

The New York Marriott Marquis has over 2,000 guest rooms and suites, sizable meeting and convention facilities, and one of the largest hotel atriums in the world. Guests will enjoy the two-story revolving rooftop restaurant and lounge. In addition, a legitimate Broadway theater, a fully equipped health club, six restaurants and lounges, and a special concierge level are on the property.

If you like cozy space, then this hotel is for you! **The Pod Hotel** (230 E 51st St, 212/355-0300, www.pickwickarms.com) has 347 guest rooms, averaging about 100 sq. ft. each. By contrast, the average hotel room size is 325 sq. ft. The big attraction here is the price, with rates that hover around the low three figures. And you get iPod docking stations, LCD television, and a rooftop bar. You *won't* find an on-site restaurant, fancy lobby, extravagant furnishings, private baths (at least in some rooms), or thick walls.

NEW YORK PALACE HOTEL
455 Madison Ave (bet 50th and 51st St)   212/888-7000
Expensive   www.newyorkpalace.com

Located close to Saks Fifth Avenue, the 896-room New York Palace offers commanding views of the city skyline, which is particularly enchanting in the evening. The public rooms encompass the 120-year-old Villard Houses, a legendary New York landmark. Rooms feature high-speed Internet access, fax machines, and safes. A comprehensive renovation added such facilities as an expansive fitness center, an executive lounge, and the two-floor Villard Center (with meeting and function rooms). The casually elegant restaurant **Istana** offers New American cuisine. A complimentary shuttle is offered to Wall Street and the Theater District.

OFF SOHO SUITES
11 Rivington St (at Second Ave)   212/979-9815, 800/633-7646
Moderate   www.offsoho.com

Looking for a downtown location? Off Soho is a European-style hotel located two blocks south of Houston Street. It offers a number of conveniences that add up to good value: exercise room, phones with Internet access, full kitchen with cookware, special rates for extended stays, self-service laundry, and large marble baths in some suites.

ON THE AVENUE HOTEL
2178 Broadway (at 77th St)   212/362-1100
Moderate to moderately expensive   www.ontheave-nyc.com

There are not many new or even particularly comfortable places to stay on the Upper West Side, making this recent arrival great for those who want to visit the legendary Zabar's, the American Museum of Natural History, Columbus Circle, and other attractions in the area. There are numerous amenities here: beautiful bed linens and towels, homemade cookies, suites with private balconies, 24-hour room service, concierge, business center, complimentary newspapers, plasma TV, and Internet connection. One of the best attractions is the 16th-floor open balcony, which has great views and comfortable chairs!

PENINSULA NEW YORK HOTEL
700 Fifth Ave (at 55th St)   212/956-2888
Expensive   www.newyork.peninsula.com

When the name "Peninsula" is mentioned, the words *quality* and *class* immediately come to mind. This is especially true of the Manhattan property, where a $45 million facelift made the property even more luxurious. The building is a 1905 landmark with 185 rooms and 54 suites, including the palatial Peninsula Suite (more than 3,000 square feet at $15,000 per night!). Room features include oversize marble bathrooms, in-room fax machines, large work desks, audiovisual systems with cable, and numerous bathroom amenities. Features of the 21st-floor Peninsula New York Spa and Health Club include an indoor pool, jacuzzi, sun decks, modern fitness equipment, and spa services. Spa menu, too! The rooftop hotspot **Pen-Top Bar and Terrace** offers dramatic views from its east and west terraces.

PIERRE HOTEL
2 E 61st St (at Fifth Ave)   212/838-8000
Expensive   www.tajhotels.com

Overlooking Central Park, this property provides 201 elegant rooms and suites with 1930s detailing, a magnificent lobby, the **Rotunda** (famous for afternoon tea and light meals), and **Cafe Pierre** (offering continental cuisine for breakfast, lunch, and dinner). Function rooms are the site of many of Manhattan's glitziest events. A fitness center, outfitted with Italian marble, provides the latest cardiovascular equipment. With a staff of over 650, you can be assured of highly personalized service.

THE PLAZA
59th St at Fifth Ave   212/759-3000
Expensive to very expensive

What a fabled career this New York landmark has had! From art-deco palace to Trump-style makeover to another complete renovation, the Plaza is nothing like what it used to be: the epitome of New York's grand hotels. After a complete overhaul that produced multimillion dollar suites on the Central Park and Fifth Avenue sides, the rest of the hotel now offers a reduced number of rooms and suites that carry a very hefty price tag. Guests can still enjoy the fabulous Plaza name and the ability to have a great Sunday brunch in the restored **Palm Court**, a drink at the fabled **Oak Bar**, and a gourmet dinner in the **Oak Room**. Eloise is less conspicuous, but who does not still thrill at the idea of a night at the Plaza? Luxury retail boutiques fill some of the grand public spaces.

RITZ-CARLTON NEW YORK, BATTERY PARK
2 West St (at Battery Park)   212/344-0800
Expensive

RITZ-CARLTON NEW YORK, CENTRAL PARK
50 Central Park S (at Ave of the Americas)   212/308-9100
Expensive   www.ritzcarlton.com

These two properties have added luster to the Manhattan hotel scene, providing all the usual amenities and outstanding service identified with this brand name. You'll find great views, top-grade lobby-level restaurants, gym and spa services, luxurious rooms and bathrooms, and business centers. Club Level guests get special treatment. The Battery Park location offers a 14th-floor bar that is a very romantic hideaway.

Need a short-term rental? Try **Affordable New York City** (21 E 10th St, 212/533-4001, www.affordablenewyorkcity.com). Ask for Susan Freschel.

ST. REGIS NEW YORK
2 E 55th St (at Fifth Ave)   212/753-4500
Expensive   www.stregis.com

The St. Regis, a historic landmark in the heart of Manhattan, is one of the crown jewels of the Starwood Hotels group, and for good reason. The hotel provides luxurious accommodations. Some rooms have been converted to condominiums. Each room has marble baths; round-the-clock butler service (including free pressing of two garments upon arrival); and 24-hour room service is available. Outstanding restaurants include **Astor Court** (breakfast, lunch, afternoon tea, dinner, and Sunday brunch) and the **King Cole Bar** (great Bloody Marys). The **St. Regis' Roof** is available for private functions.

SALISBURY HOTEL
123 W 57th St (bet Ave of the Americas and Seventh Ave)
Moderate   212/246-1300
                                               www.nycsalisbury.com

I highly recommend the Salisbury to price-savvy travelers. Capably run by Edward Oliva, it has nearly 200 rooms and suites, most of which have been redecorated. Many are outfitted with butler's pantries and refrigerators. Suites are large, comfortable, and reasonably priced. The thick walls are really soundproof! If you want to be near Carnegie Hall and other midtown attractions, the Salisbury is for you. If you've waited until the last minute for reservations, the Salisbury is a good place to call. Since it is not well-known among out-of-towners, rooms are usually available.

SHERATON MANHATTAN HOTEL

790 Seventh Ave (at 51st St)   212/581-3300, 800/325-3535
Moderate   www.starwood.com

With a convenient location, this 650-room hotel is ideal for both families and business travelers. It is within easy walking distance of Manhattan's best stores, theaters, and restaurants. The Sheraton Manhattan features a 50-foot indoor swimming pool (a rarity in midtown), a first-rate modernized health club, an excellent restaurant (**Russo's Steak & Pasta**), and 24-hour room service.

SHERATON NEW YORK HOTEL AND TOWERS

811 Seventh Ave (at 53rd St)   212/581-1000, 800/325-3535
Moderate to moderately expensive   www.starwood.com

An outstanding location in central Manhattan and a wide selection of restaurants and lounges (**Hudson's Sports Bar & Grill**, **Avenue Restaurant**, and **Library Bar**) make the Sheraton New York an excellent choice for tourists and business travelers. Sheraton Towers—the more luxurious upper floors—offers exclusive digs that include butler service. "Corporate Club" rooms come equipped with office amenities. A wide selection of package deals and seasonal specials are available.

HOTEL TIPPING GUIDE

Doorman	$1 or $2 per bag $1 or $2 for hailing a taxi
Bellhop	$1 or $2 per bag, depending on size and weight $1 or $2 for every delivery to your room
Concierge	$5 to $10 for special services, like securing theater tickets and restaurant reservations
Housekeeper	$1 or $2 a night and an additional $1 or $2 for any extra service you request
Room service	15% to 18% of the bill, before taxes (note: gratuity is often figured into the bill)

SHOREHAM HOTEL

33 W 55th St (bet Fifth Ave and Ave of the Americas)
Moderate   212/247-6700, 800/553-3347
    www.shorehamhotel.com

For those who want a well-located boutique hotel convenient to Manhattan's best shopping, the Shoreham is a good choice. Most needed amenities are offered: 24-hour concierge service, gym, a restaurant serving three meals a day, and a bar in the lobby. A modern spa, attractive original art pieces, and reasonable prices add to the appeal.

SOHO GRAND HOTEL

310 West Broadway (at Grand St)   212/965-3000
Moderately expensive   www.sohogrand.com

If business or pleasure takes you to Soho, this facility may be for you ... but at a price. The custom-designed rooms will not appeal to traditionalists, though younger guests will love them. Their bathrooms are among the best in Manhattan. Two penthouse suites with outdoor terraces are special. A fitness center, business amenities, 24-hour room service, and valet parking are available. The on-premises **Grand Bar & Lounge** offers cocktail cuisine, and **The Gallery** is an on-site restaurant.

TRIBECA GRAND HOTEL
2 Ave of the Americas (bet Walker and White St)
Moderate   212/519-6600, 877/519-6600
                                      www.tribecagrand.com

When visiting this vibrant part of Manhattan, you might consider the Tribeca Grand. With over 200 rooms, custom-designed meeting spaces, luxurious in-room amenities, flat-screen TVs, a fitness center, and valet parking, guests enjoy every comfort and convenience.

TRUMP INTERNATIONAL HOTEL AND TOWER
1 Central Park W (at 60th St)   212/299-1000
Expensive   www.trumpintl.com

Trump International is everything you'd expect from a place with The Donald's name attached. There are special amenities (fresh flowers, umbrellas, telescopes, and garment bags), 24-hour room service, complete office facilities, entertainment centers in every room, a state-of-the-art fitness center, swimming pool, and marble bathrooms. One of Manhattan's best (and most expensive) restaurants, **Jean Georges**, will pamper your taste buds.

W NEW YORK
541 Lexington Ave (bet 49th and 50th St)   212/755-1200
Moderately expensive   www.whotels.com

Located in midtown, this Starwood property has 688 rooms (including 10 spacious suites), a large ballroom, a full-service spa and health club, and 24-hour room service. The look is strictly modern. Health-food addicts will love **Heartbeat**, trendies flock to the hip **Oasis Bar** (right off the lobby), and the **Whiskey Blue Bar** is another hip oasis.

W NEW YORK—TIMES SQUARE
1567 Broadway (at 47th St)   212/930-7400
Moderately expensive   www.whotels.com

Featuring over 500 rooms in the heart of Times Square, this 57-story W flagship offers the **Blue Fin** restaurant (seafood), a classy retail store, a fitness room and spa, 24-hour room service, and other quality amenities. Ask to stay on the highest floor possible, as the views are dramatic. **The Whiskey Bar** is an underground watering hole and screening room with a coed bathroom!

THE WALDORF-ASTORIA
301 Park Ave (at 50th St)   212/355-3000
Moderately expensive   www.waldorfastoria.com

Hilton invested more than $200 million restoring their flagship property. The Royal Suite alone—used by the late Duke and Duchess of Windsor —was restored at a cost of $10 million! The work shows, and renovations are ongoing. The rich, impressive lobby is bedecked with magnificent mahogany wall panels, hand-woven carpets, and a 148,000-tile mosaic floor. The management has created larger spaces by reducing the number of units. Oversize executive business rooms are available. All-marble bathrooms have been installed in some suites. There is a fitness center, several restaurants, and deluxe rooms and suites in the Waldorf Towers/A Conrad Hotel. An event at the Waldorf is sure to be something special. Junior League members have access to rooms at substantial savings.

WASHINGTON SQUARE HOTEL
103 Waverly Place (at MacDougal St)   212/777-9515
Inexpensive to moderate   www.washingtonsquarehotel.com

Here's a find! This hotel offers good value in rooms, a capable staff, and a nice restaurant. The location is handy for those who have business at New York University or visitors who want to explore the Village. Guest rooms are done in art-deco style and comfortably equipped with good bedding and Internet connections. The fitness room is handy, and the **North Square Restaurant** is a classy venue for cocktails or dining. Discounted parking is available nearby.

THE WESTIN NEW YORK AT TIMES SQUARE
270 W 43rd St (at Eighth Ave)   212/201-2700
Moderate to moderately expensive   www.westinnewyork.com

With an exciting multicolored exterior and atrium lobby, the Westin New York brings a modern look to midtown Manhattan. The hotel is a 45-story, $300 million marvel, with 863 rooms and suites, high-speed Internet access, Westin's trademark "Heavenly" beds, a Don Shula steakhouse, and all the other amenities associated with Westin.

Alternative Housing

ABINGDON GUEST HOUSE
13 Eighth Ave (bet 12th and Jane St)   212/243-5384
Moderate   www.abingdonguesthouse.com

A charming guest house located in Greenwich Village, Abingdon Guest House consists of two landmark 1850s Federal-style townhouses, with fine examples of period architecture. All nine rooms are smoke-free, and some have a private bath and distinctive decor. Abingdon offers its guests many amenities, including daily maid service, but no food is served.

ABODE
P.O. Box 20022
New York, NY 10021   212/472-2000
Mon-Fri: 9-5   800/835-8880 (outside tri-state area)
Moderate to moderately expensive   www.abodenyc.com

Would you like to stay in a delightful old brownstone? How about a contemporary luxury apartment in the heart of Manhattan? Abode selects apartments with great care, personally inspecting them to ensure the highest standards of cleanliness, attractiveness, and hospitality. All are nicely furnished. Nightly rates begin at $145 for a studio and rise to $550 for a three-bedroom apartment. Extended stays of a month or longer receive discount rates. There is a minimum stay of four nights.

AKA CENTRAL PARK
42 W 58th St (bet Fifth Ave and Ave of the Americas)   212/753-3500
Moderately expensive   www.stayaka.com

What was once a very popular Wyndham Hotel has been renovated and renamed, and now it is a part of the Korman Communities group. With a superb location (a block from Central Park and Fifth Avenue), this facility offers a residential setting for business and leisure travelers. You will find concierge services, a state-of-the-art business center, and a private health club. Apartments are furnished in a modern style, with stone flooring and kitchens that offer the latest features.

> Having roommates can bring down the cost of housing in Manhattan. Try **Rainbow Roommates** (212/982-6265) for gay and lesbian roommate services.

BED AND BREAKFAST NETWORK OF N.Y.
130 Barrow St (bet Washington and West St), Room 508
Mon-Fri: 8-6   212/645-8134
Moderate   800/900-8134
                                          www.bedandbreakfastnetny.com

At Bed and Breakfast Network of N.Y. you have your choice of over 200 hosted and unhosted accommodations in Manhattan. The hosted rate runs from $80 to $150 a night for single or double occupancy. The weekly rate varies from $550 to $1,000. Unhosted apartments with up to two bedrooms, range from $150 to $400 a night and from $1,000 to $2,500 a week. Monthly rates are also available. Leslie Goldberg has been in business since 1986, and this is a very reliable outfit.

BROADWAY BED & BREAKFAST INN
264 W 46th St (at Eighth Ave)   212/997-9200, 800/826-6300
Moderate   www.broadwayinn.com

This is the only European country-style inn in New York City. The 41 rooms are immaculate, the atmosphere is homey, the location in the Theater District is safe, and the operation is family-owned and affordable. Amenities include a free continental breakfast, a library stocked with newspapers, and Internet access. The facility, originally built as a hotel in 1907, has been fully restored. Ask about discounted tickets for Broadway shows!

HOSTELLING INTERNATIONAL NEW YORK
891 Amsterdam Ave (at 103rd St)   212/932-2300
Inexpensive   www.hinewyork.org

Visitors over 21 are welcome here. The hostel provides over 620 beds in a newly renovated, century-old landmark. They offer meeting spaces, Internet access, cafeteria, coffee bar, airport shuttle, catering, tours, self-service kitchens, and laundry facilities to individuals and groups. Best of all, the price is right!

INN NEW YORK CITY
266 W 71st St (bet West End Ave and Broadway)   212/580-1900
Moderately expensive   www.innnewyorkcity.com

Situated in a restored, 19th-century townhouse, Inn New York City offers four suites behind a discreet exterior. Depending on which suite you choose, you may find a double Jacuzzi, extensive library, leaded glass skylights, fireplaces, baby grand piano, private terrace, or a fully-equipped kitchen stocked with hearty delights. Additional services include high-speed Internet access, cable TV, DVD, daily newspapers, maid service, and a 24-hour concierge. Personal laundry is done on request at no additonal charge.

INTERNATIONAL HOUSE
500 Riverside Dr (at 122nd St)   212/316-8436 (admissions)
Moderate   212/316-8473 (guest rooms and suites)
          www.ihouse-nyc.org

International House is a community of over 700 graduate students, interns, trainees, and visiting scholars from nearly 100 countries. Occupants spend anywhere from a day to a few years in New York City. It is located on the Upper West Side, near Columbia University and the Manhattan School of Music. Special features include a budget-friendly dining room with an international menu, 24-hour security, pub, gymnasium, and self-service laundry. Free programs for residents include ballroom dancing, lectures, a practice room for musicians, computer lab, films, recitals, and organized sports. During the summer, single-room occupancy with shared bath runs $50 per night for stays of one to ten days. The rate drops to $45 per night for stays of 11 to 20 days. Rates are less still by the semester. Reasonably priced guest rooms and suites ($125-$185 per night) with private bath, air conditioning, daily maid service, and cable television are also available.

IVY TERRACE B&B
230 E 58th St (bet Second and Third Ave)   516/662-6862
Moderate   www.ivyterrace.com

There are four guest apartments in this century-old townhouse, two with outdoor terraces. Kitchens are stocked with breakfast goodies. Hostess Vinessa (a professional actress) promises special care, including the possibility of tickets to TV-show tapings. The Ivy Terrace is gay-friendly. There is a three-night minimum and weekly rates are available. Local calls are free.

METRO HOME
515 Madison Ave (at 53rd St), 25th floor   212/813-2244, 800/987-1235
Moderate   www.metro-home.com

If you are looking for a reasonably priced, full-service, short-term furnished apartment in Soho, midtown, Murray Hill, Upper East Side, Upper West Side, Greenwich Village, Chelsea, or the Theater District, this is a good number to call. They have over 200 apartments in their inventory and offer discounts for extended stays.

92ND STREET Y (DE HIRSCH RESIDENCE)
1395 Lexington Ave (at 92nd St)   212/415-5650
Mon-Thurs: 9-7; Fri, Sun: 10-5   800-858-4692
Inexpensive   www.dehirsch.com

The De Hirsch Residence offers convenient, inexpensive, and secure dormitory housing for students, interns, and working men and women between the ages of 18 and 30. There are shared bathroom and kitchen facilities. Special discounts for Y health club memberships and single and double rooms are available. Lengths of stay can range from 30 days to one year. Admission is by application.

PHILLIPS CLUB
Lincoln Square
155 W 66th St (at Broadway)   212/835-8800
Moderate to moderately expensive   www.phillipsclub.com

This 170-unit residential hotel near Lincoln Center is designed for long-term visitors but will also take nightly customers. Suites come with fully-equipped kitchens, direct-dial phones, and stereo systems. Other impressive features include concierge, laundry and valet service, in-room safes, a handy conference room, and preferential membership at the nearby Reebok Sports Club NY.

If your residential or commercial room needs a good *trompe l'oeil* (mural), call Agnes Liptak at **Fresco Decorative Painting** (324 Lafayette St, 5th floor, 212/966-0676). You can also request decorative stucco, faux finishing, and leafing ($8 to $50 per square foot).

SOLDIERS', SAILORS', MARINES', AND AIRMEN'S CLUB
283 Lexington Ave (bet 36th and 37th St)   212/683-4353
Inexpensive   www.ssmaclub.org

Here is a great find in the Murray Hill area of Manhattan for American and allied servicemen and women—active, retired, veterans, reservists, military cadets, and Coast Guard personnel alike! Rates are extremely low (with no tax) since the club rents beds rather than rooms. If you're traveling solo, you may be assigned a roommate. Rooms have two, three, four, and six beds. Communal bathroom facilities are on each floor. There are several lounges, TVs with VCRs, and a lobby canteen with refrigerator, microwave, and coffee. A complimentary continental breakfast is available each morning.

WEBSTER APARTMENTS
419 W 34th St (at Ninth Ave)   212/967-9000
Inexpensive   www.websterapartments.org

This is one of the best deals in the city for working women with moderate incomes. It is not a transient hotel but operates on a policy developed by Charles B. Webster, a first cousin of Rowland Macy (of the department store family). Webster left the bulk of his estate to found these apartments, which opened in 1923. Residents include college students, designers, actresses, secretaries, and other business and professional women. Facilities include dining rooms, recreation areas, a library, and lounges. The Webster also has private gardens for its guests, and meals can be taken outdoors. Rates are $178 to $245 per week, which includes two meals a day and maid service. The Webster is a secret find known mainly to its residents and to readers of this book!

Looking for an architect or decorator? Here are the best of the best:

Bilhuber (330 E 59th St, 6th floor, 212/308-4888): Jeffrey Bilhuber has contemporary ideas.

David Bergman Architect (241 Eldridge St, Suite 3R, 212/475-3106): eco-conscious designer

Glenn Gissler Design (36 E 22nd St, 8th floor, 212/228-9880): Glenn Gissler works well with art.

Miles Redd (77 Bleecker St, Suite C-111, 212/674-0902): color expert

MR Architecture & Decor (245 W 29th St, 10th floor, 212/989-9300): David Mann is very practical.

Nina Seirafi (330 E 75th St, 646/382-7547): residential and commercial interiors

Ruby (41 Union Square W, Studio 705, 212/741-3380): Bella Zakarian Mancini is mindful of budgets.

Shamir Shah Design (10 Greene St, 212/274-7476): Shamir Shah's designs are modern and clean.

Specht Harpman (338 W 39th St, 10th floor, 212/239-1150): Scott Specht and Louise Harpman are pocketbook-conscious.

S.R. Gambrel (270 Lafayette St, 212/925-3380): You can't beat Steven Gambrel for detailing.

Steven Holl Architects (450 W 31st St, 11th floor, 212/629-7262): residential and commercial, worldwide

---

Interior Designers

AERO STUDIOS
419 Broome St (bet Lafayette and Crosby St)   212/966-4700
Mon-Sat: 11-6   www.aerostudios.com

Aero Studios' staff is well equipped to handle everything from a major commercial design project to a minor residential one. Be sure to visit their store for home furnishings, decor, and lighting.

ALEX CHANNING
250 W 19th St (bet Seventh and Eighth Ave), Suite 11C
By appointment   212/366-4800
                                        www.alexchanning.com

Licensed interior designer Alex Channing has built a reputation as one of Manhattan's up-and-comers. He does furniture design and custom-made furnishings, and he'll help with site selection, move-ins, and installations. Channing does both commercial and residential work.

DESIGNER PREVIEWS

36 Gramercy Park E (bet 20th and 21st St)   212/777-2966
By appointment   www.designerpreviews.com

Having a problem finding the right decorator? Designer Previews keeps tabs on over 300 of the most trustworthy and talented designers, architects, and landscaping experts in Manhattan and elsewhere. They will help you select the best, based on your style and personal requirements, through office consultation or online presentation. Karen Fisher, the genius behind this handy service, is a former design editor for *Women's Wear Daily* and *Esquire* and a member of the Interior Design Hall of Fame.

MARTIN ALBERT INTERIORS

9 E 19th St (bet Broadway and Fifth Ave)
Mon-Thurs: 9-5:30; Fri: 9-5   212/673-8000, 800/525-4637
                                          www.martinalbert.com

Martin Albert specializes in window treatments. They measure and install their product line at prices that are considerably lower than most decorators. Martin Albert offers 250,000 fabric samples, ranging from $8 to $400 a yard. Custom upholstery and slipcovers, a furniture shop, custom interior lighting, and a large selection of drapery hardware are also available. They'll deliver to all 50 states, too!

PARSONS, THE NEW SCHOOL FOR DESIGN

66 Fifth Ave (at 13th St)   212/229-5424
Mon-Fri: 9-6   www.parsons.edu

Parsons, a division of the New School University, is one of the top two schools in the city for interior design. Call for design assistance and your request will be posted on the school's career services board. Every effort is made to match clients with student decorators. Individual negotiations determine the price and length of a job, but it will be considerably less than what a practicing professional charges. Most of these students don't yet have a decorator's card, but this is a good place if you just want a consultation.

Pay attention to these up-and-coming decorators:
Ashley Whittaker Design (212/650-0024, www.ashleywhittaker design.com)
David Harris Interiors (212/219-5660, www.davidanthonyharris. com)
Kathryn Saunders Design (212/249-2903)
Michael Bargo Inc. (212/717-9936, www.michaelbargoinc.com)
Sara Story Design (212/228-6007, www.sarastorydesign.com)

RICHARD'S INTERIOR DESIGN

1390 Lexington Ave (bet 91st and 92nd St)   212/831-9000
Mon-Fri: 10-6; Sat: 10-4   www.richardsinteriordesign.net

At Richard's you'll find over 10,000 decorator fabrics, including tapestries, damasks, stripes, plaids, silks, velvets, and floral chintzes. These are all first-quality goods at competitive prices. The fabrics are imported from the same European mills used by Kravet, Lee Jofa, Robert Allen, Brunswig & Fils, and Clarence House. Richard's does upholstery, furniture, reupholstery, slipcovers, draperies, top treatments, shades, bedroom ensembles, custom furniture from North Carolina, and wall coverings. Design services, in-home consultation, and installation are available.

Jewelry Services

GEM APPRAISERS & CONSULTANTS
608 Fifth Ave (at 49th St), Suite 602   212/333-3122
Mon-Fri: 9-5 (by appointment)   www.robaretz.com

Robert C. Aretz, who owns Gem Appraisers & Consultants, is a graduate gemologist and a director and certified member of the Appraisers Association of America. He is entrusted with appraisals for major insurance companies, banks, and retail jewelry stores. His specialty is antique jewelry, precious colored stones, diamonds, and natural pearls. Aretz will do appraisals and/or consultations for estate, insurance, tax, equitable distribution, and other purposes.

RISSIN'S JEWELRY CLINIC
4 W 47th St (at Fifth Ave)   212/575-1098
Mon, Tues, Thurs: 9:30-5; closed first two weeks of July

Rissin's is indeed a clinic! The assortment of services is staggering: jewelry repair and design, antique repair, museum restorations, supplying diamonds and other stones, eyeglass repair, pearl and bead stringing, restringing of old necklaces, stone identification, and appraisals. Rissins' "Earquilizer" (an earring stabilizer) has been patented, and you can try it at the store. (Bring your own earrings.) Joe and Toby Rissin run the place. Joe's father was a master engraver, so the family tradition has been passed along. *Honesty* and *quality* are their bywords. Estimates are gladly given, and all work is guaranteed.

ZDK COMPANY
48 W 48th St (bet Fifth Ave and Ave of the Americas), Suite 1410
By appointment   212/575-1262

Zohrab David Krikorian has created original pieces for neighbors in the Diamond District, and he will also do professional work for individuals in his free time. In addition to making jewelry, ZDK mends and fixes broken jewelry as only a professional craftsman and artist can. He makes complicated repairs look easy and has yet to encounter a job he can't handle. If Zohrab can't match the stones in an antique earring or other piece of jewelry, he'll redo the item so that it looks even better than before. He loves creating contemporary designs from traditional materials, and his prices are reasonable.

Pearl stringing is a real art. One of the best practitioners in the city is Doris Kahn, at **Murrey's Jewelers** (1395 Third Ave, 212/879-3690).

Lamp Repair
THE LAMP SURGEON
Mon-Sat: 8 a.m.-10 p.m.   917/414-0426

Roy and Lois Schneit do lamp repairs and rewiring at customers' homes, offices, and apartments. Services include work on table and floor lamps, chandeliers, wall sconces, and antiques. They also offer custom lampshades. Roy has over 30 years experience in this business.

Yes, there is a reliable pawnshop in Manhattan: **New York Pawnbrokers** (177 Rivington St, 212/228-7177).

Landscape Design
AMERICAN FOLIAGE & DESIGN
122 W 22nd St (bet Ave of the Americas and Seventh Ave)
Mon-Fri: 8-5   212/741-5555
www.americanfoliagedesign.com

The focus at American Foliage is on concepts and designs for anything to do with gardens and exteriors. These folks will sell or rent live or artificial plants and props. Full service is provided, including trucking and installation.

Special Services
Chimney cleaning: **Homestead Chimney** (800/242-7668; Tues-Fri: 8-5, by appointment)
Clothing repairs: **Ban Custom Tailor Shop** (1544 First Ave, 212/570-0444)
Glass cutting: **Sundial-Schwartz** (159 E 118th St, 212/289-4969; Mon-Fri: 8-4:30)
Landscape design: **Madison Cox Design** (127 W 26th St, 212/242-4631, by appointment)
Woodwork restoration: **Traditional Line** (212/627-3555, by appointment)

Leather Repair
INNOVATION LUGGAGE & TRAVELWARE
1392 Ave of the Americas (bet 56th and 57th St)   212/586-8210
Mon-Sat: 9-6; Sun: 11-5   www.innovationluggage.com

It's a pleasure to do business with these people. Innovation Luggage is handy to most major midtown and Central Park hotels. They feature a complete line of top-brand luggage and travel accessories.

MODERN LEATHER GOODS
2 W 32nd St (bet Fifth Ave and Broadway), 4th floor   212/279-3263
Mon-Fri: 8:30-5; Sat: 8-1:30

Is a briefcase, suitcase, or handbag looking beaten up? Some people regard signs of wear on leather as a mark of class, but I like to see things looking good. Modern Leather Goods, a family business for over 60 years, is the place to go for repairs. Ask for owner Tony Pecorella. They also do needlepoint mounting, reglaze alligator bags, clean leather and suede, and repairs shoes and leather clothing.

SUPERIOR REPAIR CENTER
141 Lexington Ave (at 29th St)   212/967-0554
Mon-Fri: 10-6; Sat: 10-3   www.superiorleathernyc.com

Do you own a fine leather garment that has been damaged? Leather repair is the highlight of the services offered at Superior. Many major stores in the city use them for luggage and handbag work. They are experts at cleaning leather (suede and shearling are specialties) and repairing or replacing zippers on leather items. They can even remove ink spots. Superior has the answer to all leather problems. Just ask Gucci, Calvin Klein, Chanel, Escada, St. John, Bergdorf Goodman, and Prada!

Locksmiths

AAA LOCKSMITHS
44 W 46th St (at Ave of the Americas)   212/840-3939
Mon-Thurs: 8-5:30; Fri: 8-5   www.aaahardware.com

You can learn a lot from trying to find a locksmith in New York. For one thing, it probably has the most full-page ads of any profession in the Manhattan Yellow Pages. For another, this particular "AAA" is *not* the place to call about an automobile emergency. However, in an industry that does not often inspire loyalty or recommendations, AAA Locksmiths has been a family business for over 70 years, and that says a lot right there. They also sell residential and commercial door hardware at prices below list.

LOCKWORKS LOCKSMITHS
By appointment   212/736-3740

Got a lock problem? Give Joel at Lockworks a call. He has been in the locksmith trade for over two decades, and there isn't anything he can't unlock. This gentleman does not advertise, but he is highly regarded by some of the top businesses in Manhattan.

NIGHT AND DAY LOCKSMITH
1335 Lexington Ave (at 89th St)   212/722-1017
Mon-Fri: 9-6; Sat: 10-5 (24 hours for emergencies)

Carry Night and Day's number in case you're ever locked out! Locksmiths must stay ahead of the burglars' latest expertise and offer fast, on-the-spot service for a variety of devices designed to keep criminals out. (After all, no New York apartment has just *one* lock.) Mena Sofer, Night and Day's owner, fulfills these rigid requirements. The company answers its phone 24 hours a day, while posted hours are for the sale and installation of locks, window gates, intercoms, car alarms, safes, and keys. Inside and outside welding is a specialty.

Marble Works

PUCCIO MARBLE AND ONYX
661 Driggs Ave, Brooklyn (main office)
Mon-Fri: 8:30-4   718/387-9778, 800/778-2246
                                   www.puccio.info

Work of the highest quality is a tradition with Puccio. The sculpture and furniture designs range from traditional to sleekly modern. John and Paul Puccio show dining and cocktail tables, chairs, chests of drawers, buffets, desks, consoles, and pedestals. Custom-designed installations include foyer floors, bathrooms, kitchens, bars, staircases, fountains, and fireplaces. Retail orders are accepted. They are the largest distributor and fabricator of onyx in the country.

> Travelers to strange and exotic lands can find valuable information and obtain immunizations before a trip. They can also receive help, if necessary, after a trip:
> **Traveler's Medical Service of N.Y.** (595 Madison Ave, Suite 1200, 212/230-1020; Mon-Fri: 9-4, by appointment)
> **Travel Health Services** (50 E 69th St, 212/734-3000; daily 24-hour service)

Medical Services

BIOSCRIP
197 Eighth Ave (at 20th St)   212/691-9050
Mon-Fri: 9-9; Sat: 9-6   www.bioscrip.com

Bioscrip pharmacy provides home delivery of prescription medications, comprehensive claims management, and links to community resources and national support networks. Their specialties include prescriptions for patients with HIV or transplants. All pharmaceuticals are available, as is an extensive line of vitamins and homeopathic and holistic products. Many hard-to-find items can be provided with one-day service. They will bill insurance companies directly so that customers need not pay up front. Nationwide shipping is available.

LEAGUE FOR THE HARD OF HEARING
50 Broadway (bet Morris St and Exchange Pl), 6th floor
Mon-Fri: 9-4 (by appointment)   917/305-7700, 917/305-7999 (TTY)
                                 www.lhh.org

People of all ages who have hearing disabilities are customers of this not-for-profit organization. They dispense hearing aids, sponsor classes, and work with patients and families to find alternatives to help the hearing impaired. They come highly recommended, and their services are a real value.

N.Y. HOTEL URGENT MEDICAL SERVICES
Urgent Care Center   212/737-1212
952 Fifth Ave (bet 76th and 77th St), Room 1D   www.travelmd.com

This is one of the most valuable services in Manhattan! Dr. Ronald Primas, the CEO and medical director, is tops in his field. This outfit is locally based and has been in operation for over a decade. All manner of health care is available on a 24-hour, seven-days-a-week basis: internists, pediatricians, obstetricians, surgeons, dentists, chiropractors, physicians-on-call service, and more. Doctors will come to your hotel or apartment, arrange for tests, prescribe medications, admit patients to hospitals, and provide nurses. They also provide travel immunizations and consultations, and they are an official WHO-designated yellow-fever vaccination site. The urgent care center is also available around the clock by appointment for patients not requiring a house call. Payment is expected at the time of service; credit cards are accepted. All physicians are board-certified and have an exemplary bedside manner.

Some special pharmacies:

Anatole Pharmacy (650 First Ave, 212/481-0909): foreign prescriptions

Brodwin-Sosa Chemists (1344 First Ave, 212/879-9050): pharmaceutical information

J. Leon Lascoff & Sons, Inc. (1209 Lexington Ave, 212/288-9500): the very best pharmacy services

The Village Apothecary (346 Bleecker St, 212/807-7566): HIV/AIDS drugs and alternative medicine

---

Metal Work

ATLANTIC RETINNING AND METAL REFINISHING
532 W 25th St (bet Tenth and Eleventh Ave), 3rd floor
Mon-Fri: 9-6   973/848-0700
www.retinning.com

Jamie Gibbons has taken over a long-established Manhattan business whose specialty is retinning (which is basically tin plating). Drawing upon many years of experience, Gibbons restores brass and copper antiques, designs and creates new copperware, sells restored copper pieces, and restores lamps, chandeliers, and brass beds.

An afterhours dental emergency can be very inconvenient (and painful). Here are some numbers to call for relief on Saturday, as well as during normal hours.

Metropolitan Dental Associates (225 Broadway, 212/732-7400; Saturday 9-5): across from City Hall; walk-ins welcome

Stuyvesant Dental Associates (430 E 20th St, 212/473-4151): open on alternating Saturdays; call for appointment

---

Movers

BIG APPLE MOVING & STORAGE
83 Third Ave (bet Bergen and Dean St), Brooklyn
Mon-Fri: 9-5; Sat: 9-noon   212/505-1861, 718/625-1424
www.bigapplemoving.com

This is a handy number to have for moving and storage. Even though Big Apple Moving & Storage is located in downtown Brooklyn, they do 80% of their moving business in Manhattan. They can handle antiques, art, and high-end moves, yet manage to keep their rates reasonable. Call them for a free "no surprises" estimate. They stock every size of box and will build wood crates if needed. They also have bubble pack, plate dividers, custom paper, Styrofoam peanuts, and "French wraps" for crystal and delicate breakables. Many of the expert packers have been with Big Apple since they opened in 1979. You can save up to 50% on moving supplies by shopping at their "do-it-yourself" moving store; large orders are delivered for free. For those who need overnight or short-term storage, Big Apple will keep your loaded truck inside their high-security climate-controlled warehouse. When they handle the move, every item of furniture is fully wrapped and padded before leaving your residence. Big Apple is also equipped to handle an interstate move.

BROWNSTONE BROS. MOVING
321 Rider Ave (at 140th St), The Bronx   718/665-5000
Mon-Fri: 9:30-5   www.brownstonebros.com

Since 1977 Brownstone Bros. has been offering moving and storage services with a very personal touch by head man Bill Gross. They are highly rated by customers.

MOVING RIGHT ALONG
101-21 101st St   718/738-2468
Ozone Park, NY   www.movingrightalong.com
Mon-Fri: 9-5:30; Sat: 9-2:30

Nearly three decades of service and a top-quality reputation speak well of Moving Right Along. Moving, storage, packing, and crating are offered. A handy cleanout service will allow your residence to be ready for quick occupancy. They will also sell your pre-owned furniture. Owner Jim Rueda is a hands-on manager whose work has won accolades from numerous satisfied customers.

WEST SIDE MOVERS
644 Amsterdam Ave (bet 91st and 92nd St)   212/874-3800
Mon-Fri: 8-6; Sat: 9-4; Sun: 9-3   www.westsidemovers.com

The late Steve Fiore started West Side Movers in the kitchen of his studio apartment more than three decades ago, and it is now capably run by his wife, Joanne, a former psychotherapist. From its expanded location on Amsterdam Avenue, West Side Movers continues to offer dependable residential and office moving, specializing in fine art and antiques. Close attention is paid to efficiency, promptness, care, and courtesy. Packing consultants will help do-it-yourselfers select moving boxes and other supplies. Their boxes come in a multitude of sizes, including four specifically for mirrors. West Side Movers also rents dollies and sells moving pads.

Office Services

PURGATORY PIE PRESS
19 Hudson St (bet Duane and Reade St), Room 403   212/274-8228
Mon-Fri: by appointment   www.purgatorypiepress.com

Purgatory Pie Press is ideal for small printing jobs. They do graphic design and handset typography, hand letterpress printing, die-cutting, and hand bookbinding. They'll also create envelopes, do logos and other identity designs, and design handmade paper with unique watermarks. Specialties include printing and calligraphy for weddings and parties. They also carry limited-edition postcards and artists' books. Private lessons and small group classes are offered in letterpress printing and artist books.

WORLD-WIDE BUSINESS CENTRES
575 Madison Ave (at 57th St), 10th floor   212/605-0200, 800/296-9922
Mon-Fri: 9-5:30   www.wwbcn.com

Alan Bain, a transplanted English lawyer, has created a business that caters to executives who need more than a hotel room and companies that need a fully equipped, furnished, and staffed office in New York on short notice. The operation grew out of Bain's personal frustration in trying to put together a makeshift office. On-premises administrative, word-processing, clerical, and mail-room services are available. So are high-quality voice and data communications capabilities, including high-speed Internet access. Desk space, private offices, and conference rooms may be rented on a daily, weekly, monthly, or quarterly basis. The daily rate includes a private office, telephone answering services, and receptionists.

When it becomes necessary to look into long-term home health-care, call **Priority Home Care** (212/401-1700).

Opticians

E.B. MEYROWITZ AND DELL OPTICIANS
19 W 44th St (at Fifth Ave)   212/575-1686
Mon-Fri: 9-5:45 (till 5:30 in July, Aug); Sat: 10-4:30
(closed Sat in July, Aug)

This is the place to go for optical emergencies in the city. They do on-the-spot emergency repair of eyeglasses. You're welcome to stop by for regular optical needs, too. They stock a large frame selection, from 18-karat gold to buffalo horn. They also repair binoculars.

Painting

BERNARD GARVEY PAINTING   718/894-8272
By appointment

I am constantly asked to recommend an outstanding and reliable painter who can also do plastering and decorative finishes. Bernard Garvey Painting services residential clients, and his customers tout his reasonable prices and terrific work.

GOTHAM PAINTING COMPANY
123 E 90th St (at Lexington Ave)   212/427-5752
Mon-Fri: 8-5

If you need interior paint or wallpaper for your home, Gotham is a handy resource. They do spray work, restoration, faux painting, and plastering. More than 50 full-time painters are fully licensed and bonded. They have been in business for two decades.

Parenting Resources

PARENTING CENTER AT THE 92ND STREET Y
1395 Lexington Ave (at 92nd St)   212/415-5611
Mon-Fri: 9-5 (office hours)   www.92y.org

Just about everything the 92nd Street Y does is impressive, and its Parenting Center is no exception. It offers every kind of class you can imagine: a newborn-care class for expectant parents, a baby massage class for new parents and their infants, a cooking class for preschoolers, and so on. As this Y is a Jewish institution, Shabbat get-togethers and a Jewish heritage class for preschoolers are offered, along with workshops and seminars on a wide range of topics, from sleep to setting limits. They provide babysitting for parenting classes (as well as unrelated Y classes) and host new-parent get-togethers. Perhaps most important, they act as a resource and support center for members. The annual membership fee is $175 per couple, and benefits include discounts and priority sign-up. Non-members are welcome to take classes, too.

PARENTS LEAGUE
115 E 82nd St (bet Lexington and Park Ave)   212/737-7385
Mon-Thurs: 9-4 (Tues till 6); Fri: 9-noon   www.parentsleague.org

This nonprofit organization is a goldmine for parents in New York. In addition to putting together a calendar of events for children of all ages, the Parents League maintains extensive files on babysitters, birthday party places, tutors, summer camps, early childhood programs, and independent schools throughout the city. For a membership fee of $120 per academic year, you can access those files and attend workshops and other events. If you are the parent of a small child, you also get a copy of *The Toddler Book,* an invaluable list of almost 300 activities in New York for little ones.

SOHO PARENTING CENTER
568 Broadway (at Prince St), Suite 402   212/334-3744
Mon-Fri: 8-8 (by appointment)   www.sohoparenting.com

Soho Parenting Center is dedicated to the notion that parenting ought to be talked about and shared. It conducts workshops and group and individual discussions for parents of newborns, toddlers, and even older children. It offers play groups for children while parents discuss their experiences and challenges. Individual parent counseling is available.

Party Services

BLAIR McMILLEN
917/334-6488
www.blairmcmillen.com

Juilliard-trained Blair McMillen is one of the most sought-after concert pianists in the country. He also has his fingers on the pulse when it comes to the New York music scene. His musical tastes run from classical to blues, Broadway to bebop, Afro-Cuban to avant-garde. If you are looking for an in-house solo recital, a jazz combo for a private event, or a cabaret singer and pianist, McMillen and his musician friends can fill the bill.

BUBBY GRAM
60 E 8th St (at Broadway)   212/353-3886
Mon-Thurs: 11-8 (Fri till 5); by phone   www.bubbygram.com

If creating fun and laughter is on your mind, call this number. These folks have outrageous and humorous acts that run from simple singing telegrams to complete shows for parties or business meetings. They'll provide celebrity impersonators, roasts, magicians, psychics, belly dancers, hula shows, and much more.

Are you in need of party items? I have two suggestions:
Triserve Party Rentals (770 Lexington Ave, 212/752-7661; by appointment): stocks top-quality tents, tables, chairs, platters, china place settings, linens, and more.
Atlas Party Rentals and Chair Rentals (212/929-8888): excellent prices on chair rentals, china, and silverware

---

ECLECTIC ENCORE
620 W 26th St (at Eleventh Ave)   212/645-8880
Mon-Fri: 9-5   www.eclecticprops.com

Their name says it all. Eclectic Encore specializes in hard-to-find props for a party at home, a set for motion pictures or television, or a novel product announcement. They have been in business since 1986 and are known for an extensive collection of 18th-, 19th- and 20th-century furniture and accessories. You can find everything from an armoire to a zebra—even one of those cakes from which a scantily clad lady pops out.

EXPRESSWAY MUSIC & EVENTS
104 E 40th St (bet Park and Lexington Ave), Suite 106   212/953-9367
By appointment   www.expresswaymusic.com

If you are interested in entertainment for any kind of personal or business event, give these folks a call. Their artists include the Expressway Music Jazz Trio (modern jazz) and the Professionals (a six-piece band that plays disco, rock, dance music, swing, jazz, and more). Other ensembles include chamber music duets, trios, and quartets (for weddings, cocktail hours, and other events), and a steel drum band with up to seven pieces. They can also provide disc jockeys and karaoke services.

HIGHLY EVENTFUL
11 Fifth Ave (at 8th St), Suite 7C   212/777-3565
Daily: 10-6   www.highlyeventful.com

Since 1994, Highly Eventful has been arranging events in New York and throughout the world. These folks take charge of everything, including food, liquor, equipment rentals, tents, flowers, lighting, music, and trained personnel. They will secure prime locations, such as grand ballrooms, churches (like the Cathedral Church of St. John the Divine), museums (like the Metropolitan), and yachts. They have on-staff chefs who will do smaller dinners, specializing in Italian or Asian cuisine.

LINDA KAYE'S BIRTHDAYBAKERS, PARTYMAKERS
195 E 76th St (bet Lexington and Third Ave)   212/288-7112
Mon-Fri: 9:45-5 (parties can be scheduled for any day)
www.partymakers.com

Linda Kaye offers children's birthday parties at two of Manhattan's most desirable locations: the Central Park Zoo and the American Museum of Natural History. Zoo parties are for children from one to ten years old. Themes include Animal Alphabet Safari, Animal Olympics, Safari Treasure Hunt, and Mystery Movie Making. The Natural History parties are for children four and up, with such themes as Dinosaur Discovery, Cosmic Blast-Off, Underwater Treasure, and Safari Adventure. Kaye's website serves as a resource and shopping site for birthday party needs, listing entertainers and party locations. Partymakers also specializes in creative custom cakes (including a pop-out cake) and unique corporate events.

> There is no place like this anywhere in the world! **Fantasma Magic** (421 Seventh Ave, 2nd floor, 212/244-3633) is the largest magic venue in the world. Their midtown magic shop includes two stages, flat screens, a 3D video display, a VIP room (behind a secret door and vault), magic props, and a Houdini museum with a huge collection of his props. A private party room for birthday or special events is also available. They can accommodate 250 to 300 guests for special events or 75 seated guests for professional magic shows.

MARCY BLUM ASSOCIATES
133 W 19th St (bet Ave of the Americas and Seventh Ave), 7th floor
By appointment   212/929-9814
www.marcyblum.com

What a great lady! Marcy is so well organized that no matter what the event—wedding, reception, birthday party, bar mitzvah, or dinner for the boss—she will execute it to perfection. As anyone knows, it's the details that count, and Marcy is superb at the nitty-gritty. She has organized many celebrity weddings. Look for unusual gifts, too!

PARTY POOPERS
11 Beach St (bet Varick St and West Broadway), Suite 410
Call ahead   212/274-9955 (party planning)
                                      212/587-0734 (supplies)
www.partypoopers.com

Party Poopers is a group of entertainers who never throw the same party twice. Offering some of the best private party rooms in New York, they handle setup, clean-up, and entertainment, allowing parents to sit back and relax. Themes include fairytales, superheroes, game shows, dance parties, murder mysteries, or anything else you can dream up. They also have costume characters, magicians, and other party entertainers. The online store carries favors, paper goods, balloons, theme packs, and gifts.

PROPS FOR TODAY
330 W 34th St (bet Eighth and Ninth Ave), 12th floor   212/244-9600
Mon-Fri: 8:30-5 (appointment recommended)

www.propsfortoday.com

This is the handiest place in town when you are planning a party. Props for Today has the largest rental inventory of home decorations in New York, allowing you to distinguish your events with unique decor. Whether you want everyday china and silver or unique antiques, they've got the goods. There are platters, vases, tablecloths, and much more. They have a Christmas section, children's items, books, fireplace equipment, artwork, garden furniture, foreign items, and ordinary kitchenware. Over a million items are available! Phone orders are taken, but I'd recommend checking out the three floors of inventory for yourself.

Pen and Lighter Repair

AUTHORIZED REPAIR SERVICE
30 W 57th St (bet Fifth Ave and Ave of the Americas), 2nd floor
Mon-Fri: 8:30-5 (Wed till 6); Sat: 10-3:30   212/586-0947

www.shavers.com, www.vintagelighters.com

After more than four decades, this outfit remains incredibly busy, perhaps because it is almost without competition. Those who use fountain pens or are interested in pens or lighters (vintage and new) are devoted customers. Authorized Repair services nearly every brand and is the national service center for Alfred Dunhill, Ltd. They repair electric shavers, too! Numerous lines of pens and lighters are sold at discount. Their showroom is filled with vintage lighters from companies like Ronson, Evans, Zippo, Dunhill, and Thorens. The polite, helpful staff is well versed in the fine points of each brand.

FOUNTAIN PEN HOSPITAL
10 Warren St (bet Broadway and Church St)
Mon-Fri: 8-6   212/964-0580, 800/253-7367

www.fountainpenhospital.com

Located across from City Hall, this experienced establishment sells and repairs fountain pens of all types. It also carries one of the world's largest selections of modern and vintage writing tools.

Personal Services

A. E. JOHNSON EMPLOYMENT AGENCY
380 Lexington Ave (at 42nd St), Suite 3810   212/644-0990
Mon-Fri: 9-5   www.aejohnsonagency.com

Dating from 1890, Johnson is the oldest licensed employment agency dealing exclusively with household help in the U.S. They specialize in providing affluent clients with highly qualified butlers, cooks, housekeepers, chauffeurs, bodyguards, nannies, personal assistants, valets, maids, and couples. Both temporary and permanent workers are available, many on a moment's notice. Employment references, criminal records, and driver's licenses are checked by an independent firm.

AL MARTINO'S DOMESTICS
60 E 42nd St (bet Park and Madison Ave), Suite 2227
Mon-Fri: 9-5   212/867-1910
www.martinodom.com

Private chefs are the specialty at Al Martino Domestics, although this agency has been providing clientele with highly qualified butlers, housekeepers, cooks, estate managers, personal assistants, and chauffeurs since 1972. Look to Al Martino for party and seasonal help as well. These services do not come cheaply, but Al Martino's fees are competitive and incorporate a long-term replacement service guarantee.

> The **United States Personal Chef Association** (800/995-2138, www.uspca.com) can provide names of personal chefs. Here are two of the best in New York:
> **Belinda Clarke** (212/253-6408)
> **Bill Feldman** (212/983-2952)

BIG APPLE GREETER
1 Centre St (at Chambers St)   212/669-8159
Office: Mon-Fri: 9-5
By appointment   www.bigapplegreeter.org

Big Apple Greeter is like having a new friend show you the wonders of the city! Volunteers from all five boroughs meet groups or individuals—up to six people in all—to show them New York City through the eyes of a native. On visits of two to four hours, Greeters use public transportation or travel on foot to see neighborhoods and the city's hidden treasures. There are nearly 300 Greeters, and they speak over 25 languages between them. They are matched with visitors by language, interest, and neighborhoods requested. This service is free of charge, and tipping is not permitted. At least four weeks advance notice is required.

> Individuals who may need special protection should know about **Special Enforcers** (1 Penn Plaza, Suite 3600, 973/316-6086). These folks provide professional bodyguards for high-profile individuals, like those in the entertainment, sports, and music fields.

CELEBRITIES STAFFING SERVICES
20 Vesey St (bet Church St and Broadway), Suite 510   212/227-3877
Mon-Fri: 9-6   www.celebrities-staffing.com

Turn to Celebrities Staffing when you are looking to hire top-of-the-line baby nurses, governesses, nannies, "mannies" (male nannies), housekeepers, ladies' maids, butlers, housemen, cooks, chefs, couples, laundresses, house managers, estate managers, personal assistants, personal shoppers, chauffeurs, bodyguards, caregivers, companions, and other types of household personnel. Their services extend across the U.S. and internationally with clients who include royalty, celebrities, dignitaries, top executives, and professional families looking to hire the best.

COLUMBIA BARTENDING AGENCY
2960 Broadway (at 116th St)   212/854-4537
Mon-Fri: 10-4   www.columbiabartending.com

Columbia Bartending Agency (part of the Columbia University School of Mixology) uses students who are so expert at bartending that one wonders what profession they could possibly do as well after college. The service has been around a long time, and there is none better. They'll advise you on liquors, mixers, garnishes, and recipes for your party. Columbia also supplies wait staff and coat checkers.

CROSS IT OFF YOUR LIST
915 Broadway (at 21st St)   212/725-0122
Mon-Fri: 9-7 (or by appointment)   www.crossitoffyourlist.com

Cross It Off Your List can help you do just that! These folks will do virtually anything to help busy people: organize closets and file cabinets, manage a move, help with daily chores, plan trips, pack bags, and take care of mail.

Here is a first-class way to see this great city! James Smythe's **My Kind of Town New York** (212/754-4500, www.mykindoftown ny.com) offers private and personalized custom tours in a Mercedes-Benz sedan or SUV for one to seven guests. Special arrangements can be made for larger groups.

ETIQUETTE PROFESSIONNELLE
337 E 54th St (bet First and Second Ave)   212/751-1653
By appointment

Did you know that showing the sole of your shoe while crossing your legs is an insult in the Middle East? You'll learn this and much more from Jacqueline Baertschi, who teaches the fine points of manners and comportment in the international business community. Classes for children and members of the hospitality industry are offered, too.

FASHION UPDATE
Mon-Fri: 9-5   718/897-0381, 888/447-2846
                          www.fashionupdate.com

Sarah Gardner is a mother of three who wants the most value for every clothing dollar spent. Gardner found she could buy apparel for her family at wholesale prices from some manufacturers, so she decided to share her discoveries. She started *Fashion Update,* a quarterly publication that uncovers over 250 bargains per season in women's, men's, and children's designer clothing, accessories, and jewelry. Furniture, home accessories, and spa services, too! She also leads shopping expeditions to designer showrooms at $175 per person for 2½ hours. Ask about group rates.

FLATIRON CLEANING COMPANY
230 E 93rd St (at Second Ave)   212/876-1000
Mon-Fri: 7:30-4:30   www.flatironcleaning.com

Can you imagine how many homes and apartments these people have cleaned since opening for business in 1893? Expert services include residential house and window cleaning, installing and refinishing wood floors, and maid service, party help, laundry service, and carpet and upholstery cleaning. You might call the Rockefellers for references!

FLOOD'S CLOSET
By appointment   212/348-7257

Want to be pampered? Barbara Flood will do clothes shopping for or with you. She can even bring items to consider to your home. She can also help with closets, jewelry, decor, and other time-consuming chores.

Do you want to maximize your closet's potential? **California Closets** (1625 York Ave, 212/517-7877) will reorganize and even paint that dreary space!

IN TOWN RUN-A-ROUND
Mon-Fri: 9-6:30; Sat: by appointment   917/359-6688
www.intownrunaround.com

Owner Henry Goldstein is the man to contact if you don't have the time or desire to bring back a piece of jewelry from Rome, shop for groceries, or find a venue for your parents' 50th anniversary party. These pleasant, efficient, and reliable folks will even wait in your apartment for a repairman!

INTREPID NEW YORKER
220 E 57th St (bet Second and Third Ave), Room 2D
Mon-Fri: 9-5   212/750-0400
www.intrepidny.com

Like your author, Sylvia Ehrlich and her team delight in helping folks unravel the hassles and confusion of this great city. She provides one of the most complete services in this area and is available at any time. A corporate relocation service for people moving within a 75-mile radius is also available.

LET MILLIE DO IT!
By appointment   212/535-1539

Millie Emory is a real problem solver! She has worked for decades as a professional organizer, saving people time, money, and stress. Millie especially likes working for theatrical folks, but she can help anyone with a broad variety of tasks. She will organize and unclutter apartments, desks, files, closets, libraries, attics, basements, garages, and storage rooms. She will also pay bills, balance checkbooks, and get papers in order for a tax accountant or IRS audit. She can help with paper flow, time management, and space problems. Millie is also good at finding antiques and out-of-print books and records. She assists seniors in dismantling their homes before entering nursing facilities. When a loved one dies, Millie will handle estate liquidations, sales, and donations, leaving the space "broom clean."

NEW YORK CELEBRITY ASSISTANTS (NYCA)
459 Columbus Ave (at W 82nd St), Suite 216   212/803-5444
New York, NY 10024 (mailing address only)
www.nycelebrityassistants.org

Are you in need of a professional assistant? This outfit consists of current and former assistants to top celebrities in film, TV, theater, music, sports, philanthropy, fashion, business, and politics. NYCA provides educational forums, networking opportunities, and employment referrals.

NEW YORK'S LITTLE ELVES
151 First Ave (bet 25th and 26th St), Suite 204   212/673-5507
Daily: 8-6 (call for appointment)   www.nyelves.com

No need to worry about cleaning up! These little elves will do the job, whether it is a normal dusting or cleaning up after a big party – even a construction job. All kinds of modern cleaning equipment is used. They provide estimates, employ screened personnel, carry liability insurance, are fully bonded, and have an outstanding reputation. The elves will also subcontract for window, carpet, and upholstery cleaning.

If you need a place to store art, furniture, records, or other things, try **Sofia Storage Centers** (475 Amsterdam Ave, 139 Franklin St and 4396 Broadway, 212/873-0700). They have been family-owned since 1910.

PAVILLION AGENCY
15 E 40th St (bet Fifth and Madison Ave), Suite 400   212/889-6609
Mon-Fri: 9-5   www.pavillionagency.com

Pavillion has been a family-owned and -operated business for over 40 years. If you are in need of nannies, housekeepers, laundresses, couples, butlers, major-domos, chefs, chauffeurs, caretakers, gardeners, property managers, or personal assistants, call and ask for Keith or Clifford Greenhouse. Applicants are screened by a private firm.

RED BALL WINDOW CLEANING
221 E 85th St (bet Second and Third Ave)   212/861-7686
Mon-Fri: 8-5:30   www.redballwindowcleaners.com

These people have cleaned a lot of windows since opening in 1928! Still a family business, they specialize in residential and commercial window cleaning. The higher the windows, the happier they are.

SAVED BY THE BELL
11 Riverside Dr (bet 73rd and 74th St)   212/874-5457
Mon-Fri: 9:30-5:30 (or by appointment)

Susan Bell's goal is to take the worry out of planning and carrying out virtually any type of job for people who are too busy or need help. Bell says "doing the impossible is our specialty." Specialties include weddings, bar and bat mitzvahs, fundraising and charity benefits, party planning, tag sales, relocations, delivery arrangements, and service referrals.

SMART START
334 W 86th St (bet West End Ave and Riverside Dr)   212/580-7365
By appointment   www.smartstartny.com

There is always someone in New York to fill a special niche or need. Such a person is Susan Weinberg. She learned from experience that many expectant mothers and fathers are too busy to plan for the arrival of their little bundle of joy. So she started Smart Start, a consulting service to aid parents in pulling everything together. Her service helps provide the basic things a newborn will need, as well as interior design, storage creation, gifts, and personal shopping. In addition, Susan sells hand-painted children's furniture —everything from table and chair sets to coat hooks and toy chests. Custom cabinet work is a specialty. She is truly the stork's assistant!

TALKPOWER
333 E 23rd St (bet First and Second Ave)   212/684-1711
Mon-Fri: 9-5   www.talkpowerinc.com

Do you know that speaking in front of a group is most people's single most feared experience? If you suffer from this phobia, give these folks a call. They are true professionals who train clients to make public appearances. Personal or group sessions are available for intensive weekends. They now offer a "Golf Power" program to enhance golfers' concentration.

Oreck Clean Home Center (2003 Broadway, 212/875-0002) is devoted entirely to keeping your abode clean and healthy. We're not just talking vacuum cleaners, either!

UNAME IT ORGANIZERS
226 E 10th St (bet First and Second Ave), Suite 222   212/598-9868
By appointment   www.masterorganizers.com

Eleni Marudis claims, "As long as it is legal, we will do it!" They perform more than 200 personal services, from uncluttering your home or office to planning your wedding. They locate apartments and will even stand in line for you. In the crowded field of organizers, uName It has been in business for over two decades, which means they're doing something right.

WHITE GLOVE ELITE
39 W 32nd St (bet Fifth Ave and Broadway), Room 900
Mon-Fri: 8-8; Sat: 9-3; Sun: 10-2   212/684-4460
(cleaners available anytime)   www.whitegloveelite.com

Actors Sarah and Jim Ireland started this business as an adjunct to their stage careers. They provide trained cleaners for apartments in Manhattan, The Bronx, Brooklyn, and Queens. About half of their personnel are also actors between jobs.

ZOE INTERNATIONAL
20 Vesey St (bet Church St and Broadway), Suite 510   212/227-3880
Mon-Fri: 9-6 (24-hour emergency service)   www.zoehomecare.com

This agency specializes in the placement of nurses and nurses' aides, home health- and personal-care aides, companions, and housekeepers to work for the elderly, sick, and chronically ill. They work closely with doctors, hospitals, health care organizations, family members, friends, attorneys, estate planners, and others involved in a patient's life. Caregivers are available for live-in or live-out. They can work day or night shifts or provide 24-hour service. Specially priced packages are available for families on fixed incomes.

If you are interested in astrology, try contacting **Astrology Zone by Susan Miller** (212/360-1163). Business consulting and strategizing are specialties.

Photographic Services

DEMETRIAD CREATIVE MEDIA
1674 Broadway (at 52nd St), 4th floor   212/315-3400
Mon-Fri: 9-7   www.demetriad.com

These folks were trained as commercial photographers and have parlayed their expertise into portrait and head-shot photography, as well as digital and document system imaging and restoration of old and damaged photographs. They are pros at retouching, making a copy negative when the original is missing, and high-end portrait and editorial photography. Developing and processing can be hand-done or digital, depending on a client's preference.

HAND HELD FILMS
315 W 36th St (bet Eighth and Ninth Ave), Room 2E   212/502-0900
Mon-Fri: 9-6   www.handheldfilms.com

Hand Held Films rents motion picture equipment for feature films, commercials, music videos, and documentaries. Media composers and digital video cameras are also available. You can be assured of finding the latest equipment, lenses, and "toys," including lighting. They have an impressive list of equipment—even a 20-foot truck to haul equipment to your set.

VISKO HATFIELD
Mon-Fri: 9-5   212/979-9322, 917/544-9300
                                                 www.vhpictures.com

Visko Hatfield offers an opportunity to have a truly one-of-a-kind portrait. This talented photographer has captured images of celebrities from the literary, fashion, art, and sports scenes. You could be his next subject!

Need some cash? **Portero** (275 Madison Ave, Room 1201, 877/307-3767, www.portero.com) will visit your residence, catalog your quality items, and oversee online auctions. You will receive payment for any sold items, minus a commission.

Plumbing and Heating

KAPNAG HEATING AND PLUMBING
150 W 28th St (at Seventh Ave), Suite 501   212/929-7111
                                                 www.kapnag.com

location service is offered, free professional decorating is available, and a multilingual staff is at your service. Working with Japanese clients is a specialty. The stock is large, and delivery and setup can often be done within 48 hours. All styles of furniture and accessories are shown in their 12,000-square-foot showroom, located near Grand Central Terminal.

Furniture Repair

JOSEPH BIUNNO LTD.
129 W 29th St (bet Ave of the Americas and Seventh Ave), 2nd floor
Mon-Fri: 9-5   212/629-5630
www.antiquefurnitureusa.com

Joseph is a really nice guy! You will enjoy working with him. He restores and reproduces furniture and does metal work. There are also carvers, turners, gold leafers, finishers, and painters in his shop. Joseph is a third-generation restorer and craftsman.

Gardening

COUNCIL ON THE ENVIRONMENT OF NEW YORK CITY (CENYC)
51 Chambers St (bet Broadway and Centre St), Room 228
Mon-Fri: 9-5   212/788-7900
www.cenyc.org

It is a little-known fact that the city will loan tools to groups involved in community-sponsored open-space greening projects. Loans are limited to one week, but the waiting period is not long and the price (nothing!) is right. You can borrow the same tools several times a season. A group can be as few as four people. CENYC also runs Greenmarket—weekly farmers markets in 40 locations—and they carry a number of interesting free publications.

Haircuts

Children

COZY'S CUTS FOR KIDS
1125 Madison Ave (at 84th St)	212/744-1716
448 Amsterdam Ave (at 81st St)	212/579-2600
1416 Second Ave (at 74th St)	212/585-COZY (2699)
Mon-Sat: 10-6; Sun: 11-5	www.cozyscutsforkids.com

Cozy's takes care of kids of all ages, including the offspring of some famous personalities. What an experience: videos and videogames, themed barber chairs, balloons, candy, and free toys. They issue a "first-time" diploma with a keepsake lock of hair! Besides providing professional styling services, Cozy's is a toy boutique. There are "glamour parties" for girls, makeup and glamour art projects, and mini-manicures. Their own "So Cozy" hair-care products for children are available in-shop and online. Adults are well taken care of, too!

Family

ASTOR PLACE HAIR STYLISTS
2 Astor Pl (at Broadway)   212/475-9854
Tues-Fri: 8 a.m.-10:30 p.m.; Sat: 8-8; Sun: 9-6
www.astorplacehairnyc.com

When a reliable plumber and/or heating expert is needed, you can't do better than this outfit. They handle plumbing renovations for kitchens and bathrooms, replace toilets, repair pipes and heating equipment, expertly diagnose plumbing system problems, and more. Two dozen highly qualified workers have kept Kapnag at the top since 1935.

Portraits

CATHERINE STOCK
Mid-October through mid-May (by appointment)   917/915-6304
www.catherinestock.com

Catherine Stock has quite a life, dividing her time between France and New York. She is one of the best children's portrait artists. Stock usually paints in watercolor, requiring just one sitting. Her portraits are represented at **Magic Windows** (1186 Madison Ave, 212/289-0028), a children's boutique.

Are relatives coming to visit? Do you need pictures framed today? One-hour framing service is available at **O.J. Art Gallery** (920 Third Ave, 212/754-0123; Mon-Fri: 10-7; Sat: 11-6).

Psychic

JOANN SANDS
By appointment   212/564-2625

This talented lady has been reading people, so to speak, for most all of her life. Joann is a popular psychic who has many repeat clients and has appeared on television several times. Her fees are reasonable.

Relocation

BROWN HARRIS STEVENS
Call for appointment   917/825-4195
www.brownharrisstevens.com

Relocation expert Shelley Saxton specializes in sales and high-end leasing. She is helpful with a wide array of properties, and rental clients swear by her. Shelley is a member of both the Real Estate Board of New York and RELO, the largest network of independent residential real estate firms.

Scissors and Knife Sharpening

HENRY WESTPFAL CO, INC.
107 W 30th St (bet Ave of the Americas and Seventh Ave)
Mon-Fri: 9:30-6:30   212/563-5990

The same family has been running Henry Westpfal since 1874. They do all kinds of sharpening and repair, from barber scissors and pruning shears to cuticle scissors. They'll also work on light tools. Cutlery, shears, scissors, and tools for leather workers are sold here. They even sell lefthanded scissors!

Shipping and Packaging

THE UPS STORE
Multiple locations   800/PICK-UPS
Hours vary by store   www.theupsstore.com

UPS has over 40 store locations in New York, offering professional packaging and shipping jobs. Handy services—not all of them available at every location—include copying and printing, faxing, private mailboxes, mail forwarding, business cards, office stationery, notary and secretarial work, passport photos, laminating, rubber stamps, engraving, key duplication, computer-generated letters, and money transfers. They also sell stamps, office supplies, boxes, and packing supplies.

THE PADDED WAGON
1569 Second Ave (bet 81st and 82nd St)   212/570-5500
Mon-Fri: 9-7; Sat: 9-4; Sun: noon-5   www.paddedwagon.com

The Padded Wagon carries all sizes of boxes, paper, moving supplies, and tape, and they provide UPS and FedEx service. They are good for gift-wrapping help, too. They even offer skilled moving and storage service.

UNITED SHIPPING & PACKAGING
200 E 10th St (at Second Ave)   212/475-2214
Mon-Fri: 10:30-8; Sat: 11-6   www.uspnyc.com

United Shipping will send anything anywhere in the world! They also sell packaging supplies and boxes. Additional services include faxing, mailboxes, office supplies, and messenger services.

Shoe Repair

B. NELSON SHOE CORPORATION
1221 Ave of the Americas (at 49th St), Level C-2
Mon-Fri: 7:30-5   212/869-3552, 800/750-7669
                                           www.bnelsonshoes.com

B. Nelson is very good at repairing high-grade dress, leisure, and athletic shoes. They have performed factory-method resoling for over a century. If your Birkenstocks need repair, this is the place to bring them. Prices are excellent, and over-the-counter rates are even cheaper than online. Service is terrific, and their client list is tops.

JIM'S SHOE REPAIR
50 E 59th St (bet Madison and Park Ave)   212/355-8259
Mon-Fri: 8-6; Sat: 9-4 (closed Sat in summer)

This operation offers first-rate shoe repair, shoeshine, and shoe supplies. The shoe repair field has steadily been losing its craftsmen, and this is one of the few shops that upholds the tradition. Owner Jim Rocco specializes in orthopedic shoe and boot alterations.

TOP SERVICE
845 Seventh Ave (bet 54th and 55th St)   212/765-3190
Mon-Fri: 8-6; Sat: 9-3

Shoe repair is the main business at Top Service, but there is much more. They can cut keys, repair luggage and handbags, clean suede, and dye and clean shoes. Dance shoes are a specialty, and this source is used by many Broadway theater groups. This is a great place to keep in mind for last-minute emergencies.

Silversmiths

BRANDT & OPIS
46 W 46th St (bet Fifth Ave and Ave of the Americas), 5th floor
Mon-Thurs: 8-5; Fri: 8-2   212/302-0294

If it has to do with silver, Roland Markowitz at Brandt & Opis can handle it. This includes silver repair and polishing, buying and selling estate silver, repairing and replating silver-plated items, and fixing silver tea and coffee services. They restore combs and brushes (dresser sets) and replace old knife blades. Other services include gold-plating, lamp restoration, and plating antique bath and door hardware. In short, Brandt & Opis is a complete metal restoration specialist.

THOME SILVERSMITHS
49 W 37th St (bet Fifth Ave and Ave of the Americas), 4th floor
Wed, Thurs: 10-5   212/764-5426

Thome cleans, repairs, and replates silver. They also buy and sell some magnificent pieces. They have a real appreciation for silver and other metal goods, and it shows in everything they do. They will restore antique silver and objets d'art, repair and polish brass and copper, and repair and clean pewter, gold, and bronze. Thome can do silver- and gold-plating. They'll even restore the velvet backs of picture frames and velvet box linings.

Stained Glass Design and Restoration

VICTOR ROTHMAN FOR STAINED GLASS
578 Nepperhan Ave (at Lake Ave), Yonkers
                                212/255-2551, 914/969-0919

With over 30 years experience, this studio specializes in museum-quality stained-glass restoration. They have worked on everything from residences to churches and public buildings. Consultation is provided, and specification reports are prepared for professional and private use. Stained-glass windows can be designed and fabricated.

Dirty windows? Call **Frank's Window Cleaning Company** (212/288-4631).

Tailors

BHAMBI'S CUSTOM TAILORS
14 E 60th St (bet Madison and Fifth Ave), Suite 610   212/935-5379
Mon-Sat: 9-7   www.bhambis.com

With notice, this firm can cut custom shirts and suits in as little as two weeks. They have been in business for nearly four decades and have developed a good reputation. Next-day alterations and hand-stitching on suits are specialties. Choose from hundreds of bolts of cloth by such makers as Ermenegildo Zegna, Cerruti, Dormeuil, Holland & Sherry, and Loro Piana.

CEGO CUSTOM SHIRTMAKER
174 Fifth Ave (bet 22nd and 23rd St), 3rd floor 212/620-4512
Mon-Fri: 9:30-6; Sat: noon-4 www.cego.com

In only three weeks—faster, if it's an emergency—you can have a perfect-fitting shirt made at CEGO.

Bespoke (custom) tailoring is available from these top folks:
Bespoke Tailors (509 Madison Ave, 212/888-6887)
Nino Corvato (420 Madison Ave, 212/980-4980)
Bruno Cosentino (Dunhill, 711 Fifth Ave, 212/753-9292): English-Italian style
Eva Devecsery (201 E 61st St, Suite 1, 212/751-6091): a delightful lady whose elves can do most anything
William Fioravanti (45 W 57th St, 212/355-1540)
John Green (24 E 71st St, 212/861-9611): The fit is magnificent.
Lianna Lee (828 Lexington Ave, 212/588-9289): British power suits
Leonard Logsdail (9 E 53rd St, 212/752-5030)
Tony Maurizio (18 E 53rd St, 5th floor, 212/759-3230)
Domenico Vacca (781 Fifth Ave, 212/759-6333): He will do good things for your figure.

MOHAN'S CUSTOM TAILORS
60 E 42nd St (bet Park and Madison Ave), Suite 1753 212/697-0050
Mon-Sat: 10-7:30 www.mohantailors.com

Mohan's makes suits, coats, sports jackets, slacks, shirts, and formal wear from over 14,000 fabric samples. You can walk-in without an appointment, but don't wear jeans or T-shirts! They want classy-looking, satisfied customers. For one year after your piece is made, they offer free alterations if you lose or gain weight.

PEPPINO TAILORS
780 Lexington Ave (at 60th St) 212/832-3844
Mon-Fri: 8:30-6:30; Sat: 9-4

Joseph Peppino is a fine craftsman who has been tailoring clothes for over a quarter of a century. All types of garments, including evening wear, receive his expert attention for alterations. Delivery is offered.

Translation Services

THE LANGUAGE LAB
211 E 43rd St (bet Second and Third Ave), Suite 505 212/697-2020
www.thelanguagelab.com

The Language Lab has a thousand professional linguists at its disposal, with full IT support, printing facilities, and foreign language instruction. They can provide help with over 75 languages and dialects.

Travel Services

PASSPORT PLUS.NET
20 E 49th St (bet Fifth and Madison Ave), 3rd floor
Mon-Fri: 9:30-5   212/759-5540, 800/367-1818
                                    www.passportplus.net

Sometimes getting a passport and the proper visas can be a real pain in the neck. Passport Plus.Net takes care of these tedious chores by securing business and tourist travel documents; renewing and amending U.S. passports; obtaining duplicate birth, death, and marriage certificates; and obtaining international driver's licenses. They work closely with the U.S. Passport Agency and foreign consulates and embassies. Passport Plus.Net offers assistance in case of lost or stolen passports. These folks serve customers all over the country.

To save time and money on travel, call or log onto these useful websites:

Expedia (800/397-3342, www.expedia.com)
Hotwire (866/468-9473, www.hotwire.com)
Orbitz (888/656-4546, www.orbitz.com)
Priceline (www.priceline.com)
Travelocity (888/872-8356, www.travelocity.com)

Uniform and Costume Rentals

I. BUSS-ALLAN UNIFORM RENTAL SERVICE
121 E 24th St (bet Lexington and Park Ave), 7th floor   212/529-4655
Mon-Fri: 9-5   www.ibuss-allan.com

Because most costumes are used only once, it is far less expensive to rent than buy. At this establishment you can rent any number of costumes: doormen, police and security, firemen, maintenance, chefs, concierges, and more. They also provide uniform rentals and sell work apparel.

If you desire some sensational garment you've seen modeled on a fashion runway but cannot afford the exorbitant designer prices, here are some suggestions on where to go for copies. These houses usually quote prices from 20% to 60% less than the originals! Call for appointments.

Atelier Eva Devecsery (201 E 61st St, 212/751-6091): alterations and custom work
Dynasty Custom Tailor (6 E 38th St, 212/679-1075)
Euroco (247 W 30th St, 212/629-9665): Most of their work is theatrical costumes.
Ghost Tailor (153 W 27th St, 11th floor, 212/253-9727)

Wedding Services

WEDDING CAFÉ NEW YORK
16 E 38th St (bet Fifth and Madison Ave)   212/213-2616
Mon-Fri: 10-9; Sat: 10-7   www.weddingcafeny.com

The concept at Wedding Café is to provide a place where prospective brides can meet with vendors to discuss details of their wedding plans. They offer a wedding library, a variety of wedding products, bridal shower hostings, and networking with other brides. These folks are not salespeople. A membership fee gives access to their services.

VI. Where to Buy It: New York's Best Stores

Even some of the smaller stores in New York now have websites. Still there's nothing like actually shopping in New York! You'll find chic boutiques, sprawling department stores (like Macy's and Bloomingdale's), and everything in between. You'll also find an incredible range of prices and selections for everything from shoes to toys to art. Lots of items show up in New York long before they arrive in other parts of the country. In fact, like movies, some appear *only* in New York and never make it out to the hinterlands!

Is it possible to get a great deal in New York? Absolutely, although probably not on Fifth Avenue—unless you're shopping right after Christmas. It's also possible that you'll pay much more than you should, particularly if you get sucked into one of the perpetual "going out of business" sales in neighborhoods frequented by out-of-town visitors. Be careful. Compare prices. If it's clothing, try it on. Don't buy the first thing you see, unless you're at a flea market and you've stumbled upon a unique treasure.

New York is a shopper's paradise, so bring along some spending money and plan to do a little buying. There's something really fun about saying, "I got it in New York!"

The Best Places to Shop for Specific Items in New York: An Exclusive List

Things for the Person (Men, Women, Children)

Accessories, fashion (1890-2000): **Eye Candy** (329 Lafayette St, 212/343-4275)

Accessories, men's and women's: **Marc Jacobs Accessories** (385 Bleecker St, 212/924-6126)

Backpacks: **Bag House** (797 Broadway, 212/260-0940)

Bags, antique: **Sylvia Pines Uniquities** (1102-B Lexington Ave, 212/744-5141)

Boots, comfort and fashion: **Lord John's Bootery** (428 Third Ave, 212/532-2579)

Boots, handmade, men's and women's: **E. Vogel Boots and Shoes** (19 Howard St, 212/925-2460)

Boutique, men's: **Odin** (328 E 11th St, 212/475-0666)

Bras: **Bra Smyth** (905 Madison Ave, 212/772-9400)

Bridal wear (great assortment): **Kleinfeld** (110 W 20th St, 646/633-4300)

Bridal wear (nontraditional): **Jane Wilson-Marquis** (130 E 82nd St, 212/452-5335; appointments preferred)

Briefcases: **Per Tutti** (49 Greenwich Ave, 212/675-0113)

Buttons: **Tender Buttons** (143 E 62nd St, 212/758-7004)

Clothing and accessories, men's and women's: **Etro** (720 Madison Ave, 212/317-9096)

Clothing, children's (basics): **Lester's** (1534 Second Ave, 212/734-9292) and **Morris Bros**. (2322 Broadway, 212/724-0107)

Clothing, children's classic: **flora and henri** (1023 Lexington Ave, 212/249-1695)

Clothing, children's French: **Jacadi** (787 Madison Ave, 212/535-3200 and 1296 Madison Ave, 212/369-1616)

Clothing, children's (funky and fun): **Space Kiddets** (26 E 22nd St, 212/420-9878) and **Peanutbutter & Jane** (617 Hudson St, 212/620-7952)

Clothing, children's, party dresses and suits: **Prince and Princess** (41 E 78th St, 212/879-8989)

Clothing, children's (pricey and "Frenchy"): **Catimini** (1125 Madison Ave, 212/987-0688)

Clothing, denim: **G-Star** (270 Lafayette St, 212/219-2744)

Clothing, designer (resale): **Ina** (101 Thompson St, 212/941-4757)

Clothing, designer (samples): **Showroom Seven** (498 Seventh Ave, 212/643-4810; Feb, May, Sept, and Dec)

Clothing, hip-hop: **Mr. Joe** (500 Eighth Ave, 212/279-1090)

Clothing, imported designer: **India Cottage Emporium** (221 W 37th St, 212/685-6943)

Clothing, Japanese (high-end): **Uniqlo** (546 Broadway, 917/237-8800)

Clothing, leather: **Tannery House** (587 Fifth Ave, 212/207-3899)

Clothing, men's and boys' (traditional): **Jay Kos** (415 Park Ave, 212/319-2770)

Clothing, men's brand-name (discounted): **L.S. Men's Clothing** (49 W 45th St, 3rd floor, 212/575-0933) and **Century 21** (22 Cortlandt St, 212/227-9092)

Clothing, men's classic: **Peter Elliot** (1070 Madison Ave, 212/570-2300)

Clothing, men's custom-made: **Alan Flusser** (3 E 48th St, 212/888-4500) and **Bhambi's Custom Tailors** (14 E 60th St, Suite 610, 212/935-5379)

Clothing, men's European suits: **Jodamo International** (321 Grand St, 212/219-0552)

Clothing, men's shirts, custom-made: **Arthur Gluck Shirtmaker** (47 W 57th St, 212/755-8165)

Clothing, men's shirts and suits, custom-made: **Ascot Chang** (7 W 57th St, 212/759-3333)

Clothing, men's tuxedo shirts and accessories (discounted): **Ted's Fine Clothing** (155 Orchard St, 212/966-2029)

Clothing, men's and women's cashmere sweaters: **Best of Scotland** (581 Fifth Ave, 212/644-0415)

Clothing, men's and women's custom-made (good value): **Saint Laurie Merchant Tailors** (22 W 32nd St, 5th floor, 212/643-1916)

Clothing, men's and women's rain gear: **Paul & Shark** (772 Madison Ave, 212/452-9868)

Clothing, sportswear, brand name: **Atrium** (644 Broadway, 212/473-9200)

Clothing, T-shirts: **Eisner Bros.** (75 Essex St, 212/475-6868)

Clothing, "tween" girls': **Space Kiddets** (26 E 22nd St, 212/614-3235)

Clothing, unusual: **Gallery of Wearable Art** (34 E 67th St, 212/425-5379)

Clothing, vintage: **Bobby 2000** (104 E 7th St, 212/674-7649), **Ellen Christine** (255 W 18th St, 212/242-2457), **Reminiscence** (50 W 23rd St, 212/243-2292), and **Resurrection Vintage Clothing** (217 Mott St, 212/625-1374)

Clothing, women's: **TG-170** (170 Ludlow St, 212/995-8660)

Clothing, women's bridal and evening wear: **Reem Acra** (14 E 60th St, 212/308-8760)

Clothing, women's classic (superior): **Yigal Azrouël** (408 W 14th St, 212/929-7525)

Clothing, women's designer (resale): **Kavanagh's** (146 E 49th St, 212/702-0152) and **New & Almost New** (166 Elizabeth St, 212/226-6677)

Clothing, women's dresses, evening and wedding (made-to-order): **Jane Wilson-Marquis** (42 E 76th St, 212/452-5335)

Clothing, women's maternity (stylish): **Liz Lange Maternity** (958 Madison Ave, 212/879-2191) and **Cadeau** (254 Elizabeth St, 212/994-1801)

Clothing, women's pants: **Theory** (230 Columbus Ave, 212/362-3676)

Clothing, women's party and wedding dresses: **Mary Adams** (138 Ludlow St, 212/473-0237)

Clothing, women's post-breast surgery: **Underneath It All** (444 E 75th St, 212/717-1976 and 160 E 34th St, 212/779-2517)

Clothing, women's sportswear (good prices): **Giselle** (143 Orchard St, 212/673-1900)

Clothing, women's suits and dresses: **Blue** (137 Ave A, 212/228-7744)

Clothing, women's tops: **Joyce Leslie** (20 University Pl, 212/505-5419)

Clothing and accessories, women's: **Design in Textiles by Mary Jaeger** (51 Spring St, 212/941-5877)

Corsets and other undergarments: **Orchard Corset** (157 Orchard St, 212/674-0786)

Cuff links: **Links of London** (402 West Broadway, 212/343-8024; 535 Madison Ave, 212/588-1177; and 200 Park Ave, 212/867-0258) and **Missing Link** (40 W 25th St, Room 108, 212/645-6928)

Cuff links, vintage: **Deco Jewels** (131 Thompson St, 212/253-1222)

Denim, vintage: **What Comes Around Goes Around** (351 West Broadway, 212/343-9303)

Dungarees: **Lucky Brand Retail Store** (1151 Third Ave, 646/422-1192)

Earrings: **Ted Muehling** (27 Howard St, 212/431-3825)

Eyewear (discounted): **Quality Optical** (169 E 92nd St, 212/289-2020)

Eyewear (elegant): **Vision Fashion Eyewear** (2 W 47th St, 212/421-3750) and **Morgenthal-Frederics Opticians** (944 Madison Ave, 212/744-9444; 399 West Broadway, 212/966-0099; and 699 Madison Ave, 212/838-3090)

Fabrics: **P&S Fabrics** (355 Broadway, 212/226-1534)

Fabrics, decorator and upholstery: **Beckenstein Home Fabrics** (4 W 20th St, 212/366-5142)

Fabrics, decorator (discounted): **Harry Zarin** (318 Grand St, 212/925-6112)

Fabrics, designer (discounted): **B&J Fabrics** (525 Seventh Ave, 212/354-8150)

Fabrics, men's: **Beckenstein Men's Fabrics** (257 W 39th St, 212/475-6666)

Fabrics, Oriental: **Modern Designer** (38 Mott St, 212/349-0818)

Furs, fashion: **G. Michael Hennessy Furs** (345 Seventh Ave, 3rd floor, 212/695-7991)

Furs: **Zamir Furs** (90 W Houston St, 212/677-2332)

Gloves, custom and ready-made: **La Crasia** (15 W 28th St, 4th floor, 212/803-1600; by appointment)

Handbags (magnificent and very expensive): **Judith Leiber** (680 Madison Ave, 212/223-2999)

Handbags, custom-made: **Roberto Vascon** (140 W 72nd St, 212/787-9050)

Handbags, fashion: **Longchamp** (132 Spring St, 212/343-7444)

Handbags, vintage: **Chelsea Girl** (63 Thompson St, 212/343-1658)

Hats: **Dae Sung** (65 W 8th St, 212/420-9745)

Hats, custom-made fur: **Lenore Marshall** (231 W 29th St, 212/947-5945)

Hats, high-end: **Eugenia Kim** (347 W 36th St, 212/674-1345)

Hats, men's: **Arnold Hatters** (535 Eighth Ave, 212/768-3781), **J.J. Hat Center** (310 Fifth Ave, 212/239-4368), and **Rod Keenan** (155 W 121st St, 212/678-9275)

Hats, men's custom-made: **Young's Hat Store** (139 Nassau St, 212/964-5693; by appointment)

Hats, men's (discounted): **Makin's Hats** (212 W 35th St, 212/594-6666)

Jackets, leather bomber: **Cockpit USA** (652 Broadway, 212/254-4000)

Jeans (discounted): **O.M.G. Inc.** (428 Broadway, 212/925-5190)

Jeans, men's and women's (good-quality Dutch): **G-Star** (270 Lafayette St, 212/219-2744)

Jeans (one-of-a-kind): **Jean Shop** (435 W 14th St, 212/366-5326)

Jewelry: **Fortunoff** (681 Fifth Ave, 212/758-6660)

Jewelry, charms (baby shoe): **Aaron Basha** (680 Madison Ave, 212/935-1960)

Jewelry, costume and travel: **Lanciani** (992 Madison Ave, 212/717-2759 and 826 Lexington Ave, 212/832-2092)

Jewelry, custom-designed: **Sheri Miller** (205 E 83rd St, 212/944-2153)

Jewelry, fine: **Stuart Moore** (128 Prince St, 212/941-1023)

Jewelry, handmade: **EDGE*nyNOHO** (65 Bleecker St, 212/358-0255) and **Ten Thousand Things** (423 W 14th St, 212/352-1333)

Jewelry, Victorian: **Antique Source** (212/681-9142; by appointment)

Jewelry, vintage: **Deco Jewels** (131 Thompson St, 212/253-1222) and **Doyle & Doyle** (189 Orchard St, 212/677-9991)

Jewels (rare and historic): **Edith Weber & Associates** (994 Madison Ave, 212/570-9668)

Leather goods: **Dooney & Bourke** (20 E 60th St, 212/223-7444), **Il Bisonte** (120 Sullivan St, 212/966-8773), and **René Design Collection** (786 Madison Ave, 212/249-3001)

Leather goods, tailored: **The Leather Man** (111 Christopher St, 212/243-5339)

Leather jackets and wallets, men's and women's: **M0851** (106 Wooster St, 212/431-3069 and 748 Madison Ave, 212/988-1313)

Lingerie (discounted): **Orchard Corset** (157 Orchard St, 212/674-0786) and **Howard Sportswear** (69 Orchard St, 212/226-4307)

Lingerie, fantasy: **Agent Provocateur** (133 Mercer St, 212/965-0229)

Lingerie, fine: **Bra Smyth** (905 Madison Ave, 212/772-9400), **Jean Yu** (37 Crosby St, 212/226-0067), and **Peress** (1006 Madison Ave, 212/861-6336)

Massage oils: **Fragrance Shop** (21 E 7th St, 212/254-8950)

Millinery (one-of-a-kind): **Kelly Christy** (212/965-0686; by appointment)

Outdoor wear: **Eastern Mountain Sports** (591 Broadway, 212/966-8730)

Perfume (discounted): **R.S.V. Trading** (34 W 27th St, 11th floor, 212/481-8651)

Perfume interpretations: **Essential Products** (90 Water St, 212/344-4288)

Prescriptions: **J. Leon Lascoff & Sons** (1209 Lexington Ave, 212/288-9500)

Purses, men's: **Longchamp Paris** (713 Madison Ave, 212/223-1500)

Sandals (handmade): **Jutta Neumann** (158 Allen St, 212/982-7048)

Sewing patterns: **P&S Fabrics** (360 Broadway, 212/226-1534)

Shaving products: **The Art of Shaving** (141 E 62nd St, 212/317-8436; 373 Madison Ave, 212/986-2905; and other locations)

Shoes (discounted): **DSW** (40 E 14th St, 212/674-2146 and 102 North End Ave, 212/945-7419) and **Stapleton Shoe Company** (68 Trinity Pl, 212/964-6329)

Shoes, adult comfort and fashion: **David Z** (556 Broadway, 212/431-5450; 384 Fifth Ave, 917/351-1484; and other locations)

Shoes, athletic: **JackRabbit** (42 W 14th St, 212/727-2980)

Shoes, bridal: **Peter Fox Shoes** (105 Thompson St, 212/431-7426)

Shoes, children's (upscale): **East Side Kids** (1298 Madison Ave, 212/360-5000), **Harry's Shoes** (2315 Broadway, 212/874-2034), and **Shoofly** (42 Hudson St, 212/406-3270)

Shoes, Italian designer: **Hollywould** (198 Elizabeth St, 212/219-1905)

Shoes, large sizes: **Tall Size Shoes** (32 W 39th St, 212/736-2060)

Shoes, men's and women's (good value): **Co-Pilot** (654 Broadway, 212/475-1592)

Shoes, men's and women's custom-made: **Oberle Custom Shoes/ Mathias Bootmaker** (1502 First Ave, 212/717-4023)

Shoes, men's handmade: **E. Vogel Boots and Shoes** (19 Howard St, 212/925-2460)

Shoes, non-leather: **MooShoes** (152 Allen St, 212/254-6512)

Shoes, tennis (limited edition): **Alife Rivington Club** (158 Rivington St, 212/375-8128)

Shoes, walking: **Hogan** (134 Spring St, 212/343-7905)

Shoes, women's (small sizes): **Giordano's Shoes** (1150 Second Ave, 212/688-7195)

Soaps: **Fresh** (57 Spring St, 212/925-0099)

Swimwear, men's and boys': **Vilebrequin** (1070 Madison Ave, 212/650-0353 and 436 West Broadway, 212/431-0673)

Swimwear, women's: **Canyon Beachwear** (1136 Third Ave, 917/432-

0732), **Eres** (621 Madison Ave, 212/223-3550 and 98 Wooster St, 212/431-7300), **Malia Mills Swimwear** (199 Mulberry St, 212/625-2311; 1031 Lexington Ave, 212/517-7485; and 220 Columbus Ave, 212/874-7200), and **Wolford** (619 Madison Ave, 212/688-4850; seasonal)

Ties: **Andrew's Ties** (400 Madison Ave, 212/750-5221) and **Tie Coon** (400 Seventh Ave, 212/904-1433)

Ties, custom-made and limited-edition: **Seigo** (1248 Madison Ave, 212/987-0191)

Umbrellas: **Brella Bar** (1043 Third Ave, 212/813-9530) and **Rain or Shine** (45 E 45th St, 212/741-9650)

Uniforms, medical and housekeeping: **Ja-Mil Uniforms** (92 Orchard St, 212/677-8190)

Watchbands: **George Paul Jewelers** (1050 Second Ave, 212/838-7660)

Watches: **G. Wrublin Co.** (134 W 25th St, 212/929-8100), **Movado** (610 Fifth Ave, 212/218-7555), and **Swatch** (640 Broadway, 212/777-1002)

Watches (discounted): **Yaeger Watch** (578 Fifth Ave, 212/819-0088)

Watches, Swiss Army: **Swiss Army Soho** (136 Prince St, 212/965-5714)

Wedding rings: **Wedding Ring Originals** (674 Lexington Ave, 212/751-3940)

Wigs: **Theresa Wigs and Eyelashes** (217 E 60th St, 212/486-1693)

Yarns, luxury: **String** (130 E 82nd St, 212/288-9276)

Zippers: **Feibusch** (27 Allen St, 212/226-3964)

Things for the Home

Air conditioners: **Elgot Sales** (937 Lexington Ave, 212/879-1200)

Appliances (discounted): **Bloom and Krup** (347 E 36th St, 212/673-2760) and **Price Watchers** (800/336-6694)

Appliances (for overseas use): **Appliances & Video Overseas** (246 Eighth Ave, 3rd floor, 212/447-2008)

Appliances, kitchen: **Gringer & Sons** (29 First Ave, 212/475-0600) and **Zabar's** (2245 Broadway, 212/787-2000)

Art (great prices): **Miriam Rigler** (41 E 60th St, 212/581-5519)

Art, American Indian: **Common Ground** (55 W 16th St, 212/989-4178)

Art, ancient Greek, Roman, and Near Eastern: **Royal Athena Galleries** (153 E 57th St, 212/355-2033)

Art, antique Oriental: **Imperial Oriental Art** (790 Madison Ave, 212/717-5383)

Art deco, French: **Maison Gerard** (53 E 10th St, 212/674-7611)

Art, decorative: **Susan P. Meisel Decorative Arts** (141 Prince St, 212/254-0137)

Art, erotic: **Erotics Gallery** (41 Union Sq W, Suite 1011, 212/633-2241; by appointment)

Art, 19th- and 20th-century Western: **J.N. Bartfield Galleries** (30 W 57th St, 212/245-8890)

Art, pre-Columbian: **Lands Beyond** (1218 Lexington Ave, 212/249-6275)

Art, 20th-century dadaist and surrealist: **Timothy Baum** (212/879-4512; by appointment)

Asian furniture and accessories: **Jacques Carcanagues** (21 Greene St, 212/925-8110)

Bakeware (discounted): **Broadway Panhandler** (65 E 8th St, 212/966-3434)

Baking supplies: **New York Cake & Baking Distributor** (56 W 22nd St, 212/675-2253)

Baskets: **Bill's Flower Market** (816 Ave of the Americas, 212/889-8154)

Baskets, fruit (custom-made): **Macres** (30 E 30th St, 212/246-1600) and **Manhattan Fruitier** (105 E 29th St, 212/686-0404)

Bath and bed items: **Bed Bath & Beyond** (620 Ave of the Americas, 212/255-3550 and 410 E 61st St, 646/215-4702)

Bath fixtures (expensive): **Boffi** (31½ Greene St, 212/431-8282)

Beds: **Charles P. Rogers** (55 W 17th St, 212/675-4400)

Beds, Murphy: **Murphy Bed Center** (20 W 23rd St, 2nd floor, 212/645-7079)

Beds, sofa: **Avery-Boardman** (979 Third Ave, 4th floor, 212/688-6611)

Boxes, wooden: **An American Craftsman Galleries** (60 W 50th St, 212/307-7161)

Carpets, antique: **Art Treasury** (212/722-1235; by appointment)

Chairs, luxury massage: **Family Inada** (7 W 56th St, 212/582-8787)

Chandeliers, vintage Italian: **The Lively Set** (33 Bedford St, 212/807-8417)

China, Amari: **Bardith** (901 Madison Ave, 212/737-3775)

China (bargain pieces): **Fishs Eddy** (889 Broadway, 212/420-9020)

Christmas decor: **Christmas Cottage** (871 Seventh Ave, 212/333-7380)

Christmas decorations (discounted): **Kurt Adler's Santa World** (7 W 34th St, 212/924-0900; open for two weeks after Thanksgiving for sample sale)

Christmas ornaments: **Matt McGhee** (22 Christopher St, 212/741-3138)

Clocks, cuckoo: **Time Pieces** (115 Greenwich Ave, 212/929-8011)

Cookbooks (used): **Joanne Hendricks Cookbooks** (488 Greenwich St, 212/226-5731)

Cookware: **Bed Bath & Beyond** (620 Ave of the Americas, 212/255-3550 and 410 E 61st St, 646/215-4702)

Dinnerware, Fiesta (individual pieces): **Mood Indigo** (Showplace Antiques, 40 W 25th St, 212/254-1176)

Dinnerware, porcelain: **Bernardaud** (499 Park Ave, 212/371-4300)

Domestics: **Harris Levy** (98 Forsyth St, 212/226-3102)

Doorknobs: **Simon's Hardware** (421 Third Ave, 212/532-9220)

Electronics, vintage: **Waves** (251 W 30th St, 212/273-9616)

Fire-prevention merchandise: **Fire Zone** (34 W 51st St, 212/698-4529)

Floor coverings: **ABC Carpet & Home** (881 Broadway, 212/473-3000)

Floral designs: **Country Gardens** (1160 Lexington Ave, 212/966-2015)

Flower bouquets: **Posies** (366 Amsterdam Ave, 212/675-6190)

Flower bulbs: **Van Bourgondien** (800/622-9997)

Flowers, fresh-cut (from Europe): **VSF** (204 W 10th St, 212/206-7236)

Flowers, silk: **Pany Silk Flowers** (146 W 28th St, 212/645-9526)

Foliage, live and artificial: **American Foliage & Design** (122 W 22nd St, 212/741-5555)

Frames, picture: **A.I. Friedman** (44 W 18th St, 212/243-9000) and **Framed on Madison** (740 Madison Ave, 212/734-4680)

Furniture, classic hand-carved: **Devon Shops** (111 E 27th St, 212/686-1760)

Furniture: **Design Within Reach** (142 Wooster St, 212/475-0001; 408 W 14th St, 212/242-9449; and other locations)

Furniture and mattresses, foam: **Dixie Foam** (113 W 25th St, 212/645-8999)

Furniture, antique: **H.M. Luther Antiques** (35 E 76th St, 212/439-7919 and 61 E 11th St, 212/505-1485)

Furniture, Asian: **Jacques Carcanagues** (21 Greene St, 212/925-8110)

Furniture, children's (high-end): **Kids' Supply Company** (1343 Madison Ave, 212/426-1200)

Furniture (discounted): **Knoll** (76 Ninth Ave, 11th floor, 212/343-4000)

Furniture, handcrafted (expensive): **Thomas Moser Cabinetmakers** (699 Madison Ave, 2nd floor, 212/753-7005)

Furniture, handcrafted, 18th-century American reproductions: **Barton-Sharpe** (200 Lexington Ave, 646/935-1500)

Furniture, hardwood: **Pompanoosuc** (124 Hudson St, 212/226-5960)

Furniture, infants': **Albee Baby** (715 Amsterdam Ave, 212/662-5740) and **Schneider's Juvenile Furniture** (41 W 25th St, 212/228-3540)

Furniture, modern design (pricey): **Cassina USA** (155 E 56th St, 212/245-2121)

Furniture, outdoor: **Smith & Hawken** (394 West Broadway, 212/925-0687)

Furniture, rental: **Props for Today** (330 W 34th St, 12th floor, 212/244-9600)

Furniture, Swedish antique: **Eileen Lane Antiques** (150 Thompson St, 212/475-2988)

Gadgets: **Brookstone** (18 Fulton St, 212/344-8108 and other locations)

Garden accessories: **Lexington Gardens** (1011 Lexington Ave, 212/861-4390) and **Marston & Langinger** (117 Mercer St, 212/965-0434)

Glass, Venetian: **Gardner & Barr** (213 E 60th St, 212/752-0555) and **End of History** (548½ Hudson St, 212/647-7598)

Glassware: **67th Street Wines & Spirits** (179 Columbus Ave, 212/724-6767; glassware only)

Glassware, hand-blown: **Simon Pearce** (500 Park Ave, 212/421-8801)

Glassware and tableware: **Avventura** (463 Amsterdam Ave, 212/769-2510)

Glassware, Steuben (used): **Lillian Nassau** (220 E 57th St, 212/759-6062)

Glassware, vintage: **Mood Indigo** (Showplace Antiques, 40 W 25th St, 212/254-1176)

Home accessories: **Carole Stupell** (29 E 22nd St, 212/260-3100)

Home furnishings, primitive: **Andrianna Shamaris** (121 Greene St, 212/388-9898)

Housewares: **Dinosaur Designs** (250 Mott St, 212/680-3523) and **Gracious Home** (1217 and 1220 Third Ave, 212/517-6300 and 1992 Broadway, 212/231-7800)

Housewares (upscale): **Lancelotti** (66 Ave A, 212/475-6851)

Ice buckets (vintage): **Mood Indigo** (Showplace Antiques, 40 W 25th St, 212/254-1176)

Kitchen gadgets: **Bed Bath & Beyond** (620 Ave of the Americas, 212/255-3550 and 410 E 61st St, 646/215-4702) and **Zabar's** (2245 Broadway, 212/787-2000)

Kitchenware, professional: **Hung Chong Imports** (14 Bowery St, 212/349-3392) and **J.B. Prince** (36 E 31st St, 212/683-3553)

Knives: **Roger & Sons** (268 Bowery, 212/226-4734)

Lampshades: **Just Shades** (21 Spring St, 212/966-2757)

Lampshades, custom-made: **Oriental Lampshade Co.** (223 W 79th St,

212/873-0812 and 816 Lexington Ave, 212/832-8190) and **Unique Custom Lamp Shades** (247 E 77th St, 212/472-1140)

Lightbulbs: **Just Bulbs** (5 E 16th St, 212/228-7820)

Lighting, custom-made and antique: **Lampworks** (231 E 58th St, 212/750-1500)

Lighting fixtures: **City Knickerbocker** (665 Eleventh Ave, 212/586-3939) and **Lighting by Gregory** (158 Bowery, 212/226-1276)

Lighting fixtures, antique: **Olde Good Things** (124 W 24th St, 212/989-8401)

Lighting, photographic (purchase or rental): **Flash Clinic** (164 W 25th St, 212/337-0447)

Linens: **Bed Bath & Beyond** (620 Ave of the Americas, 212/255-3550 and 410 E 61st St, 646/215-4702) and **Nancy Koltes at Home** (31 Spring St, 212/219-2271)

Linens, Indian: **Pondicherri** (454 Columbus Ave, 212/875-1609)

Linens, vintage: **Geminola** (41 Perry St, 212/675-1994)

Linoleum, vintage: **Secondhand Rose** (138 Duane St, 212/393-9002)

Locks: **Lacka Lock and Safe** (315 W 49th St, 212/391-5625)

Mattresses (good value): **Town Bedding & Upholstery** (205 Eighth Ave, 212/243-0426)

Perfume bottles (vintage): **Gallery 47** (1050 Second Ave, 212/888-0165)

Photographs (film stars): **Movie Star News** (134 W 18th St, 212/620-8160)

Pianos, grand: **Maximiliaan's House of Grand Pianos** (305 Second Ave, Suite 322, 212/689-2177; by appointment)

Plumbing fixtures: **Blackman** (85 Fifth Ave, 2nd floor, 212/337-1000)

Posters, movie: **Jerry Ohlinger Movie Material Store** (253 W 35th St, 212/989-0869)

Posters, Broadway theater: **Triton Gallery** (630 Ninth Ave, 212/765-2472)

Posters, original (1880 to present): **Philip Williams** (122 Chambers St, 212/513-0313)

Posters, vintage: **La Belle Epoque Vintage Posters** (280 Columbus Ave, 212/362-1770)

Pottery, handmade: **Mugi Studio and Gallery** (993 Amsterdam Ave, 212/866-6202)

Pottery, paint-your-own: **Make** (1566 Second Ave, 212/570-6868 and other locations)

Prints, botanical: **W. Graham Arader** (29 E 72nd St, 212/628-3668 and 1016 Madison Ave, 212/628-7625)

Quilts: **Down and Quilt Shop** (518 Columbus Ave, 212/496-8980 and 1225 Madison Ave, 212/423-9358)

Rugs, antique: **Doris Leslie Blau** (306 E 61st St, 212/586-5511; by appointment)

Safes: **Empire Safe** (6 E 39th St, 212/684-2255)

Screens, shoji: **Miya Shoji** (109 W 17th St, 212/243-6774)

Shelves: **Shelf Shop** (1295 First Ave, 212/988-7246)

Silver (unusual): **Jean's Silversmiths** (16 W 45th St, 212/575-0723)

Silverware and holloware (good values): **Eastern Silver** (4901 16th Ave, Brooklyn, 718/854-5600)

Sofas: **Classic Sofa** (5 W 22nd St, 212/620-0485)

Sofas, vintage: **Regeneration Furniture** (38 Renwick St, 212/741-2102)

Strollers and other baby equipment: **Schneider's Juvenile Furniture** (41 W 25th St, 212/228-3540)

Tabletop merchandise: **Clio** (92 Thompson St, 212/966-8991)

Tapestries: **Lovelia Enterprises** (356 E 41st St, 212/490-0930; by appointment) and **Saint-Remy** (818 Lexington Ave, 212/486-2018)

Teaware: **Ito En** (822 Madison Ave, 212/988-7111)

Tiles: **Mosaic House** (62 W 22nd St, 212/414-2525)

Tiles, ceramic and marble: **Quarry Tiles, Marble & Granite** (132 Lexington Ave, 212/679-8889) and **Complete Tile Collection** (42 W 15th St, 212/255-4450)

Trays: **Extraordinary** (247 E 57th St, 212/223-9151)

Vacuum cleaners: **Desco** (131 W 14th St, 212/989-1800)

Wallpaper, antique: **Secondhand Rose** (138 Duane St, 212/393-9002)

Wallpaper (discounted): **Janovic Plaza** (136 Church St, 212/349-0001 and other locations)

Wrought-iron items: **Morgik Metal Design** (145 Hudson St, 212/463-0304)

Things for Leisure Time

Accordions: **Main Squeeze** (19 Essex St, 212/614-3109)

Art supplies: **Pearl Paint Company** (308 Canal St, 212/431-7932)

Athletic gear: **Modell's** (55 Chambers St, 212/732-8484 and other locations)

Athletic gear, team: **Yankee Clubhouse** (110 E 59th St, 212/758-7844 and 393 Fifth Ave, 212/685-4693) and **New York Mets Clubhouse** (11 W 42nd St, 212/768-9534)

Beads: **Beads of Paradise** (16 E 17th St, 212/620-0642) and **Beads World** (1384 Broadway, 212/302-1199)

Bicycles: **Bicycle Habitat** (244 Lafayette St, 212/625-1347)

Bicycles, track: **Trackstar** (231 Eldridge St, 212/982-2553)

Binoculars: **Clairmont-Nichols** (1016 First Ave, 212/758-2346)

Books (new, used and review copies): **Strand Book Store** (828 Broadway, 212/473-1452)

Books (rare): **Imperial Fine Books** (790 Madison Ave, 2nd floor, 212/861-6620), **J.N. Bartfield Galleries** (30 W 57th St, 212/245-8890), **Martayan Lan** (70 E 55th St, 212/308-0018), and **Strand Book Store** (828 Broadway, 212/473-1452)

Books, academic: **Labyrinth Books** (536 W 112th St, 212/865-1588)

Books, art: **Printed Matter** (195 Tenth Ave, 212/925-0325)

Books, astrology: **New York Astrology Center** (370 Lexington Ave, Suite 416, 212/949-7211)

Books, children's and parents': **Bank Street Bookstore** (610 W 112th St, 212/678-1654)

Books, exam-study and science-fiction: **Civil Service Book Shop** (89 Worth St, 212/226-9506)

Books, fashion design: **Fashion Design Bookstore** (250 W 27th St, 212/633-9646)

Books, graphic design: **Zakka** (147 Grand St, 212/431-3961)

Books, metaphysical and religious: **Quest Bookshop** (240 E 53rd St, 212/758-5521)

Books, mystery: **Black Orchid Bookshop** (303 E 81st St, 212/734-5980) and **Partners & Crime** (44 Greenwich Ave, 212/243-0440)

Books, plates (lithographs): **George Glazer Gallery** (28 E 72nd St, Room 3A, 212/327-2598)

Books, progressive political: **Revolution Books** (9 W 19th St, 212/691-3345)

Chess sets: **Chess Forum** (219 Thompson St, 212/475-2369)

Cigarettes (luxury): **Nat Sherman International** (12 E 42nd St, 212/764-5000)

Cigars: **Davidoff of Geneva** (535 Madison Ave, 212/751-9060) and **J.R. Cigars** (562 Fifth Ave, 212/997-2227)

Cigars (hand-rolled): **PB Cuban Cigars** (265 W 30th St, 212/367-8949)

Comic books, vintage: **Metropolis Collectibles** (873 Broadway, Suite 201, 212/260-4147; by appointment)

Compact discs, records, tapes, and DVDs (discounted): **Disc-O-Rama** (40 Union Sq E, 212/260-8616; 44 W 8th St, 212/477-9410; and 186 W 4th St, 212/206-8417)

Compact discs (used): **St. Mark's Sounds** (20 St. Mark's Pl, 212/677-3444)

Computer software: **J&R Music & Computer World** (15 Park Row, 212/238-9000)

Computers, Apple: **The Apple Store** (103 Prince St, 212/226-3126 and 767 Fifth Ave, 212/336-1440)

Computers, hand-held: **RCS Computer Experience** (575 Madison Ave, 212/949-6935)

Costumes and makeup: **Halloween Adventure** (104 Fourth Ave, 212/673-4546)

Dance-related items: **World Tone Dance** (230 Seventh Ave, 2nd floor, 212/691-1934)

Dolls: **Alexander Doll Company** (615 W 131st St, 212/283-5900)

Dollhouses: **Tiny Doll House** (314 E 78th St, 212/744-3719)

Drums: **Drummer's World** (151 W 46th St, 3rd floor, 212/840-3057)

Embroidery (custom-designed): **Jonathan Embroidery Plus** (256 W 38th St, 212/398-3538)

Filofax (discounted): **Altman Luggage** (135 Orchard St, 212/254-7275)

Fishing tackle: **Orvis** (522 Fifth Ave, 212/827-0698)

Fitness equipment: **Omni Fitness Equipment** (830 Broadway, 212/260-8537)

Games: **Compleat Strategist** (11 E 33rd St, 212/685-3880)

Games (*Warhammer*): **Games Workshop** (54 E 8th St, 212/982-6314)

Gifts: **Annie O** (105 Rivington St, 212/475-3490) and **Mxyplyzyk** (125 Greenwich Ave, 212/989-4300)

Gifts (pop-culture curiosities): **Exit 9** (64 Ave A, 212/228-0145)

Globes, antique (world and celestial): **George Glazer Gallery** (28 E 72nd St, Room 3A, 212/327-2598)

Golf equipment (best selection): **New York Golf Center** (131 W 35th St, 212/564-2255)

Guitars: **Carmine Street Guitars** (42 Carmine St, 212/691-8400), **Dan's Chelsea Guitars** (220 W 23rd St, 212/675-4993), **Guitar Salon** (45 Grove St, 212/675-3236; by appointment), **Ludlow Guitars** (164 Ludlow St, 212/353-1775), **Manny's Music** (156 W 48th St, 212/819-0576), **Matt Umanov Guitars** (273 Bleecker St, 212/675-2157), and **Rogue Music** (251 W 30th St, 10th floor, 212/629-5073)

Guns: **Beretta Gallery** (718 Madison Ave, 3rd floor, 212/319-3235) and **Holland & Holland** (10 E 40th St, 19th floor, 212/752-7755)

Harley-Davidson gear: **Harley-Davidson of New York** (686 Lexington Ave, 212/355-3003)

Holographs: **Holographic Studio** (240 E 26th St, 212/686-9397)

Home entertainment equipment and systems: **J&R Music & Computer World** (23 Park Row, 212/238-9000)

Horseback-riding equipment: **Manhattan Saddlery** (117 E 24th St, 212/673-1400)

Knitting: **Gotta Knit!** (498 Ave of the Americas, 2nd floor, 212/989-3030) and **Yarn Company** (2274 Broadway, 212/787-7878)

Luggage, soft: **Bag House** (797 Broadway, 212/260-0940)

Magazines: **DINA Magazines** (270 Park Ave S, 212/674-6595), **Eastern Newsstand** (many locations), and **Universal News** (977 Eighth Ave, 212/459-0932 and 676 Lexington Ave, 212/750-1855)

Magic tricks: **Tannen's Magic** (45 W 34th St, 212/929-4500)

Maps: **Hagstrom Map and Travel Center** (51 W 43rd St, 212/398-1222)

Maps and prints (antiquarian): **Argosy Book Store** (116 E 59th St, 212/753-4455)

Maps, globes, and atlases (antique): **Martayan Lan** (70 E 55th St, 212/308-0018) and **Richard B. Arkway** (59 E 54th St, 6th floor, 212/751-8135)

Marine supplies: **West Marine** (12 W 37th St, 212/594-6065)

Music (downloads for iPods): **Hungrypod** (307 Seventh Ave, 212/741-5080)

Musical gifts and souvenirs: **Backstage Memories** (1638 Broadway, 212/582-5996)

Music instruments: **Manny's Music** (156 W 48th St, 212/819-0576), **Music Inn World Instruments** (169 W 4th St, 212/243-5715), and **Sam Ash Music Store** (160 W 48th St, 212/719-2299)

New York memorabilia: **Museum of the City of New York** (1220 Fifth Ave, 212/534-1170)

Newspapers, out-of-town: **Hotalings News Agency** (630 W 52nd St, 212/974-9419)

Novelties: **Gordon Novelty** (52 W 29th St, 212/696-9664)

Outdoor gear: **Tent & Trails** (21 Park Pl, 212/227-1760)

Paper items (huge selection): **PaperPresentation.com** (23 W 18th St, 212/463-7035)

Papers (elegant): **Il Papiro** (1021 Lexington Ave, 212/288-9330)

Pens, antique and new: **Arthur Brown & Brother** (2 W 46th St, 212/575-5555)

Pet supplies (discounted): **Petland Discounts** (312 W 23rd St, 212/366-0512, and other locations)

Pets: **Pets-on-Lex** (1109 Lexington Ave, 212/426-0766)

Photo processing and frames: **Ben Ness Photo** (111 University Pl, 212/253-2313)

Photographic equipment (rental and sales): **Calumet Photographic** (22 W 22nd St, 212/989-8500)

Pipes, handmade: **Connoisseur Pipe Shop** (UBS Bldg, 1285 Ave of the Americas, concourse level, 212/247-6054)

Pool tables: **Blatt Billiards** (809 Broadway, 212/674-8855)

Quilting supplies: **City Quilter** (133 W 25th St, 212/807-0390)

Records, out-of-print: **House of Oldies** (35 Carmine St, 212/243-0500)
Records, vintage rock and roll: **Strider Records** (22 Jones St, 212/675-3040)
Robots: **Robot Village** (252 W 81st St, 212/799-7626)
Science fiction: **Forbidden Planet** (840 Broadway, 212/473-1576)
Scuba-diving and snorkeling equipment: **Pan Aqua Diving** (460 W 43rd St, 212/736-3483) and **Scuba Network** (669 Lexington Ave, 212/750-9160 and 655 Ave of the Americas, 212/243-2988)
Skateboards: **Supreme** (274 Lafayette St, 212/966-7799)
Skating equipment: **Blades Board & Skate** (156 W 72nd St, 212/787-3911; 659 Broadway, 212/477-7350; 901 Ave of the Americas, 646/733-2738; and other locations)
Snowboards: **Burton Snowboard Company** (106 Spring St, 212/966-8068)
Soccer supplies: **Soccer Sport Supply** (1745 First Ave, 212/427-6050)
Soldiers, toy: **Second Childhood** (283 Bleecker St, 212/989-6140)
Sports cards: **Alex's MVP Cards** (256 E 89th St, 212/831-2273)
Stationery: **Kate's Paperie** (561 Broadway, 212/941-9816; 1282 Third Ave, 212/396-3670; 8 W 13th St, 212/633-0570; and 140 W 57th St, 212/459-0700)
Theatrical items: **One Shubert Alley** (One Shubert Alley, 212/944-4133)
Toys (good selection): **Kidding Around** (60 W 15th St, 212/645-6337)
Toys, antique (1900-1950): **Bizarre Bazaar** (130¼ E 65th St, 212/517-2100; appointment suggested)
Toys, imported (high-quality): **Geppetto's Toy Box** (10 Christopher St, 212/620-7511)
Toys, imported Japanese: **Image Anime** (103 W 30th St, 212/631-0966)
Toys, novelties and party supplies: **E.A.T. Gifts** (1062 Madison Ave, 212/861-2544)
Toys, vintage: **Alphaville** (226 W Houston St, 212/675-6850)
Toys, young adult: **Kidrobot** (126 Prince St, 212/966-6688)
Videogames: **GameStop** (901 Ave of the Americas, 212/564-4156; 687 Broadway, 212/473-6571; and other locations)
Videos, rare and foreign (rental and sales): **Evergreen Video** (37 Carmine St, 212/691-7362) and **Mondo Kim's** (6 St. Mark's Pl, 212/598-9985)
Violins: **Universal Musical Instrument Co.** (732 Broadway, 212/254-6917)
Woodwinds: **Roberto's Woodwind Repair Shop** (149 W 46th St, 212/391-1315)
Writing instruments: **Rebecca Moss** (212/832-7671)

Factory Outlet Centers in the Tri-State Area

Merchandise at these outlet centers is generally discounted 25% to 65% from retail prices; special events afford even deeper savings.

Connecticut

Clinton Crossing Premium Outlets (20 Killingsworth Turnpike, Clinton, CT; 860/664-0700; www.premiumoutlets.com): 70 upscale outlet stores

(continued next page)

New Jersey
Flemington area:
Liberty Village Premium Outlets (1 Church St, Flemington, NJ; 908/782-8550; www.premiumoutlets.com): over 60 outlets, family shopping
Secaucus area:
This eight-to-ten-block shopping mecca includes individual factory stores and two malls:
Designer Outlet Gallery (55 Hartz Way, Secaucus, NJ; 201/726-5537; www.designeroutletgallery.com): 14 stores, upscale
Harmon Cove Outlet Center (20 Enterprise Ave N, Secaucus, NJ; 201/348-4780; www.harmonmeadow.com): 100 stores, well-known names
Other New Jersey areas:
Circle Factory Outlets (Route 35 at Manasquan Circle, Wall Township, NJ; 732/223-2300): 35 stores, values for the family
Jackson Premium Outlets (537 Monmouth Rd, Jackson, NJ; 732/833-0503; www.premiumoutlets.com): 70 stores, top retailers
Jersey Gardens (651 Kapkowski Rd, Elizabeth, NJ; 908/354-5900; www.jerseygardens.com): over 200 stores, New Jersey's largest
Marketplace Mall (Route 34, Matawan, NJ; 732/583-8700): 30 outlet and discount stores
Olde Lafayette Village (Route 15 at Route 94, Lafayette, NJ; 973/383-8323): 8 outlets, plus antique stores, specialty shops, eateries
New York
Woodbury Common Premium Outlets (498 Red Apple Court, Central Valley, NY; 845/928-4000; www.premiumoutlets.com): 220 upscale outlet stores
Pennsylvania
Franklin Mills (1455 Franklin Mills Circle, Philadelphia, PA: 215/632-1500): close to 200 manufacturers' and retail outlet stores

Things from Far Away
British clothing and shoes: **99X** (84 E 10th St, 212/460-8599)
Buddhas: **Leekan Designs** (93 Mercer St, 212/226-7226)
Chinese dinnerware: **Wing On Wo & Co.** (26 Mott St, 212/962-3577)
Chinese goods: **Pearl River Emporium** (477 Broadway, 212/431-4770) and **Chinese American Trading Company** (91 Mulberry St, 212/267-5224)
European pottery (Italian and French): **La Terrine** (1024 Lexington Ave, 212/988-3366)
Gifts and clothing, imported: **Roberta Freymann** (155 E 70th St, 212/585-3767)
Himalayan craft items: **Himalayan Crafts** (2007 Broadway, 212/787-8500)
Italian shoes (exotic skins): **Cellini Uomo** (59 Orchard St, 212/219-8657)
Japanese gift items: **Katagiri** (224 E 59th St, 212/755-3566)

Japanese kimonos: **Kimono House** (131 Thompson St, 212/505-0232)

Lampshades, Oriental: **Oriental Lampshade Company** (223 W 79th St, 212/873-0812 and 816 Lexington Ave, 212/832-8190)

Leather items, imported: **Il Bisonte** (120 Sullivan S, 212/966-8773)

Mexican imports: **Pan American Phoenix** (857 Lexington Ave, 212/570-0300)

Moroccan gifts: **Gates of Morocco** (8 Prince St, 212/925-2650)

Scandinavian imports: **Antik** (104 Franklin St, 212/343-0471)

Tibetan treasures: **Do Kham** (51 Prince St, 212/966-2404), **Tibet Bazaar** (473 Amsterdam Ave, 212/595-8487), **Vvajra** (146 Sullivan St, 212/529-4344), and **Vision of Tibet** (167 Thompson St, 212/995-9276)

Turkish carpets: **Beyond the Bosphorus** (79 Sullivan St, 212/219-8257)

Miscellaneous Other Things

Balloons: **Balloon Saloon** (133 West Broadway, 212/227-3838)

Butterflies: **Mariposa, the Butterfly Gallery** (South Street Seaport, Pier 17, 2nd floor, 212/233-3221)

Cat memorabilia: **Just Cats** (244 E 60th St, 212/888-2287)

Firefighting memorabilia: **Firestore** (17 Greenwich Ave, 212/226-3142)

Fish, tropical: **New World Aquarium** (204 E 38th St, 646/865-9604)

Flags and banners: **Art Flag Co.** (8 Jay St, 212/334-1890)

Judaica: **Manhattan Judaica** (62 W 45th St, 212/719-1918)

Office furniture (good prices): **Discount Office Furniture** (132 W 24th St, 212/691-5625)

Office supplies, Muji: **MoMA Design Store** (11 W 53rd St, 212/767-1050) and **MoMA Design Store Soho** (81 Spring St, 646/613-1367)

Optical instruments: **Clairmont-Nichols** (1016 First Ave, 212/758-2346)

Plexiglas & Lucite items: **Plexi-Craft Quality Products** (514 W 24th St, 212/924-3244)

Portfolios, custom: **House of Portfolios** (52 W 21st St, 212/206-7323)

Store fixtures: **Liberty Display & Supply** (138 W 25th St, 212/929-2777)

Travel items: **Flight 001** (96 Greenwich St, 212/989-0001)

Typewriter ribbons: **Abalon Business Machines** (60 E 42nd St, 212/682-1653)

Luxury Labels

A La Vielle Russie (781 Fifth Ave, 212/752-1727): antiques

A. Testoni (781 Fifth Ave, 212/223-0909): luxury leather goods

Abercrombie & Fitch (199 Water St, 212/809-9000): men's and women's preppy clothing and accessories

Alfred Dunhill (711 Fifth Ave, 212/753-9292): men's fashions and accessories

Ann Taylor (645 Madison Ave, 212/832-2010 and other locations): women's clothing and accessories

Asprey (853 Madison Ave, 212/688-1811): luxury jewelry and clothing

Baccarat (625 Madison Ave, 212/826-4100): crystal

Balenciaga (542 W 22nd St, 212/206-0872): men's and women's clothing and accessories

Bang & Olufsen (927 Broadway, 212/388-9792; 330 Columbus Ave, 212/501-0926; and 952 Madison Ave, 212/879-6161): home entertainment equipment

Bernardaud (499 Park Ave, 212/371-4300): elegant tableware and furniture

Bottega Veneta (699 Fifth Ave, 212/371-5511): men's and women's fashions

Botticelli (620 Fifth Ave, 212/582-6313 and 522 Fifth Ave, 212/768-1430): leather goods

Brioni (55 E 52nd St, 212/355-1940 and 57 E 57th St, 212/376-5777): Italian apparel for men and women

Brooks Brothers (666 Fifth Ave, 212/261-9440 and 346 Madison Ave, 212/682-8800): traditional fashions for men, women, and boys

Bulgari (730 Fifth Ave, 212/315-9000): jewelry and watches

Burberry (131 Spring St, 212/925-9300 and 9 E 57th St, 212/407-7100): plaid everything and more

Calvin Klein (654 Madison Ave, 212/292-9000): fashions for the body and home

Carolina Herrara (954 Madison Ave, 212/249-6552): wedding gowns and other fine attire; by appointment

Cartier (653 Fifth Ave, 212/308-0843): jewelry

Caswell-Massey (518 Lexington Ave, 212/755-2254): beauty and skin-care extravagances

Chanel (15 E 57th St, 212/355-5050; 139 Spring St, 212/334-0055; and 737 Madison Ave, 212/535-5505): classic apparel and accessories

Chopard (725 Madison Ave, 212/218-7222): jewelry and watches

Christian Dior (21 E 57th St, 212/931-2950): clothing and accessories

Christofle (680 Madison Ave, 212/308-9390): silver, crystal, and porcelain

Coach (595 Madison Ave, 212/754-0041): leather goods and shoes

Crate & Barrel (650 Madison Ave, 212/308-0011 and 611 Broadway, 212/780-0004): housewares and furniture

Crouch & Fitzgerald (400 Madison Ave, 212/755-5888): luggage and leather accessories

Daum (694 Madison Ave, 212/355-2060): crystal gifts

Dolce & Gabbana (825 Madison Ave, 212/249-4100): clothing and sunglasses

Dooney & Bourke (20 E 60th St, 212/223-7444): handbags

Donna Karan (819 Madison Ave, 212/861-1001): clothing and home furnishings

Emanuel Ungaro (792 Madison Ave, 212/249-4090): fashion clothing

Emilio Pucci (24 E 64th St, 212/752-4777 and 701 Fifth Ave, 212/230-1135): retro clothing

Ermenegildo Zegna (663 Fifth Ave, 212/421-4488): haberdashery (at 543 Madison Ave until 2008)

Escada (715 Fifth Ave, 212/755-2200): women's fashions

Etro (720 Madison Ave, 212/317-9096): men's and women's clothing

Façonnable (636 Fifth Ave, 212/319-0111): styles for men and women

Fendi (677 Fifth Ave, 212/759-4646): women's fashions

Fortunoff (681 Fifth Ave, 212/758-6660): jewelry and watches

Fretté (799 Madison Ave, 212/988-5221): bedding and accessories

Georg Jensen (125 Wooster St, 212/343-9000; 685 Madison Ave, 212/759-6457; and 125 Wooster St, 212/343-9000): silver home accessories and gifts, jewelry, and sunglasses

Gianfranco Ferré (870 Madison Ave, 212/717-5430): fragrances, men's and women's clothing, and accessories

Giorgio Armani (760 Madison Ave, 212/988-9191): men's and women's couture

Givenchy (at Barneys New York and Saks Fifth Avenue): classic clothes

Graff (721 Madison Ave, 212/355-9292): diamonds

Gucci (685 Fifth Ave, 212/826-2600 and 840 Madison Ave, 212/717-2619): sportswear, leather goods, and accessories

Harry Winston (718 Fifth Ave, 212/245-2000): serious jewels

Hermés (691 Madison Ave, 212/751-3181): scarves, ties, and fragrances

Hickey Freeman (666 Fifth Ave, 212/586-6481): menswear

Hugo Boss (717 Fifth Ave, 212/485-1800): men's and women's clothing

Issey Miyake (119 Hudson St, 212/226-0100 and 802 Madison Ave, 212/439-7822): innovative apparel

Jack of Diamonds (1196 Ave of the Americas, 212/869-7272): diamonds, of course

Jil Sander (11 E 57th St, 212/838-6100): ladies' clothing and accessories

John Lobb (680 Madison Ave, 212/888-9797): men's shoes

Jonathan Adler (47 Greene St, 212/941-8950): pottery and home furnishings

Judith Leiber (680 Madison Ave, 212/223-2999): luxury handbags and accessories

Kiehl's (109 Third Ave, 212/677-3171): men's and women's skin care products and toiletries

Lacoste (608 Fifth Ave, 212/459-2300 and 575 Madison Ave, 212/750-8115): polo shirts

Lalique (712 Madison Ave, 212/355-6550): crystal, jewelry, and leather goods

Leron (804 Madison Ave, 212/753-6700): linens for the home and lingerie

Lladro U.S.A. (43 W 57th St, 212/838-9356): porcelain figurines

Loro Piana (821 Madison Ave, 212/980-7961): men's and women's clothing and accessories

Louis Vuitton (1 E 57th St, 212/758-8877 and 116 Greene St, 212/274-9090): leather goods, fashions, and accessories

Malo (814 Madison Ave, 212/396-4721): cashmere clothing

Manolo Blahnik (31 W 54th St, 212/582-3007): sexy shoes for women

Mexx (650 Fifth Ave, 212/956-6506): men's and women's fashions

Michael C. Fina (545 Fifth Ave, 212/557-2500): silver, china, crystal, giftware, and jewelry

Michael Kors (974 Madison Ave, 212/452-4685): women's sportswear

Mikimoto (730 Fifth Ave, 212/457-4600): pearls

Missoni (1009 Madison Ave, 212/517-9339): men's and women's knit items

Montblanc-Madison (598 Madison Ave, 212/223-8888): writing instruments and accessories

Nicole Miller (780 Madison Ave, 212/288-9779): women's clothing and evening gowns

Niketown New York (6 E 57th St, 212/891-6453): athletic wear, gear, and shoes

Oscar de la Renta (772 Madison Ave, 212/288-5810): women's fashions

Oxford Clothes (717 Fifth Ave, 212/593-0204): hand-tailored menswear

Peter Elliot (1070 Madison Ave, 212/570-2300 and 1071 Madison Ave, 212/570-1551): tailored clothing and sportswear for men and women, respectively

Piaget (730 Fifth Ave, 212/246-5555): luxury watches and snazzy jewelry
Porthault (18 E 69th St, 212/688-1660): luxurious linens and gifts
Prada (575 Broadway, 212/334-8888; 724 Fifth Ave, 212/664-0010; 841 Madison Ave, 212/327-4200; and 45 E 57th St, 212/308-2332): clothing, shoes, and accessories
Pratesi (829 Madison Ave, 212/288-2315): linens, towels, and bathrobes
Ralph Lauren (867 Madison Ave, 212/606-2100; 380 Bleecker St, 212/645-5513; and other locations): fashions and accessories for the family and home
Roberto Vascon (140 W 72nd St, 212/787-9050): handbags
Salvatore Ferragamo (655 Fifth Ave, 212/759-3822): Italian shoes and clothing
Shanghai Tang (714 Madison Ave, 212/888-0111): Oriental-influenced family clothing and home fashions
St. John (665 Fifth Ave, 212/755-5252): women's wear
Steuben (667 Madison Ave, 212/752-1441): fine glassware
Swarovski (625 Madison Ave, 212/308-1710): crystal jewelry, miniatures, and figurines
Thomas Pink (520 Madison Ave, 212/838-1928 and 1155 Ave of the Americas, 212/840-9663): shirts and accessories for men and women
Tiffany & Co. (727 Fifth Ave, 212/755-8000): luxurious jewelry and gifts
Tourneau (12 E 57th St, 212/758-7300): exquisite timepieces
Turnbull & Asser (42 E 57th St, 212/752-5700): custom- and ready-made classic shirts and clothes for men and women
Valentino (747 Madison Ave, 212/772-6969): formal wear and accessories
Van Cleef & Arpels (744 Fifth Ave, 212/644-9500): classic jewelry
Wempe Jewelers (700 Fifth Ave, 212/397-9000): jewelry and watches
Yves St. Laurent Rive Gauche (855 Madison Ave, 212/988-3821 and 3 E 57th St, 212/980-2970): clothing and accessories

> One big difference between "uptown" and "downtown" stores is the hours. While those in midtown and on the East Side and West Side often open at 9 or 10 in the morning, many stores in Greenwich Village, Soho, and Tribeca don't open until 11 a.m. or noon. The same is often true of museums in those neighborhoods.

New York Stores: The Best of the Lot
Anatomical Supplies

THE EVOLUTION STORE
120 Spring St (bet Greene St and Mercer St)   212/343-1114
Daily: 11-7   www.theevolutionstore.com

Have your kids been bugging you for lollipops with edible crickets inside? Believe it or not, the Evolution Store has just such an item—and lots more, too! This store is really a natural history museum for sale. For starters, there are insects, specimens, fossils, medical models, anatomical items, minerals, seashells, and jewelry. Shopping is rarely this educational and fascinating.

MAXILLA & MANDIBLE, LTD.
451 Columbus Ave (bet 81st and 82nd St)   212/724-6173
Mon-Sat: 11-7; Sun: 1-5 (call ahead; closed some days seasonally)
                              www.maxillaandmandible.com

Henry Galiano grew up in Spanish Harlem. On the days his parents weren't running their beauty parlor, the family often went to the American Museum of Natural History. His interest in things skeletal increased when he got a job at the museum as a curator's assistant. He soon started his own collection of skeletons and bones. That, in turn, led to his opening Maxilla & Mandible (the scientific names for upper and lower jaw, respectively), which is the first and only such store in the world. How many people need complete skeletons—or even a single maxilla? More than you might think! The shop supplies museum-quality preparations of skulls, skeletons, bones, teeth, horns, skins, butterflies, beetles, seashells, fossils, meteorites, minerals, taxidermy mounts, and anatomical charts and models to sculptors, painters, interior decorators, jewelry manufacturers, propmasters, medical personnel, scientists, and educators. They also carry scientific equipment.

New York's most popular radio personality, **Joan Hamburg**, can be heard on WOR (710 AM). Joan has been sharing her encyclopedic knowledge about the city—shopping, eating, touring—for over three decades. You'll love her! Tune in 9 to 11 a.m., Monday through Friday.

Animation

ANIMAZING GALLERY—SOHO
461 Broome St (bet Greene and Mercer St)   212/226-7374
Mon-Sat: 10-7; Sun: 11-6   www.animazing.com

No one is better at showing animation than Animazing Gallery. They are New York City's authorized Disney art gallery. They showcase the *Peanuts* pop art of Tom Everhart (friend of the late Charles Schultz), and exclusively offer the work of Dr. Seuss and many other artists. Vintage and contemporary cels and drawings from all major studios are featured. Specialties include appraisals, consignments, searches, and autographed books. Special gala events, shows, and sales are held. Their space also includes 3D work, glass sculpture, Wild Home furnishings, and Art to Wear jewelry.

Antiques

Bleecker Street

Les Pierre Antiques (367 Bleecker St, 212/243-7740): French Country

Chelsea

Upstairs Downtown Antiques (12 W 19th St, 212/989-8715): eclectic, full-service

Greenwich Village

Agostino Antiques, Ltd. (979 Third Ave, 15th floor, 212/421-8820): English and French 17th-to-19th-century furniture
Donzella (17 White St, 212/965-8919): 1930s, 1940s, and 1950s furnishings
End of History (548½ Hudson St, 212/647-7598): vintage hand-blown glass

D. Barton Kyner Antiques (827 Broadway, 212/674-1000): French and English Country furniture
Hyde Park Antiques (836 Broadway, 212/477-0033): English furniture
Karl Kemp & Associates (36 E 10th St, 212/254-1877): furniture
Kentshire Galleries (37 E 12th St, 212/673-6644): English antiques
Maison Gerard (53 E 10th St, 212/674-7611): French art deco
Ritter-Antik (35 E 10th St, 212/673-2213): first-period Biedermeier

Lexington Avenue

Hayko (857 Lexington Ave, 212/717-5400): kilims
Sara (950-952 Lexington Ave, 212/772-3243): Japanese pottery and porcelain
Sylvia Pines Uniquities (1102 Lexington Ave, 212/744-5141): jewelry and handbags

Lower East Side

Billy's Antiques & Props (76 E Houston St, 917/576-6980): fun antiques

Madison Avenue

Alexander Gallery (942 Madison Ave, 212/517-4400): American and European 18th- and 19th-century paintings
Antiquarium (948 Madison Ave, 212/734-9776): jewelry and antiquities
Art of the Past (1242 Madison Ave, 212/860-7070): South and Southeast Asia
Bernard & S. Dean Levy (24 E 84th St, 212/628-7088): American furniture and silver
Cora Ginsburg (19 E 74th St, 212/744-1352): antique textiles
DeLorenzo (956 Madison Ave, 212/249-7575): art deco
Didier Aaron (32 E 67th St, 212/988-5248): 17th-, 18th-, and 19th-century pieces
Edith Weber & Associates (994 Madison Ave, 212/570-9668): rare and historic jewels
Fanelli Antique Timepieces (790 Madison Ave, Suite 202, 212/517-2300): antique timepieces
Florian Papp (962 Madison Ave, 212/288-6770): furniture
Friedman & Vallois (27 E 67th St, 212/517-3820): high-end French art deco
George Glazer Gallery (28 E 72nd St, 212/535-5706): maps, globes
Guild Antiques (1089 Madison Ave, 212/717-1810): English formal
J.J. Lally (41 E 57th St, 212/371-3380): Chinese art
John Rosselli Antiques (255 E 72nd St, 212/737-2252): cosmopolitan antiques
L'Antiquaire & the Connoisseur (36 E 73rd St, 212/517-9176): French and Italian furniture
Linda Horn Antiques (1327 Madison Ave, 212/772-1122): late 19th-century English and French antiques
Macklowe Gallery (667 Madison Ave, 212/644-6400): Tiffany
Sentimento Antiques (306 E 61st St, 6th floor, 212/750-3111): furniture, sterling silver, and desk accessories
Time Will Tell (212/787-8848; by appointment): vintage watches
Ursus Books and Prints (981 Madison Ave, 212/772-8787): books
W. Graham Arader (29 E 72nd St, 212/628-3668): rare prints

Meatpacking District

Lars Bolander N.Y. (72 Gansevoort St, 212/924-1000): 17th- and 18th-century Swedish and French antiques and reproductions

Midtown

A La Vielle Russie (781 Fifth Ave, 212/752-1727): Russian art

Chameleon (223 E 59th St, 212/355-6300): lighting

Dalva Brothers (44 E 57th St, 212/758-2297): French furniture

Doris Leslie Blau (306 E 61st St, 212/586-5511): rugs

Eric Originals & Antiques (4 W 47th St, 212/819-9595): antique diamond jewelry

Gardner & Barr (213 E 60th St, 212/752-0555): Murano glass

George N. Antiques (227 E 59th St, 212/935-4005): mirrors

Gotta Have It! (153 E 57th St, 212/750-7900): celebrity memorabilia

Gray & Davis (32 W 47th St, 212/719-4698): vintage engagement rings

Hugo, Ltd. (233 E 59th St, 212/750-6877): 19th-century lighting and decorative arts

James Robinson (480 Park Ave, 212/752-6166): silver flatware

Leo Kaplan, Ltd. (114 E 57th, 212/249-6766): ceramics and glass

Manhattan Art & Antiques Center (1050 Second Ave, 212/355-4400): 100 galleries

Martayan Lan (70 E 55th, 6th floor, 212/308-0018): 16th- and 17th-century maps

Naga Antiques (145 E 61st St, 212/593-2788): antique Japanese screens

Newel Art Galleries (425 E 53rd St, 212/758-1970): various styles and periods

Paris to Provence (207 E 60th St, 212/750-0037): French and English furniture

Philip Colleck (311 E 58th St, 212/486-7600): 18th- and early 19th-century English furniture

Ralph M. Chait Galleries (724 Fifth Ave, 10th floor, 212/758-0937): Chinese art

S.J. Shrubsole (104 E 57th St, 212/753-8920): English silver

Stephen Herdemian (78 W 47th St and 73 W 47th St, 212/944-2534): antique jewelry

Soho/Tribeca

Alan Moss (436 Lafayette St, 212/473-1310): 20th-century furniture

Art & Industry (50 Great Jones St, 212/477-0116): items from the 1940s, 1950s, and 1960s

Beyond the Bosphorus (79 Sullivan St, 212/219-8257): Turkish kilims and pillows

Bikini Bar (148-C Duane St, 212/571-6737): Hawaiian, vintage rattan, and surfboards

David Stypmann (190 Ave of the Americas, 212/226-5717): eclectic, pottery, and mirrors

Eileen Lane Antiques (150 Thompson St, 212/475-2988): Swedish art deco and Beidermeier

Gill & Lagodich Fine Period Frames (108 Reade St, 212/619-0631; by appointment): frames

Greene Street Antiques (76 Wooster St, 212/274-1076): Scandinavian and Beidermeier antiques

Lost City Arts (18 Cooper Sq, 212/375-0500): furniture and fixtures
Secondhand Rose (138 Duane St, 212/393-9002): 19th-century Moorish antiques
Urban Archaeology (143 Franklin St, 212/431-4646): architectural antiques and reproductions
WaterMoon Gallery (110 Duane St, 212/925-5556; by appointment): Chinese antiques and works of art
Wyeth (315 Spring St, 212/243-3661; by appointment): early- to mid-20th-century antiques and custom furniture

Upper East Side

Bizarre Bazaar (130¼ E 65th St, 212/517-2100): 20th-century industrial design
Evergreen Antiques (1249 Third Ave, 212/744-5664): European and Scandinavian furniture
Howard Kaplan Designs (240 E 60th St, 646/443-7170): French and English country furniture
Leigh Keno American Antiques (127 E 69th St, 212/734-2381): 17th-, 18th-, and 20th-century American furniture

Upper West Side

La Belle Epoque Vintage Posters (280 Columbus Ave, 212/362-1770): advertising posters

Architectural Antiques

OLDE GOOD THINGS
124 W 24th St (bet Ave of the Americas and Seventh Ave)
Daily: 9-7   212/989-8401
                                      www.oldegoodthings.com

What a fascinating business this is! Olde Good Things salvages significant artifacts from old buildings, offering one of the largest showings of architectural antiques and salvaged items in the country. You'll find mantels, irons, doors, stone and terra cotta, hardware, garden items, furniture, floorings, mirrors, and on and on.

> **The ShowPlace** (40 W 25th St, 212/633-6063, www.nyshowplace.com) is the largest antique center in New York, with 135 quality galleries selling jewelry, art glass, art nouveau, art deco, bronze, pottery, paintings, furniture, silver, and more on three floors. There is even a silversmith on-premises. They are open from 10 to 6 on weekdays and 8:30 to 5:30 on weekends.

Art Supplies

LEE'S ART SHOP
220 W 57th St (at Broadway)   212/247-0110
Mon-Fri: 9-7:30; Sat: 9:30-7; Sun: 11-6   www.leesartshop.com

Lee's offers an expanded stock of materials for amateur and professional artists and kids. There are architectural and drafting supplies, lamps, silk screens, art brushes, paper goods, stationery, pens, cards, gifts, and much more. Same-day on-premises framing is available, along with catalog ordering. Ask for Ricky, the very able boss.

NEW YORK CENTRAL ART SUPPLY
62 Third Ave (at 11th St)   212/473-7705
Mon-Sat: 8:30-6:15   www.nycentralart.com

Since 1905 artists have looked to this firm for fine art materials, especially unique and custom-made items. There are two floors of fine art papers, including one-of-a-kind decorative papers and over a thousand Oriental papers from Bhutan, China, India, Japan, Thailand, Taiwan, and Nepal. Amateur and skilled artisans will find a full range of decorative paints and painting materials. Their selection of brushes is outstanding. This firm specializes in custom priming and stretching of artists' canvas. The canvas collection includes Belgian linens and cottons in widths from 54" to 197".

PEARL PAINT COMPANY
308 Canal St (bet Broadway and Church St)   212/431-7932
Mon-Fri: 9-7; Sat: 10-6:30; Sun: 10-6   800/221-6845
                                              www.pearlpaint.com

The 13 retail floors at Pearl Paint contain a vast selection of arts, graphics, and crafts merchandise, plus lighting and furniture. Selections and services include fabric paint, silk-screening and gold-leaf items, drafting and architectural goods, a fine writing department, and custom framing. They provide fine-art supplies at some of the best prices in town and can ship overseas. Their **Custom Frame Factory** (56 Lispenard St, 212/431-7932, ext. 6966) sells frames at discount prices. Three other affiliated stores are **NYC Craft Center** (42 Lispenard St, 212/431-7932 ext. 3717), **NYC Home Decorating Center** (58 Lispenard St, 212/431-7932, ext. 4530), and **The School of Visual Arts** (207 E 23rd St, 212/592-2179).

SAM FLAX
900 Third Ave (bet 54th and 55th St)   212/813-6666
12 W 20th St (bet Fifth Ave and Ave of the Americas)
Mon-Fri: 9-7; Sat: 10-6; Sun: noon-6   212/620-3000
                                              www.samflaxny.com

Sam Flax is one of the biggest and best art supply houses in the business. The stock is enormous, the service special, and the prices competitive. They carry a full range of art and drafting supplies, organization and archival storage items, gifts, pens, classic and modern furniture and home decor items, and photographic products. Framing services are offered at both stores.

UTRECHT ART AND DRAFTING SUPPLIES
111 Fourth Ave (at 11th St)   212/777-5353
Mon-Sat: 9-7; Sun: 11-6

237 W 23rd St (bet Seventh and Eighth Ave)   212/675-8699
Mon-Fri: 9-8; Sat: 10-7; Sun: 11-6   www.utrecht.com

Utrecht is a major manufacturer of paint, art, and drafting supplies with a large factory in Brooklyn. At this retail store, factory-fresh supplies are sold at discount, and both quality and prices are superb. Utrecht also carries other manufacturers' lines at impressive discounts.

Autographs

JAMES LOWE AUTOGRAPHS
30 E 60th St (bet Madison and Park Ave), Suite 304   212/759-0775
By appointment

James Lowe is one of the nation's most established autograph houses. Regularly updated catalogs make visiting the gallery unnecessary, but in-person inspections are fascinating and invariably whet the appetite of autograph collectors. The gallery shows whatever superior items are in stock, including historic, literary, and musical autographs, manuscripts, documents, and 19th-century photographs (both signed and unsigned).

KENNETH W. RENDELL GALLERY
989 Madison Ave (at 77th St)   212/717-1776
Mon-Sat: 10-6 and by appointment   www.kwrendell.com

Kenneth Rendell has been in the business for over 40 years. He offers a fine collection of pieces from famous figures in literature, arts, politics, and science. Rendell shows autographed letters, manuscripts, documents, books, and photographs. All are authenticated, attractively presented, and priced according to rarity. Rendell also can arrange for evaluations and appraisals.

Bargain Stores

GABAY'S
225 First Ave (bet 13th and 14th St)   212/254-3180
Mon-Sat: 10-6:30; Sun: 11-6   www.gabaysoutlet.com

Gabay's sells designer overstocks of handbags, shoes, evening wear, suits, casual clothing, lingerie, and more at great prices. Goods come from some of Manhattan's best stores (like Bergdorf Goodman and Bendel), with items for both men and women. Designer names include Marc Jacobs, Oscar de la Renta, Yves St. Laurent, Zegna, Gucci, Ralph Lauren, and Brioni. Next door is **Gabay's Home** (227 First Ave, 212/529-4036), a home-accessories store featuring top-name housewares, linens, and furniture at 60% or more below retail.

SOIFFER HASKIN
317 W 33rd St (at Eighth Ave)   718/747-1656
Hours vary; call ahead   www.soifferhaskin.com

This is an unusual operation, selling luxury merchandise at deep discounts. The varied stock of items includes clothing, silver, gifts, housewares, linens, shoes, and more. It's a good idea to get on their mailing list for notification of special sale events.

Bathroom Accessories

A.F. SUPPLY CORPORATION
22 W 21st St (bet Fifth Ave and Ave of the Americas), 5th floor
Mon-Fri: 8-5 and by appointment   212/243-5400
www.afsupply.com

A.F. Supply offers a great selection of luxury bath fixtures, whirlpools, faucets, bath accessories, door and cabinet hardware, saunas, steam show-ers, shower doors, medicine cabinets, and spas from top suppliers.

SHERLE WAGNER INTERNATIONAL
300 E 62nd St (at Second Ave)   212/758-3300
Mon-Fri: 9:30-5:30   www.sherlewagner.com

If you desire elegance and originality, and price is no object, then come to Sherle Wagner for luxury hardware and bath accessories. You'll also find all kinds of bed and bath items, plus general furniture for your home. They've been around for over 60 years.

Where to Shop for Bargains in New York!

Asian goods: **Pearl River Mart** (477 Broadway, 212/431-4770)
Baby gear: **Buy Buy Baby** (270 Seventh Ave, 917/344-1555)
Bottled water: **Staples** (5-9 Union Square W, 212/929-6323)
Cigarettes: **CVS** (chain drugstore)
Clothing: **Old Navy** (150 W 34th St, 212/594-0115; 610 Ave of the Americas, 212/645-0663; and 503-511 Broadway, 212/226-0838)
Clothing, men's and women's (Spanish): **Zara** (580 Broadway, 212/343-1725; 101 Fifth Ave, 212/741-0555; 750 Lexington Ave, 212/754-1120; and 39 W 34th St, 212/868-6551)
Clothing for the family: **Daffy's** (3 E 18th St, 212/529-4477 and other locations), **H&M** (1328 Broadway, 646/473-1164; 558 Broadway, 212/343-2722; 640 Fifth Ave, 212/489-0390; 435 Seventh Ave, 212/643-6955; and 3190 W 125th St, 212/665-8300), and **Loehmann's** (101 Seventh Ave, 212/352-0856 and 2101 Broadway, 212/882-9990)
Clothing (upscale): **Bis Designer Resale** (1134 Madison Ave, 212/396-2760)—shoes and accessories, too!
Clothing, kids: **H&M** (1328 Broadway, 646/473-1164; 558 Broadway, 212/343-2722; 640 Fifth Ave, 212/489-0390; 435 Seventh Ave, 212/643-6955; and 3190 W 125th St, 212/665-8300)
Designer labels for the family: **SYMS** (400 Park Ave, 212/317-8200 and 42 Trinity Pl, 212/797-1199)
Discount department store: **Century 21** (22 Cortlandt St, 212/227-9092)
Discounts on everything: **Costco** (976 Third Ave, Brooklyn, 718/965-7603)
Electronics: **J&R Music** (15 and 23 Park Row, 212/238-9000)
Flowers, cut: **Wholesale Flower Market** (29th St bet Ave of the Americas and Seventh Ave)—retail and wholesale
Furniture: **Room & Board** (105 Wooster St, 212/334-4343)
Home Furnishings: **Bed Bath & Beyond** (410 E 61st St, 646/215-4702; 1932 Broadway, 917/441-9391; and 620 Ave of the Americas, 212/255-3550) and **Gabay's Home** (227 First Ave, 212/529-4036)
Hosiery: **Filene's Basement** (620 Ave of the Americas, 212/620-3100; 4 Union Sq S, 212/358-0169; and 2222 Broadway, 212/873-8000)

(continued next page)

Housewares: **National Wholesale Liquidators** (632 Broadway, 212/979-2400)
Kitchenware: **Broadway Panhandler** (65 E 8th St, 212/966-3434)
Photo: **B&H Photo-Video-Pro Audio** (420 Ninth Ave, 212/444-6600)
Quality clothes: **Find Outlet** (229 Mott St, 212/226-5167)
Sewing and upholstering notions: **M&J Trimming** (1008 Ave of the Americas, 212/391-9072)
Shoes, running: **Super Runners Shop** (360 Amsterdam Ave, 212/787-7665; Grand Central Terminal, 42nd St at Vanderbilt Ave, 646/487-1120; 1337 Lexington Ave, 212/369-6010; and 1246 Third Ave, 212/249-2133)—apparel and accessories, too!
Shoes: **Anbar** (60 Reade St, 212/227-0253), **DSW** (102 North End Ave, 212/945-7419 and 40 E 14th St, 212/674-2146), and **Payless Shoes** (187 Broadway, 212/267-2176; 415 Broadway, 212/966-9112; 513 Broadway, 212/343-1457; 600 Ave of the Americas, 212/645-1401; and 292 First Ave, 212/473-9245)
Sneakers: **Sprint Sports** (2511 Broadway, 212/866-8077)
Stationery and office products: **Jam Paper & Envelope** (135 Third Ave, 212/473-6666)
Sunglasses: **Frock** (148 Orchard, 212/594-5380)

WATERWORKS

225 E 57th St (bet Second and Third Ave)	212/371-9266
469 Broome St (at Greene St)	212/966-0605
7 E 20th St (bet Fifth Ave and Broadway)	212/254-6025
Mon-Fri: 9-6; Sat: 11-5	www.waterworks.com

If it is for the bathroom, then Waterworks has it! You'll find shower heads and curtains, all kinds of plumbing accessories, stone and glass surfacing, towels, rugs, lighting, and a large stock of soaps, candles, and scents. Many big-time designers use this store because items are so attractively displayed.

Beads

BRUCE FRANK BEADS & FINE ETHNOGRAPHIC ART
215 W 83rd St (bet Broadway and Amsterdam Ave)   212/595-3746
Daily: 11-7:30   www.brucefrankbeads.com

You'll find one of the area's best selections of beads at this store, including semiprecious stones, sterling silver, gold-plated Czech and Japanese seed beads, brass beads, contemporary glass beads, and much more. In addition to a selection of vintage and antique beads from all over the world, the store carries a large stock of supplies and findings. They also offer weekly beading classes, re-stringing, and repair. Volume discounts are available.

GAMPEL SUPPLY
11 W 37th St (bet Fifth Ave and Ave of the Americas)   212/575-0767
Mon-Fri: 8:30-5   www.elveerosenberg.com

This is the kind of esoteric business that New York does best. Request a particular kind of bead, and Gampel will invariably have it—at a cheap price, too. While single beads go for a dollar each at a department store one block away, Gampel sells them in bulk for a fraction of that price. Though they prefer to deal with wholesalers, individual customers are treated as courteously as institutions, and wholesale prices are offered to all. As for the stock—well, a visit to Gampel is an education. Pearlized beads alone come in over 20 different styles and are used for everything from bathroom curtains to earrings and flowers. Since many of its customers are craftspeople, Gampel also sells supplies for bead-related crafts. They stock needles, cartwheels, cords (in colors to match each bead), threads, chains, adhesives, jewelry tools, jewelry findings, and costume jewelry parts and pieces.

Books

Antiquarian

COMPLETE TRAVELLER ANTIQUARIAN BOOKSTORE
199 Madison Ave (at 35th St)   212/685-9007
Mon-Fri: 9:30-6:30; Sat: 10-6; Sun: noon-5   www.ctrarebooks.com

The largest collection of Baedeker Handbooks is but one feature of this store, which deals exclusively in rare, antiquarian, and out-of-print books pertaining to travel. The 12,000-book collection includes volumes on polar expeditions, adventure travel, literature, first editions, children's books, and 18th- and 19th-century maps. Books on New York are also available.

Architecture

URBAN CENTER BOOKS
457 Madison Ave (bet 50th and 51st St)   212/935-3595
Mon-Fri: 10-6:30; Sat: noon-5:30   www.urbancenterbooks.com

The Municipal Art Society is a nonprofit organization dedicated to urban planning and historic preservation. Although it is best known for exceptionally diverse and well-conceived walking tours, the organization also runs a gallery and bookstore at its headquarters in the north end of the elegant Villard Houses. The bookstore is among the best sources in the country for books, magazines, and journals on such topics as urban and land-use planning, architecture, and interior design. It also carries a wide selection of guidebooks to New York City.

Art

PRINTED MATTER
195 Tenth Ave (bet 21st and 22nd St)   212/925-0325
Tues, Wed: 10-6; Thurs-Sat: 11-7   www.printedmatter.org

The name Printed Matter is a misnomer since this store is devoted exclusively to artists' books—a trade term for portfolios of artwork in book form. They stock 24,000 titles by over 3,500 artists. The result is inexpensive, accessible art that can span an artist's entire career or focus on a particular period or theme. The store is a nonprofit operation. The idea is carried further with a selection of periodicals and audiotapes in a similar vein. Nearly all featured artists are contemporary (from 1960), so just browsing the store will bring you up-to-date on what is happening in the art world. They sell wholesale and retail, and you can browse their catalog online.

Biography

BIOGRAPHY BOOKSHOP
400 Bleecker St (at 11th St)   212/807-8655
Sun-Thurs: 11-10; Fri, Sat: 11-11

Despite the name, this is a general bookstore with bargains in overstock and remainders. If you are researching a particular person or have an interest in someone's life story, this is the place to find it. There are biographies, books of letters, autobiographies, diaries, journals, and biographies for children. They have broadened their scope into other areas, but the emphasis remains on bios.

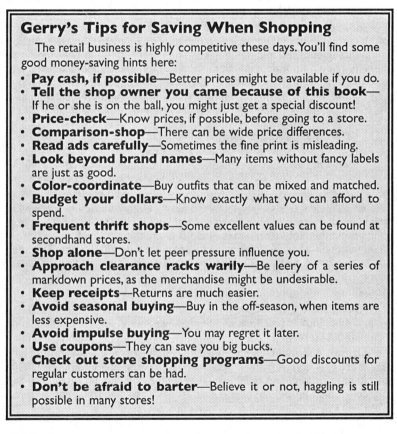

Gerry's Tips for Saving When Shopping

The retail business is highly competitive these days. You'll find some good money-saving hints here:

- **Pay cash, if possible**—Better prices might be available if you do.
- **Tell the shop owner you came because of this book**—If he or she is on the ball, you might just get a special discount!
- **Price-check**—Know prices, if possible, before going to a store.
- **Comparison-shop**—There can be wide price differences.
- **Read ads carefully**—Sometimes the fine print is misleading.
- **Look beyond brand names**—Many items without fancy labels are just as good.
- **Color-coordinate**—Buy outfits that can be mixed and matched.
- **Budget your dollars**—Know exactly what you can afford to spend.
- **Frequent thrift shops**—Some excellent values can be found at secondhand stores.
- **Shop alone**—Don't let peer pressure influence you.
- **Approach clearance racks warily**—Be leery of a series of markdown prices, as the merchandise might be undesirable.
- **Keep receipts**—Returns are much easier.
- **Avoid seasonal buying**—Buy in the off-season, when items are less expensive.
- **Avoid impulse buying**—You may regret it later.
- **Use coupons**—They can save you big bucks.
- **Check out store shopping programs**—Good discounts for regular customers can be had.
- **Don't be afraid to barter**—Believe it or not, haggling is still possible in many stores!

Children's

BANK STREET BOOKSTORE
2879 Broadway (at 112th St)   212/678-1654
                          800/439-1486 (outside New York State)
Mon-Thurs: 11-7; Fri-Sat: 10-6; Sun: noon-6
                                      www.bankstreetbooks.com

A Manhattan icon for years, this store is a marvelous source of books for children, as well as books about children, education, and parenting. Located adjacent to the Bank Street College of Education—a progressive graduate school for teachers and lab school for children—it also has a great selection of tapes, videos, and CDs. It's a treasure trove of educational toys and teacher resources. While the two-floor store is a little cramped even when it isn't crowded, the staff really knows its stock and cares enormously about quality children's literature. Make sure to check online for readings and other special events for children.

BOOKS OF WONDER
18 W 18th St (bet Fifth Ave and Ave of the Americas) 212/989-3270
Mon-Sat: 10-7; Sun: 11-6   www.booksofwonder.com

Books of Wonder is an enchanting spot with a special place in the hearts of New York children and their parents. In addition to the largest selection of books about the Land of Oz (as in *The Wizard of* . . .) in the world, this store is known for frequent "Meet the Author" events, beautiful used and often signed children's classics, a newsletter, and a story hour for young children on Sunday at noon. A special treat is the **Cupcake Cafe** (18 W 18th St, 212/465-1530), located right next door.

SCHOLASTIC STORE
557 West Broadway (bet Prince and Spring St)
Mon-Sat: 10-7; Sun: noon-6   212/343-6166, 877/286-0137
                                              www.scholastic.com/sohostore

One of two retail outlets for this educational publishing giant (the other one is in Westchester County), this is a bright, cheerful space full of familiar titles and characters. In addition to children's books, the store stocks a range of toys, puzzles, software, videos, and Klutz products, as well as a tremendous selection of parent/teacher resource books on the second floor. Ask for a calendar of events, which lists readings, workshops, and performances.

Comics

ACTION COMICS
345 E 80th St (bet First and Second Ave)   212/639-1976
By appointment

Action Comics presents the best selection of comic books in the city. There are new comics from all publishers, collectors' comics from the 1930s to the present, new and collectors' sports (and non-sports) cards, new and old collectors' action figures, magic cards, T-shirts, and collecting supplies. They will evaluate and even buy collections.

METROPOLIS COLLECTIBLES
873 Broadway (at 18th St), Suite 201   212/260-4147
Mon-Fri: 10-6 (by appointment)   www.metropoliscomics.com

Metropolis specializes in vintage comic books from the turn of the century through the 1960s, with over 100,000 vintage titles in stock. It is the largest dealer of vintage comic books in the world, with a private showroom displaying fabulous one-of-a-kind books and horror movie posters.

ST. MARK'S COMICS
11 St. Mark's Pl (bet Second and Third Ave)   212/598-9439
Mon-Wed: 10 a.m.-11 p.m.; Thurs-Sat: 10 a.m.-1 a.m.; Sun: 11-11

This unique store carries mainstream and licensed products, as well as hard-to-find small-press and underground comics. They have a large selection of back issues and claim, "If it's published, we carry it." The folks here are very service-oriented and will hold selections for you. Comic-related toys, T-shirts, statues, posters, and cards are stocked. They also carry TV- and movie-related products.

Cookbooks

KITCHEN ARTS & LETTERS
1435 Lexington Ave (at 94th St)   212/876-5550
Mon: 1-6; Tues-Fri: 10-6:30; Sat: 11-6; closed Sat in July and Aug
www.kitchenartsandletters.com

Cookbooks traditionally are strong sellers, and with all the interest in health, fitness, and natural foods, they are selling better than ever. It should come as no surprise that Nachum Waxman's Kitchen Arts & Letters found immediate success as a store specializing in food- and wine-related books and literature. Imported books are a specialty. Waxman claims his store is the only one like it in the city and that there are fewer than ten in the entire country. He is a former editor at Harper & Row and Crown publishers, where he supervised cookbook projects. Bitten with the urge to start a specialty bookshop, he identified a huge demand for out-of-print cookbooks. So while his cozy shop stocks more than 10,000 current titles, much of the business consists of finding deleted and want-listed books.

Foreign

FRENCH AND EUROPEAN PUBLICATIONS
Dictionary Store/Learn-a-Language Store
Rockefeller Center
610 Fifth Ave (bet 49th and 50th St)   212/581-8810
Mon-Sat: 10-6 (open Sun during holiday season)
www.frencheuropean.com

A short stroll through Rockefeller Center Promenade takes you to this unique foreign-language bookstore, which has occupied the same location since 1934. Inside you will find an interesting collection of French magazines and newspapers, children's books, cookbooks, best sellers, greeting cards, and recorded French music. It is on the lower level, however, where most of the treasures are found. French books are available on almost every topic. There is a Spanish bookstore, as well as French and Spanish films on video, books on cassette, a multimedia section, books and recordings for learning more than a hundred languages, and a specialized foreign-language dictionary section covering engineering, medicine, business, law, and dozens of other fields.

NEW YORK KINOKUNIYA BOOKSTORE
10 W 49th St (at Fifth Ave)   212/765-7766
Mon-Thurs: 10-7:30; Fri, Sat: 10-8; Sun: 11-7:30
www.kinokuniya.com

Kinokuniya is Japan's largest and most esteemed bookstore chain. An American branch located in Rockefeller Plaza has two floors of books about Japan. It is the largest collection of Japanese books in the city. On the first floor are 20,000 English-language books on all aspects of Japanese culture: art, cooking, travel, language, literature, history, business, economics, martial arts, comic books, and more. The rest of the floor is rounded out with Japanese-language books on the same subjects. Japanese stationery is sold on the second floor. (Note: A new store at 1073 Avenue of the Americas will open in late 2007, and the 49th Street location will be phased out.)

General

BARNES & NOBLE

105 Fifth Ave (at 18th St), main store	212/675-5500
555 Fifth Ave (at 46th St)	212/697-3048
160 E 54th St (at Third Ave)	212/750-8033
1972 Broadway (at 66th St)	212/595-6859
675 Ave of the Americas (at 22nd St)	212/727-1227
33 E 17th St (bet Broadway and Park Ave)	212/253-0810
2289 Broadway (at 82nd St)	212/362-8835
1280 Lexington Ave (at 86th St)	212/423-9900
240 E 86th St (at Second Ave)	212/794-1962
396 Ave of the Americas (at 8th St)	212/674-8780
4 Astor Pl (bet Broadway and Lafayette St)	212/420-1322
Hours vary by store	www.bnnewyork.com

For value and selection, you can't beat Barnes & Noble. Their stores are beloved by book buyers and browsers in virtually every area of the city. Generations of New York students have purchased textbooks at the Barnes & Noble main store. Barnes & Noble has opened a number of superstores with enormous stocks of books (including bargain-priced remainders), comfortable shopping conveniences (including cafes), and a large selection of magazines. Best of all, they continue to offer deep discounts on best sellers and other popular titles.

BORDERS BOOKS AND MUSIC

461 Park Ave (at 57th St)	212/980-6785
2 Penn Plaza (bet Seventh Ave and 33rd St)	212/244-1814
576 Second Ave (at 32nd St)	212/685-3938
100 Broadway (bet Pine and Wall St)	212/964-1988
10 Columbus Circle (Time Warner Building)	212/823-9775
Hours vary by store	www.bordersstores.com

Borders is one of the major national bookstore chains, offering books, CDs, DVDs, periodicals, reading areas, and cafes. The stock at Borders is wide and deep. There is plenty of well-informed help, and in-person author events draw crowds. Customer kiosks allow access to their extensive inventory via computerized searches by author, title, and keyword.

MCNALLY ROBINSON BOOKSELLERS

52 Prince St (bet Lafayette and Mulberry St)	212/274-1169
Daily: 10-10	www.mcnallyrobinsonnyc.com

Sarah McNally is a brave lady. "Brave" because opening an independent bookstore these days is a daring endeavor! But she has been successful. The store is chock full of titles in every category. Author appearances are frequent, there is a teahouse for resting between shopping and reading, and personal, informed service will help lead you to the right book.

RIZZOLI
31 W 57th St (bet Fifth Ave and Ave of the Americas)   212/759-2424
Mon-Fri: 10-7:30; Sat: 10:30-7; Sun: 11-7   www.rizzoliusa.com

When you talk about class in the book business, Rizzoli tops the list. They have maintained an elegant atmosphere that makes patrons feel as if they are browsing a European library rather than a midtown Manhattan bookstore. The emphasis is on art, architecture, literature, photography, fashion, and interior design. There is a good selection of paperbacks. Upstairs you will find Italian books, a music department, and children's books.

STRAND BOOK STORE
828 Broadway (at 12th St)   212/473-1452
Mon-Sat: 9:30 a.m.-10:30 p.m.; Sun: 11-10:30

STRAND BOOK ANNEX
95 Fulton St (at Gold St)   212/732-6070
Mon-Fri: 9:30-9; Sat, Sun: 11-8

STRAND BOOK KIOSK
Fifth Ave at 60th St
April-Dec (weather permitting)   www.strandbooks.com

This is the largest and best used bookstore in the world. Need I say more? Family-owned for eight decades, it is a fascinating place to visit and shop. The store has over 2.5 million titles in stock—that's 18 miles of books—tagged at up to 85% off list prices. They sell secondhand, out-of-print, and rare books at genuinely discounted prices. Thousands of new books and quality remainders are sold at 50% off publisher prices. An outstanding rare book department is located on the third floor. You'll find 20th-century first editions, limited signed editions, fine bindings, and much more in their enormous stock. Their mail-order and Internet business is huge. (A personal connection: Knowledgeable owner Fred Bass and daughter Nancy now have Oregon ties, as Nancy is the wife of Oregon Senator Ron Wyden.)

THREE LIVES & CO.
154 W 10th St (at Waverly Pl)   212/741-2069
Mon-Tues: noon-8; Wed-Sat: 11-8:30; Sun: noon-7
                                            www.threelives.com

Three Lives is one of the best remaining independent bookstores. Founded in 1978, it specializes in literary fiction and nonfiction, with good sections on poetry, art, New York, cooking, and gardening. The staff is knowledgeable and helpful.

Music

JUILLIARD BOOKSTORE
60 Lincoln Center Plaza (66th St bet Broadway and Amsterdam Ave)
Mon-Thurs: 9:30-7:30; Fri, Sat: 10-6   212/799-5000, ext 237
                                        www.bookstore.juilliard.edu

With over 20,000 sheet music titles and scores in stock, this bookstore claims to carry every classical music book in print! And there is more: imprinted stationery and apparel, conductors' batons, metronomes, historic recordings, and music software.

Mystery

BLACK ORCHID BOOKSHOP

303 E 81st St (bet First and Second Ave)   212/734-5980
Tues-Fri: noon-7; Sat: 11-6; Sun: noon-5 (closed Sun in summer)
                                            www.ageneralstore.com

The Black Orchid caters to all kinds of mystery readers, stocking current titles and out-of-print books. A number of signed titles are available.

Independent Bookstores

Books of Wonder (18 W 18th St, 212/989-3270): children's
Complete Traveller Antiquarian Bookstore (199 Madison Ave, 212/685-9007): travel
Crawford and Doyle (1082 Madison Ave, 212/288-6300): general bookstore
Drama Book Shop (250 W 40th St, 212/944-0595): plays, musicals, theater
East West Books (78 Fifth Ave, 212/243-5994): spirituality, holistic health, and esoteric philosophy
Forbidden Planet (840 Broadway, 212/473-1576): sci-fi, fantasy, and Japanese animation and comics
Librairie de France (610 Fifth Ave, 212/581-8810): French and Spanish books
McNally Robinson Booksellers (52 Prince St, 212/274-1160): general book-store
Mysterious Bookshop (58 Warren St, 212/587-1011): thrillers and killers
Oscar Wilde Bookshop (15 Christopher St, 212/255-8097): literature for the lesbian and gay communities
Posman Books (9 Grand Central Terminal, 42nd St at Vanderbilt Ave, 212/983-1111)
Quest Bookshop (240 E 53rd St, 212/758-5521): spirituality and esoterica
St. Mark's Bookshop (31 Third Ave, 212/260-7853): eclectic and cultural books, foreign and domestic periodicals)
Strand Book Store (828 Broadway, 212/473-1452): 18 miles of new and used books; something for everyone

---

MYSTERIOUS BOOKSHOP

58 Warren St (bet West Broadway and Church St)   212/587-1011
Daily: 11-7   www.mysteriousbookshop.com

Otto Penzler is a Baker Street Irregular, a Sherlock Holmes fan extraordinaire (an elementary deduction!), and the Mysterious Bookshop's owner. The shop is larger now, with much more stock. Mysterious stocks new hardcover and paperback books that deal with all types of mystery, and it is also stocked floor-to-ceiling with out-of-print, used, and rare books. Amazingly, the staff seem to know exactly what is in stock. If it is not on the shelves, they will order it. There is as much talk as business conducted here, and you can continue the conversation with authors who sign their works from time to time. Mysterious carries thousands of autographed books, and several store-sponsored book clubs provide autographed first editions to members.

New York

CITYSTORE
1 Centre St (at Chambers St), north plaza of Municipal Bldg
Mon-Fri: 9-4:30   212/669-8246
www.nyc.gov/citystore

This city government bookstore provides access to more than 120 official publications, all of which are dedicated to helping New Yorkers cope with their complex lives. *The Green Book* is the official directory of the city of New York, listing phone numbers and addresses of more than 900 government agencies and 6,000 officials. It includes state, federal, and international listings, as well as courts and a section on licenses. There is also a unique collection of New York memorabilia: city-seal ties, pins, and more.

Out-of-Print and Rare

ALABASTER BOOKSHOP
122 Fourth Ave (bet 12th and 13th St)   212/982-3550
Mon-Sat: 10-8; Sun: 11-8

There was a time when Fourth Avenue was known as "Bookshop Row." Back then, it was *the* place for used books in Manhattan. All that has changed with the advent of superstores and the demise of smaller entrepreneurs. Alabster's owner, Steve Crowley, has bucked the trend, offering a great selection of used and rare books in all categories, ranging from $2 paperbacks to a $1,000 first edition. Specialities include New York City, photography, and modern first editions.

ARGOSY BOOK STORE
116 E 59th St (bet Park and Lexington Ave)   212/753-4455
Mon-Fri: 10-6; Sat: 10-5 (closed Sat from May to Sept)
www.argosybooks.com

Argosy is the largest out-of-print, secondhand, and rare-volume bookstore in New York. The six-story building houses a stock of books from the 16th through the 20th centuries, including modern first editions and regional American history volumes, as well as others on art, science, and medicine. A separate autograph section includes items from a number of well-known personalities. Their print department is famous for its large collection of antique maps from all over the world, prints of every conceivable subject, and vintage posters.

BAUMAN RARE BOOKS
535 Madison Ave (bet 54th and 55th St)   212/751-0011
Mon-Sat: 10-6   www.baumanrarebooks.com

Bauman offers a fine collection of books and autographs dating from the 15th through the 20th centuries. Included are works of literature, history, economics, law, science, medicine, nature, travel, and exploration. First editions and children's books are a specialty. They also provide services from designing and furnishing libraries to locating books for customers.

IMPERIAL FINE BOOKS
790 Madison Ave (bet 66th and 67th St), 2nd floor   212/861-6620
Mon-Fri: 10:30-6; Sat: 10:30-5   www.imperialfinebooks.com

If you are in the market for books that look as great as they read, Imperial is the place to visit. You will find fine leather bindings, illustrated books, vintage children's books, unique first editions, and magnificent sets of prized volumes. Their inventory includes literary giants like Twain, Dickens, Brontë, and Shakespeare. An outstanding Oriental art gallery features Chinese, Japanese, and Korean ceramics and antiques. (They will purchase fine pieces.) Services include complete restoration and binding of damaged or aged books. A search office will locate titles and make appraisals.

J.N. BARTFIELD GALLERIES AND FINE BOOKS
30 W 57th St (bet Fifth Ave and Ave of the Americas), 3rd floor
Mon-Fri: 10-5; Sat: 10-3 (closed Sat in summer)   212/245-8890
www.bartfield.com

This shop is a spectacular hunting ground for lovers of fine paintings and rare books. Since 1937 they have specialized in masters of the American West and 19th- and 20th-century American paintings and sculptures. I have purchased outstanding collections of leatherbound books from them and can vouch for their expertise. First editions, sporting books, and high-quality antiquarian books are featured. Who wouldn't be excited to browse elegantly bound volumes that once graced the shelves of old family libraries?

Religious

J. LEVINE BOOKS & JUDAICA
5 W 30th St (bet Fifth Ave and Broadway)   212/695-6888
800/5-JEWISH (outside New York City)
Mon-Wed: 9-6; Thurs: 9-7; Fri: 9-2; Sun: 10-5 (closed Sun in July)
www.levinejudaica.com

The history of the Lower East Side is reflected in this store. Started back in 1905 on Eldridge Street, J. Levine was a fixture in the area for many years. Now it operates further uptown, just off Fifth Avenue. Being one of the oldest Jewish bookstores in the city, Levine is a leader in the Jewish-book marketplace. Though the emphasis is still on the written word, they also carry many gift items, tapes, coffee table books, and thousands of items of Judaica. You can also browse and order online.

ST. PATRICK'S CATHEDRAL GIFT STORE
15 E 51st St (bet Fifth and Madison Ave)   212/355-2749, ext 400
Daily: 10-6   www.saintpatrickscathedral.com

This store is an oasis of calm in midtown. Lovely music plays in the background as you browse books on Catholicism, displays of rosary beads, statues of saints, and related items. Proceeds benefit the cathedral.

TIMELESS TREASURES CHRISTIAN GIFT & BOOK STORE
673 Eighth Ave (bet 42nd and 43rd St)   212/582-4311
Mon-Sat: 9-9   www.timelesstreasures-ny.com

With over 20,000 titles in stock, this is a large Christian bookstore in the metropolitan area. It also stocks religious CDs, tapes, videos, and church and school supplies. A large number of these items are available in Spanish, as befits the Latino neighborhood.

Theater

DRAMA BOOK SHOP
250 W 40th St (bet Seventh and Eighth Ave)
Mon-Sat: 10-8; Sun: noon-6   212/944-0595, 800/322-0595
www.dramabookshop.com

Since 1923 this shop has been providing a valuable service to the performing arts community. Its stock includes publications dealing with theater, film, dance, music, puppetry, magic, design, costumes, and more. The Drama Book Shop is known for courteous and knowledgeable service, both in-store and by mail.

RICHARD STODDARD—PERFORMING ARTS BOOKS
By appointment   212/598-9421
www.richardstoddard.com

Richard Stoddard runs a one-man operation dedicated to rare, out-of-print, and used books, and to memorabilia relating to the performing arts. Equipped with a Ph.D. from Yale in theater history and three decades of experience as a dealer and appraiser of performing arts materials, Stoddard offers a broad range of items. He has the largest collection of New York playbills (about 20,000) for sale in the U.S., as well as books, autographs, souvenir programs, and original stage designs.

Used

HOUSING WORKS BOOKSTORE CAFE
126 Crosby St (bet Houston and Prince St)   212/334-3324
Mon-Fri: 10-9; Sat: noon-9; Sun: noon-7
www.housingworks.org/usedbookcafe

Housing Works has it all: used books, collectibles, out-of-print titles, first editions, DVDs, and audio books. The cafe features baked goods, seasonal soups, soft drinks, and beer and wine. Proceeds go to programs that provide housing, medical care, and job training for homeless people with HIV/AIDS.

Butterflies

MARIPOSA, THE BUTTERFLY GALLERY
South Street Seaport (at Fulton St), Pier 17   212/233-3221
Mon-Sat: 10-9; Sun: 11-8   www.mariposathebutterflygallery.com

At Mariposa, butterflies are regarded as art. Marshall Hill is a renowned designer in this unusual medium. Butterflies are unique, and Mariposa (the Spanish word for butterfly) displays them separately, in panels, and in groups. Butterfly farms breed and raise butterflies, which live their full one-month life spans under ideal conditions for creating this art.

Buttons

TENDER BUTTONS
143 E 62nd St (bet Lexington and Third Ave)   212/758-7004
Mon-Fri: 10:30-6; Sat: 10:30-5:30

You'll find buttons ranging in price from 60 cents to $12,000 at Tender Buttons. Millicent Safro's retail button store is complete in variety as well as size. One antique wooden display cabinet shows off the selection of original buttons, many imported or made exclusively for the store. There are buttons of pearl, wood, horn, Navajo silver, leather, ceramic, bone, ivory, pewter, and semiprecious stones. Many are antiques. Some are as highly valued as artwork; a French enamel button, for instance, can cost almost as much as a painting! Unique pieces can be made into special cuff links—real conversation pieces for the lucky owner. Blazer buttons are a specialty. They also have a fine collection of antique and period cuff links and men's stud sets. I am a cuff links buff and have purchased some of my best pieces from this shop. They also have wonderful small antiques.

Candles

OTHER WORLDLY WAXES
131 E 7th St (bet First Ave and Ave A)   212/260-9188
Tues-Sun: 2-9

www.candletherapy.com, www.otherworldlywaxes.com

In this interesting store you'll find scented candles, aromatherapy products, hand-blended oils, and incense. They also offer spiritual advice, promising that their candles "merge psychological goals with whatever spiritual framework you have." Here's a sampling of the properties associated with their oils and incense: "Cleopatra" (balm of Gilead) is a secret weapon of seduction, while "Vavoom" (coconut) promises big-time sex appeal and flair. Who knows? A visit here might change your life! Ask for Catherine Riggs-Bergesen, who is a practicing clinical psychologist. Candles are prepared as you wait, and readings are by appointment.

China, Glassware

CRATE & BARREL
650 Madison Ave (at 59th St)   212/308-0011
Mon-Fri: 10-8; Sat: 10-7; Sun: noon-6

611 Broadway (at Houston St)   212/780-0004
Mon-Sat: 10-9; Sun: noon-7   www.crateandbarrel.com

These folks are professional merchants in the best sense. Even if you aren't in the market for china, glassware, bedroom furnishings, or casual furniture, the displays will make shopping hard to resist. First, the place is loaded with attractive, quality merchandise at sensible prices. Second, it is fixtured magnificently, with every item shown to best advantage. Third, the lighting and signing are masterfully done. Finally, the store layout and number of checkout stands make for quick work in completing a purchase.

FISHS EDDY
889 Broadway (at 19th St)   212/420-9020
Mon: 10-9; Tues-Sat: 9-9; Sun: 10-8   www.fishseddy.com

Besides being treasure troves for bargain hunters, this shop is fun to browse for some of the most unusual industrial-strength china and glassware items available anywhere. Nearly everything is made in America, and the stock changes on a regular basis. Fishs Eddy is ideal for young people setting up a new residence or a business looking for unique pieces. Their tabletop collection is carried in some of the **Gracious Home** locations, as well.

Clothing and Accessories

Antique and Vintage

THE FAMILY JEWELS
130 W 23rd St (bet Ave of the Americas and Seventh Ave)
Sun-Tues: 11-7; Wed-Sat: 11-8   212/633-6020
www.familyjewelsnyc.com

Family Jewels is the place to go for vintage clothing and accessories from the Victorian era through the 1980s. The stock is well organized, the selections are huge, the service is excellent, and shopping is fun! Even the decor is 1940s, and appropriately retro music plays. Prices are reasonable. A costume and styling service is available.

FROM AROUND THE WORLD
209 W 38th St (bet Seventh and Eighth Ave), Suite 1201
Mon-Fri: 9:30-5:30 (by appointment)   212/354-6536

This is a vintage clothing archive, wardrobe lending library, and retail outlet specializing in unique, quality vintage apparel and accessories from all over the world. The continually replenished selection of designer, ethnic, military, Western, Hawaiian, work, and athletic wear includes collectible and never-worn dead-stock pieces. Items range from the 1890s to 1990s for men, women, and children.

REMINISCENCE
50 W 23rd St (bet Fifth Ave and Ave of the Americas)   212/243-2292
Mon-Sat: 11-7:30; Sun: noon-7   www.reminiscence.com

It's fun to revisit the 1950s through the 1980s at this hip emporium, created by Stewart Richer on lower Fifth Avenue. Although he is a product of this era, most of Richer's customers are between the ages of 13 and 30. The finds are unusual and wearable, with large selections of colorful vintage clothing and attractive displays of jewelry, hats, gifts, and accessories. Richer's goods, although vintage in style, are mostly new, and the company also sells what it makes to outlets all over the world. Because of its vast distribution, Richer can produce large quantities and sell at low prices.

SCREAMING MIMI'S
382 Lafayette St (bet 4th and Great Jones St)   212/677-6464
Mon-Sat: noon-8; Sun: 1-7   www.screamingmimis.com

Laura Wills presides over Screaming Mimi's, which features accessories for men and women from the 1940s through the 1980s, as well as contemporary merchandise. There is an excellent showing of handbags, shoes, jewelry, sunglasses, lingerie, and sportswear. One department also features designer and vintage couture.

TRASH & VAUDEVILLE
4 St. Mark's Pl (bet Second and Third Ave)   212/982-3590
Mon-Thurs: noon-8; Fri: 11:30-8:30; Sat: 11:30-9; Sun: 1-7:30

This place is hard to pin down, since the stock changes constantly and seems to have no boundaries. Trash & Vaudeville describes its stock as punk clothing, accessories, and original designs. "Punk clothing" means rock and roll styles from the 1950s to the present, including outrageous footwear. They also carry new clothing from Europe.

WHAT COMES AROUND GOES AROUND
351 West Broadway (bet Broome and Grand St)   212/343-9303
Mon-Sat: 11-8; Sun: noon-7   www.nyvintage.com

If vintage clothing is your thing, then don't miss this place. It claims to be one of the largest vintage outlets in the world, with over 60,000 items in stock. Many of the labels are familiar, and the prices are right. Denim and military wear are especially well represented.

Athletic

LULULEMON ATHLETICA
1928 Broadway (at 64th St)   212/712-1767
Mon-Sat: 10-9; Sun: 11-7   www.lululemon.com

This Canadian yoga-clothing outfit shows attractive and different wear for the more active members of the family. Fabrics can be quite unusual—like *luon*, which wicks away moisture—and the styling is hip.

Bridal

HERE COMES THE BRIDESMAID...
238 W 14th St (bet Seventh and Eighth Ave)   212/647-9686
Call for appointment

After walking down the aisle as a bridesmaid in 13 weddings, Stephanie Harper decided it was time that bridesmaids had a store of their own. Her establishment carries gowns from After Six, Lazaro, Jim Hjelm, and others. She also features gowns that can be hemmed and worn again to occasions other than weddings. Weekend hours make Here Comes the Bridesmaid especially convenient for working women. Call ahead for an appointment.

KLEINFELD
110 W 20th St (bet Ave of the Americas and Seventh Ave)
Tues, Thurs: 12:30-8; Fri: 11:30-6; Sat: 9:30-6; Sun: 10-5   646/633-4300
(by appointment)   www.kleinfeldbridal.com

Experience the magic! From beginning to end, the Kleinfeld experience sets the standard for all brides-to-be. The bridal business has changed a great deal in recent years. Yet little has changed at the legendary Kleinfeld—other than a new 35,000-square-foot location in Manhattan featuring the most exclusive bridal- and evening-wear designers anywhere. They are still tops in the business, and the Manhattan salon is a wonder to experience. Brides will enjoy a private dressing room with an experienced consultant who will review 1,500 styles of designer bridal gowns, including Amsale, Carolina Herrera, Monique Lhuillier, and Pnina Tornai. The perfect Kleinfeld fit will be achieved with the most experienced seamstresses. **Kleinfeld Evening-**

wear offers a great collection of designer eveningwear. Kleinfeld operates by appointment only.

Children's

Before describing what I consider to be the best children's clothing stores in New York, let me be clear about what I'm *not* including: big chains and the haughty "just so" boutiques that line Madison Avenue. That is not to say some of the chains don't have great stores here. **Baby Gap** and **Gap Kids**, **The Children's Place**, **Gymboree**, **Talbots Kids**, and even Europe's **Oilily** all have good selections, as does the cavernous "big-box" **buybuy Baby**. But unlike the stores listed below, they sell very little that you can't buy in any other city in the United States. As for the haughty boutiques, I see no reason to patronize these wildly overpriced and un-welcoming places.

BONNE NUIT
1193 Lexington Ave (at 81st St)   212/472-7300
Mon-Fri: 9-7; Sat: 10-7; Sun: noon-5

What a fun place to shop! You'll find mother and daughter pajamas, robes, and slippers; European children's wear for boys and girls (up to pre-teen sizes); old-fashioned children's books; wool and cashmere blankets; baby gifts; and fine lingerie and boudoir accessories. Very personal service is another plus.

BU AND THE DUCK
106 Franklin St (bet Church St and West Broadway)   212/431-9226
Mon-Sat: 10-6; Sun: 11-5   www.buandtheduck.com

Quality is the byword here. Come to Bu and the Duck for outstanding handmade sweaters, clothing, shoes, and accessories for infants up to eight-year olds. The fabrics are gorgeous, the designs unique, and the prices less than you might think, given the quality you'll find here.

giggle
120 Wooster St (bet Spring and Prince St)   212/334-6817
Mon-Sat: 10-7; Sun: noon-6

1033 Lexington Ave (at 74th St)   212/249-4249
Mon-Sat: 10-7; Sun: 11-6   www.giggle.com

For those about to be parents, as well as those who already are, giggle is a godsend! You'll find most every item needed to take care of the little one, including furniture for the nursery. In addition, there are clothing, toys, books, music, bath and spa items, and information on keeping baby healthy and happy. Personal shoppers are available and helpful. Customized delivery is available (that is, for the merchandise—not the baby!), and in-store parenting activities are a plus. A parents' lounge and kids' playroom are additional features.

LESTER'S
1534 Second Ave (at 80th St)   212/734-9292
Mon-Fri: 10-7; Sat: 10-6; Sun: 11-6

If you're looking for basic clothes, shoes, campwear, and/or accessories for children and don't want to leave the East Side, Lester's is your best bet.

It is large and inviting, including a downstairs section dedicated entirely to boys. In fact, you can clothe everyone from infants to teenagers here. You will even find a good selection of shoes. While its stock is not unique, and might not win any fashion awards, Lester's is just stylish enough to keep East Side moms and kids coming back.

LILLIPUT

265 Lafayette St (bet Spring and Prince St)   212/965-9567
Mon-Thurs: 11-6; Fri, Sat: 11-7   www.lilliputsoho.com

Children's clothing stores have multiplied in New York's hot shopping neighborhoods, and a lot of them start to look alike after awhile. Sometimes a good buyer with a sharp eye can set a store apart, however. In certain respects Lilliput resembles a lot of other relatively upscale children's stores, and some of what you'll find here is neither unusual nor well-priced. But look a little closer and you'll see certain items, including a wide selection from Lili Gaufreete, that make a trip here worthwhile. In addition to a wide and varied selection of infant clothes, Lilliput has a great shoe selection, unusual accessories, a few toys, and a diverse range of clothes for young children to size 8. **Lilliput Soho Kids** (240 Lafayette St, 212/965-9201), a sister store right down the block, offers clothes for girls to size 16.

LUCKY WANG

799 Broadway (bet 10th and 11th St)   212/353-2850

LUCKY WANG 2

82 Seventh Ave (bet 15th and 16th St)   212/229-2900
Mon-Sat: 11-7; Sun: noon-6

Are you looking for something unusual or unique in children's wear? These sister stores showcase colorful, contemporary kimonos, karate pants, and mandarin tops for babies and kids that are as fashionable as they are practical. A few other labels are here as well, as are accessories from shoes to blankets.

MORRIS BROS.

2322 Broadway (at 84th St)   212/724-9000
Mon-Sat: 9:30-6; Sun: noon-5:30

You can't be a parent or kid on the Upper West Side and not know about Morris Bros. Whether you're looking for a backpack, hat, tights, pajamas, jeans, underwear, or clothes for gym class and camp, this is the place to go. It's not exciting and the staff seems hassled, but it's definitely reliable for basic clothes at decent prices.

PEANUTBUTTER & JANE

617 Hudson St (at Jane St)   212/620-7952
Mon-Fri: 10:30-7; Sat: 10-7; Sun: 11-6

A friend describes this store as "very Village." In addition to a varied and fun selection of clothing, it carries funky things like ruby slippers for children, leather jackets for toddlers, and wonderfully imaginative dress-up clothes.

Indeed, almost everything is unique to the store. Unlike a lot of children's clothing stores in which older children wouldn't be caught dead, Peanutbutter & Jane appeals both to teenagers and their younger siblings. I just wish the prices weren't quite so steep!

SPACE KIDDETS
26 E 22nd St (bet Park Ave S and Broadway)   212/420-9878
Mon-Sat: 10:30-6 (Wed, Thurs till 7)   www.spacekiddets.com

This cheerful store is overflowing with funky children's clothes, shoes, and accessories. Although the location is new and the selection always seems fresh and fun, Space Kiddets actually has been around for a long time. The prices may seem a bit high if you're from out-of-town, but they're reasonable compared to some of the boutiques in trendier neighborhoods. Moreover, the sales staff is welcoming and helpful.

Costumes

ABRACADABRA
19 W 21st St (bet Fifth Ave and Ave of the Americas) 212/627-5194
Tues-Sat: 11-7 (extended hours in Oct)

www.abracadabrasuperstore.com

Abracadabra can transform you into almost anything! They rent and sell costumes and costume accessories, magician supplies, theatrical makeup, and stock props for magic tricks. It is a gagster's heaven! Come to the free magic show on Saturday afternoon. The Halloween season brings extended hours.

CREATIVE COSTUME
242 W 36th St (bet Seventh and Eighth Ave), 8th floor   212/564-5552
Mon-Fri: 9:30-4:30 (open Sat in Oct)

www.creativecostume.com

With thousands of costumes for purchase or rental, Creative Costumes can remake you into whoever you may want to be. They will even manufacture a special look for you, and alterations are included with every sale.

HALLOWEEN ADVENTURE
104 Fourth Ave (bet 11th and 12th St)   212/673-4546
Mon-Sat: 11-8; Sun: noon-7 (extended hours in Oct)

www.newyorkcostumes.com

Your kids will be the talk of the neighborhood after a visit here. You'll find wigs, costumes for adults and kids, hats, gags, magic items, props, and all manner of games and novelties. In addition, a professional makeup artist is on hand most of the time.

PARAMOUNT
52 W 29th St (bet Broadway and Ave of the Americas)   212/696-9664
Mon-Fri: 9-5

Crowns, tiaras, headpieces, false teeth, wigs, beards, eyepatches, eyelashes, swords, fake blood—name the prop or theatrical accessory, and chances are good this fading old store sells it either singly or by the dozen. The collection of masks is extensive.

Family

BLUE TREE

1283 Madison Ave (at 91st St)   212/369-2583
Mon-Fri: 10-6; Sat: 10-5; Sun: noon-5   www.bluetreeny.com

You never know what you might find at this unusual boutique! The street floor has merchandise for kids and gifts and trinkets for almost any occasion, while the second floor displays a rather exclusive collection of clothing and accessories for both men and women. A number of big-name designers are represented at Blue Tree.

Furs and Leather

BARBARA SHAUM

60 E 4th St (bet Bowery and Second Ave)   212/254-4250
Wed-Sat: 1-6

Barbara Shaum has done magical things with leather since 1963. She's a wonder with sandals, bags, sterling silver buckles, belts (with handmade brass, nickel-silver, inlaid wood, and copper buckles), jewelry, attaché cases, and briefcases. Everything is designed in the shop, and Shaum meticulously crafts each item using only the finest materials. She is regularly featured in leading fashion magazines.

FURS BY DIMITRIOS

130 W 30th St (bet Ave of the Americas and Seventh Ave)
Mon-Fri: 9-6; Sat, Sun: 10-4 (open Sun in winter only)
                                                       212/695-8469

This store is the best source for men's fur coats at wholesale prices. The racks are shaggy with furs of all descriptions and sizes for both genders. Prices are wholesale but go up slightly if the garment has to be specially ordered. This shouldn't be necessary, though, since the high-quality off-the-rack selection is the most extensive in the city.

G. MICHAEL HENNESSY FURS

345 Seventh Ave (bet 29th and 30th St), 5th floor   212/695-7991
Mon-Fri: 9:30-5; Sat by appointment

You'll find an abundance of beautiful, affordable furs here. Fur lovers should get to know Michael Hennessy and his wife, Rubye, a former fashion editor. Hennessy furs and their service are famous worldwide. The label assures you of superior pelts, great designs, and the lowest possible prices. Their showroom in the wholesale fur district stocks hundreds of furs, ranging from highly coveted minks and sables to sporty boutique furs and shearlings. You'll find all the newest fashion looks, colors, shapes, and techniques. A spectacular Italian fur collection is exclusive to Hennessy. Today's fur technology is evident in skillfully executed sheared and grooved minks, "double-face" reversible styles, and furs that weigh next to nothing but still keep you warm. No wonder the Hennessys command such a large international following. They have a huge remodeling business, turning furs that are a few years old into brand-new styles. That classic mink you've worn for years can have a second life as a sheared swingcoat or *blouson*. While this is a sizable company, you can count on Michael or Rubye being available to assist you.

GOODMAN COUTURE FURS
224 W 30th St (bet Seventh and Eighth Ave), Suite 902   212/244-7422
Mon-Fri: 10-6; Sat by appointment   www.buonuomo.com

Since 1918 the Goodmans have been creating fine fur styles. Third-generation furrier David Goodman is continuing the family tradition, offering a quality collection of fur-lined and reversible fur coats and jackets for men and women. You may choose from an array of furs, including mink, sheared mink, and fine sables. Your out-of-date or unused fur coats can be brought back to life with a new all-weather design. The Goodmans offer a custom cashmere knit collection under the label Buonuomo ("good man"), made in an Italian cashmere factory and trimmed with luxurious furs. Additionally, they have developed an innovative line of fur accessories, including scarves, collars, hats, and handbags. A full-time staff designer specializes in custom designs. Their hottest new items are feather-weight, fur-lined reversible coats.

Would you like a pair of denim jeans custom-made for you, with your own pocket design and buttons? **An Earnest Cut & Sew** (821 Washington St, 212/242-3414) will do the job for men and women. They are open daily from 11 to 7 (Sat till 8).

HARRY KIRSHNER AND SON
307 Seventh Ave (bet 27th and 28th St)   212/243-4847
Mon-Fri: 9-6; Sat: 10-5

Kirshner should be one of your first stops for any kind of fur product, from throw pillows to full-length mink coats. They will re-line, clean, alter, and store any fur at rock bottom prices. They are neither pushy nor snobbish. Harry Kirshner offers tours of the factory. If nothing appeals to a customer, a staff member will design a coat to specifications. Often, however, the factory stocks a collection of restored secondhand furs in perfect and fashionable condition. Many customers come in for a new fur and walk out with a slightly worn one for a fraction of what they expected to spend.

LIBRA LEATHER
259 W 30th St (bet Seventh and Eighth Ave)   212/695-3114
Mon-Fri: 9-5:30   www.libraleather.com

For over a half century this family-owned business has been the ultimate source for fashionable fur and leather skins. You'll find leather, suede, and shearling skins for home furnishings, women's and men's better clothing, and accessory items such as bags, belts, and shoes. The inventory is enormous —with quality skins from Italy, France, and Spain—and the staff is multilingual.

Hosiery
FOGAL
515 Madison Ave (at 53rd St)   212/355-3254
Mon-Sat: 10-6:30   www.fogal.com

Before Fogal came to New York from Switzerland, the thought of a

Madison Avenue boutique devoted to hosiery was, well, foreign. But since opening in 1982, it's hard to imagine Manhattan without it. If it's fashionable and different leg wear you're after, Fogal has it. Plain hosiery comes in nearly a hundred hues. The designs and patterns make the number of choices almost incalculable. You might say that Fogal has a leg up on the competition! Fogal also carries lingerie, bodywear, and men's socks.

Men's and Women's—General

CHRISTOPHER FISCHER
80 Wooster St (bet Broome and Spring St)   212/965-9009
Mon-Sat: 11-7; Sun: noon-6   www.christopherfischer.com

Fischer carries luxurious cashmere goods for men and women, including sweaters, blankets, shawls, and cushions. Accessories from Henry Beguelin are also available

COCKPIT USA
652 Broadway (bet Bleecker and Bond St)   212/254-4000
Mon-Sat: 11-7:30; Sun: noon-6:30   www.cockpitusa.com

What was once the Avirex store is now a bustling emporium featuring clothing from authentic contemporary flight jackets to reproductions of World War II jackets. You'll find premium contemporary Americana items, vintage clothing, antique furniture, and accessories, including Fortis watches.

DAFFY'S
3 E 18th St (bet Fifth Ave and Broadway)   212/529-4477
335 Madison Ave (at 44th St)   212/557-4422
1311 Broadway (at 34th St)   212/736-4477
462 Broadway (at Grand St)   212/334-7444
125 E 57th St (bet Lexington and Park Ave)   212/376-4477
1775 Broadway (at 57th St)   212/294-4477
50 Broadway (bet Exchange Pl and Beaver St)   212/422-4477
Hours vary by store   www.daffys.com

Daffy's describes itself as a bargain clothing outlet for millionaires. Since a lot of folks got to be millionaires by saving money, perhaps Daffy's has something going for it! Great bargains can be found in better clothing (including unusual European imports) for men, women, and children. Fine leather items are a specialty. This is not your usual "off-price" store, as they have done things with a bit of flair.

FILENE'S BASEMENT
2222 Broadway (at 79th St)   212/873-8000
620 Ave of the Americas (at 18th St)   212/620-3100
4 Union Square S (at 14th St and University Pl)   212/358-0169
Hours vary by store   www.filenesbasement.com

Anyone who has shopped in Boston knows the name Filene's Basement, which is recognized for outstanding bargains. Well, Filene's is also in New York, offering great bargains in brand-name goods for men and women. The store claims to offer savings from 30% to 60%. Sometimes it's more and sometimes less, but you can always depend on the quality. Filene's is easy to shop in, and there are huge stocks of merchandise in every category.

H&M
125 W 125th St (bet Lenox Ave and Adam Clayton Powell, Jr Blvd)

	212/665-8300
731 Lexington Ave (at 59th St)	212/935-6781
640 Fifth Ave (at 51st St)	212/489-0390
435 Seventh Ave (at 34th St)	212/643-6955
1328 Broadway (at 34th St)	646/473-1165
111 Fifth Ave (at 18th St)	212/539-1741
558 Broadway (bet Prince and Spring St)	212/343-2722
515 Broadway (bet Spring and Broome St)	212/965-8975
Hours vary by store	www.hm.com

From the day it opened, H&M has been packing them in, and it's no secret why! In a convivial atmosphere, up-to-date clothing and accessories for the young—as well as those who want to remember their carefree days —can be found at very reasonable prices. Don't come looking for pricey labels; what you will find are knockoffs of merchandise that sells for much more at boutiques and department stores. The Swedes learned quickly that American yuppies like nothing better than to fill their closets with clothing that doesn't cost very much. This is the place to get it!

Jeans come in all manner of styles, colors, fabrics, prices, and comfort levels. For the best selection try:

Anik (1122 Madison Ave, 212/249-2417 and 1355 Third Ave, 212/861-9840)

Atrium (644 Broadway, 212/473-9200)

Bloomingdale's (1000 Third Ave, 212/705-2000 and 504 Broadway, 212/729-5900)

Calvin Klein (654 Madison Ave, 212/292-9000)

Levi's Store (750 Lexington Ave, 212/826-5957 and 536 Broadway, 646/613-1847)

Scoop (532 Broadway, 212/925-2886; 861 Washington St, 212/691-1905; and 1275 Third Ave, 212/535-5577)

HARLEM UNDERGROUND
20 E 125th St (bet Fifth and Madison Ave)   212/987-9385
Mon-Thurs: 10-7; Fri, Sat: 10-8; Sun: noon-6

www.harlemunderground.com

This is a good stop for comfortable, reasonably priced, and "cool" urban wear. The merchandise has the feel of the historic area it represents. Personal or corporate embroidery is available for denim shirts and jackets, T-shirts, sweats, and caps.

HOUSE OF MAURIZIO
509 Madison Ave (at 53rd St), Room 1106   212/759-3230
Mon-Fri: 9-5

Tony Maurizio caters to men and women who like the functional and fashionable tailored look of suits. Although almost any kind of garment can be copied, this house is known for coats; two-, three-, and four-piece suits; and mix-and-match combinations. This look is favored by busy executives, artists, and journalists who have to look well-dressed but don't have hours to spend dressing. House of Maurizio's tailors create blazers or suits in a range of 2,000 fabrics, and those in silk, linen, cotton, and solid virgin wool are sensational. In addition to women's garments, they design and create coats and suits for men in the same broad range of fabrics. Tony promises fast service, expert tailoring, and moderate prices.

JEFFREY—NEW YORK
449 W 14th St (bet Ninth and Tenth Ave)   212/206-1272
Mon-Fri: 10-8 (Thurs till 9); Sat: 10-7; Sun: 12:30-6

You wouldn't expect to find a store like Jeffrey Kalinsky's in Manhattan's Meatpacking District! It offers men's and women's clothing, accessories, cosmetics, and a large selection of shoes. His Atlanta operation has been successful, and now he's brought such fashion names as Pucci, Prada, Gucci, Manolo Blahnik, and Yves St. Laurent to downtown Manhattan.

Here is a novel shop! **Nom de Guerre** (640 Broadway, 212/253-2891) can only be reached by going underground (at the Bleecker Street station of the #6 Lexington Avenue subway line).Once there you will find unusual men's T-shirts, sweat shirts, jeans, and sneakers. It's worth a visit.

LOUIS VUITTON
1 E 57th St (at Fifth Ave)   212/758-8877
Mon-Sat: 10-7 (Thurs till 8); Sun: noon-6   www.vuitton.com

In spectacular quarters at 57th and Fifth, Louis Vuitton has nearly everything you might expect: a dramatic exterior, compelling windows, a tasteful assortment of merchandise, snobby service, and inflated prices. Designer Marc Jacobs has certainly polished the label. If the LV signature is important to you, then this is the place to shop. But be warned: you are paying for four floors of very expensive real estate at Louis Vuitton.

MEXX
650 Fifth Ave (at 52nd St)   212/956-6506
500 Broadway (bet Broome and Spring St)   212/343-7954
Mon-Wed: 10-8; Thurs-Sat: 10-9; Sun: 11-7   www.mexx.com

Mexx is a global lifestyle brand with a modern European edge. For shoppers who want current styles at good prices, it is a popular destination. They have stores around the world and are quick to capitalize on hot items.

N
114 W 116th St (bet Lenox and Seventh Ave)   212/961-1036
Tues-Sat: noon-8; Sun: noon-6   www.nharlemnewyork.com

N is the first store of its kind in Harlem, raising the bar for local, national, and international designers. You'll find an exciting array of classy merchandise, including home products, cosmetics, accessories, and jewelry, all in a very attractive setting.

OSKA
415 West Broadway (bet Spring and Prince St)   212/625-2772
Mon-Sat: 11-7; Sun: noon-6   www.oska.de

For men and women who like the European look but don't want to spend a lot of money to achieve it, OSKA is the place to go. You'll find styles ranging from highly casual to very elegant.

I'm often asked where to go for French cuffed shirts and a good selection of links. Here are my answers:
Links of London (535 Madison Ave, 212/588-1177)
Missing Link (40 W 25th St, Room 108, 212/645-6928)
Thomas Pink (520 Madison Ave, 212/838-1928; 1155 Ave of the Americas, 212/840-9663; and 10 Columbus Circle, 212/812-9650)

RALPH LAUREN
867 Madison Ave (at 72nd St)   212/606-2100
872 Madison Ave (bet 71st St and Madison Ave), layette/girls
      212/434-8099
878 Madison Ave (at 72nd St), boys' store   212/606-3376
888 Madison Ave (bet 71st and 72nd St)   212/434-8000
379 West Broadway (bet Spring and Broome St)   212/625-1660
380 Bleecker St (bet Charles and Perry St), women's   212/645-5513
381 Bleecker St (bet Charles and Perry St), men's   646/638-0684
Hours vary by store   www.polo.com

Ralph Lauren has probably done as much as anyone to bring a classic look to American fashion and furnishings. His Manhattan showcase store, housed in the magnificent Rhinelander mansion, is fabulous. Four floors of merchandise for men, women, and home are beautifully displayed and expertly accessorized. You will see a much larger selection than in the many specialty boutiques in department stores. There are several things to be aware of, however. One is the haughty way some of the staff greet customers who don't look like they have big bucks. Moreover, although the clothes and furnishings are classy, one can find items of equal or better quality elsewhere at considerably lower prices. The purple-label merchandise is grossly overpriced. But shopping here does mean you can carry out your purchase in one of those popular green bags, if that matters to you.

REPLAY STORE
109 Prince St (at Greene St)   212/673-6300
Mon-Sat: 11-7; Sun: 11-6   www.replay.it

This very attractive Soho store carries dozens of different washings and fits in jeans and a variety of shirt styles. Outdoor clothing is featured. This is one of the more well-stocked stores in the area, and prices are as comfortable as the merchandise.

STEVEN ALAN
229 Elizabeth St (bet Prince and Houston St)   212/226-7482

69 Eighth Ave (at 14th St)   212/242-2677
103 Franklin St (bet Church St and West Broadway) 212/343-0692
465 Amsterdam Ave (bet 82nd and 83rd St)   212/595-8451
Hours vary by store   www.stevenalan.com

Steven Alan is a real find for men and women who have difficulty finding small or large sizes in designer merchandise. They also stock accessories, outerwear, and toiletries.

UNIQLO
546 Broadway (at Spring St)   917/237-8800
Daily: 11-9   www.uniqlo.com

This is a branch of one of Japan's largest retailers, started in 1984 in Hiroshima, Japan. You'll find high-quality casual wear for men, women, and children in a wide range of fabrics and prices. Denim and cashmere items with matching accessories are featured.

If paying four figures for sunglasses and five figures for men's shoes doesn't turn you off, then you might enjoy a look at **Tom Ford** (845 Madison Ave, 212/359-0300, www.tomford.com). This relatively new men's store is like a black and white museum, with goods in those two colors encased in glass drawers and walls. Suits can set you back as much as $8,000. What will happen to places like this when the economy takes a downturn? In the meantime, the salespeople here are pleasant and informed.

Men's Formal Wear

DANTE ZELLER TUXEDOS
201 E 23rd St (at Third Ave), 2nd floor   212/532-7320
459 Lexington Ave (at 45th St), 3rd floor   212/286-9786
1010 Third Ave (at 60th St)   212/688-0100
Hours vary by store   www.dantezeller.com

Dante Zeller Tuxedos is Manhattan's largest locally owned formalwear specialist, offering over 75 years of experience. Their wide selection includes the newest styles and colors from Calvin Klein, Ralph Lauren, Hugo Boss, Tallia Uomo, and others.

JACK AND COMPANY FORMAL WEAR
128 E 86th St (bet Lexington and Park Ave), 2nd floor
Mon-Fri: 10-7; Sat: 10-4   212/722-4609
                  www.jacktuxedos.com

Jack and Company rents and sells men's formal wear. They carry an excellent selection of sizes and names (such as After Six and Lord West), and their reputation for service dates back to 1925. In sales or rentals, Jack's can supply head-to-toe formal wear. The staff is excellent at matching outfits to customers, as well as knowing exactly what is socially required for any occasion. Same-day service is available, and the full rental price of an outfit will be applied toward its purchase!

TED'S FORMAL WEAR

155 Orchard St (bet Rivington and Stanton St)   212/966-8029
Daily: 10-6   www.tedsrocktshirts.com

Ted's is an institution on the Lower East Side. They offer reasonable prices for sales or rental of tuxedos. You'll also find a large selection of T-shirts for infants, children, and adults.

Men's—General

CAMOUFLAGE

141 Eighth Ave (at 17th St)   212/741-9118
Mon-Fri: noon-7; Sat: 11:30-6:30; Sun: noon-6

At Camouflage you'll find men's brand-name clothing, plus private label trousers, shirts, ties, and accessories. Considering some of the designers represented, prices range from reasonable to good. Camouflage can attire customers with a dignified but unique look. You definitely won't blend into the wallpaper!

EISENBERG AND EISENBERG

16 W 17th St (bet Fifth Ave and Ave of the Americas)   212/627-1290
Mon-Fri: 9-6 (Thurs till 7); Sat: 9-5; Sun: 10-4
    www.eisenbergandeisenberg.com

The classic Eisenberg and Eisenberg style dates from 1898. E&E consistently offers top quality and good prices on suits, tuxedos, coats, and sportswear. They also stock outerwear, slacks, raincoats, cashmere sport jackets, and 100% silk jackets. All are sold at considerable discounts, and alterations are available. London Fog coats are featured; no label is better known for wet-weather needs.

Looking for style on the Lower East Side? At **Blessing** (181 Orchard St, 212/378-8005), men will find a selection of unique men's wear, including furnishings, from a number of designers. The store also has a gallery displaying films, drawings, and prints that may be purchased.

FAÇONNABLE

636 Fifth Ave (at 51st St)   212/319-0111
Mon-Sat: 10-8; Sun: 11-6   www.faconnable.com

Façonnable (a French outfit) has made a name for itself in the fashion world with clothes that appeal to conservative dressers. Their New York store—which admittedly does not match the class or selection of the Beverly Hills operation—carries a good showing of men's and women's sportswear, tailored clothing, watches, suits, and shoes.

J. PRESS

380 Madison Ave (at 47th St)   212/687-7642
Mon-Sat: 9-7; Sun: noon-6   www.jpressonline.com

As one of New York's classic conservative men's stores, J. Press takes pride in its sense of timelessness. Its salespeople, customers, and attitude have changed little from the time of the founder. Styles are impeccable and distinguished; blazers are blue, and shirts are button-down and straight. Even when button-down collars were out, they never went away at J. Press.

JOHN VARVATOS

122 Spring St (at Greene St)   212/965-0700
Mon-Sat: 11-7; Sun: noon-6   www.johnvarvatos.com

Elegance is the tradition at John Varvatos, with an outstanding collection of leather and shearling outerwear, sportswear, accessories, and skincare and fragrance items. Men of all ages will feel comfortable with the Old World detailing of a line that exudes class.

Outdoorsmen will want to visit **Freemans Sporting Club** (8 Rivington St, at Freeman Alley, 212/673-3209). For comfy workwear, this is the place. (The high-priced suits are window trimming, in my view.) Oh yes, there is also a barbershop with some excellent tonsorial artists on hand to keep you looking handsomely rugged. You'll find some really neat gift items as well. You can have a delicious meal at nearby **Freemans Restaurant** (end of Freeman Alley, off Rivington St bet Bowery and Chrystie St, 212/420-0112).

L.S. MEN'S CLOTHING

49 W 45th St (bet Fifth Ave and Ave of the Americas), 3rd floor
Mon-Thurs: 9-7; Fri: 9-3; Sun: 10-4   212/575-0933
                                                  www.lsmensclothing.com

L.S. Men's Clothing bills itself as "*the* executive discount shop." I would go further and call them a must for fashion-minded businessmen. For one thing, the expansive midtown location means one needn't trek down to Fifth Avenue in the teens, which is the main area for men's discount clothing. Better still, as owner Israel Zuber puts it, "There are many stores selling $400 suits at discount, but we are one of the few in mid-Manhattan that discount the $550 to $1,500 range of suits." The main attraction, though, is the tremendous selection of executive-class styles. Within that category, a man could outfit himself almost entirely at L.S. Men's. Natural, soft-shoulder suits by name designers are available in all sizes. A custom-order department is available, with over 2,500 bolts of Italian and English goods in stock. Custom-made suits take four to six weeks and sell for around $595; sport coats are priced at $445. Custom suits by M. Freeman range from $595 to $880. They also make custom shirts by M. Freeman, with 300 swatches priced from $70 to $95. This is one of the very best destinations for top-drawer names.

PAUL STUART

350 Madison Ave (at 45th St)   212/682-0320
Mon-Fri: 8-6:30 (Thurs till 7); Sat: 9-6; Sun: noon-5
                                                  www.paulstuart.com

You'll find classy merchandise, especially in the furnishings area, at Paul Stuart. A great selection of sweaters, ties (bow ties, too!), socks, shirts, and more is shown, with ready-to-wear for women also. The men's clothing section is extensive but not exciting. As a matter of fact, the whole store is very sedate and nontrendy. Be selective when choosng a salesperson, as some of them have haughty attitudes that should be retired.

ROTHMAN'S

200 Park Ave S (at 17th St)   212/777-7400
Mon-Fri: 10-7 (Thurs till 8); Sat: 9:30-6; Sun: noon-6
www.rothmansny.com

Harry Rothman's grandson, Ken Giddon, runs this classy men's store, which offers a huge selection of quality clothes at discounts of up to 40%. In a contemporary and comfortable atmosphere, he carries top names like Canali, Hickey-Freeman, Corneliani, Joseph Aboud, Calvin Klein, Zegna, and Hugo Boss. Sizes at Rothman's range from 36 to 50 in regular, short, long, and extra long. Raincoats, slacks, sport jackets, and accessories are also sold at attractive prices.

SAINT LAURIE MERCHANT TAILORS

22 W 32nd St (bet Fifth Ave and Ave of the Americas), 5th floor
Tues-Sat: 9-6 (Thurs till 8); open Mon and closed Sat in summer
212/643-1916
www.saintlaurie.com

These folks create many items for Broadway shows! For four generations Saint Laurie has been providing quality made-to-order clothing for men and women at rack prices. Also offered is a fine selection of shirts, blouses, and accessories. A laser body scanner ensures accurate measurements. They buy directly from weavers, resulting in price savings for customers. Saint Laurie's showroom and manufacturing facility occupy the same location.

For gentlemen who don't want to pay uptown prices or suffer the haughty airs of some uptown salespeople, here are several downtown alternatives.

Memes (3 Great Jones St, 212/420-9955): cool and casual clothes
Seize Sur Vingt (243 Elizabeth St, 212/343-0476): ritzy, custom-made suits, shirts, and sweaters in beautiful fabrics from Scotland and Italy
Stussy (140 Wooster St, 212/995-8787): for the hip set
Unis (226 Elizabeth St, 212/431-5533): colorful sweaters

Men's Hats

J.J. HAT CENTER

310 Fifth Ave (at 32nd St)   212/239-4368, 800/622-1911
Mon-Fri: 9-6; Sat: 9:30-5:30   www.jjhatcenter.com

This outfit stocks over 15,000 brand-name hats and caps (to size 8) from all over the world. Founded in 1911, it is New York's oldest hat shop. Special services include free brush-up, hat stretching or tightening, custom orders, and a free catalog.

WORTH & WORTH

45-47 W 57th St (bet Fifth Ave and Ave of the Americas)
Mon, Tues, Sat: 10-6; Wed-Fri: 10-7   800/428-7467
www.hatshop.com

Your father and grandfather would love this store, which has specialized in men's hats since 1922. You'll find a good selection of fedoras, panamas, felts, caps, and berets at reasonable prices. You *won't* find baseball caps here!

Men's Shirts

CEGO CUSTOM SHIRTMAKER
174 Fifth Ave (bet 22nd and 23rd St), Room 301   212/620-4512
Mon, Tues: 9-7:30; Wed-Fri: 9-5:30; Sat: 10-3:30   www.cego.com
By appointment

For over two decades, service-oriented owner Carl Goldberg has been making quality shirts for regular people and media types. Delivery usually takes two to three weeks. If time is important, he can produce shirts in as little as two days. Prices start at less than $100 for Pima cotton broadcloth and go up for superb materials from Italy and Switzerland. CEGO also sells boxer shorts and pillow cases from his large fabric collection.

Consignment Store Shopping Hints
- Don't procrastinate; if you like it, buy it!
- You may be able to bargain on prices. Give it a try!
- Find out if returns are accepted.
- Always try on garments.
- Frequent your favorite store, as items may come in daily.
- Search online for the kind of consignment store you want.

MARK CHRISTOPHER
55 W 26th St (bet Broadway and Ave of the Americas), 35th floor
Mon-Fri: 11-6; Sat: noon-7; Sun: noon-6 (by appointment)
212/686-9190
www.markchristophercustomshirts.com

When it comes to custom-making shirts for well-dressed executives or upwardly mobile types, owner Mark Lingley is the guy to see. The classy shirts at Mark Christopher are made of fine cotton and hand-cut with superb tailoring. You pay for such special merchandise, but the service (they will make office calls) and care (the typical shirt requires about 20 measurements for a fitting) are worth the extra bucks. Shirts are the foundation of the operation, but suits and ties are also available.

SHIRT STORE
51 E 44th St (bet Vanderbilt and Madison Ave)   212/557-8040
Mon-Fri: 8-6:30; Sat: 10-5   www.shirtstore.com

The attraction of the Shirt Store is that you're buying directly from the manufacturer, so there's no middle man to hike the price. The Shirt Store offers all-cotton shirts for men (and women) in sizes from 15x32 to 18½x37. Although the ready-made stock is great, they will also do custom work and even come to your office with swatches. Additional services include mail order, alterations, and monogramming.

STATS
331 W 57th St (bet Eighth and Ninth Ave), Suite 280   212/262-5844
Mon-Fri: 8-7; weekends by appointment   www.statscustom.com

What does STATS stand for? Shirts, Ties, And Terrific Service, of course! Julie Manis sells custom-dress and casual shirts, neckwear, braces, and accessories, all custom-made in the convenience of one's office or home. She carries tailoring tools and fabrics, and can special-order fabrics not in stock. Appointments can be made to suit your busy schedule. Julie also takes the extra step of a sample shirt fitting.

Men's Ties

ANDREW'S TIES
400 Madison Ave (bet 47th and 48th St)   212/750-5221
30 Rockefeller Plaza (50th St), Room 11   212/245-4563
Mon-Fri: 9-7; Sat: 10-6; Sun: noon-6   www.andrewstiesusa.com

There are not too many really good tie stores left in New York. It's certainly not like it used to be, with great selections and bargains on the Lower East Side. But Andrew's Ties has some nice handmade Italian ties, along with ascots, pocket squares, and the like. Prices are reasonable.

Tie Care
- Always hang up ties.
- Don't rub spots.
- Use soda water to remove small spots.
- Don't iron ties.
- Don't send ties to the cleaners.
- Don't use water on stains.
- Roll ties when packing.

GOIDEL NECKWEAR
100 Clinton St (at Delancey St)   212/475-7332
Sun-Fri: 9:30-3

Since 1935 Goidel has been *the* place for bargains on ties, cummerbunds, men's jewelry, and accessories. They triple as manufacturers, wholesalers, and retailers, so savings are passed on to customers. Special note to groups: these folks will match most items brought in, usually within a week or two.

Men's Underwear

UNDER WARES
210 E 58th St (bet Second and Third Ave)   212/838-1200
Mon-Fri: 10-7; Sat: 10-6; Sun: noon-5   800/237-8641
www.underwaresforhim.com

At one time, the average fellow couldn't tell you what kind of underwear he wore and probably didn't buy it himself. All that changed when ads began featuring celebrity jocks. These days men's underwear makes a fashion statement. Under Wares sells over a hundred styles of briefs and boxer shorts. They stock the largest selection of men's undergarments in the world, carrying many top labels. There are also T-shirts, hosiery, robes, pajamas, workout wear, swimwear, and gift items. You can browse and order from their website, too.

Resale Clothing

ALLAN & SUZI
416 Amsterdam Ave (at 80th St)   212/724-7445
Mon-Sun: noon-7   www.allanandsuzi.net

This "retro clothing store" is quite an operation. You'll find current designer and vintage clothing for men and women, old and new shoes, and accessories under one roof. There are big names (like Galliano, Lacroix, Ungaro, and Versace) and labels so new you probably haven't heard of them yet. Some outfits are discounted. They are proud of the fact that they dress a number of Hollywood and TV personalities. Ask for Allan Pollack or Suzi Kandel.

DESIGNER RESALE
324 E 81st St (bet First and Second Ave)   212/734-3639
Mon-Fri: 11-7 (Thurs till 8); Sat: 10-6; Sun: noon-5
                                            www.resaleclothing.net

"Gently worn" is the concept here! Designer Resale offers previously owned ladies' designer clothing and accessories at moderate prices. Most major fashion names are represented. You might find Chanel, Armani, Hermes, or Valentino garments on the racks. If items do not sell, prices are marked down further. Call to ask about the latest bargains.

ENCORE
1132 Madison Ave (bet 84th and 85th St), upstairs   212/879-2850
Mon-Fri: 10:30-6:30 (Thurs till 7:30); Sat: 10:30-6;
Sun: noon-6 (closed Sun in July, Aug)   www.encoreresale.com

Founded in 1954, Encore can honestly be billed as a "resale shop of gently worn clothing of designer/couture quality." When you see the merchandise and clientele, you'll know why. For one thing, it is a consignment boutique, not a charity thrift shop. Its donors receive a portion of the sales price, and according to owner Carole Selig, many of the donors are socialites and other luminaries who don't want to be seen in the same outfit twice. Selig can afford to be picky, and so can you. The fashions are up-to-date and sold at 50% to 70% off original retail prices. There are over 6,000 items in stock. Prices range from reasonable to astronomical—but just think how much they sold for originally!

GENTLEMEN'S RESALE
322 E 81st St (bet First and Second Ave)   212/734-2739
Mon-Fri: 11-7; Sat: 10-6; Sun: noon-5   www.resaleclothing.org

Gentlemen interested in top-quality designer suits, jackets, and sportswear can save a bundle at this resale operation. Shopping here is like a treasure hunt, and that is half the fun. Imagine picking up a $1,000 Armani suit for $200! You might also earn a few extra bucks by consigning items from your own wardrobe.

KAVANAGH'S
146 E 49th St (bet Third and Lexington Ave)   212/702-0152
Tues-Fri: 11-6; Sat: 11-4

I can vouch highly for this designer resale shop. It is owned by Mary

Kavanagh, formerly of Bergdorf Goodman. She has superb taste! As that store's director of personal shopping, she had access to the finest labels in the world. At Kavanagh's she carries many of those same labels: Chanel, Versace, Valentino, Ungaro, Armani, Galanos, Geofrey Beene, Bill Blass, Oscar de la Renta, and many more. Chanel clothes and accessories are a specialty. Mary describes her store as a "sunny, happy spot." It is a classy shopping haven where customers come first.

MICHAEL'S, THE CONSIGNMENT SHOP FOR WOMEN
1041 Madison Ave (at 79th St)   212/737-7273
Mon-Sat: 9:30-6 (Thurs till 8)   www.michaelsconsignment.com

Is your mouth watering for one of those gowns you have seen in the papers or on TV? Would you like to dress up like one of the stars? Here's the source for pieces from top designers like Chanel, Prada, Gucci, Hermes, Yves St. Laurent, Dolce & Gabanna, Armani, and others. However, evening wear is just a small part of Michael's stock. You'll also find pant sets, skirts, suits, bags, shoes, and more. Personal attention is assured, and prices are right.

TATIANA DESIGNER RESALE
767 Lexington Ave (bet 60th and 61st St)   212/755-7744
Mon-Sat: 11-7; Sun: noon-5   www.tatianas.com

This is a unique designer consignment boutique for contemporary and vintage couture. For consigners, Tatiana offers free estimates and pickup service. For retail customers, she will try to find whatever outfit they may want. The stock is top-grade, with clothing, jewelry, bags, shoes, hats, and furs bearing top names like Chanel, Gucci, Valentino, Armani, Yves St. Laurent, and Versace.

If you have large feet, these outfits have shoes that will fit.
Johnston & Murphy (345 Madison Ave, 212/697-9375 and 520 Madison Ave, 212/527-2342): men's shoes to size 15
Stapleton Shoe Company (68 Trinity Pl, 212/964-6329): men's shoes to size 18
Tall Size Shoes (32 W 39th St, 212/736-2060): women's shoes to size 14

Shoes—Children's
EAST SIDE KIDS
1298 Madison Ave (bet 92nd and 93rd St)   212/360-5000
Mon-Sat: 10-6   www.eastsidekidsshoes.com

East Side Kids stocks footwear items up to women's size 12 and men's size 13. They can accommodate older children and juniors, plus adults with small- to average-sized feet. Of course, there is also a great selection of children's shoes in both domestic and imported styles. Frequent-buyer cards are kept on file for special discounts. The store is known for helpful service.

HARRY'S SHOES FOR KIDS
2315 Broadway (bet 83rd and 84th St)   212/874-2034
Mon, Thurs: 10-7:45; Tues, Wed, Fri, Sat: 10-6:45; Sun: 11-6:45
www.harrys-shoes.com

This popular Upper West Side shoe store is not fancy and is often wildly busy. Every single person working here knows how to fit shoes. The inventory is terrific, and the prices are often more reasonable than those at other Manhattan shoe stores. Just bring along some patience, particularly on weekends and in summer.

Notable Consignment and Thrift Shops in New York

Chelsea
Fisch for the Hip (153 W 18th St, 212/633-9053)
Goodwill Superstore (103 W 25th St, 646/638-1725)
Housing Works Thrift Shop (143 W 17th St, 212/366-0820)

East 20s
City Opera Thrift Shop (222 E 23rd St, 212/684-5344)
Goodwill Superstore (220 E 23rd St, 212/447-7270)
Housing Works Thrift Shop (157 E 23rd St, 212/529-5955)
Salvation Army Thrift Store (212 E 23rd St, 212/532-8115)
St. George's Thrift Shop (61 Gramercy Park N, 212/475-2674)

Upper East Side
Arthritis Foundation Thrift Shop (1383 Third Ave, 212/772-8816)
Bis Designer Resale (1134 Madison Ave, 2nd floor, 212/396-2760)
Cancer Care Thrift Shop (1480 Third Ave, 212/879-9868)
Council Thrift Shop (246 E 84th St, 212/439-8373)
Housing Works Thrift Shop (202 E 77th St, 212/772-8461)
Kavanagh's (146 E 49th St, 212/702-0152)
Memorial Sloan-Kettering Thrift Shop (1440 Third Ave, 212/535-1250)
Michael's (1041 Madison Ave, 212/737-7273)
Spence-Chapin Thrift Shop (1473 Third Ave, 212/737-8448)
Stuyvesant Square Thrift Shop (1704 Second Ave, 212/831-1830)

Upper West Side
Goodwill Superstore (217 W 79th St, 212/874-5050)
Housing Works Thrift Shop (306 Columbus Ave, 212/579-7566)

West Village
Housing Works Thrift Shop (245 W 10th St, 212/352-1618)

THE SHOE GARDEN
152 W 10th St (at Waverly Pl)   212/989-4320
Mon-Sat: 10-6; Sun: noon-5   www.shoegardennyc.com

This West Village newcomer has Astroturf on the floor and lizards in a terrarium. It also has a great assortment of fashionable and funky children's shoes. You'll find familiar brands like Merrell, Ecco, and Converse, as well as more unusual European names. Price takes a back seat to fashion at the Shoe Garden, although their sales are quite good.

SHOOFLY

42 Hudson St (bet Duane and Thomas St) 212/406-3270
Mon-Sat: 10-7; Sun: noon-6 www.shooflynyc.com

Shoofly carries attractive and reasonably priced imported shoes for infants to 14-year-olds. Women with tiny feet will appreciate their chic selection of footwear as well. Shoofly will take care of your shoewear needs with styles both funky and classic. The selection of tights and socks is great, too!

Shoes—Family

E. VOGEL BOOTS AND SHOES

19 Howard St (one block north of Canal St, bet Broadway and
  Lafayette St) 212/925-2460
Mon-Fri: 8-4; Sat: 8-noon (closed Sat in summer and
  first three weeks of July) www.vogelboots.com

Hank and Dean Vogel and Jack Lynch are the third- and fourth-generation family members to join this business, which has operated since 1879. They will happily fit and supply made-to-measure boots and shoes for any adult or child who can find the store. Howard is one of those streets that even native New Yorkers don't know exists. Still, many beat a path to Vogel for top-quality shoes and boots (including equestrian boots). While not inexpensive, prices are reasonable for the service involved. Even made-to-measure shoes do not always fit properly, but they do at Vogel. Moreover, once your pattern is on record, they can make new shoes without a personal visit. For craftsmanship, this spot is top-drawer. There are more than 500 Vogel dealers throughout the world, but this is the original store and the people here are super.

KENNETH COLE

597 Broadway (at Houston St) 212/965-0283
353 Columbus Ave (bet 76th and 77th St) 212/873-2061
95 Fifth Ave (at 17th St) 212/675-2550
107 E 42nd St (bet Vanderbilt and Park Ave) 212/949-8079
610 Fifth Ave (at 49th St) 212/373-5800
130 E 57th St (at Lexington Ave) 212/688-1670
Hours vary by store www.kennethcole.com

In addition to signs that induce hearty laughter at the expense of some well-known personalities, Kenneth Cole offers quality shoes, belts, scarves, watches, outerwear, and accessories at sensible prices.

LORD JOHN'S BOOTERY

428 Third Ave (bet 29th and 30th St) 212/532-2579
Mon-Fri: 10-8; Sat: 10-7 www.lordjohnsbootery.com

Lord John's Bootery has been family-owned and operated for three generations, spanning over half a century. The store has been renovated and expanded and now carries one of the largest selections of dress, casual, and comfort shoes in the area. They offer footwear for men and women from such manufacturers as Ecco, Mephisto, Paul Green, Rockport, Sebago, Birkenstock, Merrell, Camper, Kenneth Cole, Santana, and Dansko.

SHOE MANIA

853 Broadway (bet 14th St and Union Square W)	212/253-8744
331 Madison Ave (bet 42nd and 43rd St)	212/557-6627
30 E 14th St (bet University St and Fifth Ave)	212/627-0420
11 W 34th St (bet Fifth Ave and Ave of the Americas)	212/564-7319
Hours vary by store	www.shoemania.com

Shoe Mania carries men's and women's shoes for fashion, comfort, and sport at great prices. Most major brands—Hugo Boss, Adidas, Birkenstock, Converse, Kenneth Cole, Mephisto, New Balance, Rockport, Steve Madden, Via Spiga, and others—are stocked in a broad range of sizes.

T.O. DEY CUSTOM SHOE MAKERS

9 E 38th St (bet Fifth and Madison Ave), 7th floor	212/683-6300
Mon-Fri: 9-5; Sat: 9-12:30 (by appointment)	www.todeyshoes.com

T.O. Dey is a solid jack-of-all-trades operation. Though their specialty is custom-made shoes, they can also repair any kind of shoe. These folks will create men's or women's shoes based on a plaster mold of a customer's feet. Their styles are limited only by a client's imagination. They make arch supports, cover shoes to match a garment, and sell athletic shoes for football, basketball, cross-country, hockey, boxing, and running.

Shoes—Men's

CHURCH ENGLISH SHOES

689 Madison Ave (at 62nd St)	212/758-5200
Mon-Sat: 10-6; Sun: noon-4	www.churchshoes.com

Anglophiles feel right at home here, not only because of the *veddy* English atmosphere but also for the pure artistry and "Englishness" of the shoes. Church has been selling English shoes for men since 1873 and is known for classic styles, superior workmanship, and fine leathers. The styles basically remain unchanged year after year, although new designs are occasionally added as a concession to fashion. All shoes are custom-fitted, and if a style or size does not feel right, they will special-order a pair that does.

STAPLETON SHOE COMPANY

68 Trinity Pl (at Rector St)	212/964-6329
1 Rector St (bet Broadway and Trinity Pl)	212/425-5260
Mon-Thurs: 8:30-5:30; Fri: 8:30-5	

Their motto is "better shoes for less," but that doesn't begin to describe this superlative operation. Gentlemen, these stores offer Bally, Alden, Allen-Edmonds, Cole-Haan, Timberland, Rockport, Johnston & Murphy, and a slew of other top names at discount. There isn't a better source for quality shoes. They are size specialists, carrying men's sizes 5-18 in widths A-EEE.

Shoes—Women's

ANBAR SHOES

60 Reade St (bet Church St and Broadway)	212/227-0253
Mon-Fri: 9-6:20; Sat: 11-5:45	

Bargain hunters, rejoice! Anbar customers can find great deals on brand-name styles at discounts up to 80%. This is a good place to save money.

GIORDANO'S SHOES
1150 Second Ave (at 60th St)   212/688-7195
Mon-Fri: 11-7; Sat: 11-6   www.petiteshoes.com

Susan Giordano has a very special clientele. Her store stocks a fine selection of women's designer shoes in small sizes (a range that is virtually nonexistent in regular shoe stores). If you're a woman who wears shoes in the 4 to 5½ medium range, you are probably used to shopping in children's shoe departments or having shoes custom-made, either of which can cramp your style. For these women, Giordano's is a godsend. Brands carried include Anne Klein, Stuart Weitzman, Donald Pliner, Via Spiga, Rangoni, and more.

> A new designer women's shoe store, **Iris** (27 Washington St, 212/645-0950), is worth a visit.

PETER FOX SHOES
105 Thompson St (bet Prince and Spring St)   212/431-7426
Mon-Sat: 11-7; Sun: noon-6   www.peterfox.com

Peter Fox has been *the* downtown trailblazer for women's shoes. His shop carries only exclusive, limited-edition designer footwear. Perhaps because of the Soho location, Fox's designs are more adventurous than those of its competitors; the look is younger and more casual. They are well-known for their silk wedding shoes, granny boots, and hand-painted shoes. If you're looking for shoes to be seen in, this is the place to go.

TALL SIZE SHOES
32 W 39th St (bet Fifth Ave and Ave of the Americas) 212/736-2060
Mon-Sat: 9:30-6 (Thurs till 7)   www.clarotallandwide.com

Finding comfortable shoes if you are a "tall size" is not easy. This store can solve the problem, as they carry a broad selection of women's shoes to size 14 in widths from AA to extra-wide. There are custom-made women's shoes and designer names to choose from: Naturalizer, Trotters, Franco Sarto, Via Spiga, Vanelli, Sesto Meucci, Moda Spana, Costa Blanca, and many more. They also have a Cinderella department with a wide selection of shoes from size 4 on up. They will take phone orders and ship anywhere.

TE' CASAN
382 West Broadway (at Spring St)   212/584-8000
Mon-Sat: 10-7; Sun: 11-7   www.tecasan.com

When you are shopping in the Soho area, your eyes might well be directed to the windows at this classy "shoes only" store, which display shoes by a number of young designers. New designs are constantly being shown. Prices at this airy, spacious store are considerably less than uptown. Only 74 pairs of each design are made. When those are sold, that's it. So you had better buy what you like when you see it!

Sportswear

FOOTACTION USA
430 Seventh Ave (at 34th St)   646/473-1945
Mon-Thurs: 9-9; Fri, Sat: 9 a.m.-10 p.m.; Sun: 9-8
www.footaction.com

Major sports clothing and accessories can be found here! A nice selection of athletic shoes (like Michael Jordan's Nike line) and NBA fan gear is also available.

GERRY COSBY AND COMPANY
2 Pennsylvania Plaza (32nd St at Seventh Ave)   212/563-6464
Mon-Fri: 9:30-7:30; Sat: 9:30-6; Sun: 12-5   877/563-6464
                                                  www.cosbysports.com

There's a lot to like about this company. Located in the famous Madison Square Garden lobby, they are a professional business in an appropriate venue for "team sportswear"—that is, what athletes wear. They remain open for a half-hour after Rangers and Knicks home games. Gerry Cosby designs and markets protective equipment and is a top supplier of professionally licensed products. The protective equipment and bags are designed for pros but are available to the general public as well. They accept mail and phone orders for everything, including personalized jerseys and jackets.

No need to buy an around-the-world airplane ticket. Just grab a cab to **Roberta Freymann** (153 E 70th St, 212/585-3767). Roberta will tell you all about the clothes and accessories she has assembled from all over the world.

NAPAPIJRI
149 Mercer St (at Broadway)   212/431-4490
Mon-Sat: 11-7; Sun: noon-6   www.napapijri.com

The name is almost impossible to pronounce, spell, or remember, but don't let that stop you from coming here. Napapijri actually means "Arctic Circle" in Finnish. Travel and adventure are built into their men and women's sportswear apparel and accessories. Some children's wear is also shown. Soho style is paramount here.

NBA STORE
666 Fifth Ave (at 52nd St)   212/515-6270
Mon-Sat: 10-7; Sun: 11-6   www.nbastore.com

The National Basketball Association does a tremendous job of marketing itself. (I wish I could say the same for all of the NBA players!) This two-story store, occupying a prime tourist location on Fifth Avenue, is always busy with people buying team jerseys and equipment, and watching NBA videos.

NIKETOWN NEW YORK
6 E 57th St (bet Fifth and Madison Ave)   212/891-6453
Mon-Sat: 10-8; Sun: 11-7   www.niketown.com

Product innovation and Nike's sports heritage are the foundations of Niketown New York. They offer a huge selection of Nike products, including footwear, apparel (not their strongest category), items for timing and vision, and hot new tech-lab products. If you don't see your favorite athletes on the giant 36' by 22' video screen, then you might find them shopping next to you. (Oregonians like myself are proud that Nike calls the state home.)

Surplus

KAUFMAN'S ARMY & NAVY
319 W 42nd St (bet Eighth and Ninth Ave)   212/757-5670
Mon-Fri: 11-6:30 (Thurs till 7); Sat: noon-6
                                              www.kaufmansarmynavy.com

Kaufman's has long been a favorite of New Yorkers and city visitors for its extensive selection of genuine military surplus from around the globe. Over the last half-century, Kaufman's has outfitted dozens of Broadway and TV shows and supplied a number of major motion pictures with military garb. The store is a treasure trove of military collectibles, hats, helmets, uniforms, and insignias. Over a thousand military pins, patches, and medals from armies the world over are on display.

UNCLE SAM'S ARMY NAVY OUTFITTERS
37 W 8th St (bet Fifth Ave and Ave of the Americas)   212/674-2222
Mon-Sat: 10-9; Sun: noon-8:30   www.armynavydeals.com

There are a lot of Army-Navy surplus stores, but this is the only outlet in the city that gets it stock straight from the U.S. government. The quality at Uncle Sam's is very good. You'll find an excellent selection of pants, shirts, tank tops, flight jackets, watches, flags, pins, patches, and more. They will even loan out goods for a 48-hour period for various production needs— school plays and church groups, too—at no cost.

Sweaters

BEST OF SCOTLAND
581 Fifth Ave (bet 47th and 48th St), penthouse
Mon-Fri: 10-6; Sat: 10-4   212/644-0403, 800/215-3864
                                              www.cashmerenyc.com

These folks are among the very best purveyors of cashmere goods. There is a big difference in the quality of cashmere from Scotland and the Far East. At Best of Scotland you will find luxurious sweaters, baby blankets, ladies' capes, scarves, mufflers, and throws. Don't worry about sizes: you'll find ladies' sweaters up to size 48 and gentlemen's to size 59. In addition to their beautiful classic styles, you'll find multiple-ply styles with zippers and cables. Nice people, too!

GRANNY-MADE
381 Amsterdam Ave (bet 78th and 79th St)   212/496-1222
Mon-Fri: 11-7; Sat: 10-6; Sun: noon-5   www.grannymade.com

Michael Rosenberg (grandson of Bert Levy, the namesake "Granny") has assembled an extensive collection of sweaters for infants, young people, and adults, up to size 6X/7. These include handmade sweaters from all over the world, as well as some hand-loomed right here at home. The selection of women's sweaters, knitwear, dresses, skirts, slacks, soft items, and accessories is unique. They have an extensive selection of infant and toddler clothing, toys, hats, and gifts and accessories. Granny-Made has an extremely service-oriented, knowledgeable staff. They also sell "Moon and Star" cookies, made from a recipe passed down three generations!

Swimwear

CANYON BEACHWEAR
1136 Third Ave (bet 66th and 67th St)   917/432-0732
Mon-Fri: 10-8; Sat: 10-7; Sun: 11-6   www.canyonbeachwear.com

Before you dive into a pool, visit a beach, or take a cruise, come to this store. Canyon Beachwear is the ultimate in swim, sun, and vacation wear. You'll find over 1,000 swimsuits, with most major manufacturers represented. Great salespeople, also!

Goodbye, **Fine and Klein** (119 Orchard St)! This great handbag store, one of the best in the nation, has succumbed to several personal tragedies in the owning families. It was world famous, and rightfully so.

Teens

JOYCE LESLIE
20 University Pl (at 8th St)   212/505-5419
Mon-Wed: 10-9; Thurs-Sat: 10-10; Sun: 11-8

Moms like to shop here with their teenage daughters! The selection of clothing, lingerie, accessories, shoes, and handbags is very much on the inexpensive side. Most of the merchandise is trendy. There is a good showing for women who wear misses sizes.

T-Shirts

EISNER BROS.
75 Essex St (bet Broome and Delancey St)   212/475-6868
Mon-Thurs: 9:30-6:30; Fri: 8:30-3; Sun: 9-4   www.eisnerbros.com

Eisner Bros. carries a full line of licensed NBA, NFL, NHL, MLB, collegiate, and other sports, character, and novelty T-shirts and sweat shirts. Major quantity discounts are offered. You will also find police, fire, and emergency department logos, as well as Disney and Harley-Davidson. Personalizing is available on all items. They are the largest source in the area for printable corporate sportswear, T-shirts, sweat shirts, caps, jackets, work clothing, uniforms, reflective vests, tote bags, towels, aprons, umbrellas, gym and exercise equipment, team uniforms, and much more.

Uniforms

JA-MIL UNIFORMS
92 Orchard St (bet Delancey and Broome St)   212/677-8190
Mon-Thurs: 10-5 or by appointment

This is *the* bargain spot for those who must wear uniforms but do not want to spend a fortune on work clothes. There are outfits for doctors, nurses, and technicians, as well as the finest domestic uniforms and chef's apparel. Dansko clogs, Nurse Mates, and SAS shoes are available in white and colors. Mail orders are accepted.

Western Wear

BILLY MARTIN'S
220 E 60th St (bet Second and Third Ave)   212/861-3100
Mon-Sat: 11-6:30; Sun: 1-5   www.billymartin.com

If Western wear is on your shopping list, then head to Billy Martin's! They have a great selection of deerskin jackets, shirts, riding pants, skirts, hats, and parkas. They also boast one of the best collections of cowboy boots for men and women in the city. Great accessory items like bandannas, jewelry, sterling silver buckles, and belt straps complete the outfit. The items are well-tooled and well-designed, and they are priced accordingly.

Top designer clothing can be rented online from **Wardrobe** (212/302-5900, www.wardrobe-nyc.com). Most every big name is available and they will ship your outfit, which rents for about 15% of retail price.

Women's Accessories

BLUE BAG
266 Elizabeth St (bet Prince and Houston St)   212/966-8566
Mon-Sat: 11-7; Sun: noon-6

Every month you'll find a different stock of small designer bags from all over the world at Blue Bag. You likely won't find these bags in any other stores, and Blue Bag never reorders the same bag. Prices range from $65 to $500 for suedes, leathers, and other materials.

JIMMY CHOO
716 Madison Ave (bet 63rd and 64th St)   212/759-7078
Mon-Sat: 10-6 (Thurs till 7); Sun: noon-5   www.jimmychoo.com

Follow the celebrities to Jimmy Choo, where you can find classic boots, daytime and evening bags, small leather goods, fabulous designer footwear, and jeweled sandals. Bring your goldest credit card!

MARY JAEGER
51 Spring St (bet Mulberry and Lafayette St)   212/941-5877
Mon-Fri: 12:30-6:30; Sat: noon-7; Sun: noon-5   www.maryjaeger.com

Mary Jaeger's gallery-like shop carries hand-crafted collections of women's wear and interior accessories, including pillows, throws, and wall panels. Her limited-edition *shibori* T-shirts and 3D textured wraps and coats are specialties.

SUAREZ
450 Park Ave (bet 56th and 57th St)   212/753-3758
Mon-Sat: 10-6; Sun: 11-5   www.suarezny.com

Suarez has been in business for more than a half-century. In that time, they have cultivated a reputation for quality merchandise, good service, excellent selection, and reasonable prices. For years the Suarez name has been whispered by women-in-the-know as a resource for fine leather goods. They offer a great selection of exotic skin bags in a wide variety of colors.

Women's—General

ANNELORE
636 Hudson St (at Horatio St)   212/255-5574
Mon-Sat: 11-7; Sun: 11-6

Timeless fashion is key at Annelore! Everything in this charming, intimate shop is made in Manhattan. Women of all ages will find sophisticated jewelry and clothing, as well as a nice selection of soaps and candles.

BETSEY JOHNSON
248 Columbus Ave (bet 71st and 72nd St)	212/362-3364
138 Wooster St (bet Prince and Houston St)	212/995-5048
251 E 60th St (at Second Ave)	212/319-7699
1060 Madison Ave (at 80th St)	212/734-1257
Hours vary by store	www.betseyjohnson.com

In the 1960s and 1970s, Betsey Johnson was *the* fashion designer. Her designs appeared everywhere, as did Betsey herself. As an outlet for those designs not sold to exclusive boutiques, Betsey co-founded Betsey Bunky Nini, but her own pursuits led to more designing and ultimately a store in Soho. The store proved so successful that Betsey moved to larger quarters and then up and across town, as well as into such department stores as Bloomingdale's. While her style has always managed to be avant-garde, it has never been *too* far out. Johnson believes in making her own statement, and each store seems unique, despite the fact that she has over 40 of them across the country and internationally. Prices are bearable, particularly at the Soho store (which started as an outlet). Incidentally, it's hard to overlook the shops: pink with neon accents, yellow floral with gold accents, great windows, and funky, personable staff.

BEVERLY M. LTD.
By appointment   212/744-3726

Beverly Madden will design and make skirts in a selection of unusual and pure fabrics just for you. There is also a selection of silk blouses. Sizing adjustment is done at no extra cost. Delivery takes three to four weeks, depending on fabric availability.

CALYPSO
815 Madison Ave (bet 68th and 69th St)   212/585-0310
Mon-Sat: 10-7; Sun: noon-6   www.calypso-celle.com

This is the flagship store for a chain of upscale stores featuring casual fashions that are high in color and trendiness. You'll find women's and children's attire, accessories, and some home items. You will understand the merchandise when you realize that the store started in the West Indies and the designer was born in the south of France.

EDGE*nyNOHO
65 Bleecker St (bet Broadway and Lafayette St)   212/358-0255
Wed-Sun: noon-8 (Sun till 7)   www.edgeny.com

This is the place for new fashion items, accessories, and other merchandise by 65 designers. Some are just getting into the New York market, while others have already become well-known names. Located in the historic Louis Sullivan building, Edge is a fun place for those in their 20s and 30s to shop. Prices range from $25 to $6,000.

EILEEN FISHER
314 E 9th St (bet First and Second Ave)   212/529-5715
521 Madison Ave (bet 53rd and 54th St)   212/759-9888
341 Columbus Ave (bet 76th and 77th St)   212/362-3000
10 Columbus Circle (at 58th St), Room 205   212/823-9575
166 Fifth Ave (bet 21st and 22nd St)   212/924-4777
1039 Madison Ave (at 79th St)   212/879-7799
395 West Broadway (bet Spring and Broome St)   212/431-4567
Hours vary by store   www.eileenfisher.com

For the lady who likes her clothes cool, loose, and casual, look no further than Eileen Fisher. This talented designer has put together a collection of easy-care, mostly washable natural-fiber outfits in earthy colors. They travel well and are admired for their simple and attractive lines. From a small start in the East Village to six units all over Manhattan and space in some of the top stores, Eileen has produced a winner. The East Village store features discounted merchandise and first-quality goods.

ELENY
152 W 36th St (bet Seventh Ave and Broadway), Suite 504
Mon-Sat: 10-6 (by appointment)   212/245-0001

Have you dreamed about designing a dress for yourself? Well, at Eleny, this is possible. The customer-oriented personnel enjoy receiving input from their clients, and you can rest assured your evening gown will not be seen anywhere else. They will send sketches and finished gowns anywhere, and Eleny (who has been designing clothes for over two decades) gives each client her undivided attention. All fabrics are imported from Europe.

ELIZABETH CHARLES
639½ Hudson St (bet Gansevoort and Horatio St)   212/243-3201
Tues-Sat: noon-7:30; Sun: noon-6:30   www.elizabeth-charles.com

Flirty original designer clothes for all occasions from Australia and New Zealand make this a very special shop. You can even bring your boyfriend along, as the shop provides a great antique couch for patient partners!

GEMINOLA
41 Perry St (bet Seventh Ave and 4th St)   212/675-1994
Sun-Thurs: noon-7 (Mon till 6); Fri, Sat: noon-8   www.geminola.com

Geminola has an eclectic assortment of styles for the home and self. All of their clothing is made from vintage pieces, and the original designs are adapted to customer specifications.

GISELLE
143 Orchard St (bet Delancey and Rivington St)　　212/673-1900
Sun-Thurs: 9-6; Fri: 9-3　　www.giselleny.com

Women's designer sportswear, current-season goods, a large selection (sizes 4 to 20), and discount prices are among the reasons Giselle is one of the more popular shopping spots on the Lower East Side. All merchandise is first-quality. Factor in excellent service, and Giselle is well worth a trip.

LEA'S DESIGNER FASHIONS
125 Orchard St (at Delancey St)　　212/677-2043
Sun-Thurs: 9:30-5:30; Fri: 9:30-4 (till 3 in summer)

You don't have to pay full price for your Louis Feraud, Valentino, or various European designer clothes. Lea's, a popular Lower East Side outlet, discounts her merchandise up to 30% and sells the previous season's styles for 50% to 60% off. Don't expect much in the way of amenities, but you'll save enough to afford a special dinner to show off your new outfit!

> Don't miss the **Helen Wang** outlet for clothes for women and girls, and shirts for men and boys (69 Mercer St, 212/997-4180).

LINDA DRESNER
484 Park Ave (bet 58th and 59th St)　　212/308-3177
Mon-Sat: 10-6 (closed Sat in summer)　　www.lindadresner.com

You can choose from over 20 top American and European designers like Jill Sander, Chloe, Balenciaga, and Martin Margiela. The personable staff takes each customer's wishes very seriously, with all manner of special services like alterations, shipping, and messenger delivery.

MIRIAM RIGLER
41 E 60th St (bet Park and Madison Ave)　　212/581-5519
Mon-Sat: 10-6 (Thurs till 7)　　www.miriamrigler.com

Miriam Rigler is the quintessential ladies' dress shop. They have it all: personal attention, expert alterations, wardrobe coordination, custom designing (including bridal), and a large selection of sportswear, knits, and evening gowns in sizes 4 to 20. Also featured: custom headpieces, traditional and nontraditional bridal gowns, mother-of-the-bride ensembles, and debutante dresses. A subdivision now shows original paintings described as "gently priced." Despite the location, all items are discounted, including special orders. Don't miss the costume jewelry!

PALMA
463 Broome St (bet Mercer and Greene St)　　212/966-1722
Tues-Sat: 11-7; Sun: noon-6　　www.palmasoho.com

Palma has remained in business in Soho for three decades, and that is a tribute to sound retailing. This store carries designs for men and women from American, English, Italian, Canadian, French, and Spanish designers. They also provide personal wardrobe consultations.

PRADA
575 Broadway (at Prince St)   212/334-8888
Mon-Sat: 11-7; Sun: noon-6   www.prada.com

Prada is not like any other store! In rather glamorous but not easily navigated shopping spaces, the upscale Prada goods frankly look better on the racks than they do on the person. But if price is no object and you like to show off the labels you are wearing, give it a try. The architects in your family will love the decor.

REALLY GREAT THINGS
284 Columbus Ave (bet 73rd and 74th St)   212/787-5354
300 Columbus Ave (at 74th St)   212/787-5868
Mon-Sat: 11-7; Sun: 1-6

There are not many stores on the Upper West Side like these! The store at 284 Columbus Avenue is filled with high couture merchandise, while the one at 300 Columbus Avenue has a more casual feel and lower prices. Both are indeed full of really great things: clothing, bags, and accessories from the hottest European designers.

Topshop, the British fast-fashion market leader, will be opening a flagship store in Manhattan in 2008. For more information, check their website (www.topshop.com).

REBECCA TAYLOR
260 Mott St (bet Houston and Prince St)   212/966-0406
Mon-Sat: 11-7; Sun: noon-7   www.rebeccataylor.com

Here you'll find clothing, maternity wear, shoes, handbags, hosiery, and accessories. The Nolita location is a popular stop for the young and young-at-heart who are looking for whimsical merchandise.

SAN FRANCISCO CLOTHING
975 Lexington Ave (at 71st St)   212/472-8740
Mon-Sat: 11-6; Sun: noon-5   www.sanfranciscoclothing.com

The women's and children's clothing at San Francisco Clothing is just right for a casual weekend. Their merchandise is comfortable, colorful, and classy. The mature woman will find an especially good selection. Separates to go with your evening clothes are also a specialty.

TEMPERLEY LONDON
453 Broome St (at Mercer St)   212/219-2929
Mon-Sat: 11-7 (Thurs till 8); Sun: noon-6 www.temperleylondon.com

This distinctive shop was created by London fashion designer Alice Temperley. Plenty of big names shop here for women's ready-to-wear and hand-beaded bridal dresses, as well as leather and suede accessories. Champagne, wine, and more are served, as you might expect from a classy shop like this. If you want to splurge, then this is a good place to start.

TG-170
170 Ludlow St (bet Houston and Stanton St)   212/995-8660
Mon-Sun: noon-8   www.tg170.com

You won't see the clothes carried here in any other store. That is because most of the merchandise is made in small quantities especially for this store. TG-170 started as a studio where baseball hats and T-shirts were made but has grown into a retail showroom that displays unique items from young, emerging designers and some well-known ones. Freitag bags, too!

Women's—Maternity

BELLY DANCE MATERNITY
548 Hudson St (bet Charles and Perry St)   212/645-3640
Mon-Thurs: 11-7; Fri, Sat: 11-6, Sun: noon-5
www.bellydancematernity.com

Hip and fashionable moms-to-be definitely need to know about Belly Dance Maternity, a bright and funky store that's taken the West Village by storm. It is a branch of a store that started in Chicago. (Shhh! Don't tell New Yorkers that Chicago had anything first!) This is a great source for jeans, T-shirts, and cool dresses—even ultra-hip diaper bags.

CADEAU
254 Elizabeth St (bet Prince and Houston St)   212/994-1801
Mon-Sat: 11-7; Sun: noon-6   www.cadeaumaternity.com

Cadeau (French for "gift") is for moms-to-be who have a downtown sense of style and a pocketbook full of cash. Everything here is sleek and gorgeous: the fabrics, the designs, the moms, even the store itself. Cadeau has a sister store in Los Angeles.

LIZ LANGE MATERNITY
958 Madison Ave (bet 75th and 76th St)   212/879-2191
Mon-Fri: 10-7; Sat: 10-6; Sun: noon-6   www.lizlange.com

Liz Lange opened her small maternity boutique on Madison Avenue in 1996, largely in response to pregnant friends who complained they couldn't find anything fashionable to wear. She turned out to be in the forefront of a women's fashion revolution. Twelve years and two kids later, Liz's little boutique has blossomed into a three-store phenomena, with the other two in Beverly Hills and Long Island. Prices are what you would expect, given the location and high-end clothes, but the salespeople are friendly and the clothes are stylish and beautifully made.

Women's Millinery

BARBARA FEINMAN MILLINERY
66 E 7th St (bet First and Second Ave)   212/358-7092
Mon-Sat: 12:30-8; Sun: 1-7 (open later on weekends in summer)
www.barbarafeinmanmillinery.com

Although accessories are carried here, the big draw is the hats, made on-premises from original designs. If you are looking for something really funky—or, by contrast, very classy—try this spot first. Costume jewelry is also a specialty. Custom orders are welcome!

THE HAT SHOP
120 Thompson St (at Prince St) 212/219-1445
Mon-Sat: noon-7; Sun: 1-6 (closed Mon in summer)

www.thehatshopnyc.com

Owner Linda Pagan has quite a background. The boss at the Hat Shop was formerly a Wall Street broker, bartender, and world traveler. The stock reflects that diverse history, with showings from 20 local milliners. Sewn and knit hats are priced from $20 to $125; blocked hats run from $125 to $400. Custom orders are welcome.

MANNY'S MILLINERY SUPPLY COMPANY
26 W 38th St (bet Fifth Ave and Ave of the Americas) 212/840-2235
Mon-Fri: 10-5:30 www.mannys-millinery.com

This store has been in the same block since 1948! And what a stock! Row after row of drawers are dedicated to particular aspects of head adornment. The section for ladies' hatbands alone takes up almost a hundred boxes and runs the gamut from thin pearl lines to wide Western-style leather belts. There is rhinestone banding and an enormous selection of artificial flowers and feathers. The center of the store is lined with tables displaying odds and ends, as well as several bins bulging with larger items that don't fit in the wall drawers. At the front, hat forms adorn stands, and sample hats are displayed in no particular order. Manny's will help accessorize any hat with interchangeable decorations. They also sell completed hats, close-outs, and samples.

Women's Undergarments

A.W. KAUFMAN
73 Orchard St (bet Broome and Grand St)
Sun-Thurs: 10:30-5; Fri: 10:30-2 212/226-1629

Trying to find a gift for that special someone? A.W. Kaufman offers imported underwear, socks, robes, and pajamas—even nightshirts for men! For four generations, Kaufman has combined excellent merchandise with quality customer service. Among the many outstanding labels are Falke, Joelle, Chantelle, Pluto, Zimmerli, and Oscar de la Renta.

HOWARD'S
69 Orchard St (at Grand St) 212/226-4307
Sun-Fri: 9-5:30 www.shopatshellys.com

Howard transformed itself from a typical Lower East Side shop into a fashionable boutique without sacrificing the bargain prices. They carry an excellent selection of women's underwear, including top names like Hanes, Bali, Vanity Fair, Warners, Maidenform, Wacoal, Olga, Lilyette, and Jockey.

IMKAR COMPANY (M. KARFIOL AND SON)
294 Grand St (bet Allen and Eldridge St) 212/925-2459
Mon-Thurs: 10-5; Fri: 9:30-2; Sun: 10-5 (till 3 in summer)

Imkar carries pajamas, underwear, and shifts for women at roughly a third off retail prices. A full line of Carter's infants' and children's wear is also available at good prices. The store has a fine line of women's lingerie, including dusters and gowns. Featured names include Model's Coat, Vanity

Fair, Arrow, Jockey, Lollipop, and Munsingwear. Gold Toe hosiery and Arrow and Van Heusen shirts for men are also stocked.

LA PETITE COQUETTE
51 University Pl (bet 9th and 10th St)	212/473-2478
Mon-Sat: 11-7 (Thurs till 8); Sun: noon-6	www.thelittleflirt.com

Interested in a male-friendly lingerie store that will take care of your gift needs? La Petite Coquette offers a large, eclectic mix of lingerie from around the world in a diverse price range. I like their description of the atmosphere: "Flirtatious!" You'll find everything from classic La Perla to edgy designers like Ingwa Melero and Aubade. There are also old standbys like Cosabella, Hanky Panky, Mary Green, On Gossamer, Only Hearts, and Eberjey.

UNDERNEATH IT ALL
444 E 75th St (at York Ave)	212/717-1976
Mon-Thurs: 10-6	
160 E 34th St (at Lexington Ave), 4th floor	212/779-2517
Mon-Fri: 9-5	www.underneathitallnyc.com

Underneath It All is a one-stop shopping service for women who have had breast cancer or are undergoing chemotherapy. You can be assured of attentive, informed, and personal service from the staff, some of whom are breast cancer survivors. The store carries a large selection of breast forms in light and dark skin tones and in a variety of shapes, sizes, and contours. They specialize in breast equalizers and enhancers to create symmetry in your bra. There is also a complete line of mastectomy bras and name-brand bras; mastectomy and designer swimwear; sleepwear, loungewear, and body suits; and wigs and fashionable head accessories.

Boyd's of Madison Avenue no longer has a retail store. However, they do have a showroom (385 Fifth Ave, Suite 808, 212/838-6558) and website (www.boydsnyc.com) featuring cosmetics, fragrances, and gifts.

VICTORIA'S SECRET
565 Broadway (at Prince St)	212/274-9519
19 Fulton St (South Street Seaport)	212/962-8122
115 Fifth Ave (bet 18th and 19th St)	212/477-4118
901 Ave of the Americas (bet 32nd and 33rd St)	646/473-0950
1328 Broadway (at 34th St)	212/356-8380
34 E 57th St (bet Park and Madison Ave)	212/758-5592
1981 Broadway (at 67th St)	646/505-2280
1240 Third Ave (at 72nd St)	212/717-7035
2333 Broadway (at 85th St)	212/595-7861
165 E 86th St (bet Lexington and Third Ave)	646/672-9183
Hours vary by store	www.victoriassecret.com

These are some of the sexiest stores in the world! The beautiful lingerie and bedroom garb, bridal peignoirs, exclusive silks, and accessories are displayed against the most alluring backdrops. The personnel are absolutely charming as well.

Coins, Stamps

STACK'S RARE COINS
123 W 57th St (at Ave of the Americas)   212/582-2580
Mon-Fri: 10-5   www.stacks.com

Established in 1858, Stack's is the country's oldest and largest rare-coin dealer, moreover, it is still a family operation. Specializing in coins, medals, and paper money of interest to collectors, Stack's has a solid reputation for individual service, integrity, and knowledge of the field. In addition to walk-in business, Stack's conducts ten or so public auctions a year. Both neophytes and experienced numismatists can do well at Stack's.

If Mac computers, iPhones, iPod players, and related gizmos are the "Apple" of your eye, don't miss **Apple Fifth Avenue** (767 Fifth Ave, 212/336-1440). This new retail store on Fifth Avenue is identified by a stunning 32-foot tall glass tower in front of the General Motors Building. It is open 24/7 and is crowded with fascinated shoppers of all ages.

Computers
(See also "Electronics")

COMPUSA
420 Fifth Ave (bet 37th and 38th St)   212/764-6224
1775 Broadway (at 57th St)   212/262-9711
Store hours vary   www.compusa.com

There are over 5,000 computer products in stock at these computer superstores, from modern desktop models to sophisticated software. The best part of the operation, besides the selection and competitive pricing, is the service. Even though these CompUSA franchises are incredibly big and busy, the courteous sales staff will answer even the simplest questions.

RCS COMPUTER EXPERIENCE
575 Madison Ave (at 56th St)   212/949-6935
Mon-Fri: 9-7; Sat, Sun: 10-7   www.rcsnet.com

RCS is the best name to know for computers, phones and accessories, radios, and all the latest gadgets. The personnel are well-informed, the selections are vast, and the gift possibilities are endless. Customers enjoy the hassle-free environment. For those who like high-tech toys for adults (like your author), RCS is heaven!

TEKSERVE
119 W 23rd St (bet Ave of the Americas and Seventh Ave)
Mon-Fri: 9-8; Sat: 10-6; Sun: noon-6   212/929-3645
                                                      www.tekserve.com

Tekserve sells and services Macintosh computers and other Apple products. They also have a pro audio and video department, and sell all kinds of Mac accessories. On-site service and equipment rentals are offered. In business since 1987, their interest in individual customers is evidenced by the fact that Tekserve is busy all the time.

Cosmetics, Drugs, Perfumes

ESSENTIAL PRODUCTS
90 Water St (bet Wall St and Hanover Sq)   212/344-4288
Mon-Fri: 9-5

Essential Products has been manufacturing flavors and fragrances for over a century. Knowing that advertising and packaging drive up the price of name-brand colognes and perfumes, they set out to see how closely they could duplicate expensive scents at low prices. They describe their fragrances as "elegant interpretations" of designer names, sold at a fraction of the designer price. Essential features 50 perfumes and 23 men's colognes, and they offer a money-back guarantee. If you send a self-addressed stamped envelope, they will return scented cards and ordering information.

KIEHL'S
109 Third Ave (bet 13th and 14th St)   212/677-3171, 800/543-4571
Mon-Sat: 10-8; Sun: 11-6

154 Columbus Ave (bet 66th and 67th St)   212/799-3438
Mon-Sat: 10-8; Sun: 11-7   www.kiehls.com

Kiehl's has been a New York institution since 1851. Their special treatments and preparations are made by hand and distributed internationally. Natural ingredients are used in their full lines of cleansers, scrubs, toners, moisturizers, eye-area preparations, men's creams, masks, body moisturizers, bath and shower products, sports items, ladies' leg-grooming formulations, shampoos, conditioners, and treatments. Express interest in a particular product and you'll leave with a decent-size sample and extensive advice. Customers will also enjoy the unusual collection of memorabilia related to aviation and motorcycles. A Kiehl's counter is located on the street floor of Bloomingdale's.

Crafts

ALLCRAFT JEWELRY & ENAMELING CENTER
135 W 29th St (bet Ave of the Americas and Seventh Ave), Room 205
Mon-Fri: 9-5 (open late some evenings) 212/279-7077, 800/645-7124
www.allcraftonline.com

Allcraft is the jewelry-making supply store. Their catalog includes a complete line of tools and supplies for jewelry making, silver- and metal-smithing, lost-wax casting, and much more. Out-of-towners usually order from their catalog, but New Yorkers shouldn't miss an opportunity to visit this gleaming cornucopia. Call for a catalog or browse online.

CITY QUILTER
133 W 25th St (bet Ave of the Americas and Seventh Ave)
Tues-Fri: 11-7; Sat: 10-6; Sun: 11-5   212/807-0390
www.cityquilter.com

This is the only shop in Manhattan that's completely devoted to quilting. They serve everyone from beginners to professionals with classes, books, notions, thread, gifts, and 2,000 bolts of all-cotton fabrics, many hand-dyed.

CLAYWORKS POTTERY
332 E 9th St (bet First and Second Ave)   212/677-8311
Tues-Thurs: 3-7; Fri: 3-8:30; Sat: 1-8:30; Sun: 2-8:30; and by appointment (call ahead, as hours can vary)   www.clayworkspottery.com

For three decades, talented Helaine Sorgen has been at work here. If you are interested in stoneware and porcelain, then you will love Clayworks, which has a wide range for tabletop or home decor. All of Clayworks' pottery is lead-free and dishwasher- and microwave-safe. Everything is individually produced, from teapots to casseroles, mugs, and sake sets. One-of-a-kind decorative pieces include honey pots, garlic jars, pitchers, cream and sugar sets, vases, goblets, platters, and bowls. Small classes in wheel-throwing are given for adults.

GOTTA KNIT!
498 Ave of the Americas (bet 12th and 13th St), 2nd floor
Mon-Fri: 11-6 (Thurs till 8); Sat, Sun: 11-4   212/989-3030
www.gottaknit.net

At Gotta Knit! you will find luxury yarns for hand-knitting, crocheting, and custom pattern-writing for unique garments, as well as a selection of accessories, books, and buttons. Individual instructions and classes are offered.

KNITTY CITY
208 W 79th St (bet Broadway and Amsterdam Ave)   212/787-5896
Mon, Fri, Sat: 11-6; Wed, Thurs: 11-8; Sun: noon-5
www.knittycity.com

Knitty City stocks a fine selection of yarn for knitting and crocheting. Books, notions, classes, and a host of samples, too!

LOVELIA ENTERPRISES
356 E 41st St (in Tudor City Place)   212/490-0930, 800/843-8438
Mon-Fri: 9:30-5 (by appointment)

Lovelia F. Albright's establishment is one of New York's great finds. From a shop overlooking the United Nations at Tudor City Place, she dispenses the finest European Gobelin, Aubuisson, and Beauvais machine-woven tapestries at prices that are often one-third that of other places. The tapestries are exquisite. Some depict the ubiquitous unicorns cavorting in medieval scenes, while others are more modern. They come in all sizes. The latest additions include tapestries for upholstery, wool-pile miniature rugs for use under objets d'art, and an extensive line of tapestry-woven borders. They're designed by Albright and made exclusively for her in Austria and France.

WOOLGATHERING
318 E 84th St (bet First and Second Ave)   212/734-4747
Tues-Fri: 10:30-6; Sat: 10:30-5; Sun: noon-5

Woolgathering is a unique oasis dedicated to the fine art of knitting. You'll find a big selection of quality European woolen, cotton, and novelty yarns. They carry many exclusive classic and contemporary designs, a complete library of knitting magazines and books, and European-made knitting implements and gadgets. They also provide very professional finishing services, as well as crocheting and needlepoint. They will even help with your project if purchases are made at the store.

Dance Items

CAPEZIO DANCE THEATRE SHOP
1650 Broadway (at 51st St), 2nd floor   212/245-2130
www.capeziodance.com

CAPEZIO 57TH STREET
1776 Broadway (at 57th St)   212/586-5140

CAPEZIO EAST
136 E 61st St (at Lexington Ave)   212/758-8833

CAPEZIO EAST UPTOWN (children's)
1651 Third Ave (bet 92nd and 93rd St), 3rd floor   212/348-7210

ON STAGE WITH CAPEZIO (premier dancewear)
197 Madison Ave (bet 34th and 35th St)   212/725-1174
Hours vary by store   www.onstagedancewear.com

Known for service and selection, Capezio stores offer one-stop shopping for all your dance, theater, and fitness needs. Capezio Dance Theatre Shop is the largest dance and theater retail store in the world, with specialized sections for men, Flamenco, Skatewear, and a wide variety of shoes. Capezio East reflects the fashion-conscious East Side neighborhood. On Stage serves professional ballet and theater companies across the world, including the New York City Ballet. Individuals are welcome, too!

A pleasant place to rest between credit card splurges at Bergdorf Goodman (754 Fifth Ave) is **BG**, a comfortable seventh-floor dining spot with attractive fixtures and a nice view. The lunch and early evening offerings include salads, soups, seafood, and more, all served with typical Bergdorf class.

Department Stores (An Overview)

Department store closings, mergers, reincarnations, and changes of focus have taken place in recent years in Manhattan and across the nation. Some great names have disappeared: Gimbel's, B. Altman, and H. Stern. For awhile, it looked like department stores would become a relic of the past and that "big box" outlets and shopping malls would take over. However, new life has been injected into institutions that were a major part of the life and landscape of most large American cities. To a great extent, this has happened due to the vision of one man: Terry Lundgren, C.E.O. of Macy's. They (formerly Federated Dept. Stores) are the owners of the majority of department stores nationwide, including Macy's and Bloomingdale's.

In Manhattan, Bergdorf Goodman (both for women and men) is the top of the heap, quality-wise. Most major fashion names for both men and women are available at their stores (on Fifth Avenue, across from each other), with prices that can reach dizzying heights. Next down the line comes Saks Fifth Avenue, a store that has seen a constant revision in mission and presentation. There's no question about the high quality of merchandise here; the issue is whether they really know what kind of store they want to be. Next down the ladder would be Barneys, where service is spotty and too often uninformed. The uptown store is overpriced and not an easy place in which to shop. Bloomingdale's, once a great name, has slipped. They no longer carry the fabulous world merchandise imports and no longer have the spectacular model rooms. Pluses at Bloomie's include housewares and trendy apparel for women. On the down side, they have a poor men's operation – especially men's clothing. Lord & Taylor, once the epitome of American style, is trying to recover that image. How long they will remain in Manhattan is a question. Macy's, hailed as the "world's largest" store, is indeed a shopping giant, with vast selections of merchandise at just about every price level. The downstairs Cellar housewares department is spectacular. If the service matched the inventory, this would be a shoppers' paradise. Century 21 is where the New York shopper will find the best prices. Most of these department stores are open seven days a week and have varying evening hours. Unique eating facilities are featured in most, geared for quick dining between shopping splurges.

Now for the details:

Barneys New York (660 Madison Ave, 212/826-8900, www.barneys.com): Men's and women's clothing and accessories; difficult to get around the store; overpriced merchandise; attitude problem among staff.

Barneys Co-Op (236 W 18th St, 212/593-7800; 116 Wooster St, 212/965-9964; and 2151 Broadway, 646/335-0798): More comfortable prices; young designer clothes and accessories; women's clothing only at Wooster Street.

Bergdorf Goodman (754 Fifth Ave, 212/753-7300, www.bergdorfgoodman.com): Top-of-the-line clothing and accessories for women; good cosmetics department on lower level; classy home furnishings and gift selections; salespeople can treat strangers poorly.

Bergdorf Goodman Men (745 Fifth Ave, 212/753-7300): The classiest and most expensive men's store in Manhattan; most top designers show a selection of their items; great formal wear; clothing departments are better than furnishings; sales are the best time to shop; don't be intimidated by indifferent salespeople.

Bloomingdale's (1000 Third Ave, 212/705-2000, www.bloomingdales.com): Excellent women's fashions and cosmetics selection; poor showing of men's clothing; large and complete housewares and home furnishings departments; many services provided.

Century 21 (22 Cortlandt St, 212/227-9092, www.c21stores.com): Some of the best bargain hunting in Manhattan; designer labels at discount; 16 departments of children's, men's, and women's merchandise; especially good women's shoe and housewares sections; nothing fancy; friendly salespeople.

Henri Bendel (712 Fifth Ave, 212/247-1100, www.henribendel.com): Classy and expensive boutiques in beautiful surroundings, including original Rene Lalique windows; merchandise slanted to younger working women; check out the Chocolate Bar on the third floor.

Lord & Taylor (424 Fifth Ave, 212/391-3344, www.lordandtaylor.com): Now an independent store; American designers featured on 11 floors of famous-name items; main floor is unattractive; good departments for petites and larger women; service is uneven; men's departments are so-so; Christmas windows always a big draw; Signature Cafe on the sixth floor.

Macy's (151 W 34th St, Herald Square, 212/695-4400; www.macys.com):

Largest department store in the world; huge assortments of merchandise in every price category; fabulous Cellar housewares section; great home furnishings showings; one of the largest and finest cosmetics departments in the world; a visitor center concierge service is available; spectacular flower show at Easter; service can be uneven but friendly; an American icon.

Saks Fifth Avenue (611 Fifth Ave, 212/753-4000, www.saksfifthavenue. com): Store is reinvented periodically; carries top designer quality merchandise; good men's departments; very spendy street-floor boutiques; highly aggressive help in cosmetics sections.

Takashimaya (693 Fifth Ave, 212/350-0100, www.takashimaya.com): Both a museum and a gallery; attractive Japanese-made clothing, accessories, and things for the home; gracious help; top floor is a big attraction for beauty addicts.

Leave it to **davidburke & donatella** to be at the right place at the right time! On the 59th Street side of Bloomingdale's (1000 Third Ave, 212/705-3800), the hungry shopper will find a delicious array of goodies for breakfast, lunch, and early evening at two adjacent operations. One is a sit-down cafe and the other a takeout facility. You'll find soups and dumplings, big and small salads, hot sandwiches and cheeseburger sliders, hot lunches, pizzas, breakfast goodies, meatloaf, and satisfying complete dinners. Satisfying hot dinners are offered as well.

Domestic Goods

BED BATH & BEYOND
620 Ave of the Americas (bet 18th and 19th St)	212/255-3550
410 E 61st St (at First Ave)	646/215-4702
1932 Broadway (at 65th St)	917/441-9391
Daily: 9 a.m.-10 p.m.	www.bedbathandbeyond.com

Bed Bath & Beyond does things in a big way while still making every customer feel important. The selection is huge. The quality is unquestioned. The service is prompt and informed. The store on Avenue of the Americas has over 103,000 square feet of sheets, blankets, rugs, kitchen gadgets, hangers, towels, dinnerware, hampers, furniture, cookware, kiddie items, pillows, paper goods, appliances, and much more. The fine-china department is superb. Several of the stores now have health and beauty departments. The store on 61st Street has three levels jam-packed with great merchandise. The layout of the store on Broadway makes it a shopper's paradise. Prices are discounted.

D. PORTHAULT
18 E 69th St (bet Madison and Fifth Ave)	212/688-1660
Mon-Fri: 10-6; Sat: 10-5:30	www.dporthault.com

Porthault, the French queen of linens, needs no introduction. Custommade linens are available in a wide range of designs, scores of colors, and weaves of luxurious density. Wherever the name Porthault appears—for instance, on the linens at some fancy hotels—you know you're at a topnotch operation. Their printed sheets seem to last forever and are handed down from one generation to another. Porthault can handle custom work of an intricate nature for odd-sized beds, baths, and showers. Specialties include signature prints (hearts, clovers, stars, and *mille fleurs*), printed terry towels, lingerie, babies' and children's special-occasion clothing, and unique gift and fragrance items.

HARRIS LEVY
98 Forsyth St (bet Grand and Broome St)   212/226-3102
Mon-Sat: 10-6; Sun: 10-5   www.harrislevy.com

Over a century old, Harris Levy has moved into a space that was originally a premier downtown catering hall called "Pearl's Mansion," built in 1900. The building has been completely renovated, and this outstanding retailer of luxury home furnishings now includes all manner of quilts, pillows, bed linens, table accessories, bath products, candles, and fragrances —even stuffed animals for the kids. Harris Levy is a must-visit for those who want to outfit their home or apartment with goods at sensible prices.

Chocolate lovers, here is a unique suggestion! **Charbonnel et Walker** is a very old chocolate company that features handmade desserts. Located on the 8th floor of Saks Fifth Avenue, this cafe and chocolatier serves desserts on a conveyor belt. The truffle brownies are sensational!

NANCY KOLTES AT HOME
31 Spring St (bet Mott and Mulberry St)   212/219-2271
Mon-Sat: 11-7; Sun: 12-6   www.nancykoltes.com

Visit Nancy Koltes if you are interested in quality luxury home products, including beautiful bed and table linens made of the finest Italian yarns. They have a wholesale division, too.

PONDICHERRI
454 Columbus Ave (at 82nd St)   212/875-1609
Daily: 11-8   www.pondicherrionline.com

The beautiful window displays might make you think you could never afford anything inside Pondicherri. However, if you like exotic cotton prints and are looking for pillows, pillowcases, handicrafts, furniture, silks, tablecloths, quilts, curtains, bags, clothing, and the like, by all means go in. Both selection and prices are excellent! You'll find items from Tibet, India, Africa, Morocco, and other exotic spots. Because the selection is large and most items are folded on shelves, you might want to ask for help.

PRATESI
829 Madison Ave (at 69th St)   212/288-2315
Mon-Sat: 10-6   www.pratesi.com

Pratesi claims to carry the finest linens the world has to offer, and that is no idle boast. Families hand down Pratesi linens for generations. Customers who don't have affluent ancestors will wish to avail themselves of the new collections that come out in spring and fall. The Pratesi staff will help you coordinate linens to decor and to create a custom look. This three-story store has a garden that sets a mood for perusing luxurious linens.

Towels are made exclusively for Pratesi in Italy and are of a quality and thickness that must be felt to be believed. Bathrobes are magnificent, plush, and quietly understated. Cashmere pillows, throws, and blankets are available, and there is also a baby boutique.

Electronics and Appliances

DALE PRO AUDIO
22 W 19th St (bet Fifth Ave and Ave of the Americas)   212/475-1124
Mon-Fri: 9:30-5:30   www.daleproaudio.com

A family business for nearly half a century, this professional audio dealership carries the largest selection of merchandise for recording, broadcast, DJ, and sound-contracting in the country, including newly added German-made LAWO consoles. They know their stuff and are respected by customers.

For bathroom and kitchen fix-ups, several firms stand out. **Krup's Kitchen & Bath** (11 W 18th St, 212/243-5787) is a good place to go for appliances. For tiles, try **Get Real Surfaces** (37 W 20th St, 212/414-1620). The best selection of specialty glass can be found at **Bendheim** (122 Hudson St, 212/226-6370). **Simon's Hardware & Bath** (421 Third Ave, 212/532-9220) carries practically everything you could possibly want for the bathroom.

GRINGER & SONS
29 First Ave (at 2nd St)   212/475-0600
Mon-Fri: 8:30-5:30; Sat: 8:30-4:30   www.gringerandsons.com

Come to Gringer & Sons for brand-name major appliances at good prices. Gringer's informed personnel sell refrigerators, microwaves, ranges, and more to residential and commercial customers.

HARVEY HOME ENTERTAINMENT
2 W 45th St (at Fifth Ave)   212/575-5000
Mon-Fri: 10-7 (Thurs till 8); Sat: 10-6; Sun: noon-5
                                          www.harveyonline.com

Not everyone understands the finer points of the new technologies flooding the market. For those who need professional advice and individual attention, Harvey's is the place to shop. They offer state-of-the-art audio/video components, with home theater flat-screen and high-definition televisions being their specialty. Harvey has an in-home design and installation division that integrates audio and video systems into new or existing residences. There is also a Harvey outlet in **ABC Carpets & Home** (888 Broadway, 212/228-5354).

J&R MUSIC & COMPUTER WORLD
1-34 Park Row (across from City Hall)   212/238-9000, 800/221-8180
Mon-Sat: 9-7:30; Sun: 10:30-6:30   www.jr.com

This operation prides itself on being one of the nation's complete electronics and home-entertainment department stores. They carry cameras, printers and other photo accessories; all types of personal music players, including iPods; TVs and home-theater components; music and movies; and home office gear, including iPhones, phones, PDAs, faxes, multi-function printers, and desktop and laptop computers (both PCs and Macs). The place is well organized, though it can get rather hectic at times. Prices are competitive and merchandise is guaranteed. In the middle of the block, J&R has other stores with kitchenware, more small appliances, and personal-care items.

> The great majority of places written up in this book (with exception of the "Don't Bother" list in the Restaurants section) are places that I recommend. However, I must make an exception. While I believe that Sony products are generally of top quality, the flagship store **Sony** (550 Madison Ave, 212/833-8800) warrants a very strong *negative* review.
>
> In the first place, you can do better pricewise at a number of other outlets that sell Sony products. Most important, their "consumer friendly" index is about as low as it gets. Their telephone order and service line is unbelievably bad. One has a very difficult time even reaching a human being at the store. Moreover, their in-store service shows a serious lack of supervision. Orders are not filled as promised. Customers are not kept current on availability of merchandise. Finding a sales clerk is often frustrating. Why spend your hard-earned money and valuable time patronizing a place that doesn't seem especially interested in your business?

P.C. RICHARD & SON
120 E 14th St (bet Third and Fourth Ave)	212/979-2600
205 E 86th St (bet Second and Third Ave)	212/289-1700
2372 Broadway (at 86th St)	212/579-5200
53 W 23rd St (bet Ave of the Americas and Seventh Ave)	
Mon-Fri: 10-9:30; Sat: 9-9; Sun: 10-7	212/924-0200
	www.pcrichard.com

For nearly a century this family-owned and -operated appliance, electronics, and computer store has been providing superior service to customers. They offer a large inventory, good prices, delivery seven days a week, and in-house repair service. The store started as a hardware outfit, and the dedication to personalized service has been successfully passed from one generation to the next.

SHARPER IMAGE
10 W 57th St (at Fifth Ave)	212/265-2550
50 Rockefeller Plaza (bet Fifth Ave and Ave of the Americas)	
	646/557-0861
Pier 17, South Street Seaport	212/693-0477
98 Greene St (bet Prince and Spring St)	917/237-0221
Hours vary by location	www.sharperimage.com

If you are a gadget freak like me, you'll go wild at this fascinating emporium. This is truly a grown-up's toy store! The latest electronic gadgets, household helpers, sports items, games, novelties, and clothing make browsing the Sharper Image a unique experience.

STEREO EXCHANGE
627 Broadway (at Houston St)   212/505-1111
Mon-Fri: 11-7:30; Sat: 10:30-7; Sun: noon-7

www.stereoexchange.com

For high-end audio-video products, you can't do better than this outfit! They carry top names like Marantz, McIntosh, and B&W and can handle their installation. Moreover, the personnel really care about their products.

WAVES
251 W 30th St (bet Seventh and Eighth Ave)   212/273-9616
Mon-Fri: 11-6; Sat: 11-5   www.wavesllc.com

Bruce and Charlotte Mager allow the past to live on with their collection of vintage record players, radios, receivers, and televisions. They favor the age of radio over the high-tech present. Their shop is a virtual shrine to the 1930s and before. At Waves you'll find the earliest radios (still operative!) and artifacts. There are promotional pieces, such as a radio-shaped cigarette lighter. Gramophones and anything dealing with the radio age are available. Waves also rents phonographs, telephones, and neon clocks, and they will repair and appraise items.

Eyewear and Accessories

THE EYE MAN
2264 Broadway (bet 81st and 82nd St)   212/873-4114
Mon, Wed: 10-7; Tues, Thurs: 10-7:30; Fri, Sat: 10-6;
Sun: noon-5 (closed Sun in summer)   www.eyeman.com

Dozens of stores in Manhattan carry eyeglasses, but few take special care with children. The Eye Man carries a great selection of frames for young people, as well as specialty eyewear for grownups.

FABULOUS FANNY'S
335 E 9th St (bet First and Second Ave)   212/533-0637
Daily: noon-8 p.m.   www.fabulousfannys.com

I like the slogan of this outfit: "If you have to wear them, make it fun!" What they are referring to are glasses. This store has the largest and best selection of antique and vintage eyewear in the country. Men and women will be dazzled by their stock. Who doesn't want to be complimented on their glasses? It beats being told, "So, you've finally reached that age!"

GRUENEYES
599 Lexington Ave (bet 52nd and 53rd St)   212/688-3580
1076 Third Ave (bet 63rd and 64th St)   212/751-6177
740 Madison Ave (at 64th St)   212/988-5832
2009 Broadway (at 69th St)   212/874-8749
1225 Lexington Ave (bet 82nd and 83rd St)   212/628-2493
2384 Broadway (at 87th St)   212/724-0850
Hours vary by store   www.grueneyes.com

The same faces and quality care can be found at Grueneyes year after year. The firm enjoys a reputation for excellent service. They can do emergency fittings and one-day turnaround, and they carry a superb selection of specialty eyewear. Their sunglasses, theater glasses, sports spectacles, and party eyewear are noteworthy.

JOEL NAME OPTIQUE DE PARIS
448 West Broadway (at Prince St)   212/777-5888
Mon-Sat: 11-7

Service is the name of the game at this shop. Owner Joel Nommick and his crew of professionals stock some of the most fashionable specs in town.

LIGHTHOUSE STORE
111 E 60th St (bet Park and Lexington Ave)   212/821-9384
Mon-Fri: 10-6; Sat: 10-5   www.lighthouse.org

This is a wonderful place for people who are blind or partially sighted. Their vast selection includes CCTVs (desktop and pocket models), glare-free lighting, magnifying mirrors, talking products, watches, clocks, and household items. Open houses and hands-on demonstrations allow customers to learn about state-of-the-art technology.

MORGENTHAL-FREDERICS OPTICIANS
699 Madison Ave (bet 62nd and 63rd St)   212/838-3090
944 Madison Ave (bet 74th and 75th St)   212/744-9444
399 West Broadway (at Spring St)   212/966-0099
Bergdorf Goodman, 754 Fifth Ave (at 58th St)   212/872-2526
10 Columbus Circle   212/956-6402
Hours vary by store   www.morgenthalfrederics.com

If you're looking for unique eyewear and accessories, then put Morgenthal-Frederics high on your list. Owner Richard Morgenthal displays innovative styles, including exclusive designs. With Morgenthal-Frederics' various locations and attentive staff, clients are truly well serviced. They'll even make appointments for you with some of New York's best ophthalmologists.

20/20 EYEWEAR
1592 Third Ave (bet 89th and 90th St)   212/876-7676
57 E 8th St (bet Broadway and University Pl)   212/228-2192
Mon-Fri: 10-7:30; Sat: 10-6   www.twentytwentyeyewear.com

Whether you see glasses as a simple necessity, a statement of style, or both, the large selection at 20/20 will suit your needs. For over two decades 20/20 has offered trendsetting eyewear in a casual, appealing atmosphere. They provide overnight delivery, eye exams, and prescription fulfillment.

Fabrics, Trimmings

A.A. FEATHER COMPANY
(GETTINGER FEATHER CORPORATION)
16 W 36th St (bet Fifth Ave and Ave of the Americas), 8th floor
Mon-Thurs: 9-6; Fri: 9-3   212/695-9470
www.gettingerfeather.com

Do you need an ostrich plume, feather fan, or feather boa for your latest ensemble? Have you made a quilt that you'd like to stuff with feathers? Well, you're in luck with A.A. Feather (a.k.a. Gettinger Feather Corporation). The Gettingers have been in business since 1915, and first grandson Dan Gettinger runs it today. There aren't many family-owned businesses left, and there are almost no other sources for fine-quality feathers. This is a find!

A. FEIBUSCH—ZIPPERS & THREADS
27 Allen St (bet Canal and Hester St)   212/226-3964
Mon-Fri: 9-4:30; Sun: 9-2 (closed Sun in summer)
www.zipperstop.com

A. Feibusch boasts of having "one of the biggest selections of zippers in the U.S.A," as if they really believe there are zipper stores throughout the country! They stock zippers in every size, style, and color (hundreds of them), and can make zippers to order. I once saw a woman purchasing tiny zippers for doll clothes. Feibusch carries matching threads to sew in a zipper, webbing, ribbons, and other sewing supplies. Eddie Feibusch assures me that no purchase is too small or large, and he gives each customer prompt, personal service.

ALMAR FABRICS
255 W 36th St (bet Seventh and Eighth Ave), Room 401
Mon-Fri: 9-5   212/869-9616

Almar Fabrics specializes in imported men's woolens, including English cashmere and wools in qualities from super 100s to super 180s and Italian wools from the finest houses. They also carry wools for ladies, including crepes, gabardines, flannels, and imported Italian and Irish linens.

B&J FABRICS
525 Seventh Ave (at 38th St), 2nd floor   212/354-8150
Mon-Fri: 8-5:45; Sat: 9-4:45   www.bandjfabrics.com

B&J started in the fabric business in 1940 and is now run by the second and third generations of the Cohen family. They carry fashion fabrics, many imported directly from Europe. Specialties of the house: natural fibers, designer fabrics, bridal fabrics, ultra-suede, Liberty of London, and silk prints (over a thousand in stock!). Swatches are sent free of charge by specific request. You will also find a wonderful selection of hand-dyed batiks.

BECKENSTEIN MEN'S FABRICS
257 W 39th St (bet Seventh and Eighth Ave)   212/475-6666
Mon-Sat: 9-6   800/221-2727
www.fabricczar.com

Beckenstein is the finest men's fabric store in the nation. Proprietor Neal Boyarsky and his son Jonathan have been called "the fabric czars of the U.S." These folks sell to a majority of custom tailors in the country and to many top manufacturers of men's clothing, so you know the goods are best-quality. Their customer list reads like a who's who of politicians, film stars, and sports figures. You will find every kind of fabric, from goods selling for $10 a yard to fabulous pieces at $1,000 a yard. There are pure cashmeres, fine English suitings, silks, camel hair, and more.

HYMAN HENDLER AND SONS
21 W 38th St (bet Fifth Ave and Ave of the Americas)   212/840-8393
Mon-Fri: 9-5   www.hymanhendler.com

Although Hyman Hendler has passed away, the store that proudly bears his name is in the capable hands of his son-in-law. In the middle of the trimmings center of the world, it is one of the oldest businesses (established in 1900) and the crown head of the ribbon field. This organization manufactures, wholesales, imports, and acts as a wholesaler for every kind of ribbon. It's hard to believe as many variations exist as are jammed into this store.

LIBRA LEATHER
259 W 30th St (bet Seventh and Eighth Ave), 6th floor 212/695-3114
Mon-Fri: 9:30-5:30 (by appointment)   www.libraleather.com

If you are interested in leathers and skins, look no further. Libra Leather has been supplying wholesale leather to leaders in the style and fashion world for decades, and they are recognized for top quality. Now you can buy retail items, including aprons, note pads, rugs, duffels, pillows, blankets, coasters, and wine and water bottle carriers. Unfinished leather pieces, too!

LONG ISLAND FABRIC WAREHOUSE
406 Broadway (bet Canal and Walker St)   212/431-9510
Daily: 9-7

Long Island Fabric Warehouse has one huge floor of every imaginable kind of fabric and trimming. Since all are sold at discount, it's one of the best places to buy fabrics. Some of the attractions include an extensive wool collection and such dressy fabrics as chiffon, crepe, silk, and satin. Most amazing are the bargain spots, where remnants and odd pieces go for so little it's laughable. They carry an excellent selection of patterns, notions, trimmings, and dollar-a-yard fabrics.

M&J TRIMMING/M&J BUTTONS
1006 and 1008 Ave of the Americas (bet 37th and 38th St)
Mon-Fri: 9-7; Sat: 10-5; Sun: noon-5   212/391-9072
                                                   www.mjtrim.com

These folks claim to have the largest selection of trims at one location, and I'm inclined to believe them! You will find everything from imported trims, buttons, and decorator trims to various fashion accessories. One store specializes in clothing and fashion trims, and the other features interior decor trim. They have over a half century of experience in this business.

MARGOLA IMPORT CORP.
48 W 37th St (bet Fifth Ave and Ave of the Americas)
Mon-Fri: 8:30-6; Sat: 10-4 (closed Sat in summer)   212/564-2929
                                                       www.margola.com

You'll find an outstanding showing of beads and rhinestones at Margola. They will help with any phase of beading.

PARON WEST
206 W 40th St (at Seventh Ave)   212/768-3266
Mon-Fri: 8:45-5:45 (Thurs till 7); Sat: 8:45-5   www.paronfabrics.com

Paron carries an excellent selection of contemporary designer fabrics at discount prices. Many of the goods shown are available only in their store. This is a family operation, so personal attention is assured. **Paron Annex**, their half-price outlet, adjoins Paron West.

PIERRE DEUX FRENCH COUNTRY

625 Madison Ave (bet 58th and 59th St)   212/521-8012
Mon-Sat: 10-6 (Thurs till 7); Sun: noon-5 (closed Sun in summer)
                                                    www.pierredeux.com

Pierre Deux, the French Country home-furnishings company, specializes in authentic handcrafted products from the provinces of France. Everything from 18th-century antique and reproduction furniture to fabrics, brightly colored pillows, handbags, faience, pewter, lighting, wallpaper, table linens, glassware, and gourmet specialties from Le Cordon Bleu are carried here. Services include a personalized bridal registry and custom orders.

ROSEN & CHADICK FABRICS

561 Seventh Ave (at 40th St), 2nd and 3rd floors   800/225-3838
Mon-Fri: 8:30-5:45; Sat: 9-4:30   www.rosenandchadickfabrics.com

For over a half-century this family-owned business has been offering customers a huge selection of quality fabrics: silks, wools, cashmeres, linens, cottons, laces, velvets, brocades, and more. With so much interest in cashmere these days, I was particularly impressed with the selection. You can be assured of personal, attentive, and knowledgeable service. Ask for David Chadick, the hands-on owner.

SILK SURPLUS/BARANZELLI HOME

938 Third Ave (bet 56th and 57th St)   212/753-6511
Mon-Fri: 10-6 (Thurs till 7); Sat: 10-5

Silk Surplus is the exclusive outlet for Scalamandre close-outs of fine fabrics, trimmings, and wallpaper, as well as Baranzelli's own line of imported and domestic informal fabrics and trimmings. Scalamandre sells for half of retail, and a choice selection of other luxurious fabrics is offered at similar savings. There are periodic sales, even on already discounted fabrics, at this elegant fabric store. They also have custom workrooms for upholstery, drapery, pillows, and custom furniture.

TINSEL TRADING

47 W 38th St (bet Fifth Ave and Ave of the Americas) 212/730-1030
Mon-Fri: 9:45-5:30 (Sat hours vary, so call ahead)
                                                    www.tinseltrading.com

Tinsel Trading claims to be the only firm in the United States specializing in antique gold and silver metallics from the 1900s. They have everything from gold thread to lamé fabrics. Tinsel Trading offers an amazing array of tinsel threads, braids, fringes, cords, tassels, gimps, medallions, edging, banding, gauze lamés, bullions, fabrics, soutache, trims, and galloons. All are genuine antiques, and many customers buy them for accenting modern clothing. The collection of military gold braids, sword knots, and epaulets is unsurpassed. Visit the ribbon emporium at **The Store Across the Street** (64 W 38th St, 212/354-1242), where you'll find vintage and new ribbons galore in a beautiful setting.

TOHO SHOJI
990 Ave of the Americas (at 36th St) 212/868-7466
Mon-Fri: 9-7; Sat: 10-6; Sun: 10-5   www.tohoshoji-ny.com

Have you ever heard of a beads and trimmings supermarket? Only in New York will you find an establishment like Toho Shoji, which stocks all manner of items for designing and making custom jewelry: earring parts, metal findings, chains, and every kind of jewelry component. Items are well displayed for easy selection.

THE YARN COMPANY
2274 Broadway (bet 81st and 82nd St), Room 1C
Tues-Sat: noon-6 (Wed till 8)   212/787-7878, 888-927-6265
www.theyarnco.com

The largest selection of unique high-end knitting yarns in the city can be found here. You'll find cashmeres, merino wools, silks, linens, rayons, and more. The best part of this second-floor operation is the personal interest shown by the owners, who have written five knitting books. There are many samples to look at, and these folks are up to date on new yarns and designs. Workshops and classes are available.

ZARIN FABRIC WAREHOUSE
318 Grand St (at Allen and Orchard St) 212/925-6112
Sun-Fri: 9-6; Sat: 10-6   www.zarinfabrics.com

Founded in 1936, Zarin is the largest and oldest drapery and upholstery fabric warehouse in Manhattan. This "fabric heaven" occupies an entire city block stocked with thousands of designer fabrics and trims at below whole-sale prices. With the largest selection of designer fabrics in New York, Zarin is a favorite inside source for decorators, set designers, and celebrity clientele. Zarin also carries some of the finest ready-made collections of window panels, custom lampshades, lamps, and other home furnishings. Another worthy Zarin operation, **BZI Distributors** (318 Grand St, 212/966-6690), sells trimmings, fringe, and drapery and upholstery hardware.

Good shopping in Harlem!
Antiques, architectural: **Demolition Depot** (216 E 125th St, 212/860-1138)
Books: **Hue-Man Bookstore** (2319 Frederick Douglass Blvd, 212/665-7400)
Clothing, men's and women's: **N** (114 W 116th St, 212/961-1036)
Housewares: **Xukama** (11 E 125th St, 212/222-0490)
Shoes, children's: **Purple Reign** (171 Lenox Ave, 212/222-7221)
Skin-care products: **Carol's Daughter** (24 W 125th St, 212/828-6757)
Sporting goods: **Champs** (208 W 125th St, 212/280-0296)

Fans

SUPERIOR LIGHT & FAN
5 E 16th St (at Union Square W) 212/677-9191
Mon-Sat: 9-6 (Tues, Thurs till 8); Sun: noon-6   www.superiorlf.com

At Superior you will find a 5,000-square-foot showroom of contemporary lighting and ceiling fans. They are certified specialists for lighting installation and repair.

Fireplace Accessories

DANNY ALESSANDRO
308 E 59th St (bet First and Second Ave)   212/421-1928
Mon-Fri: 9-5 (open weekends by appointment)

New Yorkers have a thing for fireplaces, and Danny Alessandro caters to that infatuation. Alessandro has been in business for more than four decades. Just as New York fireplaces run the gamut from antique brownstone to ultramodern blackstone, Alessandro's fireplaces and accessories range from antique pieces to a shiny new set of chrome tools. The shop also stocks antique marble and sandstone mantelpieces, andirons, and an incredible display of screens and tool kits. In the Victorian era, paper fans and screens were popular for blocking fireplaces when not in use. The surviving antique pieces at Alessandro are great for modern decorating. They will also custom-order mantels, mantelpieces, and fireplace accessories. However, they do not repair or clean fireplaces.

WILLIAM H. JACKSON COMPANY
210 E 58th St (bet Second and Third Ave)   212/753-9400
Mon-Thurs: 9:30-5; Fri: 9:30-4   www.wmhj.com

In real estate ads "wbfp" stands for "wood-burning fireplace," and they are the rage in New York. In business since 1827, William H. Jackson is familiar with the various types of fireplaces in the city. In fact, they orginally installed many of those fireplaces. Jackson has hundreds of mantels on display in its showroom. They range from antiques and reproductions (in wood or marble combinations) to starkly modern pieces. There are also andirons, fire sets, and screens. In addition, they'll provide advice on how to enjoy your fireplace. Jackson does repair work (removing and installing mantels is a specialty), but they're better known for selling fireplace accessories. Handy item: a reversible sign that reads "Damper Is Open"/"Damper Is Closed."

Flags

ACE BANNER FLAG AND GRAPHICS
107 W 27th St (at Ave of the Americas)   212/620-9111
Mon-Fri: 7:30-4   www.acebanner.com

If you need a flag, Ace is the right place. Established in 1916, Ace prides itself on carrying the flags of every nation, as well as New York City and New York State flags in all sizes. Other kinds of flags can be made to order. They range in size from 4" by 6" desk flags to bridge-spanning banners. Ace also manufactures custom banners, from podium to building size. They offer over 45 colors of banner nylon, and quick turnaround is available for large digital graphics. If you're running for any kind of office, campaign paraphernalia can be ordered with a promise of quick delivery. They will ship anywhere. Ask for owner Carl Calo!

Floor Coverings

BEYOND THE BOSPHORUS
79 Sullivan St (bet Spring and Broome St)   212/219-8257
Tues-Sun: 11-7

Ismail Basbag, the owner of this establishment, was a kilim dealer for 12 years in Istanbul's grand bazaar before opening his shop in Soho in 1985. Anyone who could survive at that colorful, crowded, and noisy marketplace can certainly do business in Manhattan! Here you will find hand-woven Turkish kilim rugs and pillows in a variety of sizes, patterns, and colors. A line of Turkish bolsters is available. Basbag travels to Turkey several times a year to fill customers' special requests. Rug cleaning and repair are available.

COUNTRY FLOORS
15 E 16th St (bet Fifth Ave and Union Square W)   212/627-8300
Mon-Fri: 9-6; Sat: 9-5   www.countryfloors.com

Country Floors is one of New York's biggest retail success stories, no doubt because they offer a magnificent product. Begun in 1964 in a tiny, cramped basement under the owner's photography studio, Country Floors has grown to include huge stores in New York and Los Angeles. There are nearly 60 affiliates worldwide, including Canada and Australia. Country Floors carries the finest floor and wall tiles, made of stone, glass, and terra cotta. Their sources include artisans from all over the world. A visit—or at least a look at their catalogs—is necessary to appreciate the quality and intricacy of each design. Even the simplest solid-color tiles are beautiful.

ELIZABETH EAKINS
21 E 65th St (bet Fifth and Madison Ave)   212/628-1950
Mon-Fri: 10-5:30   www.elizabetheakins.com

Elizabeth Eakins is a first-class source for wool and cotton rugs. She custom-designs and makes hand-woven and hand-hooked rugs in standard and hand-dyed colors.

JANOS P. SPITZER FLOORING
131 W 24th St (bet Ave of the Americas and Seventh Ave)
Mon-Fri: 8-4:30   212/627-1818
                              www.janosspitzerflooring.com

Janos Spitzer, a Hungarian craftsman, has over four decades of experience. His top-notch flooring headquarters features installation of high-end (read: pricey) residential wooden floors, as well as expert restoration and repair. You'll find many unusual finishes here. These are highly reliable and experienced craftspeople who stock only the finest products. For large projects, they will help purchase products, hire workers, and follow up to ensure specifications have been met.

LOOM & WEAVE
1 E 28th St (bet Fifth and Madison Ave), 5th floor   212/779-7373
Mon-Fri: 10-5 (by appointment)

Loom & Weave stocks one of the largest collections of antique and semi-antique Oriental rugs in the city—over 2,000 of them! The current owners come from a family tradition of five decades in the rug business. Modern premises provide an attractive setting for discounted rugs of all sizes.

MOMENI INTERNATIONAL
36 E 31st St (bet Park and Madison Ave), 2nd floor   212/532-9577
Mon-Fri: 9-5   www.momeni.com

These people will tell you they are wholesale only, but don't let that scare you away. Those who visit their expanded showroom will be rewarded with one of the best sources for Oriental rugs in the city. Since they don't officially serve individual retail customers, prices reflect wholesale rather than retail business. That doesn't make them cheap—good Oriental rugs never are—but it does assure top quality at a fair price.

Prudence Designs (228 W 18th St, 212/691-1541, Mon-Fri: 9-6; Sat: noon-6) is a florist shop with down-to-earth prices. They specialize in weddings, bar mitzvahs, and other special events. Delivery is available, and you won't be disappointed in their exotic arrangements.

NEMATI COLLECTION
Art and Design Building
1059 Third Ave (bet 62nd and 63rd St), 3rd floor
Mon-Fri: 9-6; Sat: 10-4 (or by appointment)   212/486-6900
                                                www.nematicollection.com

The Nemati Collection was founded by Parviz Nemati, author of *The Splendor of Antique Rugs and Tapestries*. He has been dealing in antique Oriental rugs and tapestries for four decades. The tradition is carried on by his son, Darius Nemati. In addition to an extensive collection of antique Oriental rugs and period tapestries, the gallery also features modernist and contemporary rugs, as well as an exclusive collection of custom carpeting and natural-fiber flooring. Services includes a full restoration and conservation department, consulting, insurance appraisals, and professional cleaning.

PASARGAD CARPETS
180 Madison Ave (bet 33rd and 34th St)   212/684-4477
Mon-Fri: 9-6; Sat: 10-6; Sun: 11-5   www.pasargadcarpets.com

Pasargad is a fifth-generation family business established in 1904. They have one of the largest collections of antique, semiantique, and new Persian and Oriental rugs in the country. Decorating advice, repair and cleaning, and pickup and delivery service are offered. Pasargad will also buy or trade quality antique rugs.

SAFAVIEH CARPETS
153 Madison Ave (at 32nd St)   212/683-8399
238 E 59th St (at Second Ave)   212/888-0626
Mon-Fri: 9-6; Sun: noon-6

902 Broadway   212/477-1234
Mon-Sat: 10-7; Sun: 11-6   www.safavieh.com

There was a time when it was possible to visit the teeming markets of

Tehran and find some real rug bargains. At Safavieh one can still see a vast selection of these beautiful works of art, even if the setting is a little less glamorous. Safavieh has one of the finest collections of Persian, Indian, Pakistani, and Chinese rugs in this country. They're displayed in a showroom spacious enough for customers to visualize how the prized pieces would look in their homes or places of business. These rugs are truly heirlooms, and you will want to spend time hearing about their exotic origins. Prices, although certainly not inexpensive, are competitive for the superior quality represented. (Hint: It doesn't hurt to do a little haggling.)

Flowers, Plants, and Gardening Items

BLOOM
541 Lexington Ave (at 50th St)   212/832-8094
Mon-Fri: 8-7; Sat: 9-6   www.bloomflowers.com

When price is no object, you can do no better in the floral department than Bloom. Come here for a superb bouquet or arrangement when you have some special occasion to celebrate.

CHELSEA GARDEN CENTER HOME
580 Eleventh Ave (at 44th St)   212/727-7100
Mon-Sat: 9-6; Sun: 10-6   www.chelseagardencenter.com

These folks have combined their home store and outdoor garden center into one large operation. For the urban gardener this place is a dream, offering a wide selection of plants and flowers, soil, fertilizers, containers, fountains, tabletop items, lighting, candles, holiday decor, tools, indoor and outdoor furniture, garden books, and much more.

> **Shopping in Tribeca**
> Beauty products: **Lafco New York** (285 Lafayette St, 212/925-0001)
> Bikes: **Gotham Bikes** (112 West Broadway, 212/732-2453)
> Clothing: **Tribeca Issey Miyake** (119 Hudson St, 212/226-0100)
> Furniture: **Dune** (88 Franklin St, 212/925-6171)
> Home furnishings: **Baker Tribeca** (129 Hudson St, 212/343-2956)

COUNTRY GARDENS
1160 Lexington Ave (at 80th St)   212/966-2015
Mon-Fri: 8:30-6; Sat: 9-3 (closed July and Aug in summer)

The service at Country Garden is highly personalized, and they show a great selection of cut flowers and plants. They arrange everything to order and will deliver all over Manhattan.

SIMPSON & COMPANY FLORISTS
852 Tenth Ave (at 56th St)   212/772-6670
Mon-Fri: 9-5   www.simpsonflowers.com

Simpson specializes in unusual baskets, cut flowers, plants, and orchids. They will decorate for gatherings of all sizes, and their prices are very competitive.

TREILLAGE
418 E 75th St (at York Ave)   212/535-2288
Mon-Fri: 10-6   www.treillageonline.com

New Yorkers have gardens, too, although out of necessity they are small. Many times they are just patio blooms, but still they add a special charm to city living. Treillage can help make an ordinary outside space into something special. They carry furniture and accessories for indoors and outdoors, with a great selection of unusual pieces that will set your place apart. They sell everything except plants and flowers! Prices are not inexpensive, but why not splurge to enhance your little corner of the great outdoors?

VSF
204 W 10th St (bet 4th and Bleecker St)   212/206-7236
Mon-Fri: 8-5; Sat: 11-4

If you want a special look when it comes to fresh-cut flowers or dried creations, you can't do better than VSF. Their top-drawer list of clients attests to their talents for weddings and other special events. Ask for owners Jack Follmer or Todd Rigby.

ZEZÉ FLOWERS
938 First Ave (at 52nd St)   212/753-7767
Mon-Sat: 8-6 (also open holiday weekends)

Zezé came to New York several decades ago from Rio de Janeiro, a city known for its dramatic setting, and he brought a bit of that drama to the flower business in Manhattan. Zezé's windows reflect his unique talent. The exotic orchid selection is outstanding. You'll find premium fresh-cut flowers, topiaries, unique ceramics and glassware, gift items, and antiques. They offer the ultimate in personalized service, including same-day deliveries and special requests.

Frames

HOUSE OF HEYDENRYK
601 W 26th St (bet Eleventh and Twelfth Ave), Suite 305
Mon-Fri: 9:30-5; Sat: 9:30-3 (closed Sat in July and Aug)
                                               212/206-9611
                                               www.heydenryk.com

These folks have been doing frame reproductions of the highest quality since 1845 in Amsterdam (and since 1936 in Manhattan). They stock over 3,000 antique and reproduction frames, many of them Georgian-era English and American folk art. Indeed, the Heydenryk collection is one of the largest showings of period frames in the country!

Furniture, Mattresses

General

CHARLES P. ROGERS
55 W 17th St (bet Fifth Ave and Ave of the Americas)   800/561-0467
Mon-Fri: 9-8; Sat: 10-7; Sun: noon-6   www.charlesprogers.com

Rogers has been allowing folks to sleep comfortably since 1885! Their brass beds are made from heavy-gauge brass tubing with solid brass castings.

Iron beds are hand-forged, making them exceptionally heavy and sturdy. Wooden and leather beds are available, too. Rogers stocks bed linens made from the finest materials, including European linen and Egyptian cotton. All are machine washable.

COVE LANDING
995 Lexington Ave (bet 71st and 72nd St)   212/288-7597
Mon-Fri: 11-6

A collector's paradise! This miniature jewel shows carefully selected 18th- and 19th-century English and continental furniture, plus tasteful Chinese art objects from the same period.

FLOU
42 Greene St (bet Broome and Grand St)   212/941-9101
Mon-Fri: 10-7; Sun: noon-5   www.flou.it

In its U.S. flagship store, the Italian retailer Flou shows everything for the bedroom, from designer beds, mattresses, and furniture to sleepwear. This outfit is well known in Europe and Japan, where they tout the brand as promoting "the art of sleeping."

FOREMOST FURNITURE SHOWROOMS
8 W 30th St (at Fifth Ave), 5th floor   212/889-6347
Mon-Fri: 10-6 (Thurs till 7); Sat: 10-5; Sun: 11-5
                                                  www.foremostfurniture.com

Foremost provides professional design service at no cost to their customers. There are five full floors of furniture with about 250 lines represented. The personnel are friendly and helpful, making this an excellent source. The values are indeed very good, so shop around and then make Foremost one of your last stops.

GRANGE
New York Design Center Building
200 Lexington Ave (at 32nd St), 2nd floor   212/685-9057
Mon-Fri: 9-6   www.grange.fr

French furniture and accessories fill this stylish showroom. The pieces range from classic period designs to exotic and contemporary ones. All of them emphasize form, function, and comfort.

KENTSHIRE GALLERIES
37 E 12th St (bet University Pl and Broadway)   212/673-6644
Mon-Fri: 9-5   www.kentshire.com

Kentshire presents eight floors of English furniture and accessories, circa 1690–1870, with a particular emphasis on the Georgian and Regency periods. This gallery has an excellent international reputation, and the displays are a delight to see, even if prices are a bit high. There is also a collection of 18th- and 19th-century English jewelry. A Kentshire boutique at Bergdorf Goodman features antique jewelry.

LOST CITY ARTS
18 Cooper Square (Bowery at 5th St)   212/375-0500
Mon-Fri: 10-6; Sat, Sun: noon-6   www.lostcityarts.com

Lost City Arts shows mid 20th-century (1950s and 1960s) furniture and lighting fixtures, plus many other vintage items.

NORTH CAROLINA FURNITURE SHOWROOM
9 E 19th St (bet Fifth Ave and Broadway), 4th floor
Mon-Sat: 10-6 (Thurs till 7); Sun: noon-5
212/645-2524, 800/627-3503
www.ncarolinafurniture.com

You'll find over 400 famous-name brands at this showroom, and most everything is discounted. There are items for living rooms and bedrooms, dining-room tables and chairs, sofa beds, recliners, platform beds and bedding, and furniture for children's rooms. North Carolina Furniture Showroom also has a mattress gallery. For New Yorkers, who must make every square inch of apartment space count, this place is a must-visit.

Time Warner Center (10 Columbus Circle, 212/823-6300) is a brave experiment in a city that has not taken kindly to vertical malls. In a dramatic setting, on the corner of Central Park West and Central Park South, the complex offers much for well-heeled shoppers, diners, and lodgers. The shops represent some of the finest names in American retailing: **Coach**, **Cole Haan**, **Hugo Boss**, **Thomas Pink** (*really* British), **Williams-Sonoma**, and more.

The **Whole Foods Market** in the downstairs area can only be described as stupendous. It has comfortably wide aisles lined with magnificent selections of food, and there are numerous checkout stations. **Borders Books** has vast, efficiently displayed selections. The lower concourse houses **Equinox Fitness Club**.

On the upper floors, a number of fine (and expensive) restaurants offer a variety of dining experiences (see Restaurants). And the magnificent **Mandarin Oriental New York** (see Services) is a deluxe place to rest your head. All of this luxury comes at a price, and only time will tell whether New Yorkers will support the various venues. One thing is for sure: no expense has been spared in bringing a mall to Manhattan that compares with the very best in America.

OFFICE FURNITURE HEAVEN
22 W 19th St (bet Fifth Ave and Ave of the Amercas), 7th floor
Mon-Fri: 9-6
212/989-8600
www.officefurnitureheaven.com

This place has bargains in first-quality contemporary pieces for the office. Some are manufacturers' close-outs, while others are discontinued or used items that have been refurbished to look almost new. You'll find a large showroom display of refurbished Knoll Morrison work stations and new HON Initiate work stations. There are conference tables, chairs, bookcases, file cabinets, accessories, and much more.

SLEEPY'S
176 Ave of the Americas (at Spring St)   212/966-7002
874 Broadway (at 18th St)   212/995-0044
Hours vary by store   www.sleepys.com

Sleepy's sells bedding below department store prices. The byword is *discount.* Sleepy's features mattresses from Stearns & Foster, Sealy, Simmons, Serta, Kingsdown, and more. They claim to beat competitors prices by 20%. There are many locations in Manhattan, including those listed above.

234 NEW YORK
439 E 9th St (bet Ave A and First Ave)   212/228-8242
Mon-Sat: noon-8; Sun: noon-7   www.234newyork.com

Custom-made teak furniture—beds, dining-room tables, chests, chairs—is the specialty here. All pieces are designed by the owners. You'll also find lamps, tableware, and other accessories, as well as linens imported from Indonesia.

Infants and Children

ALBEE BABY
715 Amsterdam Ave (at 95th St)   212/662-5740
Mon-Sat: 9-5:30 (Thurs till 7)   www.albeebaby.com

Albee has one of the city's best selections of basics for infants and toddlers—everything from strollers and car seats to cribs and rocking chairs—and the staff can be very helpful. Organizationally, however, it's a disaster area, and it is sometimes hard to get anyone's attention in the chaos, particularly on weekends. That said, Albee Baby is very popular with Manhattan parents (and grandparents), and it's worth a visit if you're expecting.

GRANNY'S RENTALS
231 E 88th St (bet Second and Third Ave), Suite 4W   212/876-4310
By appointment   www.grannysrental.com

This is a great spot to know about! Granny's rents all sorts of things for babies and children, including strollers, cribs, breast pumps, car seats, games for kids, and popcorn, snow-cone, and cotton-candy machines. They also rent tables and chairs for children's parties. The minimum rental is for one week, and they'll deliver directly to you from their warehouse in The Bronx.

SCHNEIDER'S JUVENILE FURNITURE
41 W 25th St (bet Broadway and Ave of the Americas)
Mon-Sat: 10-6 (Tues till 8)   212/228-3540
www.schneidersbaby.com

This Chelsea store is a find for those interested in children's furniture at comfortable prices. You'll also find cribs, car seats, strollers, diaper bags, backpacks, and most everything else for infants through teens.

WICKER GARDEN'S CHILDREN
1300 Madison Avenue (bet 92nd and 93rd St), 2nd floor
Call for hours   212/410-7001
www.wickergarden.com

Pamela Scurry has a great sense of style. If you like wicker furniture, hand-painted detail, and unusual, often whimsical designs, you'll love the baby and juvenile furniture on the second floor of this East Side institution. Moms-to-be, take note: Wicker Garden's selection of comfortable, nice-looking gliders is the best in the city.

Games—Adult

COMPLEAT STRATEGIST

11 E 33rd St (at Fifth Ave)	212/685-3880, 800/225-4344
Mon-Sat: 10:30-6 (Thurs till 9)	www.thecompleatstrategist.com

The Compleat Strategist was established over a quarter of a century ago as an armory of sorts for military games and equipment. As the only such place in the city, it was soon overrun with military strategists. As time went on, the store branched into science fiction, fantasy, and murder-mystery games, as well as adventure games and books. Today, people who are re-enacting the Civil War browse the shelves alongside Dragon Masters. The stock is more than ample, and the personnel are knowledgeable and friendly. For more cerebral sorts, they have chess and backgammon sets—even good old Monopoly! Free shipping is offered on mail orders. There are special events for gamers every Saturday; call or go online for details.

VILLAGE CHESS SHOP

230 Thompson St (bet Bleecker and 3rd St)	212/475-9580
Daily: noon-midnight	www.chess-shop.com

People who enjoy playing chess do so at the Village Chess Shop for a small fee. Those searching for unique chess pieces patronize this shop as well. Chess sets are available in pewter, brass, ebony, onyx, and more. Village Chess has outstanding backgammon sets, too. In short, this should be your first stop if you're planning on moving chess pieces—either from one square to another or from the store to your home!

Gifts, Accessories

ADRIEN LINFORD

927 Madison Ave (bet 73rd and 74th St)	212/628-4500
1339 Madison Ave (at 93rd St)	212/426-1500
Daily: 11-7	

At Adrien Linford you will find an eclectic mixture of gifts, decorative home accessories, occasional furniture, lighting, jewelry, and whatever else Gary Yee finds interesting and exciting. The atmosphere and price tags are definitely upscale; you'll be impressed with the tasteful stock.

BIZARRE BAZAAR

130¼ E 65th St (bet Lexington and Park Ave)	212/517-2100
Mon-Sat: noon-6 (call for appointment)	www.bzrbzr.com

Some people collect baseball cards, while others find political buttons fascinating. I collect "Do Not Disturb" signs from hotels where I have stayed. For the discerning and serious collector, Bizarre Bazaar offers antique toys, aviation and automotive memorabilia, vintage Louis Vuitton luggage, enamel glassware, French perfume bottles, Lalique pieces, artists' mannequins, architectural miniatures, and much more of good quality.

CAROLE STUPELL

29 E 22nd St (bet Park Ave and Broadway)	212/260-3100
Mon-Fri: noon-6; Sat: 11-6	www.carolestupell.com

In my opinion, Carole Stupell is the finest home-accessories store in the country. The taste and thought that has gone into the selection of merchandise is simply unmatched. Keith Stupell, a second-generation chip-off-the-old-block, has assembled a fabulous array of china, glassware, silver, tabletop, and imported gift treasures. All are displayed in spectacular settings. In addition, they carry a large selection of china and glassware replacement patterns dating back over 30 years. Prices are not in the bargain range, but the quality is unequaled.

DE VERA
1 Crosby St (at Howard St)   212/625-0838
Tues-Sat: 11-7   www.deveraobjects.com

Federico de Vera travels the world, purchasing whatever catches his eye. The result is a unique operation, with decorative arts, antiques, Asian lacquerware, Venetian glass, and other unusual items. There's an emphasis on jewelry (vintage, one-of-a-kind, and some even designed by Federico!). A craftsman as well as a merchant, he does wonders with the most unusual items. A De Vera outlet is located on the seventh floor of Bergdorf Goodman (745 Fifth Ave).

ESTELLA
493 Ave of the Americas (bet 12th and 13th St)   212/255-3553
Mon-Fri: 11-7; Sat: 11-6; Sun: noon-5   www.estella-nyc.com

The husband and wife team of Chike and Jean operates this great shop. They go out of their way for those interested in special and unusual gifts for youngsters up to age six. Service is given with a smile, and they will even make house calls to deliver a present to a young loved one.

EXTRAORDINARY
247 E 57th St (bet Second and Third Ave)   212/223-9151
Daily: 11-10   www.extraordinaryny.com

Quite a unique jewel! An international gift selection is the draw at Extraordinary. Owner J.R. Sanders has a background in museum exhibition design, and it shows. You'll find boxes, bowls, trays, candle holders, lamps, jewelry, and other items for the home. The round-the-world theme includes merchandise from the Philippines, Japan, Thailand, China, Vietnam, India, Morocco, Ghana, Peru, and other stops.

FELISSIMO DESIGN HOUSE
10 W 56th St (bet Fifth Ave and Ave of the Americas)   212/247-5656
Mon-Sat: 11-6 (Fri till 8); by appointment   www.felissimo.com

Constructed with the senses in mind, Felissimo Design House is a venue for "design experiences in everyday life." They sell not just products but "space, inspiration, experience, and opportunity." The first four floors showcase the latest in everyday product design, while the fifth floor is an ever-changing exhibition space.

GLOBAL TABLE
107 Sullivan St (bet Prince and Spring St)   212/431-5839
Mon-Sat: noon-7; Sun: noon-6   www.globaltable.com

Affordable. Different. Fun. Worldwide in scope. These all describe the stock at this crowded tabletop and accessory store, where you will find pottery, ceramic, wood, and plastic gifts. You might find a thoughtful surprise for mom or the perfect gift to take to your next dinner party.

KIRNA ZABÊTE
96 Greene St (bet Prince and Spring St)   212/941-9656
Mon-Sat: 11-7; Sun: noon-6   www.kirnazabete.com

If you're looking for something different, Kirna Zabête surely qualifies. With a mixture of high-end designer items, candy (at $3 a bag), dog accessories, and much more, *color* and *imagination* are the bywords!

MAYA SCHAPER CHEESE & ANTIQUES
106 W 69th St (at Columbus Ave)   212/873-2100
Mon-Sat: 10-8; Sun: noon-7

Maya Schaper is one of those special personalities who knows what she likes and wants to share her interest in cheese and food-related antiques. Granted, this is an unusual combination. But Maya is an unique person. You'll find interesting gifts, gift baskets, dried flower arrangements from France, country antiques, and painted furniture. Schaper will locate special items for customers. Scenes from the movie *You've Got Mail*, starring Tom Hanks and Meg Ryan, were filmed in this shop!

MICHAEL C. FINA
545 Fifth Ave (at 45th St)   212/557-2500, 800/BUY-FINA
Mon-Thurs: 11-8; Fri: 10-7, Sat: 10-6; Sun: 11-6
                                            www.michaelcfina.com

A New York tradition for over 60 years, Michael C. Fina is a popular bridal-gift registry firm with an extensive selection (over 200 brand names) of sterling silver, china, crystal, jewelry, watches, and housewares. Prices are attractive, quality is top-notch, and the store is well organized.

ONLY HEARTS
386 Columbus Ave (bet 78th and 79th St)   212/724-5608
230 Mott St (bet Prince and Spring St)   212/431-3694
Mon-Sat: 11-7; Sun: noon-6   www.onlyhearts.com

At this "heart"-themed boutique, Helena Stuart offers romantics an extraordinary collection of European designer accessories, posh scents, soaps, and candles. She also shows a beguiling array of intimate apparel, lingerie, and women's wear.

WEDDING THINGS NEW YORK
1039 Third Ave (at 61st St)   212/308-4680
Mon-Fri: 11-7; Sat: 10-6; Sun: noon-6   www.weddingthings.com

Brides-to-be and their families will find this a very handy store. They do unique wedding invitations and carry a nice selection of unusual favors, bridal party gifts, and baby gifts.

WORKS GALLERY
1250 Madison Ave (bet 89th and 90th St)   212/996-0300
Mon-Sat: 10-6:30; Sun: noon-5 (closed Sun in summer)
www.worksgallery.com

Do you need a unique gift for a special person or occasion? At Works Gallery you will find one-of-a-kind jewelry and art-glass items handmade by talented artists. You can even have a personal piece made from your own stones. They have been in business for two decades.

THE YELLOW DOOR
4 Prince Street (bet Bowery and Elizabeth St)   212/274-0020
Tues-Sun: noon-6:30   www.theyellowdoor.com

Brooklyn has finally arrived in Manhattan via The Yellow Door! After 40 years at the Brooklyn location, Luna Zemmol and her husband, Jonathan, are on the job and in Manhattan with the same great merchandise and prices. Jewelry is their specialty, with many of the baubles made from 18-karat gold imported from Italy. You'll find such great names as Seiden Gang Designs, along with several other jewelry designers. Lalique, MacKenzie-Childs, Waterford, Baccarat, Lenox, Orrefors, and Towle are among the top names that grace the Yellow Door's superior selection of gifts, china, table accessories, and bath items. They offer a bridal registry and accept phone orders. Check with them for corporate gift needs, too.

Some say the dollar store is a relic of the past. Not so! Try **Jack's World** (110 W 32nd St, 212/268-9962; 43 W 45th St, 212/354-6888; and 16 E 40th St, 212/696-5767).

YOYA
636 Hudson St (at Horatio St)   646/336-6844
Mon-Sat: 11-7; Sun: noon-5   www.yoyashop.com

What an eclectic place is Yoya! Toys, furniture, clothing, and books for newborns to age eight. Men's grooming items. Handmade and one-of-a-kind pieces by local artists. Magnetic chalkboard paint. It all makes Yoya a fun store to shop!

Greeting Cards

UNICEF CARD & GIFT SHOP
3 United Nations Plaza (44th St bet First and Second Ave)
Mon-Sat: 10-6   212/326-7054
www.unicefusa.org

For nearly 60 years the United Nations Children's Emergency Fund (UNICEF) has been improving the lives of the world's children. One way this tremendous organization raises money for its life-saving projects and programs is through the sale of cards and gifts. If you've never seen UNICEF products before, then you're in for a treat at this well-planned and friendly store, which carries greeting cards, stationery, books and games for children, apparel, and a fascinating assortment of Nepalese paper products. It also sells cards chosen for sale in Asia, Africa, Europe, and South America. In fact, it's the only store in the U.S. that sells these exotic cards!

Hearing Aids

EMPIRE STATE HEARING AID BUREAU
25 W 43rd St (bet Fifth Ave and Ave of the Americas)   212/921-1666
Mon-Thurs: 9-5:30; Fri: 9-5   www.empirestatehearingaid.com

The late President Reagan set a shining example by not being ashamed to wear a hearing aid. The latest hearing aids are so small that most people cannot even tell they're being worn. Empire State products are up-to-date and state-of-the-art. They have been in the business for over half a century and carry all of the major manufacturers in the field: Siemens, Starkey, Oticon, and GN ReSound. Skilled personnel will test and fit quality hearing aids in a quiet, unhurried atmosphere.

Hobbies

JAN'S HOBBY SHOP
1435 Lexington Ave (bet 93rd and 94th St)   212/987-4765
Mon-Sat: 10-7; Sun: noon-5

Jan's is one of my favorite examples of New York retailing! When Fred Hutchins was young, he was obsessed with building models and dioramas, particularly on historical themes. Eventually, his parents bought his favorite source of supply. Now he runs the shop, keeping Jan's stocked with everything a serious model builder could possibly want. The store has a superb stock of plastic scale models, model war games, paints, books, brushes and all kinds of model cars, trains, planes, ships, and tanks. It also carries remote-controlled planes, sailboats, ships, and tanks. Fred himself creates models and dioramas to order for television, advertising, and private customers. He is noted for accurate historical detailing and can provide information from his vast library of military subjects. He has yet another sideline: showcase building. Because any hobbyist likes to show his wares, Fred custom-makes wood, Plexiglas, glass, and mahogany showcases.

Home Furnishings

ABC CARPET & HOME
881 and 888 Broadway (at 19th St)   212/473-3000
Mon-Fri: 10-8; Sat: 10-7; Sun: 11-6:30   www.abchome.com

If you can visit only one home furnishings store in Manhattan, ABC should be it! Starting in 1897 as a pushcart business, ABC expanded into one of the city's most unique, exciting, and well-merchandised emporiums. (It's actually two buildings located across the street from each other.) ABC is the Bergdorf Goodman of home furnishings. There are floors of great-looking furniture, dinnerware, linens, gifts, accessories, and antiques. You will see many one-of-a-kind pieces as you explore corner after corner. There is an entire floor of fabrics by the yard and an extensive selection of carpets and rugs at great prices. Don't miss their restaurant, **Pipa** (38 E 19th St, 212/677-2233), serving tapas and more. An ABC outlet store is located in The Bronx (1055 Bronx River Ave, 718/842-8772).

ABH DESIGN
401 E 76th St (bet First and York Ave)   212/249-2276
Mon-Sat: 11-6:30   www.abh-design.com

Owner and designer Aude Bronson-Howard is a very talented lady who uses her skills to offer magnificently sophisticated home furnishings and whimsical hats and clothing items. You'll find textiles, glasses, and vases from Italy; bed and bath merchandise; and fabulous gift items that are popular with the Hollywood set.

It used to be that only those holding designer's cards were admitted to some trade buildings. These days, a number of design outfits will take care of individual customers, even if the signs on their doors say "Trade Only." Listed below are some of the trade buildings worth checking out; each has a multitude of shops where you can find just about anything you need to fix up an apartment or home.

Architects & Designers Building (150 E 58th St, 212/644-2766; Mon-Fri: 9-5)

Decoration & Design Building (979 Third Ave, 212/759-5408; Mon-Fri: 8:30-5:30)—It's a good idea to bring along a decorator.

Fine Arts Building (232 E 59th St, 212/759-6935; Mon-Fri: 9-5)

Manhattan Art & Antiques Center (1050 Second Ave, 212/355-4400; Mon-Sat: 10:30-6; Sun: noon-6)

AUTO
805 Washington St (bet Gansevoort and Horatio St)   212/229-2292
Mon-Fri: 11-8; Sat: noon-7; Sun: noon-6   www.thisisauto.com

The stock at Auto includes specially designed and hard-to-find home furnishings such as pillows, ceramics, glassware, throws, and accessories. Most are handmade and one-of-kind. It's worth a visit!

BELLORA AMERICA
156 Wooster St (bet Houston and Prince St)   212/228-6651
Tues-Sat: 11-7; Sun, Mon: noon-6

Bellora America presents a superb showing of quality Italian goods: linens for the home, tabletop items like dishes and flatware, body and bath products, robes, and window treatments. They will come to your home or office, and expanded hours for designers are offered. On-site alterations are available.

CALYPSO HOME
815 Madison Ave (bet 68th and 69th St)   212/585-0310
199 Lafayette St (at Broome St)   212/925-6200
CALYPSO KIDS HOME
407 Broome St (at Lafayette St)   212/941-9700
Hours vary by store   www.calypso-celle.com

Bedrooms will look exotic with merchandise from this outlet. Calypso Home specializes in beautiful pillows, throws, textiles, furniture, and other home items, including some designer originals.

HOME DEPOT
980 Third Ave (bet 58th and 59th St)   212/888-1512
40 W 23rd St (bet Fifth Ave and Ave of the Americas)
Mon-Sat: 7 a.m.-9 p.m.; Sun: 8-7   212/929-9571
                                                            www.homedepot.com

Home Depot has two huge stores in Manhattan, featuring every modern convenience. Flat-panel touch screens will display inventories and print out product lists and how-to instructions. Expert salespeople can customize products for small spaces in Manhattan apartments. You'll find kitchen and bath items, appliances, window treatments and moldings, lighting fixtures, phones and accessories, paint, cleaning supplies, lumber and building materials, tools, plants and patio furniture (in season), and more. Same-day and next-day delivery are offered.

One of the very best design stores in Manhattan is **Moss** (150 Greene St, 866/888-6677). This emporium is internationally known for the quality and presentation of its merchandise. You'll find furniture, lighting, watches, jewelry, books, and a large showing of tabletop items. For a complete selection, visit www.mossonline.com.

KARKULA
68 Gansevoort St (bet Greenwich and Washington St) 212/645-2216
Mon-Sat: 11-7   www.karkula.com

Sexy urban contemporary furniture and home furnishings by such names as Paola Lenti, Fritz Hansen, Atlantico, and Carl Hansen are shown at Karkula. Many up-and-coming designers get their start here. Designs feature such natural materials as bronze, wood, leather, and felt. You'll also find contemporary sculpture and jewelry from Espen Eiborg and Monica Castiglioni.

PARIS APARTMENT
70 E 1st St (at First Ave)   917/749-5081
Mon-Fri: 1-6; Sat, Sun: 2-6 (or by appointment)
                                                    www.theparisapartment.com

If a visit to Paris with a stay in an exotic boudoir is on your wish list, then you should know there is an alternative right in Manhattan. The folks at Paris Apartment will transform your digs into a glorious space with sumptuous bedroom furniture and bath accessories. As you put your head on your sexy new luxury pillows, you can dream about a trip to the French capital, as guided tours (yes, really!) are offered by this outfit.

SURPRISE! SURPRISE!
91 Third Ave (bet 12th and 13th St)   212/777-0990
Mon-Sat: 10-7; Sun: 11-6   www.surprisesurprise.com

Surprise! Surprise! offers a complete line of reasonably priced items for the home. With all their stock and know-how, you can have your new apartment looking like a home in no time. You'll find a large selection of kitchenware, furnishings, patio furniture, and lamps.

TINY LIVING
125 E 7th St (bet First Ave and Ave A)   212/228-2748
Daily: 11-9   www.tiny-living.com

If you and your partner are having a tough time fitting into small spaces —not an unusual problem in New York—then a visit to this store will be very helpful. Those who are embarking on a life and career in New York will find some superb space-saving ideas at Tiny Living. Even visitors will find such items as a pocket-size map of the city to be useful and handy.

WEST ELM
112 W 18th St (bet Ave of the Americas and Seventh Ave)
Mon-Sat: 10-9; Sun: 11-7   212/929-4464
                                                     www.westelm.com

West Elm is like a Crate & Barrel store with slightly lower prices. You'll find furniture, shelving, mirrors, lamps, quilts, shams, sheets, blankets, shower curtains, bath accessories, towels, clocks, room accents, dinnerware, glassware, flatware, and much more. The store is very attractive, and merchandise is well displayed.

Top Button is a web-based company (www.topbutton.com) that informs consumers about sample, warehouse, outlet, clearance, and promotional sales. Categories include apparel, housewares, and accessories. Information can be accessed by company name, product type, and date. The service is free.

Housewares, Hardware

BRIDGE KITCHENWARE
711 Third Ave (at 45th St)   212/688-4220
Mon-Fri: 9-6; Sat: 10-4:30   www.bridgekitchenware.com

Bridge Kitchenware is a unique-to-New York store that supplies almost every restaurant within 500 miles. Named for founder Fred Bridge, the store carries bar equipment, cutlery, pastry equipment, molds, copperware, ironware, woodenware, stoneware, and kitchen gadgets. All goods are professional quality and excellent for home gourmets. Be sure to see the lines of imported French copperware, professional knives, and baking pans. After cooking with Bridge, people use no other product. Call for a catalog or look online.

BROADWAY PANHANDLER
65 E 8th St (bet Broadway and University Pl)
Mon-Sat: 11-7; Sun: 11-6   212/966-3434, 866/266-5927
                                     www.broadwaypanhandler.com

Now in a new location, Broadway Panhandler keeps up a tradition of great assortments and low prices! These folks are a pleasure to deal with. Thousands of cutlery, bakeware, tabletop items, and cookware pieces are available at sizable savings. Guest chefs make periodic appearances, and a fine selection of professional items is offered to walk-in customers and restaurant and hotel buyers.

DICK'S CUT-RATE HARDWARE
9 Gold St (at Maiden Lane)   212/425-1070
Mon-Fri: 7:30-6:30; Sat, Sun: 9-4

Really complete hardware stores like Dick's are a great conveniences for shoppers. In a Lower Manhattan location where there are few such stores, Dick's provides good prices and informed service. You will find great selections of electrical and plumbing supplies, tools, and more. They also make duplicate keys.

DOMUS NEW YORK
413 W 44th St (at Ninth Ave)   212/581-8099
Tues-Sat: noon-8; Sun: noon-6   www.domusnewyork.com

What fun it is shopping at this eclectic Hell's Kitchen housewares store! Luisa Cerutti and Nicki Lindheimer have excellent taste. They have picked out one-of-a-kind European imports, including pottery, tabletop, vintage glassware, linens, china, furniture, and unusual pieces that will catch everyone's attention. Domus (which is Latin for *home*) is a super place to shop for wedding gifts. Free gift-wrapping and delivery in Manhattan are available.

> **Sur la Table** is a famous French purveyor of high-quality kitchenware and tableware. In 2005, they opened a 5,000-square-foot store in Soho (75 Spring Street, 212/966-3375). Passionate foodies will love this place.

GARBER HARDWARE
710 Greenwich St (bet 10th and Charles St)   212/929-3030
Mon, Thurs: 8-6; Tues, Wed: 8-7; Fri, Sat: 8-5; Sun: 10-4
                                         www.garberhardware.com

This unique family business has become a New York institution. The Garbers have been operating since 1884 at the same location with this appealing motto: "Either we have it or we can get it for you." You will find a complete inventory of paints, hardware, home and garden, plumbing and electrical supplies, housewares, locks, tools, and building materials. Custom window shades, lamp repair, key-cutting, and pipe-cutting are among the many handy services offered.

GEORGE TAYLOR SPECIALTIES
76 Franklin St (bet Church St and Broadway)   212/226-5369
Mon-Thurs: 7:30-5; Fri: 7:30-4

Taylor stocks replacement plumbing parts to fit all faucets, and custom faucets can be fabricated via special order. They also offer reproduction faucets and custom designs of fittings for unique installations. Antique-style towel bars, bath accessories, and pedestal sinks are among Taylor's specialties. Founded in 1869, Taylor remains a family-run operation. Ask for father Chris, daughter Valerie, or son John.

GRACIOUS HOME

1217 and 1220 Third Ave (bet 70th and 71st St)	212/517-6300
Mon-Fri: 8-7; Sat: 9-7; Sun: 10-6	
1992 Broadway (at 67th St)	212/231-7800
Mon-Sat: 9-9; Sun: 10-7	www.gracioushome.com

For over four decades Gracious Home has been popular with savvy New Yorkers. These stores are must-visits for anyone interested in fixing up their home, establishing a new one, looking for gifts, or just browsing stores that typify the New York lifestyle. The style, expertise, and service are outstanding. You'll find appliances, wall coverings, gifts, hardware, decorative bath accessories, lighting, china, casual furniture, bedding, shelving, pots and pans, and heaven knows what else! They install window coverings, large appliances, and countertops; offer tool rental and repair services; provide a special-order department; and will deliver in Manhattan for free.

Remodelers and builders, take note! For lumber, plywood, Masonite, bricks, cork, paint, and more, **Metropolitan Lumber and Hardware** (175 Spring St, 212/966-3466 and 617 Eleventh Ave, 212/246-9090) is a good name to remember.

LEESAM KITCHEN AND BATH CENTER

501 Seventh Ave (at 37th St), Suite 408	212/243-6482
Tues-Thurs: 10-6 (by appointment)	

Since 1934 these folks have been fixing up kitchens and bathrooms. Whether you're shopping for medicine cabinets, kitchen cabinets, faucets, shower enclosures, or counters, you will see large selections of top brands from domestic suppliers. There is no excuse not to remodel your cluttered, dysfunctional old kitchen using one of their computer-designed plans.

P.E. GUERIN

23 Jane St (bet Greenwich and Eighth Ave)	212/243-5270
Mon-Fri: 9-5:30 (by appointment)	www.peguerin.com

Andrew Ward, P.E. Guerin's president, is the fourth generation to run the oldest decorative hardware firm in the country and the only foundry in the city. It was founded in 1857 and has been on Jane Street since 1892. In that time, the firm has grown into an impressive worldwide operation. The main foundry is now in Valencia, Spain (although work continues at the Village location), and there are branches and showrooms across the country and in Puerto Rico. The Jane Street location is still headquarters for manufacturing and importing decorative hardware and bath accessories. Much of it is done in brass or bronze, and the foundry can make virtually anything from those materials, including copies and reproductions. The Gueridon table has garnered design and production awards and enjoys an international reputation. No job is too small for Guerin, which operates like the hometown firm it thinks it is. They offer free estimates and can help with any hardware problems.

RESTORATION HARDWARE
935 Broadway (at 22nd St)   212/260-9479
Mon-Sat: 10-8; Sun: 11-7   www.restorationhardware.com

If you prefer a classic, quality look, then come to Restoration Hardware. You'll find a large selection of furniture, bed and bath items, drapery, lighting, bathware, and hardware. A good selection of cleaning and maintenance supplies, too! This operation is among the best in its field.

S. FELDMAN HOUSEWARES
1304 Madison Ave (at 92nd St)   212/289-7367
Mon-Sat: 9-6; Sun: 11-5   www.wares2u.com

Keep this name and address on your refrigerator door! Founded in 1929, Feldman was originally a five-and-dime store. Over the years it has changed dramatically, but it still is family-owned and -operated. You'll find housewares, cookware, home decor, gifts, tabletop items, appliances, toys, and more. Customer service is a big plus; they even provide free espresso for shoppers. With over 12,000 in-store items to choose from, this can be a true one-stop shopping spot for you and your family. They also repair vacuum cleaners.

SIMON'S HARDWARE & BATH
421 Third Ave (bet 29th and 30th St)   212/532-9220
Mon-Fri: 8-5:30 (Thurs till 7); Sat: 10-6   www.simons-hardware.com

Simon's is really a hardware supermarket, offering one of the city's finest selections of quality decorative hardware items and bath and kitchen fixtures and accessories. The personnel are patient, even if you just need something to fix a broken handle on a chest of drawers.

WILLIAMS-SONOMA
1175 Madison Ave (at 86th St)   212/289-6832
110 Seventh Ave (at 17th St)   212/633-2203
121 E 59 St (bet Park and Lexington Ave)   917/369-1131
10 Columbus Circle (Time Warner Building)   212/823-9750
Hours vary by store   www.williams-sonoma.com

From humble beginnings in the wine country of Sonoma County, California, Williams-Sonoma expanded across the nation and is referred to as the "Tiffany of cookware stores." The serious cook will find a vast display of quality cookware, bakeware, cutlery, kitchen linens, specialty foods, cookbooks, small appliances, kitchen furniture, glassware, and tableware. The stores also offer a gift and bridal registry, cooking demonstrations, free recipes, gift baskets, and shopping assistance for corporations or individuals. Especially at holiday time, their candy assortment is first-class. Ask for their attractive catalog, which includes a number of excellent recipes.

Imports
Afghan

NUSRATY AFGHAN IMPORTS
215 W 10th St (at Bleecker St)   212/691-1012
Sun-Thurs: 1-9; Fri, Sat: 1-11

Abdul Nusraty has transformed a corner of the Village into a vision of Afghanistan that is fascinating. Nusraty is one of the best sources of Afghan goods on the continent. There are magnificently embroidered native dresses and shirts displayed alongside semiprecious stones mounted in jewelry or shown individually. One area of the store features carpets and rugs, while another displays antique silver and jewelry. Nusraty has an unerring eye; all of his stock is of the highest quality and is often unique as well. The business operates on both a wholesale and retail level.

The Best of Britain!

British sweets: **Carry On Tea & Sympathy** (108-110 Greenwich Ave, 212/807-8329)

Clothes and housewares: **Eskandar** (Bergdorf Goodman, 754 Fifth Ave, 3rd floor, 212/872-8659)

Fashion designer: **Alexander McQueen** (417 W 14th St, 212/645-1797)

Leather goods and stationery: **Smythson of Bond Street** (4 W 57th St, 212/265-4573)

Purses and shoes: **Lulu Guinness** (394 Bleecker St, 212/367-2120)

Chinese

CHINESE PORCELAIN COMPANY
475 Park Ave (at 58th St)   212/838-7744
Mon-Fri: 10-6; Sat: 11-5 (closed Sat in summer)
                                                    www.chineseporcelainco.com

Come here for Chinese ceramics and works of art. There are Chinese, Tibetan, Indian, Khymer, and Southeast Asian sculptures, as well as French and continental furniture.

PEARL RIVER MART
477 Broadway (bet Broome and Grand St)   212/431-4770
Daily: 10-7:30   www.pearlriver.com

This is a true Chinese department store, with many items that were made in China. Pearl River is busy and well-stocked, and most everyone can understand what you want. A home department has recently been added.

WING-ON TRADING
145 Essex St (bet Delancey and Houston St)   212/477-1450
Mon-Sat: 10-6

There's no need to go to Hong Kong to get your Chinese porcelain or earthenware. Wing-On has a complete and well-organized stock of household goods. One of their specialties is Chinese teas at low prices.

Eskimo/Native American

ALASKA ON MADISON
937 Madison Ave (bet 74th and 75th St)   212/879-1782
Tues-Sat: 11:30-6 (or by appointment)   www.alaskaonmadison.com

This gallery is New York's most complete collection of Inuit and Northwest Coast artifacts and sculptures. Periodic shows highlight aspects of these cultures. A number of contemporary artists whose works have been shown here have gained international acclaim.

General

JACQUES CARCANAGUES
21 Greene St (bet Grand and Canal St)　　　　　212/925-8110
Tues-Sun: 11:30-7　　　　　　　　　www.jacquescarcanagues.com

After a stint in the diplomatic service, Frenchman Jacques Carcanagues decided to assemble and sell the finest artifacts he had encountered in his world travels. So while the goods are mostly Southeast Asian, this emporium is, in Jacques own words, "a complete ethnic department store, not a museum." Textiles and *tansus* (dressers) are everywhere, as are jewelry and lacquerware. It is also very appealing to Soho shoppers, who can choose among Indian, Burmese, and Thai sculptures of many periods and unusual household objects not seen elsewhere in New York. The overall effect is that of an Eastern bazaar, yet all pieces are of museum quality.

KATINKA
303 E 9th St (at Second Ave)　　　　　　　　212/677-7897
Tues-Sat: 4-7 (call ahead, as hours can vary)

Katinka is an import paradise, with jewelry, natural-fiber clothing, shoes, scarves, belts, hats, musical instruments, incense, and artifacts from India, Thailand, Pakistan, Afghanistan, and South America. The most popular items are colorful shoes and embroidered silk skirts from India. The place is small, and prices are reasonable. Jane Williams and Billy Lyles make customers feel like they have embarked on a worldwide shopping expedition!

Japanese designer Nigo has created **A Bathing Ape** (91 Greene St, 212/925-0222) for lovers of things Japanese. Offerings include unusual clothing and shoes. Fans of rock-star couture will be blown away by the merchandise.

PIER 1 IMPORTS
71 Fifth Ave (at 15th St)　　　　　　　　　212/206-1911
1550 Third Ave (at 87th St)　　　　　　　　212/987-1746
Mon-Sat: 10-9; Sun: 11-7　　　　　　　　　www.pier1.com

At Pier 1, you will find imported dining-room sets, occasional furniture, bathroom accessories, picture frames, brassware, china and glassware, floor coverings, bedding, and pillows. The goods come from exotic lands throughout Asia and the rest of the world. The selections are inviting, the prices are right, and the stores are fun to visit.

SHEHERAZADE IMPORTS
121 Orchard St (bet Delancey and Rivington St)　　　212/539-1771
Daily: 11-7　　　　　　　　　　　www.sheherazadenyc.com

Sheherazade features handcrafted merchandise imported from a number of countries. You'll find home furnishings from North Africa, the Middle East, and Asia, including antique and contemporary furniture, carpets, tapestries, chandeliers, lanterns, jewelry, and gifts. Islamic art and Oriental decorative furnishings are also featured. Custom-made furniture can be ordered.

Indian

INDIA COTTAGE EMPORIUM
221 W 37th St (bet Seventh and Eighth Ave), basement 212/685-6943
Mon-Fri: 10-6; Sat: 9-5

India Cottage features clothing, jewelry, handicrafts, and gifts imported directly from India. Moti R. Chani has a sharp eye for the finest details; the Indian clothing he sells reflects his taste and expertise. The clothing is prized by Indian nationals and neighborhood residents for its sheer beauty. The garments are made of cotton and feature unique madras patterns.

Japanese

SARA
950 Lexington Ave (bet 69th and 70th St)   212/772-3243
Mon-Fri: 11-7; Sat: noon-6   www.saranyc.com

Looking for something with a Japanese flair? Sara is the place to go for modern Japanese ceramics, glassware, tableware, cast iron, and gifts.

THINGS JAPANESE
800 Lexington Ave (bet 61st and 62nd St), 2nd floor   212/371-4661
Mon-Sat: 11-5   www.thingsjapanese.com

Things Japanese believes that the Japanese "things" most in demand are prints. So while there are all sorts of Japanese artworks and crafts, prints highlight the selection. They know the field well and will help collectors establish a grouping or assist decorators in finding pieces to round out decor. There are also original 18th- to 20th-century Japanese woodblock prints, porcelains, baskets, chests, lacquers, and books. Prices range from $10 to several thousand dollars, and every piece is accompanied by a certificate of authenticity. Things Japanese will help you appreciate both the subject matter and the artistry in the works it sells.

Middle Eastern

PERSIAN SHOP
534 Madison Ave (bet 54th and 55th St)   212/355-4643
Mon-Fri: 10-6; Sat: 10-5

Since 1940, the Persian Shop has featured unusual Middle Eastern items: end tables, chairs, frames, mirrors, and brocades sold by the yard or made into magnificent neckties for men. The jewelry selection is especially noteworthy. You'll find precious and semiprecious items, silver and gold cuff links, rings, earrings, bracelets, necklaces, and heirloom pieces. There are also Chinese vases, Russian and Greek icons, and planters. All will add a special air of interest to any setting.

Ukrainian

SURMA (THE UKRAINIAN SHOP)
11 E 7th St (at Third Ave)   212/477-0729
Mon-Fri: 11-6; Sat: 11-4   www.surmastore.com

Since 1918, Surma has functioned as the "general store of the Slavic community in New York City." Quite honestly, it seems capable of serving the entire hemisphere. This bastion of Ukrainianism makes it difficult to believe you're still in New York. The clothing is pure ethnic opulence. There are dresses, vests, shirts, blouses, hand-tooled and soft-soled leather dancing shoes, and accessories. All are hand-embroidered with authentic detailing. For the home, there are accent pieces (including an entire section devoted to Ukrainian Easter-egg decorating), brocaded linens, and Surma's own Ukrainian-style honey (different and very good). Above all, Surma is known for its educational tapes and books. Pay particular attention to the artwork and stationery, which depict ancient Ukrainian glass paintings.

Jewelry

HERMAN ROTENBERG & BILL SCHIFRIN
National Jewelers Exchange
4 W 47th St (bet Fifth Ave and Ave of the Americas), Booth 86
Mon-Fri: 10-5:30   212/944-1713, 800/877-3874
www.unusualweddingrings.com

From a booth in the National Jewelers Exchange—better known for its collection of gold, platinum, and diamond wedding and engagement rings —Bill Schifrin and son-in-law Herman Rotenberg preside over a collection of over 2,000 unusual wedding rings. Prices range from under $100 to several thousand dollars, depending upon the work's complexity and the types of metal and stones used. Bill has been doing this for over 50 years and knows the story behind each ring.

CHROME HEARTS
159 E 64th St (bet Lexington and Third Ave)   212/327-0707
Mon-Sat: 11-7   www.chromehearts.com

If you're looking for unique accessories, Chrome Hearts is the place to go! They show a broad selection of handmade jewelry in sterling silver, 22-karat gold and platinum, and precious stones; clothing in leather and fabric; gadgets for people who think they have everything; handcrafted furniture in exotic woods; great-looking eyewear; and much more.

DIAMONDS BY RENNIE ELLEN
15 W 47th St (bet Fifth Ave and Ave of the Americas), Room 503
Mon-Fri: 10-4:30 (by appointment)   212/869-5525
www.rennieellen.com

Rennie Ellen is a wholesaler offering the sort of discounts for which the city's wholesale businesses are famous. She was the first female diamond dealer in the male-dominated Diamond District. Rennie personally spent so much time and effort keeping the district straight and honest that she earned the title "Mayor of 47th Street." In other words, Ellen's reputation is impeccable. Her diamond-cutting factory deals exclusively in diamond jewelry. There are pendants, wedding bands, engagement rings, and diamonds to fit all sizes, shapes, and budgets. All sales are made under Ellen's personal supervision and are strictly confidential. Call for her $3 mail-order catalog or look online.

DOYLE & DOYLE
189 Orchard St (bet Houston and Stanton St)   212/677-9991
Tues-Sun: 1-7   www.doyledoyle.com

Antique and estate jewelry is the specialty here, with an emphasis on treasured engagement rings. Two sisters operate this shop, which also offers jewelry rentals for special events. You'll find Georgian, Victorian, Edwardian, art deco, art nouveau, and retro pieces.

FORTUNOFF
681 Fifth Ave (at 54th St)   212/758-6660
Mon-Sat: 10-6 (Thurs till 7); Sun: noon-5   www.fortunoff.com

This is one of the best stores in Manhattan devoted to quality merchandise. There is a crystal and clock department, but it is in the jewelry area (especially antique silver) that the store really shines. A jeweler is on duty at all times. Fortunoff shows one of the largest and finest collections of 14- and 18-karat gold jewelry in the city, as well as a fine selection of precious and semiprecious stones, brand-name watches, and flatware. Prices on all items are competitive.

FRAGMENTS
116 Prince St   212/334-9588
Mon-Sat: 11-7; Sun: noon-6

997 Madison Ave   212/537-5000
Mon-Sat: 10-6; Sun: noon-5

Fragments shows the latest jewelry collections from some of the country's top designers. You'll find Erica Molinari, Mizuki, Dana Kellin, and a number of others represented in their large collection. Much of the credit for the success of this outfit goes to Janet Goldman, its talented founder and CEO. A special area named **Fragments Fine Jewelry** features high-end items with precious stones and gem quality pearls. You will also find handbags and other accessories.

JENNIFER MILLER JEWELRY
972 Lexington Ave (bet 70th and 71st St)   212/734-8199
Mon-Sat: 10-5:30   www.jewelsbyjen.com

Jennifer Miller is the ultimate jewelry store! Miller specializes in contemporary, classic, and estate jewelry, in both fine and faux. The varied selection changes daily, almost guaranteeing that you will find something you can't leave without. Diamond chain necklaces in 14K yellow or white gold are classically chic, ranging from $200 to $1,800 with man-made stones and up to $61,000 with genuine diamonds. Handbags, shoes, and decorative home items round out the mix.

MAX NASS
118 E 28th St (bet Park Ave S and Lexington Ave)   212/679-8154
Mon-Fri: 9:30-6; Sat: 9:30-4

The Shah family members are jewelry artisans. Araceli is the designer and Parimal ("Perry") is the company president. Together they make and sell handmade jewelry, service and repair clocks and watches, and restore antique jewelry. They deal in virtually every type of jewelry: antique (or merely old), silver and gold, as well as semiprecious stones. Two special sales each year bring Max Nass's already low prices down even further. One is held the last three weeks in January (33% discount), and the other runs for two weeks in July (25% discount). In between, Araceli will design pieces on a whim or commission. His one-of-a-kind necklaces are particularly impressive. The store also restrings, restores, and redesigns necklaces.

MURREY'S JEWELERS
1395 Third Ave (bet 79th and 80th St)   212/879-3690
Mon-Sat: 9:30-6

I heartily recommend this shop! Family jewelers since 1936, Murrey's sells fine jewelry, watches, and giftware. In the service area, they do fine-jewelry repair, expert special-order design and manufacturing, European clock repair, engraving, pearl-stringing, and watch repair. The talented staff includes three goldsmiths, three watchmaker/clockmakers (including one of the world's best), one stringer, and one setter.

MYRON TOBACK
25 W 47th St (bet Fifth Ave and Ave of the Americas)   212/398-8300
Mon-Fri: 8-4   www.myrontoback.com

Myron Toback is ostensibly a refiner of precious metals with a specialty in findings, plate, and wire. Not very useful to the average customer, you might think, but note the address. Toback is not only in the heart of the Diamond District but is also the landlord of an arcade crammed full of wholesale artisans of the jewelry trade. Taking their cue from Toback, they are open and friendly to individual retail customers. So bookmark Toback as a source of gold, gold-filled, and silver chains sold by the foot at wholesale prices. And don't overlook the gold and silver earrings, beads, and other jewelry items sold at prices that are laughably less than those at establishments around the corner on Fifth Avenue. Tools and other materials for stringing beads and pearls are also carried. Though most customers are professional jewelers or wholesale organizations, Toback is simply charming to do-it-yourselfers, schools, and hobbyists. His son and daughter are also part of the business.

PEDRO BOREGAARD
636 Broadway (bet Houston and Bleecker St), Suite 1022
By appointment   212/826-3660
                                                        www.boregaard.com

Unusual rings, earrings, brooches, chains, and bracelets—all handmade and each a true work of art—are hallmarks of this very talented designer, who features items for both men and women. Pieces may combine rubies, sapphires, and diamonds shaded in colors from champagne to cognac, and pink, white, or yellow gold. Boregaard's credentials are impressive: apprenticeship and professional work in Germany, a jewelry workshop in England, and work with Tiffany for designers such as Angela Cummings, Elsa Peretti, and Paloma Picasso.

Ladders

PUTNAM ROLLING LADDER COMPANY
32 Howard St (bet Lafayette St and Broadway)   212/226-5147
Mon-Fri: 8:30-4   www.putnamrollingladder.com

Putnam is an esoteric shop on an esoteric street! Why, you might ask, would anyone in New York need those magnificent rolling ladders traditionally used in formal libraries? Could there possibly be enough business to keep a place like this "rolling" since 1905? The answer is that clever New Yorkers turn to Putnam to improve access to their lofts (especially sleeping lofts). Ladders come in many hardwoods and range from rolling ladders (custom-made, if necessary) to folding library ladders.

Lighting Fixtures and Accessories

CITY KNICKERBOCKER
665 Eleventh Ave (at 48th St), 2nd floor   212/586-3939
Mon-Fri: 8:30-5   www.cityknickerbocker.com

The fourth generation of the Liroff family operates this outfit, which has been in business since 1906. These folks are completely reliable when it comes to all aspects of lighting, including quality antique reproductions, glassware, and first-rate repair. The large sales inventory includes contemporary art-glass lamps. Rentals are available.

JUST BULBS
5 E 16th St (near Union Square W)   212/228-7820
Mon-Sat: 9-6 (Tues, Thurs till 8); Sun: noon-6   www.justbulbsnyc.com

This store stocks almost 25,000 types of bulbs, including some that can be found nowhere else. In addition to all the standard sizes, Just Bulbs has lightbulbs for use in old fixtures. The shop looks like an oversized backstage dressing-room mirror. Everywhere you turn, bulbs are connected to switches that customers can flick on and off. They also "refresh" light fixtures, changing bulbs and cleaning fixtures at your home or office.

JUST SHADES
21 Spring St (at Elizabeth St)   212/966-2757, 888/898-4058
Tues-Fri: 9:30-6; Sat: 9:30-5   www.justshadesny.com

Just Shades has specialized in lampshades for 40 years. They are experts at matching shades to lamps and willingly share their knowledge with retail customers. They have lampshades of silk, hide, parchment, and other materials. Their biggest peeve is customers who don't remove the protective cellophane from their shades. When left on, the cellophane actually collects ruinous dust.

LAMPWORKS
231 E 58th St (bet Second and Third Ave)   212/750-1500
Mon-Fri: 9-6   www.lampworksinc.com

You will find an extensive selection of table lamps, antiques, imports, custom lampshades, and exterior lighting fixtures at Lampworks. Over 45 lines are available, and they specialize in custom lighting.

LIGHTING BY GREGORY
158 Bowery (bet Delancey and Broome St)　　　212/226-1276
Daily: 9-5:30　　　　　　　　　　　　www.lightingbygregory.com

No false modesty here! This full-service discount lighting store claims to be the most technically knowledgeable outfit in the country. It is the largest contemporary and traditional lighting and ceiling-fan distributor in America. They are major dealers of Lightolier, Tech Lighting, and Casablanca ceiling fans, and are also experts in track lighting.

LIGHTING PLUS
680 Broadway (bet Great Jones and Bond St)　　　212/979-2000
Mon-Sat: 10-6:45; Sun: 11-6:45

Lighting Plus is a very handy neighborhood lighting store, featuring floor and table lamps, all kinds of bulbs, and extension cords.

SCHOOLHOUSE ELECTRIC
27 Vestry St (at Hudson St)　　　　　　　　212/226-6113
Mon-Fri: 11-6; Sat: 11-5　　　　　www.schoolhouseelectric.com

You'll find period lighting fixtures and glass shades at this unique store. Styles range from art deco to mid-20th century. Also available are hand-crafted solid brass lighting fixtures, made to order in many different finishes.

TUDOR ELECTRICAL SUPPLY
222-226 E 46th St (bet Second and Third Ave)　　212/867-7550
Mon-Thurs: 8:30-5; Fri: 8:30-4:30

At first glance you may feel like you need an engineering degree to patronize Tudor Electrical. However, the staff is trained to explain everything in stock. Lightbulbs are the store's forte. They are cataloged by wattage, color, and application, and the staff can quickly locate the right bulb for your needs. Some basic knowledge: quartz, tungsten, and halogen bulbs offer undistorted light, while incandescent and fluorescent lamps are best for desk work. Tudor discounts by at least 20%.

Liquidators

NATIONAL WHOLESALE LIQUIDATORS
632 Broadway (bet Houston and Delancey St)　　212/979-2400
Mon-Sat: 9:30-8:30; Sun: 9:30-6

www.nationalwholesaleliquidators.com

Here's a super place for couples who are setting up their first apartment or home in the city. Under one roof you'll find genuine bargains in furniture, electronics, toys, floor coverings, china and glassware, linens, and more.

Luggage and Other Leather Goods

DEAN LEATHER
822 Third Ave (at 50th St)　　　　　　　　212/583-0461
877 Seventh Ave (at 56th St)　　　　　　　212/581-5228
Mon-Fri: 8:30-7:30; Sat, Sun: 9-6

If it is leather, you probably can find it here: briefcases, wallets, luggage, watches, and gift items. The prices are right, and repair of luggage and leather goods is offered, too. Dean's carries many top names like Hartmann, Swiss Army, Samsonite, Briggs & Riley, Bosca, Mont Blanc, and more.

LEXINGTON LUGGAGE
793 Lexington Ave (bet 61st and 62nd St)   800/822-0404
Daily: 9-6   www.lexingtonluggage.com

If you are in the market for luggage, don't miss this place! They carry nearly every major brand at nearly wholesale prices. Luggage and handbag repairs can be done the same day. Other pluses: free same-day delivery, free monograms, and friendly personnel. You'll also find leather goods, attaché cases, pens, poker sets, trunks, and a nice gift selection.

T. ANTHONY
445 Park Ave (at 56th St)   212/750-9797, 800/722-2406
Mon-Fri: 9:30-6; Sat: 10-6   www.tanthony.com

T. Anthony handles luxurious luggage of distinction. Anything purchased here will stand out in a crowd. Luggage ranges from small overnight bags to massive steamer trunks. Their briefcases, jewelry boxes, desk sets, albums, key cases, and billfolds make terrific gifts, individually or in matched sets. Don't come looking for discount prices; however, T. Anthony's high quality and courteous service are well-established New York traditions. Exclusive products are also available through the store's website.

Magic

TANNEN'S MAGIC
45 W 34th St (bet Fifth Ave and Ave of the Americas), Suite 608
Mon-Fri: 10-5 (Thurs till 7); Sat, Sun: 10-4   212/929-4500
                                                www.tannens.com

Tannen is the world's largest supplier of magician's items, stocking more than 8,000 magic tricks, books, and DVDs. They have all that a magician of any level could possibly need. Tannen's showroom is patronized by the finest magicians in the country. The floor demonstrators are some of the best in the business—always friendly, helpful, and eager to share their knowledge with those willing to study the art of magic. Tannen also runs a "Magic Summer Camp" for boys and girls age 12 to 18. It has spawned some of today's greatest working magicians.

Maps

HAGSTROM MAP AND TRAVEL CENTER
51 W 43rd St (at Ave of the Americas)   212/398-1222
Mon-Fri: 8:30-6; Sat: 10:30-4:30

Hagstrom is the only complete map and chart dealer in the city, highlighting the maps of major manufacturers and three branches of government. There are also nautical, hiking, global, and travel guides, plus globes, atlases, and foreign-language phrase books. The staff are experts when it comes to maps and travel information.

Memorabilia

CBS STORE

1691 Broadway (at 53rd St)   212/975-8600
Mon-Sat: 10-8; Sun: noon-5   www.cbs.com

Just down the street from the Ed Sullivan Theater (where *The Late Show with David Letterman* is filmed), this store stocks T-shirts, mugs, and other merchandise with the CBS logo or images from the network's shows, such as *Criminal Minds* and *Numb3rs*.

Where to Buy New York City-Themed Merchandise

CityStore (Manhattan Municipal Building, 1 Centre St, 212/669-8246, www.nyc.gov/citystore): official City of New York merchandise

FDNY Fire Zone (34 W 51st St, 212/698-4520, www.fdnyfirezone. com): officially licensed FDNY products

Harlem Underground (20 E 125th St, 212/987-9385, www.harlem underground.com): sleek sportswear with Harlem logos and uptown attitude

Macy's Herald Square, The Cellar (151 W 34th St, 212/695-4400): unique and classy items

Metropolitan Museum of Art (Fifth Ave at 82nd St, 212/535-7710, www.metmuseum.org): posters of recent art exhibits

Museum of the City of New York (1220 Fifth Ave, 212/534-1672, www.mcny.org): ties, scarves, and umbrellas with New York-themed designs

New York City Police Museum (100 Old Slip, 212/480-3100, www.nycpolicemuseum.org): Gift items include stuffed bears and books.

New York Gifts (729 Seventh Ave, lobby, 212/391-7570)

New-York Historical Society (2 W 77th St, 212/873-3400, www. nyhistory.org): posters, prints, and holiday cards featuring scenes of old New York

Statue of Liberty (212/363-3180, www.nps.gov/stli): mini statues, books, postcards, glassware, and holiday ornaments

Steuben (667 Madison Ave, 212/752-1441, www.steuben.com): gorgeous crystal apple and the Manhattan skyline etched in crystal

Tiffany & Co. (727 Fifth Ave, 212/755-8000, www.tiffany.com): apple-themed items, including an apple key ring and Elsa Peretti-designed silver apple earrings, necklaces, and bracelets

---

FIRESTORE

17 Greenwich Ave (bet Christopher and 10th St)   212/226-3142
Mon-Thurs: 11-7; Fri, Sat: 11-8; Sun: noon-6   www.firestore.com
                                                www.ny911.com

The former New York Firefighters' Friend and New York 911 stores have merged into one mutually complementary location. Firefighters, cops, and their fans can find everything under the sun relating to these first responders. Patches, pins, T-shirts, turnout coats, caps, work shirts, FDNY memorial shirts, firefighter jackets, and even toys are available at this fascinating one-stop cop and firefighter shop!

GOTTA HAVE IT! COLLECTIBLES
153 E 57th St (bet Lexington and Third Ave)   212/750-7900
Mon-Fri: 10-6; Sat: 11-5   www.gottahaveit.com

Do you have a favorite sports star, Hollywood personality, musical entertainer, or political figure? Gotta Have It features original and unique products in these categories. There are signed photos, musical instruments, baseball bats, used sports uniforms, documents, and movie props. All items are fully authenticated and guaranteed for life.

MOVIE STAR NEWS
134 W 18th St (bet Ave of the Americas and Seventh Ave)
Mon-Thurs: 11-7; Fri: 11-6   212/620-8160
                                                       www.moviestarnews.com

Movie Star News may be the closest thing to Hollywood on the East Coast! It claims to have the world's largest collection of movie photos. Stars past and present shine brightly in this shop, which offers posters and other movie memorabilia. The store is laid out like a library. Ira Kramer, who runs the shop, does a lot of research for magazines, newspapers, and other media.

NBC EXPERIENCE STORE
30 Rockefeller Plaza (49th St bet Fifth Ave and Ave of the Americas)
Mon-Sat: 8:30-6; Sun: 9:30-4:30   212/664-3700
                                                       www.nbcuniversalstore.com

The NBC Experience Store offers walking tours that take visitors behind the scenes of NBC's studios and around one of New York's most recognizable landmarks, Rockefeller Center. The 20,000-square-foot facility is located directly across from Studio 1A, home of the *Today Show*. It stocks T-shirts, mugs, keychains, and other merchandise with the NBC logo or images from such television shows as *The Office*.

ONE SHUBERT ALLEY
One Shubert Alley (45th St bet Broadway and Eighth Ave)
                   212/944-4133, 800/223-1320 (mail order only)
Sun-Thurs: noon-8; Fri, Sat: noon-11   www.broadwaynewyork.com

Shubert Alley is often used as a shortcut between Broadway theaters. One Shubert Alley is the only retail establishment in the alley. It's a fascinating place to browse for T-shirts, posters, recordings, buttons, and other paraphernalia from current shows on and off-Broadway.

Mirrors

SUNDIAL-SCHWARTZ
159 E 118th St (bet Lexington and Third Ave)
Mon-Fri: 8-4   800/876-4776, 212/289-4969
                                    www.antiquemirror.net

The people at Sundial-Schwartz supply "decorative treatments of distinction." Anyone who has ever seen a cramped New York apartment suddenly appear to expand with the strategic placement of mirrors will understand that claim. They deal with professional decorators and do-it-yourselfers, and both benefit from the staff's years of experience. They carry tabletop glass, shower doors, and mirrors for the home, office, and showroom. In addition, Sundial-Schwartz will remodel, re-silver, and antique mirrors. They also custom-design window treatments, blinds, shades, and draperies.

Movies

VIDEOROOM

1487 Third Ave (at 84th St)	212/879-5333
300 Rector Pl (South End Ave at Thames St)	212/962-6400
Mon-Fri: 10-10; Sat: 11-11; Sun: noon-10	www.videoroom.net

VideoRoom stocks a large selection of foreign, classic, and hard-to-find films in both VHS and DVD formats. Their highly competent staff—all students of film—are motivated to help inquiring customers. There is also an in-depth selection of new releases, home pickup and delivery service ($89 per year), and a special-order departments.

Museum and Library Shops

As anybody on a mailing list knows, scores of museums across the country produce catalogs that allow people to browse their gift shops from a distance. In New York, however, you can browse in person at more than four dozen museums. Even at museums that charge an admission fee, you need not pay if you're there to shop. Rather than simply list all the museum gift shops in New York, I've chosen several particularly large or unique ones. Indeed, whether you're looking for a one-of-a-kind gift or unusual books and posters, I highly recommend shopping in the following places. Instead of Empire State Building salt-and-pepper shakers, expect to find classy, artistic, well-made items. In most cases, at least some of the wares relate directly to current and past exhibits or the museum's permanent collection. You might save money by becoming a member and taking advantage of discounts.

AMERICAN FOLK ART MUSEUM

45 W 53rd St (bet Fifth Ave and Ave of the Americas)	
Daily: 10-6 (Fri till 8)	212/265-1040
1 Lincoln Square (Columbus Ave bet 65th and 66th St)	
Tues-Sat: 11-7:30; Sun: 11-5	212/595-9533
	www.folkartmuseum.org

Both at its beautiful new home on 53rd Street and its homey branch location across from Lincoln Center, the American Folk Art Museum runs great gift shops stocked with lots of unusual handcrafted items in various price ranges. The Lincoln Square location has a particularly good selection of books about quilting, and both stores are excellent sources for books on folk and decorative arts.

AMERICAN MUSEUM OF NATURAL HISTORY

Central Park West bet 77th and 81st St	800/671-7035
Daily: 10-5:45	www.amnh.org

The museum's amazing three-level store features a wide selection of unusual merchandise related to the natural world, diverse cultures, and exploration and discovery. You'll find lots of children's books and toys on the first floor, a huge selection of books for all ages on the second floor, and jewelry, ceramics, gems, handicrafts, and other items from around the world on the third floor. Five smaller satellite shops throughout the museum offer children's toys, space-themed merchandise, and dinosaur-related items. Temporary shops are also set up to accompany some of the museum's special exhibits.

ASIASTORE
725 Park Ave (at 70th St)   212/327-9217
Daily: 11-6 (Fri till 9); closed on Mon in July and Aug
www.asiasociety.org/asiastore

The Asia Society and Museum's fabulous AsiaStore showcases the best in Asian design. Offerings include hundreds of unique items from Asia and Asian-American artists: jewelry, fashion accessories, home accents, stationery, gifts, and novelty items. A selection of books includes scores of titles on Asian art, culture, politics, and religion.

EL MUSEO DEL BARRIO
1230 Fifth Ave (at 105th St)   212/831-7272
Wed-Sun: 11-5   www.elmuseo.org

Although El Museo del Barrio is undergoing renovation and expansion as this book goes to press, I have no doubt that its charming shop will continue to be a draw. This shop is a great source for unique jewelry and handicrafts; art from local artists, Latin America, and the Caribbean; children's books in Spanish and English; and books for adults about the history, art, and culture of Latin America, the Caribbean, and immigrants from there.

FRICK COLLECTION
1 E 70th St (bet Fifth and Madison Ave)   212/547-6848
Tues-Sat: 10-5:45; Sun: 11-4:45   www.shopfrick.org

The Frick's gift shop makes the most of its small space by concentrating on exquisite cards, stationery, prints, and art books, although you will also find a small collection of paperweights, scarves, porcelains, and the like. Note that the shop closes 15 minutes earlier than the museum.

GUGGENHEIM MUSEUM STORE
1071 Fifth Ave (bet 88th and 89th St)   212/423-3615
Sat-Wed: 9:30-6:15; Thurs: 11-6; Fri: 9:30-8:30
www.guggenheimstore.org

Although much that's for sale here is ordinary—including scarves, T-shirts, prints and posters, tote bags, umbrellas, note cards and stationery, jewelry, and children's toys—the design and craftsmanship are anything but. If you're looking for an unusual clock, a great wedding present, or the right pair of earrings to set you apart from the crowd, try this store. Just be aware that prices are often through the roof. Of course, the store also carries books on modern art and exhibition catalogs. It has a great online shop as well. Unlike many other museum stores, this one is actually open before and after the museum itself closes. It is also open on Thursday, when the museum itself is closed.

INTERNATIONAL CENTER OF PHOTOGRAPHY
1133 Ave of the Americas (at 43rd St)   212/857-9725
Daily: 10-6 (Mon till 5, Fri till 8)   www.shopping.icp.org/store

This store is definitely worth a look if you're shopping for a photography buff with high-quality gifts in mind. It has an excellent collection of books about the history and technology of photography and photojournalism. You can also find coffee-table books of collected works by photographers, as well as prints, picture frames, and unusual postcards.

JEWISH MUSEUM'S COOPER SHOP
1109 Fifth Ave (at 92nd St)   212/423-3211
Sun-Wed: 11-5:45; Thurs: 11-7:45; Fri: 11-3
                                        www.jewishmuseum.org/jmuseum

This relatively large store is an excellent source for Jewish literature, decorative art, and Judaica. Its selection of menorahs is among the classiest in the city. The store also sells cards, coffee-table books, and a wide selection of children's books with Jewish themes and characters. **Celebrations**, the Jewish Museum's Design Shop, is housed in a brownstone next to the museum. It is worth a look if you're interested in high-quality ceremonial objects, jewelry, and things for the home.

METROPOLITAN MUSEUM OF ART
1000 Fifth Ave (bet 80th and 84th St)   212/570-3894
Macy's (Herald Square, 34th St at Ave of the Americas), mezzanine
                                                              212/268-7266
Rockefeller Center (15 W 49th St, bet Fifth Ave and Ave of the Americas)
                                                              212/332-1360
South Street Seaport   212/248-0954
The Cloisters (Fort Tryon Park)   212/923-3700
Hours vary by store   www.metmuseum.org/store

The two-floor store inside the Metropolitan Museum of Art is the grandfather of all museum gift shops. It specializes in reproductions of paintings and other pieces in the Met's incredible collection, as well as museum collections around the world. (For limited-edition prints, go to the mezzanine gallery or call 212/650-2910.) You can find jewelry, statues, vases, scarves, ties, porcelains, prints, rugs, napkins, and scores of other beautiful gift items. They also carry books relating to special exhibits and the museum's extensive holdings, as well as umbrellas, tote bags, and other things with the Metropolitan's name emblazoned on them. Prices range from reasonable to wildly expensive, and the salespeople are usually patient and helpful. Smaller "remote" shops can be found throughout the museum, and satellite shops are located at LaGuardia and Kennedy airports, as well as the locations in Manhattan listed above. The second floor of the main store in the Met and the satellite shop in Rockefeller Center have particularly good children's sections.

METROPOLITAN OPERA SHOP
Metropolitan Opera House   212/580-4090
Lincoln Center (Columbus Ave at 65th St)   www.metoperashop.org
Mon-Sat: 10 a.m. to end of second intermission; Sun: noon-6

Opera lovers will be in heaven! In addition to operas on video, compact discs, and other media, you'll find books, mugs, umbrellas, stationery, T-shirts, and pillows for the opera buff. Be sure to check out the Performing Arts

Shop on the lower concourse, too. And if you're looking for posters and prints from various seasons, visit The Gallery, also on the lower concourse.

MUSEUM OF JEWISH HERITAGE
36 Battery Pl (in Battery Park City)   646/437-4200
Sun-Thurs: 10-5:45 (Wed till 8); Fri: 10-3   www.mjhnyc.org

This store is a fitting companion to the museum in its celebration of Jewish art, crafts, and culture. The selection is diverse, and many items are related to the museum's collection. Everything is high quality and much of it is quite unusual. A carefully chosen section includes books and gifts for children of various ages. Elegant jewelry and Judaica are also available. The prices are remarkably good. Note that the store and the museum are closed on all major Jewish holidays.

MUSEUM OF MODERN ART DESIGN AND BOOK STORE
11 W 53rd St (bet Fifth Ave and Ave of the Americas)   212/767-1050
Daily: 9:30-6:30 (Fri till 9)

SOHO DESIGN TOO
81 Spring St (at Crosby St)   646/613-1367
Mon-Sat: 11-8; Sun: 11-7   www.momastore.org

These magnificent stores—the main one across the street from the Museum of Modern Art and a satellite shop in Soho—are dedicated to what the curators consider the very best in modern design. Furniture, textiles, vases, ties, kitchen gadgets, silverware, frames, watches, lamps, and toys and books for children are among the things you'll find. These items are not cheap, but the selection is really exceptional. You'll find books and furniture on the lower level of the Soho store.

NATIONAL MUSEUM OF THE AMERICAN INDIAN
1 Bowling Green (at the foot of Broadway)
Museum Shop   212/514-3766
The Gallery   212/514-3767
Daily: 10-5 (Thurs till 8)   www.nmai.si.edu

Like everything else about the National Museum of the American Indian, its two recently renovated gift shops are classy operations. **The Gallery**—located on the main floor to the right of the entrance—has a wide selection of books and high-quality Native American weavings, jewelry, and other handicrafts. The **Museum Shop**—down the grand marble staircase from the main entrance—is more focused on kids and families. Children's books, videos, toys, craft kits, and the obligatory arrowheads are for sale, along with T-shirts and some moderately priced jewelry. Because the museum is part of the Smithsonian Institution, both stores offer discounts to Smithsonian Associates.

THE NEUE GALERIE BOOKSTORE AND DESIGN SHOP
1048 Fifth Ave (at 86th St)   212/628-6200
Mon, Wed-Sun: 11-6 (Fri till 9)   www.neuegalerie.org

The Neue Galerie Bookstore is clearly *the* source for books on art, architecture, and cultural life in Germany, Austria, and Central Europe in the 19th and 20th centuries. The Design Shop has a small but well-chosen selection of beautiful high-end jewelry, tableware, textiles, and other decorative arts by modern German and Austrian designers. Both stores are immediately to the left of the museum's entrance.

NEW YORK PUBLIC LIBRARY SHOP
Fifth Ave bet 41st and 42nd St   212/930-0641
Tues, Wed, Sat: 11-6; Thurs, Fri: 10-6; Sun: 1-5

www.thelibraryshop.org

If ever there was a perfect gift shop for book lovers, this is it. Located just off the main lobby of the New York Public Library's main branch, it features a high-quality selection of unusual merchandise. You'll find magnets with sayings like "I Think, Therefore I'm Dangerous" and "Think for Yourself, Not for Me" and books about the library's history. The staff is particularly pleasant and helpful. The online store is a great spot to shop if you can't make it to New York!

NEW YORK TRANSIT MUSEUM
Grand Central Terminal (42nd St at Vanderbilt Ave)   212/878-0106
Mon-Fri: 8-8; Sat, Sun: 10-4   www.mta.info

This little shop and gallery make train and subway buffs downright giddy. Items for sale include books, conductor's caps, clever T-shirts, replicas of old station signs, banks for children in the shape of city buses, giant chocolate subway tokens, jewelry made from old tokens, and very classy mirrors made by one of the artists restoring the subway system's mosaics. Bus and subway maps, as well as other MTA information, are also available. Note that this shop is a branch of the much larger main store at the **New York Transit Museum** in Brooklyn (Boerum Place at Schermerhorn Street, 718/694-1868).

PERFORMING ARTS SHOP
Metropolitan Opera House
Lincoln Center (Columbus Ave at 65th St), lower concourse
Mon-Sat: 10-8; Sun: noon-6   917/441-1195

This store is lots of fun for anyone interested in opera, classical music, and ballet. Much like the Metropolitan Opera Shop on the floor above, the Performing Arts Shop also has a wide selection of music, books, instruments, and toys for children, plus an even wider selection of recordings and various ballet-related items. If you're interested in prints and posters from past seasons, walk a little farther down the hall and visit **The Gallery**.

THE SHOP AT COOPER-HEWITT NATIONAL DESIGN MUSEUM
2 E 91st St (bet Fifth and Madison Ave)   212/849-8355
Tues-Thurs: 10-5; Fri: 10-9; Sat: 10-6; Sun: noon-6

www.ndm.si.edu/shop

This terrific store is housed in the enchanting library of Andrew Carnegie's incredible mansion. It offers an eclectic mix of items that relate to the museum's extensive collection and reflect its dedication to design excellence and innovation. Pens, office items, tea cups, jewelry, clocks, vases, lamps, and plates are among the offerings. You might even find an unusual wedding present here! The store also has a pretty good collection of books and toys for children. Be sure to look around at the room (and the ceiling!) as you browse. The shop closes 15 minutes earlier than the museum.

THE SHOP AT SCANDINAVIA HOUSE
58 Park Ave (bet 37th and 38th St)   212/847-9737
Mon-Sat: noon-6 (Wed till 7)   www.scandinaviahouse.org

Tucked into the back of the first floor behind Cafe AQ, this little gem is a tribute to Scandinavian design and good taste. Household items—including vases, tableware, and glasses—are featured, as are beautiful pieces of jewelry and a small selection of children's items.

THE STORE AT THE MUSEUM OF ARTS AND DESIGN
40 W 53rd St (bet Fifth Ave and Ave of the Americas)
Daily: 10-6 (Thurs till 8)   212/956-3535, ext. 157
                                         www.madmuseum.org

The store name became a mouthful after the renaming of the American Craft Museum. However, this well-conceived shop remains a great complement to the other museum shops on West 53rd Street. Showcasing the work of exceptional artists from around the United States, it features a constantly changing collection of beautifully designed jewelry, textiles, housewares, and more.

STUDIO MUSEUM
144 W 125th St (bet Malcolm X and Adam Clayton Powell, Jr. Blvd)
Wed-Fri, Sun: noon-6; Sat: 10-6   212/864-0014
                                         www.studiomuseum.org

Located just inside the museum's entrance on the right, this store sells a wide and generally high-quality selection of jewelry, textiles, crafts, note cards, and calendars created by African and African-American artists. It also sells an unusually broad selection of cookbooks, fiction, biographies, and children's books by and about Africans and African-Americans.

UKRAINIAN MUSEUM
222 E 6th St (bet Second and Third Ave)   212/228-0110
Wed-Sun: 11:30-5   www.ukrainianmuseum.org

This store is well worth a visit if you want to find Ukrainian Easter eggs (already made and kits for do-it-yourselfers), embroidery, and other handicrafts. Be sure to ask about holiday baking, embroidery, beading, and Easter-egg classes.

UNITED NATIONS
First Ave bet 45th and 46th St   212/963-4475
Mon-Fri: 9-5; Sat, Sun: 10-5 (closed weekends in Jan, Feb)

On the lower level of the main UN building is a bookstore, post office (a real treat for stamp collectors), small UNICEF shop, and an even smaller shop run by the UN Women's Guild. That's in addition to the main gift shop, also on the lower level. The bookstore features calendars, postcards with the flags of member nations, holiday cards in dozens of languages, and a wide variety of books about the UN and related subjects. The main gift shop features a wonderful array of carvings, jewelry, scarves, dolls, and other items from all over the world. The better imports can get pricey, but it's definitely going to a good cause! One final thought: if you are interested in UNICEF cards and gifts but find the selection at the UN rather thin, then visit the store in the lobby of the nearby **UNICEF House** (3 United Nations Plaza, 44th St bet First and Second Ave, 212/326-7054).

Music

ACADEMY RECORDS & CDs

12 W 18th St (at Fifth Ave)	212/242-3000
77 E 10th St (at Fourth Ave)	212/780-9166
Mon-Sat: noon-8; Sun: noon-6	www.academylps.com

Academy Records & CDs has Manhattan's largest stock of used, out-of-print, and rare classical LPs and CDs. Emphasizing opera, contemporary classical, and early music (the Baroque period and before), Academy boasts an international reputation. Prices are fair and the staff is knowledgeable. The rock and jazz holdings are less extensive.

BLEECKER BOB'S GOLDEN OLDIES RECORD SHOP

118 W 3rd St (bet MacDougal St and Ave of the Americas)
Mon-Thurs: 11 a.m.-1 a.m.; Fri, Sat: 11 a.m.-3 a.m.   212/475-9677
www.bleeckerbobs.com

Let us sing the praises of Bleecker Bob, who is nothing if not perverse. (Name another store that's open till 3 a.m. on Christmas Day!) For one thing, although there is a real Bob (Plotnik, the owner), the store isn't on Bleecker Street. For another, Bleecker Bob is an institution to generations of New Yorkers who have sifted through his vast selection of rock, punk, and heavy metal recordings. They stock vintage rock and soul records (plus some rare jazz), and boast that they can fill any wish list. Bleecker Bob's also serves as a gathering place in the wee hours of the morning in the Village. Above all, it's a great source for out-of-print, obscure, and imported compact discs and DVDs.

FOOTLIGHT RECORDS

113 E 12th St (bet Third and Fourth Ave)	212/533-1572
Mon, Tues, Thurs, Fri: 11-7	www.footlight.com

In keeping with this outfit's passion for rare and unusual records and compact discs, the emphasis is on show tunes, film soundtracks, and jazz. Their prices are among the best around, and many of their records aren't available anywhere else. If there's an original cast album of a Broadway show, you can bet Footlight has it. They stock one of the most comprehensive collections of film scores in the country. They also carry an impressive showing of European and Japanese imports, a large selection of big band and early jazz recordings, and rock LPs.

FRANK MUSIC

244 W 54th St (bet Broadway and Eighth Ave), 10th floor
Mon-Fri: 11-5 (hours vary in summer)   212/582-1999
www.frankmusiccompany.com

Founded in 1938, this professional business has never advertised, relying instead on word of mouth. They sell classical sheet music from European and American publishers. There is an aisle for voice and violin, another for piano, and so on. Frank Music gladly fills mail orders.

JAZZ RECORD CENTER
236 W 26th St (bet Seventh and Eighth Ave), Room 804   212/675-4480
Mon-Sat: 10-6   www.jazzrecordcenter.com

Jazz Record Center is run by Frederick Cohen, a charming guy who really knows his business. It is the only jazz specialty store in the city. They deal in out-of-print and new jazz records, CDs, videos, books, posters, photos, periodicals, postcards, and T-shirts. The store buys collections, fills mail orders, and offers appraisals. They auction jazz rarities on eBay, too.

JOSEPH PATELSON MUSIC HOUSE
160 W 56th St (at Seventh Ave)   212/582-5840
Mon-Sun: 9-6   www.patelson.com

Located behind Carnegie Hall, Joseph Patelson is known to every student of music in the city. From little first graders to artists from Carnegie Hall, everyone stops here first because of the fabulous selection and excellent prices. The stock includes music scores, sheet music, music books, and orchestral and opera scores. All are neatly cataloged and displayed in open cabinets. One can easily browse a given section of interest—be it piano music, chamber music, orchestral scores, opera scores, concerts, ethnic scores, or instrumental solos. Sheet music is filed in bins the way records are elsewhere. There are also musical accessories like metronomes and pitch pipes. Patelson is an unofficial meeting place for the city's young musicians. Word goes out that "we're looking for a violinist," and meetings are often arranged in the store. Mail and phone orders are accepted.

OTHER MUSIC
15 E 4th St (bet Broadway and Lafayette St)   212/477-8150
Mon-Fri: noon-9; Sat: noon-8; Sun: noon-7   www.othermusic.com

If you can't find it elsewhere, try Other Music. They stock CDs and vinyl, hard-to-find releases, and a wide variety of imports. They will purchase or give store credit for used CDs and records.

WESTSIDER RECORDS
233 W 72nd St (at Broadway)   212/874-1588
Daily: 11-8   www.westsiderbooks.com

Westsider remains one of the few stores specializing in rare and out-of-print LPs. Compact discs have been added to the stock of 80,000 LPs. You'll also find printed music and books on the performing arts. Raymond Donnell will guide customers through his classical, jazz, rock, pop, and spoken-word holdings.

Musical Instruments

DRUMMER'S WORLD
151 W 46th St (bet Ave of the Americas and Seventh Ave), 3rd floor
Mon-Fri: 10-6; Sat: 10-4   212/840-3057
                                                        www.drummersworld.com

This is a great place, unless the patron is your teenager or an upstairs neighbor! Barry Greenspon and his staff take pride in guiding students and professionals through one of the best percussion stores in the country. Inside this drummer's paradise is everything from commonplace equipment to one-of-a-kind antiques and imports. All of the instruments are high-quality percussion items, and customers receive the same attention whether they are members of an orchestra, rock band, or rap act. The store also offers instructors and how-to books. There are esoteric ethnic instruments for virtuosos who want to experiment. Drummer's World has a catalog and will ship anywhere in the country.

GUITAR SALON
45 Grove St (at Bleecker St)   212/675-3236
By appointment   www.theguitarsalon.com

Beverly Maher's Guitar Salon NY is a unique one-person operation located in a historic brownstone in Greenwich Village. Outstanding personal service is provided by Beverly, who specializes in 19th- and 20th-century vintage instruments. You will find handmade classical and flamenco guitars for students, professionals, and collectors. Appraisals are available, and lessons are given on all styles of guitars. Even the Rolling Stones have been known to shop here!

MANNY'S MUSIC
156 W 48th St (bet Ave of the Americas and Seventh Ave)
Mon-Sat: 10-7; Sun: noon-6   212/819-0576, 866/777-6266
                                                  www.mannysmusic.com

Manny's is a huge discount department store for musical instruments. "Everything for the Musician" is their motto, and it is borne out by a collection of musical equipment so extensive that each department has its own salespeople. The emphasis is on modern music, as evidenced by the hundreds of autographed pictures of popular musicians on the walls and the huge collection of electronic instruments. All of the instruments, equipment, accessories, and supplies are sold at discount. They also have a large computer department for musical software needs.

RITA FORD MUSIC BOXES
19 E 65th St (at Madison Ave)   212/535-6717
Mon-Sat: 9-5   www.ritafordmusicboxes.com

Gerry and Nancy Wright and Joseph and Diane Tenore collect antique music boxes and have become experts in all aspects of the business. Stock consists of valuable antique and new music boxes. The main stock-in-trade is expertise; having been in business for half a century, these folks know all there is to know about music boxes. They are experts on music box scores, workings, and outer casings. Some pieces are rare antiques that are priced accordingly, while contemporary music boxes are more modestly priced. The store also does repairs and restorations.

Pets and Accessories

BARKING ZOO
172 Ninth Ave (bet 20th and 21st St)   212/255-0658
Mon-Fri: 11-8; Sat: 10-6; Sun: noon-5

You'll find quality items for your favorite canine, including knitwear, pet food, and valuable information on care of dogs and cats.

DOGGYSTYLE
100 Thompson St (bet Spring and Prince St)   212/431-9200
Mon-Sat: noon-7; Sun: noon-6

There's no fancy stuff here—just good, practical items for your pet at sensible prices. Doggystyle features boutique collars, leashes, coats, and feeding bowls, plus handy products for traveling with a pet. Dog and cat grooming is available.

PACIFIC AQUARIUM & PET
46 Delancey St (bet Forsyth and Eldridge St)   212/995-5895
Daily: 10-7:30   www.pacificaquarium.com

Goldfish are their specialty, but Pacific Aquarium & Pet also carries all types of freshwater and saltwater fish, and every kind of aquarium and supply you could imagine. They will even come to your home and maintain an aquarium while you're away.

Are you ready to get a dog? Here are a couple of suggestions to get you started. If it is a purebred you want, call the **American Kennel Club** (919/233-9767) and tell them the breed you have in mind. Another good bet is **Bide-a-Wee** (410 E 38th St, 212/532-4455). If you need to train your dog, try **Follow My Lead** (212/873-5511).

PETCO
147-149 E 86th St (at Lexington Ave)	212/831-8001
560 Second Ave (at 30th St)	212/779-4550
860 Broadway (at Union Square W)	212/358-0692
2475 Broadway (at 92nd St)	212/877-1270
Hours vary by store	www.petco.com

With a selection of over 10,000 items—including food, toys, treats, and pet-care products—this store is a pet owner's treasure trove. There are sections for cats, dogs, birds, fish, and even reptiles! Services include low-cost vaccine clinics, pet photography, dog training, and grooming.

PETLAND DISCOUNTS
132 Nassau St (bet Beekman and John St)	212/964-1821
530 E 14th St (at Ave B)	212/228-1363
312 W 23rd St (bet Eighth and Ninth Ave)	212/366-0512
137 W 72nd St (bet Columbus and Amsterdam Ave)	212/875-9785
976 Second Ave (bet 51st and 52nd St)	212/755-7228
389 Ave of the Americas (bet 8th St and Waverly Pl)	212/741-1913
734 Ninth Ave (at 50th St)	212/459-9562
2708 Broadway (at 104th St)	212/222-8851
304 E 86th St (bet First and Second Ave)	212/472-1655
56 W 117th St (bet Malcolm X Blvd and Fifth Ave)	212/427-2700
167 E 125th St (bet Ave of the Americas and Lexington Ave)	
	212/426-7193

1954 Third Ave (bet 107th and 108th St)   212/987-6714
Hours vary by store   www.petlanddiscounts.com

The pros at the New York Aquarium recommend this chain for fish and aquarium accessories. Petland also carries discount food and accessories for dogs, cats, birds, reptiles, and other pets.

Photographic Equipment and Supplies

ADORAMA CAMERA
42 W 18th St (bet Fifth Ave and Ave of the Americas) 212/741-0052
Mon-Thurs: 9-6:15; Fri: 9-1; Sun: 9:30-5:15   www.adorama.com

Adorama is one of the largest photographic mail-order houses in the country. They carry a huge stock of equipment and supplies, telescopes, and video paraphernalia, all sold at discount.

ALKIT PRO CAMERAS
222 Park Ave S (at 18th St)   212/674-1515
Mon-Fri: 8:30-6:30   www.alkit.com

If you want to shop where photographers of the Elite and Ford modeling agencies go, Alkit is the place. You don't have to be a professional to visit, however. While most establishments that deal with the pros have little time for amateurs, nothing gives Alkit's employees more pleasure than introducing the world of photography to neophytes. Alkit maintains a full line of digital and film cameras, film, and equipment. They have a one-hour processing lab on-premises. The shop repairs and rents photographic equipment. Alkit also publishes an informative catalog full of praise and gripes about particular models.

B&H PHOTO-VIDEO-PRO AUDIO
420 Ninth Ave (bet 33rd and 34th St)   212/444-6600, 800/606-6969
Mon-Thurs: 9-7; Fri: 9-2; Sun: 10-5   www.bhphotovideo.com

This is quite a store! You'll find professional and nonprofessional departments for video, pro audio, pro lighting, darkroom, film and film processing, books, used equipment, and related items. Trade-ins are welcome, and used equipment is sold. The store has been in operation since 1974 and is staffed by knowledgeable personnel. Inventory levels are high, prices are reasonable, and hands-on demo areas make browsing easy. A catalog is available.

CALUMET PHOTOGRAPHIC
22 W 22nd St (bet Fifth Ave and Ave of the Americas) 212/989-8500
Mon-Fri: 8:30-5:30; Sat: 9-5:30   www.calumetphoto.com

In business for over 60 years, this firm provides start-to-finish photographic service. Professional camera equipment, film, digital cameras and accessories, printers, and scanners are all available at good prices.

LAUMONT
333 W 52nd St (bet Eighth and Ninth Ave)   212/245-2113
Mon-Fri: 9-5:30 (evenings and weekends by appointment)
          www.laumont.com

Whether you're a professional or amateur, Laumont can take care of your photographic needs. They do excellent work producing exhibition-quality Cibachrome, Fuji, Lambda, Lightjet, Iris, and pigment prints. They are patient and understanding with those who need advice. Laumont's staff are also experienced digital retouchers and duplicators, and they can repair damaged originals or create brand new images on state-of-the-art computers. Lamination, print mounting, and framing are done on-premises.

WILLOUGHBY'S KONICA IMAGING CENTER
298 Fifth Ave (at 31st St)   212/564-1600, 800/378-1898
Mon-Fri: 9-7:30; Sun: 10-6:30   www.willoughbys.com

Established in 1898, this is New York's oldest camera store. Willoughby's has a huge stock, an extensive clientele, and a solid reputation. They can handle almost any kind of camera order, either in person or by mail order. They service cameras, supply photographic equipment, and recycle used cameras. Moreover, they sell computers, video cameras, cell phones, and other high-tech equipment.

Pictures, Posters, and Prints

JERRY OHLINGER'S MOVIE MATERIALS STORE
253 W 35th St (bet Seventh and Eighth Ave)   212/989-0869
Mon-Sat: 11-7   www.moviematerials.com

Jerry Ohlinger has a huge selection of movie posters (from the 1930s to the present) and photographs from film and TV. He also researches these items and will gladly provide a catalog.

OLD PRINT SHOP
150 Lexington Ave (bet 29th and 30th St)   212/683-3950
Tues-Fri: 9-5; Sat: 9-4   www.oldprintshop.com

Established in 1898, the Old Print Shop exudes an old-fashioned charm, and its stock only reinforces the impression of timelessness. Kenneth M. Newman specializes in Americana, including original prints, town views, Currier & Ives prints, and original maps that reflect America as it used to be. Most of the nostalgic pictures that adorned calendars and stationery were copies of prints found here. Amateur and professional historians have a field day in this shop. Newman also does "correct period framing," and prints housed in his custom frames are striking. Everything bought and sold here is original, and Newman purchases estate and single items.

PAGEANT PRINT SHOP
69 E 4th St (bet Bowery and Second Ave)   212/674-5296
Tues-Sat: noon-8; Sun: 1-7   www.pageantprintshop.com

Antique maps and prints are among the treasures you will find at this cozy, enchanting shop. The daughter of the original founder (Sidney Solomon) now runs Pageant, which has over 10,000 items.

PHILIP WILLIAMS POSTERS
122 Chambers St (bet Church St and West Broadway) 212/513-0313
Mon-Sat: 10-6   www.postermuseum.com

This is the largest poster gallery in the world, with over 50,000 poster originals for sale from 1870 to the present. Philip Williams features prints in a variety of categories, including travel, food, drink, transportation, autos, bicycles, trains, sports, magic, and films. Over 2,000 pieces of Southern folk art are available.

PHYLLIS LUCAS GALLERY & OLD PRINT CENTER
981 Second Ave (at 52nd St)   212/755-1516
Mon-Fri: 10-5; Sat, Sun: 2-5   www.phyllislucasgallery.com

You might be confused that the name on the outside is Michael Lucas Gallery; it is the same place, with Michael (the son of the founder) as the present owner. Inside is a treasure trove of engravings, prints, and photographs. As one of the oldest antiquarian print galleries in the city, this place is known for its fine decorative art and superior framing services.

TRITON GALLERY
630 Ninth Ave (bet 44th and 45th St)   212/765-2472
Mon-Sat: 10-6; Sun: 1-6   www.tritongallery.com

Theater posters are presented at Triton like nowhere else. Posters of current Broadway shows join a stock of older show posters from the U.S. and abroad. Show cards—which are the most readily available items—are the standard 14" x 22" size. Posters range in size from 23" x 46" to 42" x 84" and are priced according to rarity, age, and demand. The collection is not limited to Broadway or even American plays, and some of the more interesting pieces come from other times. Triton also does custom framing. Much of the business is conducted via mail and phone.

Plastic Goods

PLEXI-CRAFT QUALITY PRODUCTS
514 W 24rd St (bet Tenth and Eleventh Ave)   212/924-3244
Mon-Fri: 9:30-5   www.plexi-craft.com

Plexi-Craft offers anything made of Lucite and Plexiglas at wholesale prices. If you can't find what you want among the pedestals, tables, chairs, shelves, racks, stands, and cubes displayed, they will make it for you.

Rubber Goods

CANAL RUBBER SUPPLY COMPANY
329 Canal St (at Greene St)   212/226-7339, 800/444-6483
Mon-Fri: 9-5; Sat: 9-4   wwwcanalrubber.com

"If It's Made of Rubber, We Have It" is the motto at this wholesale-retail operation. There are foam mattresses, bolsters, cushions, pads cut to size, hydraulic hoses, rubber tubing, vacuum hoses, floor matting, tiles, stair treads, sheet-rubber products, and much more.

Safes

EMPIRE SAFE
6 E 39th St (bet Fifth and Madison Ave)   212/684-2255, 800/543-5412
Mon-Fri: 9-5   www.empiresafe.com

Empire shows one of the city's largest and most complete selections of safes. Their products are used in residences and businesses, with delivery and installation offered. Also on display are rare antique and art deco safes, memorabilia, old photos, and historical documents. Whether you want to protect documents in a small apartment or huge office building, these folks are able to help.

Sexual Paraphernalia

COME AGAIN
353 E 53rd St (at First Ave)   212/308-9394
Mon-Fri: 11-7; Sat: 11-6

Come Again is a one-stop shop for sexual paraphernalia. There's exotic lingerie for men and women to size 4XL, bachelorette items, adult books and magazines, "how-to" DVDs and videos, oils and lotions, gift baskets, party gifts, and toys and equipment of a decidedly prurient nature. They offer a 20% discount for readers of this book!

EVE'S GARDEN INTERNATIONAL
119 W 57th St (bet Ave of the Americas and Seventh Ave), Suite 1201
Tues-Sat: 11-7   800/848-3837
                                                    www.evesgarden.com

This is not your usual sex shop; it is particularly geared to women who wish to shop in a pleasant atmosphere. Eve's Garden is a pleasure chest of games, books, and videos to seduce the mind. A vast array of sensuous massage oils, candles, and incense will help realize your wildest fantasies. Mail orders are welcome.

Signs

LET THERE BE NEON
38 White St (bet Broadway and Church St)   212/226-4883
Mon-Fri: 9-5   www.lettherebeneon.com

Though the image of neon is modern, it harks back to 1915, when Georges Claudes captured it from oxygen. While the flashing neon sign has become the ultimate urban cliché, here it is rendered as artistic fine art. Let There Be Neon operates as a gallery with a variety of sizes, shapes, functions, and designs to entice the browser. Almost all of their sales are custom pieces. Even a rough sketch is enough for them to create a literal or abstract neon sculpture. Some vintage pieces are available.

Silver

JEAN'S SILVERSMITHS
16 W 45th St (at Fifth Ave)   212/575-0723
Mon-Fri: 9-4:45   www.jeanssilversmiths.com

Having a problem replacing a fork that went down the disposal? Proceed directly to Jean's, where you will find over a thousand discontinued, obsolete, and current flatware patterns. They specialize in antique and second-hand silver, gold, and diamond jewelry, and they also sell watches.

TIFFANY & CO.
727 Fifth Ave (at 57th St)   212/755-8000, 800/843-3269
Mon-Fri: 10-7; Sat: 10-6; Sun: noon-5   www.tiffany.com

Despite the fact that Tiffany has appeared in plays, movies, books, and songs, this legendary store really isn't that formidable or forbidding, and it can be an exciting place to shop. Yes, there really is a Tiffany diamond, and it can be viewed on the first floor. That floor also houses the watch and jewelry departments. While browsing is welcome, salespeople are quick to approach loiterers. The store carries clocks, silver jewelry, sterling silver, bar accessories, centerpieces, leather accessories, fragrances, knickknacks, china, crystal, glassware, flatware, and engraved stationery. The real surprise is that Tiffany carries an excellent selection of reasonably priced items. Many are emblazoned with the Tiffany name and wrapped in the famed blue box. A branch has opened at 37 Wall Street (between Nassau and Williams St).

Sporting Goods

Bicycles and Accessories

BICYCLE HABITAT
244 Lafayette St (bet Spring and Prince St)   212/431-3315
Daily: 10-7   www.bicyclehabitat.com

These customer-oriented folks are "geared" toward cycling buffs. They really want to get more people interested in bikes! They even sponsor repair classes—including one on roadside emergencies. They will box bikes for shipment, deliver locally, and come to your place for repairs.

BICYCLE RENAISSANCE
430 Columbus Ave (at 81st St)   212/724-2350
Mon-Fri: 10:30-7; Sat, Sun: 10-5

Biking is a way of life at Bicycle Renaissance. Services include custom-building bikes and bicycle repair, and the mechanics aim for same-day service on all makes and models. They carry racing and mountain bikes by Trek, Cannondale, and Specialized, as well as custom frames for Seven, Shimano, and others. Prices are on par with so-called discount shops.

LARRY & JEFF'S SECOND AVENUE BICYCLES PLUS
1690 Second Ave (at 87th St)   212/722-2201
Daily: 10-8   www.larrysbicyclesplus.com

Larry Duffus started fixing bicycles at age 15. He taught the art to Jeff Loewi, and together they have been operating this unique retail and repair shop since 1977. Bikes range in price from $200 to $5,000, and plenty of parts and accessories are stocked, too. Special services include a lifetime of free tune-ups with the purchase of a new bicycle, bike rentals for rides through Central Park, and free delivery.

Billiards

BLATT BILLIARDS
809 Broadway (bet 11th and 12th St)   212/674-8855
Mon-Fri: 9-6:30; Sat: 10-5   www.blattbilliards.com

Blatt's six floors are outfitted from top to bottom with everything for billiards. You can also get friendly pointers from a staff that seems, at first glance, to be all business.

Exercise Equipment

GYM SOURCE
40 E 52nd St (bet Park and Madison Ave)   212/688-4222
Mon-Fri: 9-7; Sat: 10-6; Sun: noon-5   www.gymsource.com

This is the largest exercise equipment dealer in the Northeast. They carry treadmills, bikes, stair-steppers, weight machines, rowers, and more. Over 300 top brands are available at good prices, and Gym Source's skilled technicians provide competent servicing. They also rent equipment and will even deliver items for use in Manhattan hotel rooms.

Fishing

CAPITOL FISHING TACKLE COMPANY
132 W 36th St (bet Seventh Ave and Broadway)   212/929-6132
Mon-Fri: 10-7   www.capitolfishing.com

Right in the heart of Manhattan, anglers will find the store of their dreams! These folks carry a full line of fishing gear from names like Penn, Shimano, Garcia, and Daiwa. Specials and closeouts offer good values, as these folks buy surplus inventories from bankrupt dealers and liquidators.

URBAN ANGLER
206 Fifth Ave (bet 25th and 26th St), 3rd floor   212/689-6400
Mon-Fri: 10-6 (Wed till 7); Sat: 10-5   www.urbanangler.com

Urban Angler is the only pro fly-fishing shop in Manhattan. You'll find fly-fishing tackle, high-end spin and surf tackle, and travel clothing. They offer casting and fly-tying lessons. They can even plan fishing trips locally and around the world.

General

EASTERN MOUNTAIN SPORTS (EMS)
591 Broadway (bet Prince and Houston St)   212/966-8730
Mon-Fri: 10-9; Sat: 10-8; Sun: noon-6   www.ems.com

EMS is the place for outdoor clothing and gear. Although prices can be bettered elsewhere, it is an excellent source for one-stop shopping, and the merchandise is of a higher quality than that carried in department stores. EMS covers virtually all outdoor sports, including mountain climbing, backpacking, skiing, hiking, kayaking, and camping.

G&S SPORTING GOODS
43 Essex St (at Grand St)   212/777-7590, 800/215-3947
Mon-Fri: 9-6; Sun: 10-6   www.gandsboxinggear.com

If you are looking for a place to buy a birthday or Christmas gift for a sports buff, I recommend G&S. They have a large selection of brand-name sneakers, in-line skates, boxing equipment, balls, gloves, toys, games, sports clothing, and accessory items. Prices reflect a 20% to 25% discount.

MODELL'S

1535 Third Ave (bet 86th and 87th St)	212/996-3800
51 E 42nd St (bet Madison and Vanderbilt Ave)	212/661-4242
606 W 181st St (at St. Nicholas Ave)	212/568-3000
300 W 125th St (at Eighth Ave)	212/280-9100
55 Chambers St (at Broadway)	212/732-8484
1293 Broadway (at 34th St)	212/244-4544
234 W 42nd St (bet Seventh and Eighth Ave)	212/764-7030
Hours vary by store	www.modells.com

You can't beat this outfit for quality and value! Founded in 1889, Modell's is America's oldest family-owned sporting goods chain. They specialize in sporting goods, footwear, and a large selection of apparel for men, women, and children. Make note of Modell's low price guarantee.

NBA STORE

666 Fifth Ave (at 52nd St)	212/515-NBA1
Mon-Sat: 10-8; Sun: 11-6	www.nba.com/nycstore

This attractive and well-laid-out store has the largest assortment of NBA and WNBA merchandise in the nation. A winding ramp allows full exposure to areas featuring apparel and accessories, jewelry, watches, photographs, collectibles, headwear, practice gear, basketballs, and more. The store also features multimedia presentations of game action and highlights of historic moments. An actual half-court surrounded by bleachers is a popular spot for the store's more athletic shoppers. **Hang Time Cafe**, on the lower level, is a great place to score a quick bite to eat.

PARAGON SPORTS

867 Broadway (at 18th St)	212/255-8036
Mon-Sat: 10-8; Sun: 11:30-7	www.paragonsports.com

Paragon is truly a sporting goods department store, with over 100,000 square feet of specialty shops devoted to all kinds of sports and fitness equipment and apparel. The stock is arranged for easy shopping. There are departments for team equipment, athletic footwear, skateboards, ice skates, in-line skates, racquet sports, aerobics, swimming, golf, skiing and snowboarding, hiking, camping, diving, biking, sailing, and anything else that can be done in the great outdoors. They also carry gift items.

Golf

NEW YORK GOLF CENTER

131 W 35th St (bet Seventh Ave and Broadway)	212/564-2255
Chelsea Piers, Pier 59 (West Side Hwy at 18th St)	212/242-8899
Mon-Fri: 10-8; Sat: 10-7; Sun: 11-6	888/465-7890
	www.nygolfcenter.com

New York Golf Center is the Big Apple's only golf superstore, offering goods at prices that average 20% below list. There are clubs, bags, clothing, shoes, accessories, and novelties ... everything except one's own hard-won expertise. They carry pro-line equipment such as Callaway, Taylor Made, Cleveland, Titleist, Ping, and Nike. Golfers can test demo clubs at the Chelsea Piers Driving Range! Employees couldn't be nicer or more helpful. Mention this book and receive a free sleeve of golf balls with any $20 purchase.

Guns

JOHN JOVINO GUN SHOP
183 Grand St (at Mulberry St)   212/925-4881
Mon-Sat: 10-6; Sun: 2-6   www.johnjovinogunshop.com

These folks have been in business since 1911 and are recognized leaders in the field. They carry all major brands of handguns, rifles, and shotguns, as well as ammunition, holsters, bulletproof vests, knives, and scopes. Major brands include Smith & Wesson, Colt, Ruger, Beretta, Browning, Remington, Walther, Glock, Winchester, and Sig Sauer. Jovino is an authorized warranty repair station for gun manufacturers, with a licensed gunsmith on-site.

Marine

WEST MARINE
12 W 37th St (at Fifth Ave)   212/594-6065
Mon-Fri: 10-7; Sat: 10-5; Sun: 10-4   www.westmarine.com

West sells marine supplies as if it were situated in the middle of a New England seaport rather than the heart of Manhattan. The staff sometimes looks like a ship's crew on leave in the Big Apple, and they actually are that knowledgeable. They carry marine electronics, sailboat fittings, gamefish tackle, lifesaving gear, ropes, anchors, compasses, clothing, clocks, barometers, and books. You'll also find foul-weather suits and a line of clothing for yacht owners.

Outdoor Equipment

TENT AND TRAILS
21 Park Pl (bet Broadway and Church St)   212/227-1760
Mon-Sat: 9:30-6 (Thurs, Fri till 7); Sun: noon-6   800/237-1760
                                                www.tenttrails.com

Whether you are outfitting yourself for a weekend camping trip or an ascent of Mt. Everest, Tent and Trails is the place to go! In the urban canyons near City Hall, this 6,000-square-foot store is devoted to camping. The staff is experienced and knowledgeable. There are boots from Asolo, Garmont, Lowa, Merrell, Vasque, Hi Tec, and Scarpa Footwear. They carry camping gear from all the top makers. You'll find backpacks, sleeping bags, tents, down clothing, and much more. Tent and Trails also rents camping equipment.

Running

SUPER RUNNERS SHOP
1337 Lexington Ave (at 89th St)   212/369-6010
360 Amsterdam Ave (at 77th St)   212/787-7665
1246 Third Ave (bet 71st and 72nd St)   212/249-2133
Grand Central Terminal (42nd St at Vanderbilt Ave) 646/487-1120
Hours vary by store   www.superrunnersshop.com

Co-owner Gary Muhrcke won the first New York City Marathon in 1970, and his passion became his livelihood. The stock at Super Runners Shop includes a superb selection of men's and women's running and racing shoes, as well as performance running clothes. The informed staff, who are themselves runners, believe that each person should be fitted individually in terms of sizing and need. Entry blanks for local races are available in the stores.

Skating

BLADES BOARD & SKATE
120 W 72nd St (bet Amsterdam and Columbus Ave)   212/787-3911
659 Broadway (at Bleecker St)   212/477-7350
Manhattan Mall, 901 Ave of the Americas
   (at 33rd St), Level C2   646/733-2738
Mon-Sat: 11-9 (Sun hours vary by store)

Founded in 1990 by Jeff Kabat, Blades Board & Skate has become the largest action-sports retail company in the nation. There are a number of reasons for this: a great selection of equipment for snowboarding, skateboarding, and in-line skating; a good stock of lifestyle apparel; informed service; and a 30-day price guarantee.

Skiing

SCANDINAVIAN SKI AND SPORT SHOP
16 E 55th St (bet Madison and Fifth Ave)   212/757-8524
Mon-Sat: 10-6; (Thurs till 6:30); Sun: 1-5   www.skishop.com

Despite its name, this shop is really an all-around sporting goods store. They stock a full range of goods, from skis and skiwear to bikes and skates. They also offer repairs and advice.

Soccer

SOCCER SPORT SUPPLY
1745 First Ave (bet 90th and 91st St)   212/427-6050, 800/223-1010
Mon-Fri: 10-6; Sat: 10-4   www.homeofsoccer.com

Hermann and Jeff Doss are the proprietors of this 70-year-old soccer and rugby supply company. Half their business involves importing and exporting equipment around the world. Visitors to the store have the advantage of seeing the selection in person, as well as receiving guidance from a staff that knows the field (pardon the pun) completely.

Tennis

MASON'S TENNIS
56 E 53rd St (bet Park and Madison Ave)   212/755-5805
Mon-Fri: 10-7; Sat: 10-6; Sun: 11-6   www.masonstennis.com

Mason's is the only tennis specialty store left in Manhattan. Mark Mason offers a superb collection of clothing by Fila, Polo, Nike, Ralph Lauren, and more. U.S. Open products are carried from May to December. You will also find ball machines, bags, and other tennis paraphernalia. They will match any authorized dealer on racquet prices (Babolat, Wilson, Prince, and Head), and special-order any tennis product. Same-day stringing is offered. A yearly half-price clothing sale (excluding children's wear) takes place in mid-January.

Spy Equipment

SPY TEC
44 W 55th St (bet Fifth Ave and Ave of the Americas), 3rd floor
Mon-Fri: 10-6   212/957-7400
                                                   www.spytecinc.com

These people have the security field well covered. Among their offerings:

video surveillance items, countersurveillance merchandise, network cameras, spy equipment, digital and analog recorders, wireless camera detection and location, metal detectors, and infrared sensors. All are available for residential or corporate installation. Spy Tec's highly trained personnel will discreetly take care of any need.

Stationery

JAM PAPER & ENVELOPE
135 Third Ave (bet 14th and 15th St)   212/473-6666, 800/8010-JAM
Mon-Fri: 8:30-8; Sat, Sun: 10-6   www.jampaper.com

At 7,000 square feet, this outfit has become the largest paper and envelope store in the city and perhaps the world! They stock over 150 kinds of paper, with matching card stock and envelopes. They have a vast selection of presentation folders, plastic portfolios, plastic envelopes and folders, cello sleeves, translucents, bags, tissue, and raffia—all in matching colors. Closeouts and discounted items provide excellent bargains. Ask for their free catalog!

Longtime retailer **Rebecca Moss**, whose specialty is pens, currently has no storefront. However, Moss can still fill orders by phone or online (212/832-7671, 800/INK-PENS, www.rebeccamoss.com). They are scouting locations and hope to reopen.

KATE'S PAPERIE
72 Spring St (bet Crosby and Lafayette St)   212/941-9816
8 W 13th St (at Fifth Ave)   212/633-0570
140 W 57th St (bet Ave of the Americas and Seventh Ave)
                                                          212/459-0700
1282 Third Ave (bet 73rd and 74th St)   212/396-3670
Hours vary by store   www.katespaperie.com

Here you will find one of the largest selections of decorative and exotic papers in the country. Kate's Paperie has thousands of kinds of papers, including papyrus, hand-marbled Italian, Japanese lace, recycled papers from Zimbabwe, and just about anything else you can think of. But that isn't all. There are leatherbound photo albums and journals, classic and exotic stationery, boxes, wax seals, rubber stamps, pens, and desk accessories. They will do custom printing and engraving, personal and business embossing, and custom and corporate gift selection and wrapping.

MRS. JOHN L. STRONG
699 Madison Ave (bet 62nd and 63rd St), 5th floor   212/838-3848
Mon-Fri: 10-5 (by appointment for custom work)

Several barriers must be crossed to reach this high-end stationery establishment in a fifth-floor room. First, a claustrophobic elevator. Then a locked door. When you are buzzed in, the atmosphere is strictly high-altitude, as are the noses of some of the salesladies. Strong sells very high-quality papers, invitations, and announcements—with very high prices to match. If you are looking for the best, this is the place to splurge.

PAPERPRESENTATION.COM
23 W 18th St (bet Fifth Ave and Ave of the Americas) 212/463-7035
Mon-Fri: 9-7; Sat: 11-6; Sun: 11-6   www.paperpresentation.com

Come here for a huge selection of quality paper goods. Business cards, writing paper, invitations, brochures, postcards, envelopes, folders, Oriental laser paper, bags, labels, and more are shown in quantity. Certificate plaques are also available.

PURGATORY PIE PRESS
19 Hudson St (bet Duane and Reade St), Room 403   212/274-8228
Mon-Fri: by appointment   www.purgatorypiepress.com

The people at Purgatory Pie are experts at letterpress printing from hand-set metal and wood type. In addition, they do book production, albums, custom hand bookbinding, yearly datebooks, invitations, coasters, artists' books, and handmade paper with uniquely designed watermarks. Classes are taught in hand-making books and typography.

Papyrus is a chain of upscale paper-goods stores. In all of their outlets you will find an attractive and friendly environment, superior service, custom printing, stationery, gift wrap, gift products, and a great selection of greeting cards.
- 852 Lexington Ave (bet 64th and 65th St), 212/717-0002
- 1270 Third Ave (at 73rd St), 212/717-1060
- Grand Central Terminal, 42nd St at Vanderbilt Ave, 212/490-9894 and 212/682-9359
- 2157 Broadway (bet 75th and 76th St), 212/501-0102
- 1250 Ave of the Americas (at 50th St), Suite 1, 212/265-9003

Tiles

BISAZZA MOSAICO
43 Greene St (bet Broome and Grand St)   212/334-7130
Tues-Sat: 11-7   www.bisazzausa.com

Bisazza Mosaico claims to be the world's leading glass mosaic company, with high design standards and outstanding solutions. They have large stocks of glass mosaic tile, custom mosaics, and tiles for residential, commercial, indoor, and outdoor use. They have been in business for over a half-century and carry recognized quality products.

COMPLETE TILE COLLECTION
42 W 15th St (bet Fifth Ave and Ave of the Americas) 212/255-4450
Mon-Fri: 10-6:30; Sat: 11-6

If you are shopping for quality tiles, come to Complete Tile. They carry American art tiles; glass, ceramic, concrete, metal, slate, granite, and molded tiles; marble and limestone mosaics; and a large assortment of handmade tiles. Design services are available, and the selection (800 varieties of natural stone and 400 colors of ceramic tile) is tops. They fabricate stone countertops, too!

IDEAL TILE
405 E 51st St (at First Ave)   212/759-2339
Mon-Fri: 9-5; Sat: 10-3

Ideal Tile imports ceramics, porcelain, marble, granite, and terra cotta from Italy, Spain, and Brazil. They have absolutely magnificent hand-painted Italian ceramic pottery as well. This outfit guarantees installation of tiles by skilled craftsmen. They also offer marble and granite fabrication for fireplaces, countertops, window sills, and tables.

Tobacco and Accessories

BARCLAY-REX
75 Broad St (bet Beaver and William St)   212/962-3355
70 E 42nd St (bet Madison and Park Ave)   212/692-9680
570 Lexington Ave (at 51st St)   212/888-1015
3 World Financial Center (at Winter Garden)   212/385-4632
Hours vary by store   www.barclayrex.com

Established in 1910, Barclay-Rex is the product of three generations of the Nastri family. They cater to devotees of fine cigars, pipes, tobaccos, and smoking-related gifts and accessories. Their shops are stocked with more than 200 brands of imported and domestic tobaccos. The finest tobaccos from all over the world are hand-blended and packaged under the Barclay-Rex label, and custom blending is one of their specialties. Cigars are housed in walk-in humidors at controlled temperatures. They have one of the city's best selections of pipes. You'll also find a large selection of Borsalino hats in felt, straw, and beaver.

CONNOISSEUR PIPE SHOP
1285 Ave of the Americas (bet 51st and 52nd St), concourse level
Mon-Fri: 10:15-5:30   212/247-6054

Edward Burak has a beautiful collection of hand-carved pipes that range in price from $47 to over $6,000. His store features natural unvarnished pipes, custom-made pipes, custom-blended tobacco, and expert repair. Burak will also do appraisals for insurance purposes. If your pipe came from Connoisseur, you will get admiring glances from those who know quality.

Gentlemen! Tired of searching for a place where cigar smoking is not only allowed but encouraged? At **De La Concha** (1390 Ave of the Americas, 212/757-3167), you can enjoy your stogie, a cup of coffee, and good conversation, too. High-quality imported and domestic cigars, cigarettes, pipes, and tobacco are carried here.

J.R. CIGARS
562 Fifth Ave (at 46th St)   212/997-2227, 800/JRCIGAR
Mon-Fri: 9-7; Sat: 10-5; Sun: 11-4   www.jrcigars.com

For years Lew Rothman of J.R. Cigars has claimed to offer the world's largest selection of cigars and pipe tobacco at the lowest prices. Over 3,000 styles and 300 brands of cigars are stocked. Prices are 20% to 70% off retail.

OK CIGARS
383 West Broadway (bet Spring and Broome St)   212/965-9065
Sun-Wed: 11-9; Thurs: 11-10; Fri, Sat: 11 a.m.-midnight
(call for winter hours)   www.okcigars.com

Looking for a really good cigar? Len Brunson carries some of the best in a pleasant atmosphere. Unique accessories are available, including some of the finest and most peculiar antique tobacciana to be found.

Toys and Children's Items
General

CHILDREN'S GENERAL STORE
Grand Central Terminal (42nd St at Lexington Ave Passage)
Mon-Fri: 8-8; Sat: 10-6; Sun: 11-5   212-682-0004

The emphasis at this toy store is less on space-age wizardry and battery-operated gizmos than on basic, well-made toys designed to encourage creative and imaginative play. The diverse stock is chosen by people who clearly know and love children.

DINOSAUR HILL
306 E 9th St (bet First and Second Ave)   212/473-5850
Daily: 11-7   www.dinosaurhill.com

Dinosaur Hill is a really enchanting toy store that seems to be thriving even as some of its competitors are struggling or have thrown in the towel. Maybe it's because of the diverse and consistently high-quality stock. There are marbles from England; tin windups from China; wooden toys from France, Greece, Italy, Russia, and Spain; and solid wood blocks made in the U.S. In addition, there is handmade clothing in natural-fiber fabrics for infants through four years and a wonderful assortment of games, gadgets, hats, music boxes, monkeys, moons, and mermaids! They also keep a birthday book.

EXOTICAR MODEL CO.
280 Park Ave (at 48th St)   212/573-9537
Mon-Sat: 10-7; Sun: noon-5   www.exoticar.com

For the automobile buff, Exoticar is a must-visit! You'll find all manner of collectibles, apparel, books, magazines, and accessories. Ask to see the Munster Coach, which is worth a visit in itself!

F.A.O. SCHWARZ
767 Fifth Ave (at 58th St)   212/644-9400
Mon-Sat: 10-7; Sun: 11-6   www.fao.com

Shopping here still can be a special experience! In the competitive (and sometimes unprofitable) field of toy retailing, F.A.O. Schwarz's flagship store has had its problems. Following a makeover, shopping has become a bit easier and prices are somewhat more comfortable. You'll find some merchandise that is not readily available elsewhere, and the mere fact that your purchase came from this store makes it special for many youngsters (and adults), too!

GEPPETTO'S TOY BOX
10 Christopher St (bet Ave of the Americas and Seventh Ave)
Mon-Fri: noon-7; Sat: 11-7; Sun: 12:30-5:30 (call for winter hours)
212/620-7511
www.nyctoys.com

The owners of this West Village toy store are clearly consumer-savvy, stocking trendy favorites. Yet the heart of this store is its exceptionally high-quality teddy bears, jack-in-the-boxes, European walk toys, puppet theaters, rocking horses, and other whimsical toys and games. Moreover, it's obviously run with great passion and care. You'll also find a variety of interesting items made by local artists and a small but carefully chosen selection of books. If you're a toy collector, have a child in your life, or simply like a kid's store that's run with class and grace, make a visit to Geppetto's a top priority.

KID O
123 W 10th St (at Ave of the Americas)   212/366-KIDO
Mon-Sat: 11-7; Sun: 12-6   www.kidonyc.com

Lisa Mahar has gathered products that have both a design and educational focus. She believes such items can accelerate children's development. You'll find play objects, kids' furniture, artwork, nursery items, and books. Educational materials include Montessori and Froebel gifts.

KIDDING AROUND
60 W 15th St (bet Fifth Ave and Ave of the Americas)
Mon-Sat: 10-7; Sun: 11-6   212/645-6337
www.kiddingaround.us

This bright, spacious emporium in the heart of Greenwich Village is arguably the city's best toy store. Books, toys, puzzles, balls, games, craft supplies, birthday party favors—you name it, they've got it. In addition to a wide selection of Playmobil, Brio, and Corrole dolls, Kidding Around stocks an amazing assortment of quality wooden toys for riding, building, and just having fun. The clothing section is small but well chosen, and the dress-up clothes are great, too.

MARY ARNOLD TOYS
1010 Lexington Ave (at 72nd St)   212/744-8510
Mon-Fri: 9-6; Sat: 10-5

You won't find any great bargains and likely won't see anything you haven't seen before, but Mary Arnold Toys is a spacious, well-organized, and well-stocked source for the basics. There are separate sections for games, puzzles, books, stuffed animals, craft kits and supplies, Playmobil, videos, and Madame Alexander dolls. The dress-up collection deserves a close look.

ROBOT VILLAGE
252 W 81st St (at Broadway)   212/799-7626
Tues-Fri: noon-7; Sat: 10-6; Sun: 11-5   www.robotvillage.com

Any kid who loves robots will be in heaven at this place. Anything and everything having to do with robots is available: instructions on building them, birthday parties, collectibles, educational kits, books, and more. The head robot is David Greenbaum; you'll get a kick out of meeting him.

SONS & DAUGHTERS
35 Ave A (at 3rd St)　　　　　　　　　　　212/253-7797
Mon-Tues: noon-7; Wed-Sun: 10-7

This is a toy store with a conscience! Instead of the cheap plastic toys made on assembly lines in China, you'll find all sorts of wonderful toys made from recycled cardboard and other sustainable resources by people working in decent conditions for fair wages. A trip down here will prove that you can buy great gifts and feel good about it, too.

TOYS 'R' US
1514 Broadway (at 44th St)　　　　　　　　800/869-7787
Mon-Sat: 10-10; Sun: 11-8　　　　　　　www.toysrus.com

No family trip to Manhattan is complete without a visit to Toys 'R' Us—the toy store to beat all toy stores! Set in the heart of the city, this $32 million marvel features a huge stage set with a giant Animatronic dinosaur and a 60-foot tall ferris wheel in the atrium. Each car is modeled after a different toy. Seemingly every square inch of this busy store is devoted to showing merchandise.

Once among the most famous areas of Manhattan, "Ladies' Mile" is again on the itineraries of wise shoppers. There are some great stores grouped along Avenue of the Americas between 18th and 19th streets:

Bed Bath & Beyond: a wonderful store, with huge selections of bed, bath, and home furnishings at good prices
Filene's Basement: famous for clothing bargains
Old Navy: very "in," especially with the young anti-yuppie set; clothing is fashionable and priced right
T.J. Maxx: values in clothing and accessories for the family

ZITTLES
969 Madison Ave (at 76th St), 3rd floor　　　212/737-2040
Mon-Fri: 9-8; Sat: 9-7; Sun: 10-6　　　　　www.zitomer.com

Housed on the third floor of Zitomer—an amusingly snobby drugstore-cum-department-store on Madison Avenue—Zittles has one of the most extensive selections of toys, games, stuffed animals, dolls, books, software, and videos for children in the city. There are neither bargains nor much imagination shown here, but there is a lot of space, and every inch of it is filled with all the basics and more.

Specialty and Novelty

ALPHABETS
115 Ave A (bet 7th and 8th St)　　　　　　　212/475-7250
47 Greenwich Ave (bet Charles and Perry St)　212/229-2966
Daily: noon-8　　　　　　　　　　　www.alphabetsnyc.com

These crowded spaces are a combination toy store, novelty shop, and stroll down memory lane for baby boomers. If you're looking for a Desi Arnaz wristwatch, a Gumby and Pokey piggy bank, kitschy ceramics, or a

T-shirt with the Velveeta logo on it, this is the place to visit. They also carry offbeat New York souvenirs.

BALLOON CENTER OF NEW YORK
5 Tudor City Pl (bet First and Second Ave)   212/682-0122
Call ahead for hours

The Balloon Center of New York sells balloons individually or in quantities of up to 50,000. There are graduations in diameter, thickness, style, and type (including Mylar balloons). Sizes range from peewees to blimps and extra-long shapes. Balloon clips, ribbon, and imprinting are available, as is helium. Most of this whimsical business is done for advertising campaigns and corporate and special events.

DISNEY STORE
711 Fifth Ave (at 55th St)   212/702-0702
Mon-Sat: 10-8; Sun: 11-6   www.disneystore.com

If the "malling" of New York hasn't gotten you down, this store can be a fun place to shop. Unlike the staff at many of the huge stores that have popped up all over New York, these folks really know their stock and are personable, to boot. If you don't have a Disney Store back home and are looking for kids' luggage emblazoned with Mickey Mouse, backpacks in the shape of Winnie the Pooh, or other Disney-related items, visit this three-floor maze of merchandising.

FORBIDDEN PLANET
840 Broadway (at 13th St)   212/473-1576
Sun-Tues: 10-10; Wed: 9 a.m.-midnight; Thurs-Sat: 10 a.m.-midnight

Mike Luckman's unique shop is a shrine of science-fiction artifacts. Forbidden Planet stocks sci-fi comic books and publications, videos, posters, T-shirts, cards, toys, and games.

IMAGE ANIME
103 W 30th St (at Ave of the Americas)   212/631-0966
Mon-Fri: 11-7; Sat: noon-6   www.imageanime.com

Image Anime specializes in imported Japanese toys and collectibles. If that category interests you—and a great many children and adults are almost fanatically devoted to it—then this packed little store will thrill you. Lines include Gundam, Pokémon, Transformers, Robotech, Anime, and just about every other popular Japanese line.

LOVE SAVES THE DAY
119 Second Ave (at 7th St)   212/228-3802
Daily: noon-8

Even as Starbucks franchises and new condos seem to be taking over every inch of Manhattan, unreconstructed spots like Love Saves the Day continue to thrive in the East Village. The floor-to-ceiling merchandise ranges from vintage clothing and accessories (including really great go-go boots) to *Star Wars* action figures and more Pez dispensers than I've ever seen in one place. If you're nostalgic for the 1940s and 1980s or just want to hang out with some funky folks, you're really going to groove on this place. Oddly enough, there's a branch in New Hope, Pennsylvania, as well.

MANHATTAN DOLLHOUSE
767 Fifth Ave (bet 58th and 59th St)   212/644-9400, ext 3041
Mon-Sat: 10-7; Sun: 11-6

The Manhattan Dollhouse has moved into a historic location—the former FAO Schwarz Building—while dropping at least part of what made it a unique business. I was sorry to learn that they no longer carry or repair dolls. However, they still carry a large selection of dollhouses, miniature furniture, and accessories. If you collect and decorate dollhouses, put this place on your browse list.

RED CABOOSE
23 W 45th St (bet Fifth Ave and Ave of the Americas), basement
Mon-Fri: 11-7; Sat: 11-5   212/575-0155
                                                  www.theredcaboose.com

Owner-operator Allan J. Spitz says that 99% of his customers are not wide-eyed children but sharp-eyed adults who are dead serious about model railroads. The Red Caboose claims to have 100,000 items on hand, including a line of 300 hand-finished, imported brass locomotives. The five basic sizes—1:22, 1:48, 1:87, 1:161, and 1:220, in a ratio of scale to life size—allow model railroaders to build layouts sized to fit everything from a desk drawer to a basement. They carry an extensive line of plastic kits, paints, tools, and model supplies. Red Caboose also carries die-cast airplanes (military and commercial), autos, and military vehicles.

TOY TOKYO
121 Second Ave (bet St. Mark's Pl and 7th St)   212/673-5424
Daily: 1-9   www.toytokyo.com

This store is a great example of why I love New York! Started in 2000, Toy Tokyo sells wonderful Japanese action figures and *Star Wars* collectibles. The stock changes a bit every week, and many items come straight from Hong Kong, Japan, and other points east. If you're a collector or just a curious browser, put this overflowing walkup on your list. You have to see it to believe it!

Travel Items

FLIGHT 001
96 Greenwich Ave (bet Jane and 12th St)   212/989-0001
Mon-Sat: 11-8:30; Sun: noon-6   877/FLIGHT1
                                                www.flight001.com

Traveling these days isn't always fun, but a trip to Flight 001 will make it more bearable. You will find novel and useful travel aids, including cosmetics, bags, guidebooks, stationery, luggage, and more.

Watches

TEMPVS FVGIT AT THE SHOWPLACE
40 W 25th St (bet Ave of the Americas and Broadway)   212/633-6063
Thurs, Fri: 10-5:30; Sat, Sun: 8:30-5 (or by appointment)
                                                www.tempvsfvgit.com

If you're looking for a vintage Rolex, this is the place! They also carry other top brands and watchbands at considerable savings.

YAEGER WATCH
578 Fifth Ave (at 47th St)   212/819-0088
Mon-Fri: 10-5; Sat: 10-3 (closed Sat in summer)
www.yaegerwatch.com

Over 2,000 discounted watches are carried at Yaegar. Choose from name brands retailing from $100 to $150,000. Watch repair and warranties are offered, and prices are quoted over the phone. Yaeger Watch has been owned by the same family since 1970.

Reliable New York watch stores include **Cellini Fine Jewelry** (509 Madison Ave, 212/888-0505), **Kenjo** (40 W 57th St, 212/333-7220), **Tourneau** (500 Madison Ave, 212/758-6098; 12 E 57th St, 212/758-7300; and 200 W 34th St, 212/563-6880), and **Wempe** (700 Fifth Ave, 212/397-9000).

VII. Where to "Extras"

As I research each new edition of this book, I'm always struck by the amount of information that doesn't fit neatly into any of the other chapters. That's why I came up with this chapter of "Extras": where to go dancing, take kids, spend a romantic evening, and host a special event. Those are just four of the more than a dozen subjects this chapter addresses.

ANNUAL EVENTS

While stores, museums, restaurants, and the like are open all year, some special events are held only during certain seasons or once a year. The "For More Information" section at the end of this chapter offers suggestions about how to find out what's happening in New York at any given time. *Time Out New York* is a tremendous source of up-to-date information, as are *New York* magazine and *The New Yorker*.

JANUARY
Polar Bear Club New Year's Dip (Coney Island)
Ice skating (Rockefeller Center, Central Park, and Bryant Park)
Winter Antiques Show (Seventh Regiment Armory)
Chinese New Year (January or February)

FEBRUARY
Westminster Kennel Club Dog Show (Madison Square Garden)
Empire State Run-Up (Empire State Building)
National Antiques Show (Madison Square Garden)
Kids' Night on Broadway
Valentine's Day wedding ceremony (Empire State Building)

MARCH
St. Patrick's Day Parade (Fifth Ave)
International Cat Show (Madison Square Garden)
Spring Armory Antiques Show (Seventh Regiment Armory)
Big East and NIT college basketball tournaments (Madison Square Garden)
New York Flower Show (Pier 92, Twelfth Ave at 52nd St)

Macy's Spring Flower Show
Radio City Easter Show (Radio City Music Hall)

APRIL
International Auto Show (Jacob K. Javits Convention Center)
Baseball season opens (Yankees and Mets)
New York Antiquarian Book Fair (Seventh Regiment Armory)

MAY
International Food Festival (Ninth Ave)
Ukrainian Festival (7th St in the East Village)
Fleet Week (week before Memorial Day)
Lower East Side Jewish Festival
Washington Square Outdoor Art Exhibit

JUNE
Salute to Israel Parade (Fifth Ave)
Free concerts and performances (Central Park and other city parks)
Lower Manhattan Cultural Council's Buskers Fair
Jazz festivals (Bryant Park, Carnegie Hall, and other locations)

JULY
Free concerts and performances (Central Park and other city parks)
Free movies (Bryant Park and other locations)
Fourth of July fireworks (East River and other locations)
American Crafts Festival (Lincoln Center)
Mostly Mozart (Avery Fisher Hall)
Midsummer's Night Swing (Lincoln Center)

AUGUST
Free concerts and performances (Central Park and other city parks)
Free movies (Bryant Park and other locations)
New York City Triathlon
Lincoln Center Out-of-Doors Festival (Lincoln Center)
Festival Latino (Public Theater and other locations)
U.S. Open begins (National Tennis Center)

SEPTEMBER
Autumn Crafts Festival (Lincoln Center)
Football season opens (Giants and Jets)
Third Avenue Festival
Feast of San Gennaro (Little Italy)
New York Film Festival (Lincoln Center)
Broadway Cares/Equity Fights AIDS flea market and auction (Shubert Alley)

OCTOBER
Columbus Day Parade (Fifth Ave)
Basketball season opens (Knicks and Liberty)
Hockey season opens (Rangers and Islanders)
Soho Arts Festival
Fall Antiques Show (Pier 92, Twelfth Ave at 52nd St)
Halloween Parade (Greenwich Village)
New York Marathon (late October or early November)

NOVEMBER
Home Show (Jacob K. Javits Convention Center)
Margaret Meade Film Festival (American Museum of Natural History)
Macy's Thanksgiving Day Parade (Central Park West and Broadway)
Christmas tree lighting (Rockefeller Plaza)

DECEMBER
Christmas windows (Saks Fifth Avenue, Macy's, Lord & Taylor, and other
    locations)
Messiah Sing-In (Avery Fisher Hall)
Radio City Christmas Show (Radio City Music Hall)
Holiday bazaar (Grand Central Terminal)
Menorah lighting (Grand Army Plaza)
Christmas Day walking tour (Big Onion Walking Tours)
New Year's Eve celebrations (Times Square and other locations)
First Night celebrations (Grand Central Terminal, Central Park, and other
    locations)

'Tis the Season

   Some things can only be done in New York if you're in town at the
right time. If you are planning a trip in spring or summer, get tickets to
see a **baseball game** at Yankee Stadium (www.yankees.com) or Shea
Stadium (www.mets.mlb.com). If you're in town during the summer,
find out what's going on in **Central Park** (www.centralparknyc.org).
In the fall, get tickets to the **Metropolitan Opera** (www.metoper-
afamily.org). In the winter, go **ice skating** in Rockefeller Plaza, Central
Park, or Bryant Park. And if you're in town around Christmas, take the
family to see the Christmas Show at **Radio City Music Hall**
(www.radiocity.com). It may be touristy and overpriced, but there's
really nothing like it.

WHERE TO PLAY
Films
   Like any city, New York has a multitude of theaters for first-run movies.
Indeed, most movies debut in New York and Los Angeles before opening
anywhere else. (Depending on the size of the crowds they draw, some never
do open elsewhere.) *The New Yorker, Time Out New York, New York* magazine,
and the *New York Times'* Friday Weekend section and Sunday Arts and Leisure
section are all good places to look for what is playing and where, at any given
time. You can also call 212/777-FILM (3456) for information about what
movies are showing at virtually every theater in Manhattan and to purchase
tickets by credit card at many of those theaters. If you're online, go to
www.moviephone.com or www.newyork.citysearch.com.
   If you're looking for an old movie, a foreign film, an unusual documentary,
a 3D movie, or something out of the ordinary, try calling one of the following theaters. Most numbers connect you with a recording that lists current
movies and times, ticket cost, and directions.
American Museum of Natural History's IMAX Theater (175-
    208 Central Park West, 212/769-5034)

Angelika Film Center and Cafe (18 W Houston St, 212/995-2000)
Anthology Film Archives (32 Second Ave, 212/505-5181)
Asia Society (725 Park Ave, 212/327-9276)
Austrian Cultural Forum (11 E 52nd St, 212/319-5300)
Film Forum (209 W Houston St, 212/727-8110)
Florence Gould Hall at the French Institute (55 E 59th St, 212/355-6160)
Japan Society (333 E 47th St, 212/752-0824)
Lincoln Plaza Cinema (1886 Broadway, 212/757-2280)
Loews Lincoln Square Theater (890 Broadway, 212/336-5000)
Makor (25 W 67th St, 212/601-1000)
Millennium (66 E 4th St, 212/673-0090)
Museum of Television and Radio (25 W 52nd St, 212/621-6800)
Quad Cinema (34 W 13th St, 212/255-8800)
Symphony Space (2537 Broadway, 212/864-5400)
Walter Reade Theater at Lincoln Center (165 W 66th St, 212/875-5600)
Whitney Museum of American Art (945 Madison Ave, 212/570-3676)

Like everything else, the price of movie tickets in New York tends to be higher than elsewhere in the country. The second-run theaters, film societies, and museums usually charge a little less, and Bryant Park, Seward Park, and other parks throughout the city host free movies in the summer. What fun it is to sing "Somewhere Over the Rainbow" with a thousand other people!

Of course, New York is home to dozens of popular film festivals. The best known is the Film Society of Lincoln Center's **New York Film Festival**, held in late September and early October. This annual event showcases 20 films and gets more popular every year. Call the Walter Reade Theater box office at 212/875-5600 for more information. Look in *New York* magazine, *Time Out New York*, *The New Yorker*, or any daily newspaper for information on upcoming films and festivals.

A Day in the Park
For a list of dozens of great public playgrounds in New York, go to www.nycparkgov.org and click "Things to Do," "Activities & Facilities," and "Playgrounds." My personal favorites are the playgrounds outside the Metropolitan Museum of Art in Central Park, by the Hudson River in Battery Park City, and scattered throughout Riverside Park.

Night Life

Whether you want an evening of elegant dining and dancing, rocking and rolling till the wee hours, dropping in on a set of jazz, or catching some stand-up comedy, New York's club scene offers endless choices. For descriptions of places to go and information about who is playing, look under "Night Life" in the front of *The New Yorker* or under specific listings in the back of *New York* magazine and throughout *Time Out New York*. I've listed several popular places in each category to get you started. Most levy a cover charge, many offer at least a light menu, and a very few require reservations and jackets for men. (Don't worry if you don't have one, as they'll have "loaners.") As with so many other things, it is wise to call in advance.

Cabaret Rooms

Bemelmans Bar, Carlyle Hotel (35 E 76th St, 212/744-1600)
Danny's Skylight Room (346 W 46th St, 212/265-8133)
Don't Tell Mama (343 W 46th St, 212/757-0788)
Feinstein's at the Regency, Regency Hotel (540 Park Ave, 212/339-4095)
Oak Room, Algonquin Hotel (59 W 44th St, 888/304-2047)

Comedy Clubs

Caroline's on Broadway (1626 Broadway, 212/757-4100)
Comedy Cellar (117 MacDougal St, 212/254-3480)
Comix (353 W 14th St, 212/524-2500)
Dangerfield's (1118 First Ave, 212/593-1650)
Gotham Comedy Club (208 W 23rd St, 212/367-9000)
Stand-Up New York (236 W 78th St, 212/595-0850)

Adopt-a-Bench

Central Park has almost 9,000 benches, and roughly a quarter of them have been "adopted." For $7,500, all of which goes to the Central Park Conservancy, anyone can have a brief message inscribed on a bench.

"To the world, you were one person," reads one dedicated to a victim of the terrorist attacks of September 11, 2001. "To me, you were the world."

Dancing

China Club (268 W 47th St, 212/398-3800): live music and DJs on weekends
Rainbow Room (30 Rockefeller Plaza, 65th floor, 212/632-5100)
SOB (204 Varick St, 212/243-4940): Latin and Caribbean rhythms
Supper Club (240 W 47th St, 212/921-1940): weekend ballroom dinner dances

Gay and Lesbian Clubs

Boiler Room (86 E 4th St, 212/254-7536): gay
g Lounge (225 W 19th St, 212/929-1085): gay
Henrietta Hudson (438 Hudson St, 212/924-3347): lesbian
Rubyfruit Bar and Grill (531 Hudson St, 212/929-3343): lesbian
Stonewall (53 Christopher St, 202/463-0950): historic, mostly gay

Jazz Clubs

Bill's Place (148 W 133rd St, 212/281-0777)
Birdland (315 W 44th St, 212/581-3080)
Blue Note (131 W 3rd St, 212/475-0049)
Iridium (1650 Broadway, 212/582-2121)
Jazz Standard (116 E 27th St, 212/576-2232)

Showman's Cafe (375 W 125th St, 212/864-8941)
Smoke (2751 Broadway, 212/864-6662)
Village Vanguard (178 Seventh Ave S, 212/255-4037)

Rock and Folk Clubs

Baggot Inn (82 W 3rd St, 212/477-0622): great place to discover unknowns
Bitter End (147 Bleecker St, 212/673-7030): one of the original Greenwich Village folk clubs, now with rock and blues as well
Bowery Ballroom (6 Delancey St, 212/533-2111): the city's premier rock showcase
Knitting Factory (74 Leonard St, 212/219-3132): books edgy and avant-garde acts, many very famous

---

Jazz at Lincoln Center

Well, it isn't actually at Lincoln Center anymore. **Jazz at Lincoln Center** has relocated just down the street in the Time Warner Center at Columbus Circle. Jazz trumpeter Wynton Marsalis and his orchestra are featured regularly. Look for **Dizzy's Club Coca-Cola** (212/258-9800 or www.jalc.org), too.

"Let's Have a Drink"

Aquavit (65 W 55th St, 212/307-7311)
Campbell Apartment (Grand Central Terminal, 42nd St at Vanderbilt Ave, 212/953-0409)
57, Four Seasons Hotel New York (57 E 57th St, 212/758-5757)
Grand Bar, Soho Grand Hotel (310 West Broadway, 212/965-3000)
21 Club (21 W 52nd St, 212/582-7200)
Villard Bar and Lounge, New York Palace Hotel (24 E 51st St, 212/888-7000)

Music in the Museums

Brooklyn Museum (200 Eastern Parkway, Brooklyn, 718/638-5000): free music and entertainment on the first Saturday evening of every month between 5 and 11
The Cloisters (Fort Tryon Park, 212/923-3700): frequent concerts
Frick Collection (1 E 70th St, 212/288-8700): chamber music some Sundays at 5; tickets are $25 each
Guggenheim Museum (1071 Fifth Ave, 212/423-3500): live jazz on Friday and Saturday evening in the warmer months
Metropolitan Museum of Art (Fifth Ave bet 80th and 84th St, 212/535-7710): classical music on Friday and Saturday from 4 to 8:30 in the Balcony Bar
Morgan Library and Museum (225 Madison Ave, 212/685-0008: lots of concerts, mostly classical; tickets required
Rose Center for Earth and Space (81st bet Columbus Ave and Central Park West, 212/769-5100): "Starry Nights" jazz on first Friday of every month; free with admission to museum

Recreation

Visitors sometimes see Manhattan as nothing but concrete and can't imagine what those who live here do for exercise other than walking. The people who live here, however, know that you can do just about anything in New York that can be done anywhere else—and then some! Whether it's batting cages, tennis courts, riding stables, or a driving range, chances are that New York has it if you just know where to look.

Baseball
Baseball Center NYC (202 W 74th St, 212/362-0344)
Field House at Chelsea Piers (23rd St at Hudson River, 212/336-6500)

Basketball
BasketBall City (Pier 63, 23rd St at Hudson River, 212/924-4040)
Field House at Chelsea Piers (23rd St at Hudson River, 212/336-6500)

For Young Athletes
If you have a child who wants to climb a wall, take batting practice, or kick a soccer ball, then go to the **Field House at Chelsea Piers**. Located on the far west side of Manhattan between 17th and 23rd streets, this remarkable complex has it all. Call 212/336-6500 or go to www.chelseapiers.com for more information.

Billiards
Billiard Club (344 Amsterdam Ave, 212/496-8180)
Slate Billiards (54 W 21st St, 212/989-0096)

Bowling
300 New York (Chelsea Piers, 23rd St at Hudson River, 212/835-2695)
Bowlmor Lanes (110 University Pl, 212/255-8188)
Leisure Time Bowl (Port Authority Bus Terminal, 40th Street at Eighth Ave, 212/268-6909)

Chess, Checkers, and Backgammon
Bryant Park (42nd St bet Fifth Ave and Ave of the Americas, 212/869-6057)
Chess Shop (230 Thompson St, 212/475-9580)
Washington Square Park (foot of Fifth Ave, below 8th St)

Climbing
Extra Vertical Climbing Center (61 W 62nd St, 212/586-5718)
Field House at Chelsea Piers (23rd St at Hudson River, 212/336-6500)
North Meadow Recreation Center (Central Park at 97th St, 212/348-4867)

Golf
Golf Club at Chelsea Piers (Pier 59, 23rd St at Hudson River, 212/336-6400)
Split Rock (public course in The Bronx, 718/885-1258)

Horseback Riding
Claremont Stables (175 W 89th St, 212/724-5100)

Ice Skating
Lasker Rink (Central Park at E 107th St, 917/492-3856)
The Pond at Bryant Park (Ave of the Americas at 42nd St, 866/221-5157)
Rockefeller Plaza (Fifth Ave bet 49th and 50th St, 212/632-3975)
Sky Rink at Chelsea Piers (Pier 61, 23rd St at Hudson River, 212/336-6100)
Wollman Rink (Central Park at E 63rd St, 212/439-6900)

Roller Skating
Chelsea Piers Roller Rink (23rd St at Hudson River, 212/336-6100)

Soccer
Field House at Chelsea Piers (23rd St at Hudson River, 212/336-6500)

What a Deal!

For $75 a year (just $10 for senior citizens over 55 and free for children under 18), you can join the city's wonderful recreation centers, use their indoor pools and excellent facilities, and sign up for all sorts of classes. Go to www.nycgovparks.org and then click on "Things to Do" and "Recreation Centers" for detailed descriptions of each center and its offerings.

Swimming
All-Star Fitness Center (75 West End Ave, 212/265-8200)
Asphalt Green (1750 York Ave, 212/369-8890)
Carmine Street Recreation Center (1 Clarkson St, 212/242-5418)
Vanderbilt YMCA (224 E 47th St, 212/756-9600)

Tennis
Columbus Avenue Tennis Club (795 Columbus Ave, 212/662-8367)
Sutton East Tennis Center (488 E 60th St, 212/751-3453)
Midtown Tennis Club (341 Eighth Ave, 212/989-8572)
Tennis Club at Grand Central (Grand Central Terminal, 42nd St at Vanderbilt Ave, 212/687-3841)
USTA National Tennis Center (Forest Hills, Queens, 718/760-6200)

Spectator Sports

Some people associate New York with fine food and expensive stores, while others link the city with the Yankees, the Mets, the Knicks, the Rangers, and other professional sports teams. The New York area is home to more than half a dozen professional sports teams—although only basketball's Knicks and Liberty and hockey's Rangers actually play in Manhattan. (Home field for the city's two pro football teams, the Jets and the Giants, is across the river in New Jersey).

If you want tickets to a professional sporting event, plan as far in advance as possible. Diagrams of all the area's sports stadiums appear near the front of the Manhattan Yellow Pages, and each team's website has detailed information about schedules, tickets, and how to get there.

A word of warning: New York sports fans are like no others. They are loud, rude, and typically very knowledgeable about their teams and sports in general. If you're cheering against the home team, keep your voice down—and your head, too!

Baseball
New York Mets (Shea Stadium, Queens, www.mets.com)
New York Yankees (Yankee Stadium, The Bronx, www.yankees.com)

Basketball
New York Knicks (Madison Square Garden, www.nba.com/knicks)
New York Liberty (Madison Square Garden, www.wnba.com/liberty)

Football
New York Giants (The Meadowlands, East Rutherford, New Jersey, www.giants.com)
New York Jets (The Meadowlands, East Rutherford, New Jersey, www.jets.com)

Hockey
New York Rangers (Madison Square Garden, www.newyorkrangers.com)

The **U.S. Open** returns to the Billie Jean King National Tennis Center in Flushing, Queens at the end of every summer. One of four Grand Slam tournaments in professional tennis, the U.S. Open draws tennis fans from around the world. The finals are held over Labor Day weekend. If you're interested in learning more about the National Tennis Center or getting tickets for the U.S. Open, go to www.usta.com.

WHERE TO GO
For Great Views and Photo Ops

Of course there are thousands of great views and photo opportunities in every part of New York. If you're a photographer or you just want a memorable "only in New York" photo for your album, then here are some of my favorite views and backdrops:

LOVE block (Ave of the Americas at 55th St)
Prometheus Statue (Rockefeller Plaza, west of Fifth Ave between 50th and 51st St)
Patience and Fortitude (lion statues in front of New York Public Library at Fifth Ave and 42nd St)
Statue of Liberty (off Battery Park in New York Harbor)
Wall Street bull (Broadway at Bowling Green)
Washington Arch (Washington Square Park, Greenwich Village)
Battery Park Esplanade
Roosevelt Island (anywhere on the west side, particularly Lighthouse Park)

New York Harbor (particularly from the Staten Island Ferry)
Central Park rock outcrops (just inside the park's southwest corner)
The Cloisters (Fort Tryon Park)
Morris-Jumel Mansion's grounds (65 Jumel Terrace, in Harlem Heights)
Brooklyn Bridge (anywhere along its length)

In the Middle of the Night

New York bills itself as "the city that never sleeps," and many who live here are night people. They include not only actors and artists, but also those who clean and maintain the huge office buildings, work for answering services, put together morning newspapers and newscasts, work the night shift at hospitals and other businesses that never close, and secretaries, transcribers, and editors who must make sure paperwork is ready overnight.

In general, stores and restaurants in Soho, Tribeca, and Greenwich Village stay open later than those in the rest of the city. The restaurants and mom-and-pop operations along Broadway on the Upper West Side and on Lexington and Third avenues on the Upper East Side also tend to keep late hours. As with everything else, call before setting out to make sure they are still keeping late hours.

Up Late and Looking for Something to Do?
  Barnes & Noble (2289 Broadway, 212/362-8835 and other locations)
    Bowlmor Lanes (110 University Pl, 212/255-8188)
    Cafeteria (119 Seventh Ave, 212/414-1717)
    Chess Shop (230 Thompson St, 212/475-9580)
    Crunch Fitness (404 Lafayette St, 212/614-0120)
    Slate Billiards (54 W 21st St, 212/989-0096)

Need Help in the Middle of the Night?
  Animal Medical Center (212/838-8100)
  Doctors on Call (212/737-2333)
  Moonlight Courier (212/473-2246)

Where to Go with the Kids

When I first began writing this book, I did so from the perspective of an adult who comes to New York without children. I quickly learned that many people bring kids to New York, whether they're coming for business or pleasure. That's more true now than ever before. The number of kids living in New York has also increased dramatically over the years. Restaurants, hotels, museums, theaters, and other tourist venues have noted this trend and adjusted their offerings to this growing audience. Always ask about special deals and events for children and families.

Remember that New York can be totally overwhelming for children. (The same is true for adults!) Don't push too hard and retreat to quiet spaces from time to time. Remember, too, that New York can be a wonderland for all ages, if you know where to go. The "Kids" pages in the back of New

York magazine and *Time Out New York* are great places to look for children's events and activities. Look inside toy stores and bookstores for seasonal calendars, and get hold of *Big Apple Parent* or one of the other free parenting magazines published in New York. A couple of good websites for families and children in New York are:

- www.gocitykids.com
- www.parentsknow.com
- www.newyorkkids.net
- www.ny.com/kids

I've listed some suggestions for things to do with kids in several categories: entertainment, museums, and sights; restaurants; and toy and bookstores. In many cases, these places are described in detail in other parts of this book. Of course, children's interests can vary dramatically, so I've inevitably included places that one child will love and another might find boring. I'll let you be the judge of that! I also recommend looking under Children's Books, Children's Clothing Stores, and Toy Stores in Chapter III.

> If you have your heart set on **ice skating** at Rockefeller Center, I suggest going on a weekday morning. There's no wait and relatively few people will be watching in case you hit the ice!

Entertainment, Museums, and Sights

Busy Little Ones

Bryant Park Carousel (Ave of the Americas at 42nd St)
Central Park Carousel (behind The Arsenal in Central Park at E 64th St)
Central Park Zoo (behind The Arsenal in Central Park at E 64th St, 212/439-6500)
Children's Museum of the Arts (182 Lafayette St, 212/941-9198)
Donnell Library Children's Center (20 W 53rd St, 212/621-0636)
Helmbold Family Children's Learning Center (Scandinavia House, 58 Park Ave, 212/879-9779)
92nd Street Y (Parenting Center, 1395 Lexington Ave, 212/427-6000)
Little Sports (10 E 38th St, 212/576-1018)
Playspace at the Cathedral (Cathedral Church of St. John the Divine, 1047 Amsterdam Ave, 212/316-7530)

Museums with a Family Focus

American Museum of Natural History (Central Park West bet 77th and 81st St, 212/769-5100)
Children's Museum of Manhattan (212 W 83rd St, 212/721-1234)
Dyckman Farmhouse Museum (4881 Broadway, 212/304-9422)
Fraunces Tavern Museum (54 Pearl St, 212/425-1778)
Liberty Science Center (Liberty State Park, Jersey City, NJ, 201/200-1000)
Lower East Side Tenement Museum (90 Orchard St, 212/431-0233)
Madame Toussaud's (234 W 42nd St, 212/512-9600)
Museum of the City of New York (1220 Fifth Ave, 212/534-1672)

New York City Fire Museum (278 Spring St, 212/691-1303)
New York City Police Museum (100 Old Slip, 212/480-3100)
Sony Wonder Technology Lab (550 Madison Ave, 212/833-8100)
South Street Seaport Museum (east end of Fulton St, 212/732-7678)

For Tweens and Teens

Dylan's Candy Bar (1011 Third Ave, 646/735-0078)
Field House at Chelsea Piers (23rd St at Hudson River, 212/336-6500)
Leisure Time Bowl (Port Authority Bus Terminal, 40th St at Eighth Ave, 212/268-6909)
Madame Toussaud's (234 W 42nd St, 212/719-9440)
Museum of Television and Radio (25 W 52nd St, 212/621-6800)
Scene on TV Tours (www.sceneontv.com)
Shark Speedboat Harbor Ride (South Street Seaport, 866/925-4631, www.circlelinedowntown.com)
Sony Wonder Technology Lab (500 Madison Ave, 212/833-8100)

New York Classics

Bronx Zoo (The Bronx, 718/367-1010)
Ellis Island (New York Harbor, 212/363-7620)
Empire State Building (Fifth Ave bet 33rd and 34th St, 212/736-3100)
New York Hall of Science (4701 111th St, Queens, 718/699-0005)
Statue of Liberty (New York Harbor, 212/363-3200)
United Nations (First Ave bet 45th and 46th St, 212/963-7713)
Yankee Stadium (The Bronx, 212/307-1212)

> Do you want to hear Woody Allen (yes, *that* Woody Allen) tooting the clarinet in a Dixieland jazz band? He plays most Monday nights at **Cafe Carlyle**, in the Carlyle Hotel (35 E 76th St, 212/570-7189), but call ahead to be sure.

Plays, Movies, and TV

IMAX Theater (American Museum of Natural History, Central Park West bet 77th and 81st St, 212/769-5034)
Kaye Playhouse (Hunter College, 68th St at Lexington Ave, 212/772-4448)
Museum of Television and Radio (25 W 52nd St, 212/621-6600)
NBC Experience Studio Tour (50th St bet Fifth Ave and Ave of the Americas, 212/664-7174)
New Amsterdam Theater/*The Lion King* (214 W 42nd St, 212/282-2900)

Boats and Other Transportation

Circle Line Sightseeing Tours (Pier 83, 43rd St at Hudson River, 212/563-3200)
New York Transit Museum (Boerum Pl at Schermerhorn St, Brooklyn, 718/243-3060)
Roosevelt Island Tram (Second Ave bet 59th and 60th St)

Staten Island Ferry (Whitehall Terminal, south end of Manhattan)

Restaurants

Good for Grownups, Too

Shake Shack (Madison Square Park, Madison Ave at 23rd St)
Tavern on the Green (Central Park West at 67th St, 212/873-3200)
Union Square Cafe (215 E 16th St, 212/243-4020)

Great Basics

EJ's Luncheonette (447 Amsterdam Ave, 212/873-3444 and other locations)
Jackson Hole Burgers (232 E 64th St, 212/371-7187 and other locations)
John's Pizzeria (278 Bleecker St, 212/243-1680 and other locations)
Lombardi's (32 Spring St, 212/941-7994)
Two Boots Pizza (37 Ave A, 212/505-2276 and other locations)

Comfort Station

New York's Parks Department has placed more than 600 "comfort stations" inside its parks. While many languish in disrepair, several dozen have been significantly improved, thanks in part to revenue from selling advertising space in some of them. By far the nicest is in Bryant Park, behind the main branch of the New York Public Library.

Great Desserts

Blue Smoke (116 E 27th St, 212/447-7733)
Bubby's (120 Hudson St, 212/219-0666)
Cafe Lalo (201 W 83rd St, 212/496-6031)
Peanut Butter & Co. (240 Sullivan St, 212/677-3995)
Piece of Cake (1370 Lexington Ave, 212/987-1700)
Serendipity 3 (225 E 60th St, 212/838-3531)

Theme Restaurants

Barking Dog Luncheonette (1678 Third Ave, 212/831-1800 and other locations)
Brooklyn Diner USA (212 W 57th St, 212/977-1957)
ESPN Zone (1472 Broadway, 212/921-3776)
Hard Rock Cafe (1501 Broadway, 212/489-6565)
Jekyll & Hyde (1409 Ave of the Americas, 212/541-9505 and other locations)

Toy Stores and Bookstores

Bookstores

Bank Street Bookstore (2875 Broadway, 212/678-1654)
Books of Wonder (16 W 18th St, 212/989-3270)
Scholastic Store (557 Broadway, 212/343-6166)

Toy Stores

E.A.T. Gifts (1062 Madison Ave, 212/861-2544)

F.A.O. Schwarz (767 Fifth Ave, 212/644-9400)
Kid O (123 W 10th St, 212/366-KIDO)
Kidding Around (60 W 15th St, 212/645-6337)
Toys "R" Us (Times Square, 514 Broadway, 800/869-7787)
West Side Kids (498 Amsterdam Ave, 212/496-7282)

Want to Rent a Bike?

New York's parks are full of bike paths, including a 6.2-mile loop in Central Park and a 5.5-mile route that runs along the Hudson River down to Battery Park. Go to www.transalt.org/info/bikeshop.html for an extensive list of shops throughout the city that rent bikes. This website belongs to **Transportation Alternatives**, a terrific advocacy group that supplies extensive maps and useful information to bicyclists, pedestrians, and mass-transit riders.

Just as some things are fun to do with kids, there are others that you should *not* do with them. A few museums—such as the Frick Collection and the Neue Galerie—are not places to bring small children. Indeed, children under 16 are not allowed on the tour of the Federal Reserve Bank, children under 12 are not welcome at the Neue Galerie, and children under 10 are not allowed in the Frick. Children under 6 can't go on the NBC Studio Tour, and those under 5 are not welcome on the tour of the United Nations. If you're going shopping at a perpetually crowded place like Zabar's or Fairway, don't take kids or keep a firm grip on their hands if you do. The latter holds true just about everywhere in New York—it's easy for a young one to get lost in a crowd! And remember that kids tire more quickly than adults. Chances are you'll do a lot of walking, and they're taking two or three steps for every one of yours! As the *New York Times* once put it, "Baby miles are like dog years."

Finally, be forewarned that it's a real challenge to tote an infant or toddler in New York. While hundreds of thousands of children are born and raised in the city, visitors who are accustomed to carting their children through malls in strollers and around town in car seats may have trouble here. Many places, including the subway system, are not exactly stroller-accessible, and the United Nations, the Forbes Magazine Galleries, the Metropolitan Museum of Art (on Sundays), and the Museum of Jewish Heritage ban them altogether. (However, the Museum of Jewish Heritage offers free backpacks and Snugglies during your visit.) Taxis with functioning seatbelts have become much easier to find in recent years, but ones with car seats are a rarity. Only a few public restrooms have changing tables, and I've yet to hear of a store that has followed the Nordstrom chain's example and set aside space for nursing mothers. The good news is that up to three children under 44 inches tall ride free with a fare-paying adult on buses and subways.

For Free

There's no way to get around it: New York is expensive. Even the most frugal and resourceful visitors often feel as if they're bleeding money. ("Didn't we just get $200 out of the cash machine!?") Still, you can find some good deals and do a lot of sightseeing for free. Look in *Time Out New York*'s tremendous weekly listings of events for boxes noting free ones. You can also go to www.nycvisit.com and click "Visitors," "Things to Do," and "NYC for Free."

Two Ways to Save

If you're planning to visit certain prime tourist spots in New York and want to save a little money, consider getting a **New York Pass**. You can buy passes for one, two, three, or seven days that allow free or reduced admission to dozens of museums and tours, including the American Museum of Natural History, the NBC Studio Experience Tour, and Madame Tussaud's Wax Museum. It also gives you discounts at restaurants and stores. Prices start at $65 for adults and $45 for children between 2 and 12, although I would say the three- and seven-day passes are a better deal if you're really planning to visit a lot of spots on the list. Call 877/714-1999 or go to www.newyorkpass.com for more information. Another money-saving option is the **CityPass**. Good for nine days, it covers admission at five very popular spots, including the American Museum of Natural History, the Museum of Modern Art, and the Empire State Building. It costs $53 for adults and $44 for children. Go to www.citypass.com for more information.

Museums and Sights

The Museum of Modern Art broke through the $20 ceiling for admission to museums a couple years ago, and now other museums are following suit. Still, you can find some free museums and sights in New York. They include:

Cathedral Church of St. John the Divine
Drawing Center
Federal Hall National Memorial
Forbes Magazine Galleries
General Grant National Monument
Museum at FIT
National Museum of the American Indian
New York Public Library
Sony Wonder Technology Lab
Tibet House
Transit Museum Gallery (Grand Central Terminal)
Trinity Church
Whitney Gallery and Sculpture Court at Altria

It used to be that all the museums along Museum Mile on Fifth Avenue offered free admission one night a week. Unfortunately, that tradition lives on only one night a year, in late June. Still, some museums do offer pay-as-you-wish admission on certain evenings. They include:

Brooklyn Museum: Friday from 5 to 11
China Institute: Tuesday and Thursday from 6 to 8
Guggenheim Museum: Friday from 6 to 8
International Center of Photography: Friday from 5:45 to 7:45

Jewish Museum: Thursday from 5 to 8
Morgan Library and Museum: Friday from 7 to 9
Mr. Morgan's Library and Study: Tuesday from 3 to 5 and Sunday from 4 to 6
Museum of Arts and Design: Thursday from 6 to 8
Museum of Modern Art: Friday from 4 to 8
New Museum of Contemporary Art: Thursday from 6 to 8
Studio Museum: first Saturday of every month
Whitney Museum of American Art: Friday from 6 to 9

Many places admit children under 12 for free. Active duty military personnel in uniform are admitted free to the Empire State Building, and Smithsonian Associates are admitted free to the Cooper-Hewitt. Although it definitely isn't free, you can tour both The Cloisters and the Metropolitan Museum of Art on the same day for one admission price. You can also get a discount on admission to the Jewish Museum if you show a ticket stub from the Museum of Jewish Heritage (and vice versa).

Note: If you're interested in visiting any of the places listed here, you will find addresses, phone numbers, and more information in Chapter III.

I'm often asked about reliable ticket brokers. For over 80 years **Americana Tickets** (800/833-3121, 212/581-6660, www.americana tickets.com) has been cited over and over for outstanding service. The third generation of the Radler family are outstanding people to deal with! Just a few of the advantages: premium seating for theater, entertainment, concert, and sporting events in New York and worldwide; expert, professional agents; unique cancellation and exchange privileges; special offers for individuals and groups; conveniently located ticket desk in the Marriott Marquis; great hours (8 a.m. to 8 p.m., seven days a week); and complimentary hotel, restaurant, limousine, and sightseeing reservations.

You can rely on **Surftix.com** (877-SURFTIX, www.surftix.com) for all of your worldwide entertainment needs. They have sold over 16 million tickets and offer more than 10,000 events worldwide at any given time. When backed by such a successful business as Americana Tickets, they've got to be good.

For Tickets

Nowhere else in the world will you find such a wealth of performing arts. And no trip to New York is complete without taking in at least one play, musical, ballet, concert, or opera.

The trick, of course, is getting tickets. People have written entire books about how and where to get tickets, and others have made lucrative careers out of procuring them for out-of-towners. I've provided a variety of approaches for getting theater tickets and to find out about other performances. Keep your eye out for student and other discounts, but be aware that good deals for the best shows and performances are few and far between.

> ## Hot Deals
>
> Every theater does things differently, so you really need to get accurate, up-to-date information if you want to get hot tickets at a lower price. Some theaters have **lotteries** a couple of hours before each performance for seats in the first few rows. Some have **Standing Room Only** (SRO) tickets available. Some give discount tickets only to students, while others have so-called **rush** tickets available for certain performances. To make sense of it all, go to www.talkingbroad way.com and click "On the Boards/Rush & SRO." Be sure to bring along lots of patience and enough cash to cover the cost of whatever tickets you end up buying.

BROADWAY

People often have different things in mind when they say they want to see a show. Some may have their hearts set on great seats at a Saturday night performance of the hottest show on Broadway, while others are willing to sit anywhere to see anything. A lot of people fall somewhere between those extremes. In addition, some are willing to pay whatever it takes to see the show they want, while others just won't go if they can't pay less than full price. If the main purpose of your visit to the city is to see a particular show (or shows), make sure you have the tickets you want before leaving home so you're not disappointed.

Look in the Sunday Arts and Leisure section or the Friday Weekend section of the *New York Times*, the front pages of *The New Yorker*, the Theater section of *Time Out New York*, or the back pages of *New York* magazine to find out where the play or musical you want to see is being performed. The front section of the Manhattan Yellow Pages has a list of Broadway and off-Broadway theaters and a map of the Theater District. **The Broadway Line** (888/276-2392 or 212/302-4111) tells what is playing and where, and also gives quick plot summaries.

> ## Bring the Kids!
>
> It used to be that everyone dressed up for the theater and nobody would think of bringing a young child. Disney's *The Lion King* changed all that, and now the pre-teen set is often seen in almost every Broadway theater. Some even supply booster seats! One word from this adult: please try to choose productions your child will like and leave promptly if your little one behaves disruptively. I know you paid a lot for that ticket, but so did the rest of us!

Box Offices and Phone Orders—If you want to save money and pick your seat, go directly to the theater's box office with cash or a major credit card. Ask to see a diagram of the theater if it isn't posted, although most theaters are small enough to ensure that every seat has a good view. The best time to try is midweek. You can also ask the box office if it releases day-of-performance cancellations or rush tickets (see "Hot Deals" box, above).

If you're willing to spend a little extra and let a computer pick what is in theory the "best available" seat, call the number or go to the website listed and have your credit card ready. Most numbers will be for **Telecharge** (212/239-6200, www.telecharge.com) or **TicketMaster's Broadway Performance Line** (212/307-4100, www.ticketmaster.com). Both services charge a handling fee in addition to the ticket price.

Be forewarned: full-price tickets to Broadway shows typically cost $50 and sometimes fetch well over $100. Moreover, if the play or musical you want to see is really hot, it may be sold out the entire time you're in New York. In fact, a few really hot ones may be sold out months in advance.

What Are Those Unique Flags Flying Over New York?

The presence of the United Nations means that flags of many countries fly in New York. However, two flags flown over the city can't be found in any world atlas. The white one with the green maple leaf is the New York City Parks and Recreation Department's flag, while the blue, white, and orange one is the official flag of New York City.

CareTix—If you have your heart set on a particular show and cost is no obstacle, Broadway Cares/Equity Fights AIDS sells house seats for sold-out Broadway and off-Broadway shows for twice the box-office price. The extra money goes to a good cause and is a tax-deductible contribution. Call 212/840-0770 and ask for CareTix.

TKTS Outlets—If you want to see a Broadway show, are flexible, and have some free time, go to one of the TKTS outlets in Manhattan. Operated by the Theater Development Fund, these outlets sell whatever tickets happen to be left for various shows on the day of performance for half price or less (plus a $3 per-ticket charge). The most popular TKTS outlet is temporarily located at the Marriott Marquis Hotel (46th St between Broadway and Seventh Ave) while a new building is constructed on Duffy Square (47th St at Broadway). It's open from 3 to 8 Monday through Saturday (but not for evening tickets at these times), from 11 to 3 for Sunday matinees, and from 3 until half an hour before the latest curtain time of a ticket being sold that day. A less crowded TKTS outlet is at the intersection of Front and John streets, just below South Street Seaport's main plaza. It's open Monday through Friday from 11 to 6, Saturday from 11 to 7, and Sunday in summer months from 11 to 6. Matinee tickets at this location go on sale only the day *before* a performance. The problem with the TKTS outlets is that you won't know until you get there what is available. A list of shows available is posted at each outlet, and chances are that the hottest tickets won't be among them. You can go to the Theater Development Fund's website (www.tdf.org) to see which tickets were available *last* week. You must pay with cash or travelers' checks at both locations.

The Theater Development Fund also offers extremely good deals to its members on tickets to theater and other performances. If you're a student, member of the clergy or armed forces (serving or retired), teacher, union member, or performing artist, go to the Fund's website (www.tdf.org) for more information. All Broadway theaters offer a small number of deeply discounted tickets to people in wheelchairs and their companion or attendant. Call the theater box office directly for more information.

Hi Art!

Cyndie Bellen-Berthezene offers young children—even very young ones—and their families innovative exposure to art, dance, and music through museum and gallery visits, studio workshops, and classes. For more information, call 212/362-8190 or go to www.hiartkids.com.

Off-Broadway and off-off-Broadway—In part because staging a Broadway production has become almost prohibitively expensive, off-Broadway and off-off-Broadway theaters have really taken *off*. Thanks to a glut of talented actors and actresses in New York, such theater is typically excellent and often innovative. The front section of the Manhattan Yellow Pages lists off-Broadway theaters. Descriptions of what's playing off-Broadway and off-off-Broadway are published every Sunday in the *New York Times* Arts and Leisure section, in the back of *New York* magazine, and in *Time Out New York*. Tickets for off-Broadway and off-off-Broadway productions tend to be significantly less expensive. TKTS outlets sometimes offer discounts, and "twofers"—two tickets for the price of one—may be available.

Some theater productions close almost as soon as they open and others run for only a couple months. But **Tony 'n' Tina's Wedding** has been going on since 1987. It's theater with a twist: you follow the couple from their wedding (St. Luke's Church, 308 W 48th St) to the reception (Edison Hotel, 221 W 46th St), complete with a pasta dinner, champagne, and wedding cake. Intrigued? Call 212/352-3101 or go to www.tonylovestina.com for more information.

OPERA AND CLASSICAL MUSIC

No other city in the world has as much music to choose from as New York! *Time Out New York* has an excellent listing of classical and opera performances, including locations, times, and ticket prices. Many New York-related websites, including several listed in the "For More Information" section of this chapter, have comprehensive listings as well. Contact the **92nd Street Y** (212/996-1100, www.92y.org) if you're interested in chamber music or recitals by top performers. Otherwise, here's how to find schedule and ticket information at New York's top venues:

Carnegie Hall—Individual musicians, out-of-town orchestras, and chamber music ensembles perform at Carnegie Hall all year. Visit the box office at 57th Street and Seventh Avenue between 11 and 6 (noon to 6 on Sunday). For detailed information about performances, go to www.carnegie hall.org. For information about rush tickets and same-day student and senior discounts, call 212/247-7800. A limited number of partial-view seats are available for $10 at noon on the day of each performance.

Metropolitan Opera—The internationally renowned Met's season runs from fall through spring, and ticket sales are broken into three periods. Try the Met's box office (212/362-6000, www.metopera.org) at Lincoln Center between 10 and 6 (noon to 6 on Sunday). Be aware that choice seats can cost as much as $300! If you have a little time on your hands, there are bargains to be had. Two hundred orchestra seats are sold for $20 each two hours before curtain time for performances during the week. Full-time students under 30 with identification can buy tickets for $25 ($35 for Friday and Saturday performances) at 10 a.m. on the day of a performance. Standing Room Only ("SRO") tickets are also often available. All reduced-price tickets must be paid for in cash, and no more than two can be purchased at a time.

Take My Money . . . Please!

American Girl Place (609 Fifth Ave, at 49th St) is a restaurant, theater, store, and giant credit-card bill all wrapped up into one. A relative newcomer, you'll know it by the line of dressed-up little girls coming and going. If you're familiar with the American Girl Doll phenomenon, I need explain no more. If you're not, you don't want to know! A whole-day dream package starts at $270 for one child over six and an accompanying adult. Call 877/247-5223 or go to www.americangirl.com for more information. You might also try the wildly popular **Build-a-Bear Workshop** on the corner of Fifth Avenue and 46th Street. Call 212/871-7080 or go to www.buildabear.com/nyc.

New York City Opera—The season for this exceptional but often overshadowed opera runs through summer and early fall. For schedule and ticket information, visit the opera's website (www.nyopera.com) or go to the New York State Theater's box office at Lincoln Center. Special student discounts are often available, including a limited number of rush tickets sold at 4 on the day of each performance for $16. Call in advance (212/870-5630) to learn about availability.

New York Philharmonic—The Philharmonic's season runs from September through June at Avery Fisher Hall in Lincoln Center. For schedule and ticket information, go to the Philharmonic's website (www.newyorkphil harmonic.org) or call 212/875-5656. If you would rather attend a performance during the day and save a bit, ask about $15 tickets to open rehearsals. Rush tickets may also be available.

DANCE AND BALLET

Ballet and dance companies have experienced tough times financially, but New York is still home to several world-class companies and a great many smaller ones. They include:

Alvin Ailey American Dance Theater (212/767-0590, www.alvin ailey.org)

American Ballet Theater (212/362-6000, www.abt.org)

Dance Theater Workshop (212/691-6500, www.dtw.org)

Dance Theatre of Harlem (212/690-2800, www.dancetheatreof harlem.org)

New York City Ballet (212/870-5570, www.nycballet.com)

Paul Taylor Dance Company (212/431-5562, www.ptdc.org)

Time Out New York has a particularly good section on dance, including reviews and a day-by-day calendar of large and small performances by local and visiting companies. A number of major companies perform at the **City Center of Music and Dance** (131 W 55th Street). The Alvin Ailey American Dance Theater is now in its **Joan Weill Center for Dance** (405 N 55th St). Call **CitiTix** (212/581-1212), go to the **City Center** website (www.citycenter.org), or visit an individual dance company's website for information about tickets and upcoming performances.

TELEVISION SHOW TAPINGS

Fine arts aside, there is one other kind of ticket everybody wants to get in New York: those that allow you to become part of the television studio audience for one of the many talk shows filmed here. I've listed some of the most popular shows and rules for getting free tickets.

The Daily Show with Jon Stewart—These tickets must be ordered well in advance, but the system for getting them is wonderfully straightforward. Simply go to Comedy Central's website (www.comedycentral.com) and click his show. There's an online reservation system that will tell you what days are available. Tickets are sometimes available this way for **The Colbert Report**, though when I checked at press time, only stand-by tickets were available. To get on the waiting list, go to Comedy Central's studio at 513 W 54th Street (between Tenth and Eleventh Ave). You must be at least 18 and have identification.

Look for NBCs **Today Show** crowd on the sidewalk along 49th Street between Fifth Avenue and Avenue of the Americas. People show up before dawn, although cameras don't starting rolling until 7 a.m.

Late Nite with Conan O'Brien—Tickets are available only by calling 212/664-3056. You can request up to four tickets every six months. Everyone attending must be at least 16. While they don't guarantee admission, standby tickets are distributed one per person at 9 a.m. on taping days under the "NBC Studios" sign on the 49th Street side of 30 Rockefeller Plaza.

Late Show with David Letterman—These remain one of the hottest tickets in town, and you must be at least 18 to qualify for them. You can apply by filling out a form at www.lateshowaudience.com or going in person to the Ed Sullivan Theater box office (Broadway between 53rd and 54th streets) between 9:30 and 12:30 on weekdays or 10 to 6 on weekends. Expect to wait at least six to eight months and probably longer. Standby tickets are sometimes distributed at 11 on the morning of a show by calling 212/247-6497 (not in person, as used to be the case). If you hear a recording, you'll know tickets have run out. Shows are taped Monday through Thursday. Bring a picture ID and jacket, as Dave insists that the theater be kept at a chilly 52° all year! They are sticklers for the rules and won't let you use anyone else's tickets.

Saturday Night Live—Year in and year out, these are the hardest tickets of all to get. A lottery is held every August from emails collected during the preceding 12 months, and each winner gets two tickets. If you want to be included in the lottery, send an e-mail to snltickets@nbc.com. Send only one email per household, and realize there is no guarantee that you will get tickets in the following year. Standby tickets for the 8 p.m. dress rehearsal and the 11:30 p.m. live show are available at 7 a.m. on the day of the show (but show up around 5 a.m. if you really want them) at the 49th Street entrance to 30 Rockefeller Plaza. Be sure you're certain there's a live show planned for the time you are in New York, and expect a long line if there's a popular host. They do not guarantee entrance, and only one ticket is distributed per person over 16.

The View—This women's gabfest is taped Monday through Thursday at the ABC Studios on Manhattan's Upper West Side (320 W 66th St). If you're planning well in advance and live outside New Jersey, New York, Connecticut, and Pennsylvania, go to www.abc.go.com/daytime/theview/tickets to request tickets for a specific date at least three months in advance. (If you live in one of those four states, ABC will simply assign a date to you.) If you're in town and feel lucky, go by the studio between 8:30 and 10 a.m. on a day they're taping and pick up a stand-by number. When you return at 10:20, they'll let you know what numbers they're taking that day. You must be at least 16 years old to attend. The show airs from 11 to noon.

Test Your New York IQ

Here's an eclectic list of questions about New York that even a native New Yorker probably wouldn't know:

1. Where was George Washington's inauguration held in 1789?
2. When was the first ticker-tape parade and why was it held?
3. What do Ella Fitzgerald, the Rolling Stones, Mark Twain, and Eleanor Roosevelt all have in common?
4. Why are triads, nautiluses, and Poseidon himself carved in stone outside the Bowling Green Post Office?
5. Where does the red star associated with Macy's come from?

Answers: 1. In a building on the corner of Wall and Nassau streets, now home to the Federal Hall National Memorial 2. The throwing of a ticker-tape happened spontaneously in October 1886 during a parade to celebrate the dedication of the Statue of Liberty. 3. They all appeared in front of sold-out crowds at Carnegie Hall. 4. The building, on Broadway at Bowling Green, was home of the Cunard Steamship Line. 5. Rowland Hussey Macy, who started the store in 1858, had a red star tattooed on his hand from his days as a Nantucket whaler.

For a Romantic Interlude

Whether you're falling in love for the first time or celebrating a wedding anniversary, New York can be one of the most romantic places in the world. If you're in the mood for love or want to create a mood that's just right for romance, try the following:

- Drinks by the fireplace followed by dinner at **One If By Land, Two If By Sea** (17 Barrow St)
- A summertime dinner in the garden at **Barbetta** (321 W 46th St)

- Dinner at the discreet and classy **Le Périgord** (405 E 52nd St)
- Dinner at **Tavern on the Green**'s sparkling Crystal Room (in Central Park off 67th St)
- Drinks in **Campbell Apartment,** an elegant spot tucked away in Grand Central Terminal (just east of Vanderbilt Ave)
- A late-night visit to the **Empire State Building Observation Deck** (Fifth Ave between 33rd and 34th St)
- A walk across the **Brooklyn Bridge** is a must!
- Watching the sun rise from the **Brooklyn Bridge**, the **Battery Park Esplanade**, **Lighthouse Park** on Roosevelt Island, or the deck of the **Staten Island Ferry**
- A visit to the restored **Winter Garden** (World Financial Center)
- A teatime interlude at **Payard Patisserie** (1032 Lexington Ave)
- A picnic lunch looking out over the Hudson River from **The Cloisters**
- A stroll through the splendid lobby of **The Waldorf-Astoria**
- An early evening spent listening to classical music from the balcony of the **Metropolitan Museum of Art**'s Great Hall or jazz at the **Guggenheim Museum**
- A rowboat or gondola ride on **Central Park Lake** or a nighttime sail around Manhattan
- An evening carriage ride through **Central Park** after a fresh snow has fallen or a springtime stroll on some of the park's less traveled paths

For Parties and Special Events

If you're looking for the perfect place to hold a wedding reception, bar mitzvah, or gala event for thousands, New York inevitably has the right place ... and the people to put it together for you. The trick, of course, is finding them. The other trick is paying for them!

Note that you will not find museums, restaurants, or hotels in the following list. Many museum spaces, including the **Mount Vernon Hotel Museum & Garden**, the **Cooper-Hewitt National Design Museum**, and the **Roosevelt Rotunda** at the **American Museum of Natural History** (complete with its dinosaur display) can be rented for parties and other events. Many restaurants have spaces for private parties, as do most hotels.

Some of my favorite private party rooms in New York are at **Barbetta** (321 W 46th St), **Firebird** (365 W 46th St), **Four Seasons** (99 E 52nd St), **Gramercy Tavern** (42 E 20th St), the **Hudson River Club** (World Financial Center), **Le Périgord** (405 E 52nd St), **Lutèce** (249 E 50th St), **Montrachet** (239 Broadway), **One If By Land, Two If By Sea** (17 Barrow St), **Primavera** (1578 First Ave), **Serendipity 3** (225 E 60th St), **Tavern on the Green** (Central Park W at 67th St), **The Terrace** (400 W 119th St), **The Tonic** (108 W 18th St), and **Tribeca Grill** (375 Greenwich St). If you want to throw a party at your favorite museum, restaurant, hotel, or bar, by all means ask.

Some venues available for special events take care of all the catering, while others simply provide the space. Among the former are the **Art Club** (100 Reade St), the **Burden Mansion** (7 E 91st St), **New York Public Library** (Fifth Ave at 41st St), the **Puck Building** (295 Lafayette St, at Houston St), and **Studio 450** (450 W 31st St). Among the latter are **Astra** (979 Third Ave), **The Boathouse** (in Central Park), **Glorious Foods**

(522 E 74th St), the **Museum Club at Bridgewaters** (South Street Seaport), **Pier 60** (at Chelsea Piers), and **Upper Crust 91** (91 Horatio St). Catering is optional at the **New York Botanical Garden** (in The Bronx) and the **Pratt Mansion** (1026 Fifth Ave). This list should give you an idea of the breadth of spaces available.

Before you forge ahead with planning a party in New York, be forewarned that it's going to cost a great deal of money. I'm talking *really* big bucks. You can save money by avoiding Saturday evening, holding your numbers down, and throwing your party in the off months of July and August or between January and early April. Some places and services will negotiate on price. But don't expect any great or even particularly good deals. And make your reservations at least two months and as far as two years in advance.

Going Underground?

Manhattan has some interesting spots for you to visit! One of the best known is the **Grand Central Oyster Bar Restaurant** (Grand Central Terminal, 42nd St at Vanderbilt Ave, 212/490-6650) plus other eateries in the Food Court in the same building. **Decibel** (240 E 9th St, 212/979-2733) is a restaurant and sake bar, but it is not the kind of place you would want to spend a whole evening. **Pravda** (281 Lafayette St, 212/226-4696) is a bit more visitor friendly, with lots of vodka available. For good comedy, the **Village Vanguard** (178 Seventh Ave, 212/255-4037) is the place to go "down under." A surprise underground venue is **Zankel Hall** (Carnegie Hall, 881 Seventh Ave, 212/247-7800). It is a 600-seat concert theater that most New Yorkers have never heard of!

For Restrooms

Nothing can ruin a trek around New York more quickly than not being able to find a bathroom when one is needed. By law, public buildings are required to have public restrooms. They are not, however, required to be clean and safe.

Following is a list of bathrooms that meet at least a minimum standard of safety and cleanliness. You may need to ask for directions or a key at some of them, but all are free to the public. As a general rule, try hotel lobbies, department stores, schools, theaters, municipal goverment buildings, churches, libraries, and even hospitals. **Barnes & Noble** and **Starbucks** locations throughout the city are also good bets. Of course, if you have small children in tow, just about any store or restaurant will likely take pity.

Wherever you end up, be sure to follow a few safety tips. Leaving anything on the floor in a public restroom is a mistake, as purses, packages, and everything else have a bad habit of disappearing while you're occupied! The same is true of items left hanging on the back of a stall door. Avoid deserted bathrooms, as well as those in parks (unless listed below) and most subway stations.

Below 14th Street

- **Castle Clinton** (inside Battery Park)
- **National Museum of the American Indian** (1 Bowling Green)

- **Trinity Church** (Broad St at Wall St)
- **Federal Hall National Memorial** (Wall St at Nassau St)
- **South Street Seaport** (Fulton at Water St)
- **The Hotel at Rivington** (107 Rivington)
- **Essex Street Market** (120 Essex St)
- **New York City Fire Museum** (289 Spring St, bet Hudson and Varick St)
- **Kmart** (Lafayette at 8th St)
- **Strand Book Store** (Broadway at 12th St)

Between 14th and 42nd streets

- **Loehmann's** (Seventh Ave at 17th St)
- **ABC Carpet & Home** (Broadway at 19th St)
- **Supreme Court of the State of New York** (25th St bet Madison and Park Ave)
- **Macy's** (Herald Square, Broadway at 34th St)
- **Science, Industry, and Business Library** (Madison Ave at 34th St)
- **Sheraton Park Avenue Hotel** (Park Ave and 37th St)
- **New York Public Library** (Fifth Ave bet 40th and 42nd St)
- **Bryant Park** (42nd St bet Fifth Ave and Ave of the Americas)
- **Grand Hyatt Hotel** (42nd St bet Park and Lexington Ave)
- **Grand Central Terminal** (42nd St at Vanderbilt Ave)

Midtown

- **United Nations** (First Ave bet 45th and 46th St)
- **The Waldorf-Astoria** (Park Ave at 50th St)
- **Saks Fifth Avenue** (611 Fifth Ave, bet 49th and 50th St)
- **Rockefeller Center** (concourse level, bet Fifth Ave and Ave of the Americas from 49th to 51st St)
- **Fendi** (677 Fifth Ave)
- **Park Avenue Plaza** (55 E 52nd St)
- **Henri Bendel** (712 Fifth Ave)
- **Omni Park Central** (870 Seventh Ave)
- **Sony Wonder Technology Lab** (56th St at Madison Ave)

Upper East Side

- **McDonald's** (Third Ave bet 57th and 58th St)
- **Bloomingdale's** (1000 Third Ave, at 59th St)
- **Asia Society** (725 Park Ave, at 70th St)
- **Ralph Lauren** (867 Madison Ave, at 72nd St)
- **Marimekko** (1263 Third Ave, at 73rd St)
- **92nd Street Y** (1395 Lexington Ave, at 92nd St)
- **Charles A. Dana Discovery Center** (in Central Park, Fifth Ave at 110th St)

Upper West Side

- **Avery Fisher Hall** (Lincoln Center, 64th St at Broadway)
- **New York Public Library for the Performing Arts** (Lincoln Center, 65th St at Broadway)
- **Barnes & Noble** (Broadway at 82nd St)
- **Cathedral Church of St. John the Divine** (Amsterdam Ave at 114th St)

311 is New York City's all-purpose information number. Do you need to know how to rent a baseball field in Central Park, how to sign up for a tour of Gracie Mansion, or how to pay a parking fine? Operators are standing by!

For More Information

I suggest doing a few things before packing your bags for New York. Contact **NYC & Company** (800/692-8474, 212/484-1222, www.nyc visit.com), the city's marketing arm, to request a free copy of the official **NYC Guide**. (For $5.95, they'll send you the guide, plus a map and lots of brochures, but the guide is sufficient for most people.) Second, look through both the "Tours" section of Chapter III and the "Tickets" section of this chapter to find out which things you want to do that require advance reservations. Third, write the **New York City Transit Authority** (Attention: Customer Services, 370 John Jay Street, Brooklyn, NY 11201) for maps and brochures about the mass-transit system so you can hit the ground (or subway) running.

Whether you're planning in advance or already sitting in your hotel room, get copies of *The New Yorker*, *New York* magazine, *Time Out New York*, and the *New York Times*. All but *Time Out New York* are generally available throughout the country (although the various out-of-town editions of the *New York Times* are abridged). *The New Yorker* (in the front), *New York* magazine (in the back), and *Time Out New York* (throughout) carry detailed information about current theater productions, movies, gallery and museum exhibitions, concerts, dance, and New York nightlife. Be advised that the free magazines in hotel rooms are paid for by advertisers and therefore are not particularly useful or unbiased (although maps and information about current museum exhibitions can be helpful).

If you don't have everything planned when you arrive, drop by one of several visitor information centers in Manhattan. They include:

- **Chinatown Visitor Kiosk**—Walker, Canal, and Baxter streets (weekdays and Sunday from 10 to 6, Saturday from 10 to 7)
- **NYC Heritage Tourism Center**—Broadway at Park Row (weekdays from 9 to 6, weekends from 10 to 6)
- **Embassy Theater Information Center**—Seventh Ave bet 46th and 47th St (daily 10 to 6)
- **Federal Hall National Memorial "Gateway to America"** —This is a great source for information about National Parks and other federally run attractions in New York. Located at 26 Wall Street, it's open weekdays (except federal holidays) from 9 to 5.
- **Harlem Visitor Information Center**—Located in the Apollo Theater at 253 W 125th Street (bet Frederick Douglass and Adam Clayton Powell, Jr. Blvd), it's open weekdays from 11 to 5.
- **NYC & Company**—810 Seventh Ave, just off 53rd St (weekdays from 8:30 to 6, weekends from 8:30 to 5)

The front section of the Manhattan Yellow Pages is a good place to look for information and ideas. In addition to useful telephone numbers, it includes diagrams of major concert halls and sports stadiums. It also includes a short calendar of major annual events and maps of the subway and bus systems.

> ## Over the Bridge
>
> As I explained in the first chapter, New York to me means Manhattan. The moment I leave "the city," I'm definitely out of my element. For many years, no self-respecting Manhattanite would even think of crossing the bridge to any other burrough. But in recent years, Brooklyn has become increasingly appealing and lots of folks, even tourists, are heading that way. The **Brooklyn Museum of Art** (718/638-5000, www.brooklynmuseum.org) is a world-class art museum and well worth a visit. The **Brooklyn Botanic Garden** (718/623-7200, www.bbg.org) and **Prospect Park** are within walking distance of each other and of the museum. Of course some folks come to Brooklyn for the great shops and restaurants in Park Slope, Carroll Gardens, Williamsburg, and other Brooklyn neighborhoods. Among those I recommend are **Blue Ribbon Brooklyn** (280 Fifth Ave, 718/840-0408), **Beast** (638 Bergen St, 718/399-6855), and the amazing **Brooklyn Ice Cream Factory** (Fulton Ferry Landing, 718/246-3963). If you just want a taste of what makes Brooklyn so appealing that folks are willing to stay on the F train, go take a walk along Smith and Court streets south of Atlantic Avenue.

Finally, the Internet has made accessing tourist information about New York as easy as clicking a mouse. Typing "New York City" into a search engine will generate several million hits. Here are the most useful sites:

- **www.ci.nyc.ny.us**: The official site of the city of New York has great information for residents and visitors alike, including transportation resources, links to attractions and events, and the New York Yellow Pages.
- **www.centralparknyc.org**: The official site of the Central Park Conservancy offers a huge array of information about this remarkable park.
- **www.cityguidemagazine.com**: restaurant reviews and numerous links to tours, museums, and other sites
- **www.gocitykids.com**: helpful ideas for parents about parks, restaurants, play spaces, stores, and babysitting services
- **www.mta.nyc.ny.us**: The official site of the Metropolitan Transportation Authority has helpful information about the bus and subway systems.
- **www.newyork.citysearch.com**: current schedules for plays, concerts, and movies, good descriptions of clubs, lots of opinions, and a weekly calendar
- **www.nycgovparks.org**: extensive information about parks and recreation centers in all five boroughs
- **www.nycvisit.com**: The NYC & Company site lets you request publications, maps, and event calendars.
- **www.nymag.com**: information from *New York* magazine
- **www.nytoday.com**: Produced by the *New York Times*, this site provides access to its reviews, calendars, and classified ads.
- **www.timeout.com/newyork**: This is a great source of reviews, information about exhibits and tours, and other updates from *Time Out New York*.

If you're coming to New York in a wheelchair, you ought to know about a couple of resources. First, make sure to get a copy of "Access for All," an exceptional guide to the city's cultural institutions that describes in detail facilities for people in wheelchairs, as well as the blind and deaf. This invaluable guide is available from **Hospital Audiences** (www.hospaud.org). This organization also runs a hotline (888/424-4685) on weekdays. Second, the **New York City Transit Authority** has a special phone number (718/596-8585) for information about routes accessible to people in wheelchairs and postage-paid fare envelopes for disabled riders. The **City of New York's Office for People with Disabilities** (212/788-2830, www.nyc.gov/html/mopd) is also a great resource. Finally, many Broadway theaters offer deeply discounted tickets for people in wheelchairs and their companions. Call individual theaters for more information.

The New York Philharmonic's marketing tag line sums up my philosophy perfectly: "**Expect the Extraordinary. This Is New York.**"

Index

(Note: Bolded page numbers indicate major listings' main entries; index is in strict alphabetical order.)

NOTES

NOTES

NOTES

NOTES

NOTES

NOTES

NOTES

NOTES